Mental Health Practice in Today's Schools

Raymond H. Witte, PhD, NCSP, is trained and licensed as a school psychologist and provided educational and psychological services to the Jessamine County School System in Nicholasville, Kentucky, the Albert Chandler Medical Center in Lexington, Kentucky, and Midway College in Midway, Kentucky, before joining the faculty at Miami University in Oxford, Ohio, in 1993. Dr. Witte's professional training and current instruction focus on individual and system assessment and intervention, transition services, and diversity awareness, along with mental health provision in the schools. During his 21 years at Miami University, Dr. Witte has given undergraduate and graduate instruction in the areas of educational assessment and evaluation, psychological assessment and intervention, and practicum supervision, along with program design and evaluation. He has completed two textbooks in the area of assessment: *Assessment in Special Education* (2014) and *Classroom Assessment for Teachers* (2012). He is also currently working with the Cincinnati Children's Medical Center on assessing the effectiveness of their employee diversity-training program.

G. Susan Mosley-Howard, PhD, is trained and licensed as a psychologist in the state of Michigan and a professional clinical counselor in the state of Ohio, and has provided educational and psychological services in various educational and mental health settings. Dr. Mosley-Howard joined the faculty at Miami University in Oxford, Ohio, in 1988 after her work in Miami's Student Counseling Services from 1983 to 1988. Dr. Mosley-Howard's professional training and current instruction focus on mental health and academic intervention, and minority help-seeking, along with mental health provision in the schools. During her 31 years at Miami University, Dr. Mosley-Howard has given undergraduate and graduate instruction in the areas of counseling and mental health intervention, human development and learning, educational measurement, minority mental health, and practicum supervision, along with research methods. She is currently completing manuscripts on identity development of Native American students. Dr. Mosley-Howard has filled several administrative positions at Miami, most recently serving as dean of students for 10 years, responsible for institutional emergency response, student support, transition and residential services, and student conduct processes at the university.

Mental Health Practice in Today's Schools

Issues and Interventions

Raymond H. Witte, PhD, NCSP

G. Susan Mosley-Howard, PhD

Editors

SPRINGER PUBLISHING COMPANY
NEW YORK

Springer Publishing Company, LLC
11 West 42nd Street
New York, NY 10036
www.springerpub.com

Acquisitions Editor: Nancy S. Hale
Production Editor: Shelby Peak
Composition: Amnet
Cover Artwork: Ashleigh Witte

ISBN: 978-0-8261-9645-3
e-book ISBN: 978-0-8261-9642-2

14 15 16 17 / 5 4 3 2 1

The author and the publisher of this Work have made every effort to use sources believed to be reliable to provide information that is accurate and compatible with the standards generally accepted at the time of publication. The author and publisher shall not be liable for any special, consequential, or exemplary damages resulting, in whole or in part, from the readers' use of, or reliance on, the information contained in this book. The publisher has no responsibility for the persistence or accuracy of URLs for external or third-party Internet websites referred to in this publication and does not guarantee that any content on such websites is, or will remain, accurate or appropriate.

Library of Congress Cataloging-in-Publication Data

Witte, Raymond H.
  Mental health practice in today's schools : issues and interventions / Raymond H. Witte, PhD, NCSP, G. Susan Mosley-Howard, PhD.
      pages cm
  Includes bibliographical references and index.
  ISBN 978-0-8261-9645-3 (print : alk. paper) — ISBN 978-0-8261-9642-2 (e-book : alk. paper)
  1. School children—Mental health services. 2. School psychology. I. Title.
  LB3430.W57 2015
  370.15—dc23
                                                                                    2014024529

Special discounts on bulk quantities of our books are available to corporations, professional associations, pharmaceutical companies, health care organizations, and other qualifying groups. If you are interested in a custom book, including chapters from more than one of our titles, we can provide that service as well.

For details, please contact:
Special Sales Department, Springer Publishing Company, LLC
11 West 42nd Street, 15th Floor, New York, NY 10036-8002
Phone: 877-687-7476 or 212-431-4370; Fax: 212-941-7842
E-mail: sales@springerpub.com

Printed in the United States of America by Gasch Printing.

Contents

Contributors

Chizara Ahuama-Jonas, PhD
Department of Psychology
University of Cincinnati
Cincinnati, Ohio

Sheri Bauman, PhD
Department of Disability and Psychoeducational Studies
University of Arizona
Tucson, Arizona

Kristin W. Bolton, PhD
Department of Social Work
University of North Carolina Wilmington
Wilmington, North Carolina

Ann Kathleen Burlew, PhD
Department of Psychology
University of Cincinnati
Cincinnati, Ohio

Mona Burts-Beatty, PhD
Hamilton County Educational Service Center
Cincinnati, Ohio

Dewey G. Cornell, PhD
Clinical and School Psychology
University of Virginia
Charlottesville, Virginia

Susan C. Davies, PhD
Department of Counselor Education and Human Services
University of Dayton
Dayton, Ohio

Dorothy L. Espelage, PhD
Department of Educational Psychology
University of Illinois
Champaign, Illinois

Cynthia Franklin, PhD
School of Social Work
University of Texas
Austin, Texas

Jennifer H. Green, PhD
Department of Psychology
Miami University
Oxford, Ohio

Michelle Flaum Hall, EdD
Department of Counseling
Xavier University
Cincinnati, Ohio

Joshua Hersh, MD
Staff Psychiatrist
Miami University
Oxford, Ohio

Shannon Flaum Horvath, PhD
Pickaway County Educational Service Center
Pickaway, Ohio

Mary Kay Klimesh, JD
Seyfarth Shaw LLP Law Firm
Chicago, Illinois

Cheryl Kornfeld, MS
Center for Psychological Studies
Nova Southeastern University
Fort Lauderdale–Davie, Florida

Caravella McCuistian, MS
Department of Psychology
University of Cincinnati
Cincinnati, Ohio

Terri L. Messman-Moore, PhD
Department of Psychology
Miami University
Oxford, Ohio

G. Susan Mosley-Howard, PhD
Department of Educational Psychology
Miami University
Oxford, Ohio

Amanda B. Nickerson, PhD
Counseling, School and Educational Psychology
University at Buffalo, the State University of New York
Buffalo, New York

Amity L. Noltemeyer, PhD
Department of Educational Psychology
Miami University
Oxford, Ohio

Deborah Pergament, JD
Children's Law Group
DePaul University College of Law
DePaul University
Chicago, Illinois

Bridgette J. Peteet, PhD
Department of Psychology
University of Cincinnati
Cincinnati, Ohio

Scott Poland, PhD
Center for Psychological Studies
Nova Southeastern University
Fort Lauderdale–Davie, Florida

Todd A. Savage, PhD
Department of Counseling and School Psychology
University of Wisconsin–River Falls
River Falls, Wisconsin

Raymond H. Witte, PhD
Department of Educational Psychology
Miami University
Oxford, Ohio

Scott A. Woitaszewski, PhD
Department of Counseling and School Psychology
University of Wisconsin–River Falls
River Falls, Wisconsin

Robert E. Wubbolding, PhD
Center for Reality Therapy
Xavier University
Cincinnati, Ohio

Preface

Mental health professionals who work in today's schools face the challenge of addressing the social, emotional, and cognitive needs of millions of children while attempting to serve as effective consultants who address systemic educational issues. Although the task is daunting, school-based mental health professionals can draw upon myriad resources to enhance their knowledge, form interdisciplinary teams to leverage diverse points of view and expertise, and amass a variety of emerging tools to inform their work.

Never before have the skills possessed by mental health professionals been so important. By most measures, approximately 20% of young people experience a significant mental health problem; environmental issues of poverty, violence, and familial stress impact children and adolescents in ways that hinder their educational performance (Merikangas et al., 2010). Most of these children do not receive mental health services; for the majority of them school serves as the only potential source of support services (Merikangas et al., 2011). At the same time, never before has the educational system been so demanding, requiring children and educators alike to acquire skills and demonstrate those skills on high-stakes tests or employee assessments and statewide rating reports. Diminished funding, increased accountability, and psychosocial stressors complicate the picture even more.

While the aforementioned issues compete for attention, mental health status remains an all-important imperative. Professionals operating within schools need to become skilled at how to address children's mental health issues and this text is designed to assist with building that awareness. Fortunately, mental health and educational research has never been so rich. Emerging trends in evidence-based practice, therapeutic interventions, and academic strategies have come together to form highly effective tools. *Mental Health Practice in Today's Schools: Issues and Interventions* provides an understanding of some of these strategies and knowledge bases to enhance practice. This textbook examines key mental health issues and challenges that practitioners encounter when administering services in the school setting. Across the chapters, the Response to Intervention (RTI) model with tiered intervention is followed, along with the necessity of integrating therapeutic services and practices into the daily instruction of the classroom. This professional reference serves as a valuable resource for mental health professionals including school psychologists, clinical psychologists, guidance counselors, school social workers, and other community mental health providers, as well as professional educators including teachers, principals, and district school administrators.

We hope that this resource helps you to complete your professional mission of helping all children under your care. As we all know, mental health matters!

The goals of this text are to:

- Provide understanding of the relationship among mental health intervention, support, and impact within the school setting
- Examine the tiered intervention model and how mental health services and behavior support can be delivered to all students based on their level of need
- Supply knowledge and awareness of mental health screening instruments and how they can be used to help identify at-risk students
- Provide awareness and sensitivity to cultural issues and practices that influence mental health counseling and consultation services
- Disperse knowledge and awareness of evidence-based mental health practices for use in the schools
- Expand the practitioner's knowledge and skills regarding high-need issues and challenges relating to students' mental health

REFERENCES

Merikangas, K. R., He, J., Burstein, M. E., Swanson, S. A., Avenevoli, S., Cul, L., . . . Swendsen, J. (2010). Lifetime prevalence of mental disorders in U.S. adolescents: Results from the national co-morbidity study-adolescent supplement (NCS-A). *Journal for the American Academy of Child and Adolescent Psychiatry, 49*(10), 980–989.

Merikangas, K. R., He, J., Burstein, M. E., Swendsen, J., Avenevoli, S., Case, B., . . . Olfson, M. (2011). Service utilization for lifetime mental disorders in U.S. adolescents: Results from the national co-morbidity survey adolescent supplement (NCS-A). *Journal for the American Academy of Child and Adolescent Psychiatry, 50*(1), 32–45.

Acknowledgments

The editors express deep appreciation to all of the chapter authors, an array of highly skilled and accomplished scholars and practitioners who are advancing mental health practice in significant ways. We thank school-based partners Linda Milholland, Susan Witte, Kelsey Janning, Claire Kunesh, and Kristin Willis for their case contributions. In addition, we acknowledge the superb editorial skills of Susan Treadway, and Libby, Jonathan, and MacKinzie at Miami University. And, finally, we are grateful to the Springer Publishing Company team (Nancy S. Hale, Pete Feely, Joanne Jay, Shelby Peak, Jacob Seifert, and Alina Yurova).

Raymond H. Witte
G. Susan Mosley-Howard

CHAPTER 1

Response to Intervention and Mental Health Intervention

BRIDGETTE J. PETEET

ANN KATHLEEN BURLEW

CHIZARA AHUAMA-JONAS

CARAVELLA McCUISTIAN

LEARNING OUTCOMES

On completion of this chapter, the reader should be able to:

- Describe the Response to Intervention (RTI) Model and its potential application to student problems that affect academic outcomes
- Use a decision-making process to select an appropriate RTI classification level
- Understand the need to consider both the problem severity and effectiveness of evidence-based treatments (EBTs) with specific racial/ethnic groups when implementing RTI
- Comprehend the implications and challenges of utilizing an RTI-approach to address problem behaviors

The need for mental health support in schools has never been so great. Nearly 20% of youths have or report a mental health problem or emotional and behavioral disorders (EBDs; Merikangas et al., 2010). Children with EBDs have high suspension rates and low graduation rates (Merikangas et al., 2010; U.S. Department of Education, 2005). Addressing mental health issues that impact students is an intricate and essential requirement for improving academic performance.

An increasing number of effective approaches can be used to improve student mental health outcomes. Yet, despite the growing number of existing EBTs to meet the mental health needs of kindergarten through 12th-grade students, these interventions are not always organized in a manner that would enable school officials to select the most appropriate intervention(s) for a specific student and/or behavioral problem. RTI, a decision-making method aimed at matching students to appropriate services, has the potential to address this limitation. Schools nationwide have successfully used RTI to improve the academic and behavioral problems of children (Denton et al., 2013).

The aim of this chapter is to demonstrate the application of RTI to mental health issues that may originate outside the classroom but can directly affect academic performance in the classroom. In addition, strategies for considering the needs of diverse school-age youths are illustrated. The chapter defines RTI and presents its core components followed by a presentation of the current status of RTI work including some challenges with using the model. This chapter outlines mental health interventions related to the core components of RTI. Next, each intervention level of or tier in the RTI approach is described and demonstrated through a vignette. Along with the vignettes, a decision tree is introduced to facilitate the decision-making process required to address a student's needs. Finally, the implications, challenges, and future directions for applying RTI are discussed.

BACKGROUND ON RESPONSE TO INTERVENTION

RTI, a multilevel, district-wide system for identifying and addressing early learning or behavioral difficulties, is aimed at preventing school failure by matching students to appropriate interventions or support services based on the severity of the problem. RTI affords educators and school-based mental health professionals an opportunity to identify, intervene with, and support students with learning and behavior issues. Using RTI to address behavioral problems relies on identifying the target behavior(s) and augmenting the intensity of the intervention (e.g., primary, secondary, or tertiary) based upon assessment data and the needs of a specific student (National Center on Response to Intervention, 2010).

The RTI process begins with quality instruction (academic context), universal screening, and positive behavioral supports (PBS; mental health context). The core of the RTI approach includes leveraging effective intervention strategies, progress monitoring, and data-based decision making (National Center on Response to Intervention, 2010). Data-based decision making refers to the use of ongoing objective data to make determinations regarding students and their appropriate treatment

(Gresham, 2007). Throughout the entire RTI process, the underlying principles include high-quality instruction, research-based academic and behavioral intervention, progress monitoring, and an integrative or collaborative team approach (Hawken, Vincent, & Schumann, 2008). Focusing on tier intensity, treatment efficacy, and individual student attributes are all critical to strengthening the RTI approach. (For more on cultural responsive treatment and universal screening issues, refer to the description of culturally sensitive mental health services in Chapter 5 and the discussion of screening at-risk students in Chapter 2.) For that reason, identifying not only the intensity of the interventions needed by students but also matching the students to interventions with proven efficacy within the context of their personal attributes (e.g., age, gender, culture, language) may maximize RTI outcomes.

Gresham (2007) contended that an RTI approach has the following four advantages. First, the emphasis on the early identification of behavioral difficulties increases the likelihood of extinguishing problem behaviors before they escalate in severity. Second, an RTI approach stresses a risk versus a deficit treatment model. A risk model approach assumes the intervention will ameliorate the student's problem, whereas a deficit model too often simply adjusts services to the student's functioning without the expectation of change. The third benefit, the use of standardized screening procedures, potentially reduces the likelihood that referrals are more a reflection of teacher biases rather than student needs. Fourth, the assignment of students to EBTs increases the probability of positive outcomes over procedures that simply place students in programs established for those with a higher likelihood of school failure (e.g., special education).

Despite the growing popularity of RTI, several specific implementation gaps are evident. First, the focus has been on managing challenging behaviors in the school setting (e.g., conduct problems, bullying, calming an agitated student, bus conduct, behavior with substitute teachers). Efforts to apply RTI to behaviors or problems that originate outside the school setting (e.g., mental health disorders) yet negatively impact academic performance are restricted. Second, previous applications of RTI to behavioral problems were primarily limited to identifying the intensity of the intervention (e.g., primary, secondary, or tertiary) appropriate for a specific student. However, that focus ignores that the efficacy of a specific EBT may vary across racial/ethnic groups. Therefore, identifying not only the intensity of the interventions needed by students but also matching the students to interventions with proven efficacy for their racial/ethnic group may improve RTI outcomes even further. Finally, no universal algorithm is available to assist busy school officials in matching students' needs with the appropriate EBTs.

The next sections address these issues by describing in more detail the process used in a RTI approach. Because selecting interventions to use with groups or individual students can be daunting, the school team may find it useful to craft a decision-making process or a *decision tree* to provide a consistent frame of reference to undergird the intervention selection process. Vignettes are also presented to illustrate the use of a decision tree and to assist with selecting an appropriate intervention for each tier. These examples are intended to illustrate how the RTI process might be used to make uniform decisions about appropriate interventions for students.

RESPONSE TO INTERVENTION TIERS

An RTI approach assumes that students vary in the intensity of the services they require. As established earlier, the RTI approach usually consists of three intervention levels. Accordingly, the interventions appropriate for students at one level of need may be inappropriate for those at a different level. The three RTI levels of intervention are referred to as Tier 1 (primary), Tier 2 (secondary), and Tier 3 (tertiary; Figure 1.1; National Center on Response to Intervention, 2010).

Students enter into the RTI process in many ways including (a) schools may implement a RTI Tier 1 intervention curriculum for all students without incorporating intervention screens (e.g., drug prevention intervention); or (b) schools may screen students and place them into an appropriate tier intervention

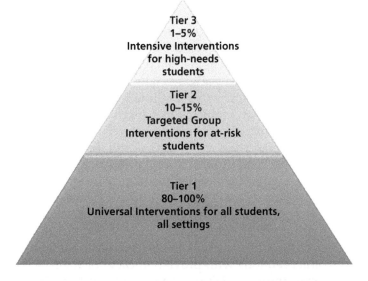

FIGURE 1.1 Visual depiction of the tiers. Each tier shares certain common aspects (i.e., accessible to all students, monitored progressively, evidence-based) and sometimes requires interdisciplinary collaboration.

depending on the assessment of the severity of the problem (e.g., drug prevention intervention for students at risk for current or future substance abuse). Another tool that may assist with the application of the RTI process is a decision-tree approach. School staff members are often bombarded with multiple tasks. Within this overwhelmingly busy environment, it is easy to make judgments that lack the methodical process needed for quality intervention decisions. A decision-tree approach is offered here to illustrate how schools can streamline and systematize intervention decisions for students (Figure 1.2; Evans, Serpell, Schultz, & Pastor, 2007; Farrell, Meyer, & White, 2001; Henggeler et al., 1991; Horn, Dino, Kalsekar, & Fernandes, 2004; Liddle et al., 2001; Marsiglia, Ayers, Gance-Cleveland, Mettler, & Booth, 2012; Masia-Warner et al., 2005; Stevens, Leybas-Amedia, Bourdeau, McMichael, & Nyitray, 2006; Winters, Fahnhorst, Botzet, Lee, & Lalone, 2012). This decision-tree approach has been used in both clinical and field settings with beneficial impact in standardizing and systematizing the intervention decision-making process. A more detailed description of each tier and decision-tree use follows with examples of evidence-based interventions along with vignettes illustrating the application of RTI to a mental health problem.

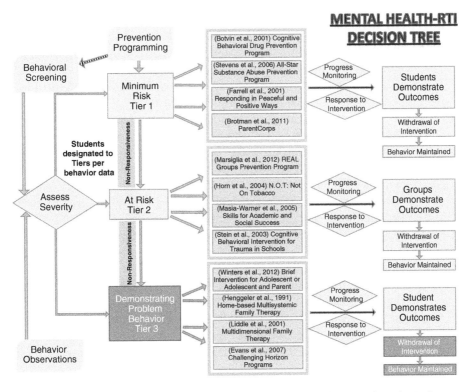

FIGURE 1.2 Visual representation of EBT selection process that can be adapted within a school system.

Tier 1 Interventions

Tier 1 interventions are the least intensive of the three intervention levels. These interventions are universal and designed to be appropriate for all students. In Tier 1 (primary level), the instruction, screening, PBS, or behavioral curriculum are delivered to the largest number of students (80%–100%) and provide all students with universal supports within the general education classroom. Tier 1 behavioral intervention examples include *social skills* programs and psychoeducational programs designed to teach targeted skills (e.g., stress reduction, anger management). Data screening in this tier may include school-wide climate surveys, incidence mapping, and rating scales for emotional risk and social skills (e.g., Behavioral and Emotional Screening System [BESS] or Youth Risk Behavioral Survey [YRBS]).

The Life Skills Training Middle School (LST-MS) Program is an intervention that can function as a Tier 1 level substance use intervention. LST-MS is a universal curriculum appropriate for all middle-school adolescents between the ages of 11 and 14. The aim of LST-MS is to arm adolescents with both knowledge and social skills for resisting social pressures to use drugs, alcohol, or cigarettes. LST-MS was developed to be effective for all adolescents but later was culturally adapted to be appropriate for African American and other ethnic minority adolescents (Botvin et al., 1989; Botvin & Botvin, 1992). The intervention utilizes cognitive-behavioral techniques to address social and psychological factors associated with early onset substance use. The three major components—drug-resistance skills, personal self-management skills, and general social skills—are helpful for reducing substance use among adolescents.

Botvin, Griffin, Diaz, and Hill-Williams (2001) examined the efficacy of LST-MS in an urban majority African American school district. The 29 participating schools were categorized as high-, medium-, or low-smoking prevalence schools. Entire schools within each category were then randomly assigned to either the control condition or to the LST intervention, which included 15 sessions in the seventh grade and 10 booster sessions in the eighth grade. Classroom teachers delivered the intervention. The students in schools implementing the intervention later reported less smoking, drinking, drunkenness, inhalant use, and poly-drug use than controls. Although most students respond well to these broad-based experiences, some students may not respond adequately. Should that occur, these students could be referred to receive more intensive interventions (e.g., Tier 2). The following case of Keisha illustrates a situation in which a Tier 1 intervention was appropriate.

Tier 1 Vignette

Keisha is an African American girl in the seventh grade at an inner-city school in the northeastern region of the United States. She had no reported behavioral problems in school and was considered a "gifted" student by all of her teachers. There was no evidence that she ever experimented with drugs. Noticing the increasing drug trends in the surrounding community, the school decided to implement a district-wide prevention program. Using the school's decision tree as shown in Figure 1.2, the school selected a culturally adapted version of LST-MS intervention because the EBT was appropriate as a Tier 1 intervention and had demonstrated efficacy with African American students. Keisha participated with the rest of her class. Every week for 15 weeks, Keisha's teacher Ms. Jones implemented this curriculum for Keisha and her classmates. During each class session, Keisha participated in group discussions and received homework assignments about drug prevention skills to practice outside of the classroom. At the conclusion of the drug prevention intervention, Keisha continued to exhibit positive behavior in school and reported no use of cigarettes, alcohol, or any other illegal substance.

Tier 2 Interventions

Tier 2 interventions are mid-range interventions appropriate for students whose at-risk status mandates more than a Tier 1 intervention and for students whose target behavior(s) was not responsive to Tier 1 efforts. Tier 2 interventions are targeted toward those students in need of more support (approximately 10%–15% of all students). Tier 2 interventions may include prevention groups focused on identified problem areas (e.g., anger management, substance abuse, parental divorce). Tier 2 data-gathering practices might include classroom observations, or functional behavioral assessment (FBA) with a particular student (to determine environmental contributors, antecedents, sustaining factors, frequency, patterns across subjects or time-of-day and task demands, self-monitoring, or reinforcement plans), or behavioral reports of student conduct or behavior. Again, data are obtained to monitor or determine intervention impact (e.g., anxiety scale, observation data, etc.).

Tier 2 interventions are typically provided in an adult-led, small-group format (National Center on Response to Intervention, 2010). Cognitive-Behavioral Intervention for Trauma in Schools (CBITS) is a mental health intervention that could be used as a Tier 2 intervention. This school-based, 10-session group intervention addresses posttraumatic stress disorder (PTSD), depression, or anxiety symptoms related to exposure to trauma. The sessions include a combination of didactic presentations, cognitive-behavioral group activities, and games, as well as the completion of individual worksheets. Stein et al. (2003) implemented CBITS in two middle schools in a largely Latino, socio-economically disadvantaged school district in East Los Angeles. Trained clinicians screened all sixth-grade students and selected those who met the following criteria for potential participation: exposure to three or more violent events, clinically significant PTSD symptoms, willingness to discuss their exposure to violence in a group setting, and not demonstrating behavior that would disrupt the group. Eligible participants were randomly assigned to either the CBITS condition or to a wait-list control. Three months after baseline, CBITS participants self-reported fewer PTSD and depressive symptoms than the wait-list control group. The parents of CBITS participants also reported less psychosocial dysfunction in their children than parents of the wait-list control group. The following vignette examines a Tier 2 intervention for symptoms of PTSD.

Tier 2 Vignette

Carlos is a 12-year-old Latino boy in the sixth grade. He attends an inner-city school and lives in the nearby urban community. Carlos lives with his mother and two siblings in a small apartment building. One year ago, Carlos's mother allowed her younger brother, David, to move into their home. David was heavily involved in local gang activities and, at times, would get into altercations with other gang members in the parking lot outside of the apartment complex. Carlos participated in a school-wide Tier 1 program. (The school implemented the GREAT [Gang Resistance Education and Training] from the Bureau of Justice Assistance and the Office of Juvenile Justice and Delinquency Prevention [OJJDP].) However, his teacher referred him to the school counselor because he reported on his GREAT survey that he had witnessed gang violence and because his teachers and mother noted academic and behavioral struggles. Carlos witnessed rival gang members brutally attack his uncle on at least three occasions, resulting in multiple arrests and hospital visits. Carlos had nightmares about the fights and worried constantly about the next attack.

The teacher's referral also included a note indicating that Carlos had been repeatedly sleepy and jumpy in class. After explaining his nightmares, the counselor referred Carlos to the CBITS program at his school. Using the decision tree, the counselor along with the school team selected CBITS because the school's decision-making process suggested that CBITS is effective as an intervention for reducing PTSD symptoms among Latino adolescents who are at the Tier 2 level of risk. Carlos participated in 10 weekly sessions with seven of his peers who had similar traumatic experiences. Themes of the sessions included education on trauma, ways to combat anxiety, coping strategies, and social problem solving. The group also completed homework assignments each week. At the conclusion of treatment, Carlos's anxiety and stress scores were lower than his prescores, and he reported feeling less stressed and was having fewer nightmares.

Tier 3 Interventions

Tier 3 interventions, the most intensive of the RTI model, are aimed at a small number (about 1%–5%) of students who either are not responding adequately to a Tier 2 intervention or are already demonstrating significant levels of the target behavior(s). Students placed in Tier 3 receive the most intensive support. Tier 3 interventions are usually individualized to meet the needs of the target child/adolescent. Common strategies explored at Tier 3 are specific behavior plans, individualized counseling (greater frequency and intensity), collaboration with outside agencies (clinicians, family therapists, juvenile justice systems, physicians for psychotropic medication, etc.), and parent conferences. Throughout the intervention, data progress monitoring occurs, including using scales, behavior charting, observation, and psychological assessment to determine student response to intervention. The education professional (e.g., teacher, counselor) continuously monitors a student's progress to determine the need for modification in the intervention plan. When the school-based mental health teams are making these decisions, multiple issues must be considered (see Figure 1.2 for a representation of this process). The following vignette, however, is an example of a student who received multitiered interventions as his behavior escalated.

Tier 3 Vignette

Aaron is a Caucasian boy who attended eighth grade in a school district that offered the generic LST program to all students. During his ninth grade, a teacher found what looked like marijuana in the boys' bathroom, and Aaron was one of a group suspected of flushing more of the drug down the toilet. Their counselor completed a substance abuse assessment indicating that all the boys' substance abuse attitudes placed them at risk of substance abuse involvement. Consequently, using the decision-tree process, the school team assigned all the boys to the Tier 2 Strengthening Families Program (SFP; Kumpfer, DeMarsh, & Child, 1989). By high school, Aaron tested positive for methamphetamines, when the school conducted random drug tests for his soccer team. At that time, Aaron admitted to using methamphetamines regularly. The counselor conducted a substance abuse and family assessment that revealed some family challenges possibly contributing to his drug use. Aaron lived with his father and younger sister. His older brother had recently been sentenced to prison for drug possession. Aaron's father worked two jobs to support the family. Aaron's mother, suffering from bipolar disorder (BD), had been in and out of psychiatric hospitals for the past decade and had minimal contact with the family. The counselor also noted that Aaron's grades were low and that he had just been placed on probation for frequent truancy and bullying.

The school determined that the Tier 2 intervention had been inadequate. Aaron was now appropriate for a Tier 3 level intervention. The school officials referred Aaron to the Multidimensional Family Therapy (MDFT) Program because MDFT has demonstrated efficacy in treating White school-aged youths (adolescents) with significant substance abuse problems. A trained therapist met with Aaron, his father, and his sister in their home for 2 hours on a weekly basis over a 6-month period. The therapist conducted an assessment to identify factors that contributed directly and indirectly to the target problems. She found that Aaron's dad worked third shift and did not return home in time to ensure that his children attended school. In addition, friends of Aaron's older brother had been providing Aaron with methamphetamines. Thus, limited parental supervision was a direct factor and his older brother's drug problem was an indirect factor. The therapist worked with the family to increase supervision and support for Aaron. After the intervention, Aaron experienced

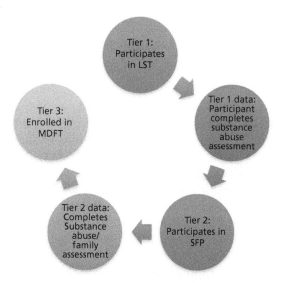

FIGURE 1.3 RTI (Response to Intervention) process starting with Tier 1 through Tier 3 interventions.
LST, Life Skills Training; MDFT, Multidimensional Family Therapy; SFP, Strengthening Families Program

less truancy and drug use, and his grades were improving. (See Figure 1.3 for a representation of how Aaron transitioned through the tiers.)

In each vignette, school-aged youths with different issues were assigned to interventions based on their level of risk. Matching the student to the appropriately tiered EBT proved to be a significant factor in the successful outcome of these cases. An additional aspect in all three cases was the continued monitoring and data collection regarding progress to ensure that each youth was getting the correct level of care. In Aaron's case, when his problems escalated, he advanced to Tier 2 and, subsequently, to Tier 3 interventions.

EVIDENCE-BASED TREATMENTS, RESEARCH, AND PRACTICE IN RESPONSE TO INTERVENTION

RTI interventions are required and expected to be EBTs regardless of the tier. This section describes three specific questions inherent in using EBTs. The first question is: What criteria must an intervention meet to be classified as evidence-based? In addition, an EBT may be efficacious with one racial/ethnic group but not another. Accordingly, the second question is: What criteria render an EBT appropriate for a specific target group? Beyond determining whether an intervention is evidence-based and efficacious, RTI school districts must have an efficient method for selecting appropriate EBTs. Therefore, the third question is: What is the best way to organize the information so that school officials can easily select the most appropriate intervention?

Nathan and Gorman (2002) classified EBTs into six types, according to the strength of the research design in the outcome paper. Type I research designs randomly assign participants into treatment and control groups, use measures with demonstrated reliability and validity, and conduct appropriate statistical analyses. In Type II studies, at least one of the aforementioned Type I criteria is absent but the design is not considered to have a fatal flaw. Since the remaining four classifications are weaker designs, the extent to which they meet the criteria for an EBT is questionable.

The American Psychological Association (APA) Presidential Task Force on Evidence-Based Practice (2006) maintained that cultural appropriateness should be considered in selecting appropriate EBTs. Huey and Polo (2008) operationalized APA's recommendation by establishing the conditions necessary to conclude that the evidence supports the efficacy of an intervention for a specific target group. Specifically, Huey and Polo proposed that studies demonstrating effectiveness for a specific group must meet at least one of the following conditions: (a) at least 75% of the sample must be members of the target group; (b) data for the target group must be analyzed in separate statistical analyses; or

(c) moderation analyses must demonstrate no racial/ethnic differences in the effectiveness of the treatment on target outcomes. Once EBTs meet the requirements for both scientific design and cultural effectiveness, a classification system may foster appropriate decision making.

A decision tree provides an efficient visual approach to enable school officials to select an appropriate EBT. Figure 1.2 is an example of a decision tree with three steps. The target behavior(s) for the intervention must first be identified. Since the level of intervention (i.e., Tier 1, 2, or 3) depends on the severity of the presenting problem, selecting the appropriate level of severity ranging from minimal risk to demonstrating the problem behavior is an important next step. Finally for Tier 3, specific interventions can then be selected while considering the demographic characteristics of the student (e.g., age, gender, race/ethnicity, and language of the target participants). Following this framework potentially enables EBTs to be easily mapped onto a model that can become a useful resource for teachers, school-based mental health professionals, and administrators within the school setting.

SUMMARY

The discussion so far has focused on strategies for utilizing RTI to develop district-wide approaches to addressing student mental health issues. Much of the existing RTI work focuses on behaviors or academic performance that occur in the classroom. Resources for applying RTI to behavioral concerns that may extend beyond the school (e.g., externalizing, internalizing, ADHD, substance abuse, mental health) are somewhat limited. Consequently, while this approach may be new to some school settings, RTI can be used with academic and behavioral-oriented issues. This section describes several implications, challenges of utilizing an RTI approach, and necessary future directions for moving RTI into new areas.

Implications

Our review suggests that RTI, a framework originally designed to address academic issues, can be extended to developing school district–wide plans for addressing behaviors and problems that, although they may originate outside of the school setting, certainly influence academic outcomes. Earlier, we presented examples of using an RTI approach to address substance involvement and PTSD symptoms. However, RTI may also be useful for selecting appropriate EBTs to address mental health issues (e.g., anxiety, social anxiety) and risky behaviors (e.g., sexual risk behaviors) other than substance abuse and PTSD symptoms. (See Chapter 18, "Mental Health Intervention Case Studies.")

In addition, the vignettes described earlier demonstrated that busy school staff might benefit from a decision-tree format. The decision tree provides an efficient method for selecting the most appropriate EBT for a specific adolescent. Our cases illustrated the use of an RTI decision tree to select an appropriate EBT for two very specific concerns: substance use and PTSD symptoms. Obviously, each school system will need to develop its own decision tree tailored to the needs of its students and the EBTs available to their schools.

Challenges

Despite the benefits of an RTI approach, school systems implementing RTI may encounter several significant challenges. First, some EBTs may not fit neatly into the RTI format. In addition, some EBTs that focus on more than one behavior (e.g., substance abuse and conduct disorder) may not be appropriate for adolescents requiring a Tier 1 intervention for one problem but a Tier 3 intervention for the other. For example, MDFT has demonstrated effectiveness for students with Tier 3 level substance abuse and acting out behaviors (e.g., anger control, impulsive behaviors). Therefore, the appropriateness of MDFT for an individual demonstrating acting out behaviors but no substance use is unclear.

A second challenge facing an RTI approach is the selection of EBTs demonstrating effectiveness for diverse classrooms. Tier 1 and Tier 2 interventions are, by definition, meant for larger groups of students (perhaps even entire classrooms). If these groups are ethnically diverse, it may be difficult to identify a specific EBT with demonstrated efficacy for each ethnic group. Furthermore, it may be unfeasible for a school to select separate Tier 1 and/or Tier 2 interventions for the different ethnic groups. Instead, the school might select an intervention proven effective for the largest number of students. Since Tier 3 interventions are more likely to be individually tailored, classroom diversity is less of an issue.

A third challenge is that a small number of interventions appropriate for most students may be less effective for a specific subgroup. For example, Dishion (1995) found that participating in a small group, Tier 2 type, substance abuse prevention EBT actually had the iatrogenic effect of reinforcing deviant behavior in a group of at-risk Caucasian youth. This may be a particular concern when implementing school-wide Tier 1 interventions.

The training required to deliver EBTs is another challenge to implementing an RTI in school systems. Teachers and other school personnel typically implement Tier 1 and 2 interventions. Conceivably, however, an appropriate EBT may require more training in mental health than most teachers and other school officials have acquired. For example, among those articles in our decision tree reporting the amount of time required to train teachers or counselors to implement the EBT, the minimal amount of training required was 8 hours. The costs (e.g., teacher or counselor salaries and trainer costs) of providing adequate training may exceed the training budgets of many school systems. Moreover, the costs of providing Tier 3 interventions that are typically individualized and require mental health specialists may be even higher.

We have argued for the use of RTI to match students to interventions appropriate for their individual needs. Educators and mental health professionals need to take considerable care in assessing, determining an appropriate tiered intervention, monitoring, and validating the RTI-EBT efficacy for the target student(s).

Future Directions

Our overall conclusion is that an RTI approach may assist school systems in meeting the mental health needs of their students. However, several steps may facilitate the future use of RTI to address problems that originate outside the classroom but affect academic outcomes. First, classifying EBTs as appropriate Tier 1, 2, or 3 interventions is an essential task for the future. Classifying EBTs at the national level would be much more efficient than relying on individual school systems to accomplish that task.

Second, an important component of leveraging RTI-EBTs is ensuring their appropriateness for the target students. (This is discussed further in Chapters 2 and 18.) Therefore, developing decision trees that inform school staff about the efficacy of an intervention is of paramount importance. However, more research examining the efficacy of EBTs with specific target groups is required to develop such decision trees.

CONCLUSION

The first aim of this chapter was to demonstrate the application of RTI to mental health issues that originate outside the classroom but may affect academic performance. A second aim was to expand the application of RTI by illustrating a strategy for considering the needs of diverse children and adolescents.

Prior evidence has demonstrated that using the RTI framework to match students to appropriate EBTs for school-based problems is effective and has successfully improved adolescent outcomes. This chapter expands RTI to include problem behaviors that originate outside the school setting but also influence academic outcomes. Categorizing interventions according to problem, target student demographic characteristics, and efficacy are all important. Use of algorithms such as the proposed decision tree can benefit school officials deciding which EBT best fits a student.

Future research is needed to determine the most effective EBT for specific target groups. The evidence for using RTI in other applications is strong, and this chapter aids in broadening its use for mental health.

RESOURCES

RTi success.org

Life Skills Training Middle School (LST-MS)

Botvin, G. J., Batson, H., Witts-Vitale, S., Bess, V., Baker, E., & Dusenbury, L. (1989). A psychosocial approach to smoking prevention for urban black youth. *Public Health Reports, 104*, 573–582.

Botvin, G. J., & Botvin, E. M. (1992). Adolescent tobacco, alcohol, and drug abuse: Prevention strategies, empirical findings, and assessment issues. *Journal of Developmental and Behavioral Pediatrics, 13*, 290–301.

Botvin, G. J., Griffin, K. W., Diaz, T., & Hill-Williams, M. (2001). Drug abuse prevention among minority adolescents: Posttest and one-year follow-up of a school-based preventative intervention. *Prevention Sciences, 2*(1), 1–13.

Cognitive-Behavioral Intervention for Trauma in Schools (CBITS)

Stein, B. D., Jaycox, L. H., Katoaka, S. H., Wong, M., Tu, W., Elliot, M. N., & Fink, A. (2003). A mental health intervention for school children exposed to violence. *Journal of the American Medical Association, 290*(5), 603–611.

Multidimensional Family Therapy (MDFT)

Liddle, H. A., Dakof, G. A., Parker, K., Diamond, G. S., Barrett, K., & Tejeda, M. (2001). Multidimensional family therapy for adolescent drug abuse: Results of a randomized clinical trial. *American Journal of Drug and Alcohol Abuse, 27*(4), 651–688.

REFERENCES

Adelman, H. S., & Taylor, L. (2010). *Mental health in schools: Engaging learners, preventing problems and improving schools.* Thousand Oaks, CA: Corwin Press.

APA Presidential Task Force on Evidence-Based Practice. (2006). Evidence-based practice in psychology. *American Psychologist, 61*(4), 271–285.

Blondin, C. A., Skinner, C. H., Parkhurst, J., Wood, A., & Snyder, J. (2010). Enhancing on-task behavior in fourth-grade students using a modified color wheel system. *Journal of Applied School Psychology, 28*, 37–58. doi:10.1080/15377903.2012.643756

Botvin, G. J., Batson, H., Witts-Vitale, S., Bess, V., Baker, E., & Dusenbury, L. (1989). A psychosocial approach to smoking prevention for urban black youth. *Public Health Reports, 104*, 573–582.

Botvin, G. J., & Botvin, E. M. (1992). Adolescent tobacco, alcohol, and drug abuse: Prevention strategies, empirical findings, and assessment issues. *Journal of Developmental and Behavioral Pediatrics, 13*, 290–301.

Botvin, G. J., Griffin, K. W., Diaz, T., & Hill-Williams, M. (2001). Drug abuse prevention among minority adolescents: Posttest and one-year follow-up of a school-based preventative intervention. *Prevention Sciences, 2*, 1–13.

Brotman, L. M., Calzada, E., Huang, K., Kingston, S., Dawson-McClure, D., Kamboukos, D., & Petkova, E. (2011). Promoting effective parenting practices and preventing child behavior problems in schools among ethnically diverse families from underserved, urban communities. *Child Development, 82*, 258–276.

Denton, C. A., Tolar, T. D., Fletcher, J. M., Barth, A. E., Vaughn, S., & Francis, D. J. (2013). Effects of Tier 3 intervention for students with persistent reading difficulties and characteristics of inadequate responders. *Journal of Educational Psychology, 105*, 633–648. doi:10.1037/a0032581

Dishion, T., & Andrews, D. (1995). Preventing escalation in problem behaviors with high risk young adolescents: Immediate and 1-year outcomes. *Journal of Consulting and Clinical Psychology, 63*, 538–548.

Evans, S. W., Serpell, Z. N., Schultz, B. K., & Pastor, D. A. (2007). Cumulative benefits of secondary school-based treatment of students with attention deficit hyperactivity disorder. *School Psychology Review, 36*, 256–273.

Farrell, A. D., Meyer, A. L., & White, K. S. (2001). Evaluation of responding in peaceful and positive ways (RIPP): A school-based prevention program for reducing violence among urban adolescents. *Journal of Clinical Child Psychology, 30*, 451–463.

Franklin, C. G. S., Kim, J. S., Ryan, T. N., Kelly, M. S., & Montgomery, K. L. (2012). Teacher involvement in school mental health interventions: A systematic review. *Child and Youth Services Review, 34*(5), 973–982.

Gresham, F. (2007). Response to intervention and emotional and behavioral disorders. *Assessment for Effective Intervention, 32*, 214–222.

Hawken, L. S., Vincent, C. G., & Schumann, J. (2008). Response to intervention for social behavior: Challenges and opportunities. *Journal of Emotional and Behavioral Disorders, 16*, 213–225.

Henggeler, S. W., Borduin, C. M., Melton, G. B., Mann, B. J., Smith, L., Hall, J. A., . . . Fucci, B. R. (1991). Effects of multisystemic therapy on drug use and abuse in serious juvenile offenders: A progress report from two outcome studies. *Family Dynamics of Addiction Quarterly, 1*, 40–51.

Horn, K. A., Dino, G. A., Kalsekar, I. D., & Fernandes, A. W. (2004). Appalachian teen smokers: Not on tobacco 15 months later. *American Journal of Public Health, 94*, 181–184. Retrieved from http://dx.doi.org/10.2105%2FAJPH.94.2.181

Huey, S., & Polo, A. (2008). Evidence-based psychosocial treatments for ethnic minority youth: A review and meta-analysis. *Journal of Clinical Child and Adolescent Psychology, 37*(1), 262–301.

Kumpfer, K. L., DeMarsh, J. P., & Child, W. (1989). *Strengthening families program: Children's skills training curriculum manual, parent training manual, children's skills training manual, and family skills training manual.* Salt Lake City, UT: University of Utah, Social Research Institute.

Liddle, H. A., Dakof, G. A., Parker, K., Diamond, G. S., Barrett, K., & Tejeda, M. (2001). Multidimensional family therapy for adolescent drug abuse: Results of a randomized clinical trial. *American Journal of Drug and Alcohol Abuse, 27*, 651–688.

Marsiglia, F. F., Ayers, S., Gance-Cleveland, B., Mettler, K., & Booth, J. (2012). Beyond primary prevention on alcohol use: A culturally specific secondary prevention program for Mexican heritage adolescents. *Prevention Sciences, 13*, 241–251. doi:10.1007/s11121-011-0263-0

Masia-Warner, C., Klein, R. G., Dent, H. C., Fisher, P. H., Alvir, J., Albano, A. M., & Guardino, M. (2005). School-based intervention for adolescents with social anxiety disorder: Results of a controlled study. *Journal of Abnormal Child Psychology, 33*, 707–722. doi:10.1007/s10802-005-7649-z

Merikangas, K. R., He, J., Burstein, M. E., Swanson, S. A., Avenevoli, S., Cul, L., . . . Swendsen, J. (2010). Lifetime prevalence of mental disorders in U.S. adolescents: Results from the national co-morbidity study-adolescent supplement (NCS-A). *Journal for the American Academy of Child and Adolescent Psychiatry, 49*, 980–989.

Nathan, P. E., & Gorman, J. (2002). Efficacy, effectiveness, and the clinical utility of psychotherapy research. In P. E. Nathan & J. Gorman (Eds.), *A guide to treatments that work* (2nd ed., pp. 642–654). New York, NY: Oxford University Press.

National Center on Response to Intervention. (2010). Essential components of RTI—A closer look at response to intervention. Retrieved from http://www.RTI4success.org

Shapiro, E. S. (2011). *Academic skills problems: Direct assessment and intervention* (4th ed.). New York, NY: Guilford.

Stein, B. D., Jaycox, L. H., Katoaka, S. H., Wong, M., Tu, W., Elliot, M. N., & Fink, A. (2003). A mental health intervention for school children exposed to violence. *Journal of the American Medical Association, 290*, 603–611.

Stevens, S., Leybas-Amedia, V., Bourdeau, B., McMichael, L., & Nyitray, A. (2006). Blending prevention models: An effective substance use and HIV prevention program for minority youth. *Child and Adolescent Social Work Journal, 23*, 4–23. doi:10.1007/s10560-005-0027-4

U.S. Department of Education. (2005). *27th annual report to Congress on the implementation of the Individuals with Disabilities Education Act, 2004.* Washington, DC: Author.

Winters, K. C., Fahnhorst, T., Botzet, A., Lee, S., & Lalone, B. (2012). Brief intervention for drug-abusing adolescents in a school setting: Outcomes and mediating factors. *Journal of Substance Abuse Treatment, 42*, 279–288. doi:10.1016/j.jsat.2011.08.00

CHAPTER 2

Screening At-Risk Students for Mental Health Intervention

AMITY L. NOLTEMEYER

LEARNING OUTCOMES

On completion of this chapter, the reader should be able to:

- Understand the nature and prevalence of risk factors for student mental health challenges and the rationale for mental health screening
- Comprehend the screening process used to identify students who may be at risk for mental health conditions
- Compare and contrast screening instruments that can be used within a school-based multitiered system of support
- Identify steps needed to construct and implement a universal screening process in the schools

Between 12% and 27% of young people experience externalizing behavior problems, depression, and anxiety; however, only one sixth to one third of these youths receive mental health treatment (Weist, Rubin, Moore, Adelsheim, & Wrobel, 2007). Unfortunately, unaddressed mental health issues can contribute to several unfavorable individual and societal outcomes, including suicide (Fried, Williams, Cabral, & Hacker, 2013) and criminal arrest (Copeland, Miller-Johnson, Keeler, Angold, & Costello, 2007; Greenbaum et al., 1996). In order to prevent and address these circumstances through early identification and treatment, the New Freedom Commission on Mental Health (2003) recognized mental health screening as one of six goals for transforming mental health care in America.

Universal mental health screening serves an ameliorative function, given evidence that significant disabilities can be prevented for at-risk children who are identified through a screening process and consequently receive appropriate classroom-based supports (U.S. Department of Education Office of Special Education and Rehabilitative Services, 2002). However, only 2% to 3% of schools engage in mental health screening, and many schools that do so fail to effectively link screening results to intervention (Vannest, 2012). This chapter aims to address this need by reviewing school-based mental health screening practices that can be used to identify students for appropriate supports, thereby minimizing unfavorable developmental trajectories.

Students entering schools experience a variety of conditions that place their social–emotional development at risk. Poverty, food insecurity, learning disabilities, exposure to violence, poor parental monitoring, peer rejection, residential instability, and engaging in drug/alcohol use all have the potential to disrupt normal child development (see Hanson & Carta, 1995; Noltemeyer, 2014, for a review of some of these risks). Unfortunately, data suggest these risks are ubiquitous. For example, 28% of students reported being a victim of bullying at school (Robers, Zhang, Truman, & Snyder, 2012). Beyond school, 9.8% of children and adolescents had witnessed an assault in their families; 18.6% reported having been victims of maltreatment themselves; and 28.7% reported having witnessed a community assault during their lives (Finkelhor, Turner, Ormrod, & Hamby, 2009). Additionally, roughly 20% of children live in poverty, and these figures are substantially higher for children living in single-parent homes and those who were African American and Latino (RAND Corporation, 2005). These are merely a few indicators that reveal the complex challenges students and educators face in the classroom. In order to address this risk-saturated milieu, schools are increasingly using a multitiered system of support (MTSS) to identify student needs and provide supports to prevent risks and enhance functioning.

A three-tiered model, based on the public health model, is a commonly utilized MTSS for preventing and addressing student behavioral and mental health concerns. In Tier 1 (also known as primary prevention), all students receive high-quality core instruction in social–emotional competencies concurrent with school-wide programming designed to prevent or minimize risk factors. In this tier, students may also participate in school-wide screenings to identify those who may be at risk for concerns. Students identified as being at risk enter Tier 2 (also known as secondary prevention), where they are provided with supplemental targeted instruction in the areas of need. Progress monitoring data are also collected to examine these students' performance trends and responses to the interventions. Those who are not sufficiently responding to Tier 2 supports may progress to Tier 3 (also known as tertiary prevention), where they receive highly individualized and research-based interventions. These students continue to be progress-monitored, and interventions are intensified as needed based on the data. Across all these tiers, as much as possible, supports should be evidence-based, data-driven, and culturally responsive; additionally, they may focus on teaching skills and coping mechanisms, minimizing risk factors, or enhancing protective factors (Noltemeyer, 2014).

Because students at risk for mental health problems could benefit from prevention and early intervention initiatives within this MTSS, psychometrically rigorous universal screening tools are needed to effectively and efficiently identify these young people and their needs. Although this chapter focuses exclusively on Tier 1 social–emotional/mental health screening, it is important to note that mental health risk often exists concurrent with academic deficits. For this reason, integrated multitiered models of behavior and academic support may be more effective than either academic or behavior models in isolation (McIntosh, Chard, Boland, & Horner, 2006; Stewart, Benner, Martella, & Marchand-Martella, 2007). Therefore, readers are encouraged to supplement this chapter with resources focusing on the integration of academic and behavioral screening data (Kalberg, Lane, & Menzies, 2010; Lane, Menzies, Oakes, & Kalberg, 2012).

EVIDENCE-BASED RESEARCH AND PRACTICE

Population-based screening is a cost-effective way to identify individuals who may be at risk for developing mental health concerns (Dever, Raines, & Barclay, 2012). These types of screenings minimize the likelihood that students "fall through the cracks," failing to be considered for needed services. For example, Huskey et al. (2011) found that school-based mental health screening identified a significantly greater percentage of youths in need of mental health services than did traditional referral procedures. Refuting initial speculation that mental health screening may be viewed as intrusive or unacceptable by stakeholders, recent data suggest that screening programs are generally acceptable and do not produce undue distress for participants (Robinson et al., 2011).

Despite the relatively recent emergence of mental health screening in the schools, several types of screening systems can be utilized within Tier 1 of a MTSS. Brief descriptions of select multiple-gating, single-stage, and specialized systems are provided in the following sections. Supplementary information on each of these screening tools can be found in Table 2.1.

TABLE 2.1 Comparison of Several Mental Health Screening Instruments/Systems

Instrument	Description	Target Population	Informants	Number of Items and/or Time to Complete	Additional Information
Behavioral and Emotional Screening System (BESS; Kamphaus & Reynolds, 2007)	Rating scale designed to assess behavioral and emotional risk	Preschool (ages 3–5) and child/adolescent (Grades K–12) forms	Teacher, parent, and student forms (student forms only for Grades 3–12)	25–30 items, depending on the form; roughly 5 minutes–10 minutes per student	Electronic and online scoring options are available; Spanish versions of the parent and student forms; component of a larger system of assessment/intervention products
Columbia SuicideScreen (CSS; Shaffer et al., 2004)	Measures suicide risk via suicidal ideation, suicide attempts, negative mood, and substance abuse	Intended for high school students (Shaffer et al., 2004), but has been studied on populations as young as age 11 (Scott et al., 2009)	Student	11 items	The 11 items are embedded within 36 general health/relationship items to avoid the focus on suicide risk
Early Screening Project (ESP; Walker, Severson, & Feil, 1995)	Three-stage screening process for internalizing and externalizing concerns; involves student nomination/ranking, behavior rating scales, and observation	Ages 3–5	Teacher (Stages 1 and 2), Parent (Stage 3), and other trained professional (Stage 3)	Less than 1 hour per class for Stages 1 and 2 (Lane et al., 2012)	Modeled after the Systematic Screening for Behavior Disorders (SSBD; Walker & Severson, 1990); available for no cost* at esp.ori.org
Office Disciplinary Referrals (ODRs)	A record of student misbehavior resulting in referral to the school administrator	All students attending schools that use ODRs as a disciplinary consequence	Teachers and/or other school staff	Depends on the method used to track ODRs, which could require varying amounts of information about the incident	

Instrument	Description	Population	Administered by	Items/Time	Notes
School-Wide Positive Behavior Support (SWPBS) expectations	School-developed rating scale where items are the school's SWPBS expectations	All students attending schools implementing SWPBS	Teachers and/or other school staff	Depends on the number of SWPBS expectations at the school, but typically between 3–5 items	
Social Skills Improvement System (SSIS; Gresham & Elliott, 2008)	Rating scale that assesses prosocial behavior, motivation to learn, reading skills, and math skills	Ages 3–18 (preschool, elementary, and secondary versions)	Teachers	Approximately 25 minutes–30 minutes to screen a classroom	Part of a system that also includes more intensive rating scales and intervention guides; electronic scoring available
Strengths and Difficulties Questionnaire (SDQ; Goodman, 1997)	Behavior rating scale that assesses internalizing problems, externalizing problems, and prosocial behavior	Ages 3–16 for the informant report; ages 11–16 for the self-report	Teacher, parent, and adolescent forms	25 items	Available for no cost* in more than 50 languages
Student Risk Screening Scale (SRSS; Drummond, 1994)	Rating scale that assesses primarily antisocial and externalizing behaviors	Initially developed for Grades K–6, but preliminary evidence supports use in Grades 6–12	Teacher	7 items; approximately 10 minutes–15 minutes to complete on an entire class	No cost*
SSBD (Walker & Severson, 1990, 2014)	Three-stage process to identify students at risk for emotional or behavioral disorders; involves student nomination/ranking, behavior rating scales, and observation (third stage is optional, but recommended)	Initially designed for Grades 1–6, but validation studies have been conducted on middle school students as well	Teacher (Stages 1 and 2) or other trained professional (Stage 3)	Less than 1 hour per class for Stages 1 and 2	A revised and updated version of the SSBD will be available in 2014 as part of the Screening, Identification, and Monitoring System (SIMS); option for online administration and scoring

*No cost other than labor, printing (when necessary), and so forth.

Multiple-Gating Systems

Multiple-gating systems use several stages of increasingly individualized assessment to identify students who need additional supports. One three-stage system, the Systematic Screening for Behavior Disorders (SSBD; Walker & Severson, 1990, 2014), is designed to identify students at risk for emotional or behavioral disorders. A revised and updated version of the SSBD, including a new 7,000-norm sample with the option for online administration/scoring, will be available in 2014 as part of the Screening, Identification, and Monitoring System (SIMS). In Stage 1 of the SSBD, teachers identify 10 students in the class whose behavior is most like recognized internalizing behaviors (and subsequently 10 different students whose behavior is most like externalizing behaviors), and rank order how much they are like these behaviors. The three highest ranked students on the internalizing behaviors and the three highest ranked on the externalizing behaviors progress to Stage 2, where the teachers complete two more detailed behavioral rating scales on each student. Students who pass through Stage 2 can be considered to have at least moderate risk (McKinney, Montague, & Hocutt, 1998, as cited in Walker, Cheney, Stage, & Blum, 2005). Finally, for those students with elevated Stage 2 scores, a trained professional who is not the classroom teacher conducts two direct systematic observations in two settings for each student. Extensive research evidence has been accumulated documenting multiple forms of reliability and validity of the SSBD, suggesting it is effective at screening for both clinically recognized externalizing and internalizing problems (see Walker & Severson, 2014, for a thorough review).

The Behavioral and Emotional Screening System (BESS; Kamphaus & Reynolds, 2007) can also be used as an initial step in a multiple-gating process that is followed by more comprehensive and individualized assessments. A component of the Behavior Assessment System for Children-2 (BASC-2) family of assessments, the BESS is a rating scale designed to assess behavioral and emotional risk. The BESS consists of two teacher forms (preschool for ages 3–5 and child/adolescent for grades K–12), one student self-report form (child/adolescent for grades 3–12), and two parent report forms (preschool for ages 3–5 and child/adolescent for grades K–12). Respondents read each item and answer whether the statement *never, sometimes, often,* or *almost always* applies to the child. Results are reported in T-scores to identify students who are in the normal range, elevated risk range, and extremely elevated risk range. It is recommended that students with elevated BESS scores have the more intensive BASC-2 rating scales (Reynolds & Kamphaus, 2004) administered; those who evidence elevated scores on the BASC-2 should be identified for Tier 2 intervention (Kamphaus & Reynolds, 2007). In addition to strong reliability and validity data presented in the manual

(Kamphaus & Reynolds, 2007), the BESS has been shown to significantly predict student behavioral outcomes (Chin, Dowdy, & Quirk, 2013).

Single-Stage Assessments

Unlike these multiple-stage processes, some screening systems involve a single-stage application. For example, the Student Risk Screening Scale (SRSS; Drummond, 1994) is a no-cost, teacher-completed rating scale that assesses primarily antisocial and externalizing behaviors. The SRSS, comprised of seven items, takes approximately 10 to 15 minutes to complete on an entire class. Teachers use a 4-point Likert scale (i.e., *never, occasionally, sometimes, frequently*) to rate each child on the following behaviors: steals; lies, cheats, sneaks; behavior problems; peer rejection; low achievement; negative attitude; and aggressive behavior. A total score is derived that places students into low-, moderate-, and high-risk categories. In addition to being used as a screening assessment, the SRSS can also be used to examine changes in student risk status over time (Lane, Kalberg, Bruhn, Mahoney, & Driscoll, 2008). The instrument has been found to have excellent accuracy predicting externalizing and internalizing behavior problems (Lane et al., 2009). Although specificity and sensitivity were both found to be excellent for externalizing behavior, and specificity was also excellent for internalizing behaviors, sensitivity was poor for internalizing behaviors.

The Strengths and Difficulties Questionnaire (SDQ; Goodman, 1997) is another no-cost, single-stage assessment. Unlike the SRSS, the SDQ can be completed by parents (for ages 3–16), teachers (for ages 3–16), and students (for ages 11–16). Although it originally had five subscales, recent research by Goodman, Lamping, and Ploubidis (2010) suggested a three-subscale division is better for screening typical populations: internalizing problems (emotional and peer symptoms, 10 items), externalizing problems (conduct and hyperactivity symptoms, 10 items), and the prosocial scale (5 items). When completing the SDQ, the informant reads each item and responds whether it is *not true, somewhat true,* or *certainly true* about the child. Total raw scores on each scale are used to place children in *normal, borderline,* and *abnormal* ranges. Research has suggested that when given to multiple informants (parents, teachers, older children), the SDQ has a specificity of 80% and a sensitivity of 85% in identifying individuals with psychiatric diagnoses (Goodman, Ford, Corbin, & Meltzer, 2004).

Local Data Systems

Although nationally standardized behavior rating scales such as those just described often provide desirable levels of psychometric rigor for a mental health screening system, locally created data can also be used to screen students. For example, Office Disciplinary Referrals (ODRs), an index of student misbehavior that leads to a referral to the building administrator, can be used to identify students who need Tier 2 support. Although varying guidelines on the use of ODRs for this purpose have been reported, McKevitt and Braaksma (2008) suggested that Tier 2 intervention may be warranted for a student with three to five ODRs in a year but who isn't displaying significantly dangerous behaviors; in contrast, Tier 3 support may be needed for a student with six or more ODRs in a year or one who demonstrates dangerous or significantly disruptive behaviors. Despite the ease and potential utility of using ODRs as a screening mechanism, particularly for students who have multiple ODRs, caution is also warranted. For example, relying *only* on ODR data could be problematic because ODRs have been found to have a high degree of false negatives (i.e., failure to detect a concern when it exists), particularly under-identifying students with internalizing behavior concerns (McIntosh, Campbell, Carter, & Zumbo, 2009; Nelson, Benner, Reid, Epstein, & Currin, 2002).

Researchers have also recently begun to explore the use of School-Wide Positive Behavior Support (SWPBS) expectations as a screening alternative to behavior rating scales and ODRs (Burke et al., 2012). SWPBS is a tiered model of support in which Tier 1 consists of establishing school-wide behavioral expectations, teaching them, encouraging expected behaviors, discouraging problematic behaviors, and using data to drive decisions (Lewis & Sugai, 1999). In schools implementing SWPBS, a brief rating scale can be developed where the items are the school's SWPBS expectations and teachers are asked to rate the degree to which each student meets each expectation. Although this does not assess the entire spectrum of mental health or behavioral issues, it does allow schools to screen children based on local normative behavioral expectations. Results have documented moderate to strong relationships among SWPBS expectation ratings and outcome measures of externalizing problems, school problems, and adaptive skills, but not internalizing problems (Burke et al., 2012). This method has the benefit of providing schools with a screening option congruent with local initiatives (Burke et al., 2012). However, because very little research has examined this use of SWPBS expectations, limited reliability and validity data have been produced.

Specialized Instruments

Although the reviewed screening tools represent viable options for schools to consider, they do not constitute an exhaustive list of measures available for more specialized concerns and populations. For instance, the Columbia SuicideScreen (CSS; Shaffer et al., 2004) is used to screen populations for suicide risk; and the

Social Skills Improvement System (SSIS; Gresham & Elliott, 2008) focuses primarily on social skills. In addition, the Early Screening Project (ESP; Walker, Severson, & Feil, 1995) is specifically designed to assess risk in preschool children.

RECOMMENDATIONS FOR CRAFTING THE SYSTEM IN YOUR SCHOOL

Schools interested in establishing mental health screening should adopt a systematic process for planning, implementing, and evaluating the system. Although this process should be individualized to align with context-specific needs and resources, the following six steps can provide direction.

Step 1: Establish School Leadership Team

A building leadership team (BLT[1]) should be assembled to help plan and evaluate the screening process. This team, working collaboratively with grade-level teacher teams to translate plans into practice, should include diverse representation. At a minimum, the BLT should be composed of at least one mental health service provider with a strong background in mental health and assessment (e.g., school psychologist), one administrator, one regular education teacher, and one special education teacher. Ideally, team members should have different backgrounds and work with students across the age spectrum. Within the BLT, individuals should be assigned roles to ensure effective and efficient processes (e.g., facilitator, note-taker, timekeeper).

Step 2: Identify Key Areas to Screen and Select Appropriate Screening Instrument(s)

The BLT should identify the key foci of its screening based on the needs of the school and any extant data. For example, is externalizing behavior a concern? Is a broad measure of functioning desired? After identifying the foci of the screening, according to Glover and Albers (2007), research should be conducted to evaluate potential screening instruments on a variety of dimensions: (a) *appropriateness* for the intended use (e.g., alignment with constructs of interest, population fit); (b) *technical adequacy* (e.g., reliability, validity); and (c) *usability* (e.g., feasibility of administration, acceptability, utility of outcomes).

Step 3: Plan for Implementation

After selecting the screening instrument(s), school-based teams should carefully plan for implementation. One consideration during this planning phase involves parental consent. State and district policies on consent vary, with some utilizing passive consent and others requiring active consent (see Lane et al., 2012).

For more details, see Chapter 4 covering law, ethics, and school policy. It is important to consult district, state, and professional laws and ethical guidelines to ensure consent is obtained ethically and legally. In addition, it is critical to consider which informants to use in the screening process (e.g., teachers, parents, children). In deciding upon informants, the BLT should consider student age, student and rater characteristics, and what is being screened for, in addition to any practical considerations (Dowdy & Kim, 2012). Professional development and training are also essential to take into account. It is important that school staff understand the reason for the screening, the procedures, and the anticipated outcomes. Finally, logistics should be systematically planned for. Who will conduct the screening? When? Where? How? Schools vary in how screenings are conducted to make them most effective and efficient. Some schools administer teacher report screenings during professional development events or planning time, and handle student report screenings during a homeroom period (Dever et al., 2012).

Step 4: Administer Screening

The screening should be administered in accordance with the developed plan. Assessment proctors should use scripts to ensure standardized administration (Dever et al., 2012). Plans should be in place to address any unanticipated events that may occur (e.g., student becomes emotional during the screening). In addition, if screening unearths concerns that put a student at immediate risk, action must be taken at once to ensure student safety and comply with legal and ethical guidelines. Finally, a team of trained professionals should score the assessments in accordance with the scoring guidelines. Across these procedures, the fidelity of implementation should be spot-checked by trained observers who can provide supportive feedback to improve implementation (e.g., if scoring errors are found, the observer can model appropriate scoring).

Step 5: Use Results to Drive Intervention

After the screening has been administered and scored, the BLT should reconvene to examine the results. Vannest (2012) recommended a four-phase process when using the results to drive intervention:

1. *Determine who to serve*—Various criteria can be used to identify students in need of more intensive services, and staff should have the opportunity to review the resulting list of students for validity to ensure appropriate identification for Tier 2 services.

2. *Determine when to serve*—Provide results and services within a responsible time frame following the screening.
3. *Determine what services to provide*—Identify evidence-based interventions that match the school's composition, philosophical orientation, and capacity.
4. *Decide who will provide the intervention services and identify what support they will need to do so*—Identify who has the skill set and resources to implement the intervention(s), and plan for a rapid follow-up to provide feedback and discuss implementation progress.

Although a full review of evidence-based interventions that may be selected as part of this process extends beyond the scope of this chapter, readers are referred to repositories that house rigorous effectiveness data. For example, the National Registry of Evidence-based Programs and Practices (nrepp.samhsa.gov/Index.aspx) and the What Works Clearinghouse (ies.ed.gov/ncee/wwc) both include searchable data-based reviews of a variety of school-based mental health interventions.

Step 6: Evaluate Progress

In order to determine if interventions require modifications or alterations in intensity, it is important to collect frequent and repeated measurement of target behavior(s). This can be accomplished in a variety of ways (e.g., direct behavior ratings, repeated systematic observations, intervention results), depending on the focus and nature of the intervention, but should be methodologically and psychometrically defensible.

CASE STUDY

A case study is presented to illustrate a process that might be used to plan for, implement, and evaluate a school-based mental health screening program.

Reason for Referral

Educators at Smith Elementary School were concerned about the increasing number of student externalizing problem behaviors (fights, classroom aggression and disruptions, bullying) observed in the school.

Background/History

Attended by 648 students in the first grade through fifth grade, Smith Elementary serves an ethnically and economically diverse community on the fringe of an urban area in the Midwest. In response to teacher concerns about student behavior, 2 years ago the principal at Smith began systematically analyzing its discipline data. A clear upward trend in problematic behaviors emerged; the number of ODRs per 100 students per day increased from 0.50 to 2.65 between 2010 and 2013, compared to the state average of 0.41 per 100 students per day. The number of suspensions was similarly increasing, and a downward trend in achievement scores emerged concurrent with the upward trend in behavioral issues. As a result of these concerns, the principal and several teachers recently attended a workshop on positive behavior supports implemented within a MTSS, and became interested in implementing the model.

Overview of Current Practices

In addition to academic screenings conducted three times per year, Smith teachers currently collect ODR data using office referral forms created by the principal. The forms ask for the student's name, date, time of incident, and narrative description of the incident. The information on the number of disciplinary referrals from these forms, as well as the number of any subsequent suspensions and expulsions, are entered into a database maintained by the school; however, this information is mainly used for state reporting purposes. Most often, students with repeated referrals receive punitive consequences (e.g., after-school detention, in-school suspension, out-of-school suspension) rather than skill-building interventions. There is no systematic method for determining who receives intervention supports or what types of supports they receive, and these decisions are often based on what one teacher described as a "squeaky wheel gets the oil" approach.

Conceptualization

The BLT met in August and identified externalizing behavior problems as its primary target. Team members reviewed data such as disciplinary records, bully reports, teacher referrals for disruption, and wished they possessed more school climate survey data. When considering the current process for identifying students in need of supports in this area, they identified the following immediate needs: (a) a systematic method for identifying which students would benefit from further mental health intervention; and (b) a school-wide curricular initiative to prevent large numbers of students from needing supplementary intervention services. Based on these needs, the BLT identified its initial goals as developing (a) a mental health screening program, focusing primarily on externalizing behaviors; and (b) a universal SWPBS program.[2] Although they sought to accomplish the former using methods that were psychometrically rigorous, they also recognized significant financial and personnel constraints that inhibited the cost and time-intensive nature of the work that could initially be undertaken.

Assessment Goals and Plan

Planning for the mental health screening program, the BLT first inventoried current practices and extant data. The team agreed that ODR data could be useful within this screening process, although modifications to the data collection and analysis procedures were warranted. They decided to alter the ODR forms to include additional information about the type of misbehavior, location, and time of misbehavior so that data could be disaggregated by these characteristics and subsequently be used to inform intervention decision making. In addition, they established a plan for more systematically tracking and using the ODR information. Specifically, it was decided that the BLT would compile ODR data quarterly and a representative would be assigned to review the information with grade-level teams (GLTs) at quarterly data meetings.[3]

The BLT also determined that ODRs in isolation did not provide the amount of depth or psychometric rigor they sought in a screening system. They extensively researched available rating scales that could be used in conjunction with ODRs to drive decision making. After comparing several options, they selected the SRSS (Drummond, 1994) due to its focus on externalizing behaviors, strong technical properties, ease of use, and cost. The BLT decided to begin with a twice yearly SRSS administration, so that they could present the results concurrent with the ODR facts at two of the four quarterly GLT data meetings.

After making the decision to move forward with these two measures, the BLT planned for collecting consent, training staff, and implementing the assessments. The new ODR forms were implemented in December, and the SRSS was completed in January during a teacher in-service day. The SRSS was scored the subsequent day by a team of trained scorers.

Efficacy Measures/Intervention Assessment

The BLT met a week after the SRSS administration to review the data. One team member presented tables and graphs with both aggregated (i.e., entire school) and disaggregated (i.e., grade levels, classrooms, individual students) data for ODRs and the SRSS. The BLT established the following criteria to identify students for Tier 2 intervention: (a) those who fell within the medium-risk category on the SRSS and had more than one ODR; (b) those who fell within the high-risk range on the SRSS, regardless of whether they had an ODR; and (c) those who had at least six ODRs. Social validity was also checked via teacher confirmation to minimize the likelihood of false positives or false negatives. For example, a few students did not meet these criteria but were strongly considered to be at risk by the classroom teachers based on infrequent but very extreme behaviors. After this vetting process, a BLT representative met with each GLT to determine what intervention supports were warranted from the data and plan for implementation and progress monitoring. Each GLT developed its own intervention and progress-monitoring plan, which was reviewed within its own GLT meetings monthly.

Case Prognosis/Summary/Referral or Future Direction

The BLT was pleased overall with this initial screening experience, and resolved to continue using ODRs and the SRSS the following year. However, the team experienced some difficulty linking assessment to intervention and decided to focus more the following year on professional development to assist with identifying appropriate Tier 2 and Tier 3 supports informed by data. In conjunction with GLTs, they also decided to develop an "intervention menu" at each grade level specifying several ongoing Tier 2 interventions and decision criteria for students to enter them. Additionally, the BLT decided to track the overall percentage of students identified as having elevated scores across the year, in order to determine whether the Tier 1 programming was effective. Finally, due to several teachers expressing concerns about the potential for the SRSS and ODRs to overlook students with internalizing behaviors, the BLT also made plans to explore whether to append the SRSS with a few school-developed items to assess internalizing behavior problems.

SUMMARY

Mental health screening in the schools is one mechanism for ensuring that students at risk for social–emotional difficulties are identified and receive appropriate services. There are a variety of assessments that can be used to screen students for mental health risk, each with its own characteristics and strengths. In order to effectively implement a mental health screening program, schools should establish a leadership team, identify key area(s) to assess, select a high-quality screening instrument, plan for implementation, implement the screening, use the results to drive intervention, and evaluate progress. Throughout this process, the focus should be on using the information to learn more about how to support students in a way that can prevent the development of pathology and support positive functioning.

As such, screening for mental health risk should be considered one piece of a larger MTSS that is designed to prevent mental health concerns and address student needs.

RESOURCES

Kamphaus, R. W. (Guest Ed.). (2012). Emotional and behavioral screening [Special issue]. *School Psychology Forum, 6*(4). This special issue, guest edited by Dr. Randy W. Kamphaus, is entirely devoted to the topic of emotional and behavioral screening in schools. Among other topics, the six articles included cover the social validity of screening, choosing informants when screening, practical considerations, and progress monitoring subsequent to screening.

Lane, K. L., Menzies, H. M., Oakes, W. P., & Kalberg, J. R. (2012). *Systematic screenings of behavior to support instruction: From preschool to high school.* New York, NY: Guilford. This book contains high-quality, user-friendly information on a variety of issues related to social–emotional screening in schools. The authors provide detailed information on many screening tools and utilize case studies to demonstrate their uses.

Illinois PBIS Network. (2013). *Universal screening for behavior.* Retrieved from http://www.pbisillinois.org/curriculum/ universalscreening. The Illinois PBIS (Positive Behavior Interventions and Supports) Network website contains a variety of information on universal screening for behavior, including an overview of the topic, implementation tools, scoring tools, and publications. Although some of the information is specific to this state initiative, the utility of much of it could be expanded to other areas.

NOTES

The author is grateful to Jessica Robertson, graduate student at Miami University, for her assistance with editing and formatting this chapter. The author also thanks Dr. G. Susan Mosley-Howard for her guidance and ideas.

1. The BLT may go by another name and likely engages in planning related to the entire MTSS process school-wide for both academics and behavior. In some schools, the BLT plans for these initiatives but a school-based data team evaluates the results and uses them to drive intervention. However, for this chapter, the BLT is conceptualized to engage in all aspects of the planning, implementation, and evaluation process.

2. The focus of this chapter is on the screening process. Although a universal SWPBS program should accompany this, the remainder of this case study focuses on the goal of implementing a mental health screening program.

3. In addition to the quarterly data meeting with the BLT representative, the GLTs meet among themselves once a week to review student progress and make curricular adjustments.

REFERENCES

Burke, M. D., Davis, J. L., Lee, Y.-H., Hagan-Burke, S., Kwok, O., & Sugai, G. (2012). Universal screening for behavioral risk in elementary schools using SWPBS expectations. *Journal of Emotional and Behavioral Disorders, 20*(1), 38–54. doi:10.1177/1063426610377328

Chin, J. K., Dowdy, E., & Quirk, M. P. (2013). Universal screening in middle school: Examining the behavioral and emotional screening system. *Journal of Psychoeducational Assessment, 31*(1), 53–60. doi:10.1177/0734282912448137

Copeland, W. E., Miller-Johnson, S., Keeler, G., Angold, A., & Costello, E. J. (2007). Childhood psychiatric disorders and young adult crime: A prospective, population based study. *American Journal of Psychology, 164*(11), 1668–1675.

Dever, B. V., Raines, T. C., & Barclay, C. M. (2012). Chasing the unicorn: Practical implementation of universal screening for behavioral and emotional risk. *School Psychology Forum: Research in Practice, 6*(4), 108–118.

Dowdy, E., & Kim, E. (2012). Choosing informants when conducting a universal screening for behavioral and emotional risk. *School Psychology Forum: Research in Practice, 6*(4), 98–107.

Drummond, T. (1994). *The student risk screening scale (SRSS)*. Grants Pass, OR: Josephine County Mental Health Program.

Finkelhor, D., Turner, H., Ormrod, R., & Hamby, S. L. (2009). Violence, abuse and crime exposure in a national sample of children and youth. *Pediatrics, 24*(5), 1411–1423. doi:10.1542/peds.2009-0467

Fried, L. E., Williams, S., Cabral, H., & Hacker, K. (2013). Differences in risk factors for suicide attempts among 9th and 11th grade youth: A longitudinal perspective. *The Journal of School Nursing, 29*(2), 113–122. doi:10.1177/1059840512461010

Glover, T. A., & Albers, C. A. (2007). Considerations for evaluating universal screening assessments. *Journal of School Psychology, 45*(2), 117–135. doi:10.1016/j.jsp.2006.05.005

Goodman, A., Lamping, D. L., & Ploubidis, G. B. (2010). When to use broader internalising and externalising subscales instead of the hypothesised five subscales on the strengths and difficulties questionnaire (SDQ): Data from British parents, teachers and children. *Journal of Abnormal Child Psychology, 38*(8), 1179–1191. doi:10.1007/s10802-010-9434-x

Goodman, R. (1997). The strengths and difficulties questionnaire: A research note. *Journal of Child Psychology and Psychiatry, 38*(5), 581–586.

Goodman, R., Ford, T., Corbin, T., & Meltzer, H. (2004). Using the strengths and difficulties questionnaire (SDQ) multi-informant algorithm to screen looked after children for psychiatric disorders. *European Child & Adolescent Psychiatry, 13*(2), 25–31. doi:10.1007/s10802-010-9434-x

Greenbaum, P. E., Dedrick, R. F., Friedman, R. M., Kutash, K., Brown, E. C., Lardieri, S. P., & Pugh, A. M. (1996). National Adolescent and

Child Treatment Study (NACTS): Outcomes for children with serious emotional and behavioral disturbance. *Journal of Emotional and Behavioral Disorders, 4*(3), 130–146.

Gresham, F. M., & Elliott, S. N. (2008). *Social skills improvement system (SSIS).* Minneapolis, MN: Pearson Assessments.

Hanson, M. J., & Carta, J. J. (1995). Addressing the challenges of families with multiple risks. *Exceptional Children, 62*(3), 201–212.

Huskey, M. M., Kaplan, A., McGuire, L., Flynn, L., Chrostowski, C., & Olfson, M. (2011). Identifying adolescents at risk through voluntary school-based mental health screening. *Journal of Adolescence, 34*(3), 505–511. doi:10.1016/j.adolescence.2010.05.018

Kalberg, J. R., Lane, K. L., & Menzies, H. M. (2010). Using systematic screening procedures to identify students who are nonresponsive to primary prevention efforts: Integrating academic and behavioral measures. *Education and Treatment of Children, 33*(4), 561–584.

Kamphaus, R. W., & Reynolds, C. R. (2007). *Behavior Assessment System for Children–Second Edition (BASC-2): Behavioral and Emotional Screening System (BESS).* Bloomington, MN: Pearson.

Lane, K. L., Kalberg, J. R., Bruhn, A. L., Mahoney, M. E., & Driscoll, S. A. (2008). Primary prevention programs at the elementary level: Issues of treatment integrity, systematic screening and reinforcement. *Education and Treatment of Children, 31*(4), 465–494.

Lane, K. L., Little, M. A., Casey, A. M., Lambert, W., Wehby, J., Weisenbach, J. L., & Phillips, A. (2009). A comparison of systematic screening tools for emotional and behavioral disorders. *Journal of Emotional and Behavioral Disorders, 17*(2), 93–105. doi:10.1177/1063426611417627

Lane, K. L., Menzies, H. M., Oakes, W. P., & Kalberg, J. R. (2012). *Systematic screenings of behavior to support instruction: From preschool to high school.* New York, NY: Guilford.

Lewis, T. J., & Sugai, S. (1999). Effective behavior support: A systems approach to proactive schoolwide management. *Focus on Exceptional Children, 31*(6), 1–24.

McIntosh, K., Campbell, A. L., Carter, D. R., & Zumbo, B. D. (2009). Concurrent validity of office discipline referrals and cut points used in schoolwide positive behavior support. *Behavioral Disorders, 34*(2), 100–113.

McIntosh, K., Chard, D. J., Boland, J. B., & Horner, R. H. (2006). Demonstration of combined efforts in school-wide academic and behavioral systems and incidence of reading and behavior challenges in early elementary grades. *Journal of Positive Behavior Interventions, 8*(3), 146–154.

McKevitt, B. C., & Braaksma, A. D. (2008). Best practices in developing a positive behavior support system at the school level. In A. Thomas & J. Grimes (Eds.), *Best practices in school psychology* (5th ed., pp. 735–748). Bethesda, MD: National Association of School Psychologists.

Nelson, J. R., Benner, G. J., Reid, R. C., Epstein, M. H., & Currin, D. (2002). The convergent validity of office discipline referrals with the CBCL-TRF. *Journal of Emotional and Behavioral Disorders, 10*(3), 181–188.

New Freedom Commission on Mental Health. (2003). *Achieving the promise: Transforming mental health care in America. Final report* (DHHS Pub. No. SMA-03-3832). Rockville, MD: Department of Health and Human Services.

Noltemeyer, A. (2014). Best practices in fostering student resilience. In A. Thomas & P. Harrison (Eds.), *Best practices in school psychology* (6th ed., pp. 225–238). Bethesda, MD: National Association of School Psychologists.

RAND Corporation. (2005). *Children at work: Consequences for school readiness and beyond* (RB-9144-PNC). Santa Monica, CA: Author.

Reynolds, C. R., & Kamphaus, R. W. (2004). *Behavior assessment system for children* (2nd ed.). Circle Pines, MN: AGS.

Robers, S., Zhang, J., Truman, J., & Snyder, T. D. (2012, February). *Indicators of school crime and safety: 2011.* Retrieved from National Center for Education Statistics website: http://www.eric.ed.gov/PDFS/ED529642.pdf

Robinson, J., Yuen, H. P., Martin, C., Huges, A., Baksheev, G. N., Dodd, S., . . . Yung, A. (2011). Does screening high school students for psychological stress, deliberate self-harm, or suicidal ideation cause distress—And is it acceptable? *Crisis, 32*(5), 254–263. doi:10.1027/0227-5910/a000087

Shaffer, D., Scott, M., Wilcox, H., Maslow, C., Hicks, R., Lucas, C. P., . . . Greenwald, S. (2004). The Columbia SuicideScreen®: Validity and reliability of a screen for youth suicide and depression. *Journal of the American Academy of Child and Adolescent Psychiatry, 43*(1), 71–79. doi:10.1097/01.chi.0000096370.43887.68

Scott, M. A., Wilcox, H. C., Schonfeld, I. S., Davies, M., Hicks, R. C., Turner, J. B., & Shaffer, D. (2009). School-based screening to identify at-risk students not already known to school professionals: The Columbia Suicide Screen. *American Journal of Public Health, 99*(2), 334–339.

Stewart, R. M., Benner, G. J., Martella, R. C., & Marchand-Martella, N. E. (2007). Three-tier models of reading and behavior: A research review. *Journal of Positive Behavior Interventions, 9*(4), 239–253. doi:10.1177/10983007070090040601

U.S. Department of Education Office of Special Education and Rehabilitative Services. (2002). *A new era: Revitalizing special education for children and their families.* Retrieved from http://education.ucf.edu/mirc/Research/President's%20Commission%20on%20Excellence%20in%20Special%20Education.pdf

Vannest, K. J. (2012). Implementing interventions and progress monitoring subsequent to universal screening. *School Psychology Forum: Research in Practice, 6*(4), 119–136.

Walker, B., Cheney, D., Stage, S., & Blum, C. (2005). Schoolwide screening and positive behavior supports: Identifying and supporting students at risk for school failure. *Journal of Positive Behavior Interventions, 7*(4), 194–204.

Walker, H. M., & Severson, H. H. (1990). *Systematic Screening for Behavior Disorders (SSBD).* Longmont, CO: Sopris West.

Walker, H. M., & Severson, H. H. (2014). *Systematic Screening for Behavior Disorders (SSBD) technical manual.* Eugene, OR: Pacific Northwest.

Walker, H. M., Severson, H. H., & Feil, E. G. (1995). *The early screening project: A provident child find process.* Longmont, CO: Sopris West.

Weist, M. D., Rubin, M., Moore, E., Adelsheim, S., & Wrobel, G. (2007). Mental health screening in schools. *Journal of Health, 77*(2), 53–58.

CHAPTER 3

Mental Health Integration and Collaboration Within Communities

SUSAN C. DAVIES

LEARNING OUTCOMES

On completion of this chapter, the reader should be able to:

- Define benefits of partnerships among schools, families, agencies, and religious institutions
- Understand challenges to family/school/community collaboration
- Conduct a needs assessment to identify valuable and meaningful activities for students, families, schools, and community members
- Identify evidence-based practices that effectively increase family and community involvement in schools
- Describe specific programs that facilitate integration of schools, families, agencies, and religious institutions

Children's development depends on numerous ecological systems: families, schools, communities, local agencies, and places of worship. To varying degrees, each system offers a distinctive opportunity for cognitive, social, emotional, academic, and spiritual development. Positive collaboration among the systems, however, not only improves individual student development, but also strengthens each of the collaborative entities. This is particularly true when examining professional collaboration for mental health services.

It is estimated that 1 in 5 children and adolescents (20%) has a mental disorder (Centers for Disease Control and Prevention [CDC], 2013; U.S. Department of Health and Human Services [HHS], National Institute of Mental Health [NIMH], 2013), yet many of these children do not receive adequate identification or treatment. Although the school is a logical place to locate and serve students with mental health needs, components of mental health services in schools have historically been marginalized, fragmented, or unnecessarily duplicated (Taylor & Adelman, 2000).

Alliances among schools, families, agencies, and places of worship can help address nonschool issues that affect students' educational performance. Certainly the school can serve as the lead agency in communicating among these entities and coordinating services. The school is a logical location for such services because a school requires attendance, is accessible to children and families, and may be less stigmatizing than private or public mental health clinics. In collaboration with local hospitals or community-based mental health venues, the school can also maximize resources, providing a range of prevention and treatment-oriented mental health services (Weist, Lever, & Stephan, 2004).

Such a collaborative effort is mutually beneficial. As schools acquire more support through additional staff and financial contributions, agencies can reach youths they might not otherwise serve. The school, family, and agency may all experience reduction of stress as well. When working alone, each is likely to perceive itself as the sole provider of mental health care; collaboration builds shared responsibilities.

Of course, such an undertaking requires that stakeholders think outside the box to enlist professionals from agencies and parents for support (Weist, Ambrose, & Lewis, 2006). It also demands an initial understanding of both benefits and barriers to effective collaboration, as well as the identification of specific evidence-based practices and programs that increase positive collaborative efforts. This chapter provides a description of the history and current trends in collaboration for school-based mental health care, obstacles to successful home–school–community collaboration, and research-based strategies for overcoming such challenges.

BACKGROUND

Historical Trends in Collaboration

The notion of family–school–community collaboration is not a new one. An examination of past research and of historical trends in collaborative programming provide background and reasoning for the contemporary practice of professional collaboration. Hundreds of years ago, parents generally assumed control of children's schooling; however, the idea that the school should direct academic endeavors became popular about 60 years ago in the United States (Hiatt-Michael, 2006). In fact, this tension between parent control and school control of academic endeavors exists around the world, and there is lively debate about ultimate responsibility.

In the 1960s a large research study was conducted as a direct response to the Civil Rights Act of 1964 (Coleman, 1966). Coleman's report to the U.S. Department of Education provided results from a national survey focusing on problems related to academic achievement experienced by children from lower socioeconomic homes. These data provided evidence of significant differences in academic achievement among students from different socioeconomic levels: Students from middle- and upper-class families had higher GPAs and graduated from high school and college at higher rates. The data also showed that the effect of factors outside of the school on student academic achievement was greater than the effect of factors in the school. The Coleman Report sparked dialogue on the value of parental involvement in school, political action, and novel educational research. Federal legislation during the following decade addressed ways to fund programs at schools with high numbers of underachieving and economically disadvantaged students. These programs included Head Start and Title 1.

In 1973, Don Davies promoted organized activity for family–community development by founding the Institute for Responsive Education (Hiatt-Michael, 2006). This was a forerunner of family–school collaboration action research. During that same decade, the Community Schools Act signaled government interest in the idea of schools as the center of the community. This act was designed to increase community involvement within the public school system and to allow community-based agencies, including mental health agencies, to utilize the schools' facilities.

In the 1980s, Joyce Epstein from Johns Hopkins University brought the National Network of Partnership Schools together. Epstein has been an influential figure in family–school–community collaboration for decades. In her popular research model on overlapping spheres of influence (2011), she described how the role of schools should be a shared enterprise among the family, the school, and the community—with the individual child at the center. This model is reflected throughout this chapter. During that same decade, the Robert Wood Johnson Foundation funded the first national school-based health initiative. Although that effort was primarily concerned with physical health care, recognition of the need to integrate mental health services into school-based programs followed. These expanded school mental health (ESMH) programs provide comprehensive mental health services to youths and families within the school setting, including assessment, treatment, prevention, case management, and consultation (Acosta, Tashman, Prodente, & Proescher, 2002).

In the late 1990s, after-school programs garnered federal support, which brought financial backing to school-linked services. In 2004, more than six million school-aged children participated in after-school programs (Dodd & Bowen, 2011). Recent policy statements from the federal government also support the expansion of school-based mental health services.

Contemporary Practice

The 2003 report from the President's New Freedom Commission on Mental Health (NFCMH) provided impetus for those involved in child and adolescent mental health to consider ways to improve the system of care. The commission emphasized the importance of a full continuum of community-based services for children and families, as well as a recommendation to improve and expand school mental health programs. The tiered model of school-based services, when paired with links to the home and community, is an ideal way of providing this full continuum of services.

In most states, learning about parent involvement is part of the required standards for teacher licensure. Parent involvement is also part of the No Child Left Behind Act (U.S. Department of Education, 2001). This bolsters the idea that there is broad support for educators to embrace parents as an important part of the educational process. However, rather than focusing solely on increasing parent involvement, contemporary practice in collaboration requires consideration of more comprehensive school-based mental health service delivery.

BENEFITS OF PARTNERSHIPS

Summaries of research on parent and community involvement (e.g., Epstein, 2011; Henderson & Mapp, 2002) confirm its importance across cultures, school types, and geographic areas and illustrate the following general benefits.

Benefits for Students and Schools

Collaborative partnerships among schools, families, and agencies can result in improved student performance, particularly in reading and math (Epstein & Dauber, 1991; Henderson & Mapp, 2002; Sheldon, 2003). Students whose parents meet various criteria for *involved* and who live in communities that provide support programs within the school also tend to have better attendance, more positive attitudes and behavior, improved goal-setting, higher self-esteem, and more pride in school work (Bryan, 2005; Darsch, Miao, & Shippen, 2004; Jeynes, 2003). Their learning needs are better supported, and often school is made to be more relevant in their lives. For schools, there is often a more efficient use of funds and less redundancy of programs and services.

Benefits for Families

Families who feel welcome and valued in their local schools tend to have higher satisfaction with the schools (Sheldon, 2003). Those who benefit from school-based services often become more interested in "giving back" to their school and community; they might provide social support for other students and families, participate in decision making within the school, and help create a fuller sense of community.

Benefits for Community Members

Community groups can bring a wealth of resources to the school by creating school-linked programs that provide services for children and families. Such groups include social service agencies, faith-based institutions, businesses, safety and security agencies, cultural groups and museums, legal services, health services, and higher education institutions. Formalizing these connections can restore community vitality. For example, families may patronize local restaurants that contributed t-shirts to a school walk-a-thon fundraiser. Adolescents may remember the friendly police officer who visited their school and exhibit greater respect for law enforcement. Parents may appreciate church or temple members who volunteered to tutor their children and attend worship services at their religious institutions. Elementary school students may have volunteers from the nature center conduct a program at their school and use a voucher provided by the center to gain discounted admission over the weekend. Such mutually beneficial collaborations can help keep all stakeholders invested in continuing to build relationships. This community of caring within and outside of the school is vital to students' mental health and well-being.

CHALLENGES TO SUCCESSFUL PARTNERSHIPS

Many families, schools, community agencies, and religious organizations experience similar challenges when attempting collaboration: Scarcity of time and resources are overarching themes. The following sections describe some of the specific challenges experienced by each stakeholder, as well as additional issues that may be encountered.

Challenges in Families

Various challenges, including economic constraints, lack of transportation, an unwelcoming school environment, and narrow concepts of parent involvement, contribute to minimal parent participation at school (Christenson, Godber, & Anderson, 2005; Friend & Cook, 2010; Johnson, Pugach, & Hawkins, 2004). Many families have two working parents who may work long and/or erratic hours, making it difficult for them to come to school during the day or to evening events. Further, the "need it now" culture in the United States has led to a shift in many occupations requiring workers to be available at all hours. Some parents have positions that require extensive travel or late hours to accommodate global business needs. Often parents are required to take personal days or unpaid days to come to school for meetings or events. Some parents may feel they lack the skills to help their children. For example, parents who speak English as a second language may have difficulty helping their children with homework and therefore feel disconnected from the children's school and educational experience. Whereas technological changes in communication—such as e-mails, texting, and newsfeeds—often facilitate home–school collaboration, they can be overwhelming for some families who feel inundated by technological communications and feel dissatisfied by this type of social interaction. This could also prove difficult for families without access to technology or those who do not speak English.

Challenges in Schools

Although the No Child Left Behind Act (2001) addressed the importance of parent involvement, this same act has also led to a focus among educators and administrators on standards and testing. Often this is at the expense of what are perceived as noneducational student needs, including mental health needs. School-based mental health providers are often limited by competing demands. For example, the school psychologist may be overwhelmed by assessment work, the school counselor by academic guidance, and the school social worker by truancy issues. Whereas most schools provide some type of mental health services, these are often limited to students who are eligible for special education or referred for special education evaluation.

Some educators are concerned that parents are not involved enough in addressing their children's academic or behavioral challenges. Other teachers define parental involvement only as the parents' complying with their requests; such teachers see themselves as the experts and may overlook the value of eliciting input and two-way communication/collaboration with the parents. Still other teachers may be wary of working with parents perceived as difficult or angry. In fact, many educators have cited problematic interactions with parents as a reason for their departure from the teaching profession (Smithers & Robinson, 2003). Distant teacher–parent relationships may often be rooted in teacher resistance and fear of dealing with the unknown. For example, the new ninth-grade teacher may hesitate to call the parents of a student who seems withdrawn because she knows the parents are highly educated and significantly older than she.

Or the veteran third-grade teacher may reject the idea of reaching out to the parents of a misbehaving student because the parents speak English as a second language and the teacher is wary of the language difference.

In addition to perceiving a lack of parental involvement, educators sometimes must deal with incongruence between their own values and those of the parents. These might include rules at home, discipline types and consistency, goal-setting, or how parents model behavior. For example, the parents—and the community in which the school resides—may accept physical discipline, a form of discipline that goes against the teacher's moral code. Or a child may be told by his parents that if he is hit, he should hit back, although this same behavior would likely have him suspended from school. This, in turn, can lead to a contentious relationship between the home and school.

Few teacher preparation programs beyond special education and early childhood include specific coursework or activities related to parent involvement (Bingham & Abernathy, 2007; Epstein, 2011; Greenwood & Hickman, 1991; Harris, Jacobson, Hemmer, & Harvard Family Research Project, 2004; Zygmunt-Fillwalk, 2006). Thus, many new teachers may enter their profession unprepared to resolve a variety of situations with parents. This is especially problematic for teachers who enter their first classrooms to teach students from cultures different from their own. The principal is typically central in faculty selection and may choose faculty members who are not well trained in working with families. In other scenarios, schools with apathetic administrators or high principal turnover may find weak leadership another barrier to family–school–community involvement.

Challenges in Agencies and Religious Organizations

Community agencies and places of worship face some challenges similar to those experienced by schools—lack of time, lack of resources, and difficulty coordinating services with other providers. Traditional community settings such as mental health centers and private practices many find clients have difficulty transporting themselves to sessions. They may also have to deal with insurance obstacles and bureaucracy, such as arduous paperwork and confusing policies. Religious institutions wishing to become more involved in schools may be uncertain about their roles and about boundaries related to separation of church and state.

Fractured Services

Various professionals, organizations, programs, and providers may be serving the same child or family with little or no collaborative efforts. Further, a family may have children attending multiple schools within the community (e.g., elementary, middle, and high schools). If several children in the family are having problems, each child likely works with staff from each school—staff who never develop a cohesive intervention plan or work with the family in a unified way. Special "add-on" after-school or summer programs are well intended but may also lack collaboration with classroom teachers in order to enhance what is happening every day in the classroom (Taylor & Adelman, 2000). Such piecemeal approaches, without a coordinating provider, interfere with initiatives to prevent and ameliorate childhood mental health problems.

Fractured Relationships

Most school-based professionals have heard of or participated in the what-we-hate-about-parents conversation. They may feel the parents are neglectful or difficult, or they may feel parents make excuses for their children's poor schoolwork or behavior. This may be rooted in a hidden standard or expectation that all parents should behave in a certain manner. Or professionals may have an unexplored bias against families who do not value education in the same way they do, and assume that parents who appear uninvolved in their children's education do not love their children. Teacher educators report that many preservice teachers have unacceptable stereotypes of parents with low income, parents who do not speak fluent English, and parents from other marginalized groups (Epstein, 2013). Teachers who have such negative attitudes toward children or their families may, in fact, contribute to their failure.

Likewise, most parents have heard of or participated in the what-we-hate-about-teachers conversation. They might complain about their children's homework load or inconsistent discipline in the classroom. Or they might recount their own negative experiences with a harsh or incompetent teacher and describe symptoms of anxiety upon reentering a school building, now on their children's behalf. Such parents might be resistant to attending back-to-school nights, parent conferences, and open houses. Successful team-building often requires a level of collaboration with which families and educators may be unfamiliar.

Turf Issues

In addition to challenges in relationships between educators and families, coordinated school-based mental health services can raise concerns of school personnel about threats to job security. School employees may be concerned that their district will contract out support services. Others may have proprietary worries about their roles or their kids in the school being served by outsiders.

A number of professionals can provide mental health services in schools: school psychologists, school counselors, school social workers, clinical psychologists, clinical social workers, counseling psychologists, nurses, and child psychiatrists. The expanded school mental health framework calls for these disciplines to increasingly interact with each other. Such cross-disciplinary work is challenging because it requires a new mind-set and, in many cases, new skills.

EVIDENCE-BASED RESEARCH AND PRACTICE

Although a number of research studies have been published in academia on the positive effects of professional collaboration and family involvement in school (Bryan, 2005; Darsch et al., 2004; Epstein, 2013; Henderson & Mapp, 2002), many of these findings are not evident in public practice. The following practices overcome the aforementioned challenges and barriers to effective integration of school, home, and community. Whereas the mental health services that end up being provided by community and school-based mental health providers likely involve targeted (Tier 2) or intensive, individualized (Tier 3) therapeutic techniques, the following evidence-based practices generally involve universal supports for all students, staff, and settings (Tier 1).

School-Linked Services

Connecting social service agencies to physical school sites can generate a number of benefits (Clayton, Chin, Blackburn, & Echeverria, 2010; Dryfoos, 2005; Weist et al., 2006). The concept of school-based service integration centers (also referred to as full-service schools or school-linked services) involves placing the school at the center of the community as a place where social services, health and dental care, and mental health counseling might be received. Such programs might also provide before- and after-school programs, legal aid, provision of referral for such basic needs as food, clothing, and shelter, and even English classes and job training for parents. Public and private agencies work collaboratively with schools toward a shared goal of meeting the whole child's needs. Models vary in their composition, the intensity of services provided, and the mode of delivery (Bryan & Henry, 2012; Epstein, 1995; Epstein & Van Voorhis, 2010).

One example of school-linked mental health services is MindPeace in southwestern Ohio. The goal of this organization is to help children in the community gain access to mental health care. MindPeace links key community partners, including the children's hospital, the county board of mental health, the community learning center, and pediatricians with families and schools. This organization has partnered with a number of districts serving a diverse student population. The community mental health personnel provide services directly in schools. They accept Medicare or private insurance, depending on the student's circumstances. They can ensure continuity of care during school breaks and when students transition from elementary to high school.

Action Team

A team of stakeholders can form an action team to serve as an advisory committee or strategic planning group (Epstein et al., 2009, 2011; Sanders, 1996). This team facilitates the development, planning, and coordination of comprehensive school-based mental health resources. In an ongoing forum, the team can discuss issues such as unmet needs or gaps in services. Members of this team would include staff from different disciplines and agencies, such as school-based mental health providers (school psychologists, school counselors, school social workers), school nurses, special education staff, others who provide referrals and primary care, community members who provide school-linked services (clinical mental health therapists, volunteer tutors), a site administrator, representatives of enrichment and recreation programs, parents, and youths. The different professionals could help increase the others' knowledge of strategies and resources.

There might be significant overlap between this team and the school-based intervention assistance team that focuses on individual students' presenting problems, as well as overlap with school-based safety and crisis intervention teams. However, the purpose of this team is to focus on systems and resources and how they are functioning. Thus, the savvy administrator might use time efficiently by having an existing team expanded and charged with resource coordination.

The action team can identify unmet needs and evaluate what resources exist, how well they are used, what services might be redundant, and what services must be prioritized. For example, the school-based mental health providers might determine that the number of counseling groups needs to be increased so more students can begin treatment soon after referral. They might also find that multiple and fragmented volunteer tutoring programs exist within the school district and therefore charge one of the church volunteers with helping coordinate and schedule all volunteer tutors. Other existing programs that show promise or have been deemed effective can be similarly evolved by sharing space, sharing information, and building relationships.

Representatives from school-based action teams can then report to a *district-wide* or *regional council* to provide linkages among the schools. This is helpful when schools in the same area that share similar concerns and often interact with the same families can share resources, minimizing redundancy and cutting costs. This can also help integrate and improve the range of activities and address barriers to effective school-based mental health services. The district-wide council may also assist in identifying both training and funding opportunities for community collaboration, such as grants and business partnerships.

Needs Assessment

The action team can conduct a needs assessment to clarify specific barriers or challenges in a community or school district. In addition to exploring student and family needs, it is important for those involved in school-based mental health initiatives to evaluate the necessities of school systems, personnel, and relevant community entities. Unfortunately, needs assessments often overemphasize deficits and deemphasize assets, thereby ignoring system resources. A sound assessment should involve mapping supports and services that are already in place, analyzing cost and current resource use, redeploying resources that are not well used, and defining strategies to fill in gaps over time (Taylor & Adelman, 2000). Evaluators can map existing services and programs along a continuum (e.g., from Tier 1 to Tier 3, or from a range of mental health services of increasing intensity, as discussed in a following section).

Cohesive Policy Framework

Howard Adelman and Linda Taylor, codirectors of the Center for Mental Health in Schools at the University of California, Los Angeles, have spearheaded a workgroup that has developed research-based frameworks for guiding the expansion of school-based mental health services. Their comprehensive and multifaceted approach to blending public and private resources helps improve delivery of mental health services to students by combining parallel programs, connecting families across schools (e.g., elementary, middle, and high schools), and connecting agency resources to schools. In addition, according to Adelman and Taylor (1997) a range of services should be provided, from primary prevention (Tier 1: including quality after-school programs and positive behavior supports), to early intervention (Tier 2: encompassing parent-support groups, programs for students who are at risk), to treatment of severe mental health problems (Tier 3: including counseling, case management, referrals to agencies and programs).

By mapping and analyzing all resources, stakeholders can better understand what is already in place, use resources more efficiently, and avoid unnecessary duplication of services or programs. Newly developed services should complement existing programs and resources, evolving into a comprehensive, multifaceted, and integrated approach (Adelman & Taylor, 2002). A memorandum of understanding can help formalize mutual expectations of a professional collaboration.

Epstein's Keys to Success

Epstein (2009, 2011, 2013) describes six types of involvement as keys to successful partnerships among school, family, and community. These keys are italicized, followed by specific school-based mental health examples:

1. *Parenting—Assist families with parenting skills and setting home conditions to support children as students. Also, assist schools to better understand families.* Hold evening parent-education workshops, such as a workshop on how to tell when a child is ready to stay home alone and a workshop on how to manage defiant adolescents.

2. *Communicating—Conduct effective communications from school to home and from home to school about school programs and student progress.* Provide a folder in which the school can send communications to parents and vice versa; provide e-mail addresses for sending digital communications.

3. *Volunteering—Organize volunteers and audiences to support the school and students. Provide volunteer opportunities in various locations and at various times.* Initiate an after-school program staffed by community volunteers *that lets students choose from various interests, such as crafts, drama, gardening, cooking, reading, or homework help.* Such a program can help students build meaningful relationships with both peers and adults, creating positive links between the school and community members.

4. *Learning at home—Involve families with their children on homework and other curriculum-related activities and decisions.* Create a parent–child book group in which the parents and children read a specific book at home together and then come in to discuss the book. Select a book that tells a story of a child who experiences some social or emotional challenges that students can relate to.

5. *Decision making—Include families as participants in school decisions, and develop parent leaders and representatives.* Establish a principal's advisory committee to formalize a way for parents to engage in dialogue and decision making with school leaders.

6. *Collaborating with the community—Coordinate resources and services from the community for families, students, and the school, and provide services to the community.* Allow after-school groups, such as parent support groups, running clubs, and book clubs, to meet in the school after hours. Encourage school organizations, such as the band or choir, to provide free performances or services to nursing homes and hospitals in the community.

Teacher Training

Teacher preparation programs and professional development for certified teachers related to home–school–community collaboration can include sessions on communication skills, using volunteers in the school, making home visits, and more. Ideally, educating teachers to work with families and community members should start in their preservice education programs. Such instruction can focus on developing basic skills in working with diverse families in the school community.

This training cannot be expected to occur only on the job. Teachers can seek additional professional development in this crucial area, such as workshops or in-service trainings that prepare them to interact with parents (e.g., role-playing team meetings and conferences). Such training can focus on interpersonal skills such as empathy, verbal and nonverbal communication, and writing effective classroom newsletters. Professional development opportunities might also deepen teachers' understanding of a child's entire ecological system by addressing the culture of the student's community, working with family liaisons, and gaining knowledge about students' home lives that might affect their educational performance.

Paradigm Shift

Every school has a unique culture, and no guide can provide a foolproof, step-by-step way of developing effective collaborative school-based mental health services. It is important that any initiative takes into account the norms of the school and district, determining how to surmount the complexity of each setting. Following are five paradigm shifts that facilitate the development of effective professional collaborations.

Help the Disadvantaged Acquire Social Capital

In his historic research, French sociologist Bourdieu (1989) stressed that both *cultural capital*—a shared set of norms and insider information—and *social capital*—social connections—are needed to succeed within educational institutions. If students from minority cultural groups do not have equal access to cultural or social capital, they are at a disadvantage. This theory explains elitist, exclusionary practices that maintain class distinctions and privilege.

Acquiring social capital can help decrease educational inequality. This process requires a paradigm shift, including groups' trusting each other, forming a group or organization, and sharing common goals and belief systems (Putman, 2000). Sometimes parents, educators, and community groups are actively involved in building social and cultural capital but do not act in concert toward a shared goal of student well-being. Streamlining efforts among groups can fortify their activities; viewing community groups—particularly those representing ethnic minority groups—through a strength-based lens can facilitate use of community resources and bode well for their future (Martinez & Ulanoff, 2013).

Two-Way Communication

Effective school reformers invite and respond to voices from all stakeholders (Bryan, 2005; Bryan & Henry, 2012; Epstein, 1995; Epstein & Van Voorhis, 2010). Such bidirectional communication allows families to have their voices heard in school decisions affecting their children's lives and allows community members to share their concerns and suggestions (Bryan & Henry, 2012). This also involves mutual respect, rather than the usual setup in which school personnel are the experts who tell parents, the nonexperts, what their children need. Skills in this two-way communication can be built through role-plays in teacher training or professional development sessions. It is important that all participants develop cultural competence to maximize collaborative interactions. This involves understanding the sociocultural realities of different cultural, religious, and ethnic groups and being cognizant of how such differences might affect communication. In other words, what one participant sees as poor communication may, in fact, be a factor of another individual's personal background and manner of relaying information or feelings.

Administrators as Leaders

The development of the school administrator as a positive, collaborative leader can also set the tone of the school as a community rather than as a dictatorship. Although the teacher sets the tone for parent involvement in the classroom, it is essential that the building principal and district superintendent establish the climate for parent and community involvement. Administrators' willingness to connect to families and the community—to address their concerns and to share decision making—can be a significant factor in unlocking barriers to effective collaboration. The principal is also central in supporting community activities, connecting the school to community agencies, and coordinating such resources. This leader can also be a key player in adding new partners who can help connect all the pieces of school-based mental health services. A strong alliance between school leaders and leaders in community agencies is an effective way to build a sustainable professional collaboration (Auerbach, 2011; Sanders & Sheldon, 2009). Overall, successful school administrators can anticipate factors that inhibit effective home–school–community collaboration and can discern ways to effectively soften their impact. They can also promote evidence-based strategies that increase collaborative involvement.

Transdisciplinary Work

Professionals involved in collaborative school mental health efforts can advocate for role release—in which they work across disciplines. This reflects recent trends toward blended role training (Weist et al., 2006). Within this model it is important that existing providers not be displaced; instead, participants can mutually decide who does what. Equally crucial is avoiding typecasting people from other disciplines, which can pigeonhole them in unnecessarily narrow roles. For example, the generalization that school psychologists are testers overlooks their value as consultants and as systems change agents. And thinking of school principals as only disciplinarians ignores their talents in public relations and mediation.

Focus on the Positive

Having a strength-based lens can help dispel misguided perceptions educators may have about the families of their students and the communities in which they work (Martinez & Ulanoff, 2013). In fact, in most cases teachers will find that families and communities have a genuine interest in the education of their children; they may just not know how to be involved. By being culturally responsive to students and looking at family assets rather than deficits, educators can help increase student success. School-Wide Positive Behavior Support (SWPBS) is a tiered framework of prevention and intervention that involves teaching and encouraging prosocial behaviors. Data-based problem solving is used to address behavior concerns by providing students who continue to exhibit problems with progressively intensive services. Family–school–community collabration efforts can complement positive behavioral supports (PBS) initiatives in schools; relationship-building opportunities can be created and nurtured at all tiers in the process (Minke & Anderson, 2005).

One example of such positive efforts involves more formalized programs in character and civic education. Such initiatives bring together families, schools, and communities and can, in turn, enhance students' feelings of self-worth, as well as diminish community problems—particularly with adolescents. Such programs might involve cooperative learning, a service project, or a program in conflict resolution. Like SWPBS, such programs can lead to a reduction in number and severity of discipline problems (Berkowitz & Bier, 2004). To illustrate, a student who has vandalized school property would most likely be required to clean up what was defaced and might be required to complete a community service project instead of being suspended from school. Although a number of character and civic education programs exist in the United States, few have a specific component that involves parents; therefore, future collaborative efforts should consider remedying such a gap.

Program Evaluation

It is crucial that the action team document accomplishments and share the information with others through flyers or resource lists circulated among appropriate groups. This marketing technique can help sustain involvement and enthusiasm for school-based mental health collaborations. The team can also complete evaluation tools to plan programs and assess the quality of their practices. These might include questionnaires for all stakeholders (parents, students, teachers, community members) to obtain information about attitudes toward the school, partnerships, experiences, and expectations for future family and community involvement. These can also involve measures to assess annually the efficacy of specific activities and how well the action team is working together, as well as to document progress, discuss program strengths and weaknesses, and improve the program for the following year.

A program evaluation is a powerful mechanism for monitoring services. Rather than reporting only on how much various stakeholders *like* a collaborative opportunity, a program evaluation provides a more formal and more substantive approach to assessing the quality of a professional collaboration (e.g., by evaluating achievement of best-practice principles, performance on quality indicators, and student outcomes) and then pinpointing potential areas for improvement. By providing objective documentation of outcomes, the action team can better enhance program quality, while also holding providers accountable for their work (Weist et al., 2004). This type of sound program evaluation can help to define and sustain strong features of a professional collaboration that can endure even in times of tenuous funding.

CASE STUDY

Reason for Referral

Nick Z., 8 years old, exhibited somatic concerns including headaches and stomachaches, as well as disruptive behavior in the classroom. His third-grade teacher indicated he acted impulsively, was verbally and physically aggressive toward classmates, and did not complete assignments. He complained daily of physical ailments and visited the school nurse two to three times per week.

Background/History

Nick lived with his grandmother, Mrs. Z., and two younger brothers. Nick's grandmother reported that Nick and his brothers were left in her care by their mother 1 year earlier. Nick's father was in jail, serving a life sentence, and his mother had been in and out of treatment facilities for drug abuse since Nick's birth. She was currently living in another city with her boyfriend and his 2-year-old daughter. Nick's grandmother described him as a sweet but rambunctious boy and stated that she had difficulty managing the three young children. Nick received average grades and test scores from kindergarten through second grade but was now struggling to keep up with grade-level material in all subjects. Mrs. Z., a retired food service worker, expressed financial concerns, stating she was not receiving any financial support for the three children. She considered returning to work to help support the children, but stated she could not afford childcare for Nick's younger brothers. Mrs. Z. spoke English as her second language and had no knowledge of community resources. She lived in a one-bedroom mobile home in a trailer park. Her limited English proficiency hampered her ability to help Nick with his homework. Further, Mrs. Z did not have legal custody of Nick and his brothers.

Overview of Current Intervention(s)

Nick's teacher, Mrs. Q, is currently using Tier 1 behavior supports in the classroom, including the Good Behavior Game, to reinforce the entire class for following the rules and demonstrating appropriate behavior. Data collected during the first 6 weeks of the school year indicated Nick required more intensive behavior management.

Conceptualization

Classroom observation across dates and settings indicated Nick was off-task 68% of the time; typical same-age boys were off-task only 12% of the time. Nick's off-task behaviors included being out of his seat, calling out in class, and talking to other students during instruction. Interviews with his grandmother and teacher noted he often appeared tired (putting his head down, closing his eyes). His teacher mentioned he seemed hungry; he took food from other students' plates at the lunch table. Behavioral checklists showed elevated levels of hyperactivity, attention problems, and aggression, as well as poor social skills. However, evaluation of background data, observations, and interviews suggested these behavior patterns emerged only over the past year. Thus, rather than focusing exclusively on possible within-child variables (e.g., a neurological disorder), it was hypothesized that Nick's behaviors may have been exacerbated by ecological factors, including the absence of his parents and the uncertain financial situation in his grandmother's home. This was supported by the fact that he was relatively successful in kindergarten through second grade.

Intervention Goals and Plans

- The school counselor will include Nick in her social skills group. Sessions involve direct instruction, role-plays, and cognitive-behavioral strategies that focus specifically

on students' keeping their hands to themselves, asking others to play, and decreasing inappropriate verbal outbursts.
- Because she does not have legal custody, Nick's grandmother cannot sign consent for educational services. His case manager and the Department of Children's Services (DCS) worker will collaborate to obtain physical custody forms for Mrs. Z and help to transfer Aid to Families with Dependent Children benefits from Nick's biological mother to Mrs. Z.
- Nick will receive a full medical evaluation by the community-based physician who contracts with the school to rule out medical factors for his behaviors.
- The teacher will provide appropriate academic modifications, including extended time on tests, cues to pay attention, and self-monitoring of work completion.
- Nick's grandmother, with the assistance of the DCS, will begin formal guardianship proceedings.
- The school social worker will assist Mrs. Z with completing the necessary paperwork to gain legal custody and to apply for permanent government-subsidized housing. He has already helped Mrs. Z enroll in a local English as a second language (ESL) class.
- Nick will attend the after-school homework club coordinated by the local church, where he can complete homework with assistance and receive a snack.

Efficacy Measures/Intervention Assessment

- The efficacy of the intervention will be evaluated by time on-task, quarterly grades, and behavior checklists.

Case Prognosis/Summary/Referral or Future Direction

Nick's case involved close collaboration among the school, Nick's family, school-based mental health providers, the Department of Mental Health (DMH), the DCS, and community volunteers. Nick now exhibits greater self-control, reduced somatic symptoms, and appears happier at home and school. Nick, his brothers, and their grandmother are receiving counseling services from a community mental health therapist at the school to deal with emotional issues related to the absence of Nick's mother and father. Because of a referral from the school to a community support group, Nick's grandmother also attends a support group for caretakers of children with attention deficit hyperactivity disorder (ADHD), where she can share experiences with other parents and guardians and receive parenting support. She has also enrolled in a 6-week parenting course offered at the school by a local agency. The collaborative support provided by the school, local agencies, and church have helped not only Nick but also his grandmother and younger brothers. Once Nick's brothers were in school, Mrs. Z decided she wanted to "give back" and began serving as a school-based tutor for children who spoke English as a second language.

SUMMARY

There is clearly a need for schools, students' families, community agencies, and places of worship to merge efforts and resources to better meet the mental health needs of children and adolescents. Appropriate policy, planning, programs, and services can be integrated into schools and communities to better address barriers to effective mental health services and implement systemic change.

Schools have historically held a central role in communities. In addition to educating students, they can serve as community learning centers that offer educational, social, and recreational activities to both children and adults. They can serve as an ideal location for providing integrated mental health services. Improvement in student achievement can be facilitated through school-based mental health services that are multifaceted and comprehensive. Action teams can help districts understand the needs and resources that exist for children and how they can be used more effectively. Continued attention and collective efforts in practices designed to improve how school and community members communicate, lead, and perceive others can facilitate effective reforms in delivering mental health services to children.

RESOURCES

The University of Maryland's Center for School Mental Health administers the Baltimore School Mental Health (www.schoolmentalhealth.org) Technical Assistance and Training Initiative. This website offers resources for clinicians, educators, families, students, and individuals who work with children in foster care. It also provides web-based trainings on Trauma-Focused Cognitive-Behavioral Therapy; presentations on specific traumas; newsletters; and PowerPoint presentations on various topics related to working with children and adolescents.

The Center on School, Family, and Community Partnerships (www.csos.jhu.edu/p2000/center.htm) conducts and distributes research regarding collaboration among schools, families, and communities and its effect on student learning and development. The website offers links to research articles, textbooks, and other materials on the importance of collaboration.

The National Network of Partnership Schools (www.csos.jhu.edu/p2000) works with the Center on School, Family, and

Community Partnerships and advocates for collaboration among schools, states, and organizations to create programs that will foster family and community involvement. The website also disseminates important research results regarding collaboration, legislative updates, and information regarding professional development workshops.

Communities in Schools (www.communitiesinschools.org) is an organization that facilitates relationships with local agencies, businesses, and service providers who offer resources to promote learning for all students, especially those at risk of dropping out. The website offers links to publications, ways to donate or help, and success stories.

The National Coalition for Parent Involvement in Education (NCPIE; www.ncpie.org) works at the national level to advocate for family involvement in education. The website provides key resources and important legislative updates regarding education and how families can get involved to enhance student learning and success. The website also details how partnerships with communities and schools can greatly enhance students' educational experiences.

REFERENCES

Acosta, O. M., Tashman, N. A., Prodente, C., & Proescher, E. (2002). Establishing successful school mental health programs: Guidelines and recommendations. In H. S. Ghuman, M. D. Weist, & R. M. Sarles (Eds.), *Providing mental health services to youth* (pp. 57–94). New York, NY: Brunner-Routledge.

Adelman, H. S., & Taylor, L. (1997). Mental health in schools and system restructuring. *Clinical Psychology Review, 19*, 137–163.

Adelman, H. S., & Taylor, L. (2002). Building comprehensive, multi-faceted, and integrated approaches to address barriers to student learning. *Childhood Education, 78*(5), 261–268. doi:10.1080/00094056.2002.10522738

Auerbach, S. (2011). *School leadership for authentic family and community partnerships: Research perspectives for transforming practice.* New York, NY: Routledge.

Berkowitz, M. W., & Bier, M. C. (2004). Research-based character education. *The Annals of the American Academy of Political and Social Science, 591*, 72–85. doi:10.1177/0002716203260082

Bingham, A., & Abernathy, T. V. (2007). Promoting family-centered teaching: Can one course make a difference? *Issues in Teacher Education, 16*(1), 37–60.

Bourdieu, P. (1989). Social space and symbolic power. *Sociological Theory, 7*, 14–25.

Bryan, J. (2005). Fostering educational resilience and achievement in urban schools through school–family–community partnerships. *Professional School Counseling, 8*, 219–227.

Bryan, J., & Henry, L. (2012). A model for building school–family–community partnerships: Principles and process. *Journal of Counseling and Development, 90*, 408–420.

Centers for Disease Control and Prevention. (2013). *Mental health surveillance among children—United States, 2005–2011*. Morbidity and Mortality Weekly Reports (MMWR), *62*(suppl, 2013, May 16), 1–35. Retrieved from http://www.cdc.gov/mmwr/preview/mmwrhtml/su6202a1.htm

Christenson, S. J., Godber, Y., & Anderson, A. R. (2005). Critical issues facing families and educators. In E. N. Patrickakaou, R. P. Weissberg, S. Redding, & H. J. Walberg (Eds.), *School-family partnerships for children's success* (pp. 21–39). New York, NY: Teachers College Press.

Clayton, S., Chin, T., Blackburn, S., & Echeverria, C. (2010). Different setting, different care: Integrating prevention and clinical care in school-based health centers. *American Journal of Public Health, 100*(9), 1592–1597. doi:10.2105/AJPH.2009.186668

Coleman, J. S. (1966). *Equality of educational opportunity*. Washington, DC: U.S. Government Printing Office.

Darsch, C., Miao, Y., & Shippen, P. (2004). A model for involving parents of children with learning and behavior problems in the schools. *Preventing School Failure, 48*(3), 24–35.

Dodd, A. T., & Bowen, L. M. (2011). 21st century community learning centers—improving the academic performance of at-risk students: A Bronx tale. *Journal of Health and Human Services Administration, 34*(1), 11–41.

Dryfoos, J. (2005). Full-service community schools: A strategy—not a program. *New Directions for Youth Development, 107*, 7–14. doi:10.1002/yd.124

Epstein, J. L. (1995). School/family/community partnerships: Caring for the children we share. *Phi Delta Kappan, 76*, 701–712.

Epstein, J. L. (2011). *School, family, and community partnerships: Preparing educators and improving schools* (2nd ed.). Boulder, CO: Westview Press.

Epstein, J. L. (2013). Ready or not? Preparing future educators for school, family, and community partnerships. *Teaching Education, 24*(2), 115–118. doi:10.1080/10476210.2013.786887

Epstein, J. L., & Dauber, S. L. (1991). School programs and teacher practices of parent involvement in inner-city elementary and middle schools. *The Elementary School Journal, 91*, 289–305.

Epstein, J. L., & Van Voorhis, F. L. (2010). School counselors' roles in developing partnerships with families and communities for student success. *Professional School Counseling, 14*, 1–14.

Epstein, J. L., Sanders, M. G., Sheldon, S., Simon, B. S., Salinas, K. C., Jansorn, J. R., . . . Williams, K. J. (2009). *School, family, and community partnerships: Your handbook for action* (3rd ed.). Thousand Oaks, CA: Corwin Press.

Friend, M., & Cook, L. (2010). *Interactions: Collaboration skills for school professionals* (6th ed.). Upper Saddle River, NJ: Pearson Education.

Greenwood, G. E., & Hickman, C. W. (1991). Research and practice in parent involvement: Implications for teacher education. *The Elementary School Journal, 91*(3), 279–288.

Harris, M. M., Jacobson, A., & Hemmer, R. (2004). *Preparing teachers to engage parents.* Cambridge, MA: Harvard Family Research Project.

Henderson, A. T., & Mapp, K. L. (2002). *A new wave of evidence: The impact of school, family, and community connections on student achievement.* Austin, TX: Southwest Educational Development Laboratory.

Hiatt-Michael, D. (2006). Reflections and directions on research related to family–community involvement in schooling. *The School Community Journal, 16*(1), 7–30.

Jeynes, W. H. (2003). A meta-analysis: The effects of parental involvement on minority children's academic achievement. *Education and Urban Society, 35,* 202–218.

Johnson, L. J., Pugach, M. C., & Hawkins, A. (2004). School–family collaboration: A partnership. *Focus on Exceptional Children, 36*(5), 1–12.

Martinez, E., & Ulanoff, S. (2013). Latino parents and teachers: Key players building neighborhood social capital. *Teaching Education, 24*(2), 195–208. doi:10.1080/10476210.2013.786891

Minke, K. M., & Anderson, K. J. (2005). Family-school collaboration and positive behavior support. *Journal of Positive Behavior Interventions, 7*(3), 181–185.

President's New Freedom Commission on Mental Health. (2003). *Achieving the promise: Transforming mental health care in America—final report* (DHHS publication SMA-03-3832). Rockville, MD: U.S. Department of Health and Human Services.

Putman, R. D. (2000). *Bowling alone: The collapse and revival of American community.* New York, NY: Simon & Schuster.

Sanders, M. G. (1996). Building family partnerships that last. *Educational Leadership, 54,* 61–66.

Sanders, M. G., & Sheldon, S. B. (2009). *Principals matter: A guide to school, family, and community partnerships.* Thousand Oaks, CA: Corwin Press.

Sheldon, S. B. (2003). Linking school–family–community partnerships in urban elementary schools to student achievement on state tests. *The Urban Review, 35*(2), 149–165.

Smithers, A., & Robinson, P. (2003). *Factors affecting teachers' decisions to leave the profession* (Research Report No. RR430). Liverpool, England: University of Liverpool, Centre for Education and Employment Research, Department of Education and Skills.

Taylor, L., & Adelman, H. S. (2000). Toward ending the marginalization and fragmentation of mental health in schools. *Journal of School Health, 70,* 210–215. doi:10.1111/j.1746-1561.2000.tb06475.x

U.S. Department of Education. (2001). *No child left behind act.* Retrieved October 1, 2013, from http://www.ed.gov/policy/elsec/leg/esea02/index.html

U.S. Department of Health and Human Services, National Institute of Mental Health. (2013). *Any disorder among children.* Retrieved from http://www.nimh.nih.gov/statistics/1anydis_child.shtml

Weist, M. D., Ambrose, M. G., & Lewis, C. P. (2006). Expanded school mental health: A collaborative community-school example. *Children and Schools, 28*(1), 45–50. doi:10.1093/cs/28.1.45

Weist, M. D., Lever, N. A., & Stephan, S. H. (2004). The future of expanded school mental health. *Journal of School Health, 74*(6), 191–227. doi:10.1111/j.1746-1561.2004.tb07925.x

Zygmunt-Fillwalk, E. M. (2006). The difference a course can make: Preservice teachers' perceptions of efficacy in working with families. *Journal of Early Childhood Teacher Education, 27*, 327–342. doi:10.1080/10901020600996026

School-Based Law, Ethics, and Mental Health Services

DEBORAH PERGAMENT

MARY KAY KLIMESH

LEARNING OUTCOMES

On completion of this chapter, the reader should be able to:

- Understand the legal framework that guides providing mental health services to youths and families within the educational setting
- Recognize the intersection of law, ethics, and school policy
- Define basic elements of professional practice such as duty, confidentiality, privilege, privacy, and informed consent
- Know how standards of care are impacted by select educational and health laws
- Comprehend the ethical decision-making process that guides the work of mental health services' delivery
- Recognize when professional supervision or legal counsel should be sought in response to an ethical or legal issue

Mental health professionals working in schools frequently must consider a confusing array of professional codes of ethics, federal and state laws, and school policies that govern their professional activities and obligations. They must recognize and respect the rights of students and families under the U.S. Constitution and federal and state statutory laws. As school employees or agents, school-based mental health service providers may have legal and ethical obligations to take steps to protect all students and other individuals from reasonably foreseeable risks of harm. This requires an understanding of how the law works to balance the authority of parents and guardians to make decisions about their children, the rights and needs of children, and the purpose and authority exercised by schools.

This chapter provides a general understanding of some of the basic ethical and legal principles that concern mental health professionals and how those principles relate to the provision of mental health services within primary- and secondary-grade educational settings. The chapter is based on an understanding that mental health services within educational settings encompass school-wide interventions, professional consultations, identification, assessment and evaluation, and services to both groups of students and individual students and their families. Mental health professionals engaged in any of these activities must comprehend how local, state, and federal laws regulate the education of school-aged students and define their professional responsibilities. Therefore, included here is an overview of the intersection of the American legal system and public education, and general descriptions of several of the federal laws that most concern mental health professionals working in schools.

This chapter is designed to provide a framework for understanding the ethical and legal challenges that may arise within the school setting and the professional responsibilities that may result. The focus is on the commonalities among ethical guidelines and consideration of professional responsibilities in very general terms and not within the context of standards unique to one profession. This is not a comprehensive treatment of specific legal or ethical issues. It is purposefully general in nature when discussing potential differences among the laws and regulations of different states and the policies and procedures of schools and school districts. It emphasizes applied law—law that is usable and applicable in solving the problems that mental health professionals working in schools are likely to encounter. The chapter should not be viewed as legal advice or counsel. Readers are encouraged to seek professional supervision and legal counsel regarding specific matters, at all times.

AN OVERVIEW OF PROFESSIONAL ETHICS

The various mental health professions represented among professionals in school settings may each have a unique history and philosophy, employ different terminology, and emphasize different areas of knowledge and theoretical constructs. Ethical codes developed by professional organizations tend to emphasize a discipline-specific understanding of an issue and may provide guidance that reflects the theoretical approach and terminology that guides that specific discipline. The professions and disciplines, however, are similar in that they share the intent of providing services designed to address needs that may arise from emotional, behavioral, social, educational, or other challenges of those being served.

Ethics are standards of values and guiding principles that define acceptable behavior and conduct of an individual. The formal principles that professional organizations use to promote and encourage the proper conduct of a professional are known as *professional ethics*. The purpose of these principles is to protect the public and those who receive professional services, such as mental health services, by sensitizing professionals to the ethical aspects of their work, educating them about appropriate conduct, helping them monitor their own behavior, and providing standards to be used in the resolution of complaints of unethical conduct. Ethics are benchmarks that guide or help to determine behavior. Ethics reflect the "common good." Ethical standards within the context of mental health professions are guidelines designed by professional mental health organizations or bodies for the purpose of establishing parameters for an "ethic of care" and professional practice. These guidelines vary among professional organizations but are generally grounded in core thematic areas and emphasize truthfulness, forthrightness, respecting law, and encouraging ethical conduct.[1] These thematic areas are broadly defined as beneficence and nonmaleficence, fidelity and responsibility, integrity, justice, and respect for people's rights and dignity.

The principles of beneficence and nonmaleficence emphasize the doctrines that mental health professionals endeavor to benefit those being served and take care to "do no harm." The tenets of fidelity and responsibility reflect an awareness of the relationships of trust mental health professionals form with both those who receive services and those with whom the professional interacts within the school and larger community. The precept of integrity incorporates the expectations that mental health professionals seek to promote accuracy, honesty, and truthfulness in the practice of their profession. The standard of justice reflects the idea that mental health professionals should endeavor to provide equal access and quality in the process, procedures, and services being offered, and that they exercise reasonable judgment and precautions to ensure that potential biases and limitations of their competence or expertise do not result in or condone unjust practices. The principle of respect for people's rights and dignity emphasizes the importance of the dignity and worth of all people and the rights of individuals to privacy, confidentiality, and self-determination. This doctrine also reflects the importance of mental health professionals being aware of and respecting cultural, individual, and role differences that exist between the professional and the individual or groups that the professional is serving. These differences result from the wide variations among individual human beings and communities and may include age, gender, gender identity, race, ethnicity, culture, national origin, religion, sexual orientation, disability, language, and socioeconomic status (American Psychological Association [APA], 2010).

Many ethical issues faced by mental health professionals working in schools also raise legal questions. In many instances, the ethical standards of a professional organization are consistent with legal requirements and provide guidance about how to comply with the applicable law. When there is a conflict, mental health professionals should determine whether they understand their legal responsibilities and the actions that are permitted under the law. Various professional organizations have different standards that provide guidance about how to reconcile the difference between professional ethics and the law and how then the professional might take responsible action to address the problem. If there are questions about how to respond to an issue because of conflicts between the law and ethical standards, professionals should obtain appropriate professional supervision and legal guidance (Knapp, Gottlieb, Handelsman, & Berman, 2007, pp. 54, 58).

A BRIEF OVERVIEW OF THE AMERICAN LEGAL SYSTEM AND THE ROLE OF THE LAW IN EDUCATION

There are many different ways to define the word *law* and terms that are used to describe legal concepts. This chapter uses various legal terms when describing the ethical and legal challenges that mental health professionals working in schools may encounter. Therefore, it is important to understand how the term is being used in that specific context.

In general, laws are a body of principles, standards, rules, and requirements intended to govern the actions of government entities and the behavior of individual citizens by creating obligations as well as rights and by imposing penalties (Garner, 2009, p. 362). The American legal system is a highly complex system of constitutional, statutory, regulatory, and common laws. There are three levels of law: The federal level affects the activities of the entire nation; state law is specific to each individual state; and local law regulates activities of a specific area such as a city. Educational institutions must follow all of the applicable federal laws and the laws that are specific to their state or municipality. The laws that educational institutions must follow are augmented or interpreted by state and federal agency guidance documents such as memoranda and letters. The court system plays an important role by interpreting all of these requirements as they apply to specific situations and reviewing the constitutionality of laws and regulations. There are several types of courts at each level and forms of law that govern the activities of educational organizations and professionals working within them. At each level, the legal requirements that structure the activities of mental health professionals and the schools and agencies they work within can come from multiple jurisdictions and sources, some with more significance than others depending on the situation or issue.

Statutory law is a written form of law and includes the formal acts of a legally constituted body (Garner, 2009, p. 1547). Examples of statutory laws are the federal and state constitutions, acts of the U.S. Congress, state codes, and municipal ordinances. The term *common law* refers to laws and legal principles embodied primarily in judicial decisions based on custom and precedent rather than from statutes or constitutions (Garner, 2009, p. 313). These principles form the basis of the English legal system that guided the development of the federal court system and the legal systems of all the state court systems in the United States except in Louisiana, where the historical development of the state's legal system reflects the French tradition of codified civil law. Whereas common law does rely on some principles that may be written into statutes, it is largely precedent-based. Precedents are judicial decisions that have already been made in similar cases and are documented in collections of case law (Garner, 2009, p. 1295). The precedents that are applied in a case are determined by the presiding judge. The common law tradition is an adversarial system because common law precedents largely arise from cases involving conflicts between two or more opposing parties before a judge who moderates. In some cases, a jury of citizens without legal training decides on the facts of the case.

Administrative law is comprised of the formal regulations and decisions of various federal and state governmental agencies, as well as decisions made by administrative judges (Garner, 2009, p. 51). The two federal agencies that have the most significant effect on schools are the Department of Education (DOE) and the Department of Justice (DOJ). The DOE is responsible for the administration of most federal education programs. The DOJ often becomes involved in legal controversies concerning public schools involving claims of systemic discrimination.

The methods of implementation and administration by the DOE include promulgating federal regulations; issuing agency guidance documents, policy statements, and interpretive letters; and taking enforcement actions. These agency rules or regulations have the force and effect of law and must be followed by states and schools in order to maintain federal funding. Agency guidance documents generally provide the DOE's interpretation and explanation of what the law means, or how the department will enforce the law's requirements. In addition, the DOE enforces the laws over which it has jurisdiction through agency hearings and orders and state compliance monitoring. Orders generally come as part of an adjudicatory hearing or investigation of potential violations. For example, the DOE's Office for Civil Rights (OCR) can receive a complaint by parents that a school did not follow the provisions of Section 504 of the Rehabilitation Act of 1973 (Section 504) regarding their child's participation in classroom or standardized tests. The agency will investigate this complaint and may issue a remedial order if it finds a violation. The DOE also requires states to submit plans and reports delineating how they will comply with the conditions of laws like the Individuals with Disabilities Education Improvement Act of 2004 (IDEA). The DOE reviews these documents and may reject a state's plan or require states to make changes in order to receive or to maintain federal funding.

The texts of federal laws can be found in the United States Code (U.S.C.). These are the laws that are the written record of the legislation passed by the U.S. Congress. The Code of Federal Regulations (C.F.R.) is the codification of the general and permanent rules that govern the actions of the executive agencies that are authorized to interpret and enforce the laws that Congress has made and the U.S. president has signed. The regulations contained in the C.F.R. may specify the actions that state school systems (referred to as state educational authorities) and individual school districts (referred to as local educational authorities) must follow to comply with the requirements of the federal law. Although the names that are used may vary among the states, each state also has similar systems of statutes and codes that regulate activities in that state, such as how schools are supposed to function. At the local level, school districts may draft and implement policies and procedures that define how schools carry out everyday activities in ways that comply with the federal and state laws that must be followed.

As noted, federal, state, and local laws all govern education. There is a hierarchy of law, with federal law being at the top under the Supremacy Clause of the U.S. Constitution (U.S. Const. art. VI, § 2). In the United States, however, there is no single national public school system. The U.S. Constitution does not contain any specific mention of education and schools. The 10th Amendment states that "powers not delegated to the United States by the Constitution, nor prohibited by it to the States, are reserved to the States respectively, or to the people" (U.S. Const. amend. X). The 10th Amendment has been interpreted as making state governments directly responsible for establishing and maintaining public school systems, resulting in each state forming and operating a public education system within its state boundaries. Public school systems are created and governed by state constitutional and legislative mandates. Because each state has control over its public school system, individual state school codes and interpreting court decisions may vary among the states and should be consulted regarding a situation that arises within a specific state.

In the past century, beginning with *Brown v. Board of Education* (1954), a child's right to gain access to a public education has through court action become a legal entitlement. The U.S. Supreme Court established that "education is perhaps the most important function of state and local governments . . . where the

State has undertaken to provide it, is a right which must be available to all on equal terms" (347 U.S. at 492). Since the 1950s, the federal government has exercised growing influence in educational matters, primarily through federal court decrees, congressional enactments, and agency regulations and guidelines. When the federal government is involved in education, it is primarily acting under Article I, Section 8 of the U.S. Constitution, which states that Congress has the power to tax and to spend so as to "provide for the common defense and general welfare of the United States" (U.S. Const. art. I, § 8). In addition, the federal government's involvement in education stems from the authority to assure due process and equal protection under the 14th Amendment.

Despite the increasingly prominent role the federal government plays in education, public education remains primarily a state and local function. Each individual state regulates the schools and activities that occur within them through statutes, state agency regulations, and actions. The majority of states have statutes that create state departments of education that oversee the activities of local school districts and local schools. At the local level, most states have provided powers to local public school boards that are composed of members elected or appointed. Public school boards typically exercise all three types of governmental power: legislative, judicial, and executive. Public school boards exercise legislative powers when they create policies or approve tax levies or bond issues. They exercise judicial or adjudicatory powers when they serve as decision makers in hearings to determine whether students or staff violated particular policies such as in student expulsion or teacher employment termination matters. School boards exercise executive powers in the management of the school system through budgeting and other managerial functions.

In addition to interacting with laws that govern the actions of schools as a whole, providers of mental health services in schools must also consider state licensure laws governing their professional activities and any additional requirements imposed on professionals in their official capacities. The majority of school-based mental health services are provided by school-employed or contracted counselors, psychologists, and social workers. Requirements for certification or licensure vary among the states. In most states, the certification or licensure for practice in the schools is typically issued by the state's department of education. Throughout the country, community mental health providers work in public schools through interagency agreements. These providers may hold professional credentials issued by state departments of health or professional regulation. Regardless of licensure or whether employed by the school district or a community agency, all mental health providers working in schools should only practice within the scope of their training, qualifications, and experience; adhere to the professional code of ethics for their disciplines; and hold the appropriate state licensure or certification credentials.

LEGAL CONCEPTS IMPORTANT IN THE DELIVERY OF MENTAL HEALTH SERVICES TO YOUTHS

Duty

Under the law, a duty is an obligation that is owed or due to another and that needs to be satisfied; it is an obligation for which somebody else has a corresponding right (Garner, 2009, p. 580). The failure to fulfill such a duty can result in civil or criminal sanctions. Legal duties are distinct from moral or ethical duties such as the ones delineated in professional codes of ethics. Although a duty may be both legal and ethical, only legal duties may be enforced by the judicial system or an administrative agency. Legal duties can be created in several ways and by different types of law. Case law decisions rendered by a judge can create a legal duty. Statutes, codes, and administrative regulations can also impose a legal duty on individuals or entities within the jurisdiction that the law applies. When a mental health professional obtains a professional license or credential, this individual assumes specific responsibilities under the laws and regulations that are designed to regulate the activities professionals with specific credentials undertake. Generally, when acting in a professional capacity, the individual is expected to provide due care by exercising a level of care that is standard in the profession. Such care is defined as ordinary, reasonable, and prudent. This means that the care reflects what is recognized as ordinary customary practice; the professional took reasonable action based on appropriate and adequate professional knowledge and judgment; and the care reflects a prudent exercise of caution in maintaining adequate safeguards.

The Duty to Practice Reasonably and Competently

The duty to practice in a reasonable and competent manner should be considered to apply to all practice situations and settings. The specific parameters of the duty are typically defined by individual licensing standards and other state laws including judicial decisions and statutes and codes. This includes, but is not limited to, service providers fulfilling their obligations to draft appropriate documentation, maintain adequate records, and follow applicable laws and policies regarding records. A competent professional is expected to follow the standards of professionals working within the specific discipline (e.g., social work, counseling, school psychology, or other mental health profession). If a professional has a particular area of specialization, it is expected that the provider's actions should conform to the standards of professionals working within that specialty. When working within an institutional setting such as a school or community agency, a competent professional endeavors to understand his or her roles and responsibilities with regard to his or her status as an employee, contractor, or agent. A competent professional working in a school also seeks to understand how to balance professional ethical obligations to individual students and families with the responsibilities and obligations to the entire student body, the school and school system, and the general community. This means that the mental health professional recognizes the extent and limits of the training and has an understanding of any physical or mental and ethical and legal limitations affecting the capacity and ability to practice. A reasonable and competent professional also demonstrates a comprehension of when it is necessary to seek supervision, consultation, or transfer the responsibility for the provision of service to another professional to prevent or address ethical or legal issues.

The Duty to Obtain Informed Consent

It is an essential professional responsibility to obtain informed consent prior to providing services. Generally, consent means a person's agreement to allow something to happen, made with full knowledge of the risks involved and the alternatives (Garner, 2009, p. 346). Informed consent means more than just someone signing a consent or release form. Informed consent means that consent was given voluntarily and freely. The term *informed consent* also encompasses the quality and completeness of the information provided by the mental health professional that forms the basis of consent. That information must allow the recipient to have an understanding of the benefits and risks of the services including, but not limited to, the risks associated with the disclosure of data. Informed consent also requires that the person giving consent has the capacity to understand this information. Capacity means both the legal capacity and mental capacity. This means that the person is recognized as capable of giving consent under the law and does not have any mental or cognitive disabilities that impair judgment or the ability to make decisions (Garner, 2009, p. 235). This is particularly important when considering the capacity of minors to consent. When a parent or guardian provides consent that means the person is doing so pursuant to representative capacity because the adult is in the legal position of standing or acting for another (Garner, 2009, p. 235).

Laws that control informed consent for the provision of mental health services to minors reflect the importance of parental authority and autonomy. This results from historical precedents and legal definitions of competency and capacity to make legally binding decisions. The rights of minors are protected under the U.S. Constitution; however, their rights are not protected to the same degree as adults. There are three reasons that minors are not afforded the same constitutional rights as adults: the vulnerability of children, their limited decision-making capacity, and the role parents play in making decisions for their children. State laws that limit the rights of minors reflect the complex balance required to protect the state interest in protecting the welfare of the greater community, the interests of parents, and the interests of minors. State laws have traditionally recognized the rights of parents to make health care decisions on their children's behalf based on the presumption that before reaching the age of majority (age 18 in most states), children and adolescents lack the experience and judgment to give informed consent. There have been long-standing exceptions to this rule, such as medical emergencies when there is no time to obtain parental consent and when minors are legally emancipated by marriage or another circumstance and legally considered able to make decisions on their own behalf. Some state courts have also adopted the so-called "mature minor rule," which allows a minor who is deemed sufficiently intelligent and mature to understand the nature and consequences of a proposed treatment to consent without consulting with parents or obtaining their permission.

The provision of mental health services in schools raises unique concerns that reflect the intersection of mental health practice and the legal requirements that schools must follow. The considerable control that state and federal laws afford parents over the legal rights of their children may conflict with the standards of practice provided by professional ethical codes. Difficulties may arise because of mental health professionals' struggle to balance what they perceive as the best interests of the child, practice standards within their profession, the legal and ethical guidelines related to the minor and parents' rights, and the legal obligations that may apply to professionals working in schools. It is significant to recognize that the informed consent rights of minors have expanded in recent years and many states now allow adolescents to consent to outpatient mental health and substance abuse services. These laws vary in the age at which minors may consent to treatment and the types of services that do not require parental consent (Boldt, 2012; Hill, 2012).

Mental health professionals providing services to school-aged students may also have to confront issues related to disclosures of information or requests for services pertaining to contraception and abortion, sexually transmitted diseases including but limited to HIV/AIDS, prenatal care, adoption, and medical care for a minor's own child. There are specific state and federal laws that should be considered with regard to both information and the ability to consent for services dealing with these issues. Mental health professionals should obtain information about their specific responsibilities in these situations under both federal law and the law of the state in which the service is being provided.[2]

Privacy, Confidentiality, and Privilege

Personal privacy and individual autonomy are central values in American society. A right to privacy is not mentioned in the Constitution, but the Supreme Court has said that several of the amendments create this right (Rideout, 2010, pp. 156–157). As described later, the importance of privacy with regard to disclosures of personally identifiable information is one of the fundamental components of the federal law governing education records. Mental health professionals frequently struggle with issues surrounding the rights of minors to confidentiality and the rights of parents to obtain information about their children or limit disclosures of information related to their children and sensitive family matters regardless of the setting in which treatment is provided. These concerns may arise in all practice settings but the school setting may present unique challenges. Mental health professionals should be cognizant of the limitations imposed on confidentiality and the differences in how information may be used in the educational settings versus other settings with regard to disclosures made by both students and their family members during the course of evaluations and other assessments and psychotherapeutic and counseling interaction.

Generally, confidentiality is the obligation not to disclose willingly any information obtained in confidence (Garner, 2009, p. 339). Confidentiality is based on four basic principles: respect for an individual's right to privacy, respect for human relationships in which personal information is shared, the appreciation of the importance of confidentiality to both individuals and society, and expectations that those who pledge to safeguard confidential information will do so. The fundamental intent is to protect a client's right to privacy by ensuring that matters disclosed to a professional are not relayed to others without the informed consent of the client. Confidentiality of information that has been obtained through a mental health professional–client relationship is afforded legal status throughout the United States through licensing laws for counselors, with several states specifically granting the right of privileged communication to school mental health professionals. It should be noted that this privilege belongs to the client/service recipient and not the professional. Breach of confidence is considered unprofessional conduct and is grounds for disciplinary action and sometimes legal action. Neither privacy nor confidentiality, however, is an absolute right, especially in the case of minors. There are fundamental exceptions, which are defined in the following paragraphs.

Privileged communication is a legal concept that applies to communications that originate in a confidential relationship. It addresses legal rights protecting clients from having their disclosures to certain professionals revealed during legal proceedings without their informed consent (Garner, 2009, p. 1316). Legal determinations regarding who the client is (e.g., whether minors or their parents hold the "privilege") and limitations on clients' rights to privileged communication are the basis for legal exceptions to maintaining confidentiality. In 1996, the U.S. Supreme Court held that communications between psychotherapists trained at the master's degree level, not just psychiatrists and doctoral level psychologists, and their patients are privileged and do not have to be disclosed in cases heard in federal court (*Jaffee v. Redmond*, 518 U.S. 1, 1996). Some states have recognized a similar specific right of privileged communication for school mental health professionals, others have not. In general, mental health professionals working in schools should understand the policies and procedures that govern the maintenance of records and the written and oral disclosures of potentially privileged information. When faced with a situation that raises issues of privileged communication, mental health professionals working within schools should endeavor to seek appropriate professional supervision and legal counsel with regard to what information may and may not be disclosed on response to requests for records, a subpoena to testify, or any other legal action designed to obtain information about a student or family member.

Duty to Warn/Duty to Protect

As noted, mental health professionals are encouraged by ethical standards and often required by law to maintain the confidentiality of information disclosed by patients or clients in the course of the treatment relationship. With some exceptions codified in state and federal law, health professionals can be held civilly liable for breaching confidentiality. One exception that governs mental health treatment, regardless of the age of the client, results from efforts to protect potential victims from a patient's or client's violent behavior. The defining cases regarding these issues were decided in 1974 and 1976 by the California Supreme Court in *Tarasoff v. The Regents of the University of California*. The 1974 case (referred to as *Tarasoff I*) held that a therapist must disclose information that is confidential because of the patient–psychotherapist relationship in instances when the disclosure is essential to avert danger to others; that is, the duty to warn (529 P.2d 553, Cal. 1974). The 1976 ruling (*Tarasoff II*) held that a therapist has a duty to exercise reasonable care to protect the foreseeable victim from harm (551 P.2d 334, Cal. 1976). This imposed a legal duty on psychotherapists, enforceable by a civil suit for damages, to warn a person who may become a victim of a violent act by a patient.

Other court decisions and state laws followed that resulted in legal precedents or actual state laws that either require the disclosure of confidential information—if the mental health professional determines that such disclosures are necessary to warn third parties about potential harm—or permit mental health professionals to make such disclosures without fearing that they could result in a civil law suit or action to suspend or revoke a professional's license. Most states now have laws that require (i.e., impose a duty) mental health professionals to disclose information about clients who may become violent or threaten others.

The specifics of the laws imposing the duty to warn vary from state to state but the general formulation is that a mental health professional is obligated to notify promptly either the potential victim and/or the police when a client makes a specific threat of serious physical harm against a readily identifiable third party. Some variations of the law include what kinds of mental health professionals have the duty, whether there is a duty to hospitalize the patient, whether the duty is triggered by threats of suicide, and whether the duty also extends to threats against real property.

In school-based mental health practice, the ethical obligations to keep information confidential may conflict with the legal obligations created by the duty to protect students and others from harm. A professional confronting this situation may have to consider the necessity of sharing information disclosed by a minor student within the parameters of the professional obligations as a school employee or contractor responsible for protecting students from risk of harm.

Duty to Report

The vast majority of American states and territories mandate that mental health professionals report child maltreatment. The circumstances under which a mandatory reporter must make a report vary from state to state. Readers should know the exact reporting requirements, procedures, and resources applicable in the state in which they provide mental health services.[3] Typically, a report must be made when documenters, in their professional capacities, credibly suspect or have reasons to believe that a child has been abused or neglected. Another standard that may apply is that reports should be made regarding situations in which the reporter has knowledge of or observes a child being subjected to conditions that would reasonably result in harm to the child. Reasonable cause to suspect child abuse or maltreatment means that, based on observations, professional training, and experience, the reporter believes the parent or person legally responsible for a child has harmed that child or placed that child in imminent danger or harm.

Mandatory reporting statutes may not recognize mental health professional–client privilege as a justification for failure to report. Some states also assign civil and criminal liability to professionals who fail to fulfill their mandated reporter duties. If a mandated reporter makes a good faith report, that individual is immune from any criminal or civil liability. This immunity is not available where the liability results from willful misconduct or gross negligence by the reporter and most states have laws against malicious and false reports.

A question that frequently arises when mental health professionals suspect abuse or neglect is: What must the professional do to make a report and after making the report? How a report is actually made, whether the reporter may remain confidential, and the documentation that a reporter may be required to submit are dependent on state and local requirements. For example, depending on the state law and school district or agency policies and procedures, an administrator may serve as the designated reporter or agency reporter for a school or agency, meaning that person makes all reports to the local or state child protection authorities. Whereas state laws may allow a person without actual knowledge to play this role, merely informing a supervisor, even if designated as the agency reporter, may not fulfill the duty to make a mandated report. Fulfillment of the duty may only occur once the report has actually been made to the child protection authorities.

Mental health professionals often have questions about what constitutes appropriate professional action and behavior after a report of child endangerment is made. It is important for all school personnel to understand that child protection authorities are charged with investigating the abuse. Further investigation is not the responsibility of the reporter and may result in unforeseen ethical and legal consequences related to interfering with the investigation. Mental health professionals working in schools may also need to consider if they should continue to interact with the child and family during the investigation and afterwards and the appropriate limits on those interactions. Such issues may include determining whether they are legally and ethically obligated to participate in the investigation or court proceedings. Another issue that may arise is whether it is legally permissible or appropriate, from both an ethical or clinical perspective, to interact with the parent or other family members or provide information about why the report was made. Mental health professionals providing individual direct services may also need to consider whether or not responsibility for services should be transferred to another professional during the investigation and how the report and its aftermath may be addressed during service-based interactions. Professionals may want to address these very challenging interpersonal issues with an appropriate supervisor and also consider the legal mandates and school policies and procedures that

4: SCHOOL-BASED LAW, ETHICS, AND MENTAL HEALTH SERVICES

should be followed regarding interacting with child protection investigators, family members, and the child.

Liability and Immunity

Liability is the quality or state of being legally obligated or held accountable (Garner, 2009, p. 997). When people use the colloquial term *being sued* it generally means that someone is a defendant in a civil or criminal case and the result may be a finding of liability. Mental health professionals working in schools are often concerned that they will be held liable for violating a student's legal rights or failing to comply with laws, such as those mandating the reporting of child abuse and neglect.

At the federal level, public elementary and secondary schools are subject to federal civil rights laws, including laws that prohibit discrimination based on disability, race, religion, national origin, and gender. These laws include the Americans with Disabilities Act of 1990 (ADA; 42 U.S.C. § 12101 *et seq.*; 28 C.F.R. Part 35) and Section 504 of the Rehabilitation Act of 1973 (29 U.S.C. § 701 *et seq.*; 34 C.F.R. Part 104); Titles IV and VI of the Civil Rights Act of 1964 (42 U.S.C. § 2000d *et seq.*; 34 C.F.R. Part 100); and Title IX of the Education Amendments of 1972 (20 U.S.C. § 1681 *et seq.*; 34 C.F.R. Part 106). State civil rights laws and local ordinances may also extend protections to certain groups against discrimination in the state or a city. In addition, law suits may arise from allegations that a student or family member suffered a personal injury as a result of inaction (negligence) or an action undertaken by a mental health professional in a school setting.

Under certain circumstances, a professional working in a school is immune from civil or criminal liability. Immunity is any exemption from a duty, liability, or service of process (Garner, 2009, p. 817). The Paul D. Coverdell Teacher Protection Act of 2001, 20 U.S.C. § 6731, *et seq.*, provides a limitation on liability for school professionals when they undertake reasonable actions to maintain order, discipline, and an appropriate educational environment. The Act states that no punitive damages can award against a school professional for any harm that results from an action or omission if the school professional was acting on behalf of the school, within the scope of authority, in furtherance of efforts to maintain order in the school, and if the actions conformed to federal, state, and local laws. The immunity does not apply if there is clear and convincing evidence that shows that harm was proximately caused by willful or criminal misconduct by the school professional or is a result of conscious, flagrant indifference to the rights or safety of the individual harmed (20 U.S.C. § 6736(a)(4)).

Whether a mental health professional would be named in a lawsuit is highly dependent on the statute the case is brought under and whether that law allows for the naming of individuals as defendants. The potential liability of the school district, school officials, and professionals working in the school is also dependent on facts surrounding the allegations of civil rights' violations or personal harm and the legal status of the professionals providing services within a school. The importance of mental health professionals acting within the scope of professional duties as an employee, agent, contractor, or other defined legal relationship with a school is an essential part of basic ethical and legal sound practice. Therefore, readers are encouraged to understand the parameters of any agreements, policies, and procedures that may govern their work as mental health professionals in schools. Moreover, when questions arise about whether an action or inaction might result in a legal action against professionals, they are encouraged to obtain appropriate professional supervision and legal counsel.

FERPA and HIPAA

The laws governing student records have been profoundly affected by congressional enactments. School officials and other professionals working in schools frequently find themselves balancing the need to disclose information about an individual student against the student's interest in keeping the information confidential.[4] These decisions are guided by the federal Family Educational Rights and Privacy Act of 1974, commonly known as FERPA or the Buckley Amendment (20 U.S.C. § 1232g; 34 C.F.R. Part 99).

FERPA is intended to protect the confidentiality of student records from access by unauthorized third parties and also affords parents, guardians, and students (within specific age limitations) with rights to review and to challenge the accuracy of the information contained in the student records. The passage of FERPA also resulted in states enacting statutes and regulations governing the storage, access, and dissemination of student records including records of mental health services. The need to comply with FERPA and other state and federal laws regulating the maintenance and disclosure of student records has resulted in most school districts developing systems of record keeping and policies and procedures. Mental health professionals working in schools should endeavor to understand and to follow these practices and procedures and to seek appropriate professional consultation and legal guidance if questions arise.

FERPA affords parents[5] and eligible students[6] with the right to inspect and review records, to seek amendment of records, and to consent to the disclosure of personally identifiable information (PII) from education records, except as specified by law. FERPA applies to educational agencies and institutions that receive funds under any program administered by the DOE. This would include all public schools and school districts and most private and public colleges and universities. Private and religious elementary and secondary schools generally do not receive funds from the DOE. Therefore, they are not subject to FERPA. A private school is not made subject to FERPA just because its students and teachers receive services from a local school district or state educational agency that receives funds from the DOE.

An important question is: What is actually considered an *education record?* The term includes all records, files, and documents, and other materials that are (a) directly related to the student and (b) maintained by an education agency or institution or by a party acting for that agency or institution (34 C.F.R. § 99.3). This includes all records regardless of medium including, but not limited to, handwriting, videotape or audiotape, electronic or computer files, film, print, microfilm, and microfiche. For elementary and secondary students, the definition of education record includes medical and health records that the school creates, collects, or maintains. It also includes disciplinary records and any official letters regarding a student's status in school.

Records that schools maintain on special education students, including records concerning services provided to students under IDEA, are also education records under FERPA. This includes records of services provided by school psychologists, social workers, counselors, behavioral analysts, and any other type of mental health professional providing services to students as part of an Individualized Education Program (IEP). This is because these records are (a) directly related to a student, (b) maintained by the school or a party acting for the school, and (c) not excluded from the definition of education records (34 C.F.R. § 99.3). It makes no difference whether the information is located in the student's official record, in the special education office, or in the central office. By contrast, observations that a school employee makes about a student but does not record are not education records. Moreover, records that instructional, supervisory, and administrative personnel make and keep for themselves as memory aids (known as "sole possession notes") are not education records. Notes made by mental health professionals are not considered education records if they are (a) kept in the sole possession of the maker, (b) not accessible or revealed to any other person except as a temporary substitute, and (c) used only as a memory aid (34 C.F.R. § 99.3). Any information placed in a student's education record including information that in other settings might be considered privileged due to the professional–client relationship would be accessible under FERPA (20 U.S.C. § 1232g).

A question that is of specific concern for psychologists and others who conduct evaluations using standardized test instruments is whether FERPA affords parents the right to inspect and review test protocols. Related questions include whether it is permissible to make copies given the obligation to respect copyrights and uphold the integrity of the test instrument. The DOE's Office for Special Education Programs (OSEP) and OCR have determined that a student's psychological test protocol that records answers provided by the student is an education record under FERPA and IDEA because these records contain PII (e.g., Letter to Carroll Independent School District, 2005). Parents have a right to inspect and review those responses. They do not have a right to blank test protocols nor does the school have the right to redact or destroy records to avoid complying with a request under FERPA (e.g., Letter to Carroll Independent School District, 2005). Moreover, under IDEA parents of students receiving special education services must be informed when any PII that is collected, maintained, and used in accordance with IDEA-Part B is destroyed (34 C.F.R. § 99.10(e)). FERPA requires copies of records only when a parent is unable, because of unusual circumstances, to physically inspect records. However, fair use and specific agreements with test providers would likely allow the copying of an individual protocol to fulfill a request under FERPA, and making a copy may also be the most prudent approach when the request may result from an acrimonious personal situation or as part of a contemplated or actual litigation. Mental health professionals should also be aware that FERPA and IDEA require that schools respond to a parent's request for an explanation of the child's education records (34 C.F.R. § 99.10(c)). This requirement may be an important part of developing and implementing school policies regarding providing and explaining test protocols and interpretation of test results to parents.

FERPA has specific requirements regarding the release of a student's education records. Schools must annually notify parents and eligible students of their rights under FERPA, and must include in this notification the criteria for whom constitutes a school official and what constitutes a legitimate educational interest. An educational agency or institution that is subject to FERPA may not have a policy or practice of disclosing the education records of students, or PII from education records with a parent or eligible student's written consent (34 C.F.R. § 99.30). FERPA contains several exceptions to this rule. An eligible student is a student who is at least 18 years of age or who attends a postsecondary institution at any age (34 C.F.R. §§ 99.3 and 99.5(a)). The consent of special education students over 18 years of age who have not delegated education rights to their parents or guardians or do not have a guardian may also be required to release education records. Under FERPA, parents and eligible students have the right to inspect and review the students' education records and to seek to have them amended in certain circumstances (34 C.F.R. §§ 99.10–99.12 and §§ 99.20–99.22).

School officials with a "legitimate educational interest" may access student records under FERPA. Generally, this term refers to individuals employed by the school district who need to know information in a student's education record in order to perform their professional responsibility. Interest, concern, or curiosity about a student or groups of students is not a legitimate educational interest. FERPA considers legitimate educational interests to include federal, state, and local education agencies that must collect data or student information to audit, evaluate, or enforce educational programs (20 U.S.C. § 1232g(b)(1)). Organizations conducting certain studies for or on behalf of a school to develop, validate, or administer predictive tests, student aid programs, or improve instruction may also receive education records but only under specific conditions (20 U.S.C. § 1232g(b)(1)). The school may disclose information for such studies only if the study methodology does not permit the personal identification of parents and students by anyone other than researchers and their representatives, the information is not used for any purpose other than to complete the study, and the information is destroyed when it is no longer needed for the stated purposes of the study (20 U.S.C. § 1232g(b)(1)(F)).

There are other important exceptions that may directly affect the work of mental health professionals. Schools must release information requested by a judicial order or legal subpoena. The school, however, must make a reasonable effort to notify the parent or eligible student in advance of compliance, unless the court or other issuing agency has ordered that the contents of the subpoena not be disclosed or that the protected education records not be included (34 C.F.R. § 99.31(a)(9)(1)). If state law permits, schools may release information to state and local juvenile justice authorities after receiving written certification that the information will not be disclosed to any other agency, organization, or third party without the parent's permission, except as allowed in state law (20 U.S.C. § 1232g(b)(1)(E)). School officials must balance safety interests and student privacy interests and FERPA contains exceptions to the general consent requirement, including the "health or safety emergency exception." Schools have discretion to determine what constitutes a health or safety emergency; if there is an articulable and significant threat to the health or safety of a student or other individuals, a school may disclose information from education records to any person whose "knowledge of the information is necessary to protect the health or safety of the student or other individuals" (34 C.F.R. § 99.36).

HIPAA

In 1996, Congress passed the Health Insurance Portability and Accountability Act (HIPAA) to ensure continued health insurance coverage to individuals who change jobs and to establish national standards regarding the electronic sharing of health information. HIPAA and its implementing regulations, commonly known as the HIPAA Privacy Rule and the HIPAA Security Rule, protect the privacy and security of individually identifiable health information, called protected health information (PHI), held by health plans, health care clearinghouses, and most health care providers, collectively known as covered entities, and their business associates (entities that have access to individuals' health information to perform work on behalf of a covered entity; 45 C.F.R. § 160.103). "Health care providers" include institutional providers of health or medical services, such as hospitals, as well as noninstitutional providers, such as physicians, dentists, and other practitioners, along with any other person or organization that furnishes health care, bills for health care, or is paid for health care in the normal course of business. Covered transactions are those for which the U.S. Department of Health and Human Services (HHS) has adopted a standard, such as health care claims submitted to a health plan (45 C.F.R. § 160.104; Part 162, Subparts K–R). The Privacy Rule, or Standards for Privacy of Individually Identifiable Health Information, establishes national standards to protect the privacy of individuals' identifiable health information. It requires covered entities to protect individuals' health records and other identifiable health information by warranting appropriate safeguards to protect privacy, and setting limits and conditions on the uses and disclosures that may be made of such information without patient authorization. Under this rule, patients have rights to examine and obtain a copy of their health records and to request corrections.

In the case of minors, the HIPAA Privacy Rule generally allows a covered entity to disclose PHI about the child to the child's parent, as the minor child's personal representative, when the disclosure is not inconsistent with state or other law (45 C.F.R. § 164.502(g)).

Technically, schools and school systems that provide health care including mental health care services to students may qualify as "covered entities" under HIPAA. However, the final regulations for the HIPAA Privacy Rule exclude information considered "education records" under FERPA from HIPAA privacy requirements (HHS, 2008, p. 3). This includes student health records and immunization records maintained by an education agency or institution, or its representative, as "education records" under FERPA (HHS, 2008, p. 3). These records are not subject to HIPAA privacy requirements. This would include school nurse or other health records maintained on students receiving services under the IDEA. Parents and guardians accustomed to interacting with health care service providers outside of the educational setting may be confused or even angry when they are informed that HIPAA may not apply to mental health information maintained by their child's school. Both school administrators and mental health professionals may need to explain the distinction between HIPAA and FERPA to parents and also the policies and procedures the school follows with respect to mental health and other health information.

In most cases, the HIPAA Privacy Rule does not apply to an elementary or secondary school because the school either is

(a) not a HIPAA covered entity or (b) a HIPAA covered entity but maintains health information on students only in records that are by definition "education records" under FERPA, and therefore is not subject to the HIPAA Privacy Rule (HHS, 2008, p. 3). There are instances when HIPAA and FERPA may intersect. It is important to remember that even if a school employs psychologists, social workers, nurses, physicians, or allied health care providers, the school is not generally a HIPAA covered entity because the providers do not engage in any of the covered transactions, such as billing a health plan electronically for the services that are provided to students.

Some schools may be HIPAA covered entities because they employ a health care provider who conducts one or more covered transactions electronically, such as transmitting health care claims to a health plan for payment. In this case, the school is a HIPAA covered entity and must comply with the HIPAA Transactions and Code Sets and Identifier Rules with respect to such transactions. However, many schools would not be required to comply with the HIPAA Privacy Rule because they maintain health information only in student health records that are "education records" under FERPA and therefore not PHI under HIPAA (45 C.F.R. § 160.103). For example, if a public school district employs health care providers who bill Medicaid electronically for services provided to students under IDEA, the school is a HIPAA covered entity and would be subject to the HIPAA requirements concerning transactions. However, if the school district maintains health information only in what are education records under FERPA, the school is not required to comply with the HIPAA Privacy Rule. Instead, the school would have to comply with FERPA's privacy requirements with respect to the contents of students' education records, including the requirement to obtain parental consent in order to disclose to Medicaid billing information about a service provided to a student.

The legal relationship between mental health professionals and the school may be an important consideration when determining whether FERPA or HIPAA applies to elementary or secondary student health records. If a person, private company, or community organization acting on behalf of a school subject to FERPA maintains student health records, these records are education records under FERPA, just as if the school maintained the records directly. This is true regardless of whether the students receive services on school grounds or off-site. As education records, the information is protected under FERPA and not HIPAA.

When outside parties such as community agencies provide services directly to students and are not employed by, under contract to, or otherwise acting on behalf of the school, the records containing information about the mental health services students receive are not education records subject to FERPA. This is true even if the services are provided on school grounds because the party creating and maintaining the records is not acting on behalf of the school. A school that wishes to disclose any PII from education records to such outside party would have to comply with FERPA and obtain parental consent (34 C.F.R. § 99.30). Even when student health records maintained by a health care provider are not education records protected by FERPA, the HIPAA Privacy Rule would apply to such records only if the provider conducts one or more HIPAA transactions electronically (e.g., billing a health plan electronically for the services provided).

There are some unique circumstances in which an elementary or secondary school would be subject to the HIPAA Privacy Rule for some students and to FERPA for other students. If a private school is required to comply with the HIPAA Privacy Rule and enrolls students who are placed by either parents or a public school district, the records of the students placed privately are subject to HIPAA, and the education records containing individually identifiable health information of publicly placed students held by the school district would be subject to FERPA.

Protection of Pupil Rights Act (PPRA)

This federal statute should be understood by mental health professionals providing school-wide mental health interventions or seeking to assess mental health needs through the use of surveys and other assessments. Written parental consent is required before a minor student participates in a survey, analysis, or evaluation project funded through the U.S. DOE that reveals information about the student or family members' political affiliations; mental or psychological problems; sexual behavior or attitudes; illegal, antisocial, self-incriminating, and demeaning behavior; critical appraisals of other individuals with whom the student has a close family relationship; legally recognized privileged or analogous relationships, such as those of physicians, lawyers, or ministers; and income—except for that information required to determine eligibility for financial assistance (20 U.S.C. § 1232h(b)). The statute does not apply to information gathering that is entirely voluntary (20 U.S.C. § 1232h(e)). Curricula or classroom management techniques are also exempt from the regulations (20 U.S.C. § 1232h(c)(4)).

SECTION 504 OF THE REHABILITATION ACT OF 1973, AMERICANS WITH DISABILITIES ACT OF 1990, AND INDIVIDUALS WITH DISABILITIES EDUCATION IMPROVEMENT ACT OF 2004

The current approach to educating students with disabilities results from dramatic shifts in disability law and public policy over the past 50 years. The first major federal law to prohibit disability-based discrimination and require affirmative measures to address the needs of disabled students was Section 504 of the

Rehabilitation Act of 1973 (29 U.S.C. § 794(a)). Its application is limited to those programs operated by recipients of federal funds, including elementary and secondary schools. Shortly thereafter, in 1975, Congress passed Public Law No. 94-142, which is codified at 20 U.S.C. § 1401 *et seq.*, and at the time of enactment was entitled the Education for All Handicapped Children Act. This law comprehensively and specifically addresses a public school's obligations to eligible children with disabilities, including the specific means to identify, evaluate, program for, and place such students. In 1990, the Americans with Disabilities Act (ADA) was passed and extended the nondiscrimination prohibitions of Section 504 to all employers and public accommodations, including private schools, childcare centers, and preschools. These laws have continued to evolve and their reach is now deeply embedded in how services are brought to disabled children. Public Law No. 94-142 has been reauthorized over time, and is presently titled the Individuals with Disabilities Education Improvement Act of 2004 but remains commonly referred to as IDEA throughout the education sector. Finally, the ADA Amendments Act (ADAAA) took effect January 1, 2009 and clarified the ADA's and Section 504's expansive scope of coverage by making clear who is eligible for the benefits and protections of these statutes.[7]

IDEA and Section 504 are widely credited with improving access to education for children and youths with disabilities by establishing an infrastructure for educating them in public schools and promoting inclusion of these children alongside their nondisabled peers. The legal issues surrounding special education are numerous because of the complex rules and regulations governing the rights of parents and students and the obligations of schools and public school districts. Legal disputes addressing the broad scope of obligations relating to the education of students with disabilities have generated a large body of decisions from state and federal courts, which provide guidance to the obligations of public schools and their professionals to their special education students. In fact, as of the date of publication of this book, the Supreme Court has decided 14 cases involving legal disputes under the IDEA since the statute was enacted. There are also ever-evolving numbers of print and online resources providing guidance to school administrators, educators, and other professionals working in schools and with parents of children with disabilities.

Because Section 504's regulatory framework specifically pertains to elementary and secondary education and its protections for students are similar to the ADA's mandates, schools generally address their general nondiscrimination mandates to qualified students with disabilities by referring to their obligations under Section 504. For those students who qualify for special education services under IDEA, the legal mandates of Section 504 and the ADA are generally considered to have been met if the substantive and procedural requirements of IDEA have been met (Jacob, Decker, & Hartshorne, 2011, p. 131). For these reasons, more specifically addressed here are the requirements of Section 504 and IDEA that are most applicable to the day-to-day responsibilities of mental health professionals working in or for elementary and secondary schools. This section provides a very general overview of Section 504 and the IDEA and the basic responsibilities mental health professionals must fulfill under these laws. Readers are encouraged to consult other resources devoted specifically to the topic of special education law and seek appropriate professional supervision and legal counsel to answer specific questions.

SECTION 504

Section 504 provides:

> No otherwise qualified individual with a disability in the United States, as defined in section 7(20) [29 U.S.C. § 705(20)] shall, solely by reason of her or his disability, be excluded from the participation in, be denied the benefits of, or be subjected to discrimination under any program or activity receiving Federal financial assistance. (29 U.S.C. § 794(a))

All students covered by Section 504 are protected from discrimination under the general nondiscrimination regulatory provisions implementing these statutes, which cover program and physical accessibility requirements as well as protection from harassment[8] and retaliation (34 C.F.R. § 104 *et seq.*). These regulatory requirements establish the general legal parameters of a school's substantive obligations to identify, program for, place, and accommodate students with disabilities as well as a public elementary and secondary program's obligations to implement procedural safeguards (34 C.F.R. §§ 104.31-36).

Students Protected by and Eligible Under Section 504

At the elementary and secondary educational level, an "otherwise qualified student with a disability" is a student with a disability who is at an age at which students without disabilities are provided elementary and secondary educational services, is at an age at which it is mandatory under state law to provide elementary and secondary educational services to students with disabilities, or is a student to whom a state is required to provide a free appropriate public education under the IDEA[9] (34 C.F.R. § 104.3(l)(2)). A disabled student who is protected by the nondiscrimination requirements of Section 504 is any student who (a) has a physical or mental impairment that substantially limits one or more of such student's major life activities, (b) has a record of such an impairment, or (c) is regarded as having such an impairment (29

U.S.C. § 705(20)(B)). The definition of impairment under Section 504 would likely encompass students receiving mental health services in schools because it includes, but is not limited to, any mental or psychological disorder, such as mental retardation, organic brain syndrome, emotional or mental illness, and specific learning disabilities (28 C.F.R. § 41.31(b)(1)).

The determination of whether a student has a physical or mental impairment that substantially limits a major life activity must be made on the basis of an individual inquiry. In considering substantial limitations, students must be measured against their same-age, nondisabled peers in the general population and without benefit of medication or other mitigating measures such as learned behavioral or adaptive neurological modifications, assistive technology, or accommodations.[10]

Taking into account the term "major life activities," the ADAAA is applicable to the meaning of this term in Section 504 and contains two nonexhaustive lists of major life activities including: caring for oneself, performing manual tasks, seeing, hearing, eating, sleeping, walking, standing, lifting, bending, speaking, breathing, learning, reading, concentrating, thinking, communicating, and working (42 U.S.C. § 12102(2)(A)). The ADAAA also specifies a list of "major bodily functions" that are now considered major life activities, which include but are not limited to functions of the immune system; normal cell growth; and digestive, bowel, bladder, neurological, brain, respiratory, circulatory, endocrine, and reproductive functions (42 U.S.C. § 12102(2)(B)). An impairment that is episodic or is in remission is a disability if, when in an active phase, it would substantially limit a major life activity. The DOE's OCR counsels that "a student with bipolar disorder would be covered if, during manic or depressive episodes, the student is substantially limited in major life activities (e.g., thinking, concentrating, neurological function, or brain function)" (U.S. Department of Education, 2012).

A vital consideration for mental health care professionals is how Section 504 addresses drug and alcohol use. Section 504 excludes from the definition of a student with a disability, and from Section 504 protection, any student who is currently engaging in the illegal use of drugs when a covered entity acts on the basis of such use with the exception of individuals in rehabilitation programs who are no longer engaging in the illegal use of drugs. Section 504's definition of a student with a disability does not exclude users of alcohol; however, Section 504 allows schools to take disciplinary action against students with disabilities using drugs or alcohol to the same extent as students without disabilities.[11]

Under Section 504, a public school program is required to conduct an evaluation of a student who needs or is believed to need special education or related services (34 C.F.R. § 104.34). Therefore, determining whether an elementary or secondary school student is a qualified disabled student under Section 504 begins with the evaluation process. Section 504 requires the use of evaluation procedures that ensure that children are not misclassified, unnecessarily labeled as having a disability, or incorrectly placed, based on inappropriate selection, administration, or interpretation of evaluation materials (34 C.F.R. § 104.35). The amount of information required should be determined by a multidisciplinary committee of professionals who meet for the purpose of evaluating the student.[12] Section 504's regulatory provisions require schools to evaluate the student before determining the student's eligibility for Section 504 services or a Section 504 Plan (discussed in the following section). Federal law does not require a medical diagnosis or a diagnosis pursuant to the *Diagnostic and Statistical Manual of Mental Disorders* (5th ed.; *DSM-5*; American Psychiatric Association, 2013) for a school district to make a determination that a student has a disability. Schools should consider the findings of a medical evaluation if shared by the parents during the eligibility determination process. Furthermore, if the school determines that a medical evaluation is necessary to determine eligibility, this must be provided without cost to the parent.

The Section 504 Plan

A Section 504 Plan documents the plan to accommodate and support a student with a disability in the educational setting. The Section 504 plan is written for those disabled students who are not eligible for special education services under IDEA and do not have an IEP, as the IEP is the written plan that documents the school program and supports for IDEA-eligible students. The Section 504 plan should be designed to help a student with special needs participate fully in school. Section 504 regulations require a school district to provide a free appropriate public education (FAPE) to each qualified student with a disability who is in the school district's jurisdiction, regardless of the nature or severity of the disability (34 C.F.R. § 104.33). Under Section 504, FAPE consists of the provision of regular or special education and related aids and services designed to meet the student's individual educational needs as adequately as the needs of nondisabled students are met (34 C.F.R. § 104.33(b)). Typically, a Section 504 Plan is developed for a student placed in general education classes who is not otherwise eligible for special education services under IDEA. A Section 504 Plan lists accommodations related to the student's disability and required by the student to enable participation in the general classroom setting and educational programs.

Procedural Safeguards Under Section 504

Section 504 requires schools and school districts to develop and implement procedural safeguards with respect to the identification, evaluation, and educational placement of students who need or may need special education or related services because of a disability (34 C.F.R. 104.36). These procedural safeguards must include notice, an opportunity for the parents or guardian of the child to examine relevant records, an impartial hearing with the opportunity for participation by the student's parents or guardian, representation by counsel, and a review procedure. It is important that a school's procedural safeguards under Section 504 are distributed to parents.

Disability Harassment and Discrimination Under Section 504

It is also important to note that Section 504 is considered an anti-discrimination statute not an entitlement program. Section 504 prohibits disability-based harassment, retaliation, and discrimination. The DOE's Office for Civil Rights (OCR) is charged with investigating such complaints.

The DOE has identified disability harassment as an important issue, noting that "[d]isability harassment can have a profound impact on students, raise safety concerns, and erode efforts to ensure that students with disabilities have equal access to the myriad of benefits that an education offers" (U.S. Department of Education, 2012). The DOE has defined and described disability harassment as:

> intimidation or abusive behavior toward a student based on disability that creates a hostile environment by interfering with or denying a student's participation in or receipt of benefits, services, or opportunities in the institution's program. Harassing conduct may take many forms, including verbal acts and name-calling, as well as nonverbal behavior, such as graphic and written statements, or conduct that is physically threatening, harmful, or humiliating. (U.S. Department of Education, 2012)

Mental health providers must understand that disability harassment is unacceptable and that they should take prompt and effective action to end harassment that does occur and prevent it from recurring and to otherwise assist in remedying the effects of any harassment. Schools typically have policies and procedures that address harassment and bullying in the school setting, including harassment and bullying on the basis of a student's disability. Mental health providers should be familiar with these policies and implementation procedures.

IDEA

IDEA requires public school districts to meet very specific statutory obligations. These obligations require school districts to make a FAPE available to all children with disabilities between

the ages of 3 and 21, inclusive, who reside within their jurisdictions (20 U.S.C. § 1412(a)). IDEA's reach is broad and obligates
the public school district to reach children with disabilities who
are homeless or wards of the state and, to a more limited degree
as specified in IDEA's implementing regulations, children with
disabilities attending private schools.

FAPE is defined under IDEA to mean "special education
and related services that [are] provided at public expense, under
public supervision and direction, and without charge . . . [and]
are provided in conformity with the individualized education
program required . . . " (20 U.S.C. § 1401(9)). IDEA defines "special education" to mean:

> specially designed instruction, at no cost to parents, to meet
> the unique needs of a child with a disability, including
> (A) instruction conducted in the classroom, in the home,
> in hospitals and institutions, and in other settings; and
> (B) instruction in physical education. (20 U.S.C. § 1401(29))

IDEA has defined "related services" as

> transportation and such developmental, corrective, and
> other supportive services as are required to assist a child
> with a disability to benefit from special education, and in-
> cludes speech-language pathology and audiology services,
> interpreting services, psychological services, physical and
> occupational therapy, recreation, including therapeutic
> recreation, counseling services, including rehabilitation
> counseling, orientation and mobility services, and medical
> services for diagnostic or evaluation purposes. Related ser-
> vices also include school health services, school nurse ser-
> vices designed to enable a child with a disability to receive a
> free appropriate public education as described in the IEP of
> the child, social work services in schools, and parent coun-
> seling and training. (20 U.S.C. § 1401(26)(A))

The list of related services is not exhaustive and may include
other types of related services as may be necessary to provide a student with a FAPE. IDEA's implementing regulations
provide definitions for each related service listed at 34 C.F.R.
§ 300.34(c).

IDEA's statutory framework and implementing regulations provide a detailed and complex scheme for school districts
to follow when meeting the basic obligations already described.
A mental health provider—who works in a school setting or has
been retained to address the needs of a student with a disability
who qualifies for special education services—should be particularly cognizant of IDEA's mandates for determining eligibility of
a student for special education services, developing the IEP, and

certain procedural safeguards related to the discipline of students with disabilities. The discussion in this chapter is nonexhaustive with respect to these obligations; however, it should provide the mental health provider with a general understanding of a school district's and a school professional's obligations in these important areas to the provision of special education services to IDEA-eligible students.

Students Eligible for Special Education Services Under IDEA

IDEA and its implementing regulations set the parameters that guide mental health professionals in understanding the scope of IDEA's coverage and the meaning of its mandates. Importantly, IDEA's definition of "child with a disability" provides the basis for determining which students are eligible for special education services under IDEA. The term "child with a disability" is defined by IDEA (20 U.S. C. § 1401(3); 34 C.F.R. § 300.8) to mean a child

(i) with intellectual disabilities, hearing impairments (including deafness), speech or language impairments, visual impairments (including blindness), serious emotional disturbance (referred to in this chapter [and the implementing regulations] as "emotional disturbance"), orthopedic impairments, autism, traumatic brain injury, other health impairments, or specific learning disabilities; and

(ii) who, by reason thereof, needs special education and related services.

IDEA also provides for a general category of "development delay" to be used for children ages 3 through 9 to be identified as eligible for special education services at the discretion of the state and local school district (20 U.S.C. § 1401(3)(B); 34 C.F.R. § 300.8(b)). IDEA's coverage therefore leads to a two-question inquiry when determining eligibility of students for special education services under IDEA:

1. Does the student have a disability that falls into one of the categories identified in IDEA?
2. Does the student need special education and related services as a result of such disability?

In order to ensure that children with disabilities in need of special education services are identified, located, and evaluated, IDEA imposes a "child find" obligation on school districts (34 C.F.R. § 300.111). When applying this "child find" obligation and evaluating children suspected of being in need of special education services, IDEA provides for certain procedures to be followed. These procedures include referring a child for an evaluation

(34 C.F.R. § 300.301(b)), reviewing existing evaluation data regarding the student to determine whether further evaluation is required (34 C.F.R. § 300.305(a)), deciding upon the evaluation's components (34 C.F.R. § 300.305), and ensuring that parental consent is sought prior to conducting the evaluation (20 U.S.C. § 1414(a)(1)(D); 34 C.F.R. § 300.300).

IDEA's procedures require that the evaluation must be completed within 60 days of receiving parental consent or within the time frame established by state law (20 U.S.C. § 1414(a)(1)(C)(i)(I); 34 C.F.R. § 300.301(c)(1)).

The student should be assessed in all areas related to the suspected disability including, if appropriate, health, vision, hearing, social and emotional status, general intelligence, academic performance, communicative status, and motor abilities (20 U.S.C. § 1414(b)(3)(B); 34 C.F.R. § 300.304(c)(4)), and the evaluation components should be sufficiently comprehensive to identify all of the student's special education and related service needs, whether or not commonly linked to the disability category in which the child has been classified (34 C.F.R. § 300.304(c)(6)). As under Section 504, the IDEA does not require a medical diagnosis or a diagnosis pursuant to the *DSM-5* for a school district to make a determination that a student has a disability. Schools should consider the findings of a medical evaluation if shared by the parents during the eligibility determination process. Furthermore, if the school decides that a medical evaluation is necessary to determine eligibility or develop an IEP for the student, this must be provided without cost to the parent.

When conducting an evaluation, IDEA and its implementing regulations mandate that a school district use

- A variety of assessment tools and strategies to gather relevant functional, developmental, and academic information (20 U.S.C. § 1414 (b)(2)(A); 34 C.F.R. § 300.304(b)(1))
- Technically sound instruments that may assess the relative contribution of cognitive and behavioral factors in addition to physical or developmental factors (20 U.S.C. § 1414(b)(2)(C); 34 C.F.R. § 300.304(b)(3))
- Assessments and other evaluation materials that are nondiscriminatory, are administered in the child's native language or other mode of communication, are used for the purposes for which the assessments or measures are valid and reliable, are given by trained and knowledgeable personnel, and are delivered in accordance with any instructions provided by the producer of the measures (20 U.S.C. § 1414(b)(2)(3); 34 C.F.R. § 300.304(c)(1))
- Appraisals and other evaluation materials that include those tailored to review specific areas of educational need and not merely those that are designed to provide a single general intelligence quotient (34 C.F.R. § 300.304(c)(2))

- Assessments that are selected and administered so as best to ensure that if an evaluation is given to a child with impaired sensory, manual, or speaking skills, the appraisal results accurately reflect the child's aptitude or achievement level or whatever other factors the test purports to measure, rather than reflecting the child's impaired sensory, manual, or speaking skills, unless those skills are the factors that the test purports to measure (34 C.F.R. § 300.304(c)(3))
- Assessment tools and strategies that provide relevant information and directly assist persons in determining the educational needs of the child (20 U.S.C. § 1414(b); 34 C.F.R. § 300.304(c)(7))

Any evaluation conducted should meet these requirements and, thereafter, must be considered by the IEP team, including the child's parents, which ultimately determines whether the child is eligible for special education and related services under the IDEA (34 C.F.R. § 300.304).

If the parents disagree with an evaluation obtained by a school district, they have the right to request that the district conduct an independent educational review at public expense (34 C.F.R. § 300.502(b)(1)). If the parents obtain an independent educational assessment of their child at their own expense, the written evaluation results must be considered by the IEP team if the parents request a meeting to consider the results (34 C.F.R. § 300.502(c)).

Reevaluations of IDEA-eligible students should be conducted if the school district decides that a reevaluation is warranted or if the child's parent or teacher requests a reevaluation (20 U.S.C. § 1414(a)(2)(A); 34 C.F.R. § 300.303(a)). However, there must be a reevaluation at least once every 3 years unless the parent and the school district agree otherwise (20 U.S.C. § 1414(a)(2); 34 C.F.R. § 300.303(b)). Additionally, a school district must conduct an assessment of a child with a disability before determining that the child no longer qualifies for special education and related services under the IDEA unless the eligible student with a disability has graduated from high school with a regular diploma or has aged out of IDEA eligibility (20 U.S.C. § 1414(c)(5); 34 C.F.R. § 300.305(e)).

Individualized Education Program

The individualized education program (IEP) of an IDEA-eligible student is the basic plan that guides the delivery of programming and services to the student. It is the written document that contains the information supporting the basis for and the provision of a special education program to the eligible student. The IEP must be in writing and must be developed, reviewed, and revised by the student's IEP team, which includes qualified educators, related service providers, the parents, and individuals with knowledge of the child that the parents may bring to the IEP conference (e.g., therapists working with the child outside of the educational setting). The IEP is at the core of developing and delivering services to special education students. IDEA carefully and specifically describes what an IEP should contain, how it is to be developed, and the means by which it should be implemented.

Under IDEA, an IEP must include (20 U.S.C. § 1414(d))

- A statement of the child's present levels of academic achievement and functional performance (34 C.F.R. § 300.320(a)(1))
- A statement of measurable annual goals, including academic and functional goals (34 C.F.R. § 300.320(a)(2))
- A description of how and when the child's progress toward meeting these annual goals is to be measured and when periodic reports on the progress the child is making toward meeting the annual goals will be provided (34 C.F.R. § 300.320(a)(3))
- A statement of the special education and related services and supplementary aids and services—based on peer-reviewed research to the extent practicable—to be provided to the child or on behalf of the child, and a statement of the program modifications or supports for school personnel that are to be provided (34 C.F.R. § 300.320(a)(4))
- An explanation of the extent, if any, to which the child should not participate with nondisabled children in the regular class and activities (34 C.F.R. § 300.320(a)(5))
- A description of any individual appropriate accommodations necessary to measure the academic achievement and functional performance of the child on state- and district-wide assessments (34 C.F.R. § 300.320(a)(6))
- The projected date for beginning the services and modifications, and the anticipated frequency, location, and duration of those services and modifications (34 C.F.R. § 300.320(a)(7))
- Beginning not later than the first IEP to be in effect when the child is 16 (or sooner, if required by state law), a transition plan designed to address a student's transition from school to postsecondary school education, employment, and/or independent living as appropriate (34 C.F.R. § 300.320(b))

It is important for school personnel, including mental health providers, to follow IDEA's procedures for developing the IEP, especially inclusion of parent participation in the process. In addition to specifying the components of the IEP, these procedures establish requirements for the frequency of IEP meetings, the individuals who need to attend an IEP meeting, the nature of IEP meeting discussions, and the process by which notice should be provided to parents about their rights and their child's special education program. IDEA requires that the following participants be included in the IEP team: the parents, at least one regular education teacher, at least one special education teacher, a qualified school district representative with knowledge of the available district resources, a professional who can interpret evaluation results, others at the discretion of the parent or the agency who have knowledge or special expertise regarding the child, and, as appropriate, the child with the disability (20 U.S.C. § 1414(d)(1)(B); 34 C.F.R. § 300.321). A school district must hold an IEP team meeting at least annually (34 C.F.R. § 300.324(b)(1)(i)).

Certain matters must be considered at the IEP team meeting, including a discussion of the child's strengths, parental concerns for enhancing the education of their child, the results of the child's initial evaluation or most recent evaluation, and the child's academic, developmental, and functional needs (20 U.S.C. § 1414(d)(3)(A); 34 C.F.R. § 300.324(a)). In certain circumstances that may exist when a mental health provider is supporting a school district or parent, the IEP team must consider special factors. For example, in the case of a child whose behavior impedes the child's learning or that of others, the IEP team must consider the use of positive behavioral interventions and supports, and other strategies, to address the child's behavior (20 U.S.C. § 1414(d)(3)(B)(i); 34 C.F.R. § 300.324(a)(2)(i)).

The IEP team determines the student's placement and the program in which the student is to receive special education and related services. The placement must be consistent with the child's IEP, must be where the student can realize a FAPE (34 C.F.R. § 300.101), and must ensure that the student is placed in the least restrictive environment because IDEA provides that "to the maximum extent appropriate, children with disabilities, including children in public or private institutions or other care facilities, are educated with children who are nondisabled" (34 C.F.R. § 300.114). The school district must ensure parental involvement in any decision regarding the educational placement of their child (34 C.F.R. §§ 300.327, 300.501(b), 300.501(c)).

Discipline of Students With Disabilities Under IDEA

Mental health providers who work in public schools or with parents of children in public schools should be aware that IDEA's procedures afford students with disabilities certain protections when a student's behavior is of concern or discipline is contemplated and/or imposed. IDEA addresses the suspension and expulsion of special education students as well as the obligation of school districts to develop and implement behavior intervention strategies to address student behavior. Certain procedures also allow for the removal of a student to an interim alternative educational placement for 45 school days in certain circumstances.

IDEA does not prohibit a school district from suspending an IDEA-eligible special education student for up to 10 consecutive school days so long as such a disciplinary measure would have been applied to a student without a disability. IDEA states that

> [s]chool personnel under this subsection may remove a child with a disability who violates a code of student conduct from their current placement to an appropriate interim alternative educational setting, another setting, or suspension, for not more than 10 school days (to the extent such alternatives are applied to children without disabilities). (20 U.S.C. § 1415(k)(1)(B))

If services are not provided to a child without disabilities who has been similarly removed, the school district does not need to provide services for the first 10 cumulative days of suspension during a school year (34 C.F.R. § 300.530(d)(3)).

However, other guarantees of IDEA address a disciplined student's right to FAPE requiring that services be provided during the suspension period beginning on the 11th cumulative day of suspension during the school year (34 C.F.R. § 300.530(b)(2)). These services must be provided "so as to enable the child to continue to participate in the general education curriculum, although in another setting, and to progress toward meeting the goals set out in the child's IEP" (34 C.F.R. § 300.530(d)(1)(i)). The determination of which services are to be provided beginning on the 11th day of suspension is made by school personnel.

An IDEA-eligible special education student can only be removed from school for more than 10 consecutive school days, or expelled, if certain procedures are followed and only if the school district continues to provide services during the period of the special education student's disciplinary removal (expulsion) from school. Those IDEA procedures require that within 10 school days of a recommendation or decision to expel a student with a disability, or otherwise change a disabled student's placement for disciplinary reasons, a manifestation determination review (MDR) meeting must occur (20 U.S.C. § 1415(k)(1)(E)).

An MDR is a meeting of relevant members of a child's IEP team who must review the special education student's alleged misconduct as well as all relevant information in the student's file, including the child's IEP, any teacher observations, and any relevant information provided by parents to determine (34 C.F.R. § 300.530(e))

- If the conduct in question was caused by, or had a direct and substantial relationship to, the child's disability
- If the conduct in question resulted directly from the school district's failure to implement the IEP

If the student's conduct was caused by, or had a direct and substantial relationship to, the child's disability or if the student's conduct directly resulted from the school district's failure to implement the IEP, then the conduct must be determined to be a manifestation of the child's disability and the student cannot be expelled from school (20 U.S.C. § 1415(k)(1)(E); 34 C.F.R. § 300.530(e)). If the student's behavior subject to disciplinary action is determined not to have been a manifestation of the disability, the school district may expel the student from school in the same manner as it would students without disabilities (20 U.S.C. § 1415(k)(1)(C); 34 C.F.R. § 300.530(c)). However, if a special education student is expelled, the student must continue to receive educational services so as to enable the student to continue to participate in the general education curriculum, although in another setting, and to progress toward meeting the goals set out in the child's IEP (the IEP team determines the placement/services to be provided). In addition, the expelled special education student shall receive, as appropriate, a functional behavioral assessment (FBA), behavioral intervention services, and modifications designed to address the behavioral violation so that it does not recur (20 U.S.C. § 1415(k) (1)(D); 34 C.F.R. § 300.530(d)(1)).

There are certain circumstances in which a special education student can be removed from the student's school placement to an interim alternative educational setting for up to 45 school days even if the student's behavior is a manifestation of his or her disability (20 U.S.C. § 1415(k)(2); 34 C.F.R. § 300.530(g)). Those circumstances include instances when:

- A student carries a weapon to or possesses a weapon at school, on school premises, or to or at a school function (34 C.F.R. § 300.530(g)(1)
- A student knowingly possesses or uses illegal drugs, or sells or solicits the sale of a controlled substance, while at school, on school premises, or at a school function (34 C.F.R. § 300.530(g)(2)
- A student has inflicted serious bodily injury upon another person while at school, on school premises, or at a school function (34 C.F.R. § 300.530(g)(3)

FAPE must continue to remain available to these students in the interim alternative educational setting, which is determined by the student's IEP team (20 U.S.C. § 1415(k)(2); 34 C.F.R. 300.530(d)(5)).

Other important protections relating to the discipline of special education students involves the school district's obligations to develop and implement behavior intervention plans. Under IDEA, an FBA should be conducted and a behavior intervention plan (BIP) developed when a student is suspended for more than 10 cumulative school days during a school year, is expelled, or is placed in an interim alternative educational setting for not more than 45 school days (34 C.F.R. § 300.530(d)(ii)). If a student is suspended for more than 10 school days during a school year, the child must "[r]eceive, as appropriate, a functional behavioral assessment, and behavioral intervention services and modifications that are designed to address the behavior violation so that it does not recur." Further, if the student's conduct is determined to be a manifestation of a disability, the IEP team must conduct an FBA and develop a BIP unless it has already been developed; if a BIP exists, it should be reviewed and modified as necessary to address the behavior (20 U.S.C. § 1415(k)(1)(F); 34 C.F.R. § 300.530(f)).

Procedural Safeguards Under IDEA

Districts must provide the parents of a child with a disability with notice of the procedural safeguards that the IDEA establishes on a yearly basis, that specific notice must be provided in certain circumstances including when an initial referral is made for a child to be considered for an evaluation to determine eligibility for special education services, in accordance with disciplinary procedures, and when parents request a copy (34 C.F.R. § 300.504(a)). The notice of procedural safeguards afforded students and parents/guardians under IDEA must address the following (34 C.F.R. § 300.504(c)):

- Independent educational evaluations
- Prior written notice
- Parental consent
- Access to educational records
- Opportunity to present complaints to initiate due process hearings
- Child's placement during pendency of due process proceedings
- Procedures for students who are subject to placement in an interim alternative educational setting
- Requirements for unilateral placement by parents of children in private schools at public expense
- Mediation
- Resolution meetings
- Due process hearings, including requirements for disclosure of evaluation results and recommendations
- State-level appeals (if applicable in the state)
- Civil actions
- Attorney's fees

The procedural safeguards notice must be written in a language that is understandable to the general public and in the parent's/guardian's native language, unless it is clearly not feasible to do so (34 C.F.R. § 300.504(d)).

DECISION-MAKING FRAMEWORK FOR ADDRESSING LEGAL AND ETHICAL ISSUES

Numerous models and decision-making frameworks have been developed to help mental health professionals resolve legal and ethical dilemmas. Professional codes of ethics often provide a framework to analyze problems and determine an appropriate course of action. The following is a decision-making framework that reflects a general understanding of the legal obligations of individual mental health professionals working in educational settings. It is premised on a pragmatic approach that all mental health practice dilemmas should be addressed by considering, under appropriate professional supervision and, if necessary, the assistance of legal counsel, the legal implications and consequences of a particular action (Israel, 2010, pp. 13–30).

The framework emphasizes the importance of understanding the policies and procedures that school districts develop to define the roles and responsibilities of mental health professionals working within schools:

1. Define and describe the situation.
2. Identify the potential ethical and legal issues involved.
3. Determine all of the parties involved in the situation and the potential parties that may be involved. Carefully consider what federal and state laws and school policies must be followed and the professional ethical standards that may apply. These include, but may not be limited to, the laws and policies governing education and mental health records, confidentiality, informed consent, special education, and civil rights.
4. Decide upon the nature of the professional relationships that may exist with the parties and the duties that have arisen or may arise from those relationships. This analysis should include identifying the students who may be involved and determining the nature of their family relationships to ensure that the legally recognized parent(s) receive any required notices and that the parent(s) are afforded the opportunity to exercise any rights they may have under the applicable state and federal laws and school or agency policies. This analysis should also consider the professional duties and responsibilities that may involve the educators and other professionals working within the schools, as well as members of the general community.
5. Develop a list of the actions that should be undertaken to address the situation and the possible consequences of each course of action. This evaluation should consider the immediate and future consequences of the action from an educational, clinical, and legal perspective.

6. Determine and implement the chosen course of action.
7. At all stages, maintain appropriate documentation and comply with applicable policies governing education records and personally identifiable health information.
8. Seek necessary and appropriate professional supervision and legal counsel at all stages.

SUMMARY

Mental health services to students and their families within educational settings encompass a range of professional activities including school-wide interventions, professional consultations, identification, assessment and evaluation, and services to both groups of students and individual students and their families.

Mental health professionals working within schools must

- Recognize and respect the rights of students under the U.S. Constitution and federal and state statutory laws
- Balance the authority of parents and guardians to make decisions about their children, the rights and needs of children, and the purpose and authority exercised by schools
- Fulfill the professional legal and ethical duties that arise from the licensure or certification they may hold and the code of ethics that govern their chosen profession
- Understand the policies and procedures that govern their actions as employees, agents, or independent contractors providing mental health services in school settings
- Seek necessary and appropriate professional supervision and legal counsel

RESOURCES

Ethics and Law for School Psychologists is a comprehensive textbook for understanding and delivering ethically and legally sound services. Its authors are Professor Susan Jacob, PhD, Professor Dawn Decker, PhD, NCSP, and Professor Timothy Hartshorne, PhD (2010, Wiley).

School Psychology for the 21st Century: Foundations and Practices is a book written by Professor Kenneth Merrell, PhD, Professor Ruth Ervin, PhD, and Professor Gretchen Peacock, PhD. It is an introductory text describing the role of school psychologists in promoting academic, behavioral, and emotional achievements for students. The text includes coverage of the impact of IDEA and professional ethics (2011, Guilford).

Ethical, Legal, and Professional Issues in the Practice of Marriage and Family Therapy, written by Allen Wilcoxon, Professor Theodore Remley Jr., PhD, and Samuel Gladding, is a book for students, educators, supervisors, and practitioners that considers the legal, ethical, and professional issues that marriage and family therapists face daily (2011, Pearson).

Counseling and Psychotherapy with Children and Adolescents: Theory and Practice for School and Clinical Setting covers major approaches to counseling children and adolescents including information on ethical and legal issues involved with treating children and adolescents. This book is edited by Professor H. Thompson Prout, PhD and Douglas T. Brown, PhD (2007, Wiley).

Ethical, Legal, and Professional Issues in Counseling, written by Professor Theodore Remley Jr., PhD and Professor Barbara Herlihy, PhD, is a book that explores issues in counseling from both an ethical and a legal point of view. It includes recent federal court cases that pose ethical and legal matters in counseling today (2013, Pearson).

The Center for Mental Health in Schools at UCLA has developed a series of continuing education materials in order to address barriers to student learning through a comprehensive approach that recognizes the roles played by school, home, and community life. Information presented includes legal and ethical issues faced by schools providing mental health services. *Addressing Barriers to Learning: New Directions for Mental Health in Schools* (smhp.psych .ucla.edu/pdfdocs/contedu/conted.pdf) and *Confidentiality and Informed Consent* (smhp.psych.ucla.edu/pdfdocs/confid/confid .pdf) are two of these publications.

The DOE has published policy guidance regarding FERPA available on its website (www2.ed.gov/policy/gen/guid/fpco/ brochures/elsec.html) entitled *Balancing Student Privacy and School Safety: A Guide to the Family Educational Rights and Privacy Act for Elementary and Secondary Schools*. This document provides an overview of what FERPA permits and requires of school districts.

The DOE has also published an informational sheet (www 2.ed.gov/policy/gen/guid/fpco/brochures/parents.pdf) with answers to frequently asked questions regarding FERPA.

The American Counseling Association produces an online publication called VISTAS Online. An article written by M. Sherrill, Luther Pitcairn, and Kristi Ann Phillips entitled *Ethics, Laws, and Adolescents: Confidentiality, Reporting, and Conflict* (www.counseling .org/docs/disaster-and-trauma_sexual-abuse/ethics-laws-and-adolescents_confidentiality.pdf?sfvrsn=2) provides a brief overview of how to approach the issues of confidentiality, mandated reporting, and the conflicting needs of the child, the school, the parents, and the law.

The HHS Administration for Children and Families provides information and resources (www.childwelfare.gov) for child welfare and related professionals. The information is designed to help protect children and strengthen families, including how to prevent and respond to child abuse and neglect.

Several professional associations provide information online regarding ethical principles, legal resources, overviews of IDEA, guidance from DOE, and relevant laws and case law.

These include the following:

- American Psychological Association
  www.apa.org/ethics/code/index.aspx
- American School Counselor Association
  www.schoolcounselor.org/asca/media/asca/Resource%
  20Center/Legal%20and%20Ethical%20Issues/Sample%
  20Documents/EthicalStandards2010.pdf
- American Mental Health Counselors Association
  www.amhca.org/about/codetoc.aspx
- American Counseling Association
  www.counseling.org/knowledge-center/ethics
- National Association of Social Workers
  www.socialworkers.org/pubs/code/default.asp
- National School Boards Association
  www.nsba.org/SchoolLaw/Issues/Health
- The AASA, the School Superintendents Association
  www.aasa.org/Default.aspx
- American School Health Association
  netforum.avectra.com/eWeb/DynamicPage.aspx?Site=
  ASHA1&WebCode=WhatisSchoolHealth
- The Center for Health and Health Care in Schools
  www.healthinschools.org
- School-Based Health Alliance
  www.sbh4all.org/site/c.ckLQKbOVLkK6E/b.7505827/
  k.2960/About_SchoolBased_Health_Alliance.htm
- National Dissemination Center for Children with Disabilities (NICHCY)
  nichcy.org/schools-administrators
- American Bar Association, Center on Children and the
  Law
  www.americanbar.org/groups/child_law/tools_to_use.
  html
- Bazelon Center for Mental Health Law
  www.bazelon.org/Where-We-Stand/Success-for-All-
  Children/Mental-Health-Services-for-Children.aspx
- National Center for Youth Law
  www.youthlaw.org/health

NOTES

1. There are several professional organizations that represent and support mental health professionals working in schools. A list of some of these institutions and citations to codes of professional ethics for each group are included in the Resources section at the end of the chapter.
2. The Guttmacher Institute provides resources and information (www.guttmacher.org/sections/adolescents.php and www.guttmacher.org/statecenter/spibs/spib_OMCL.pdf) regarding minors' rights and responsibilities and an overview of state policies regarding consent in matters related to reproduction, contraception, and sexuality and the rights of pregnant and parenting teens.
3. The HHS (www.childwelfare.gov) provides state-specific guidance and resources including the texts of statutes for specific states and territories, state child abuse reporting numbers, and other resources concerning child abuse and neglect.
4. The discussion in this chapter should be considered an overview. For more information, the reader may wish to consult materials developed by the American Academy of Pediatrics (AAP). The AAP provides online overviews and commentary, easily understood by readers without legal training (www.nationalguidelines.org/guideline.cfm?guideNum=0-03 and www.nationalguidelines.org/guideline.cfm?guideNum=4-25), regarding confidentiality of student health records and maintaining and protecting records that include health, mental health, and family health.
5. FERPA defines parent as a parent of a student (natural parent, guardian, or an individual acting as a parent in the absence of parent or guardian; 34 C.F.R. § 99.3). Parental separation, divorce, and custody status do not affect the right to inspect records absent a court order or legally binding agreement specifically limiting or revoking the right to access records (34 C.F.R. § 99.4).
6. An eligible student is a student who is at least 18 years of age or who attends a postsecondary institution at any age (34 C.F.R. §§ 99.3 and 99.5(a)). The consent of special education students over 18 years of age who have not delegated education rights to their parent or guardian or do not have a guardian may also be required to release education records.
7. The ADAAA amended not only the ADA but also Section 504 through a conforming amendment (42 U.S.C § 12102).
8. The U.S. DOE's OCR has recently issued guidance (www2.ed.gov/about/offices/list/ocr/docs/disabharassltr.html) to school officials and professionals that addresses a disabled student's right to be free from "harassment" in the school setting. OCR's guidance is entitled Reminder of Responsibilities under Section 504 of the Rehabilitation Act of 1973 and Title II of the ADA.
9. Students can be considered otherwise qualified only if they are able to meet all requirements to be a part of a program despite their disability. See *Southeastern Community College v. Davis*, 442 U.S. 397, 406 (1979; "An otherwise qualified person is one who is able to meet all of a program's requirements in spite of his handicap.")
10. The ADAAA makes clear that the term "substantially limits" must be interpreted without regard to consideration of mitigating

measures other than ordinary eyeglasses or contact lenses (42 U.S.C. § 12102(4)(E)).

11. The DOE's OCR (www2.ed.gov/about/offices/list/ocr/504faq. html) addresses users of alcohol and disciplinary actions available.

12. In its *Frequently Asked Questions About Section 504 and the Education of Children with Disabilities*, the OCR states that the "committee should include persons knowledgeable about the student, the meaning of the evaluation data, and the placement options."

REFERENCES

American Psychiatric Association. (2013). *Diagnostic and statical manual of mental disorders* (5th ed.). Washington, DC: Author.

American Psychological Association. (2010). *Ethical principles of psychologists and code of conduct.* Retrieved from http://www.apa.org/ethics/code/index.aspx?item=3

Americans with Disabilities Act, 42 U.S.C. § 12101, *et seq.*; implementing regulations 28 C.F.R. § 35.

Boldt, R. (2012). Adolescent decision making: Legal issues with respect to treatment for substance misuse and mental illness. *Journal of Health Care Law and Policy, 15,* 75–128.

Brown v. Board of Educ., 347 U.S. 483 (1954).

Family Educational Rights and Privacy Act of 1974, 20 U.S.C. § 1232g; implementing regulations 34 C.F.R. Part 99.

Garner, B. (2009). *Black's law dictionary* (9th ed.). Eagan, MN: West.

Health Insurance Portability and Accountability Act, 42 U.S.C. § 300gg, 29 U.S.C. § 1181 *et seq.*, 42 U.S.C. 1320d *et seq.*; implementing regulations 45 C.F.R. §§ 144, 146, 160, 162, 164.

Hill, B. J. (2012). Medical decision making by and on behalf of adolescents: Reconsidering first principles. *Journal of Health Care Law and Policy, 15,* 37–87.

Individuals with Disabilities Education Act, 20 U.S.C. § 1401 *et seq;* implementing regulations 34 C.F.R. Part 300.

Israel, A. (2010). *Using the law: Practical decision making in mental health.* Chicago, Il: Lyceum Books.

Jacob, S., Decker, D., & Hartshorne, T. (2010). *Ethics and law for school psychologists* (6th ed.). Hoboken, NJ: Wiley.

Jaffee v. Redmond, 518 U.S. 1 (1996).

Knapp, S., Gottlieb, M., Handelsman, M., & Berman, J. (2007). When laws and ethics collide: What should psychologists do? *Professional Psychology: Research and Practice, 38*(1), 54–59.

Protection of Pupil Rights Act, 20 U.S.C. § 1232h.

Rideout, J. C. (2010). Penumbral thinking revisited: Metaphor in legal argumentation. *Journal of the Association of Legal Writing Directors, 7,* 155–198.

Section 504 of the Rehabilitation Act of 1973, 29 U.S.C. § 701 *et seq.*; implementing regulations 34 C.F.R. Part 104.

Tarasoff v. The Regents of the University of California (Tarasoff I), 529 P.2d 553 (Cal. 1974).

Tarasoff v. The Regents of the University of California (Tarasoff II), 551 P.2d 334 (Cal. 1976).

Title VI of the Civil Rights Act of 1964, 42 U.S.C. § 2000d *et seq.*; implementing regulations 34 C.F.R. Part 100.

Title IX of the Education Amendments of 1972, 20 U.S.C. § 1681 *et seq.*; implementing regulations 34 C.F.R. Part 106.

U.S. Const. amend. X.

U.S. Const. art. I, § 8.

U.S. Const. art. VI, § 2.

U.S. Department of Education. (2005). *Letter to Carroll independent school district re: destruction of student test data.* Retrieved from http://www2.ed.gov/policy/gen/guid/fpco/ferpa/library/carrollisd091305.html

U.S. Department of Education. (2012, January 19). *Dear colleague letter.* Retrieved from http://www2.ed.gov/about/offices/list/ocr/letters/colleague-201109.html

U.S. Department of Health and Human Services, U.S. Department of Education. (2008). *Joint guidance on the application of the Family Educational Rights and Privacy Act (FERPA) and the Health Insurance Portability and Accountability Act (HIPAA) of 1996 to student health records.* Retrieved from http://www2.ed.gov/policy/gen/guid/fpco/doc/ferpa-hipaa-guidance.pdf

CHAPTER 8

Culturally Sensitive Mental Health Services

ANN KATHLEEN BURLEW

G. SUSAN MOSLEY-HOWARD

LEARNING OUTCOMES

On completion of this chapter, the reader should be able to:

- Comprehend mental health issues facing ethnic minority youths
- Define relevant models/methods for culturally adapting evidence-based treatments (EBTs)
- Understand the core elements of cultural adaptation as it relates to mental health and evidence-based practice (EBP)

INTERSECTION OF CULTURE AND MENTAL HEALTH INTERVENTION

In this increasingly diverse world, the need to consider cultural context within mental health practice is more important than ever. Currently, the United States has a population that is 37% minority, and five states have a population where the minority is the majority (California, District of Columbia, Hawaii, New Mexico, and Texas). Further, according to a U.S. Bureau of the Census report, of the 79 million children and adults enrolled in U.S. schools (pre-K–college), 25% had at least one parent who was foreign-born, 11.8 million school-age children (ages 5–17) spoke a language other than English at home (mostly Spanish), and U.S. schools today have a 44% minority student body population (U.S. Bureau of the Census, 2013).

At the same time, mental health practice along with all medical and social service practice are moving toward evidence-based and culturally relevant frameworks. EBT, evidence-based intervention (EBI), or EBP in the mental health arena is generally perceived to be an integration of three pillars: (a) scientific evidence of a treatment's efficacy; (b) inclusion of expert clinical opinion and expertise; and (c) a provision of high-quality services sensitive to client/caregiver perspectives, values, needs, and choices (Sackett, Straus, Richardson, Rosenberg, & Haynes, 2000). This third pillar (sensitive to client needs) is generally thought to include cultural context. In addition, partly in response to the nation's changing demographics, cultural competence guidelines from each major professional mental health organization (American Psychological Association, American Psychiatric Association, American Counseling Association, National Association of Social Workers, National Association of School Psychologists), along with the National Alliance on Mental Illness goal 3, and APA's Council of National Psychological Association for the Advancement of Ethnic Minority Interests 2003 report, have highlighted the mental health status of the U.S. ethnic minority population. These organizations also draw attention to limited access to mental health treatment and the critical importance of culturally sensitive practice.

Because this chapter focuses on cultural dynamics related to EBT with school-age clients within the Response to Intervention (RTI) framework, it is important to review mental health issues present among the ethnic minority population of school-age children. Youths in general experience developmental milestones that lead to acquiring self-sufficiency, individuation, and cultivating talents, skills, and relationships—all a part of the child to adult journey. Being surrounded by supportive adults is of significant benefit to the child development process. Schools house some of those supportive adults who play a key role in the success of today's youths. Yet the developmental journey of 21st century youths is filled with challenges unfamiliar to youths from earlier decades. Psychological, academic, physiological, and social needs, dynamics, and events (fueled and accelerated by our highly technological and socially orchestrated world) are unfolding at paces unseen by past youths. Young people of today face a myriad of issues requiring coping mechanisms they may not yet possess. Add a cultural or socioeconomic dimension to that developmental pathway, and we may have a recipe leading to disparities between youths from the cultural minority versus youths socialized in the cultural majority.

A review of the literature on health and mental health status of North American children and youths suggests that overall the status of this nation's youths is sound in comparison to the global context. However, despite all of these advantages that U.S. youths enjoy, they still exhibit symptoms of mental illness over their lifetimes. According to Merikangas et al. (2010), 13% of 8- to 13-year-old children experience diagnosable mental disorders, whereas the statistics are 20% for youths ages 13 to 18 (mostly mood and anxiety/impulse issues). A Health and Human Services (HHS) report presents data highlighting that U.S. youths' self-report of *not feeling healthy* ranks 7th highest for boys and 10th highest for girls in global comparisons; U.S. youths were among the highest for those *not feeling happy* (7th for boys and 11th for girls), and were in the top four nations for *feeling low*. U.S. youths were first and second highest in reports of backache, stomachache, headache, and third highest in reports for feeling tired when going to school (U.S. Department of Health and Human Services, 2003). According to Kessler, Berglund, Demler, Jin, and Walters (2005), suicide is the third leading cause of death among U.S. adolescents and young adults. Further, based upon Centers for Disease Control and Prevention (CDC) data, the National Institute for Mental Health (NIMH) reported that one half of youths from ages 8 to 15 with a mental illness reportedly received no services in the previous year (National Institute of Mental Health, 2012). To further support this trend, Merikangas et al. (2011) reported that approximately 36% of youths with an identified mental disorder over their lifetimes received mental health intervention services, and most of those children were in treatment for fewer than six sessions. Given this overall picture of mental health need among youths, a focused look at mental health specifically for ethnic minority youths is important, particularly in regard to the implementation of approaches in the field such as understanding cultural adaptation.

Ethnic minority youth are impacted by a multitude of environmental factors, such as socioeconomic status and ethnicity. Culture and cultural context can be seen as an asset, as well as viewed as contributing to mental health challenges. As an asset, culture creates and gives space to social support, kinship bonds, affirmation, heritage, spirituality, sense of self, resilience, and intergenerational and indigenous ways of coping. Jackson, Forsythe-Brown, & Govia (2007) noted the benefit of indigenous cultural practices and experiences as contributors to well-being. Culturally infused mental health intervention relies on these inherent strengths to ameliorate the challenges brought by mental illness. Cultural context however can also play a role in the manifestation of mental health symptoms. Pumariega, Rogers, and Rothe (2005) made the observation that some culturally laden child rearing practices, communication styles, role expectation, beliefs about illness, and other variables that impact development may influence the mental health status of ethnic minority youths.

Although there is a need for continued epidemiological study to determine more about the mental health status of ethnic minority youths, following is a partial list of what is currently known (refer to Table 5.1). The data in this table are from a comprehensive survey of mental health status (Mental Health Surveillance Among Children) conducted by the U.S. CDC (2013). This study used a variety of mental health measures, databases, and surveys; among these are Diagnostic Interview Schedule for Children (DISC-IV), National Health Interview Survey (NHIS), National Survey of Children's Health (NSCH), National Health and Nutrition Examination Survey (NHANES), National Survey on Drug Use and Health (NSDUH), Youth Risk Behavior Survey (YRBS), and the Patient Health Questionnaire (PHQ-9). Some data also stem from the American Community Survey (ACS; U.S. Bureau of the Census, 2006), National Center for Children in Poverty (NCCP), and National Alliance on Mental Illness (NAMI) resources.

A summary of these data indicate that overall the most prevalent disorders among all youths nationwide are attention deficit hyperactivity disorder (ADHD), depression, behavioral and conduct disorders, anxiety, and substance use/abuse. Differences emerge along ethnic/racial categories for some disorders. Unless otherwise indicated, data in Table 5.1 are from the previously mentioned CDC (2013) study.

To add to the mental health picture, the CDC's School Health Programs (2011) report cited health risks across ethnic minority youths (CDC, 2011). For example, African American youths reported lower levels of drinking and driving, tobacco use, and bullying than White/Caucasian youths (YRBS, 2012). Yet African American youths were more likely to engage in sexual intercourse, whereas Latino youths were more likely to have engaged in drinking and driving, felt sad or hopeless, made a plan for suicide, and drank before the age of 13.

These health-oriented CDC data, coupled with the CDC mental health data, generally suggested that ethnic minority youths were susceptible to health and environmental dangers that might place them at risk for death, illness, or in need of social or educational intervention. Multiracial (non-Hispanic) youths had higher incidences of ADHD, depression, and substance abuse. Latinos had the lowest rate of ADHD diagnoses, but higher prevalence of substance issues. African American youths had higher rates of behavioral and conduct disorder diagnoses, but lowest comparatively speaking on alcohol abuse. Autism spectrum disorder (ASD) and anxiety prevalence tended to be higher for White, non-Hispanic youths.

Given the dynamics of a shifting demography, the distinctive mental health and educational issues facing children and ethnic minority youths, and the increased call for efficacious mental health practice, mental health providers need to embrace and infuse culturally relevant practice. Examined next are effectiveness of cultural interventions, various models of culturally based practice, and case study applications.

TABLE 5.1 Mental Health Disparities

Disorder type	Asian American youths	Native American youths	Latino youths	African American youths	Multiethnic youths
Attention deficit hyperactivity disorder (ADHD)	Prevalence of reported ADHD was highest among ethnic minority children (compared to White children).			Prevalence of reported ADHD was highest among ethnic minority children (compared to White children). *This was true especially among African American male youths.*	
Depression			On YRBS, close to 30% of all students between ages 14–18 (28.5%) reported that they felt so sad or hopeless almost every day for more than 2 weeks in a row, they stopped usual activities. *The rate was 32.6% for Latino AND 4% for non-White Latino youths who reported "ever having been diagnosed with depression."*	YRBS covers self-report youth data, and close to 30% of all students between ages 14–18 (28.5%) reported that they felt so sad or hopeless almost every day for more than 2 weeks in a row, they stopped usual activities. *24.7% were Black, non-Latino youths.*	According to parent report data from NSCH, *ethnic minority stats did not vary from the general stats with the exception of non-Latino children of multiple races. Of that group, 5.9% reported "ever having been diagnosed with depression."*
Suicide		*Death rate for Native American female youths was four times higher than for White female youths* (HHS, 2011).	*Suicide attempts among Latino female youths were 70% higher than for White female youths* (HHS, 2011).	In the last 20 years, there was a > 200% increase in the African American suicide rate for youths between ages 10–14 (compared to a 120% increase for White youths ages 10–14; NAMI [National Alliance on Mental Illness], 2012). The rate was higher for African American female youths with lower income (Joe, Baser, Neighbors, Caldwell, & Jackson, 2009).	

(continued)

109

TABLE 5.1 Mental Health Disparities (*continued*)

Disorder type	Asian American youths	Native American youths	Latino youths	African American youths	Multiethnic youths
Alcohol		20% of select Native American middle-school youths attempted suicide at twice the rate of the general U.S. teenage population. *Suicidal ideation was tied to substance abuse and depression* (Yoder, Whitbeck, Hoyt, & LaFromboise, 2006).	According to 2010–2011 data, 4.2% of adolescents (in general) were dependent on or abused alcohol in the past year *(these rates were slightly higher for Latino youths)*. 4.7% of youths had illicit drug use disorder *(higher for Latino youths)*, with marijuana being the most used drug.		
Immigration	*The likelihood for mental health disorders was increased for Asian teenagers born in the U.S. and for those who immigrated to the U.S. before age 12*, as measured by the National Latino and Asian American Study (NLAAS; Abe-Kim et al., 2007).		For Latinos *past age 7 immigrating to the U.S., the older the age at immigration the later the onset of mental health disorders* (Alegria & Takeuchi, 2009).		

Note: CDC, Centers for Disease Control and Prevention; HHS, U.S. Department of Health and Human Services; NSCH, National Survey of Children's Health; stats, statistics; YRBS, Youth Risk Behavior Survey.

Sources: Centers for Disease Control and Prevention (2011). National Alliance on Mental Illness (NAMI; 2012). Joe et al. (2009). Yoder et al. (2006). Abe-Kim et al. (2007). Alegria and Takeuchi (2009).

CULTURAL CONTEXT: WHY AND WHEN TO MODIFY THE INTERVENTION

Two alternative schools of thought provide quite different viewpoints regarding the development of appropriate interventions of ethnic minority children. A universalist perspective, sometimes referred to as a "one-size fits-all" approach, posits that designing interventions for specific subgroups is unfeasible and unnecessary (Elliott & Mihalic, 2004; Kazdin, 2000). Moreover, a universalist approach cautions that modifying an EBI to fit a specific group risks potentially diminishing program effectiveness by altering the active ingredients of the intervention (DePue et al., 2010). Alternatively, those who favor the design of specific interventions for specific groups argue that a one-size-fits-all approach ignores the substantial influence of culturally different traditions and social practices on behavior. For example, a universalist approach to substance use may not adequately consider that treatment outcomes may be affected by racial/ethnic differences in specific drugs used (Moselhy & Telfer, 2002), pathways to treatment (Iguchi, 2005; Shillington & Clapp, 2003), patterns of treatment engagement and retention (Campbell, Weisner, & Sterling, 2006; Jackson-Gilfort, Liddle, Tejeda, & Dakor, 2001), attitudes about mental health treatment (Buser, 2009) along with differences in the health consequences of substance use (Iguchi, 2005), and in the relation of acculturative stress to alcohol (Ornelas, Eng, & Perreira, 2011) and substance use (Ortega, Rosenheck, Alegria, & Desai, 2000). Those challenging the universalist approach (cultural adaptation proponents) advance the notion that human beings are, to a great extent, the products of cultural socialization and that cultural context cannot be separated from intervention. So, what is culture?

Culture is typically defined as a set of traditions and customs, beliefs, history, language, and experiences inherent within and shared by a group and transmitted to subsequent generations. Ogbu (1995) frames it this way: It is who we are (identity, codes of conduct), what we do (what we build and produce), and how we interact (social patterns). Although much attention is paid to ethnic culture, this can also relate to gender (male vs. female socialization) or age (teenagers vs. older adults, etc.). In this chapter the focus is on ethnicity–race. This cultural context, according to cultural adaptation proponents, should be connected to mental health adaptations.

If mental health practice or interventions infuse cultural adaptations, they will reflect the client's language, culture, and context (cultural patterns, meaning, and values; Bernal, Jimenez-Chafey, & Domenech-Rodriguez, 2009). This approach has been used with various ethnic groups from Chinese American families (Hwang, 2009), to African Americans dealing with substance abuse and prevention issues (Burlew, Copeland, Ahuama-Jones, & Calsyn, 2013), to Latino youths with internalizing and externalizing disorders (Huey & Polo, 2008). This technique also involves the clinician being culturally competent ("a set of congruent behaviors, attitudes, and policies that come together in a system, agency, or among professionals that enables effective work in cross-cultural situations" Cross, Bazron, Dennis & Issacs, 1989, p. 13), engaging in a systematic exploration of the client's presenting issues (using the EBT system grounded in a therapeutic framework), and conducting a careful collaboration with the community being served (client as informant or epistemological partner sharing indigenous beliefs, values, and data).

According to cultural adaptation proponents, EBT should be modified for all clients for two major reasons: (a) to adhere to ethical practice that compels addressing a client's cultural background to ensure respect and responsive treatment, and (b) because research suggests that considering culture increases the chances that interventions are more impactful. This is even more important within a school setting because of the wide array of students/children and families served within the community.

An example of EBT modification is explored by Huey and Polo (2010), who stated that some generic psychotherapy is moderately effective for many problems of ethnic minority youths but multisystem therapy shows efficacy with reducing negative behaviors with criminally offending African American delinquent youths. Multisystem therapy, if used with ethnic groups, should be delivered in homes or schools with specially trained therapists. In general, therapy that is highly structured, time-limited, pragmatic, and goals-oriented shows promise with ethnic minority youths. Over the past several decades, culturally modified modes of health and mental health treatment have repeatedly been shown to have significant impact on diverse clients (Huey & Polo, 2008). For example, Botvin, Baker, Dusenbury, Botvin, and Diaz (1995) using augmented Life Skills Training (LST) and Brody et al.'s (2006) Strengthening Families Program (SFP) impacted the onset of smoking and substance use respectively in African American youths.

Barrera, Castro, Strycker, and Toobert (2013) identified substantial differences even among those who favor the development of interventions that better match the characteristics of the target audience. The curriculum in several approaches emphasizes cultural norms, traditions, and values of either the subgroup (culture-specific, culturally targeted) or even the individual (culturally tailored). However, two other approaches either supplement the EBT with activities aimed at enhancing engagement and retention (cultural attunement) or modify an existing EBT in order to design a more appropriate curriculum for the target group (cultural adaptation; Barrera et al., 2013).

The focus here is on culturally adapted interventions for several reasons. First, a culturally adapted approach represents a middle ground between a universalist approach and the approaches designed for specific groups or individuals: culture-specific, culturally tailored, and culturally targeted. Second, more and more schools, agencies, and funders are requiring mental health and education staff to use EBTs. Accordingly, prior to obtaining evidence of effectiveness of the culturally tailored or the culturally adapted intervention, an educational institution or agency proposing to use a culturally adapted intervention may have a better chance of gaining external support and collaboration with other support entities because of the evidence supporting the generic EBT. And third, most schools have a diverse student body whose needs may be more adequately met using this culturally adapted approach. The focus of this section is on the frameworks and models for culturally adapting interventions. So, what exactly is cultural adaptation? How does one go about augmenting an EBT to be more in line with a student's or client's culture or lived experience? These questions are addressed in the paragraphs that follow.

Cultural Adaptation

A culturally adapted approach retains the core components of an EBT but translates the EBT to better match the ideas, values, beliefs, norms, attitudes, and knowledge of the target group (Copeland, 2006; Falicov, 2009). The science of cultural adaptation has evolved substantially over the past two decades, and numerous frameworks and models of cultural adaptation are now available. These models are described in the remainder of this section.

Cultural Adaptation Frameworks

The frameworks that guide cultural adaptation generally support the inclusion of human social dynamics and contextually influenced behavior such as culture and ethnicity. Perhaps the two most widely cited frameworks are the Ecological Validity Framework (EVF; Bernal, Bonilla, & Bellido, 1995; Bernal & Saez-Santiago, 2006) and the Cultural Sensitivity Framework (CSF; Resnicow, Soler, Braithwaite, Ahluwalia, & Butler, 2000).

The EVF, grounded in ecological systems theory (Broffenbrenner, 1989), identifies the following eight potential domains to include in the adaptation: (a) language, (b) persons, (c) metaphors, (d) content, (e) concepts, (f) goals, (g) methods, and (h) context. The CSF, a bidimensional concept, organizes cultural adaptations into two broad categories: surface and deep structural interventions. Surface adaptations alter the presentation of intervention activities (e.g., case scenarios using characters from the target group, using treatment staff from the target group) and modify those activities to be more acceptable or familiar to the target group. Changes made to the language used in a Cognitive-Behavioral Therapy (CBT) intervention protocol (in order to make the content more appropriate for Haitian youths) are an example of a CSF surface adaptation (Nicolas, Arntz, Hirsch, & Schmiedigen, 2009; Nicolas & Schwartz, 2012). Similarly, Trevino, Hernandez, Yin, Garcia, and Hernandez (2005) altered the activities in a program aimed at promoting physical fitness to include a familiar game and salsa dancing. However, they left the original message embedded in the activity unchanged.

Unlike surface adaptations, deep structural adaptations can involve actual changes to the curriculum to better align the curriculum with the culture, social experiences, and values of a particular racial ethnic group (Resnicow et al., 2000). Deep structural adaptations may also promote behavioral change by incorporating cultural strengths and rituals into the curriculum. For example, the addition of a rites of passage program, an African-centered program aimed at marking youths' transition from one stage to another by connecting them to their cultural heritage, is an example of a deep structural adaptation.

Mier, Ory, and Medina (2010) reviewed the modifications to 18 interventions aimed at promoting better nutrition and exercise for Latinos. The team classified the modifications as either surface or deep structural activities. The surface modifications included (a) the use of bilingual and bicultural materials and delivery agents, (b) inclusion of ethnic foods, (c) working with community health workers, and (d) delivering the intervention in familiar group settings. The deep structural modifications included (a) involving the family in interventions, (b) adjusting the curriculum to the literacy level of participants, (c) use of social support and networks, and (d) incorporation of Latino cultural values (e.g., familial) in intervention design or implementation.

METHODS OF CULTURAL ADAPTATION

Recently, Burlew et al. (2013) reviewed 14 different models used to adapt mental health interventions. The three most common approaches included (a) community involvement (involving members of the community and/or target group in modifying the intervention), (b) conducting research and/or reviewing existing literature and research on the target group to identify the areas to address in the culturally adapted version, and (c) consultation from experts in either cultural adaptation or on the problem behavior of the target group. The case study that follows illustrates cultural adaptation with community involvement.

CASE STUDY

The Strong African American Families Program (SAAF) is a culturally adapted version of the Strengthening Families Program: For Parents and Youth 10-14-Revised (SFP 10-14-R; Molgaard, Kumpfer, & Fleming, 1996). Both parent and adolescent participants in the SFP 10-14-R meet weekly for 7 weeks. The weekly sessions include separate sessions for parents and adolescents along with a joint family session. The SFP 10-14-R parent sessions include skill building on clarifying expectations, establishing appropriate discipline, managing emotional responses to the child, and effective communication. Some topics in the adolescent sessions are similar to the topics in the parent sessions. In addition, however, the adolescent sessions also address peer resistance and peer relationships. The family sessions enable family members to practice conflict resolution and effective communication skills but also include activities aimed at fostering family cohesion. Much of the content is delivered via videotape. A modified version of the intervention has demonstrated effectiveness with urban African Americans (Spoth, Guyll, Chao, & Molgaard, 2003). However, Gene Brody and his team were the first to adapt the intervention specifically for rural African American adolescents (Brody et al., 2006).

Prior research demonstrated the interrelationships of alcohol use and early sexual activity within this rural African American adolescent group (Brody et al., 2004). Moreover, both alcohol and sexual behavior have been demonstrated to contribute to other negative outcomes for this group (Brody et al., 2006). Accordingly, Brody's team began by conducting research aimed at identifying "malleable protective factors" that could be changed to delay the onset of alcohol use and sexual activity. Their research revealed both parental and adolescent protective factors. The parent protective variables included a regulated, communicative home environment characterized by parental involvement and monitoring, racial socialization, parent–child communication about sex, and clear expectations about alcohol use. The adolescent protective variables included negative attitudes about early sexual activity or alcohol use, negative perceptions of youths who drink, peer resistance skills, a goal-oriented future orientation, and openness to parental influence.

The research findings were translated into an intervention that, similar to the generic version, included seven 2-hour weekly meetings with separate sessions for parents and adolescents. The adapted version of the parent sessions in SAAF included parent training on establishing a regulated, communicative parenting approach such as parental training on monitoring, limit setting, strategies for setting clear expectations about alcohol use, strategies for communicating about sex, and strategies for teaching racial socialization. Based on the original research, the adolescent sessions in the adapted SAAF included discussions on the importance of complying with family rules, strategies for addressing racism, and practice in setting goals and making plans for a positive future. The adolescent sessions also included discussions on the differences between themselves and their classmates who engage in negative behaviors as well as strategies for resisting peer pressure. Each session included a joint session with both parents and adolescents, in which the two groups practiced communication skills and conducted activities aimed at engaging the adolescents into the family.

The findings in an evaluation of SAAF revealed that African American families who participated in SAAF increased both regulated-communicative parenting practices and youth protective processes in the 8 months between the pretests and posttests. Moreover, the SAAF adolescents were less likely to use alcohol than control participants (Brody et al., 2006).

Other Adaptation Models

Two additional stage models for cultural adaptation have also received considerable attention. Barrera's stages include (a) information gathering, (b) preliminary adaptation design, (c) preliminary adaptation tests (case or pilot studies providing tentative evidence of the efficacy of the intervention), (d) adaptation refinement, and (e) a trial of the cultural adaptation intervention (Barrera et al., 2013). The ADAPT-ITT (Assessment, Decision, Administration, Production, Topical Expects, Integration, Training, Testing) model uses the term *phases* instead of stages (Wingood & DiClemente, 2008). The first phase (a) assessment involves the collection of data from members of the target population, key stakeholders, and is similar to the first stage in the Barrera model. However, the next phases in the ADAPT-ITT model involve the (b) decision: selection of the appropriate EBT; (c) administration: a unique "theater" testing of the generic intervention aimed at eliciting feedback from members of the target group, key stakeholders, and other experts; (d) production: the development of a draft of an adapted intervention; (e) topical experts: consultation with experts on the adapted version; (f) integration: incorporation of feedback from experts into the design of the intervention, other checks to ensure that the intervention is appropriate (e.g., readability); and (g) training: train staff to conduct the adapted intervention. Similar to the Barrera model, the ADAPT-ITT ends with (h) testing: pilot test the adapted intervention and analyze results.

SUMMARY

School Mental Health Application

Within the practice of mental health, it is essential to ensure the efficacy of mental health intervention while also considering cultural factors, and cultural adaptation provides the platform from which to accomplish this balance. This chapter on culturally sensitive mental health intervention supplies the reader with the context for providing culturally sensitive EBI and sample strategies for implementation. The reader is invited to consider the impact on practice in schools.

Although the culturally sensitive and adaptive approach is relevant in all school settings, it is especially appropriate in urban school settings where children and families with diverse lived experiences disproportionately reside. The approach of RTI itself requires an analysis of instruction and student need and learner performance/behavior, and this process intersects nicely with cultural adaptation. Further, researchers emphasize culturally responsive education that requires rigor, relevance, and relationship building (Ladson-Billings, 1994; Morales-James, Lopez, Wilkins, & Fergus, 2011). The connection of RTI with culturally responsive education and cultural adaptation provides a rich recipe for powerful interventions that create desired outcomes for diverse learners. The power of this intervention approach is substantiated by a meta-analysis indicating that culturally adapted treatments have a greater impact than the universal method and are more effective (Smith, Domenech-Rodriguez, & Bernal, 2011). How can this be of benefit in schools? By leveraging EVF or CSF approaches in a school setting, one can provide a method for including parents and the broader school community (along with other networks and agencies that support students' daily activities) and reap dividends by enhancing treatment fidelity and eliciting community buy-in needed for an effective school as well as effective intervention.

The intervention examples highlighted in this chapter are reminders of some key lessons (Bernal & Domenech-Rodriquez, 2012; Ripp, Jean-Pierre, & Fergus, 2011), such as:

- Building meaningful and respectful relationships is vital. These relationships are needed for family, school community, and broader community consultation. Further, inclusion of the target group in treatment modification is essential to being culturally adaptive and instructionally responsive.
- There is often dual impact when culturally responsive treatments are used. Both behavior and academic achievement are impacted.
- Professional development, cultural competence, and self-awareness are important. Consider working in teacher–mental health intervention pairs to enhance effective practice.

- Don't be afraid to examine school practices for inclusiveness. Deep and surface adaptation may lead to needed changes in the curriculum or school practice. Don't forget to consult with the school-age children themselves to inform thinking.
- A balance of maintaining the core of the EBT with the adaptations is possible and desirable when examining mental health intervention.

RESOURCES

National Network to Eliminate Disparities in Behavioral Health is a helpful online guide (www.nned.net/index-nned.php/cbt) to various cognitive therapy approaches. Open discussions, resources, and best-practice strategies are presented.

A Toolkit for Applying the Cultural Enhancement Model to Evidenced-Based Practice is a helpful application manual (depts.washington .edu/pbhjp/downloads/projectsD/models_for_changeD/Toolkit Cultural Enhancement Model.pdf) filled with resources and information on cultural competence and the cultural enhancement model. It also contains EBP strategies and assessment protocols.

Evidence Based Practices with Latino Youth is a manual containing a rich overview (depts.washington.edu/pbhjp/downloads/projectsD/models_for_changeD/EBP%20with%20Latino%20Youth%20-%20 A%20Literature%20Review.pdf) of the demographic, acculturation, and mental health status of Latino youth. Cultural adaptations are presented to guide mental health intervention.

Evidence Based Practices and Multicultural Mental Health-NAMI is a valuable tool (www.nami.org/Template.cfm?Section=Fact_ Sheets1&Template=/ContentManagement/ContentDisplay .cfm&ContentID=63974) to use to find useful intervention tools designed with cultural context in mind.

A seminal and collaborative piece created by representatives of the Asian American Psychological Association, the Association of Black Psychologists, the National Latina/o Psychological Association, and the Society of Indian Psychologists, *Psychological Treatment of Ethnic Minority Populations* was written for the Council of National Psychology Associations for the Advancement of Ethnic Minority Interests (a group comprised of leaders of national psychology organizations who meet to address issues of importance to ethnic minorities and to the advancement of ethnic minority interests; www.apa.org/pi/oema/ resources/brochures/treatment-minority.pdf) and remains one of the definitive theoretical and empirical underpinnings of cultural competence and recommendations for mental health treatment (2003).

REFERENCES

Abe-Kim, J., Takeuchi, D. T., Seunghye, H., Zane, N., Sue, S., Spencer, M., . . . Alegria, M. (2007). Use of mental health services among immigrant and U.S.-born Asian Americans: Results from the national Latino and Asian American study. *American Journal of Public Health, 97*(1), 91–98.

Alegria, M., & Takeuchi, D. (2009). *National Latino and Asian American study (NLAAS), 2002–2003.* Retrieved from http://www.icpsr.umich.edu/icp-srweb/ICPSR/studies/00191

Barrera, M., Castro, F., Strycker, L., & Toobert, D. (2013). Cultural adaptations of behavioral health interventions: A progress report. *Journal of Consulting & Clinical Psychology, 81*, 196–205.

Bernal, G., Bonilla, J., & Bellido, C. (1995). Ecological validity and cultural sensitivity for outcome research: Issues for the cultural adaptation and development of psychosocial treatments with Hispanics. *Journal of Abnormal Child Psychology, 23*(1), 67–82.

Bernal, G., & Domenech-Rodriguez, M. (2012). Cultural adaptation in context: Psychotherapy as a historical accounting of adaptations. In G. Bernal & M. Domenech-Rodriguez (Eds.), *Cultural adaptations: Tools for evidence-based practice with diverse populations* (pp. 3–22). Washington, DC: American Psychological Association.

Bernal, G., Jimenez-Chafey, M. I., & Domenech-Rodriguez, M. (2009). Cultural adaptations of treatments: A resource for considering culture in evidenced-based practice. *Professional Psychology, Research and Practice, 40*(4), 361–368.

Bernal, G., & Saez-Santiago, E. (2006). Culturally centered psychosocial interventions. *Journal of Community Psychology, 34*(2), 121–132.

Botvin, G., Baker, E., Dusenbury, I., Botvin, E., & Diaz, T. (1995). Long-term follow-up results of a randomized drug abuse prevention trial in a white middle-class population. *Journal of the American Medical Association, 273*, 1106–1112.

Brody, G., Murry, V., Gerrard, M., Gibbons, F., Molgaard, V., McNair, L., . . . Neubaum-Carlan, E. (2004). The strong African American families program: Translating research into prevention programming. *Child Development, 75*, 900–917.

Brody, G. H., McBride-Murry, V. M., Gerrard, S. M., Gibbons, M., Molgaard, F. X., Brown, V., . . . Ashby, T. (2006). The strong African American families program: A cluster-randomized prevention trial of long-term effects and a mediational model. *Journal of Consulting and Clinical Psychology, 74*, 356–366.

Broffenbrenner, U. (1989). Ecological stems theory. *Annals of Child Development, 6*, 187–249.

Burlew, A. K., Copeland, V., Ahuama-Jones, C., & Calsyn, D. (2013). Does cultural adaptation have a role in substance abuse treatment? *Social Work in Public Health, 28*(3), 1–21.

Buser, J. K. (2009). Treatment-seeking disparity between African Americans and Whites: Attitudes toward treatment, coping resources, and racism. *Journal of Multicultural Counseling and Development, 37*(2), 94–104.

Campbell, C. I., Weisner, C., & Sterling, S. (2006). Retention. *The Journal of Adolescent Health, 38*, 343–350.

Centers for Disease Control and Prevention. (2011). *School health programs: Improving the health of our nation's youth at a glance.* Retrieved from http://www.cdc.gov/chronicdisease/resources/publications/AAG/dash.htm

Centers for Disease Control and Prevention. (2013). Mental health surveillance among children—United States, 2005–2011. Supplements. *Mortality and Morbidity Weekly Report, 62*(2), 1–35. Retrieved from http://www.cdc.gov/media/dpk/2013/dpk-child-mental-health.html

Copeland, V. (2006). Disparities in mental health service utilization among low-income African American adolescents: Closing the gap by enhancing practitioner's competence. *Child and Adolescent Social Work Journal, 23*, 407–428.

Cross, T. L., Bazron, B. J., Dennis, K. W., & Issacs, M. R. (1989). *Towards a culturally competent system of care: A monograph on effective services for minority children who are severely emotionally disturbed* (Vol. I). Washington, DC: Georgetown University Child Development Center, CASSP Technical Assistance Center.

DePue, J. D., Rosen, R. K., Batts-Turner, M., Bereolos, N., House, M., Held, R. F., . . . McGarvey, S. (2010). Cultural translation of interventions: Diabetes care in American Samoa. *American Journal of Public Health, 100*, 2085–2093.

Elliott, D. S., & Mihalic, S. (2004) Issues in disseminating and replicating effective prevention programs. *Prevention Science, 5*(1), 47–52.

Falicov, C. J., (2009). Commentary: On the wisdom and challenges of culturally attuned treatments for Latinos. *Family Process, 48*, 292–309.

Huey, S., & Polo, A. (2008). Evidenced-based psychosocial treatments for ethnic minority youth: A review and meta-analysis. *Journal of Clinical Child Adolescent Psychology, 37*(1), 262–301.

Huey, S. J., & Polo, A. J. (2010). Assessing the effects of evidence-based psychotherapies with ethnic minority youth. In J. R. Weisz & A. E. Kazdin (Eds.), *Evidenced-based psychotherapies for children and adolescents* (2nd ed., pp. 451–465). New York, NY: Guilford.

Hwang, W.-C. (2009). The formative method for adapting psychotherapy (FMAP): A community-based developmental approach to culturally adapting therapy. *Professional Psychology, Research and Practice, 40*(4), 369–377.

Iguchi, M. (2005). How criminal system racial disparities may translate into health disparities. *Journal of Health Care for the Poor and Underserved, 16*(4), Supplement B, 48–56.

Jackson, J. S., Forsythe-Brown, I., & Govia, I. O. (2007). Age cohort, ancestry, and immigrant generation influences in family relations and psychological well-being among Black Caribbean family members. *Journal of Social Issues, 63*(4), 729–743.

Jackson-Gilfort, A., Liddle, H. A., Tejeda, M. J., & Dakor, G. A. (2001). Facilitating engagement of African American male adolescents in family therapy: A cultural theme process study. *Journal of Black Psychology, 27*(3), 321–340.

Joe, S., Baser, R., Neighbors, H., Caldwell, C., & Jackson, J. (2009). 12-month and lifetime prevalence of suicide attempts among black adolescents in the national survey of American life. *Journal of American Academy of Child and Adolescent Psychiatry, 48*(3), 271–282.

Kazdin, A. E. (2000). Perceived barriers to treatment participation and treatment acceptability among antisocial children and their families. *Journal of Child and Family Studies, 9*, 157–174.

Kessler, R. C., Berglund, P., Demler, O., Jin, R., & Walters, E. E. (2005). Lifetime prevalence and age of onset distribution of *DSM-IV* disorders in the national co-morbidity survey replication. *Archives of General Psychiatry, 62*, 593–602.

Ladson-Billings, G. (1994). *The dreamkeepers: Successful teachers of African American children.* San Francisco, CA: Jossey-Bass.

Merikangas, K. R., He, J., Burstein, M. E., Swanson, S. A., Avenevoli, S., Cul, L., . . . Swendsen, J. (2010). Lifetime prevalence of mental disorders in U.S. adolescents: Results from the national co-morbidity study-adolescent supplement (NCS-A). *Journal for the American Academy of Child and Adolescent Psychiatry, 49*(10), 980–989.

Merikangas, K. R., He, J., Burstein, M. E., Swendsen, J., Avenevoli, S., Case, B., . . . Olfson, M. (2011). Service utilization for lifetime mental disorders in U.S. adolescents: Results from the national co-morbidity survey adolescent supplement (NCS-A). *Journal for the American Academy of Child and Adolescent Psychiatry, 50*(1), 32–45.

Mier, N., Ory, M., & Medina, A. (2010). Anatomy of culturally sensitive interventions promoting nutrition and exercise in Hispanics: A critical examination of existing literature. *Health Promotion Practice, 11*(4) 541–554.

Molgaard, V. K., Kumpfer, K., & Fleming, E. (1996). *The strengthening families program: For parents and youth 10-14-revised.* Ames: Iowa State University Extension Service.

Morales-James, C., Lopez, L., Wilkins, R., & Fergus, E. (2011). RTI Action Network. *Cultural adaptations when implementing RTI in urban settings.* Retrieved from http://www.rtinetwork.org/learn/diversity/cultural-adaptations-when-implementing-RTI-in-urban-settings

Moselhy, H., & Telfer, I. (2002). The pattern of substance misuse among ethnic minorities in a community drug setting. *The European Journal of Psychiatry, 16*, 240–247.

National Alliance on Mental Illness (NAMI). (2012). *African American community mental health fact sheet.* Retrieved from http://www.nami.org/Template.cfm?section=fact_sheets1&template=/contentmanagement/contentdisplay.cfm&contentID=53812

National Institute of Mental Health (NIMH). (2012). *Use of mental health services and treatment among children.* Retrieved from http://www.nimh.nih.gov/statistics/1NHANES.shtml

Nicolas, G., Arntz, D., Hirsch, B., & Schmiedigen, A. (2009). Cultural adaptation of a group treatment for Haitian American adolescents. *Professional Psychology, Research and Practice, 40*, 378–384.

Nicolas, G., & Schwartz, B. (2012). Culture first: Lessons learned about the importance of the cultural adaptation of cognitive behavior treatment interventions for Black Caribbean youth. In G. Bernal & M. Domenech-Rodriguez (Eds.), *Cultural adaptations: Tools for evidence-based practice with diverse populations* (pp. 71–90). Washington, DC: American Psychological Association.

Ogbu, J. (1995). Cultural problems in minority education: Their interpretations and consequences. Part one: Theoretical background. *The Urban Review, 27*(3), 189–205.

Ornelas, I. J., Eng, E., & Perreira, K. M. (2011). Perceived barriers to opportunity and their relation to substance use among Latino immigrant men. *Journal of Behavioral Medicine, 34*(3), 182–191.

Ortega, A. N., Rosenheck, R., Alegria, M., & Desai, R. A. (2000). Acculturation and the lifetime risk of psychiatric and substance use disorders among Hispanics. *Journal of Nervous & Mental Disease, 188*(11), 728–735.

Pumariega, A. J., Rogers, K., & Rothe, E. (2005). Culturally competent systems of care of children's mental health: Advances and challenges. *Community Mental Health Journal, 41*(5), 539–555.

Resnicow, K., Soler, R., Braithwaite, R. L., Ahluwalia, J. S., & Butler, J. (2000). Cultural sensitivity in substance abuse prevention. *Journal of Community Psychology, 28*, 271–290.

Ripp, A., Jean-Pierre, P., & Fergus, E. (2011). RTI Action Network. *Promising examples of RTI practices in urban settings.* Retrieved from http://www.rtinetwork.org/learn/diversity/promising-examples-of-rti-practices-for-urban-schools

Sackett, D. L, Straus, S. E., Richardson, W. S., Rosenberg, W., & Haynes, R. B. (2000). *Evidence-based medicine: How to practice and teach EBM* (2nd ed.). Edinburgh, Scotland: Churchill Livingstone.

Shillington, A. M., & Clapp, J. D. (2003). Adolescents in public substance abuse treatment programs: The impact of sex and race on referrals and outcomes. *Journal of Child and Adolescent Substance Abuse, 12*(3), 69–79.

Smith, T., Domenech-Rodriguez, M. M., & Bernal, G. (2011). Culture. *Journal of Clinical Psychology, 67*(2), 166–175.

Spoth, R., Guyll, M., Chao, W., & Molgaard, V. (2003). Exploratory study of a preventive intervention with general population African American families. *Journal of Early Adolescence, 23*, 435–468.

Trevino, R. P., Hernandez, A. E., Yin, Z., Garcia, O. A., & Hernandez, I. (2005). Effect of the Bienestar health program on physical fitness in low-income Mexican American children. *Hispanic Journal of Behavioral Sciences, 27*(1), 120–132.

U.S. Bureau of the Census. (2006). *American community survey 2005.* Retrieved from http://www.census.gov/acs/www/data_documentation/pums_documentation

U.S. Bureau of the Census, Department of Commerce. (2013). *Profile America facts for features: Back to school 2013–2014.* Retrieved June 19, 2013, from www.census.gov/newsroom/releases/archives/facts_for_features_special_editions/cb13-ff17.html

U.S. Department of Health and Human Services. (2011, January 14). CDC health disparities and inequalities report-United States. *Morbidity and Mortality Weekly Report, S60*, 47–109. Retrieved from http://www.cdc.gov/mmwr/pdf/other/su6001.pdf

U.S. Department of Health and Human Services, Health Resources and Services Administration. (2003). *U.S. teens in our world.* Rockville, MD: Author. Retrieved from http://mchb.hrsa.gov/mchirc/_pubs/us_teens

Wingood, G. M., & DiClemente, R. J. (2008). The ADAPT-ITT model: A novel method of adapting evidence-based HIV interventions. *JAIDS Journal of Acquired Immune Deficiency Syndromes, 47*(Suppl. 1), S40–S46.

Yoder, K. A., Whitback, L. B., Hoyt, D. R., & LaFromboise, T. (2006). Suicidal ideation among American Indian youth. *Archives of Suicide Research, 10*(2), 177–190.

Youth Risk Behavior Survey. (2012). *Selected 2011 national health risk behaviors and health outcomes by race/ethnicity.* Retrieved from http://www .cdc.gov/healhtyyouth/yrbs/pdf/us_disparityrace_yrbs.pdf

CHAPTER 6

Micro-Skills: Daily Practice for Mental Health Providers

MICHELLE FLAUM HALL

SHANNON FLAUM HORVATH

LEARNING OUTCOMES

On completion of this chapter, the reader should be able to:

- Define counseling micro-skills and understand the main types of micro-skills
- Differentiate the use of various micro-skills according to the tiered intervention model
- Appreciate how effective use of micro-skills can positively impact relationships with students, parents, administrators, and colleagues
- Understand how micro-skills can bolster multicultural understanding and sensitivity

THE RESPONSE TO INTERVENTION MODEL AND SCHOOL-BASED MENTAL HEALTH

The Response to Intervention (RTI) Model of service delivery has fundamentally changed the manner in which schools provide services to students. RTI refers to a school-wide system of instructional delivery with the overarching goal of achieving successful academic outcomes for all students and, most notably, for those who are struggling academically or behaviorally. Originally stemming from the perspective that the traditional IQ-discrepancy formula fails in its attempt to validly identify those students who are learning disabled, RTI is widely considered a model for preventing and remediating academic, behavioral, and emotional concerns or issues. The National Center on Response to Intervention (NCRTI) cites that 45 of 48 states have RTI components in their state performance plans; and 48 states permit RTI processes as a method for identifying students with a specific learning disability (National Center on Response to Intervention, 2010). The American School Counselor Association's (ASCA) position declaration on RTI explicitly states that

> Professional school counselors are stakeholders in the development and implementation of the Response to Intervention (RTI) process. Professional school counselors align with the RTI process through the implementation of a comprehensive school counseling program designed to improve student achievement and behavior. (ASCA, 2008, p. 37)

Those particular skills employed by mental health professionals may vary, according to the intensity of interventions defined by the tiers within the RTI model. Ockerman, Mason, and Hollenbeck (2012) indicate that RTI and school counseling programs share three primary components: a tiered service delivery model, the use of data and empirically based assessments, and a foundation emphasizing social advocacy (p. 4).

RTI was designed with the dual purpose of *preventing* academic and behavioral problems through early identification, remediation, and use of research-based educational practices, and as a mechanism for *identifying* students with disabilities (Fuchs et al., 2007; Gresham, 2001). Within the scope of prevention, RTI consists of a school-wide service of delivery designed to address academic and behavioral difficulties before they escalate into such severity that remediation is difficult. This system of intervention is available to all students, and may include professional development, enhanced classroom instruction, supplemental instruction, or school-wide behavioral supports (Denton, Fletcher, Anthony, & Francis, 2006). With prevention methods in place, those children who continue to struggle are identified as needing intensive supports that may include the provision of special education services.

Although some variation exists in the conceptual model of RTI service delivery, most researchers and educators agree with the overarching philosophy. Graner, Faggella-Luby, and Fritschmann (2005) describe an RTI "archetype" composed of eight primary features:

- High-quality classroom instruction
- Research-based instruction
- Classroom performance measures
- Universal screening
- Continuous progress monitoring

- Research-based interventions
- Progress monitoring during interventions
- Fidelity measures

The five secondary features are

- Multiple tiers, transitioning from least intensive to most intensive instruction
- Implementation of differentiated curriculum
- Instruction delivered by paraprofessionals and other staff
- Varied duration, time, and frequency of interventions
- Categorical or noncategorical placement decisions

This model of service delivery generally is conceptualized on a continuum that ranges in intensity in a tiered or phase format, although variations exist in both the number and nature of tiers utilized (Mastropieri & Scruggs, 2005).

As mentioned, it has been well established that the skills and interventions employed by school-based mental health professionals will likely vary according to the specific tier of intervention within the RTI model; however, what has not been established is how the micro-skills of effective therapeutic communication fit within the three tiers of intervention in the RTI model and how these skills can be useful to school-based mental health professionals in ensuring that students receive the necessary and appropriate services to meet their academic and behavioral needs.

WHAT ARE MICRO-SKILLS?

Simply put, micro-skills are the building blocks of effective therapeutic communication and they "break down" the complexity of counseling into distinct and learnable skills (Ivey, 1971). Whereas it has been widely accepted that micro-skills do not encompass the entire therapeutic skill set, they are useful and accessible in the early stages of counselor training. Combined with cultural considerations, theoretical orientation, conceptualization, and affective skills, micro-skills are an important component of training mental health professionals (Ridley, Kelly, & Mollen, 2011). Unlike intervention skills that are based on specific theoretical orientations (such as Cognitive-Behavioral Therapy [CBT], Reality Therapy [RT], or Solution-Focused Brief Therapy [SFBT]), micro-skills are *transtheoretical*, or used across all theories. They are the ingredients of the therapeutic process, and the theoretical framework is the recipe. To take the cooking metaphor a bit further, anyone who has spent time in the kitchen knows that it is not enough to have quality ingredients and a good recipe to create a good dish: It also takes a conscientious cook who is skillful, flexible, creative, and adaptable to accomplish the recipe and make the dish delicious.

Effective therapeutic communication in the schools requires many of these same characteristics; for it is not enough that a mental health practitioner be *technically* adept. Being truly effective as a school-based mental health practitioner requires not only micro-skills and a sound theoretical framework, but also an authentic desire to help children and their families flourish. In their meta-analyses of the factors that contribute to positive therapeutic outcomes, Duncan, Miller, Wampold, and Hubble (2010) inform us that the quality of the therapeutic relationship, including the therapeutic alliance and collaboration, has twice the impact of the specific theoretical techniques used by a mental health clinician. In other words, in the field of mental health, relationships—and micro-skills of effective communication are the building blocks of those relationships.

This chapter focuses on the basic micro-skills of effective school-based mental health communication across three tiers of intervention in the kindergarten through 12th-grade settings. Although there has been much debate about what sufficiently encapsulates counseling micro-skills (Ridley, Mollen, & Kelly, 2011), the focus here is on the most salient skills encountered across numerous counseling resources (Chen & Giblin, 2002; Ivey, Ivey, & Zalaquett, 2010; Young, 2009). To provide context, an overview of the three tiers of intervention in the RTI model is presented. Next, foundational micro-skills, or skills useful in all tiers of intervention, are highlighted, followed by specific skills employed in each tier of intervention.

THE RESPONSE TO INTERVENTION MODEL: THREE TIERS OF INTERVENTION

Typically, RTI is conceptualized as a three-tiered pyramid in which the base represents universal supports available to all children (Mellard, McKnight, & Jordan, 2010; Vaughn, 2003). Because the three-tiered model is well documented in the literature (Martinez, Nellis, & Prendergast, 2006; Stecker, 2007; Vaughn, 2003; Vaughn & Roberts, 2007) and in Chapter 1 of this text, it is summarized here.

Tier 1

Often termed in literature as the *primary* level of service delivery, Tier 1 is represented by the wide base of the pyramid, and includes those universal programs and system-wide supports accessible to all students. Generally, interventions within Tier 1 are considered large scale, and grouping is flexible and classroom-centered. At the heart of the primary tier is the incorporation of core curricula and instructional practices deemed by well-designed, scientifically based research methods as effective in increasing educational and behavioral outcomes. With a sound, research-based curriculum in place, school personnel must then gather data on the school-wide effectiveness of the programs as they operate within the general education setting. At this level, teachers are usually the first line of defense in identifying those students not experiencing success and requiring more targeted, individualized supports. Within Tier 1, school counselors or school psychologists often serve students and staff through school-wide training on a variety of topics: for example, social skills, bullying, and conflict resolution.

Tier 2

Tier 2, sometimes referenced as the *secondary* level of service delivery, targets an estimated 15% of students considered at risk for academic or behavioral difficulties and for whom universal supports are deemed insufficient. Tier 2 services are markedly more individualized than those implemented in Tier 1 because specific needs of students are identified and prescriptive measures are put into place. At this level, building level teams, incorporating staff from many disciplines, collaborate and select appropriate prescriptive measures designed to augment existing Tier 1 supports. Grouping in Tier 2 may include small groups of students requiring intervention of a similar type, with interventions implemented several times a week for roughly 20 minutes to 30 minutes per session. Throughout Tier 2, progress monitoring assessments, designed to evaluate the effectiveness of selected interventions, form a critical piece of the decision-making process. Mental health professionals may use formative as well as summative assessments, such as pretests and posttests, surveys, and/or curriculum-based measures in assessing intervention effectiveness (Ockerman et al., 2012). Upon review of the student's progress, the team may advise continuing the intervention, modifying the intervention, or progressing to Tier 3. It is recommended that students proceed to the next tier if any of the following apply: (a) the student has participated in two rounds of Tier 2 instruction and has not made sufficient progress after the intervention has been modified, for a total of 20 weeks or 100 sessions; (b) the student has demonstrated a marked lack of progress after one round of Tier 2, and further instruction in Tier 2 is considered insufficient; or (c) the student has received previous Tier 3 instruction and has returned to Tier 2 (Vaughn, 2003). Within Tier 2, mental health professionals may provide more intensive services: for example, small-group counseling or interventions designed to address a target behavior.

Tier 3

Tier 3, often referred to in the literature as the *tertiary* level, is markedly more intensive and individualized than Tier 2. Students who continue to struggle with the additional support provided in Tier 2 are referred for this third level of service. At the Tier 3 level, homogeneous, small-group, or individualized instruction is provided to students, generally for a minimum of two 30-minute sessions per day in addition to the 90 minutes of core instruction provided in Tier 1. Progress monitoring is conducted at least twice per month but more often weekly and, in some cases, daily. The duration of the intervention in Tier 3 is considerably longer, and may span months or perhaps years. Students who fail to make adequate progress with intensive intervention are often referred for special education evaluation to rule out other disabilities, such as a cognitive disability or emotional disturbance (Fuchs & Fuchs, 2005). These services "may be delivered by the school counselor in such forms as individual counseling, behavior improvement plans, or coordination with community resources" (Gruman & Hoelzen, 2011, p. 184).

It is clear from the descriptions of the three tiers of intervention that the nature and intensity of services change as a student transitions from one tier to the next; therefore, it stands to reason that school-based mental health professionals will differentiate their skills and approach according to the specific tier of intervention. Whereas some skills could be considered more universal, other skills are more appropriately used at more intensive levels of intervention. In the next section, the differentiated uses of micro-skills are elaborated upon across the three tiers of intervention.

FOUNDATIONAL MICRO-SKILLS USED ACROSS ALL TIERS OF INTERVENTION

Before discussing how specific micro-skills are used in the more intensive levels of intervention (Tiers 2 and 3), the authors first present the skills they believe to be foundational and applicable to all levels of intervention with students.

Creating a Positive First Impression

Mental health practitioners in the schools have the opportunity to meet students in many contexts: formally in large-group guidance lessons, in small counseling groups, in individual counseling, or informally in the hallways, at special events, or in common areas such as the cafeteria or gymnasium. It is helpful to remember that a relationship with each student begins at the first meeting—regardless of the context. Similarly, meeting and forming relationships with parents, family members, and instructional or administrative staff span across context and time. School-based mental health professionals strive to project an image of a professional, caring, and trustworthy adult who is warm and approachable. This means ensuring that the communication style is inviting, which includes maintaining comfortable eye contact, a warm facial expression, and a friendly tone of voice. Written communications should be welcoming and not intimidating or wrought with jargon; and the office environment should create feelings of comfort, safety, and privacy by providing age-appropriate seating options and resources, uplifting messages on wall art and signs, and sound screens to ensure confidentiality.

Building Rapport

During classroom guidance lessons and other classroom-based activities, school-based mental health professionals have the opportunity to establish rapport with several students at one time. Think about how one might break the ice with them, considering their developmental level. Establishing rapport with groups of students is similar to establishing rapport with individuals, in that one should think in terms of what they might be interested in and comfortable talking about. Given their ages, what might they be willing to share? For children in the primary grades, asking about topics like animals/pets, family/siblings, and favorites (such as colors, foods, or cartoon characters) are appropriate ways to get to know students and to set a positive tone. Children often *wear* their interests, so clothing can give clues as to what they like. For older elementary students, asking about hobbies/interests, family, pets, and favorites (such as music, foods, and television shows) can help ease into a conversation. For adolescents, beginning with a discussion about a current event (either at school, locally, or perhaps nationally/globally), or inquiring about favorite music, hobbies, or other extracurricular interests could be helpful transitioning to the specific purpose of the meeting.

Whether one is building rapport with a student or a classroom full of students, it helps to be genuine, positive, and engaged. School-based mental health professionals have many opportunities to interact with students, and can use rapport-building skills to increase their effectiveness in building comfort and trust in those interactions. Although more individualized attention can require a lengthier rapport-building phase (and possibly the addition of an activity—such as a game—to help the student feel more comfortable talking), even Tier 1 interventions can benefit from the process.

Basic Attending Skills

Active listening skills are the foundation of the helping professions (Ivey et al., 2010). Solid therapeutic relationships begin with respectful, engaged professionals who take the time and energy to be attentive to students, parents, and other professionals. When using basic attending skills, nonverbal messages are sent that one is listening, such as a slight lean forward, comfortable eye contact, intermittent head nodding and verbal utterances (e.g., mmm-hmmm). Although these skills are certainly basic, they are critical for demonstrating that one is actively attending to the conversation at hand—plus they help build the trust needed to form effective therapeutic relationships.

Observation Skills

A set of skills applicable to all levels of intervention are observation skills. Ivey et al. (2010) identify many elements worth observing in clients, including both verbal and nonverbal behaviors. Keen observation skills on the part of school-based mental health professionals, teachers, and administrators can mean the difference between students getting or not getting the services they need. At the Tier 1 level, mental health professionals can look for nonverbal and verbal behaviors that can signify a strong emotional reaction to the content or even disengagement, which taken in context may be indicative of a specific need. At Tier 2 or 3 levels, professionals pay close attention to both nonverbal and verbal behaviors in an effort to understand in more depth the students and their needs.

Multicultural Sensitivity

When one enumerates all of the ways in which human beings can differ, it makes sense to assume that every encounter with others is in some way multicultural—if one considers culture broadly to include not only culture but also race, ethnic heritage, gender, age/generation, religion, sexual orientation, ability, regional differences, family characteristics, and so forth. It can be important to have discussions about cultural differences with clients, rather than pretending that these differences do not exist. As Richardson (2001) states:

> Longer term relationships (counseling, friendship, supervision) have been enhanced by such discussions if: (1) they are approached with the goals of improved understanding, communication, and appreciation, and (2) we remember that as humans, we are more alike than different. (p. 45)

Whereas respectful, open, and direct communication about differences is critical for building trust in the therapeutic relationship, it requires that mental health professionals have multicultural competencies such as self-awareness, knowledge of one's own culture and of those who are different, and the skill set for communicating effectively (Arredondo et al., 1996).

Micro-Skills for More Intensive Interventions—Tier 2 and Tier 3

Empathy Skills

Without empathy, there is truly no foundation on which to build trust in a therapeutic or collegial relationship. From an emotional perspective, empathy is feeling what others feel as one listens to and connects with their stories; however, from a micro-skills perspective, empathy is so much more. It requires that mental health providers not only understand their clients but also that they *demonstrate* that understanding. When practitioners use the micro-skills of empathy, they are basically saying to others: *I'm here; I'm listening; I'm putting myself in your shoes; and I'm validating your experience.* As Chen and Giblin (2002) so clearly articulate, "empathy is the embryo of therapy" (p. 73). The authors would go a step further and suggest that empathy is the embryo of all positive professional relationships.

Providers demonstrate empathy to their clients using several different skills. Basic skills such as minimum utterances (e.g., *mmm-hmmm*) and repeating key words send a signal to clients that practitioners are keeping up with them and are alert to their stories. From there let's move to *paraphrase*, which is a distilled version of what the client has been saying—but using one's own words to relay the basic meaning. Providers typically paraphrase the content of the client's story, or the facts of the situation as understood by the client. Although professionals listen to understand the facts, they also listen to understand the emotional experiences of their clients. By listening for the emotional context of a client's story and watching nonverbal communication for additional clues, providers begin to more fully grasp a client's unique circumstances and reactions to those circumstances.

Professionals cannot forget that sometimes being a fully present, caring adult who listens with a sensitive ear is truly enough. Sometimes there are no solutions to construct and no plans to be made. Sometimes what children and teenagers need most is to tell their stories to people who will really listen and understand them. Employing empathy does not mean one is admiring or prolonging a problem; in fact, using empathy facilitates growth and healing. Of using empathy with challenging youth, Richardson (2001) reminds one that "if you are having a hard time connecting with a challenging youth, quit talking and start listening" (p. 55).

Whereas technically empathy is needed at all levels of intervention, the skills are most often used at the more intensive levels of Tier 2 and Tier 3. Empathy helps connect with clients and understand their concerns in order that they can be matched to the appropriate services. Active listening and empathy during classroom guidance lessons alert providers to individual students' concerns that may be addressed with more intensive, targeted services. Empathy is used to validate the unique emotional experiences of clients in smaller group settings and with individual clients during one-on-one counseling. Empathy skills are vital when meeting with parents, especially when giving reports that could be surprising or upsetting. Empathy also helps in communicating more effectively with teachers and administrators in that it helps foster caring professional relationships. By using active listening skills and working to understand each participant in the conversation, the school-based mental health practitioner (whether a school counselor, school psychologist, or school-based social worker or clinical counselor) will consistently communicate respect, compassion, and a willingness to engage with others in a positive manner.

As mentioned, empathy builds the foundation of the helping process. The skills allow mental health professionals to reflect what others have stated in order to demonstrate understanding. Providers use them to help reach greater and greater depths of understanding: basic empathy, such as *paraphrase*, allows practitioners to reflect the facts, or shallow most layer of the clients' stories; the *reflection of feeling* skill is used to mirror the emotional content of the clients' stories, yet it is difficult to gain an accurate understanding of emotions before the facts are understood; and *reflection of meaning* helps understand the central meaning of the clients' stories, or what is most important to them (such as a value, belief, or dream/goal). It is difficult to accurately comprehend meaning unless a basic understanding of the problem is first grasped, including its emotional impact on the client.

Inquiry Skills

Many therapists would argue that empathy and unconditional positive regard are necessary, but not sufficient, to achieving positive therapeutic outcomes. Mental health practitioners rely on their ability to ask meaningful questions to focus the conversation and uncover important details to facilitate the helping process. Questions such as "What would you like to talk about today?" or "Can you tell me more about how you have been feeling lately?" can also provide an invitation to clients to share their stories. Chen and Giblin (2002) describe three main types of inquiry skills: focusing questions to zero in on specific feelings or problems; probing questions to uncover specific details, meaning, patterns, and to understand the client's perspective and experience; and clarifying statements that help better understand what the client has related. When used effectively, inquiry provides structure and direction to each therapeutic conversation.

Influencing Skills

It is often heard that a goal of effective counseling is to provide a balance of challenge and support. If counseling were solely about support, then clients might feel safe and validated but perhaps might not be willing to take the necessary steps to grow and change. Enter *influencing skills*. When clients' stories are understood, counselors are in a better position to actively influence clients' perspectives, choices, and actions. Although empathy and inquiry skills are used to gain that understanding, influencing skills are used to participate more directly in the counseling process. Skills such as confrontation of problematic thinking or behavioral patterns, psychoeducation, immediacy, self-disclosure, advanced empathy (e.g., reflecting implicit emotions or patterns), and feedback can encourage a client to take the steps necessary for change.

Now that a cursory review of micro-skills has been provided, the examination can continue by differentiating their use across the three tiers of intervention. This is followed by a case study illustrating the use of micro-skills in the kindergarten through 12th-grade settings.

EVIDENCED-BASED RESEARCH AND PRACTICE

Micro-Skills in Three Tiers of Intervention

Tier 1

Classroom guidance:

- Foundational skills—Creating a positive first impression, establishing rapport, basic attending skills, observation skills, and multicultural sensitivity
- Observation skills
- Classroom management skills

Tier 2

Counseling group (Kottler & Englar-Carlson, 2010):

- Foundational skills
- Inquiry skills
- Influencing skills
- Group counseling skills
  - Linking or making connections among group members
  - Cuing or giving an invitation for a group member to speak
  - Blocking or obstructing a group member from engaging in unhelpful behaviors
  - Supporting or reinforcing positive interactions in the group
  - Energizing or drawing members in to participate

Tier 3

Individual short-term counseling:

- Foundational skills
- Use of advanced empathy (e.g., reflecting feeling and meaning, summary)

- Use of advanced inquiry skills (e.g., focusing and probing questions to shape the session and encourage processing)
- Influencing skills
- Conceptualization and intervention skills

Intervention skills move beyond basic micro-skills to include techniques from specific theoretical orientations. Whereas micro-skills are transtheoretical, intervention skills are predicated on a specific theory (such as CBT, SFBT, RT, Motivational Interviewing [MI], Systems, or mindfulness-based approaches, to name a few).

To examine how micro-skills can be used at each level of intervention, a case study following a young student (Gabriela in third grade) through the three tiers of the RTI model is provided. After the case study, there is a brief summary of the specific micro-skills used along with a rationale.

CASE STUDY

Reason for Referral

Gabriel was initially included in a whole-class social skills program, then referred to Tier 2 intervention after insufficient progress from the Tier 1 intervention.

Background, Case History, and Intervention Process

Gabriela is an 8-year-old Hispanic girl in Mrs. Smith's third-grade class at Mountaintop Elementary School. Her parents are both from Mexico (her father is deceased), and this is her first year going to Mountaintop. During the summer, Gabriela, her mother, and Gabriela's three sisters moved to town to live with her aunt, uncle, and three cousins following her father's death the previous spring. Gabriela speaks English proficiently because she studied it at her old school; however, her mother's fluency is quite limited. Mountaintop school counselor Ms. Brown visited Mrs. Smith's class to teach a guidance lesson on friendship. Because Ms. Brown had not yet visited Mrs. Smith's class, she spent the first few minutes establishing rapport by asking students about their costumes for the upcoming school Halloween parade. This prompted a lively discussion among the students, and the laughter throughout the room was a nice icebreaker before the guidance lesson. The first topic in the lesson was friendship; and Ms. Brown asked the students to talk at their tables about what makes a good friend. Ms. Brown noticed that while other students were engaging in discussion, Gabriela sat quietly at her desk, looking out the window at the parking lot below. During the second small-group activity, Gabriela exhibited the same behavior, which prompted Ms. Brown to approach.

Ms. Brown:	Hi, Gabriela. I noticed that you aren't talking with your group about the topic. Is everything okay?
Gabriela:	*(head down-turned with arms crossed)* I . . . I guess . . . so *(in a barely audible voice).*
Ms. Brown:	Okay, well I just wanted to check since you seemed quiet. Would you like to work with Hannah *(who sits right next to Gabriela)* for the last few minutes of the activity?
Gabriela:	*(nods her head slowly and turns to Hannah)*

After the lesson, Ms. Brown approached Mrs. Smith and described Gabriela's apparent reluctance to engage with her peers. Mrs. Smith responded that she too has observed similar behavior because Gabriela often remains isolated even during nonstructured activities (e.g., lunch and recess). Ms. Brown suggested changing the arrangement of desks from rows to units of four, and placing Gabriela with a group of girls known to be friendly and accepting. Ms. Brown also recommended peer tutoring, should it appear that Gabriela's socially isolating behavior was beginning to negatively affect her ability to work collaboratively on academic tasks. Since data collection forms a critical piece of the decision-making process within RTI, Mrs. Smith decided to conduct daily interval observations during a group activity to record the frequency in which Gabriela initiated interactions with peers. As a basis of comparison, Mrs. Smith additionally collected baseline data prior to implementing the interventions suggested by Ms. Brown. Mrs. Smith indicated that she would track Gabriela's performance for 3 weeks and report upon her progress.

Three weeks after implementing these changes, Mrs. Smith approached Ms. Brown to report on Gabriela's progress. As they reviewed the data, it became apparent that the frequency with which Gabriela initiated contact with peers was not significantly improving. In fact, during group work she had become increasingly withdrawn and her academic performance had dropped remarkably. Mrs. Smith shared that she had approached Gabriela numerous times throughout these 3 weeks asking if Gabriela was okay, and that Gabriela always nodded her head *yes* but didn't elaborate. Upon consultation with Ms. Brown, Mrs. Smith decided to refer Gabriela to the school's Intervention Assistance Team (IAT) to collaborate with staff in identifying those factors hindering Gabriela's social engagement and develop an intervention plan for Gabriela. The IAT collected information from a variety of sources (e.g., Gabriela's cumulative file, academic performance, ESL [English as a second language] status, medical information) and examined it in conjunction with data collected by Mrs. Smith. Upon review, the IAT determined that Gabriela might benefit from Tier 2 intervention services in the form of a social skills group. Ms. Brown stated that she was just in the process of forming a group and was happy to include Gabriela. The IAT decided to implement the intervention twice a week, for 20 minutes per session, over the course of 6 weeks. Over the course of the intervention, Ms. Brown conducted biweekly classroom observations to monitor the frequency in which Gabriela initiated social interactions with peers. Additionally, Ms. Brown conducted observations during lunch and recess to determine if Gabriela generalized skills beyond the classroom setting. At the beginning and end of the 6-week intervention, Ms. Brown asked Gabriela to complete preprogram and postprogram surveys to assess changes in Gabriela's confidence and comfort in engaging with peers.

In the third week of the social skills group, the Feelings and Friends Club, Gabriela makes a statement that indicates she might be struggling with some anxiety/posttraumatic stress disorder (PTSD).

Ginger:	Sometimes it's hard for me to talk with other kids because I think they won't talk back.
Ms. Brown:	It sounds like you feel scared sometimes about how other kids will respond to you. It sure can be tough to do things that are scary. . . .
Gabriela:	Yeah (barely audible).
Ginger:	Did you say something, Gabriela?

Ms. Brown turns to Gabriela and allows silence as Gabriela begins to speak. She calmly motions to Jacob to be quiet because he is about to interject (something he does often). With a warm expression and gentle voice, she responds: Gabriela?

Gabriela:	I used to have to go to my little sister's room when she was crying because my uncle was hitting my aunt and she was screaming . . . but now he's in jail so that doesn't happen anymore. . . .
Ms. Brown:	That does sound scary, Gabriela. You were very brave to go to your little sister's room to help her. . . .
Gabriela:	I had to be brave lots of times. . . .
Ms. Brown:	What is another time you've had to be brave, Gabriela?
Gabriela:	Like when my dad died . . . in the accident. He had blood all over and I had to sit with him (*Gabriela looks down, gets very quiet*). I don't want to talk about it anymore. . . .
Ms. Brown:	That's okay, Gabriela.

When the IAT reconvened in 6 weeks, Ms. Brown shared her findings with the team. She noted that Gabriela responded positively to the intervention over the course of the first 2 weeks, but the frequency of her social interactions sharply decreased from weeks 3 through 6. Further, examination of Gabriela's responses on the preprogram and postprogram administration of the social skills survey revealed that Gabriela's perceived comfort and competence when engaging with peers did not improve. Ms. Brown indicated that for the first 2 weeks of the Feelings and Friends Club, Gabriela listened attentively but did minimal sharing. In the third week, she shared about the domestic violence incident between her uncle and aunt, as well as witnessing the death of her father, but seemed to shut down following these disclosures. For the remaining 3 weeks of the group, Gabriela remained quiet, despite several attempts by her peers to draw her into discussion.

In addition, Mrs. Smith reported that Gabriela's academic performance had declined remarkably; she was now failing those courses in which she exhibited strengths during her initial enrollment at Mountaintop. Given Ms. Brown's concerns that Gabriela's anxiety and PTSD clearly appeared to be affecting more than her social functioning, she suggested that Gabriela might benefit from Tier 3 services, in the form of intensive individual counseling with Mrs. Fleming, the school-based clinical counselor. Mrs. Fleming is part of the Emotional and Behavioral Intervention and Support Services (EBISS) program that is funded partially by a federal grant.

Relying on the evidence provided about the efficacy of CBT approaches with children (and with immigrant children), Mrs. Fleming met with Gabriela once a week for 40-minute sessions and focused on helping Gabriela learn skills for managing her anxiety (Compton et al., 2004; Kataoka et al., 2003). Mrs. Fleming took the first few sessions to establish rapport, talking about Gabriela's love of animals and her favorite Mexican foods. Gabriela seemed to become more comfortable with Mrs. Fleming and responded well to her friendly demeanor. Therapy progressed well, with Gabriela telling Mrs. Fleming about the traumas she had experienced and expressing extreme sadness about the loss of her father. Gabriela learned how to verbalize her feelings in healthy ways with the help of Mrs. Fleming and learned specific techniques for managing her stress and anxiety. Over several weeks of individual counseling, Gabriela improved her grades markedly, but she was still struggling to form friendships with her peers. Because of their strong therapeutic relationship, Mrs. Fleming felt that she could now begin to challenge Gabriela about her reluctance to engage with others. Up until this time, Mrs. Fleming had relied on her use of empathy skills to validate Gabriela and to help her feel safe. She used inquiry skills to learn more about Gabriela's cultural context and family dynamics, as well as her experience with anxiety. To challenge Gabriela to use her new skills for interacting with her peers, Mrs. Fleming used influencing skills.

Mrs. Fleming:	So, Gabriela . . . how have things been going with your classmates?
Gabriela:	*(arranging the stuffed animals by height on Mrs. Fleming's table)* What do you mean?
Mrs. Fleming:	I mean, remember when we talked last week about how you would ask Hannah if she would like to play at recess?
Gabriela:	Yes, I remember. Mrs. Fleming . . . I didn't want to. I'm afraid that Hannah will say no and run away from me.
Mrs. Fleming:	Gabriela, I can understand that you are afraid, but I want to remind you of something. Remember when you told me that Hannah has asked you twice if you would like to sit with her during quiet reading time?
Gabriela:	Yes.
Mrs. Fleming:	What do you think that says about Hannah?
Gabriela:	That she wanted to sit with me.
Mrs. Fleming:	Yes . . . and what else have you noticed about Hannah?
Gabriela:	That she seems really nice.
Mrs. Fleming:	Yes, I think it does, too. Gabriela, I think you've noticed that Hannah is a nice girl, and maybe it's time that you step out and ask her to play. You've mentioned that you really like her, and that you're getting tired of playing by yourself at recess. Why not give it a try?
Gabriela:	Ok, I'll do it this afternoon! *(Gabriela smiles.)*

Gabriela asked Hannah to play at recess, and Hannah agreed. They have since become friends and play every day at recess and sit together at lunch. Mrs. Fleming terminated weekly sessions with Gabriela after 6 months of working with her to treat acute symptoms of PTSD and help her with social anxiety. Mrs. Fleming met with Gabriela's mother twice during the 6 months of counseling in order to check on her progress at home and to help support efforts to ensure that Gabriela practiced many of her anxiety-reduction techniques at home. Mrs. Fleming relied on her ability to establish rapport, her use of empathy, and her multicultural competencies in order to build an alliance with Gabriela's mother. Mrs. Fleming tapered her sessions with Gabriela to once per month, then reassessed toward the end of the school year. Both her classroom teacher Mrs. Smith and her school counselor Ms. Brown monitored Gabriela to ensure that she continued to make gains throughout the remaining weeks of the school year.

Throughout this intervention, the use of micro-skills was critical in achieving a positive outcome for Gabriela and connecting with the mother. By closely observing Gabriela's behavior in the classroom and establishing rapport with the student, the teacher and school counselor were able to identify an appropriate service and encourage Gabriela to participate in a small-group experience. When in the group, the school counselor used the skills of empathy and group leadership skills such as linking, cuing, and blocking to give Gabriela the space to share. As a result of her disclosures, the school counselor identified that individual counseling would be an appropriate referral for the student. Finally, while working individually with Gabriela, the school-based clinical counselor used rapport, empathy skills, inquiry, and influencing skills in addition to specific techniques to help Gabriela improve academically, socially, and behaviorally. It is also important to note that throughout the three tiers of intervention, every mental health practitioner approached Gabriela in a way that affirmed her culture and unique family circumstances.

SUMMARY

This chapter presents micro-skills of effective therapeutic communication across the three tiers of intervention in the kindergarten through 12th-grade settings. Although many skills are broad and can be applied in all levels (e.g., establishing rapport, creating a positive first impression, using basic attending skills, and approaching students with multicultural sensitivity), other skills can be especially effective when used at the more intensive levels, or Tier 2 and Tier 3. Empathy skills are a key to building trust and validating the feelings and experiences of others, whereas effective use of inquiry and influencing skills help to better understand problems and facilitate growth and change. Although specific interventions create the structure of the helping process, micro-skills give practitioners the communication tools necessary to realize positive outcomes.

RESOURCES

The American School Counselor Association website (www.schoolcounselor.org) provides publications and various resources on RTI and the role of the school counselor.

Textbooks and videos on learning counseling micro-skills can be found by browsing catalogs from the American Counseling

Association website (www.counseling.org/publications/pub-lications-catalog) or by going to the American Psychological Association website (www.apa.org) and searching the key words *counseling skills*.

Visit the Association for Multicultural Counseling and Development website (www.multiculturalcounseling.org) to learn more about multicultural counseling skills.

The Association for Specialists in Group Work (ASGW) website (www.asgw.org/index.htm) provides books and training videos highlighting group counseling skills.

REFERENCES

American School Counselor Association. (2008). *The professional school counselor and response to intervention*. Retrieved from www.schoolcounselor.org

Arredondo, P., Toporek, M. S., Brown, S., Jones, J., Locke, D. C., Sanchez, J., & Stadler, H. (1996). *Operationalization of the multicultural counseling competencies*. Alexandria, VA: Association for Multicultural Counseling and Development.

Chen, M., & Giblin, N. (2002). *Individual counseling: Skills and techniques*. Denver, CO: Love.

Compton, S. N., March, J. S., Brent, D., Albano, A. M., Weersing, R., & Curry, J. (2004). Cognitive-behavioral psychotherapy for anxiety and depressive disorders in children and adolescents: An evidence-based medicine review. *Journal of the American Academy of Child & Adolescent Psychiatry, 43*(8), 930–959.

Denton, C. A., Fletcher, J. M., Anthony, J. L. & Francis, D. J. (2006). An evaluation of intensive intervention for students with persistent reading difficulties [Electronic version]. *Journal of Learning Disabilities, 39*(5), 447–466.

Duncan, B., Miller, S., Wampold, B., & Hubble, M. (2010). *The heart and soul of change: Delivering what works in therapy*. Washington, DC: American Psychological Association.

Fuchs, D., & Fuchs, L. (2005). *Operationalizing response-to-intervention (RTI) as a method of LD identification*. Retrieved January 15, 2008, from http://www.tennessee.gov/education/speced/sefuoperti-faq.pdf

Fuchs, D., Fuchs, L. S., Compton, D. L., Bouton, B., Caffrey, E., & Hill, L. (2007). Dynamic assessment as responsiveness to intervention: A scripted protocol to identify young at-risk readers [Electronic version]. *Teaching Exceptional Children, 39*(5), 58–63.

Graner, P. S., Faggella-Luby, M. N., & Fritschmann, N. S. (2005). An overview of responsiveness to intervention: What practitioners ought to know [Electronic version]. *Topics in Language Disorders, 25*(2), 93–105.

Gresham, F. (2001). *Responsiveness to intervention: An alternative approach to the identification of learning disabilities*. Washington, DC: Department of Education Office of Special Education Programs.

Gruman, D. H., & Hoelzen, B. (2011). Determining responsiveness to school counseling interventions using behavioral observations. *Professional School Counseling, 14*(3), 183–190.

Ivey, A. (1971). *Microcounseling: Innovations in interviewing training.* Springfield, IL: Charles C. Thomas.

Ivey, A., Ivey, M., & Zalaquett, C. (2010). *Intentional interviewing and counseling: Facilitating client development in a multicultural society* (7th ed.). Belmont, CA: Brooks/Cole.

Kataoka, S. H., Stern, B. D., Jaycox, L. H., Wong, M., Escudero, P., Tu, W., . . . Fink, A. (2003). A school-based mental health program for traumatized Latino immigrant children. *Journal of the American Academy of Child & Adolescent Psychiatry, 42*(3), 311–318.

Kottler, J., & Englar-Carlson, M. (2010). *Learning group leadership: An experiential approach* (2nd ed.). Thousand Oaks, CA: Sage.

Martinez, R. S., Nellis, L. M., & Prendergast, K. A. (2006). Closing the achievement gap series: Part II response to intervention (RTI)-basic elements, practical applications, and policy recommendations [Electronic version]. *Education Policy Brief, 4*(8), 1–6.

Mastropieri, M. A., & Scruggs, T. E. (2005). Feasibility and consequences of response to intervention: Examination of the issues and scientific evidence as a model for the identification of individuals with learning disabilities [Electronic version]. *Journal of Learning Disabilities, 38*(6), 525–531.

Mellard, D., McKnight, M., & Jordan, J. (2010). RTI tier structures and instructional intensity. *Learning Disabilities Research and Practice, 25*(4), 217–225.

National Center on Response to Intervention. (2010). *RTI state database: The state chart.* Retrieved from http://state.rti4success.org/

Ockerman, M. S., Mason, E. C. M., & Hollenbeck, A. F. (2012). Integrating RTI with school counseling programs: Being a proactive professional school counselor. *Journal of School Counseling, 10*(15), 1–37.

Richardson, B. (2001). *Working with challenging youth: Lessons learned along the way.* New York, NY: Routledge.

Ridley, C., Kelly, S., & Mollen, D. (2011). Microskills training: Evolution, reexamination, and call for reform. *The Counseling Psychologist, 39*(6), 800–824.

Ridley, C., Mollen, D., & Kelly, S. (2011). Beyond micro-skills: Toward a model of counseling competence [Electronic version]. *The Counseling Psychologist, 39*, 825–864. doi:10.1177/0011000010378440

Stecker, P. M. (2007). Tertiary intervention: Using progress monitoring with intensive services [Electronic version]. *Teaching Exceptional Children, 39*(5), 50–57.

Vaughn, S. (2003, December). *How many tiers are needed for response to intervention to achieve acceptable prevention outcomes?* Paper presented at the National Research Center on Learning Disabilities Responsiveness-to-Intervention Symposium, Kansas City, MO.

Vaughn, S., & Roberts, G. (2007). Secondary interventions in reading: Providing additional instruction for students at risk. *Teaching Exceptional Children, 39*(5), 40–46.

Young, M. (2009). *Learning the art of helping: Building blocks and techniques* (4th ed.). Upper Saddle River, NJ: Pearson.

CHAPTER 7

Solution-Focused Brief Therapy

CYNTHIA FRANKLIN

KRISTIN W. BOLTON

LEARNING OUTCOMES

On completion of this chapter, the reader should be able to:

- Understand the core elements of Solution-Focused Brief Therapy (SFBT)
- Define models and applications of SFBT in school settings
- Comprehend the evidence base of SFBT in school settings

SFBT was developed during the late 1970s at the Brief Family Therapy Center in Milwaukee, Wisconsin, by Steve de Shazer, Insoo Kim Berg, and a team of therapeutic collaborators. SFBT evolved out of Systemic and Brief Family Therapy. It is a strengths-based and future-oriented intervention that focuses on working with the client or student to solution build rather than problem solve. Specifically, the solution-building process directs clients toward exploration of resources, past successes, and the identification of goals and future hopes as opposed to present and past problems.

At the core of SFBT is the collaborative relationship between the student and the mental health professional, with a focus on letting clients or students discover or co-create their own solutions. SFBT also makes use of solution talk and co-construction of meaning in the conversations between students and mental health professionals, which is a major therapeutic mechanism for change (Bavelas, 2012). This means that mental health professionals practicing SFBT position questions and dialogue in ways that help students think and feel differently about their current

problems. Mental health professionals practicing SFBT challenge the client/student to identify present competencies and
new behaviors that can be enacted in the future and that have
the potential to accomplish desired goals (De Jong & Berg, 2008;
Franklin, Kim, & Tripodi, 2009b).

To date, SFBT has been used in a variety of practice settings
with diverse client populations across age groups and with internalizing and externalizing behavioral problems. Over the last
decade, there has been an increase in the number of outcome studies examining the effectiveness of SFBT with children and adolescents in schools, clinics, juvenile courts, and child-welfare settings
(Bond, Woods, Humphrey, Symes, & Green, 2013; Franklin, Kim, &
Tripodi, 2009a; Franklin, Trepper, Gingerich, & McCollum, 2012;
Jordan et al., 2013). For example, SFBT has been implemented in
the amelioration of behavioral and emotional issues, academic
problems, and dropout prevention (Berg & Shilts, 2005; Franklin,
Biever, Moore, Clemons, & Scamardo, 2001; Franklin & Hopson,
2009; Franklin, Streeter, Kim, & Tripodi, 2007; Kral, 1995; Metcalf,
1995; Murphy, 1996; Murphy & Duncan, 2007; Sklare, 1997; Webb,
1999). As indicated by a recent review of the National Registry
of Evidence-Based Programs and Practices (www.nrepp.samhsa
.gov), the increase in research studies has also resulted in SFBT
being recognized as a promising, evidence-based practice.

According to recent reviews of the literature, one of the most
promising areas of intervention for SFBT is with children, adolescents, and teachers in school settings (Bond et al., 2013; Kim
& Franklin, 2009). This chapter summarizes how SFBT is used
in schools, including assessment and intervention strategies, and
the research supporting the use of SFBT in schools. The chapter
also discusses the specific solution-focused techniques that are
used in schools and illustrates them with a case study. Finally, the
chapter further shows how SFBT has been applied at different
levels of intervention and therefore may be used within an RTI
(Response to Intervention) framework.

SOLUTION-FOCUSED BRIEF THERAPY IN SCHOOLS

The application of SFBT in schools occurred during the early 1990s
and was followed by the emergence of associated publications
and preliminary research studies in the mid-1990s (e.g., Kral, 1995;
LaFountain & Garner, 1996; Metcalf, 1995; Murphy, 1996; Sklare,
1997). Since that time, the research and scholarly literature on the
use of SFBT in schools has grown across disciplines such as school
social work, counseling, and psychology (e.g., Berg & Shilts, 2005;
Franklin & Gerlach, 2007; Kelly, Kim, & Franklin, 2008; Metcalf,
2008; Murphy, 2008; Murphy & Duncan, 2007; Webb, 1999), with
reports of SFBT interventions and programs implemented in
schools in the United States, Canada, Europe, Australia, South
Africa, and in the provinces of mainland China and Taiwan

(e.g., Daki & Savage, 2010; Fitch, Marshall, & McCarthy, 2012; Kelly, Kim, & Franklin, 2008; Zhang et al., in press).

SFBT school interventions may be delivered in a variety of different modalities including individual, group, family, and even organizational level interventions and have the potential to serve as universal, secondary, and tertiary prevention purposes (Metcalf, 2010). To date, a variety of school-based interventions have been applied at different grade levels and with varying groups (teachers, parents, and students) within the school environment. For example, past SFBT programs and interventions have included

- Individual, group, parent, and family counseling and teacher consultations to assist with students who have behavioral problems and may also be at risk for school failure and dropout (Franklin et al., 2001; Franklin, Moore, & Hopson, 2008; Franklin et al., 2007; Metcalf, 2008; Murphy, 2008). SFBT counseling and consulting interventions have been used with elementary school, middle school, and high school students.
- Intervention for Hispanic pregnant and parenting adolescent mothers (Harris & Franklin, 2008), with a focus on increasing problem-focused versus emotion-focused coping, improving grades, school attendance, social support, and parenting efficacy.
- Bullying prevention for youth as part of an antibullying initiative (Young & Holdorf, 2010).
- A classroom management and coaching program known as Working on What Works (WOWW), developed for special education teachers to use "solution-building" in classroom settings to improve behavioral and attendance problems (Kelly et al., 2008). Similar SFBT classroom coaching interventions known as Lip-Focus have also been developed for classrooms and used in Sweden and other European nations by two special education teachers (Mahlberg & Sjoblom, 2013).
- Classroom group interventions for students with reading difficulties, with a focus on improving academic and emotional difficulties associated with learning disabilities (Daki & Savage, 2010)
- Training or coaching program for all school faculty and staff in an effort to incorporate SFBT techniques into the entire school environment (Franklin, Montgomery, Baldwin, & Webb, 2012; Franklin & Streeter, 2003; Kelly et al., 2008). This training was accomplished in a public, alternative high school for dropout prevention, and the high school has sustained its solution-focused training and practices for the past 13 years. See Franklin and Montgomery (2012) for a review of the Garza High School program.

Franklin and Gerlach (2007) further identified three important reasons why SFBT may be a useful and expedient intervention for school settings, and those reasons also show the potential for use of SFBT across different tiers of intervention. First, SFBT is a student-centered method that allows for a high degree of flexibility and transportability to the whole school and can be applied with other educational and therapeutic models to improve a student's academic and behavioral performance. The principles of SFBT, for example, can be taught to teachers and used in classrooms and in conversations between counselors, students, teachers, and administrators. Since the SFBT philosophy, relationship, and coaching skills can be taught to different personnel in a school, the intervention may serve as a cost-effective method for improving school climate. A student's engagement with the school, social cognition, and sense of personal competencies may improve, for example, because of the strategic use of positive language, an increase in positive social interactions, and achievement of personal goals that is accomplished by the use of the SFBT intervention.

Second, SFBT was initially developed as a method while being delivered in a mental health clinic serving high-risk populations who also often had contacts with the social services. This makes the approach a good match for schools that often serve involuntary and high-risk groups who may need additional Tier 2 or Tier 3 interventions to help them progress in school (i.e., the homeless, teenage parents, those with externalizing behaviors, etc.). SFBT is a brief intervention that emphasizes achievement of practical goals through building on strengths and facilitating collaboration with those involved in the student's life. SFBT therefore provides a practical focus on addressing day-to-day issues that may hinder educational achievement, such as the relationship with the teacher, attendance problems, transportation issues, or family problems. Teachers and student support teams may deliver interventions that assist in practical solution building. For example, a teacher may use supportive relationship skills, solution talk, and goal-setting to assist a student who repeatedly shows up to the classroom late and emotionally upset. A school social worker or counselor may further be involved in helping both the teacher and student find ways to resolve issues impacting the student's tardiness and family and interpersonal problems that are associated with these responses.

Finally, as has been suggested, the applications of solution-focused interventions and programs in schools vary, and several different school personnel may become involved in the delivery of these interventions. For instance, interventions can be tailored to students in either an individual or group setting, or entire classrooms may employ solution-focused techniques throughout the school year. Regardless of the setting, there are a number of specific techniques used in a SFBT intervention or program that tend to be universal to the therapeutic model. SFBT methods are based on careful listening to what the client says and for strengths and competencies that may exist, creating cooperative relationships, and inspiring hope. SFBT practitioners further reflect on client competencies and on what clients want to happen, including their goals and aspirations. The strategic use of communication and social interactions, sometimes referred to as solution-building conversations, are most important for facilitating positive emotional and behavioral changes (Kelly et al., 2008; Kim & Franklin, in press).

SOLUTION-BUILDING CONVERSATIONS

Specific types of questioning and communication methods have been associated with solution-building conversations (Kelly et al., 2008). Methods such as purposefully using the client's or student's language, grounding understanding in communication exchanges, and the awareness that questions and language are not neutral but shape perceptions and outcomes have been explored in process studies and determined to be important to SFBT change strategies (Solution-Focused Brief Therapy Association Research Committee, 2013). A nonconfrontational and collaborative approach to counseling is a part of the SFBT intervention, and for this reason the counselor follows closely the responses of the student using reflective listening and inquisitive and tentative language such as maybe, perhaps, suppose, and adopts an accepting, nonjudgmental, and conversational approach (Kelly et al., 2008). Examples of SFBT questions and counseling methods follow.

QUESTIONS AND REFLECTIONS THAT BUILD COOPERATIVE RELATIONSHIPS FOR SOLUTION BUILDING

- How can I be helpful to you?
- What has been going well in your life?
- How would you know if our talk would make a big difference?
- Tell me what accomplishments you are most proud of.
- How did you know that was the right thing to do?
- What I am hearing is that you are able to. . . .
- What I see about you is that you are good at. . . .

Exception Questions

Exception questions are questions that allow the practitioner and student to explore points in the student's life where an identified problem could have but did not occur.

- Tell me a time when this problem does not occur.
- What was different then?
- What's been better?

- What has changed?
- What has been your best day?
- What are you good at?
- Tell me about a time that you avoided getting in trouble. How did you do that?

Relationship Questions

Relationship questions are questions that allow students to reflect on how others in their lives perceive them and to notice different behaviors and social interactions that may lead to different responses. A counselor might say, for example, "Let's just suppose that you were able to stay awake in class even though you are so tired from working and taking care of your baby—how would that make a difference? What would the teacher say? Who else would notice?"

Miracle Question

The miracle question provides clients with an opportunity to reconstruct their stories by identifying a preferred future without perceived problems (Berg & De Jong, 1996; De Jong & Berg, 2001). There are many adaptations to the miracle question but the one that was first developed by Berg, de Shazer, and colleagues is as follows:

> I would like to ask you a very strange question. The strange question is this: After you leave here today, you go home, follow your regular routine, whatever that may be, and eventually go to bed. While you are sleeping, a miracle happens and the problems you are experiencing today are solved! But, you did not know it because you were sleeping. So, when you wake up in the morning, what would be the first thing that you would notice that is different? (DeJong & Berg, 2008, p. 84)

Goal Setting

Goal setting is a fundamental element of the solution-focused process. In order to set an appropriate goal, the counselor has a conversation with students or clients about how they want their lives to be different. Questions include: "What has to happen for it to be worth your time to come here today? Suppose after we talk today that your life would be different, what would have to happen? What do you want to happen instead?" This conversation may also involve ways that others want the student to change even if the student does not agree with those changes. "So, what would your teacher say that you need to do differently?" A goal-directed conversation should lead to the identification of a goal that is stated in behavioral and practical terms that can specify who will do what, when, how, and where to create a solution. The goal should be self-determined and be important to the client. The counselor should also ask the student to make a commitment to work toward the goal and emphasize that this will be hard work (De Jong & Berg, 2008).

Importantly, in SFBT, goal setting is viewed as a beginning of change, and goals allow the counselor and student to negotiate reasonable, observable tasks that lead to the preferred future. As a part of envisioning the goal, it is also important for the student to identify new behaviors, to become aware of different types of social interactions, and to become very mindful of what is needed to achieve the goal. Many times goals are identified through the miracle question. This allows the counselor to ask students detailed questions about how they want their lives to be different and to identify "pieces of the miracle" that may already be present, as well as the changes that are needed in their everyday lives.

Scaling Questions

Scaling questions provide students with the opportunity to examine or evaluate progress toward identified goals and also serve as a method for envisioning the next steps needed to build a solution. This process allows both the student and practitioner to quantify progress and to identify the next steps to change by using a numeric rating scale (usually ranging from 0 or 1 through 10, with 0 or 1 as the lowest and 10 as the highest). Many different issues can be scaled from student progress, to hope for change, to commitment toward making the changes. For example, a counselor might say: "On a scale from 1 through 10, with 1 being all the problems we have discussed the worst they have ever been, and 10 being that a miracle has occurred and they are all solved, where would you rate yourself today?" If the C student says "a 4," the counselor might say: "How come a 4 and not lower? How will you get to a 5? On a scale of 1 through 10, how much hope do you have right now that things will improve?" (e.g., "a 3." "Really, that high? What kept you from giving yourself a 1?" "How will you get to a 4?"). In another example, the counselor might say: "On a scale of 1 through 10, with 1 being that you are not coping so well with this issue, and 10 being that you are coping well, where would you rate yourself?" . . . and so forth.

Compliments

Compliments serve as positive student feedback from the counselor; they highlight what the student is doing well and what is working. It is important for compliments to be genuine and for the counselor to notice and point out student strengths and competencies such as persistence, coping, social skills, and special abilities. Compliments are often offered in a manner that asks students to also reflect on their own strengths and to view themselves differently. For example, a student might say: "I left the class because I was pissed and she would not leave me alone. I was going to lose my temper and I wanted to throw something." A counselor might respond with: "You left the class because you were going to blow up at her?" Student exclaims: "Yeah!" Counselor: "And you came back?" Student: "Yeah!" Counselor: "Where did you learn that type of self-control? Some kids would have just cursed her out. That is amazing that you chose to leave instead of throwing something at the teacher. Really, where did you learn that type of self-control?"

Breaks for Planning Feedback

Breaks are often taken near the end of a session. This gives the counselor a moment to collect thoughts and develop compliments and to also think of the next steps, tasks, or experiments to propose to the client. In schools this could just be a pause for 2 minutes to 3 minutes or a 5-minute break to get some water.

Homework

At the end of a session, the counselors frequently suggest a possible assignment or experiment based on something the clients are already doing (exceptions) or an important new task that the clients have identified in the session that may move them toward their goals.

CASE STUDY

According to Franklin, Kim, and Tripodi (2013), solution-focused interviews are suggested to occur in a 50-minute session. However, given the nature of schools, solution interviews may be shorter in length (i.e., 20 minutes–40 minutes). This case study provides practical application of the aforementioned techniques of a solution-focused conversation between a student and a mental health counselor and is adapted, with permission, from a case written by Robert Blundo. The conversation is one that would take place during the first session between a client and counselor and is divided into three parts. The first segment of the solution-focused interview is spent making small talk and building rapport in an effort for the counselor to learn about the student's life. The second segment of the session involves discussing the problem, looking for exceptions, and formulating goals. Finally, the last segment of the session includes compliments, homework, and a follow-up plan.

Reason for Referral

Emma is a 10th-grade student who was referred to the school mental health counselor by her guidance counselor. Emma is at risk for failing out of high school primarily due to attendance. She has not responded to the standard school protocol for managing absent students, and her teachers believed she needed this additional help to continue in school and to graduate on time; therefore, this Tier 3 intervention was leveraged. Exhibit 7.1 presents a segment from the first session between Emma and the school mental health counselor. Notice, the counselor uses a number of solution-focused techniques throughout the conversation with Emma.

EXHIBIT 7.1 Case Study Dialogue

Counselor:	Hello, I am glad you came to see me. I have read the note from Mr. Bowers. He has asked that you come here because he says you have not been attending enough classes and may not graduate. Would you help me understand what has to happen to make that different for you?	
Emma:	I don't know. . . . School sucks and I don't like having to be here.	
Counselor:	"School sucks." Tell me about what makes it suck so that you don't want to be here.	
Emma:	I don't like getting up early and I don't like most of my classes. They are stupid.	
Counselor:	So, you do not like *most* of your classes; you feel they are stupid but that is not all of your classes? Which classes do you like a little that are not stupid?	Exception
Emma:	I don't know; maybe art and English are okay.	
Counselor:	You must be good at art and English!	
Emma:	Maybe a little. I like drawing and using colors and poetry.	
Counselor:	Poetry too?!	
Emma:	Yeah. . . .	
Counselor:	So art and English are something you like to do. What is it about those two classes that make them a little better for you?	
Emma:	I like the teachers; they help me to understand better and I like making things in art class.	
Counselor:	I would like to hear more about what you like about these two teachers and about the work.	
Emma:	Well, Mr. Chagall in art is very interested in what I am doing and is always available to all of us in the class to help us with our projects. He also lets us work on our own ideas. Mr. Wolf has helped me learn to write down my ideas in poetry . . . like rap versions. He also seems to really care when I am down or having issues.	
Counselor:	So you like being creative and English and art are classes where you can do some interesting learning and express yourself. It is also nice to have a teacher who you feel cares about you.	
Emma:	Yeah, I guess so. . . .	

(continued)

EXHIBIT 7.1 Case Study Dialogue (*continued*)

Counselor:	Let me make sure I understand this. You attend these two classes most of the time, is that correct?	
Emma:	Yes, I am usually late or miss my other classes, like history and math.	
Counselor:	So even though they are not your favorites and you think they are stupid, you make it to those classes too at times?	Exception
Emma:	Yeah, I guess so. . . . But not enough and the teachers are not understanding like Mr. Wolf.	
Counselor:	So, what has kept you coming to school, even though you have been late, even missing history and math sometimes?	
Emma:	I don't know; I guess I want to graduate. It is just hard to make myself come all the time and I don't like some classes.	
Counselor:	You want to graduate? Is that something you really want? Yes? So, that is what makes you come even though you do not like some classes; you come to school and attend the ones you like and others sometimes because you would like to graduate?	
Emma:	Yeah. . . .	
Counselor:	Wow! That takes some motivation to make yourself come when you do not want to come. How do you do that? How are you able to get up and come to class even when you don't want to or don't like some of the classes? That is not easy to do. How do you do that?	
Emma:	I never thought about it that way. I guess, I like some classes and when I am working on a project I want to come to finish it and talk with my teachers in art and English. Once I am here, I stay and go to the other classes and can do okay in them at times. I really want to graduate and be the first in my family to finish high school.	
Counselor:	You mentioned that you wanted to graduate and be the first one. What is important about graduating? What would that mean to you?	
Emma:	I don't know . . . maybe go to art school or write poetry. Get a better job and be able to do what I want to do.	
Counselor:	You really do like art and poetry and I see that you enjoy doing those. So, graduating would mean being able to do more of what you want to do and maybe go to art school?	
Emma:	Yeah . . . if I could get into a school or the community college.	
Counselor:	Go to community college, huh? What would you need to do to make that happen?	
Emma:	Just attend classes and get the work done on time.	
Counselor:	From what Mr. Bowers said to me, you have the grades to graduate but you may not because you are not attending enough classes. So, I agree with you, if you want to keep learning art and poetry then you would need to attend classes and complete the work.	
Emma:	Yeah. . . .	
Counselor:	From what you have told me, you are able to do that most of the time, particularly in art and English; and even in math and history you are passing and do well when you are there. Let me ask you a strange kind of question. Okay?	
Emma:	Okay.	
Counselor:	On a scale of 0 to 10, with 0 = not interested in attending school and graduating and 10 = I want to graduate and I want to do well in my classes, in particular art and English, where would you place yourself on that scale this very moment?	Scaling

EXHIBIT 7.1 Case Study Dialogue (*continued*)

Emma:	I guess somewhere around a 4 and maybe a 5.
Counselor:	Wow, that is nearly halfway to graduating and attending classes. What would it take to make that a definite or a good solid 5? A 5 meaning you want to really start to make graduating and going on to the community college in art and English your goal?
Emma:	Just make myself get to class and do my work like I do for art and English.
Counselor:	That would really make a difference for you here at school. What would it take for you to do each day to make that happen? What would you need to tell yourself that would get you up and to school each day?
Emma:	I guess think about what I want to do . . . like art and poetry and to graduate.
Counselor:	Each morning telling yourself that your goal is to graduate so that you can study art and English would help?
Emma:	Yeah.
Counselor:	Now, I would like to ask you a strange kind of question that takes imagination and creativity. Okay?
Emma:	Sure.
Counselor:	Let's say that when you and I are finished talking today, you go on about whatever you need to do at school today and then you go do whatever you do after school. With me so far *(pause for response)*? Now, at some time when you are at home, you finish up whatever you usually do before going to bed. You're tired and you fall asleep. But this is a special night and a magical thing happens during the night while you are sleeping. That magical thing that happens is that all of the uncertainty and challenges you have been having about graduating and attending classes has disappeared, vanished. You are at a 9 on the scale we used before. When you awoke, what would be the very first thing you would notice that would tell you *something was different*, that would tell you this *magical thing had happened*?	Miracle
Emma:	Magical and different. . . . I would be thinking of my work and my projects in English and art. . . . Also my other classes because I would be planning to apply to the community college and have things around that I was filling out. I would be different . . . like have more energy and I would not be worrying so much about my boyfriend. He usually stays out late and I am not sure if he will get up and go to work. He left school and got a job to help his mom pay the rent.
Counselor:	Hum, that is tough to have a boyfriend who worries you. What would you do instead of worrying though?
Emma:	I would eat breakfast and get ready for school.
Counselor:	And what would your family notice that was different about you so they would think: "Wow, what in the world happened last night?"	Relationship
Emma:	I would be up *(laughs)* and getting dressed and eating breakfast on time. They would be surprised. My mom would be asking me questions about what had happened to me, not yelling at me to get up and calling me names, like slut. I think she would be smiling. I would tell her I was going to graduate.
Counselor:	And would your mom be proud of you for saying that?
Emma:	Oh yeah, she would not believe it but she would be proud.

(continued)

EXHIBIT 7.1 Case Study Dialogue (*continued*)

Counselor:	How would that be for you, your mom smiling, not yelling, and asking questions?
Emma:	Different. Better. She would be calmer and I would feel better.
Counselor:	Then when you get to school, what would others notice that was different about you. . .? Like what in the world happened to Emma?
Emma:	Some of my friends who go to school on time would be surprised that I was at school so early and ask what I was doing there. I guess my teachers would not be real surprised but maybe a little in my math and history classes. Ms. Jones would probably say she was glad I could make it.
Counselor:	What else would be different for you and different for others?
Emma:	I guess it would be an easier day and I could get through the class stuff.
Counselor:	You mentioned that you would be completing forms for the community college after the magic. Tell me a little about that.
Emma:	I do have some of the forms but haven't filled them out. So I guess I would just get them done. It is getting late.
Counselor:	How would that make things different for you?
Emma:	I would feel like I was making something happen and getting out of high school.
Counselor:	From what you have said to me it seems that you would really like to finish and start your English or art studies in the community college. Let me ask you a different kind of question. Let's say that on a scale of 0 to 10, with 0 meaning you have absolutely no interest in going on with your studies and no confidence that you will do it, and 10 meaning that you are absolutely sure that you will make this happen and are absolutely confident that it will happen; where would you place yourself?
Emma:	I guess now I would say at about a 7 or 8. I feel like I want to go to community college and I need to get going on that.
Counselor:	That is a lot of confidence and determination that you are going to make this happen. What are some first steps you can take to stay at 7 or 8? Because, like you said, some days it is hard to come to some classes.
Emma:	I guess, I just have to focus on what I want to do and make sure I do what I have to do so I can finish school, like go to classes and get in my applications.
Counselor:	So, how will you focus? What will be different?
Emma:	I won't stay out late with my boyfriend and get in a fight with my mom when I come home.
Counselor:	What will you do instead of fighting with your mom?
Emma:	Come home when she says.
Counselor:	So, that would be really different and helpful for you to come home when she says?
Emma:	Yeah.
Counselor:	And what tells you that you are able to come home on time?
Emma:	(*Silence. . . .*) Uh, not sure. . . .
Counselor:	How do you know? You obviously know you can do this?

The word "Scaling" appears in the right margin next to the Counselor's scaling question.

EXHIBIT 7.1 Case Study Dialogue (*continued*)

Emma:	Yeah, I come home on time sometimes. I have to make up my mind and tell my boyfriend I am not going to stay.
Counselor:	That might be hard to not stay with your boyfriend? Are you sure you want to do this, leave and come home on time so you won't fight with your mom and can get up for school on time?
Emma:	Yeah, it's hard but I want to do it.
Counselor:	Can he take no for an answer?
Emma:	Yeah, he might be mad but he'll get over it.
Counselor:	That is good to know that you can say no to him and that you are so determined. You can stand up for yourself and what you want. *(Emma nods, yes.)* You seem like a very smart and determined person. Is that right? Can you do things that you make up your mind to do?
Emma:	*(smiles)* Yeah.
Counselor:	I bet you can! From what you have said and what the school has told me, attending your classes will be the key to graduating and moving on. You are already halfway there and this is what you want to be doing. You have talent in art and poetry and really want to continue studying those subjects at the community college. So, if it is okay with you, I would like to stay in touch to see how you are doing. Would you be willing to come back to see me next week to check in and maybe bring some of the filled out paperwork?
Emma:	Sure.
Counselor:	I will contact you to set up a time and, in the meantime, you can also come by and see me any time I am free.
Emma:	Okay.

Created by Robert Blundo, Professor, University of North Carolina at Wilmington.

Case Process

Subsequent meetings between Emma and the counselor continued to use progress monitoring and emphasize movement toward the goal of improved attendance and graduation and applying to the community college. Continued use of scaling questions, compliments, and tasks promotes ongoing movement toward goal achievement.

GROWING EVIDENCE BASE FOR SOLUTION-FOCUSED BRIEF THERAPY IN SCHOOLS

Outcome studies examining the effectiveness of SFBT using experimental and quasi-experimental designs have increased exponentially over the last several decades. Similarly, several meta-analyses (Kim, 2008; Stams, Dekovic, Buist, & De Vries, 2006) and systematic reviews (Bond et al., 2013; Gingerich & Peterson, 2013; Kim & Franklin, 2009) have emerged in the literature with supporting evidence that SFBT is a promising intervention and

TABLE 7.1 Study Summary

Study	Tier	Study theme	Study design	Outcome measure	Sample size	Sample population
Springer, Lynch, & Rubin (2000)	2	Internalizing behavior	Quasi-experimental	Hare Self-Esteem Scale	10	Hispanic elementary students
Franklin et al. (2001)	3	Externalizing behavior	Single case	Conners' Teacher Rating Scale	7	Middle school students ages 10–12
Newsome (2004)	2	Academic outcomes	Quasi-experimental	Grades; attendance	52	Middle school students
Corcoran (2006)	3	Externalizing behavior	Quasi-experimental	Conners' Parent Rating Scale; Feelings, Attitudes, and Behaviors Scale for Children	86	Students ages 5–17
Franklin, Moore, & Hopson (2008)	2/3	Behavioral problems Internalizing behavior	Quasi-experimental	Achenbach Child Behavior Checklist (CBCL)—Youth Self-Report (YSR) Form—Internalizing and CBCL Externalizing; Teachers Report Form (TRF)—Internalizing and Externalizing Score	67	Middle school students
Franklin, Streeter, Kim, & Tripodi (2007)	1	Academic outcomes	Quasi-experimental	Grades; attendance	85	At-risk high school students
Froeschle, Smith, & Ricard (2007)	3	Behavior problems Self-esteem Academic performance Substance abuse	Experimental design	American Drug and Alcohol Survey; Substance Abuse Subtle Screening Inventory Adolescent Version 2; Knowledge exam on physical symptoms of drug use; Piers-Harris Children's Self-Concept Scale Version 2; Home and Community Social Behavior Scales; School Social Behavior Scales Second Edition; Grade point average (GPA)	65	8th-grade female students

Source: Kim and Franklin (2009).

works in a variety of settings. In a recent systematic review, Bond et al. (2013) examined 38 RCTs (randomized controlled trials) and quasi-experiments on SFBT that explored the effectiveness of SFBT on children and families with internalizing, externalizing, and other problems, and concluded that SFBT was a promising intervention. In particular, SFBT showed efficacy for early intervention and when problems were not too severe; this also suggests that SFBT might be used in schools to prevent more severe behavioral and academic problems.

Kim and Franklin (2009) conducted a systematic review of the literature on SFBT in schools within the United States. This review examined seven methodologically rigorous solution-focused studies that used experimental or quasi-experimental designs and standardized outcome measures (Table 7.1 contains a summary of the studies that were included in the review).

Some of the same studies were subsequently analyzed in the Bond et al. (2013) review. Of the studies in the Kim and Franklin review, sample sizes ranged from 7 to 86 and spanned different age groups and grade levels. In addition, studies utilized a variety of SFBT techniques with a number of problems, including externalizing behaviors, internalizing behaviors, and academic outcomes (e.g., attendance, credits, and graduation rates). Findings from the studies that were included in the review are summarized in the following sections.

Outcome Studies on SFBT in Schools

Corcoran (2006) and Franklin et al. (2001) examined the application of SFBT with students who had serious behavioral problems. Corcoran (2006) explored the effectiveness of SFBT related to aggression, conduct problems in schools, and impulsivity and included 86 students ages 5 to 17. Participants were either enrolled in a SFBT intervention or treatment as usual (TAU; family treatment program premised on cognitive-behavioral techniques) and were assessed by the Conners' Parent Rating Scale and the Feelings, Attitudes, and Behaviors Scale for Children. Findings demonstrated improvement for the SFBT group and the TAU group; however, statistical significance was not found when comparing group differences. Corcoran (2006) asserted that the lack of difference between the SFBT group and the TAU group might be attributed to the fact that the TAU group used components of an empirically validated technique. Overall, the study had high attrition rates; however, the SFBT had better treatment engagements and fewer dropouts than the TAU (Corcoran, 2006).

Franklin et al. (2001) examined the effectiveness of SFBT with middle school students with learning disabilities or behavioral problems. The treatment protocol included use of the miracle question, exception questions, and scaling questions, as well as consultations with teachers using components of the collaborative meeting process developed by Metcalf (1995). Students received anywhere from 5 sessions to 10 sessions, lasting 30 minutes to 45 minutes. Behavioral changes were assessed using the Conners' Teacher Rating Scale. Findings demonstrated an improvement on previously clinically significant subscales of the Conners' Teacher Rating Scale for five of the seven students. Specifically, hyperactivity, conduct problems, emotional indulgence, and asocial behavior were outcomes that moved out of a clinical range.

In addition to behavioral problems, several studies examined the effectiveness of SFBT as it relates to internalizing problems. One study, conducted by Springer, Lynch, and Rubin (2000), investigated the effectiveness of SFBT on improving self-esteem of children whose parents or family members were incarcerated. A total of 10 elementary school students participated in an experimental wait-list control group design. The intervention involved six group sessions and employed SFBT techniques, such as scaling questions and the miracle question. Self-esteem was assessed using the Hare Self-Esteem Scale. Study results revealed that the students in the SFBT group had a statistically significant increase in scores, whereas the wait-list comparison group's scores remained unchanged.

Franklin et al. (2008) conducted a quasi-experimental design study with 67 middle school students in an effort to examine both behavioral outcomes and internalizing outcomes. Outcomes were assessed by the Teachers Report Form (TRF) and Youth Self-Report (YSR) of the Achenbach Child Behavior Checklist (CBCL). Findings demonstrated that the SFBT group declined below the clinical level at the time of posttest and remained there at follow-up for both the internalizing and externalizing scores for the TRF. The comparison group demonstrated little change between the pretest, posttest, and follow up. The results showed no difference between the SFBT and comparison groups for the internalizing score; however, the externalizing score of the SFBT group dropped below the clinical level and continued to decline at follow up.

Franklin et al. (2007) and Newsome (2004) used SFBT in an effort to improve school and academic outcomes. Newsome (2004) examined the effectiveness of SFBT on middle school students classified as at risk in relation to academic and attendance problems. A total of 52 students participated in the quasi-experimental pretest–posttest comparison group design. In the SFBT group, 26 students met for one class period (35 minutes) for a total of 8 weeks. During the sessions, the SFBT group facilitator used several different SFBT techniques including scaling questions, miracle questions, goals, and homework tasks. Findings indicated that students in the SFBT group increased their overall GPA from the pretest to the posttest. There was, however, no statistical significance between the comparison and control groups for the variable of attendance.

Similarly, Franklin et al. (2007) conducted a quasi-experimental design study in an effort to examine the effectiveness of SFBT in relation to credits earned, attendance, and graduation rates in a high school population. The intervention was employed at an alternative school with the idea of exploring the effectiveness of a SFBT program specific to dropout prevention. The SFBT group consisted of 46 students, whereas the comparison group consisted of 39 students from another school with similar at-risk characteristics. Findings revealed change over time in the number of credits earned as a proportion of credits attempted in both the SFBT group and the comparison group. Although both groups demonstrated an increase in the proportion of credits earned, the SFBT group exhibited a statistically significant higher average proportion of credits earned to credits attempted than the comparison group. The comparison group, however, performed better in terms of attending classes than the students in the SFBT group. Franklin et al. (2007) posited that the comparison of attendance between the two groups was problematic because the SFBT group worked on a self-paced curriculum and was able to decrease attendance once the curriculum was completed. Therefore, the use of attendance as a variable may not serve as an accurate measure for assessing the effectiveness of the intervention.

In the same study, Franklin et al. (2007) examined graduation rates by highlighting all of the students in the sample who were classified as 12th graders during the spring semester of 2004. Of the 37 students classified as 12th graders, 23 graduated from the SFBT group and 27 graduated from the comparison group. Of the 14 students in the SFBT group that did not graduate in the spring of 2004, 9 remained enrolled in high school during the fall of 2004 and 7 graduated the following school year. Finally, of the remaining 5 students, 3 were attending another alternative school and 1was attending a public high school (Franklin et al., 2007).

Finally, Froeschle, Smith, and Ricard (2007) conducted a randomized experimental design study in order to examine the effectiveness of SFBT in relation to behavior problems, self-esteem, academic problems, and substance abuse. This intervention included SFBT group sessions, mentorship, and action learning techniques in an effort to reduce substance use and behavioral problems among adolescent girls. Findings revealed a statistically significant change on drug use, attitudes toward drugs, knowledge of physical symptoms of drug use, and competent behavior scores in favor of the SFBT group. Some improvement was found on the American Drug and Alcohol Survey, Substance Abuse Subtle Screening Inventory Adolescent Version 2, and the Community Social Behavior Scale Measure, whereas the Knowledge exam and the School Social Behavior Scales Second Edition both demonstrated great improvement. Finally, no group differences were found between the SFBT and comparison groups on negative behaviors as measured by office referrals.

Based on the studies included in Kim and Franklin's (2009) review, SFBT is a promising and useful approach in working with at-risk students in a school setting. Some of the positive findings included improved academic achievement, reduction in the intensity of negative feelings, and reduced drug use. The overall results from the review were mixed; however, enough positive outcomes were found indicating SFBT is in fact a promising intervention in a school setting. Additionally, the effect sizes calculated and reported in the review show SFBT to be promising, with most studies having medium to large effect sizes.

Continued research is required in order to further establish the evidence base of SFBT in school settings. Replication of past empirically tested interventions and development and empirical testing of future interventions will continue to expand the evidence base, as well as generate additional understanding of the effectiveness of SFBT in schools settings. SFBT interventions are complex and applied in different modalities including individual, group, family, and organizational. Future studies will be useful in determining what levels of SFBT interventions are in fact the most effective.

Outcome Assessment for SFBT

When administering any intervention, including SFBT, it is important to assess changes in the client prior to the intervention and across time after the intervention. This allows the counselor the ability to quantify areas of growth and/or decline. The studies described in this chapter, for example, use a range of standardized measures when examining the effectiveness of SFBT in school settings. Some of the most common measures used include the CBCL (Achenbach System of Empirically Based Assessment) and the Conners' Teacher Rating Scale (Conners, 2014). Bowen and colleagues developed the School Success Profile (SSP; Bowen, Richman, & Bowen, 2002), a comprehensive tool for assessing youths' strengths and needs in the context of their social environment. This measure is also very compatible with SFBT assessment and intervention and has been used in some studies.

When using assessment measures in SFBT, it is also important to consider when and how to conduct an assessment. Previous studies described in this chapter assess students before and after the implementation of the SFBT intervention and at follow-up periods. These types of discreet measurements are often associated with research studies and may be helpful in determining the effectiveness of an intervention. In the actual practice of SFBT, however, it may be more helpful to assess the specific client behaviors more frequently to gauge clinical progress. For example, it may be more helpful to know how often a student comes to school in a given week than to show changes on school engagement measure. Conducting direct behavioral observations in the classroom and other settings is a valuable assessment for SFBT and provides rich information on students' behavior and the social context that shapes that behavior. Schools use an array of measures in assessing and reporting school outcomes. Academic outcomes such as test scores, graduation rates, attendance, GPA, and academic credits earned are also very important. Understanding the specific outcome measures within an individual school setting is useful in formulating and assessing outcomes for SFBT programs and interventions and will also help with demonstrating accountability of SFBT practices.

Selecting appropriate assessment and outcome measures should relate to the identified problem and be able to measure associated behavioral changes and provide client and counselor feedback about the progress being made. Brief and rapid assessment tools that are self-reporting or rating scales that can be used to assess session-by-session changes are useful to measuring outcomes in SFBT. Murphy and Duncan (2007) discuss, for example, the use of the Outcome Rating Scale that can be customized to client assessment and is useful for monitoring and providing feedback to clients. This type of assessment is helpful for improving the change process and serves a function similar to the scaling questions used in SFBT. Another useful resource in identifying outcome assessment measures is a book written by Simmons and Lehmann (2013). This text contains a number of measures capable of assessing a variety of outcomes generally associated with strengths'-based interventions like SFBT. Additionally, the text shows how to use goal attainment scales that are also useful in SFBT sessions to demonstrate client progress during the course of an intervention. Other resources for strengths'-based assessment and fidelity measurement are also reviewed in Franklin et al. (2012), including measures that were developed specifically for SFBT assessment such as the Solution-Building Inventory. Corcoran and Fischer (2013) further review several rapid assessment measures that may be used to measure problems and to monitor different outcomes with children and families, and these types of assessment tools may be used in SFBT outcome monitoring and assessment, as well as the strengths'-based measures.

SUMMARY

This chapter summarizes how SFBT is used in schools, including covering assessment and intervention strategies and the research supporting the use of SFBT in schools. Specific SFBT counseling techniques that are used in schools are described and illustrated, and a case study demonstrates how to conduct a solution-building conversation with a student who has attendance problems. This chapter further shows how SFBT has been applied at different levels of intervention, including with individual students, groups, classrooms, families, teachers, and school staff, and in organizational level interventions. SFBT may be used by a number of different school personnel, including teachers, and is adaptable for use with other academic and behavioral approaches. It has been used to change academic and nonacademic outcomes, and has been applied to both internalizing and externalizing behavioral problems. It is also a practical and brief intervention that is cost effective. Although additional studies are needed, SFBT is gaining a good amount of research that supports its effectiveness.

RESOURCES

Garza High School (www.austinschools.org/garza) is an alternative high school that operates on the principles and practices of Solution-Focused Brief Therapy. This high school has been in operation for 14 years and has a training manual that describes its practices.

School Social Work and Research Special Interest Group (www.luc.edu/sswsig) provides ongoing information about the research and development on school-based practices including studies about Solution-Focused Brief Therapy.

Solution-Focused Brief Therapy Association (SFBTA; www.sfbta.org) is a North American group of practitioners and researchers that focus on the practice and development of Solution-Focused Brief Therapy. SFBTA provides a treatment manual and videos and holds an annual conference.

REFERENCES

Bavelas, J. B. (2012). Connecting the lab to the therapy room: Micro-analysis, co-construction, and solution-focused brief therapy. In C. Franklin, T. Trepper., W. Gingerich, & E. McCollum (Eds.), *Solution-focused brief therapy: A handbook of evidence-based practice* (pp. 144–162). New York, NY: Oxford University Press.

Berg, I. K., & De Jong, P. (1996). Solution-building conversation: Co-constructing a sense of competence with clients. *Families in Society, 77*(6), 376–391.

Berg, I. K., & Shilts, L. (2005). *Classroom solutions: WOWW approach.* Milwaukee, WI: Brief Family Therapy Center.

Bond, C., Woods, K., Humphrey, N., Symes, W., & Green, L. (2013). The effectiveness of solution focused brief therapy with children and families: A systematic and critical evaluation of the literature from 1990–2010. *Journal of Child Psychology and Psychiatry, 54,* 707–723.

Bowen, G. L., Richman, J. M., & Bowen, N. K. (2002). The school success profile: A results management approach to assessment and intervention planning. In A. R. Roberts & G. J. Greene (Eds.), *Social workers' desk reference* (pp. 787–793). New York, NY: Oxford University Press.

Conners, K. C. (2014). *Conners* (3rd ed.). Toronto, Ontario: Multi-Health Systems Inc.

Corcoran, J. (2006). A comparison group study of solution-focused therapy versus "treatment-as-usual" for behavior problems in children. *Journal of Social Service Research, 33*(1), 69–81.

Corcoran, K., & Fischer, J. (2013). *Measures for clinical practice and research: Families and children.* New York, NY: Oxford University Press.

Daki, J., & Savage. R. S. (2010). Solution-focused brief therapy: Impacts on academic and emotional difficulties. *The Journal of Educational Research, 103*(5), 309–326.

De Jong, P., & Berg, I. K. (2001). Co-constructing cooperation with mandated clients. *Social Work, 46,* 361–381.

De Jong, P., & Berg, I. K. (2008). *Interviewing for solutions* (3rd ed.). Pacific Grove, CA: Brooks/Cole.

Fitch, T., Marshall, J., & McCarthy, W. (2012). The effect of solution-focused groups on self-regulated learning. *Journal of College Student Development, 53*(4), 586–595.

Franklin, C., Biever, J., Moore, K., Clemons, D., & Scamardo, M. (2001). The effectiveness of solution-focused therapy with children in a school setting. *Research on Social Work Practice, 11*(4), 411–434.

Franklin, C., & Gerlach, B. (2007). Clinical applications of solution-focused brief therapy in public schools. In T. S. Nelson & F. N. Thomas (Eds.), *Handbook of solution-focused brief therapy: Clinical applications* (pp. 168–169). Philadelphia, PA: Haworth Press.

Franklin, C., & Hopson, L. (2009). Involuntary clients in public schools: Solution-focused interventions. In R. Rooney (Ed.), *Strategies for work with involuntary clients* (2nd ed., pp. 322–333). New York, NY: Columbia University Press.

Franklin, C., Kim, J. S., & Tripodi, S. J. (2009a). A meta-analysis of published school social work intervention studies: 1980–2007. *Research on Social Work Practice, 19*(6), 667–677.

Franklin, C., Kim, J. S., & Tripodi, S. J. (2009b). Solution-focused brief therapy interventions for students at-risk to dropout. In A. R. Roberts (Ed.), *The social worker's desk reference* (2nd ed., pp. 1020–1030). New York, NY: Oxford University Press.

Franklin, C., Kim, J. S., & Tripodi, S. J. (2013). Solution-focused brief therapy interventions for students at risk to drop out. In C. Franklin, M. B. Harris, & P. Allen-Meares (Eds.), *The school services sourcebook: A guide for school-based professionals* (2nd ed., pp. 419–432). New York, NY: Oxford University Press.

Franklin, C., Montgomery, K., Baldwin, V., & Webb, L. (2012). Development and research on a solution-focused high school. In C. Franklin, T. Trepper, W. J. Gingerich, & E. McCollum (Eds.), *Solution-focused brief therapy: A handbook of evidence based practice* (pp. 371–389). New York, NY: Oxford University Press.

Franklin, C., Moore, K., & Hopson, L. (2008). Effectiveness of solution-focused brief therapy in a school setting. *Children & Schools, 30,* 15–26.

Franklin, C., & Streeter, C. L. (2003). Solution-focused alternatives for education: Training manual for Garza High School. Austin: University of Texas, Hogg Foundation for Mental Health.

Franklin, C., Streeter, C. L., Kim, J. S., & Tripodi, S. J. (2007). The effectiveness of a solution-focused, public alternative school for dropout prevention and retrieval. *Children & Schools, 29*(3), 133–144.

Franklin, C., Trepper, T., Gingerich, W. J., & McCollum, E. (2012). *Solution-focused brief therapy: A handbook of evidence-based practice.* New York, NY: Oxford University Press.

Froeschle, J. G., Smith, R. L., & Ricard, R. (2007). The efficacy of a systematic substance abuse program for adolescent females. *Professional School Counseling, 10*(5), 498–505.

Gingerich, W. J., & Peterson, L. T. (2013). Effectiveness of solution-focused brief therapy: A systematic qualitative review of controlled outcome studies. *Research on Social Work Practice, 23*(3), 266–283.

Harris, M. B., & Franklin, C. (2008). *Taking charge: A school-based life skills program for adolescent mothers.* New York, NY: Oxford University Press.

Jordan, C., Lehmann, P., Bolton, K. W., Huynh, L., Chigbu, K., Schoech, R., . . . Bezner, D. (2013). Youthful offender diversion project: YODA. *Best Practices in Mental Health, 9*(1), 20–30.

Kelly, M. S., Kim, J. S., & Franklin, C. (2008). *Solution-focused brief therapy in schools: A 360-degree view of the research and practice principles.* New York, NY: Oxford University Press.

Kim, J. S. (2008). Examining the effectiveness of solution-focused brief therapy: A meta-analysis. *Research on Social Work Practice, 18*(2), 107–116.

Kim, J. S., & Franklin, C. (2009). Solution-focused brief therapy in schools: A review of the literature. *Children and Youth Services Review, 31*(4), 464–470.

Kim, J. S., & Franklin, C. (in press). The use of positive emotion in solution-focused brief therapy. *Best Practices in Mental Health.*

Kral, R. (1995). *Solutions for schools.* Milwaukee, WI: Brief Family Therapy Center.

LaFountain, R. M., & Garner, N. E. (1996). Solution-focused counseling groups: The results are in. *Journal for Specialists in Group Work, 21*(2), 128–143.

Mahlberg, K., & Sjoblom, M. (2013). *Lip-focus.* Retrieved from http://www.sfe4u.org

Metcalf, L. (1995). *Counseling toward solutions: A practical solution-focused program for working with students, teachers, and parents.* San Francisco, CA: Jossey-Bass.

Metcalf, L. (2008). *A field guide to counseling toward solutions.* San Francisco, CA: Jossey-Bass.

Metcalf, L. (2010). *Solution-focused RTI: A positive and personal approach.* San Francisco, CA: Wiley.

Murphy, J. J. (1996). Solution-focused brief therapy in the school. In S. D. Miller, M. A. Hubble, & B. S. Duncan (Eds.), *Handbook of solution-focused brief therapy* (pp. 184–204). San Francisco, CA: Jossey-Bass.

Murphy, J. J. (2008). *Solution-focused counseling in schools.* Alexandria, VA: American Counseling Association.

Murphy, J. J., & Duncan, B. S. (2007). *Brief interventions for school problems* (2nd ed.). New York, NY: Guilford.

Newsome, S. (2004). Solution-focused brief therapy (SFBT) groupwork with at-risk junior high school students: Enhancing the bottom-line. *Research on Social Work Practice, 14*(5), 336–343.

Simmons, C. A., & Lehmann, P. (2013). *Tools for strength's-based assessment and evaluation.* New York, NY: Springer Publishing Company.

Sklare, G. B. (1997). *Brief counseling that works: A solution-focused approach for school counselors*. Thousand Oaks, CA: Sage.

Solution-Focused Brief Therapy Association Research Committee (SFBTRC). (2013). *Solution focused brief therapy treatment manual for working with individuals*. Retrieved from http://www.sfbta.org/

Springer, D. W., Lynch, C., & Rubin, A. (2000). Effects of a solution-focused mutual aid group for Hispanic children of incarcerated parents. *Child & Adolescent Social Work Journal, 17*, 431–432.

Stams, G. J. J. M,. Dekovic, M., Buist, K., & De Vries, L. (2006) Effectiviteit van oplossingsgerichte korte therapie: een meta-analyse [Efficacy of solution-focused brief therapy: A meta-analysis]. *Tijdschrift voor gedragstherapie, 39*, 81–94.

Webb, W. H. (1999). *Solutioning: Solution-focused interventions for counselors*. Philadelphia, PA: Accelerated Press.

Young, S., & Holdorf, G. (2010). Using solution focused brief therapy in individual referrals for bullying. *Educational Psychology in Practice, 19*(4), 272–282.

Zhang, Y., Liu, X., Franklin, C., Qu, Y., Chen, H., & Kim, J. S. (in press). The practice of solution-focused brief therapy in Mainland China. *Health and Social Work*.

Reality Therapy and School Practice

ROBERT E. WUBBOLDING

LEARNING OUTCOMES

On completion of this chapter, the reader should be able to:

- Identify the foundational principles of Choice Theory and Reality Therapy (RT)
- Examine the utility of RT as a tool for mental health intervention in the schools
- Understand how to apply WDEP (Wants, Direction, Self-Evaluation, Plan) to create systems of change and support for students within a school setting
- Differentiate the use and implementation of Choice Theory and RT within a three-leveled intervention system

It is often said that students function below their ability level and fail to achieve a desirable level of competency because their needs are unsatisfied. These unsatisfied needs can create feelings of low self-worth and inner conflict that students exhibit through actions inconsistent with school policy or that fall below standards needed for a well-functioning school. RT and Choice Theory, founded by William Glasser, provide an explanation and interventions to address these issues. As a therapeutic approach, RT has been integrated into many systemic interventions such as the Deming Total Quality Movement (Glasser, 1990; William Glasser Institute, 2013), management and supervision (Wubbolding, 1996), stages of recovery from addictions (Wubbolding & Brickell, 2005), parenting (Buck, 2013), and couples counseling (Robey, Wubbolding, & Carlson, 2012). In this chapter, Choice Theory and RT are presented as vehicles for guiding mental health interventions designed to bring about behavioral change that enhances student achievement and functioning.

Choice Theory is an underlying explanation of human thinking and behavior. It advances the notion that humans are motivated to satisfy five basic needs (to survive, to love and belong, to be powerful, to be free, and to engage in fun). And thus, motivation is internal *not* based on rewards and punishments. As opposed to seeing human beings as externally controlled, Choice Theory contends that humans exercise more internal control via life choices made. These choices are connected with needs and the key concepts of the "quality world" (how we want our world to look). Glasser states that RT, a closely tied partner of Choice Theory, is the train whereas Choice Theory is the track (Glasser & Glasser, 2008). This approach has been widely used in schools especially to address behavioral challenges posed by children (Mason & Duba, 2009). Numerous empirical studies have established the efficacy of RT approaches on students' sense of self (Omizo & Cubberly, 1983), self-regulation and choices (Kim, 2002; Kim & Hwang, 2001), and general cognitive and behavioral change (Passaro, Moon, Wiest, & Wong, 2004; Yarbrough & Thompson, 2002). In this chapter, the principles of this approach are presented and the implementation shown through a case study.

PRINCIPLES OF CHOICE THEORY

William Glasser (1988) once stated that counseling was just one person helping another with a problem; and that wasn't too difficult if the other person wanted to be helped. Most students want and desire help when confronted with life's challenges and problems. Both teachers and mental health providers are uniquely positioned to be able to provide daily help, support, and guidance to students within the school setting. However, in order to better understand basic human needs and wants and the role personal choice plays, a brief examination of Choice Theory is needed. The following principles summarize Choice Theory, as a motivational, behavioral, and perceptual system developed by William Glasser (1998a) and extended by Robert Wubbolding (2000, 2011).

1. Human motivation originates from five driving forces: generic and universal needs. These include *survival or self-preservation, love and belonging, power or inner control, freedom or independence,* and *fun or enjoyment.* These needs or human motivators are generic in that they are like salad bowls that individuals fill with *specific* wants or desires developed from infancy to death. They are universal in that they motivate *all* behavior for all human beings. Consequently, human needs are common to students from every culture. They are the all-prevailing basic sources of human behavior.

2. As human beings interact with the world around them and find that people, experiences, ideas, and things satisfy their needs, they retain them in their minds as positive and need-satisfying. They are specific, unique to each individual and referred to as *wants*. The collection of wants is called the "quality world" because each want has quality for the individual. The practical implication of this principle is that mental health providers and educators need to ask themselves: "Are my current behavior, my attitude, my interactions with the students helping me to become part of their quality worlds and thus helping the students to put intervention and/or instructional content and skills into their quality worlds?"

   Additionally, and even more specifically, when human beings do not satisfy the quality world wants, they then become internally motivated to generate behaviors. A metaphor that the person has an out-of-balance scale helps visualize and clarify the discrepancy between a want satisfied and a want unsatisfied. This discrepancy energizes and generates specific behaviors.

3. Human behavior is dealt with as chosen. This principle does not mean that people have total control over every aspect of behavior. Choice is predicated primarily of actions even though intense emotions can impinge upon actions thereby diminishing responsibility. Wubbolding (2015) advises educators, counselors, and all who implement Choice Theory and RT to treat actions "as if" they are choices even if they don't seem to be thoroughly thought out by the agent of the action. Further, all human behavior has a purpose. According to Glasser (1998a, 2011), human behavior is an attempt to impact the person's external world, to shape it as a sculptor molding clay so that the external world matches the desired perception of the sculptor. Wubbolding (2000, 2011) has added a second purpose. Behavior is also an attempt to send a signal or to communicate a message to the outside world. Often a student wishing to be "left alone" sends a very ineffective signal to teachers, administrators, parents, and others by acting out, ignoring rules, and in general rebelling against the reasonable expectations of society. Adults applying this principle of Choice Theory to individuals or to groups help students describe the message that they wish others would receive and then evaluate the effectiveness of their behavior.

4. From the perspective of Choice Theory, there are four components that constitute human behavior: actions, cognition, emotion, and even physiology. Please note

that the word *behavior* means more than does its customary connotation—actions. Two analogies help to understand this meaning of behavior: the suitcase and the car. Inside each human being is a packed suitcase with four levels or layers of behavior: actions, cognition, emotion, and physiology. The handle of the suitcase is attached to the top level or layer of behavior—the actions. Someone lifting the suitcase by the handle lifts the entire suitcase and its contents. This illustrates that when human beings change their actions they thereby alter their total behavior. They also have more direct control over the second level of behavior contained in the suitcase—cognition, than over the lowest levels of behavior—emotion and physiology. Similarly, visualizing a car with the front wheels as action and cognition and the rear wheels as emotion and physiology teaches that people have more direct control over their actions and cognition than over their emotions and physiology. And yet, choosing alternative actions often requires time and continued effort in order to improve feelings and physiology. For example, engaging in exercise or leisure-time activities, developing and improving human relationships, experiencing success in school entail consistent effortful choices made over varying periods of time.

5. Because behavior is a person's purposeful attempt to impact the world in order to gain something, the question remains, "What is the *something* that is gained?" The answer is that human beings seek perceptions. Human beings know and are aware of their perceptions. When people view their external worlds (i.e., their environment), they insert images into their perceptual frame of reference from those worlds. For mental health intervention a practical implication of this concept is that students perceive their control either as originating from within or from outside them. Rotter (1954) referred to this principle as "locus of control." When mental health advocates intervene at Tier 1, Tier 2, or Tier 3 they help students examine their source of control. They guide them in determining what they have control of and what they do not have control of. For example, when students describe themselves as helpless or unable to achieve, the significant adult intervenes with such questions as "What do you have control over?" "Is it really true that there is nothing you can do about your situation?" Such questions are designed to operationalize the theoretical principle that human beings possess a storehouse of perceptions. Many are images relating to their sense of

personal control or, in contrast, to their sense of living at the mercy of the world around them, often an unmerciful and inflexible controlling world.

RELATIONSHIPS

Healthy human relationships occupy a central place in mental health, effective teaching, family life, the workplace, and community living. Virtually every diagnostic category listed in the *Diagnostic and Statistical Manual of Mental Disorders, 5th Edition* describes a relationship issue connected with each diagnosis (American Psychiatric Association, 2013). For example, among the symptoms for hyperactivity and impulsivity is "often leaves seat in situations when remaining seated is expected" (p. 60). Other symptoms include running about when it is inappropriate, talking excessively, and interrupting others. Similarly, several diagnostic criteria for a major depressive disorder are appearing excessively tearful, markedly diminished interest in activities, loss of energy, diminished ability to concentrate, and many others. Clearly, these examples indicate a disruption in human relationships. And although not all school-based staff members engage in mental health intervention, the school staff can enhance their relationships with children, thereby indirectly facilitating improvement in student mental health. Also, warm and safe human relationships in the classroom and in the school building, workplace, and community create an atmosphere in which students want to learn, disrupt less, and believe that the school is a joyful place for them (Glasser, 1990, 1998b; Ludwig & Mentley, 1997; McClung & Hoglund, 2013). The use of RT formulated as the WDEP system is eminently useful for addressing the needs of students at every level of intervention: enhancing core instructional interventions (Tier 1), adding to the effectiveness of targeted group interventions (Tier 2), and helping to structure intensive individual instruction (Tier 3).

WDEP DELIVERY SYSTEM

The WDEP formulation of RT is a refinement and extension of the original eight steps described in the early development of RT (Glasser, 1972). The WDEP system outlines a practical and teachable structure and direction for enlivening and delivering the principles of Choice Theory. These procedures provide for the individualized application of Choice Theory: the five human needs or motivators, quality world, out-of-balance scales as a proximate cause of behavior, choosing purposeful behaviors aimed at sending signals to the outer world, and impacting it to gain want and need fulfilling perceptions.

The intent of associating RT with four letters (WDEP) is to present a structure for utilizing procedures described by Glasser

(2005). Glasser and Glasser (2008) detail the key role of procedures in learning and practicing RT:

> We wish to state publicly that teaching the procedures, the WDEP system, continues to be an integral part of training participants wishing to learn choice theory and reality therapy . . . this system helps to formulate and deliver questions and offer mental health workers, educators, criminal justice personnel, organizations and others a practical method facilitating solutions that are internally motivational. (p. 1)

Each letter of the WDEP system represents neither a step to be used in a lock-step fashion, nor a single attempt to elicit a fragment of information, but rather a cluster of possible interventions for use in an artful and empathic manner.

W—Exploring Wants, Needs, Perceptions, Locus of Control, and Level of Commitment

A frequently omitted discussion with students is the identification, clarification, and exploration of student wants and their needs as described in Choice Theory, as well as their perceived locus of control and their level of commitment. Mental health interventionists can facilitate such discussions with the entire class or small groups, as well as individual students. Questions focusing on the W include:

- What do you want to accomplish today, this week, this month, this year, or even what do you want to accomplish in the next 15 minutes?
- What do you want to derive from the lesson that we are about to study? How will this information satisfy one of the recognized needs (in WDEP language) and learning objectives and/or outcomes (in instructional language) that we've posted in our classroom?
- What level of quality work interests you: low quality, mediocre quality, or high quality?
- What do you want from me, your teacher/counselor/psychologist? What do you want from yourself? In other words, how hard are you willing to work at learning today, this week, and so forth?
- What do you want from your fellow students, your learning team? What kind of support do you want from your parents?
- Look at the three levels of commitment that we've posted. What is your level of commitment for today, this week, and so forth? Is it the lowest level, "I won't," the middle level "I'll try, I might," or is it the highest level, "I will"?

- How much energy or effort are you willing to expend to achieve a high level of quality?
- How will you know or recognize your level of commitment? How will you want me to acknowledge your level of commitment?
- Talk about what you have control over in the classroom, in how you study the topic, and how you will work with your team members.
- If you feel that you would like to read at a higher level, what will it take for you to achieve it?
- What do you think needs to be done by you regardless of whether you want to do it?

As with all questions and requests, mental health support should be stated and presented in language that students can understand. Thus, just as the teacher of second-grade students gears the questions to their vocabulary, as does the teacher at the senior high school level, so must the mental health interventionist speak in student-centered language.

D—Exploration of Total Behavior—Actions (Determining Direction and Doing), Cognition, Emotions, and Physiology

The discussion of total behavior focuses primarily on student actions. This conversation is more efficacious after mental health interventionists have explained the analogy of the suitcase and the car. All behavior involves actions, thinking, feelings, and physiology. Changing actions and thinking results in altering the movement of the car and the location of the entire suitcase. Questions focusing on D include

- Describe what you did yesterday or last night to learn the lessons taught.
- Explore with me or with your intervention team exactly what you have been doing, how you have been spending your time.
- What thoughts have you had about the lessons to be done? About your grades? About the consequences of your actions or choices?
- What kind of feeling do you get when you follow through on your plans? When you work as a team? When you produce a high-quality product or meet conduct expectations?
- What is your feeling when you come to believe that you have a positive friendship, a loyal friend, someone you can confide in, a healthy relationship with another student or with a teacher?

One tool that aids with students engaging in this exploration of behavior is helping them examine their inner thoughts or "inner talk." Wubbolding (2000) has identified ineffective self-talk statements as well as effective or positive self-talk statements derived from Choice Theory. Ineffective self-talk is represented by such sentences as "No one is going to tell me what to do." "I am powerless." "Even though what I am doing is not helping, I will continue to choose the same behavior." On the other hand, more effective self-talk statements are "I am happiest when I live within reasonable boundaries." "I have choices." "If what I am doing is not helping me, I will choose another course of action" (p. 107).

A paradox among the four components of behavior is that human beings are more aware of their feelings and thoughts than their actions. And yet, they have more direct control over actions. A person is often aware of feeling guilt, shame, anger, or frustration and less aware of the thinking and especially the actions that accompany these feelings. RT reflects the 12-Step axiom used in addictions recovery programs: "You can act your way to a new way of thinking and feeling easier than you can think or feel your way to a new way of acting." Changing the actions modifies total behavior.

E—Self-Evaluation—Keystone in the Arch of Behavioral Change and Improvement

Self-evaluation occupies a central place among the interventions summarized in Figure 8.1. It is the keystone in the arch. Without the keystone an arch crumbles and becomes rubble. Effective RT

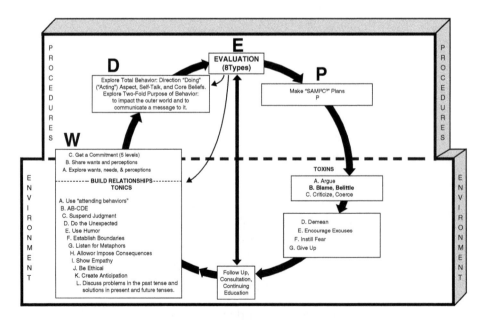

FIGURE 8.1 The cycle of counseling and managing.

Source: Wubbolding (2011).

places heavy emphasis on helping students and clients conduct a searching internal evaluation of behavior, quality world, and one's perceptual system. Glasser (2005) describes self-evaluation as the core of RT. Wubbolding (2011) states, "The process of self-evaluation, the most typically representative set of interventions for reality therapy, is a *sine qua non*, a necessary pre-condition for behavioral change" (p. 89).

Educators assisting students to evaluate their academic behavior as well as their social behavior need to recognize and utilize both internal and external standards. The following probing questions illustrate the utilization of *internal standards* focusing on behavior.

- Is what you're doing getting you what you want?
- Is your current overall direction satisfying to you or not?
- Is what you're doing in line with the teacher's expectations?
- Is what you're doing helping you or hurting you?
- Are your current actions helpful or hurtful for your fellow students?
- Are your current actions adding to or taking away from the classroom atmosphere?

Other self-evaluation comparisons utilizing *external standards* include

- Are your current actions congruent with the rules or against the rules?
- Is what you're doing against the unwritten rules?
- Are your current actions acceptable in the school environment?
- What are the consequences of your current actions or your current overall direction?

Evaluation of student self-talk or cognition provides an additional avenue for assisting students with evaluating their total behavior. Several possible questions are

- Which is better for you, to tell yourself "I can't" or to tell yourself "I can"?
- How does repeating such statements to yourself as "I don't like school," or "The teacher picks on me," and so forth, impact your feelings of happiness in this school?
- Does the preoccupation with the thoughts "nobody should tell me what to do," or "I want to be left alone," help you achieve your goals?

Although not emphasized as a self-evaluation element, with the help of a mental health interventionist students can evaluate the usefulness of their emotions. Examples of questions focusing on emotions include

- You mentioned that you are angry and upset about your class. What impact will this upsetness have on you in the classroom or at home when you do your independent school work? What impact could it have on the members of your learning team?
- Which is better for you, to encourage yourself to feel bad or to let some of the feelings go and to replace them with happier feelings?
- What kind of feelings will help you and what kind of feelings will hold you back from getting along with your classmates?

The questions described provide samples of possible ways for assisting students to assess their specific actions and the overall trajectory of their accumulated actions. This list is not exhaustive but intended to trigger interventions geared to specific classroom situations.

Another form of self-evaluation indicated by the arrow (Figure 8.1) pointing toward the *W* of the WDEP system consists in assessing several aspects of wants related to human needs. For instance, students are asked to evaluate the realistic attainability of their wants and whether their wants or desires are truly beneficial to them:

- You stated that you want people to leave you alone. I've heard you say it several times, "I want people to get off my back." How realistic do you think it is for you to be completely on your own? Have you ever been free of adults telling you that you have to go to school, that you must study, and do your homework?
- You said that you want to learn mathematics. How realistic is it for you to learn it without working and contributing to your learning team?
- I know you want to go home and not come to school. Is it possible for us to allow you to stay home when you are required to be here?
- You want people to leave you alone. You want to learn mathematics. You said you want to remain at home and not come to school. Tell me whether these wants are truly helpful to you? If you were able to satisfy these wants would your life *really* be better?

Part of self-evaluation listed under the *W* of the WDEP system can be gently challenging students to examine their perceptions of the world around them, especially their locus of control.

- Is it really true that you have no choices?

- Of all the events that you have no control over, is there any one of them that you could gain at least partial control over?
- You can receive classroom help in studying your mathematics. When you are part of the instructional group do you believe you are in charge of your own actions or do you believe that the other students and the teacher control you? In others words, what can you control and what can you not control?

These questions are samples of possible ways and questions to include in a counseling session to use when implementing the self-evaluation component of the WDEP system. As with all interventions, classroom teachers, counselors, and administrators gear the questions to specific situations and formulate them so as to apply to the appropriate developmental level of the students.

P—Formulating a Plan of Action

Developing a plan of action appears to be the culmination of the WDEP system. And yet it constitutes the initial stage of behavioral change and improvement. "To fail to plan is to plan to fail" summarizes the process of interventions often used by educators and parents. The simple question, "What is your plan now?" asked of students at Tier 1, Tier 2, or Tier 3 intervention levels has the effect of initiating or continuing healthy change. The impression made on students often surprises them and even startles them, leaving them momentarily speechless. Students feeling powerless and victimized derive an implicit and unspoken message, a subliminal suggestion that they have choices for empowering themselves and improving their current situations. Positive plans designed to replace ineffective behaviors ideally consist in several characteristics summarized by the acronym $SAMI^2C^3$:

- *S Simple*. The plan is uncomplicated, and is easily understood.
- *A Attainable*. A realistically doable plan signals a behavioral reversal and creates strategies more achievable by the student. British writer G. K. Chesterton remarked that "trifles make perfection and perfection is no trifle." A seemingly trivial plan can be the beginning of significant change.
- *M Measurable*. Successful plans answer the question "When will you do it?" Additional measurable questions include "Where, how often, and who will help you with your plan?" "What might interfere with the implementation of your plan?" "How will you detour around barriers that might present themselves?" In other words, the

plans should be objective and the change must be documentable using some system of collection (listing the frequency of behaviors in charts, graphs, etc.).

- *I Immediate.* Implementation should be as soon as possible. Sometimes plans can even be rehearsed. Students can practice more courteous responses to others during group or individual sessions, thereby replacing disrespectful behaviors previously directed toward teachers or other students.

- *I Involved.* If necessary, the adult is involved with the plan. This involvement cannot be part of *every* plan but it could include, occasionally, a teacher providing extra attention to a student. In his lectures Glasser was accustomed to advising educators, "When you meet [a] difficult student[s] at the door of the building or the classroom, give them ten seconds of courteous attention." If several teachers conspire to treat such a student in this manner, the result is likely to be noticeable after several weeks.

- *C Controlled by the planner.* Successful accomplishment of the plan depends on the planner not on students' environments. When human beings deal with the world around them in a new and different way, their external worlds rarely respond quickly to such change. At first, persons in the students' environments might not even notice an improvement. Such disappointments for students provide opportunities to teach a lesson central to Choice Theory and RT by asking, "Can you really regulate or control the behavior of other people?" "Whose behavior can you control?"

- *C Consistent.* Even though plans are realistically doable (i.e., performed one time), the goal of planning is the establishment of repetitive plans. The following philosophy formulated by an unknown author fits: "Sow an act and reap a habit. Sow a habit and reap a character. Sow a character and reap a destiny."

- *C Committed to.* The adult assists in helping students to write down the plan and to be firmly committed to its accomplishment. Students often report back to the teacher, the counselor, or to another student and answer a question such as, "How did it go?"

Effective planning does not occur automatically. Although the question, "What's your plan?" is a necessary component for improvement, self-evaluation constitutes a necessary precondition. Individuals and groups alter their behavior only when they decide that their current choices are not satisfying one or more of their five needs. And so, questions focusing on evaluation of plans include "Is your current behavior, your actions, helping you or hurting you?" "Is it having a positive effect on the people around you?" "If you continue to make the same choices, where will they take you today, this week, in the next several months?"

CLASSROOM AND CONFERENCING ENVIRONMENT

Foundational for the effective use of the WDEP system is the environment or the atmosphere in the relationship between adult and student (Figure 8.1). Toxic behaviors create a poisonous atmosphere in relationships. On the other hand, the use of tonic behaviors facilitates relationships that serve as prerequisites for continuous improvement.

Toxins

Human reluctance to change, student resistance to learning, and even reticence to receiving help increase if relationships are characterized by toxic behaviors (Figure 8.1). These behaviors include the following:

A. Arguing about behavior, rules, and perceived change in routine.
B. Blaming and belittling also diminish motivation and cooperation, similar to belittling.
C. Criticizing students rarely has a salutary effect because students often see it as a personal attack on them. This admonition does not include critiquing their work or developing the skill to think critically.
D. Demeaning is a more severe form of belittling.
E. Encouraging excuses often includes asking students why they failed to study or why they misbehaved. Frequently "why" questions elicit reasons that are beyond the students' control. "They *made* me do it." or "I have too many responsibilities at home." are answers that, although often accurate, allow little room for effective planning.
F. Instilling fear by threats or punishment serves only to create distance between the adult and the learner. Throughout the process the adult adheres to the following mental axiom.
G. "Don't give up." "Be faithful to the intervention system and have confidence in both your own skill and the students' ability to improve." But this is difficult for a student if giving up is a possible option.

Parents often ask teachers, counselors, and administrators, "What can I do at home to help my child?" Because toxic behaviors poison human relationships, school personnel often suggest that parents *at least* lessen if not avoid toxic behaviors—especially *arguing belittling,* and *criticizing* students overtly or unconsciously during discussions about their behavior.

Tonics

The following tonics, especially using empathy to establish a cordial atmosphere, set the stage for students to insert the adult, socioemotional, and behavioral expectations, and the curriculum into their quality worlds.

Tonic behaviors include utilizing the tools and suggestions listed in Figure 8.1:

A. Nonverbal communication or *attending* behaviors. The adults' nonverbal behaviors such as tone of voice and facial expression communicate an engaging attitude.
B. AB-CDE as a tonic behavior means *always* be *courteous, determined, and enthusiastic.*
C. *Omitting a judgmental attitude,* simple courteous statements, a determined and confident belief, as well as an enthusiastic search for positive behaviors and successes are many times D as below.
D. *Unexpected* by students and positively contribute to the atmosphere.
E. Regarding the *use of humor,* comedian Victor Borge observed that the shortest distance between two people is a laugh.
F. Adults also enhance relationships by communicating relationship *boundaries,* classroom rules, and school policies. This is done in a matter-of-fact and unequivocal manner.
G. In conversations, human beings often employ *metaphors.* A student might remark, "Everybody is on my back." A careful listener uses this metaphor as a motivational tool by responding, "We have a program for helping you to get people off your back."
H. *Consequences* are essential for helping motivate students. The adult describes both positive and negative results from student choices. A major tool for effective communication is to see the world as the other person sees it. Developing this skill requires effort, practice, forethought, and a willingness to learn from mistakes.
I. *Showing empathy* does not mean agreeing with another person. It means communicating appreciation for another human being's plight.
J. Part of *ethical* practice means knowing one's own limitations as well as strengths, and communicating students' responsibilities to them is a core ethical principle in the practice of RT. This principle and the entire body of professional ethics permeate the use of RT.
K. *Creating a sense of anticipation* for the students (i.e., something new and different is going to happen for you if you are willing to make the effort) can be a source of hope and self-confidence for the students. Additionally, hope and confidence are implicitly present when:

L. problems are presented in the *past tense* and solutions in the *present* and *future tenses*. This style of language provides a basis for taking necessary next steps: study partnering, tutoring, small support groups, and many other possibilities.

The effective use of RT by mental health interventionists and generating positive student growth by educators include establishing and maintaining a trusting atmosphere and relationship. This relational environment is the basis for RT-based mental health interventions summarized with four generic questions made specific to each situation: *W*—what do you *want*? *D*—what are you *doing*? *E*—how is your behavior helping or hurting you (*evaluation* process)? *P*—what is your *plan* for improvement?

The Art of Questioning

Much of the suggested RT-based intervention detailed is formulated as questions. However, RT is not limited to questioning. Targeted and focused questions represent the most significant style for helping students examine their inner motivations. These nonpunitive questions always spring from a relationship-building, empathic attitude on the part of the adult. They serve several purposes:

1. To become part of the students' quality world. Asking students what they want from the world around them, how they are spending their time, and other inquiries based on the WDEP system enable the teacher to communicate respect for the student. Honoring the students' current motivation and behavior deepens the interpersonal relationship that is a prerequisite for behavioral change.
2. To elicit information. Assisting students to improve academic or social behavior requires gathering at least a minimal amount of information. How students see their current circumstances or how they evaluate their behavior provides data for the adult seeking to facilitate more effective learning and improved behavior.
3. To heighten student awareness. When students describe their wants and especially their actions, they become more aware of them. Paradoxically, human beings are more aware of feelings and less aware of actions and yet have more direct control over actions. Asking students to describe their actions and to evaluate them helps them raise their awareness about what they can control and what they cannot control.
4. To help students make more appropriate choices. The result of the psychologist's, counselor's, or teacher's

effort to be seen as a helpful adult, to gather information, and to increase student awareness of effective ways
to satisfy their needs leads to choices acceptable to the
students themselves and to the school community.

Consequently, the artistic interweaving of the WDEP procedures
results in heightened motivation on the part of the students,
as well as behavioral and academic improvements. Nevertheless, users of the WDEP system need not fear using the system
mechanically as they learn. Practicing the suggested interventions eventually leads to a more spontaneous and natural skill
set aimed at the enhancement of school atmosphere. McClung
and Hoglund (2013) described major improvements gained from
the use of Choice Theory and RT principles. They reported major
improvements in student achievement and virtual elimination
of discipline problems with occasional discipline incidents. They
stated, "The school's average suspensions per 100 students was
1.7 compared to the district elementary school average of 3.0 suspensions per 100 students" (p. 57). Findings such as these are not
uncommon; dating back to the 1990s meta-analyses of RT have
consistently shown an impact on therapeutic and behavioral
outcomes in the schools (Graham, Sauerheber, & Britzman 2012;
Passaro et al., 2004; Radtke, Sapp, & Farrell, 1997; Yarbrough &
Thompson, 2002).

INTEGRATING REALITY THERAPY WITH TIERED INTERVENTION

A tiered-intervention approach lends itself to the addition of the
WDEP system of RT. Due to its universal applicability and therapeutic potential, RT can provide a daily mental health framework
to support and enhance Response to Intervention (RTI) Tier 1 and
Tier 2, as well as Tier 3 interventions. The WDEP formulation of
RT can assist educators in delivering differentiated instruction
regarding all students' needs in the general classroom as well
as assist mental health professionals with the delivery of school-
wide Tier 1 prevention or early intervention support. The WDEP
intervention process can further assist teachers in putting responsibility for action on the class as a whole as well as for "at-risk"
or high-priority individuals aimed at improving their academic
achievement and classroom behavior (Tier 2). The self-evaluation component of RT applies especially to Tier 3 intervention as
individual students learn to self-question, self-assess, and help
themselves by asking key questions of themselves such as, "Is
what I'm doing helping or hurting me?" "Are my current decisions and choices assisting or impeding the development of my
relationships with my classmates and with my teacher?" Practitioners of Choice Theory and RT must apply these questions in
a vocabulary and a manner appropriate for the developmental
level of students.

Throughout the process of intervening, it is important that every educator and mental health professional remain cognizant of the five needs foundational to Choice Theory and the practice of RT or, as it is known in schools, Lead Management. Adhering to this approach increases the opportunities for establishing a fair, firm, yet supportive learning environment.

Since both Choice Theory and RT intersect at many points within a tiered-intervention approach, following is a summary of several suggestions about how this can be accomplished.

Tier 1

Tier 1 can be a multifaceted process involving such tasks as gathering and interpreting data, using data for making instructional changes, and evaluating the process to ensure the success of the interventions (Metcalf, 2013; Passaro et al., 2004). A leadership team coordinates these processes utilizing the following questions: (a) What is the problem? (b) Why is the problem occurring? (c) What should we do about the problem? and (d) Did our solution work? For the sake of simplicity, following are several questions that the team might use at the system level and/or at the student level. Additional questions based on the WDEP system of RT could complement Metcalf's four basic questions.

- What do we want from the students, from the class, from ourselves that we are getting and that we are *not* getting?
- What is the level of commitment needed to ensure success?
- How will we know that we are getting what we want and that our commitment level is sufficient?
- What have we been doing that has been working and *not* working?
- How would a visitor to the school know that we are engaged in a process of continuous improvement?
- What kind of SAMI^{2}C^3 plans can the team formulate? . . . can the class members formulate?

These are seminal questions designed to trigger additional questions applicable to specific team situations and student situations.

Tier 2

According to Johnson (2013) "Tier 2 is meant to provide a limited but targeted support system for students who struggle to meet grade level performance standards." Tier 2 involves small-group "clearly articulated intervention implemented with fidelity." Johnson emphasizes that many schools do not have sufficient resources to implement this level of intervention. From the point of view of RT it would be helpful for teachers, volunteers, and counselors trained in the WDEP system to lead small groups on a regular basis. Adequate, ongoing, and thorough training in the questioning process that springs from each component of the WDEP system helps to ensure the success of small-group work. Many of the same questions described in Tier 1 and Tier 3 can also be used. Moreover, small groups could take the form of the proven quality school intervention known as class meetings (Glasser, C., 2009) or the direct teaching of the principles of Choice Theory and RT (Glasser, C., 1996a, 1996b). The goal of these two interventions is to enhance the involvement of students in the learning process by helping them satisfy their four psychological needs: belonging, power or achievement, freedom or independence, and fun or enjoyment. When students learn the essentials of Choice Theory and the basics of the WDEP system of RT, they gain information that is congruent with and complements the tiered approach.

Tier 3

Ervin (2013) states, "Practitioners can guide their decision making by adhering to a self-questioning process." Questions focus on: Who is experiencing a problem? What intervention strategies can be used? Did the problem go away or lessen. The WDEP system provides an appropriate intervention model compatible with Tier 3. Although it is not practical to describe every possible intervention for use at Tier 3, the following dialogue represents a conversation between a student and a tutor, counselor, or teacher.

CASE STUDY: USING A TIER 3 REALITY THERAPY-WDEP INTERVENTION APPROACH

Reason for Referral

Lee was referred because of expressed frustration with reading and subsequent disruptive behavior when he is disengaged in class.

Background and History

Lee is a fourth-grade White 10-year-old boy who experiences difficulty in reading. Lee has one younger and one older sibling at home; his parents are divorced and he spends some after-school time with his grandmother. Lee has been in his current school system since kindergarten and has exhibited an average performance throughout this time. He has a keen interest in mechanical types of toys and loves to construct things. Little information was reported on his medical history, and his attendance record shows very few absences from school.

Case Conceptualization, Goal, and Mental Health Intervention Approach

The general goal is to enhance Lee's reading capacity, while also attending to his disruptive classroom behavior, reported lack of school engagement, yet reported desire to participate in the classroom experience.

Lee's reading performance is falling under the DIBELS (Dynamic Indicators of Basic Early Literacy Skills) benchmark criteria by reading 85 words correctly per minute in the winter term of the third grade. He will receive tutoring as part of Tier 3 and his teacher believes that his underachievement results from a lack of skill and, even more so, lack of interest, personal motivation, and the consequent acting out in class. The following interaction represents the initiation of the reality-based WDEP intervention of an adult professional. In the conversation, the interventionist is not only attempting to establish rapport but is (a) signaling what Lee *can* do; (b) determining Lee's "wants" and level of desire and willingness to engage; (c) letting him know that he has a committed partner; and (d) beginning to build a simple, attainable, and measureable plan that addresses Lee's total behavior.

Adult professional:	Lee, I noticed that you are able to read and so I'm here to help you increase your reading accuracy. To begin, I'd like to ask you a few questions. Is that okay with you?
Lee:	Uh-huh. I guess so.
Adult professional:	They're not really hard questions. They help us to get to know each other. I've found that having a little conversation helps the tutoring go better.
Lee:	That's okay with me.
Adult professional:	Good, thank you. Tell me, Lee, do you like to read?
Lee:	No, there are too many words that I don't understand.
Adult professional:	And yet I hear you can read some of the material that's given to you.
Lee:	If it's easy enough. But most of the time I don't care.
Adult professional:	I believe if we work together I can help you enjoy reading more than you do now.
Lee:	I don't know about that. Sounds too hard.
Adult professional:	If it would be not too hard, maybe even fun, would you be willing to put some energy into our time together?

Lee:	What do you mean?
Adult professional:	I mean would you be willing to work hard at making progress in your reading level?
Lee:	How hard?
Adult professional:	There are three levels of effort posted on the wall in your classroom: "I won't make any effort." "I'll try; I might." and "I will do my best." As you sit here now with me, you know the purpose of our meetings. Are you willing to at least say, "I'll try"? And, for my part, I will work hard to make the lessons enjoyable for you.
Lee:	That sounds okay to me.
Adult professional:	Let me ask you this: What could you do that will help you "try"?
Lee:	It would help if I'd sit and listen. I don't always do that in class.
Adult professional:	So, listening would help. What do you think would stand in the way of you making progress?
Lee:	Not trying, messing around during the lesson.
Adult professional:	So you know what would help and what would hurt. Let's work together and build up whatever will help.
Lee:	You'd help me do that?
Adult professional:	Yes, I will. And my commitment is "I'll do my best." Okay?
Lee:	Okay.
Adult professional:	Alright, let's get started with today's work and let's work together to make it enjoyable and successful for both of us. Oh yes, one more thing: If you learned to read even a little bit better, would you feel better inside?
Lee:	It would be nice.

In this dialogue, the adult sets a safe, friendly, and welcoming atmosphere in the conversation by discussing the problem and the initial solution as they relate to Lee's internal needs: fun and belonging and power or achievement. The adult (mental health interventionist) attempts to begin a relationship with Lee and perceives the problem and progress for dealing with the problem as closely connected to Lee's need for belonging. The adult believes that a pleasant, respectful, and of course professional relationship serves as the basis for focusing on Lee's two presenting issues:

lagging behind in reading achievement and insufficient motivation. The adult does not directly address behavioral problems. It would be appropriate to confront such issues in a nonpunitive way; however, at this point the adult chooses to put Lee's acting-out behaviors on hold and deal with them as necessary at a later time. Lee might be surprised by this seeming omission at this point. And so Lee's expectation, based on previous conversations with adults, is appropriately and temporarily unmet. If another adult inquires about the rationale behind this conversation, a good response would be, "We'll deal with that issue indirectly, maybe directly, but in due time."

SUMMARY

Choice Theory has been applied to school settings and has an impact on students, classroom climate, management, and learning (Sullo, 2009). In this framework, the teacher or mental health professional is viewed as a caring adult who helps students see that choosing to engage in the learning environment is a good choice and can be consistent with what they need and want (will add quality to their lives). Teachers craft lessons that are need-satisfying and facilitate classrooms where students feel powerful, are validated, and have positive relationships. Mental health professionals craft interventions that create opportunities for children's needs to be met and for them to gain a sense of efficacy in obtaining their goals. In these kinds of classrooms, students perform because they want to, not because they have to (Bucher & Manning, 2001; Erwin, 2003). Sullo (2009) suggests that in schools where Choice Theory is applied there is no coercion, teachers build positive connections with students, there is a focus on quality instruction and mastery is emphasized, and students take ownership. One of Glasser's (1998b) central points is that students must see immediate and future satisfaction from their education.

Although a widely used tool in education, the principles of Choice Theory and RT explain all human behavior. They are universal and multicultural in that all people are motivated to satisfy five innate drives. They seek to fulfill the needs for survival or self-preservation; belonging or love; power or accomplishment and all its nuances such as recognition, self-worth, and many others; freedom or independence; and fun or enjoyment. If mental health interventionists in the tiered schools explain these needs to students, everyone gradually comes to see that human beings are internally motivated. They realize the futility of using punishment, fear, and coercion as forms of motivation. They infuse their school environment with Choice Theory and RT methodologies by creating a firm, fair, and friendly environment—thus utilizing tonic behaviors while lessening toxic behaviors.

In implementing three systemic tiers of intervention, mental health interventionists can choose to infuse the art of using the

WDEP system: exploring their own as well as students' wants and goals; describing three levels of behavior, especially actions; most importantly, emphasizing the tool of self-evaluation; and culminating in specific SAMI²C³ plans for improvement (simple, attainable, measureable, immediate, involved, controlled, consistent, committed to).

RESOURCES

Choice Theory: Using Choice Theory and Reality Therapy to Enhance Student Achievement and Responsibility, written by Sylinda Gilchrist Banks, is a helpful book filled with lessons and activities designed to enhance individual and small-group interventions. It is available (www.schoolcounselor.org/advertiseexhibit/publications-(1)/resource-series) through the ASCA (American School Counselor Association) on their website.

Comprehensive but user-friendly websites to obtain resources on RT and WDEP (www.wglasser.com and www.realitytherapy-wub.com) are valuable options offered by the Glasser Institute and the Center for Reality Therapy.

Counselling With Reality Therapy, written by Robert E. Wubbolding and John Brickell, is a comprehensive discussion of applications of RT to education and relationships, as well as a discussion of how to use paradoxical techniques with difficult behaviors. It is published by Speechmark Press, Milton Keynes, United Kingdom.

A meta-analysis (www.realiteettiterapia.fi/wp-content/uploads/2013/12/CTRT-Research-list.pdf) of Choice Theory and RT efficacy research can be obtained from the website listed here.

REFERENCES

American Psychiatric Association. (2013). *Diagnostic and statistical manual of mental disorders* (5th ed.). Washington, DC: Author.

Bucher, K., & Manning, L. (2001). Exploring the foundations of middle school classroom management: The theoretical contributions of BF Skinner, Fritz Redl and William Wattenberg, William Glasser and Thomas Gordon. *Childhood Education, 78*(2), 84–90.

Buck, N. (2013). *How to be a great parent*. New York, NY: Beaufort Books.

Ervin, R. (2013). *Considering tier 3 within a response-to-intervention model*. Retrieved October 4, 2013, from http://www.RTINetwork.org

Erwin, J. C. (2003). Giving students what they need. *Educational Leadership, 61*, 19–23.

Glasser, C. (1996a). *My quality world workbook*. Los Angeles, CA: William Glasser.

Glasser, C. (1996b). *The quality world activity set*. Los Angeles, CA: William Glasser.

Glasser, C. (2009). *Glasser class meeting kit: Choice theory curriculum*. Los Angeles, CA: William Glasser.

Glasser, W. (1972). *The identity society*. New York, NY: Harper & Row.

Glasser, W. (1988). *Choice theory in the classroom*. New York, NY: HarperCollins.

Glasser, W. (1990). *The quality school*. New York, NY: HarperCollins.

Glasser, W. (1998a). *Choice theory*. New York, NY: HarperCollins.

Glasser, W. (1998b). *The quality school teacher*. New York, NY: HarperCollins.

Glasser, W. (2005). *How the brain works chart*. Tempe, AZ: The William Glasser Institute.

Glasser, W. (2011). *Take charge of your life*. Bloomington, IN: iUniverse.

Glasser, W., & Glasser, C. (2008). Procedures: The cornerstone of institute training. *The William Glasser Institute Newsletter*, Summer, 1–2. Chatsworth, CA: The William Glasser Institute.

Graham, M. A., Sauerheber, J. D., & Britzman, M. J. (2012). Choice theory and family counseling: A pragmatic, culturally sensitive approach. *Family Journal, 21*(2), 230–234.

Johnson, E. (2013). How to develop an effective tier 2 system. Retrieved October 4, 2013, from http://www.RTINetwork.org

Kim, K. (2002). The effect of a reality program on the responsibility of elementary school children in Korea. *International Journal of Reality Therapy, 22*(1), 30–34.

Kim, R. I., & Hwang, M. G. (2001). The effect of internal control and achievement motivation in group counseling based on RT. *International Journal of Reality Therapy, 20*(2), 12–15.

Ludwig, S., & Mentley, K. (1997). *Quality is the key*. Wyoming, MI: Educational Services.

Mason, C., & Duba, J. (2009).Using reality therapy in schools. *International Journal of Reality Therapy, 29*(1), 5–12.

McClung, C., & Hoglund, R. (2013). A Glasser quality school leads to choosing excellence. *International Journal of Choice Theory and Reality Therapy, 32*(2), 54–64.

Metcalf, T. (2013). *What's your plan? Accurate decision making within a multi-tier system of supports: Critical areas in tier 1*. Retrieved October 4, 2013, from: http://www.RTINetwork.org

Omizo, M., & Cubberly, W. E. (1983). The effects of reality therapy classroom meetings on self-concept and locus of control among learning disabled children. *The Exceptional Child, 30*(3), 201–209.

Passaro, P. D., Moon, M., Weist, D. J., & Wong, E. H. (2004). A model for school psychologists practice: Addressing the needs of students with emotional and behavioral challenges through the use of an in-school support room and reality therapy. *Adolescence, 39*(155), 503–517.

Radtke, L., Sapp, M., & Farrell, W. (1997). Reality therapy: A meta-analysis. *International Journal of Reality Therapy, 14*(2), 29–36.

Robey, P., Wubbolding, R., & Carlson, J. (2012). *Contemporary issues in couples counseling*. New York, NY: Routledge, Taylor & Francis Group.

Rotter, J. B. (1954). *Social learning and clinical psychology*. New York, NY: Prentice-Hall.

Sullo, B. (2009). *The motivated student: Unlocking the enthusiasm for learning*. Alexandria, VA: Association of School Counseling & Development.

The William Glasser Institute. (2013). *The Glasser approach: Quality schools*. Retrieved October 26, 2013, from http://wglasser.com

Wubbolding, R. (1996). *Employee motivation*. Knoxville, TN: SPC Press.

Wubbolding, R. (2000). *Reality therapy for the 21st century*. Philadelphia, PA: Brunner Routledge.

Wubbolding, R. (2011). *Reality therapy: Theories of psychotherapy series*. Washington, DC: American Psychological Association.

Wubbolding, R. (2015). *Reality therapy training manual* (16th Rev. ed.). Cincinnati, OH: Center for Reality Therapy.

Wubbolding, R., & Brickell, J. (2005). Reality therapy in recovery. *Directions in Addiction Treatment & Prevention, 9*(1), 1–10.

Yarbrough, J. L., & Thompson, C. L. (2002). Using single-participant research to assess counseling approaches on children's off-task behavior. *Professional School Counseling, 5*(5), 308–314.

CHAPTER 9

Mental Health for Educators

RAYMOND H. WITTE

LEARNING OUTCOMES

On completion of this chapter, the reader should be able to:

- Acknowledge that stress can be a significant work-related mental health issue
- Understand that effective mental health and wellness practices are critical for teachers and the students they teach
- Realize that the leveled Response to Intervention (RTI) Model is designed to address the behavioral and mental health needs of all students
- Comprehend the necessity that all teachers must deal with their own mental health needs before they can help and address the needs of their students
- Recognize the importance of the construction of an Individualized Mental Health Plan (IMHP) to address each educator's particular mental health needs

Mental health matters for everyone in every community (Jorm, 2012). The importance is readily apparent when watching the evening news as multiple instances of mental health-based problems emerge from the reported stories. It's not just the sensationalized cases, however, that bear these connections. For instance, the issue of work stress and its connection to a variety of stress-related diseases and clinical conditions such as heart disease and/or heart attack (Belkic, Landsbergis, Schnall, & Baker, 2004; Marmot, Bosma, Hemingway, Brunner, & Stansfeld, 1997), depression (LaMontagne, Keegel, Louie, & Ostry, 2010; Sanderson & Andrews, 2006; Wang, Schmitz, Dewa, & Stansfeld, 2009), alcoholism (Crum, Muntaner, Eaton, & Anthony, 1995; Harris & Fennell, 1988), anxiety disorders (Michie & Williams, 2003; Strazdins, D'Souza, Lim, Broom, & Rodgers, 2004), suicide (Bottomley, Dalziel, & Neith, 2002), as well as many other health events represent a significant life issue for anyone who works. Chronic occupational stress is recognized as a significant factor in physical health outcomes (Noblet & LaMontagne, 2006). In addition, life stressors, and in particular work stress, are associated with common mental disorders and conditions that impair the overall effectiveness and productivity of workers (LaMontagne et al., 2010).

Is stress a significant impact factor for educators? The answer, in a word—yes. Current research findings indicate that teaching is acknowledged as a high-stress occupation (Johnson et al., 2005; Kyriacou, 2001). Approximately 40% of new teachers leave the profession during their first 5 years of teaching (Ingersoll, 2002). Various reasons have been identified in this exodus including factors such as job satisfaction, workload, challenging students, as well as other issues that can be connected to insufficient resources and/or ineffective school system support services (Adelman & Taylor, 2010; Stockard & Lehman, 2004).

Stress and its negative impact, however, is not an automatic outcome for teachers. Many of the harmful outcomes of stress are preventable if appropriate mental health procedures and supports are put in place and employees are armed with essential knowledge and skill sets (LaMontagne et al., 2010). Through deliberate and comprehensive professional development trainings and workshops, educators can develop a broad mental health knowledge base along with effective strategies and skill sets that can be used to enhance their general well-being and capacity to handle challenging work and life events.

ADDRESSING THE NEED

Understanding the role of mental health and its impact on the quality of one's life is critical, and that is true for young people as well as the educators who instruct them (Witte, 2006a). Unfortunately, at the present time no one can receive a "how-to-develop-and-maintain-effective-mental-health" neural program that is conveniently absorbed into one's brain. Until that day arrives, mental health advocates need to continue the mental health conversation and facilitate educational programs that develop awareness and effective skills designed to promote everyone's well-being; that work needs to take place in the school setting since it is the most likely location for students to receive and benefit from mental health services (Capella, Frazier, Atkins, Schoenwalk, & Glisson, 2008; Nastasi, Moore, & Varjas, 2004; Reinke, Stormont, Herman, Puri, & Goel, 2011; Rones & Hoagwood, 2000).

Mental health education, just like academic content, requires instructional time and practice. However, as Adelman and Taylor (1998) stated more than 15 years ago, "Despite widespread acknowledgement of the need for interventions related to mental health and psychosocial concerns, such activities are not a primary item on a school's agenda. This is not surprising. After all, schools are not in the mental health business. Their mandate is to educate" (p. 175).

Although schools may not technically be in the mental health business, educators certainly acknowledge the challenges and mental health barriers (e.g., lack of services, support, and mental health training) that exist for students and that interfere with their ability to function in society and learn effectively in the classroom (World Health Organization [WHO], 2004). In addition, schools are uniquely situated to address the interconnection between mental health practices and school performance (Reinke et al., 2011). Given this reality, educators certainly recognize the value of mental health curriculum and intervention programs that are designed to address the comprehensive learning needs of today's learner (Hoagwood et al., 2007; Weissberg, Kumpfer, & Seligman, 2003).

The RTI model that is now recognized across the country is fundamentally designed to address both academic as well as behavioral concerns in the classroom (see Figure 9.1). Schools are now mandated to provide instruction and/or support at all intervention levels in regard to behavioral needs, and the inclusion of mental health practices can be used in that endeavor (Graczyk, Domitrovich, Small, & Zins, 2006; Rones & Hoagwood, 2000; Weissberg et al., 2003). Tier or leveled intervention (e.g., three-tier or level intervention model) can provide a range of support based on the needs of all students within a building and/or district.

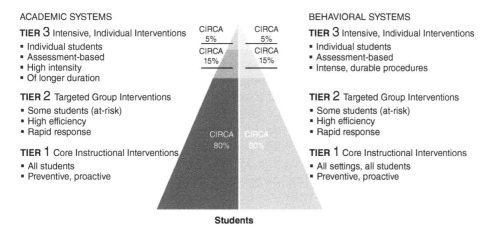

FIGURE 9.1 Three tiered intervention model.

Reprinted with permission from the National Association of State Directors of Special Education (NASDSE).

For example, at the Tier 1 level mental health instruction theoretically is directed toward all students in order to educate them and hopefully eliminate or minimize the likelihood of future problems and/or the occurrence of particular events (e.g., stress-related health problems). To illustrate, if a district decides to focus on teaching its students effective anger management skills, activities would be designed around educating the students on this topic and the development of skills dealing with the effective management and/or reduction of anger. For students who require more time and practice and/or are at a higher risk of having difficulties in acquiring these skills, Tier 2 level services would likely be more appropriate, most likely in the form of small-group instruction during scheduled times during the week. For students who need individual help and practice, as well as perhaps additional instructional strategies and supports, Tier 3 services could be made available to them. Clearly the purpose is to provide *the level of service to the student(s) that is required based on the need and skills of that student(s).*

Although recognized primarily for academic intervention and focus, the RTI model is certainly expected to address student behavior. This is done to provide students with functional, life-based skills that also facilitate academic success in the classroom. With orderly and engaged learning behavior, classroom management procedures and operations have a better chance of running smoothly, allowing for more focused attention toward academic goals and outcomes in the school environment. There is certainly a desire to model, teach, and enhance appropriate or desired behavior patterns in the school setting. This same approach can and should be followed with mental health training. Since good behavior facilitates academic progress and success, the role of mental health education and wellness cannot be overstated.

SUPPORT FOR ALL

As Adelman and Taylor (1998) have indicated, the mandate for schools is to educate and that is why the school setting is the ideal place for teaching, modeling, and practicing effective mental health practices (Greenwood, Kratochwill, & Clements, 2008). A *whole-child* education is exactly what is needed in order to prepare students for the challenges of the 21st century, and a mental health curriculum is just as essential as academic content. However, according to Adelman and Taylor (2010), a systematic "reculturing" is necessary in order for a mental health curriculum to exist and optimally operate in the schools, and that process involves several key actions including

1. Creating and maintaining a caring supportive environment
2. An effective mentoring (and modeling) program for teachers

3. Teaming opportunities
4. Collegial supports including personalized staff development and shared decision making

Given that a uniform mental health curriculum and the desired
system changes connected to it have yet to emerge across the
nation's school districts, educators are faced with the reality of
dealing with and addressing mental health issues as best they
can. Also, if educators and educational opportunities are to be
utilized in the delivery of mental health services (Lynn, McKay, &
Atkins, 2003), it is important to review the potential levels of
impact. The tiered RTI model previously mentioned is actually
based on the earlier work of Gerald Caplan.

Caplan's (1964) mental health consultation model involves
three levels of intervention (primary, secondary, and tertiary)
support. Theoretically, primary intervention is provided to all,
and is preventive in nature, because the group receiving the intervention is not viewed as possessing the problem or it is at a level
that it is not adversely affecting the members of that group. The
goal here is to lessen the occurrence of the disorder or problem
through direct education and/or skill development. At the secondary level, the intervention is centered on individuals who are
identified as being "at risk" to demonstrate problems if more concentrated resources are not provided, or have already started to
demonstrate undesired behaviors or characteristics. Due to their
status, these individuals as a collective group receive more and/or
repeated opportunities in order to enhance their knowledge
and/or skill set(s). At the tertiary level, direct and often individual intervention is provided in order to reduce the frequency,
duration, and/or the intensity of the maladaptive conditions or
behavior(s). Here the approach is to minimize the effect of the
condition to those affected by it.

A leveled intervention approach has been advocated for
some time as a mental health–school model (Adelman & Taylor,
1998) where levels of school support to students involve early
prevention and/or education (Tier 1), early intervention for those
who need extra help and/or are at high risk (Tier 2), as well as
individuals who demonstrate severe needs and individualized
support (Tier 3). A tiered-intervention approach is also evidenced
with public health regarding job-stress intervention. In particular, three basic levels of support are recognized for workers in
regard to work-stress problems (LaMontagne, Keegel, Louie,
Ostry, & Landsbergis, 2007; LaMontagne, Keegel, & Vallance,
2007). Primary intervention can be directed toward the entire
working system or organization as well as the individual workers. The approach at this level is designed to eliminate or reduce
job stressors. For example, at the organization level it might be
the work of health and safety committees and the recommendations generated from such committees. At the individual level, it

could be staff trainings to enhance worker skills in specific areas such as conflict management. Secondary intervention focuses on altering the ways individuals perceive or respond to job stressors. Training can be provided to help workers minimize their stressful situations on the job, such as the use of relaxation techniques during high-stress periods. Finally, at the tertiary level, intervention attempts to treat, compensate, and rehabilitate workers with job stress-related illness. The focus here is to treat and minimize the long-term effects of the stress-related problems. This would likely involve counseling or other rehabilitation-focused programs.

As reported in Adelman and Taylor (2010), in order to address the anticipated stress and potential burnout (i.e., a chronic stress condition that significantly diminishes an individual's ability to cope and function on a daily basis) that can accompany teaching, three essential intervention areas for educators need to be recognized:

1. Reducing environmental stressors
2. Enhancing job supports
3. Increasing personal capabilities

Reducing work stressors and increasing/enhancing job supports are important for teachers and their professional work satisfaction. Both of these are connected to the school system, however, and are typically beyond the individual control of a teacher or any other school-based professional for that matter. That is not the case with the third area because increasing and developing an educator's personal capabilities and supports are under the direct control of every educator.

School-based professionals are faced with the reality of learning and acquiring new skills and enhancing those they already possess. Teacher preparation programs almost exclusively focus on professional content and instructional delivery with little, if any, instruction devoted to mental health and wellness (Koller & Bertel, 2006; Koller, Osterlind, Paris, & Weston, 2004). A focus on self-care is essential (Barnett & Cooper, 2009) for all individuals, and that includes educators who operate and must succeed in high-stress environments. As Adelman and Taylor (2010) have stated,

> It should surprise no one that school staff might find it difficult to attend effectively to the needs of students when their own needs are ignored. Addressing staff well-being through promoting a caring, supportive, learning community at a school is basic to helping all of the school's stakeholders maintain a sense of balance, perspective, and hope. (p. 200)

Teachers are well prepared in the process of content preparation and instructional delivery. For them to be effective, however, career-directed educators need to learn and immerse themselves into productive mental health and self-care practices to benefit both themselves and the students they instruct.

MANDATE TO EDUCATE

As lifelong learners, students need to understand what mental health is and what steps need to be taken in order to maintain it throughout their lives. This learning outcome is as essential as any academic goal they will attain. Teachers, due to their daily contact, are in a position to directly impact students in regard to their mental health practices. This can occur from both an instructional as well as a modeling/demonstration perspective. Yet an important issue must be acknowledged and recognized. This delivery approach is predicated on the belief and assumption that educators are knowledgeable and effective with their own mental health practice, and also have the knowledge and skills to support their students.

Recent research suggests that although teachers may agree that schools should address the mental health needs of their students, a majority of teachers report that they lack the knowledge and skills necessary to support their students (Koller & Bertel, 2006; Kratochwill & Shernoff, 2004; Reinke et al., 2011). Teachers view this professional content as falling outside of their normal training, and based on the majority of current teacher preparation programs that is accurate (Koller & Bertel, 2006). Nevertheless, educators enter their profession with the understanding that they will always be learning; however, that is typically connected to academic content, instructional techniques, or maybe technology. Receiving formal instruction and/or being involved in self-instruction in the area of mental health may represent an instructional first for many educators.

To effectively teach, one must be knowledgeable in a subject matter and have the skills that effectively transmit that knowledge and skill to the intended learners. That is understood as one of the fundamental premises of teaching. Therefore, educators should demonstrate and model the mental health knowledge and skills that are desired of their students in the classroom. Beyond the obvious need for good instruction with students, there is a more basic and self-centered reason for making sure educators are well versed in effective mental health practices, and it's quite straightforward—you can't help others unless you take care of yourself *first*. This sounds selfish, and it is, but it's for all the right reasons.

As a former mental health disaster team leader for the American Red Cross, the author and all team members based their actions and decisions on a few core principles and procedures. For example, we always made sure that the lines of communication were operational. Checking in and taking account of everyone and their actions and/or location were essential, especially just after a natural disaster. But an even more essential operating principle was making sure of taking care of oneself. In fact, the mantra was "take care of yourself first and then someone else" and it was followed for good reason. You can't help anyone if you aren't ready and secure in your mental health status. So what may sound self-centered is absolutely essential if you are to help others.

Educators and school staff need to follow this disaster team mind-set. Teachers can only help students when they are truly secure and functioning well relative to their own mental health. Obviously that is easier said than done, but it represents a basic and foundational principle and requirement that educators and staff must acknowledge from the start. Furthermore, mental health like one's physical health is not a static condition; it can and will change over time. Nevertheless, if good mental health practices are followed on a daily basis then a consistent sense of well-being is likely to follow for an extended period of time. For example, if you eat well, exercise on a routine basis, get adequate sleep, stay active, and avoid passive activities you will likely enjoy better physical and mental health just because of those consistent decisions and actions.

ENHANCING MENTAL HEALTH: DEVELOP A PLAN

For all education professionals, as well as for everyone else, generating and maintaining an effective mental health program involves the development and implementation of a comprehensive and individualized plan. As mentioned previously, recognizing the importance of mental health is a keystone for any long-term professional development plan. That recognition has to exist before any meaningful plan can be developed. Also, adhering to evidence-based practices promotes the well-being of educators as well as promoting important mental health outcomes for their students (Reinke et al., 2011).

According to Witte (2006b), educators need to take responsibility for their mental health status, and the development of an IMHP is a major step toward that professional outcome. Functioning similar to that of an Individualized Education Program (IEP), an IMHP represents the important steps and actions that each individual takes in order to obtain and maintain an effective mental health foundation. Each professional needs to decide what those steps and actions will be and how they will be implemented. As stated in Witte (2006b),

> For an IMHP to be effective it should include several components:
>
> 1. Mental health awareness including knowledge of stress, its potential impact, and the specific, key stressors that operate within an individual's life pattern
> 2. Skill and technique knowledge and mental wellness research

3. Opportunities to practice and refine these skills in natural settings under authentic conditions
4. Evaluation of the effectiveness and benefit of these skills to determine the best collection for each individual's plan of action (p. 172)

Regardless of the individual components that are selected to make up an individual's IMHP, it is important to understand that it needs to be centered on the important process of mental health problem solving. As part of that process, educators must be able to identify key stressors in their work and life environment and distinguish effective and workable intervention strategies that can be faithfully implemented and monitored. They must also be able to objectively evaluate the effectiveness of the strategies and plan through the collection of meaningful data, and then maintain the plan if successful and, if not, consider other options.

To help illustrate this process consider the following information. According to the research of Reinke et al. (2011), the top professional areas and issues that teachers believe they need additional knowledge and training in include the following:

(a) strategies for working with children with externalizing behavior problems, (b) recognizing and understanding mental health issues in children, and (c) training in classroom management and behavioral interventions. A large number of teachers also reported the need for training in engaging and working effectively with families. (p. 7)

Since these issues likely represent high need or concern areas for teachers, it is reasonable to assume these areas represent potential stressors for a majority of teachers.

To address this, on both an individual as well as a system level, it is important to obtain professional material and training to deal with these classroom challenges. First, are these or will they likely become key stressors that will impact a teacher's work setting? Could these stressors also impact one's personal life experience? If the answer to either of these potential outcomes is *yes*, then it is an important issue and a potential stressor for a teacher.

Second, what information and development opportunities can and should be obtained in order to develop both competency and confidence for the teachers? They would need to refine and enhance their knowledge and skill sets to the point that these identified "concern areas" no longer matter and do not represent stressors for the teachers. This continuing professional development could be part of the teacher's IMHP and also part of the district's attempt to provide meaningful in-service training and skill development for its faculty and staff. The following case study is one teacher's attempt to focus on and address the recognized stressors in her professional career.

CASE STUDY

Background and Professional Goals

Mrs. Smith is a fourth-grade teacher who has taught in Washington City School District for the last 5 years. As a seasoned teacher, she recognizes the importance of taking care of herself so that she can effectively take care of her students. She wants to provide the best for her students and that includes academic instruction as well as the personal care and support of her students.

As part of her continuing professional development plan, Mrs. Smith has constructed a list of professional outcomes for herself. Those outcomes include the following:

- Reach an exemplary or master level teaching status within 10 years
- Pursue and complete a graduate program, resulting in obtaining a Master's degree or higher
- Develop an extensive intervention knowledge base and skill set, especially for students with special learning needs and English Language Learners (ELL) students
- Provide excellent and effective instruction for all her students

Current Professional Plan

Mrs. Smith recognizes that the enhancement of her teaching qualifications includes both professional areas (e.g., use of apps and tablets in her classroom) and personal health improvement (e.g., general wellness practices). Presently, her targeted professional development opportunities for this academic year include the following:

- Attend a workshop on the latest technology programs and apps (supported by evidence-based research and findings) designed for and used by special needs and ELL students
- Attend a workshop or take an online course designed to further develop her understanding of professional burnout and stress triggers in the workplace as well as at home

IMHP

Mrs. Smith already has a working mental health plan and program that she follows, or tries to follow, during the school year. She recognizes the benefit of exercise, consistent and restful sleep-cycle issues, and deep-breathing and relaxation techniques in order to more appropriately deal with stress events during work as well as at home. She participates in and assisted in organizing specific school-wide activities to help her colleagues along with herself. For example, she was successful in getting a yoga instructor to come and visit the school for after-school instruction every Tuesday and Thursday. Also, during lunchtime she leads a group of teachers and staff on an exercise-focused walk-around on the school track. This happens Mondays through Thursdays (except in inclement weather), and anywhere from 5 to 15 individuals participate depending on their schedules.

Extension of Professional Plan into the Classroom

In addition to helping herself, Mrs. Smith also embeds personal wellness and mental health instruction into the classroom curriculum. For example, Mrs. Smith teaches all her students a simple but effective problem-solving process. She uses the KidsMatter website (www.kidsmatter.edu.au) associated with Australia's mental health and wellbeing initiative for early childhood and primary schools. A basic 5-step problem-solving process is followed with Mrs. Smith's students. The basic steps are

1. What is the problem?
2. How do you feel?
3. Make a plan
4. Take action
5. Check and review the results

When she reviews this process, Mrs. Smith explains to her students that they first must know what the problem is before they can try to solve it. They must also identify their feelings that are connected to the problem. They are encouraged to think of several different solutions to solve the identified problem. Next they must select a solution they think will work and implement it. They must see if it works or gets better, and if it doesn't work they must not give up but then try another solution.

Instead of denying or avoiding stress in the classroom setting, she actively promotes that her students address stress-related issues and follow effective problem-solving strategies to eliminate and/or minimize those issues in their young lives. In essence, they are encouraged to practice and develop this lifelong skill. Also, since this is taught to everyone as part of the classroom curriculum, it falls within a primary or Tier 1 level experience. For students who have more difficulty understanding and following through with the steps, extra examples are provided and practiced. This sometimes happens in the class during independent seat time or during some class specials. This constitutes more of a Tier 2 type of instructional experience and usually only involves a few students.

Mrs. Smith follows best practices when it comes to mental health. First, she is focused on enhancing and maintaining her own mental health status. This is essential if she is going to help others, namely her students. She presents as an excellent role model because she goes beyond the *talk* and definitely does the *walk* in regard to good mental health practices. She also doesn't wait for mental health instruction to happen somewhere else. She blends it into her daily instruction and uses classroom events as "learning experiences" for finding good solutions to problems. Perhaps the most significant feature is that the students are practicing a skill that will serve them now as well as in the future; that definitely constitutes instructional impact.

MENTAL HEALTH FOUNDATION

As affirmed by President Obama during the National Conference on Mental Health (June 2013), mental health wellness is part of the national agenda for today's youth. Due to continued public and legislative initiatives, an increased emphasis and expectation on mental health training and intervention now exists for professional educators. Without question, teachers are now expected to know more about mental health. Moreover, they are also expected to be able to identify potential mental health problems and issues that may be presented by students.

This professional expectation is predicated on teachers' being knowledgeable about mental health and demonstrating effective mental health practices. Therefore, in order for teachers to be secure in their own mental health practices, continued research on effective mental health strategies is needed. Several key components of effective mental health that educators can utilize are examined in the following paragraphs.

As was mentioned earlier in this chapter, an essential intervention area for teachers involves increasing their personal capacities and skills. Each teacher needs to recognize and maintain homeostatic or physiological balance as this is challenged with daily events and conflicts. But what are effective evidence-based stress reducing techniques? What basic elements, if any, should exist as part of any effective plan? The most basic categories in dealing with stress reduction and for promoting overall good mental health planning are briefly reviewed.

EVIDENCE-BASED RESEARCH AND PRACTICE

In the author's former private practice, many new clients were often found to be physically and mentally exhausted. They indicated a variety of reasons for their rundown condition. Most justifications fell into the broad categories of either bad luck or life events that were beyond their control. After encouraging and sometimes insisting for clients to accept responsibility for their actions and decisions, an IMHP was developed for each client and/or family. As part of every therapy plan, each client/family had to agree to meet three essential foundational components of physical/mental health (i.e., adequate sleep, proper nutrition, and daily/weekly exercise). Also, a concrete plan to monitor the intended progress of each of these mental health components had to be developed.

Sleep

Establishing and maintaining a consistent sleep schedule is essential for every individual's daily functioning. Research has indicated that a poor and/or inconsistent sleep cycle negatively impacts social life and interactions, normal physiological processes, essential daily cognitive operations, and general quality of life (Lee et al., 2009; Willingham, 2013). More severe instances of prolonged sleep deprivation (i.e., 4 hours–5 hours or less a night) have been associated with significant medical conditions such as obesity and diabetes (Knutson, 2012) as well as cardiovascular problems and psychiatric illness (Grandner, Jackson, Gerstner, & Knutson, 2013). According to the National Sleep Foundation, approximately 7 hours to 9 hours of sleep for adults is required on a nightly basis in order to ensure normal daily functioning. Unfortunately, in this 24/7 continuously-on world, getting the required amount of sleep each night is a challenge, but one that must be met if mental health is a priority and a desired personal/professional goal.

Nutrition

Along with the need for sufficient restorative sleep, proper and adequate nutrition is needed for the establishment and maintenance of the physical body and basic health in general (Ross, Caballero, Cousins, Tucker, & Ziegler, 2014). In addition to eating at specific intervals during the day (e.g., three or four times), it is also important to eat nutritious food. Research has established that foods lower in nutritional value (e.g., high in saturated fats—and that includes most processed foods) provide less essential nutrients for the body resulting in lower metabolic efficiency, greater fatigue, less resistance to pathogenic agents, and higher reported stress levels (Story, Kaphingst, Robinson-O'Brien, & Glanz, 2008; U.S. Department of Health and Human Services [HHS], 1988). With minimal nutrition, the body and mind cease to function at an optimal level resulting in decreased student performance in school (Taras, 2005). As would be expected, this poor performance effect is not limited to just students with a deficient nutritional history. Adults are just as likely to demonstrate poor work performance and potential health issues due to inadequate nutritional intake (Ross et al., 2014).

Exercise

In addition to successful sleeping and eating practices, exercise is also necessary as part of everyone's daily life pattern. It comes as no surprise that physical exercise is a cornerstone to a solid mental health foundation (Morgan & Goldston, 1987; Statho-poulou, Powers, Berry, Smits, & Otto, 2006). Contrary to popular belief and contemporary practice, humans are not designed to exist as passive, sedentary creatures (Morgan & Goldston, 1987). An inactive lifestyle is a relatively new phenomenon and experience (since the middle of the 20th century) because humans over the centuries have lived active, physically challenging lives. Sitting and working at a desk all day is a recent change compared to our ancestors of just two or three generations ago.

In addition to avoiding or minimizing a sedentary lifestyle, active aerobic activity with the prolonged intake of oxygen into the human body helps to reduce many stress-related problems (Edenfield & Blumenthal, 2011; Hamer, Taylor, & Steptoe, 2006; Tsatsoulis & Fountoulakis, 2006). Exercise has a double stress-reduction effect on the body. Regular exercise actually lowers the secretion of stress hormones into the body while at the same time increases the release of endorphins, which are designed to reduce the effects of stress on the body (Sapolsky, 2004; Tsatsoulis & Fountoulakis, 2006).

What is extremely encouraging is that an intensive exercise program is not needed in order to derive therapeutic effects. For example, Orsega-Smith, Mowen, Payne, and Godbey (2004) found that just exercising (e.g., walking) in a park setting can help reduce stress and tension among adults. In fact, research has demonstrated that moderate exercise routines (e.g., 30 minutes–60 minutes of exercise a day for three or more times a week) can help significantly reduce the impact of stress on the human body (Berger & Owen, 1988; Jin, 1992; King, Baumann, O'Sullivan, Wilcox, & Castro, 2002).

ON-THE-CLOCK SKILLS

Getting restful sleep, eating well, and exercising daily all serve as a collective and essential mental health foundation base for everyone. However, possessing this mental health foundation certainly doesn't ensure a stress-free environment and work experience. In fact, daily challenges will always take place and that is why teachers need to also focus on resources and techniques that can serve them while they are on the job directly confronting stressful events or situations. The following represent a few essential skills and resources for any teacher in the classroom.

Relaxation Techniques

Research has demonstrated that relaxation techniques (e.g., deep breathing, yoga meditation) are effective in reducing muscle tension, mental fatigue, and fostering a more productive and relaxed state of mind (Hartfiel et al., 2012; Matsumoto & Smith, 2001; Paul, Elam, & Verhulst, 2007; Stueck & Gloeckner, 2005). Other *therapeutic approaches* such as mindfulness (i.e., making a person aware of internal and external experiences that coexist during a particular event) have demonstrated stress-reduction effects (Baer, 2003; Grossman, Niemann, Schmidt, & Walach, 2004; Praissman, 2008; Shapiro, Brown, & Biegel, 2007). Given that a variety of techniques and approaches are available and effective, it is up to each individual to decide what *fits* best. Classroom-oriented approaches can also be used to benefit the students, such as the use of music to decrease arousal and increase attention to tasks (Pelletier, 2004).

Social Support

Having a support group and/or individuals to talk to regarding work and other stress-related conditions helps minimize the effects of stress (Viswesvaran, Sanchez, & Fisher, 1999). Research has shown the importance of support and/or companionship for individuals under high-stress conditions (Cairney, Boyle, Offord, & Racine, 2003). Talking about events and issues can serve a cathartic purpose and can also help in identifying and clarifying issues, potential decisions, and possible intervention options.

Problem Solving

Findings clearly demonstrate that individuals who follow some kind of problem-solving plan or system report less stress and greater perceived control of life events (D'Zurilla, 1990; Largo-Wight, Peterson, & Chen, 2005). The IMHP is a clear example of how teachers can follow a professional plan of action designed to address mental health needs and issues in the workplace. Adhering to a recognized approach and model provides a framework that can be preventive and proactive in nature, and allows for greater personal control and more effective responding to stress-related events and challenges.

SUMMARY

The importance of creating and maintaining a IMHP for educators cannot be overstated. It is an essential professional skill area that needs to be well developed for all teachers. With a stronger mental health foundation, a teacher becomes more confident regarding instructional skills, demonstrates greater professional flexibility and resiliency, and consequently is more likely to stay in the profession.

RESOURCES

The U.S. government mental health website (www.mentalhealth.gov) provides considerable information on mental health services in addition to providing links to help individuals receive direct help and support for mental health problems and issues.

Mental Health America (MHA; www.mentalhealthamerica.net) is an advocacy organization dedicated to helping individuals across the nation successfully deal with a wide variety of mental and substance-use issues and problems. This organization has been in existence for almost 100 years and currently has 240 affiliates in 41 states.

The UCLA School Mental Health Project (smph.psych.ucla.edu/) is a comprehensive mental health site that provides information on current resources and publications including a practitioner's toolbox. Information on new initiatives and system approaches is also provided. This is one of the most complete resource sites for school mental health anywhere.

REFERENCES

Adelman, H. S., & Taylor, L. (1998). Mental health in schools: Moving forward. *School Psychology Review, 27*(2), 175–190.

Adelman, H. S., & Taylor, L. (Eds.). (2010). *Mental health in schools: Engaging learners, preventing problems, and improving schools.* Thousand Oaks, CA: Corwin Press.

Baer, R. A. (2003). Mindfulness training as a clinical intervention: A conceptual and empirical review. *Clinical Psychology: Science and Practice, 10*(2), 125–143.

Barnett, J. E., & Cooper, N. (2009). Creating a culture of self-care. *Clinical Psychology: Science and Practice, 16*(1), 16–20.

Belkic, K. L., Landsbergis, P. A., Schnall, P. L., & Baker, D. (2004). Is job strain a major source of cardiovascular disease risk? *Scandinavian Journal of Work, Environment & Health, 30*(2), 85–128.

Berger, B. G., & Owen, D. R. (1988). Stress reduction and mood enhancement in four exercise modes: Swimming, body conditioning, hatha yoga, and fencing. *Research Quarterly for Exercise and Sport, 59*(2), 148–159.

Bottomley, J., Dalziel, E., & Neith, M. (2002). *Work factors in suicide.* Praham East, Australia: Creative Ministries Network (formerly Urban Ministry Network).

Cairney, J., Boyle, M., Offord, D. R., & Racine, Y. (2003). Stress, social support and depression in single and married mothers. *Social Psychiatry and Psychiatric Epidemiology, 38*(8), 442–449.

Capella, E., Frazier, S. L., Atkins, M. S., Schoenwald, S. K., & Glisson, C. (2008). Enhancing schools' capacity to support children in poverty: An ecological model of school-based mental health services. *Administration and Policy in Mental Health and Mental Health Services Research, 35*(5), 395–409.

Caplan, G. (1964). *Principles of preventive psychiatry.* Oxford, England: Basic Books.

Crum, R. M., Muntaner, C., Eaton, W. W., & Anthony, J. C. (1995). Occupational stress and the risk of alcohol abuse and dependence. *Alcoholism: Clinical and Experimental Research, 19*(3), 647–655.

D'Zurilla, T. J. (1990). Problem-solving training for effective stress management and prevention. *Journal of Cognitive Psychotherapy, 4*(4), 327–354.

Edenfield, T. M., & Blumenthal, J. A. (2011). Exercise and stress reduction. In R. J. Contrada & A. Baum (Eds.), *The handbook of stress science: Biology, psychology, and health.* New York, NY: Springer Publishing Company.

Graczyk, P., Domitrovich, C., Small, M., & Zins, J. (2006). Serving all children: An implementation model framework. *School Psychology Review, 35*(2), 266–274.

Grandner, M. A., Jackson, N., Gerstner, J. R., & Knutson, K. L. (2013). Dietary nutrients associated with short and long sleep duration. Data from a nationally representative sample. *Appetite, 64*, 71–80.

Greenwood, C. R., Kratochwill, T. R., & Clements, M. (2008). *Schoolwide prevention models: Lessons learned in elementary schools.* New York, NY: Guilford.

Grossman, P., Niemann, L., Schmidt, S., & Walach, H. (2004). Mindfulness-based stress reduction and health benefits: A meta-analysis. *Journal of Psychosomatic Research, 57*(1), 35–43.

Hamer, M., Taylor, A., & Steptoe, A. (2006). The effect of acute aerobic exercise on stress related blood pressure responses: A systematic review and meta-analysis. *Biological Psychology, 71*(2), 183–190.

Harris, M. M., & Fennell, M. L. (1988). A multivariate model of job stress and alcohol consumption. *The Sociological Quarterly, 29*(3), 391–406.

Hartfiel, N., Burton, C., Rycroft-Malone, J., Clarke, G., Havenhand, J., Khalsa, S., & Edwards, R. (2012). Yoga for reducing perceived stress and back pain at work. *Occupational Medicine, 62*(8), 606–612.

Hoagwood, K., Olin, S., Kerker, B., Kratochwill, T., Crowe, M., & Saka, N. (2007). Empirically based school interventions targeted at academic and mental health functioning. *Journal of Emotional and Behavioral Disorders, 15*(2), 66–92. doi:10.1177/10634266070150020301

Ingersoll, R. M. (2002). The teacher shortage: A case of wrong diagnosis and wrong prescription. *National Association of Secondary School Principals (NASSP) Bulletin, 86*(631), 16–31.

Jin, P. (1992). Efficacy of tai chi, brisk walking, meditation, and reading in reducing mental and emotional stress. *Journal of Psychosomatic Research, 36*(4), 361–370.

Johnson, S., Cooper, C., Cartwright, S., Donald, I., Taylor, P., & Millet, C. (2005). The experience of work-related stress across occupations. *Journal of Managerial Psychology, 20*(2), 178–187.

Jorm, A. F. (2012). Mental health literacy: Empowering the community to take action for better mental health. *American Psychologist, 67*(3), 231–243.

King, A. C., Baumann, K., O'Sullivan, P., Wilcox, S., & Castro, C. (2002). Effects of moderate-intensity exercise on physiological, behavioral, and emotional responses to family caregiving: A randomized controlled trial. *The Journals of Gerontology Series A: Biological Sciences and Medical Sciences, 57*(1), M26–M36.

Knutson, K. L. (2012). Does inadequate sleep play a role in vulnerability to obesity? *American Journal of Human Biology, 24*(3), 361–371.

Koller, J. R., & Bertel, J. M. (2006). Responding to today's mental health needs of children, families and schools: Revisiting the preservice training and preparation of school-based personnel. *Education and Treatment of Children, 29*(2), 197–217.

Koller, J., Osterlind, S., Paris, K., & Weston, K. (2004). Differences between novice and expert teachers' undergraduate preparation and ratings of importance in the area of children's mental health. *International Journal of Mental Health Promotion, 6*(2), 40–46.

Kratochwill, T., & Shernoff, E. (2004). Evidence-based practice: Promoting evidence-based interventions in school psychology. *School Psychology Review, 33*(1), 34–48.

Kyriacou, C. (2001). Teacher stress: Directions for future research. *Educational Review, 53*(1), 27–35.

LaMontagne, A. D., Keegel, T., Louie, A. M., & Ostry, A. (2010). Job stress as a preventable upstream determinant of common mental disorders: A review for practitioners and policy-makers. *Advances in Mental Health, 9*(1), 17–35.

LaMontagne, A. D., Keegel, T., Louie, A. M., Ostry, A., & Landsbergis, P. A. (2007). A systematic review of the job-stress intervention evaluation literature, 1990–2005. *International Journal of Occupational and Environmental Health, 13*(3), 268–280.

LaMontagne, A. D., Keegel, T., & Vallance, D. (2007). Protecting and promoting mental health in the workplace: Developing a systems approach to job stress. *Health Promotion Journal of Australia, 18*(3), 221–228.

Largo-Wight, E., Peterson, P. M., & Chen, W. W. (2005). Perceived problem solving, stress, and health among college students. *American Journal of Health Behavior, 29*(4), 360–370.

Lee, M., Choh, A. C., Demerath, E. W., Knutson, K. L., Duren, D. L., Sherwood, R. J., . . . Czerwinski, S. A. (2009). Sleep disturbance in relation to health-related quality of life in adults: The Fels longitudinal study. *JNHA-The Journal of Nutrition, Health and Aging, 13*(6), 576–583.

Lynn, C. J., McKay, M. M., & Atkins, M. S. (2003). School social work: Meeting the mental health needs of students through collaboration with teachers. *Children & Schools, 25*(4), 197–209.

Marmot, M. G., Bosma, H., Hemingway, H., Brunner, E., & Stansfeld, S. (1997). Contribution of job control and other risk factors to social variations in coronary heart disease incidence. *Lancet, 350*(9073), 235–239.

Matsumoto, M., & Smith, J. C. (2001). Progressive muscle relaxation, breathing exercises, and ABC relaxation theory. *Journal of Clinical Psychology, 57*(12), 1551–1557.

Michie, S., & Williams, S. (2003). Reducing work related psychological ill health and sickness absence: A systematic literature review. *Occupational and Environmental Medicine, 60*(1), 3–9.

Morgan, W. P., & Goldston, S. E. (1987). *Exercise and mental health.* New York, NY: Hemisphere.

Nastasi, B. K., Moore, R. B., & Varjas, K. M. (2004). *School-based mental health services: Creating comprehensive and culturally specific programs.* Washington, DC: American Psychological Association.

Noblet, A., & LaMontagne, A. D. (2006). The role of workplace health promotion in addressing job stress. *Health Promotion International, 21*(4), 346–353.

Orsega-Smith, E., Mowen, A. J., Payne, L. L., & Godbey, G. (2004). The interaction of stress and park use on psycho-physiological health in older adults. *Journal of Leisure Research, 36*(2), 232–256.

Paul, G., Elam, B., & Verhulst, S. J. (2007). A longitudinal study of students' perceptions of using deep breathing meditation to reduce testing stresses. *Teaching and Learning in Medicine, 19*(3), 287–292.

Pelletier, C. L. (2004). The effect of music on decreasing arousal due to stress: A meta-analysis. *Journal of Music Therapy, 41*(3), 192–214.

Praissman, S. (2008). Mindfulness-based stress reduction: A literature review and clinician's guide. *Journal of the American Academy of Nurse Practitioners, 20*(4), 212–216.

Reinke, W. M., Stormont, M., Herman, K. C., Puri, R., & Goel, N. (2011). Supporting children's mental health in schools: Teacher perceptions of needs, roles, and barriers. *School Psychology Quarterly, 26*(1), 1–13. doi:10.1037/a0022714

Rones, M., & Hoagwood, K. (2000). School-based mental health services: A research review. *Clinical Child and Family Psychology Review, 3*(4), 223–241. doi:10.1023/A:1026425104386

Ross, A. C., Caballero, B., Cousins, R. J., Tucker, K. L., & Ziegler, T. R. (Eds.). (2014). *Modern nutrition in health and disease.* Baltimore, MD: Lippincott Williams & Wilkins.

Sanderson, K., & Andrews, G. (2006). Common mental disorders in the workforce: Recent findings from descriptive and social epidemiology. *Canadian Journal of Psychiatry, 51*(2), 63–75.

Sapolsky, R. M. (2004). *Why zebras don't get ulcers* (3rd ed.). New York, NY: Henry Holt.

Shapiro, S. L., Brown, K. W., & Biegel, G. M. (2007). Teaching self-care to caregivers: Effects of mindfulness-based stress reduction on the mental health of therapists in training. *Training and Education in Professional Psychology, 1*(2), 105–115.

Shapiro, S., Schwartz, G., & Bonner, G. (1998, December). Effects of mindfulness-based stress reduction on medical and premedical students. *Journal of Behavioral Medicine, 21*(6), 581–599.

Stathopoulou, G., Powers, M. B., Berry, A. C., Smits, J. A., & Otto, M. W. (2006). Exercise interventions for mental health: A quantitative and qualitative review. *Clinical Psychology: Science and Practice, 13*(2), 179–193.

Stockard, J., & Lehman, M. B. (2004). Influences on the satisfaction and retention of 1st-year teachers: The importance of effective school management. *Educational Administration Quarterly, 40*(5), 742–771.

Story, M., Kaphingst, K. M., Robinson-O'Brien, R., & Glanz, K. (2008). Creating healthy food and eating environments: Policy and environmental approaches. *Annual Review of Public Health, 29*, 253–272.

Strazdins, L., D'Souza, R., Lim, L., Broom, D., & Rodgers, B. (2004). Job strain, job insecurity, and health: Rethinking the relationship. *Journal of Occupational Health Psychology, 9*(4), 296–305.

Stueck, M., & Gloeckner, N. (2005). Yoga for children in the mirror of the science: Working spectrum and practice fields of the training of relaxation with elements of yoga for children. *Early Child Development and Care, 175*(4), 371–377.

Taras, H. (2005). Nutrition and student performance at school. *Journal of School Health, 75*(6), 199–213.

Tsatsoulis, A., & Fountoulakis, S. (2006). The protective role of exercise on stress system dysregulation and comorbidities. *Annals of the New York Academy of Sciences, 1083*(1), 196–213.

U.S. Department of Health and Human Services (HHS). (1988). *The surgeon general's report on nutrition and health: Summary and recommendations.* Washington, DC: U.S. Government Printing Office.

Viswesvaran, C., Sanchez, J. I., & Fisher, J. (1999). The role of social support in the process of work stress: A meta-analysis. *Journal of Vocational Behavior, 54*(2), 314–334.

Wang, J., Schmitz, N., Dewa, C., & Stansfeld, S. (2009). Changes in perceived job strain and the risk of major depression: Results from a population-based longitudinal study. *American Journal of Epidemiology, 169*(9), 1085–1091.

Weissberg, R. P., Kumpfer, K. L., & Seligman, M. E. (2003). Prevention that works for children and youth: An introduction. *American Psychologist, 58*(6/7), 425–432. doi:10.1037/0003-066X.58.6-7.425

Willingham, D. (2013). Are sleepy students learning? *American Educator, 36*(4), 35–39.

Witte, R. (2006a). Psychopathology is alive and well. In A. Wang & R. Witte (Eds.), *Selected topics on educational psychology and school psychology* (pp. 115–122). Dalian, China: Liaoning Normal University Press.

Witte, R. (2006b). Have a plan. In A. Wang & R. Witte (Eds.), *Selected topics on educational psychology and school psychology* (pp. 169–190). Dalian, China: Liaoning Normal University Press.

World Health Organization (WHO). (2004). *Prevention of mental disorders: Effective interventions and policy options.* Geneva, Switzerland: Author.

CHAPTER 10

Bullying

DOROTHY L. ESPELAGE

LEARNING OUTCOMES

On completion of this chapter, the reader should be able to:

- Define bullying and recognize the primary correlates of bully perpetration and victimization
- Acknowledge the ecology and systems of impact with bullying involvement
- Identify the main school-based bullying prevention approaches used in the United States as well as throughout the world
- Distinguish the attributes of several evidenced based school-based social–emotional learning (SEL) programs

Bullying is regarded as a significant problem in the United States among school-aged youth. The Centers for Disease Control and Prevention (CDC) estimate that approximately 20% of high school youth report being bullied by other students in their school each year (Eaton et al., 2012). National estimates with middle school-aged students demonstrate higher rates—more than 30% (Robers, Kemp, & Truman, 2013). Over time, bullying trends have remained stagnant (Eaton et al., 2012), and only a few programs are showing promise in reducing bullying in U.S. schools (Farrington & Ttofi, 2011). However, we know even less about how exposure to bullying as a perpetrator, victim, or bully–victim negatively affects child and adolescent development over time.

DEFINITION

A rigorous debate has emerged about how best to define bullying and how to distinguish it from other forms of aggression and peer victimization (American Educational Research Association [AERA], 2013; Rodkin, Espelage, & Hanish, under review). One of the first predominant definitions of bullying that continues to be used in the literature and in the legal arena is as follows: "A student is being bullied or victimized when he or she is exposed, repeatedly and over time, to negative actions on the part of one or more students" (Olweus, 2010, p. 11). More recent definitions of bullying emphasize observable or non-observable aggressive behaviors, the repetitive nature of these behaviors, and the imbalance of power between the individual/group perpetrator and victim (Gladden, Vivolo-Kantor, Hamburger, & Lumpkin, 2014; Ybarra, Espelage, & Mitchell, 2014). An imbalance of power exists when the perpetrator or group of perpetrators have more physical, social, or intellectual power than the victim. In a recent examination of a nationally representative study, early and late adolescents that perceived their perpetrator as having more power reported greater adverse outcomes (e.g., depression, suicidal ideation) than victims who did not perceive a power differential (Ybarra et al., 2014).

In 2010, the Department of Education and the CDC collaborated to develop a uniform *research* definition. This group defined bullying as follows:

> Bullying is any unwanted aggressive behavior(s) by another youth or group of youths who are not siblings or current dating partners that involves an observed or perceived power imbalance and is repeated multiple times or is highly likely to be repeated. Bullying may inflict harm or distress on the targeted youth including physical, psychological, social, or educational harm. (Gladden et al., 2014)

These behaviors include verbal and physical aggression that ranges in severity from making threats, spreading rumors, and social exclusion, to physical attacks causing injury. As defined, bullying can occur face to face and through technology (e.g., cell phones, computers). Previous meta-analyses of cross-sectional studies found that relations between bully perpetration and victimization differed depending on whether the assessment was self- or teacher-report (Card et al., 2008; Cook et al., 2010).

CROSS-SECTIONAL AND LONGITUDINAL CORRELATES OF BULLY PERPETRATION AND VICTIMIZATION

Academic Outcomes

Several national and international research studies relying on cross-sectional data have documented that experiences of being victimized or bullying other students are associated with decreased academic achievement. For example, findings from a sample of 7th-, 9th-, and 11th-graders in an urban public school district also revealed that for each 1-point increase in grade point average, the odds of being a victim versus a bystander decreased by 10% (Glew et al., 2008). These associations are also found when students are followed over time in longitudinal studies (e.g., Juvonen, Wang, & Espinoza, 2011; Schwartz, Gorman, Nakamoto, & Toblin, 2005). Juvonen and colleagues (2011) documented that peer victimization can account for an average 1.5–letter grade decrease in one academic subject (e.g., math) across 3 years of middle school. Moreover, the researchers found that greater self-reported victimization was associated with lower grades and lower teacher-rated academic engagement. However, a meta-analytic review of 33 cross-sectional studies conducted by Nakamoto and Schwartz (2010) reported that empirical research on this association has produced an incongruent pattern of findings and modest correlations. In fact, these authors reported a small but significant negative correlation between peer victimization and academic achievement under both a random effects model ($r = -.12$, $p < .001$) and the fixed-effects model ($r = -.10$, $p < .001$). Friendship quality and peer social support appear to have a complex moderating role in the association between peer victimization and academic performance (Schwartz, Gorman, Dodge, Pettit, & Bates, 2008).

Psychiatric Disorders, Depression, and Suicidality

Few studies directly assess the relation between bullying and mental health disorders (e.g., Copeland et al., 2013; Fanti & Kimonis, 2013; Kumpulainen, Räsänen, & Puura, 2001). Kumpulainen et al. (2001), using an epidemiological sample of second graders from Finland, found that children who were classified as bullies (children who bully others but are not bullied themselves) and bully–victims (children who both bully and are bullied) had high rates of psychiatric disorder relative to noninvolved children, largely for externalizing behaviors like attention deficit hyperactivity disorder, oppositional defiant disorder, and conduct disorder. In particular, bully–victims were likely to have more severe problems and to have used mental health services. Similar findings emerge in Copeland et al.'s (2013) U.S. Great Smoky Mountain study: Children and youth who self-reported involvement in bullying were more likely than uninvolved youth to be diagnosed via child- and parent-reports with disruptive and substance use disorders; bully–victims were additionally at risk for internalizing disorders, including depression and suicidality. These youth were later assessed for psychiatric disorders between the ages of 19 and 26, including for depression, suicidality, anxiety, panic disorder, agoraphobia, antisocial personality disorder, and alcohol and marijuana abuse (Copeland et al., 2013). Youth who bullied during childhood were no different from children not involved in bullying on any of the nine long-term outcomes examined for except antisocial personality disorder. Other studies support these findings, indicating that victims of bullying report significant psychosomatic problems (Gini & Pozzoli, 2009) and report depression later in life (Ttofi et al., 2011).

The majority of extant research indicates that involvement in bullying in any capacity is associated with higher rates of suicidal ideation and behaviors, with cross-sectional studies finding increased odds ratios of 1.4–10.0 (the corresponding statistical increase in ideation due to bullying; Kim & Leventhal, 2008). Most of the research on the links between bully/peer victimization and suicidal behaviors has been conducted outside the United States, but a 2009 paper examined the association between peer victimization and suicidal ideation and attempts across three nationally representative samples of U.S. adolescents (Kaminski & Fang, 2009). Youth victimized by their peers were 2.4 times more likely to report suicidal ideation and 3.3 times more likely to report a suicide attempt than youth who reported not being bullied.

Although there is fairly consistent evidence that there is increased suicide risk for those involved in bullying, evidence suggests that risk might vary for youth who are bullies perpetrators, victims, and bully–victims. For instance, some studies have shown that the association between suicidal ideation and bullying is stronger for targets of bullying than for perpetrators (e.g., Rigby & Slee, 1999). However, another study found that after controlling for depression, the association between bullying and suicidal ideation was strongest for bully perpetrators (Kaltiala-Heino, Rimpela, Marttunen, Rimpela, & Rantanen, 1999). Another study of middle school youth reported that the bully–suicide association was minimized when depression and delinquency were considered for all youth (Espelage & Holt, 2013). Whereas multiple studies have found that bully–victims report more suicidal ideation and behaviors than uninvolved youth, victims, or perpetrators (e.g., Klomek et al., 2007), there are other studies that do not support this pattern. For instance, Herba and colleagues (2008) found that there were no differences in levels of suicidal ideation between bully–victims and uninvolved youth. These studies point to the complexity of assessing suicide risk based on the level of involvement youth play in the bully–victim dynamic.

Similarly, mixed findings exist with regard to whether the association between bullying and suicidal ideation varies by sex. Klomek and colleagues (2009) found that bullying victimization at age 8 was associated with later suicide attempts and completed suicides after controlling for depression and conduct problems, but only for girls. The authors speculate that this sex difference might have emerged because girls are more likely to experience relational victimization (e.g., indirect, manipulative, social- or emotion-based) whereas boys are more likely to experience physical victimization (physical aggression, fights), and relational victimization might have more long-lasting effects. On the other hand, other studies have found that boys might be at greater risk. For instance, male bullies showed higher than average levels of suicidal ideation in one study of a community population (Rigby & Slee, 1999), and in a sample of Italian youth seeking psychological help suicidal ideation was predicted by being bullied at school only for boys (Laukkanen et al., 2005). According to Poteat and Rivers (2014), research comparing sexual and gender minority and heterosexual youth has consistently shown that sexual minority youth report higher levels of suicidality (Eisenberg & Resnick, 2006; Remafedi, French, Story, Resnick, & Blum, 1998; Robinson & Espelage, 2011; Russell & Toomey, 2012).

Delinquency, Criminal Activity, and Alcohol/Drug Use

Only recently have studies examined the link between bullying involvement and later delinquency or criminal behavior. In a 2011 meta-analysis, bullying perpetration at age 14 led to higher violent conviction rates between ages 15 and 20, lower job status at age 18, increased drug use from ages 27 to 32, and relationship problems by age 48 (Farrington & Ttofi, 2011). Furthermore, Hemphill and colleagues (2011) found that greater bullying perpetration among Australian youth in year 7 of school was associated with a twofold increase in binge drinking and marijuana use when these students were in year 10 of school. From the U.S.-based Raising Healthy Children project, childhood bullying in grade 5 was associated with heavy drinking and marijuana use at age 21 (Kim, Catalano, Haggerty, & Abbott, 2011). Other studies have shown longitudinal associations between bullying among older adolescents and associations with heavy drinking and marijuana use into adulthood, but these studies often enter family variables as covariates and do not build mediation models.

ECOLOGY OF BULLYING INVOLVEMENT

In his classic 1977 *American Psychologist* essay, Bronfenbrenner (1977) introduced the ecology of human development model in an attempt to push the field of developmental science forward. He articulated the importance of conducting experimental studies in naturally occurring environments (e.g., schools) alongside controlled laboratory experiments. Over the years, Bronfenbrenner and colleagues offered several reformulations of the ecology model, including the bioecological model (Bronfenbrenner & Morris, 1998) and the introduction of chaos theory into this model (Bronfenbrenner & Evans, 2005). Numerous aggression scholars resonated with this model, recognizing that youth are situated in systems that have direct, indirect, and dynamic influences on development and behavior.

In the area of school bullying and peer victimization, this model has often been called a social–ecological model and focuses on understanding how individual characteristics of children interact with environmental contexts or systems to promote or prevent victimization and perpetration (Espelage, 2012; Hong & Espelage, 2012). Structures or locations where children have direct contact are referred to as the *microsystem*, including peers, family, community, and schools. The interaction between components of the microsystem is referred to as the *mesosystem*. An example of a mesosystem is the interrelations between the family and school, such as parental involvement in their child's school. The *exosystem* is the social context with which the child does not have direct contact, but that affects him or her indirectly through the microsystem. Examples would be teacher or staff perceptions of the school environment and opportunities for professional development around bullying, school violence, or school climate. The *macrosystem* level is commonly regarded as a cultural "blueprint," which may determine the social structures and activities in the various levels (Bronfenbrenner, 1977). This level includes organizational, social, cultural, and political contexts, which influences the interactions within other system levels (Bronfenbrenner 1977). The final level of the ecological framework, the *chronosystem* level includes consistency or change (e.g., historical or life events) of the individual and the environment over the life course (e.g., changes in family structure). In the following sections, the literature on the various components of the social–ecological model will be reviewed, and that will be followed by a description of the sample participants, the measures that are available in the dataset, and the research hypothesis and data analysis plan.

Individual Characteristics (Microsystem)

Sociodemographic characteristics, such as age, gender, and race/ethnicity, are frequently examined predictors of bullying behavior in school. Many studies report that boys, in general, are more likely to engage in bullying than girls (Espelage, Low, Rao, Hong, & Little, 2013; Nansel et al., 2001; Varjas, Henrich, & Meyers, 2009). During the 1990s, much research supported the notion that girls are socialized to exercise more relational forms of aggression or social bullying, whereas boys engage in multiple forms of aggression (Neal, 2007). Despite this, several studies have failed to document significant sex differences in relational aggression or social forms of bullying (Crick, Casas, & Mosher, 1997; Card, Stuckey, Sawalani, & Little, 2008).

What perhaps is more important than gender differences is the notion that bullying is a gendered phenomenon whereby youth are targeted by either same- and other-sex peers in attempts to gain social status (Faris & Felmlee, 2011; Rodkin & Berger, 2008) or to marginalize lesbian, gay, bisexual, and gender-nonconforming youth (Espelage, Aragon, Birkett, & Koenig, 2008; Robinson & Espelage, 2011). Furthermore, developmental trends indicate that bullying is a precursor to the use of homophobic epithets that is in turn associated with sexual harassment during middle school (Espelage, Basile, & Hamburger, 2012; Espelage & De La Rue, 2013) and with teen dating violence in high school (Espelage et al., 2014; Miller et al., 2013).

Like gender, race/ethnicity and immigrant status are demographic variables of interest in this research, but findings have differed across studies. Inconsistent findings are likely a result of variability in sample characteristics and narrow definitions of race/ethnicity. For Hispanic/Latino and Asian youth, immigrant status and language/cultural barriers appear to be significant predictors for peer victimization in school (Peguero, 2009; Qin, Way, & Rana, 2008). Collectively, the association between race/ethnicity and bullying is complex and appears to be influenced by the racial/ethnic composition of the classroom, school, or community (Juvonen, Nishina, & Graham, 2000).

Health status and psychological functioning can also place youth at risk for experiences of bullying at school (Cook, Williams, Guerra, Kim, & Sadek, 2010). First, studies report that overweight and obese youth of both genders are at increased risk of peer victimization in school (e.g., Puhl, Peterson, & Luedicke, 2013). Second, Fekkes et al.'s (2005) study found that children with depressive symptoms were significantly more likely to be victimized by their peers than were children without a history of depression.

Finally, disability status and poverty are both significant predictors of peer victimization. Students with disabilities have been consistently overrepresented within the bullying dynamic as bullies, victims, and bully–victims (see Rose, Monda-Amaya, & Espelage, 2011 for literature review). With respect to poverty, few studies in the United States have examined poverty as a risk factor for bullying and peer victimization (Carlson, 2006; Crockett, 2003). These studies found that impoverished youth were significantly more likely to be exposed to peer violence in school (Carlson, 2006) and to identify with a culture of bullying (Crockett, 2003).

Family Characteristics (Microsystem)

Consistent parental monitoring has long been recognized as a protective factor (for future victimization or violent perpetration) for youth development (Li, Fiegelman, & Stanton, 2000). Bullies tend to have parents who do not provide adequate supervision or who are not actively involved in the lives of their children

(Espelage, Bosworth, & Simon, 2000; Georgiou & Fanti, 2010; Low & Espelage, 2013). In other instances, parents may encourage the use of aggressive and retaliatory behaviors. In a recent longitudinal study, exposure to family conflict (sibling aggression, yelling) was associated with greater bully perpetration for a large sample of middle school students (Espelage, Low, Rao, Hong, & Little, 2013). Furthermore, children who are victims of bullying more often come from families with histories of abuse or inconsistent parenting (Espelage et al., 2012; Georgiou & Fanti, 2010).

Supportive familial relations can also buffer the effects of involvement with bully experiences. When victims of bullying have warm relationships with their families, they have more positive outcomes, both emotionally and behaviorally (Bowes, Maughan, Caspi, Moffitt, & Arseneault, 2010; Holt & Espelage, 2007). These positive parent–child interactions provide children with the opportunity to talk about their bullying experiences and can provide guidance on how to cope with these events. Bowes and colleagues (2010) also found that supportive relationships with siblings could serve to aid in bully–victims' resilience.

Peers (Microsystem)

Bullying and peer victimization rarely takes place in isolated dyadic interactions, but instead often occurs in the presence of other students (Espelage, Holt, & Henkel, 2003). Youth who have friends who bully will bully more (Salmivalli, 2010), and those who have friends who engage in homophobic name-calling will use this language (Birkett & Espelage, 2014). In a recent meta-analysis, Cook and colleagues (2010) found that youth in middle school who bullied other students had greater social status among peers, whereas younger children who bullied were socially rejected. Furthermore, students may serve to perpetuate bullying by actively joining in or passively accepting the bullying behaviors, whereas on the other hand students can intervene to stop bullying or defend the victim (Espelage, Green, & Polanin, 2012).

Increasingly, school-based bullying prevention programs and social media campaigns are focusing their attention on encouraging bystanders to intervene (e.g., individuals not directly involved in bullying). A growing literature base is emerging that demonstrates the complexity of bystander or defender behaviors. Girls are more likely than boys to intervene on behalf of victims (Gini, Albiero, Benelli, & Altoe, 2007), and youth with high self-efficacy (e.g., perceived ability to intervene), positive attitudes toward the victim, affective empathy, and personal responsibility to intervene (Pozzoli & Gini, 2010) will also intervene. In a recent meta-analysis, researchers found that programs were effective at changing bystander intervening behavior when they included opportunities for youth to discuss reasons why they do not intervene to help victims, develop understanding of others, and practice effective bystander intervention skills (Polanin, Espelage, & Pigott, 2012).

Interactions among Microsystems (Mesosystem)

Mesosystem encompasses interrelations among two or more microsystems, each containing the individual (Bronfenbrenner, 1977). These interactions are between and among family, peers, and schools. Relations among students, teachers, and administrators matter. There is no doubt that teachers and school officials can influence students' relationships with their peers and their perceptions of the school environment (Lee, 2009). One study found that teachers' positive involvement in their students' academic and social lives significantly decreased the degree to which students feel unsafe in their school (Hong & Eamon, 2011). It is also important to note that students are more willing to seek help from teachers or school officials when teachers intervene in students' peer conflicts (Aceves et al., 2009). Finally, in a recent multilevel study of over 4,000 middle school students across 36 schools students reported less bullying, physical fighting, victimization, and greater willingness to intervene in schools where staff reported that they felt supported by their administration to address bullying in their classrooms and schools (Espelage, Polanin, & Low, 2014).

Another example of a mesosystem structure is the influence of family functioning on peer friendship selection or the interaction between family characteristics and individual attributes. For example, a longitudinal study of middle school youth found that parental monitoring buffered the effects of community violence exposure on bully perpetration and victimization through reduced involvement in deviant behavior (Low & Espelage, 2014). In contrast, impulsivity exacerbated the effects of community violence exposure on bully perpetration by elevating involvement in deviant behavior. This study demonstrates the utility of the ecology model where multiple systems influence each other.

SCHOOL-BASED BULLYING PREVENTION APPROACHES

Recognizing that the majority of the bully prevention programs have not been rigorously evaluated, what data are available indicate that the efficacy of school violence and bullying prevention programs have varied across countries and contexts (Espelage, 2012; Ttofi & Farrington, 2011). The most comprehensive meta-analysis that applied the Campbell Systematic Review procedures included a review of 44 rigorous program evaluations and randomized clinical trials (RCTs; Ttofi & Farrington, 2011). Almost two-thirds of the studies were conducted outside the

United States or Canada, and one-third of the programs were based on the Olweus Bully Prevention Program (Limber, Riese, Snyder, & Olweus, 2015; Olweus, 2003). Farrington & Ttofi, (2011) found that the programs, on average, were associated with a 20–23% decrease in perpetration of bullying and a 17–20% decrease in victimization (Farrington & Ttofi, 2011); however, smaller effect sizes were found for RCT designs in comparison to non-RCT designs. Specific program elements that were associated with decreases in *bully perpetration* included (Farrington & Ttofi, 2011) parent training/meetings, improved playground supervision, disciplinary methods, classroom management, teacher training, classroom rules, whole-school antibullying policy, school conferences, information for parents, and cooperative group work (all these involve multiple school-based professionals). Furthermore, number of elements and the duration and intensity of the program for teachers and children were significantly associated with a decrease in bullying, and the programs worked best with older children (aged 11 and older), and in studies in Norway and Europe in general. Of note, programs inspired by the work of Dan Olweus (see next section) had the highest effect sizes.

Decreases in *victimization* were associated with the following special program elements: disciplinary methods, parent training/meetings, use of videos, and cooperative group work. In addition, the duration and intensity of the program for children and teachers were significantly associated with a decrease in victimization. Work with peers (e.g., peer mentoring, peer mediation) was associated with a decrease in victimization (e.g., Farrington & Ttofi, 2011).

Next, we highlight three programs that worked best across this meta-analysis.

Olweus Bully Prevention Program

The Olweus Bully Prevention Program (OBPP) was first implemented in Norway schools and has the goal of reducing existing bullying concerns, preventing the development of new incidents of bullying, and improving peer relationships at school (Limber et al., 2015). This is accomplished with the restructuring of the school environment so as to reduce opportunities and rewards for bullying behavior, shift social norms to create expectations of inclusion and civility, and build a sense of community among students and adults in the school (Limber et al., 2015). OBPP is based on the need for adults in the school environment to show warmth and positive interests and to be involved with the students, to set firm limits, to consistently use nonhostile negative consequences when rules are broken, and to function as authorities and positive role models (Olweus & Limber, 2010). Typically the components of the program are implemented across the whole school and include specific interventions that are directed at the school, classroom, individual, and community levels (Olweus & Limber, 2010).

There have been many evaluations of the OBPP conducted in many different countries. The studies have produced mixed results, including both positive and negative (null) results, but it is unclear whether the implementation of the OBPP in all of these studies was consistent with the original OBPP (Olweus & Limber, 2010).

The Peaceful Schools Project

The Peaceful Schools Project, developed in 2000 (Twemlow et al., 2001), is a philosophy, rather than a program (Twemlow, Fonagy, & Sacco, 2004). The goals are consistent with the SEL framework by the inclusion of developing healthy relationships between all stakeholders in the educational setting and altering the school climate in permanent and meaningful ways. The project includes five main components. First, schools embark on a positive climate campaign that includes counselor-led discussions and the creation of posters that help alter the language and the thinking of everyone in the school (i.e., "Back off, bullies!" or "Stop bullying now!"). All stakeholders in the school are flooded with an awareness of the bullying dynamic, and bullying is described as a social relationship problem. Second, teachers are fully supported in classroom management techniques and are taught specific techniques to diffuse disruptive behavior from a relational perspective rather than from a punishment perspective. Third, peer and adult mentors are used to help everyone in the school resolve problems without blame. These adult mentors are particularly important during times when adult supervision is minimal (i.e., in hallways and on the playground). The fourth component is called the "gentle warrior physical education program." It uses a combination of role-playing, relaxation, and defensive martial arts techniques to help students develop strategies to protect themselves and others. These are essentially confidence-building skills that support positive coping. Fifth, reflection time is included in the school schedule each day. Teachers and students talk for at least 10 minutes at the end of the day about bully, victim, and bystander behaviors. By engaging in this dialogue, language and thinking about bullying behaviors can be subtly altered (Twemlow, Fonagy, & Sacco, 2005). In an RCT, elementary students whose schools participated in the Peaceful Schools Project had higher achievement scores than students from schools without the program; there were also significant reductions in suspensions for acting out behavior in the treatment schools, whereas the comparison schools had a slight increase in suspensions for problem behavior (Fonagy et al., 2009).

KiVa National Antibullying Programme in Finland

The KiVa program, developed in Finland for elementary through high school students, is a universal school-based program that includes addressing bullying at school by working with teachers, parents, families, community leaders, and students. Teacher training, student lessons, and virtual learning environments are all crucial aspects of this multicomponent program (Salmivalli, Poskiparta, Tikka, & Pöyhönen, 2009; Salmivalli, Pöyhönen, & Kaukiainen, 2009). Teachers use a manual for classroom instruction, which is supplemented by an antibullying computer game for primary school children and an Internet forum, KiVa Street, for secondary school students. On KiVa Street, students can access information pertaining to bullying or watch a short film about bullying. Both are designed to motivate students to apply learned skills. Early data show significant decreases in self-reported bullying and self- and peer-reported victimization in 4th- to 6th-graders (Kärnä et al., 2011) and increases in empathy and antibullying attitudes.

Social–Emotional Learning Programs

School-based violence prevention programs that facilitate social and emotional learning skills, address interpersonal conflict, and teach emotion management have shown promise in reducing youth violence and disruptive behaviors in classrooms (Wilson & Lipsey, 2007). This is especially the case for programs that target peer violence in a coordinated fashion across different microcontexts of the school ecology (e.g., individual, classroom, school, community; Steps to Respect; Brown, Low, Smith, & Haggerty, 2011). Many of these social–emotional and social–cognitive intervention programs target risk and protective factors that have consistently been associated with aggression, bullying, and victimization in cross-sectional and longitudinal studies (Basile, Espelage, Rivers, McMahon, & Simon, 2009; Espelage, Basile, & Hamburger, 2012; Espelage, Holt, & Henkel, 2003), including anger, empathy, perspective-taking, respect for diversity, attitudes supportive of aggression, coping, intentions to intervene to help others, and communication and problem-solving skills.

SEL programs can be quite diverse in format and intensity, but all have a goal of promoting youth development by building competencies and fostering skills that enable students to flexibly respond to demands and opportunities in their environments (Durlak, Weissberg, Dymnicki, Taylor, & Schellinger, 2011). SEL approaches focus on students' acquiring skills that allow them to recognize and manage emotions, take the perspectives of others, establish and maintain positive relationships and handle interpersonal conflicts appropriately (Elias et al., 1997). SEL programs offer schools, after-school programs, and youth community centers a research-based approach to building skills and promoting positive individual and peer attitudes that can contribute to the prevention of bullying. The theory of reasoned action, problem behavior theory, and social–cognitive theory (e.g., Greenberg et al., 2003; Hawkins et al., 2004).

School-based SEL programs developed to prevent school violence, including bullying, are predicated on the belief that academic skills are intrinsically linked to children's ability to manage emotions, regulate emotions, and to communicate and problem-solve challenges and interpersonal conflicts (Durlak et al., 2011). Within the SEL framework there are five interrelated skill areas: self-awareness, social awareness, self-management and organization, responsible problem-solving, and relationship management. Within each area, there are specific competencies supported by research and practice as essential for effective social–emotional functioning, including emotion recognition, stress-management, empathy, problem-solving, or decision-making skills (Elias, 2003; Elias et al., 1997). Self-regulated learning is both directly and indirectly targeted in these programs. As students are better able to control their feelings, thoughts, and actions, especially under emotional demands, academic learning is optimized. Furthermore, exercises and opportunities to practice these skills and competences differ in their level of cognitive-emotional complexity across development in order to ensure that SEL skills are sustainable. SEL programs use social skill instruction to address behavior, discipline, safety, and academics to help youth become self-aware, manage their emotions, build social skills (empathy, perspective-taking, respect for diversity), build friendship skills, and make positive decisions (Zins et al., 2004).

Research support for SEL programs is growing. A recent meta-analysis including more than 213 SEL-based programs found that if a school implements a high-quality SEL curriculum, that school can expect better student behavior and test scores that are 11 percentile points higher than schools with no SEL programming (Durlak et al., 2011). Schools elect to implement these programs because of the gains that schools see in achievement and prosocial behavior. Students exposed to SEL activities feel safer and more connected to school and academics and build work habits in addition to social skills, and youth and teachers build strong relationships (Zins et al., 2004).

In summary, SEL approaches to prevention are showing promise in reducing aggression and promoting prosocial behavior (Brown et al., 2011; Espelage, Low, Polanin, & Brown, 2013; Frey et al., 2005). This success is largely because SEL school-based programs parallel the hallmarks of the prevention science framework. First, these programs draw from the scientific literature on the etiological underpinnings of aggression, bullying, school violence, and other problematic behaviors among children and adolescents (Merrell, 2010). Second, risk (e.g., anger, impulse control) and promotive (e.g., empathy, communication skills) factors are identified from the etiological literature and targeted through direct instruction of skills and opportunities to use skills in different contexts. Third, in relation to bystander intervention, these programs include discussions and content about the barriers or challenges (e.g., fear of being targeted, losing friends) that youth face when they attempt to intervene on behalf of a victim of aggression.

Several RCTs of bullying prevention programs (based on SEL framework) have attended to the rigorous evaluation of the intervention effects (Brown et al., 2011; Espelage et al., 2013), which is an additional hallmark of prevention science. RCTs of SEL programs have identified implementation as a critical component of producing reductions in aggression and increases in prosocial behavior. However, in order to have public health effects, we must move beyond efficacy to focus on adoption, implementation, and sustainability. As schools are increasingly pressed to find time in the day to address psychosocial issues, SEL programs that prevent victimization and its correlates (e.g., social rejection) and also simultaneously improve academic engagement should be rigorously evaluated to make convincing arguments to educators and school administrators that the use of these resources will produce noticeable benefits.

PROGRAM-BASED CASE STUDY

Several school-based programs with strong efficacy data are now highlighted. These represent just a small sample of programs or approaches that are available to schools and communities (see www.casel.org for reviews of SEL programming) to help students reduce their chances of being victims of bullying and to help establish more positive and productive social interactions in the school setting.

CASE STUDY: EVIDENCE-BASED SCHOOL-BASED SEL PROGRAMS

Steps to Respect: A Bullying Prevention Program

Steps to Respect: A Bullying Prevention Program© is designed to help students build supportive relationships with one another (STR; Committee for Children, 2001). The Steps to Respect program uses a whole-school approach to bullying prevention by addressing factors at the staff, peer group, and individual levels. Intervening at multiple levels is the most effective way to reduce school bullying considering the complex origins, forms, and maintenance factors associated with bullying. Empirical support has shown reductions in playground bullying, acceptance of bullying behavior, and argumentative behavior. At the same time, it has demonstrated increases in agreeable interactions and perceived adult responsiveness in comparison with control schools (Frey et al., 2005). More recently, it has demonstrated reductions in physical perpetration, destructive bystander behavior, and increases in bystander behavior and positive social school climate (Brown et al., 2011), especially among schools with high student engagement in the program (Low, Van Ryzin, Brown, Smith, & Haggerty, 2013) Steps to Respect relies heavily on adults to deliver scripted training from a curriculum and to continually emphasize those lessons throughout the school year.

Primary bullying prevention strategies address risk factors from a systemic perspective that will influence the maximum number of students. Knowing that primary-level interventions have the potential to reach approximately 80% of students in a school encourages school officials and stakeholders to invest time and effort into these systemic efforts (Walker & Shinn, 2002). For example, the first component of the Steps to Respect program is staff training for "all adults" in the school building, emphasizing that the term includes janitors, bus drivers, mentors, receptionists, school nurses, volunteers, licensed staff, administrators, teachers, assistants, and other adults at school who are involved in the daily lives of students. Training meetings include a scripted training session that provides basic information on the Steps to Respect program, information on bullying, and training on how to receive bullying reports from students. Administrators, teachers, or counselors who will work directly with students who have been bullied or who are bullying others receive additional training.

The Steps to Respect curriculum includes lessons to increase students' social–emotional competence and positive social values. Specifically, the program addresses three general skills: First, students learn skills of perspective-taking and empathy as well as how to manage their emotions. Second, academic skills are also encouraged by incorporating themes of friendship and bullying into literature unit activities such as oral expression, writing composition, and analytical reasoning. Third, the curriculum addresses students' social values by encouraging students' sense of fairness, and attempts to instill a desire for rewarding friendships. As Frey and colleagues demonstrated (2005) a 25% reduction in playground bullying incidents, compared with a control group, and a decrease in bystanders to bullying episodes who encouraged it. Furthermore, the effects of the Steps to Respect program were most pronounced among students who were observed to do the most bullying before program implementation. Another study results included less observed victimization of all children who had previously been victimized and less destructive bystander behavior among all children who had previously been observed contributing to bullying as bystanders (Hirschstein et al., 2007). In a more recent randomized clinical trial evaluation of Steps to Respect in 33 California schools indicated that participation in a SEL bully prevention program was associated with higher social skills, reductions in aggression, and reductions in bystanders assisting the bully among elementary school children (3rd–6th–graders) (Brown et al., 2011).

Second Step: Student Success Through Prevention (Second Step–SSTP)

Second Step: Student Success Through Prevention (Second Step–SSTP; Committee for Children, 2008) is the middle school version of the K–8th-grade Second Step Program curriculum. Second Step is an SEL program that also focuses on bullying prevention, sexual harassment, bullying in dating relationships, and substance abuse prevention. The program is composed of 15 lessons at grade 6 and of 13 lessons each at grades 7 and 8. Lessons are delivered in one 50-minute or two 25-minute classroom sessions, taught weekly or semiweekly throughout the school year. Through skill building and skill practice, the program targets risk and protective factors linked to aggression, violence, and substance use. Curriculum developers also incorporated classic developmental research on risk and protective factors that address simultaneously multiple problems, reducing the need for a separate program for each concern (Hawkins, Catalano, Kosterman, Abbott, & Hill, 1999). The program targets the following risk factors: inappropriate classroom behavior (e.g., aggression and impulsivity), favorable attitudes toward problem behavior (e.g., violence, substance abuse), friends who engage in the problem behavior, early initiation of the problem behavior, peer rewards for antisocial behavior, peer rejection, and the following protective factors: social skills, empathy, school connectedness, and adoption of conventional norms about drug use.

Lessons are scripted and highly interactive, incorporating small group discussions and activities, class discussions, dyadic exercises, whole class instruction, and individual work. Delivery of the lessons is structured and supported through an accompanying DVD, which contains rich media content including topic-focused interviews with students and video demonstrations of skills. Manualized training covers not only the curriculum and its delivery, but also an introduction to child developmental stages as related to targeted skills. Lessons are skills-based, and students receive cueing, coaching, and suggestions for improvement on their performance. Lessons are supplemented by homework that reinforces the instruction, extension activities, academic integration lessons, and videos. Lessons are supplemented by "transfer of training" events in which the teacher connects the lessons to events of the day, reinforces students for displaying the skills acquired, identifies natural reinforcement when it occurs, and asks students whether they used specific skills during the day's events. The program is designed to address directly a range of bullying and violent behaviors, including physical, relational, and verbal aggression, in peer and dating relationships, as well as sexual harassment.

The curriculum targets the peer context for bullying through expanding students' awareness of the full range of bullying behaviors, increasing perspective-taking skills and empathy for students who are bullied, educating students on their influence and responsibility as bystanders, and education and practice on the appropriate, positive responses students can use as bystanders to remove peer support for bullying. Students are taught and practice a range of positive bystander behaviors from refusing to provide an audience to directly intervening to stop bullying. By decreasing both active and tacit peer support for bullying, the program is designed to change the peer context, removing the social support that is such a critical driver of bullying and other violent behavior.

Recent research suggests that this program is reducing aggression, homophobic teasing, and sexual harassment. More specifically, an RCT in 36 middle schools found that participants who received SEL instruction via Second Step (Committee for Children, 2008) were 42% less likely to report engaging in physical fights after 1 year in comparison to students in control schools (Espelage, Low, et al., 2013) after the 6th-grade curriculum (15 weeks). Furthermore, after 2 years of SEL curriculum, students in the Second Step schools were 56% less likely to report homophobic victimization and 39% less likely to report sexual violence perpetration than students in the control condition. These findings are particularly important considering the elevated risk of suicidal ideation and behaviors among youth who are targets of homophobic language, including gender-nonconforming and lesbian, gay, and bisexual youth (Espelage, Aragon, Birkett, & Koenig, 2008; Robinson & Espelage, 2012).

Promoting Alternative Thinking Strategies

The Promoting Alternative Thinking Strategies (PATHS) program, designed for children in kindergarten through sixth grade, was designated a Blueprints model program by the Office of Juvenile Justice and Delinquency Prevention (Kusche & Greenberg, 1994). The PATHS program is based on the ABCD (affective, behavioral, cognitive, dynamic) model of development and places primary importance on the developmental integration of affect and the development of emotion and cognitive understanding as they relate to social and emotional competence (Kelly, Longbottom, Potts, & Williamson, 2004). The PATHS curriculum builds from a model of development in which children's behavior and internal regulation is a function of their emotional awareness and control, their cognitive abilities, and their social skills (Curtis

& Norgate, 2007). Specifically, the PATHS model posits that during the maturational process, emotional development precedes most forms of cognitive development (Kelly et al., 2004). Following the universal prevention model, PATHS was developed to integrate into existing curricula. Goals of the program include enhancing social and emotional competence and reducing aggression. Some program components are targeted at parents, but classroom teachers, who are initially trained by PATHS project staff, deliver most of the curriculum. The PATHS framework posits that interventions are most effective when the environment promotes opportunities to use the skills learned (Curtis & Norgate, 2007) and accordingly promotes full-school implementations.

The PATHS curriculum consist of 101 lessons divided into three major units, each containing developmentally sequenced lessons to integrate and build from previous lessons (Curtis & Norgate, 2007). The units include readiness and self-control, feelings and relationships, and problem solving (Kelly et al., 2004). There is also an additional supplementary unit that contains 30 lessons. Each unit contains aspects of five themes: self-control, emotional understanding, interpersonal problem-solving skills, positive self-esteem, and improved peer communication/relationships.

Several randomized trials of PATHS have indicated positive outcomes, including a reduction in aggressive solutions to problems and increases in prosocial behaviors (Greenberg et al., 1998; Greenberg et al., 2003).

Recognizing, Understanding, Labeling, Expressing, and Regulating (RULER) Approach

RULER is a multiyear program available for kindergarten through grade 8 youth, with units that extend across the academic year (Hagelskamp, Brackett, Rivers, & Salovey, 2013). The design of RULER is based on the achievement model of emotional literacy (Rivers & Brackett, 2011) and includes the development of skills to recognize emotions in oneself and others, understand the causes and consequences of emotions, accurately label emotions, and express and regulate emotions appropriately (Hagelskamp et al., 2013). Emotional literacy is acquired through the acquisition of emotion-related knowledge and skills, learning skills in a safe and supportive environment in which the adults model RULER skills, and consistent opportunities to practice using the RULER skills, using feedback to help them become refined and automatic. RULER builds social and emotional skills by focusing on the teaching and learning of emotion-related concepts or "feeling words" and by introducing tools for leveraging emotions in the learning environment (Hagelskamp et al., 2013).

An important component of the RULER approach is the inclusion of comprehensive professional development for school leaders and teachers (Hagelskamp et al., 2013). Together, teachers and students analyze the emotional aspects of personal experiences, academic materials, and current events; evaluate how various people, characters, and historical figures feel and manage their feelings; and discuss techniques and use tools for identifying, problem solving about, and regulating their own and others' emotions (Hagelskamp et al., 2013; Rivers & Brackett, 2011).

Evaluation research shows support for distal outcomes of RULER. Students in classrooms that integrated RULER had greater academic and social achievements compared to students in comparison classrooms (Brackett, Rivers, Reyes, & Salovey, 2012). Additionally, longitudinal research has shown that RULER does have sustained impacts on socioemotional processes in the classroom and that after prolonged implementation, RULER's effects on classroom quality broadened to include positive effects on the classroom's instructional quality and organization (Hagelskamp et al., 2013).

SUMMARY

The literature reviewed here supports a multisystem approach to bullying prevention. At the most basic level, all adults in schools should participate in professional development opportunities to understand bullying, including how to recognize and intervene to support youth. In addition, staff and students should work together to gain knowledge and skills to reduce bullying and promote prosocial behaviors. But simply working with staff and students will not bring about the real changes in bullying behaviors. School staff and administration must partner with others to affect the ecology. First, schools should include parents on their school safety committees and work together to coordinate "parent nights" to involve other parents, providing transportation, babysitting, and food. Newsletters and email blasts should also be used to communicate with parents and community members. Second, many schools have partnered with community agencies and faith-based organizations to address bullying and to make sure youth and their families know where they can seek help. Some schools hold events on the topic of bullying at family recreational centers, museums, and street festivals. Third, school administrators should work closely with local media to highlight their bully prevention initiatives and to promote community involvement. This would be particularly useful during October of each year, for Bullying Awareness Month. Youth leaders should also be actively engaged in bully prevention efforts in order to create effective bystander intervention. Interventions should target students who are chronically victimized, or who bully other youth, through social–emotional approaches.

RESOURCES

A number of education-based and mental health-based professional organizations offer antibullying information and training options. Check with your respective professional association for more information about those options.

The Department of Health and Human Services provides a website rich with resources and antibullying (cyber-, etc.) intervention strategies, including Spanish-language versions. (www .stopbullying.gov).

The National Bullying Prevention Center provides a range of educational resources that can be used in school-based programs for bully prevention (www.pacer.org/bullying).

The U.S. Office of Justice offers an array of reports and resources on antiviolence programs for schools (ojp.gov/programs/yvp_ schools.htm).

The Centers for Disease Control provide a wealth of evidence-based studies, reports, and program-oriented interventions designed to address violence prevention in schools (www .cdc.gov/violenceprevention/index.html).

REFERENCES

Aceves, M. J., Hinshaw, S. P., Mendoza-Denton, R., & Page-Gould, E. (2009). Seek help from teachers or fight back? Student perceptions of teachers' actions during conflicts and responses to peer victimization. *Journal of Youth and Adolescence, 145,* 784–789.

American Educational Research Association. (2013). *Prevention of bullying in schools, colleges, and universities: Research report and recommendations.* Washington, DC: Author.

Basile, K. C., Espelage, D. L., Rivers, I., McMahon, P. M., & Simon, T. R. (2009). The theoretical and empirical links between bullying behavior and male sexual violence perpetration. *Aggression and Violent Behavior, 14*(5), 336–347.

Birkett, M., & Espelage, D. L. (2014). Homophobic name-calling, peer-groups, and masculinity: The socialization of homophobic behavior in adolescents. *Social Development.* doi:10.1111/sode.12085

Bowes, L., Maughan, B., Caspi, A., Moffitt, T. E., & Arseneault, L. (2010). Families promote emotional and behavioural resilience to bullying: evidence of an environmental effect *Journal of Child Psychology and Psychiatry, 51*(7), 809–817.

Brackett, M. A., Rivers, S. E., Reyes, M. R., & Salovey, P. (2012). Enhancing academic performance and social and emotional competence with the RULER feeling words curriculum. *Learning and Individual Differences, 22*(2), 218–224.

Bronfenbrenner, U. (1977). Toward an experimental ecology of human development. *American Psychologist, 32,* 513–531.

Bronfenbrenner, U., & Evans, G. W. (2005). Developmental science in the 21st century: Emerging questions, theoretical models, research designs and empirical findings. *Social Development, 9*(1), 115–125.

Bronfenbrenner, U., & Morris, P. A. (1998). *The ecology of developmental processes*. Hoboken, NJ: Wiley.

Brown, E. C., Low, S., Smith, B. H., & Haggerty, K. P. (2011). Outcomes from a school-randomized controlled trial of STEPS to RESPECT: A bullying prevention program. *School Psychology Review, 40*, 423–443.

Card, N., Stuckey, B., Sawalani, G., & Little, T. (2008). Direct and indirect aggression during childhood and adolescence: A meta-analytic review of gender differences, intercorrelations, and relations to maladjustment. *Child Development, 79*, 1185–1229.

Carlson, K. T. (2006). Poverty and youth violence exposure: Experiences in rural communities. *Children and Schools, 28*, 87–96.

Committee for Children. (2001). *Steps to Respect: A bullying prevention program*. Seattle, WA: Author.

Committee for Children. (2008). *Second Step: Student Success through Prevention Program*. Seattle, WA: Author.

Cook, C. R., Williams, K. R., Guerra, N. G., Kim, T. E., & Sadek, S. (2010). Predictors of bullying and victimization in childhood and adolescence: A meta-analytic investigation. *School Psychology Quarterly, 25*, 65–83.

Copeland, W. E., Wolke, D., Angold, A., & Costello, E. J. (2013). Adult psychiatric outcomes of bullying and being bullies by peers in childhood and adolescence. *JAMA Psychiatry, 70*(4), 419–426.

Crick, N. R., Casas, J. F., & Mosher, M. (1997). Relational and overt aggression in preschool. *Developmental Psychology, 33*, 579–588.

Crockett, D. (2003). Critical issues children face in the 2000s. *School Psychology Quarterly, 18*(4), 446–453. doi:http://dx.doi.org/10.1521/scpq.18.4.446.26997

Curtis, C., & Norgate, R. (2007). An evaluation of the promoting alternative thinking strategies curriculum at key stage 1. *Educational Psychology in Practice, 23*, 33–44. doi:10.1080/02667360601154717

Durlak, J. A., Weissberg, R. P., Dymnicki, A. B., Taylor, R. D., & Schellinger, K. B. (2011). The impact of enhancing students' social and emotional learning: A meta-analysis of school-based universal interventions. *Child Development, 82*, 405–432.

Eaton, D., Kann, L., Kinchen, S., Shanklin, S., Flint, K. H., Hawkins, J., . . . Wechsler, H. (2012). Youth Risk Behavior Surveillance—United States, 2011. *Morbidity and Mortality Weekly Report, 61*(SS-4), 1–162.

Eisenberg, M. E., & Resnick, M. D. (2006). Suicidality among gay, lesbian and bisexual youth: The role of protective factors. *Journal of Adolescent Health, 39*(5), 662–668.

Elias, M. J. (2003). Enhancing school-based prevention and youth development through coordinated social, emotional, and academic learning. *American Psychologist, 58*(6-7), 466.

Elias, M. J., Zins, J. E., Weissberg, K. S., Greenberg, M. T., Haynes, M., Kessler, R., . . . Shriver, T. P. (1997). *Promoting social and emotional learning: Guidelines for educators*. Alexandria, VA: Association for Supervision and Curriculum Development.

Espelage, D. L. (2012). Bullying prevention: A research dialogue with Dorothy Espelage. *Prevention Researcher, 19*(3), 17–19.

Espelage, D. L., Aragon, S. R., Birkett, M., & Koenig, B. W. (2008). Homophobic teasing, psychological outcomes, and sexual orientation among high school students: What influences do parents and schools have? *School Psychology Review, 37,* 202–216.

Espelage, D. L., Basile, K. C., & Hamburger, M. E. (2012). Bullying experiences and co-occurring sexual violence perpetration among middle school students: Shared and unique risk factors. *Journal of Adolescent Health, 50,* 60–65.

Espelage, D. L., Basile, K., Low, S., Anderson, C., & De La Rue, L. (2014). Bullying, sexual harassment, and teen dating violence across middle and high school. Paper to be presented at the Annual Meeting of the Society for Prevention Research.

Espelage, D. L., Bosworth, K., & Simon, T. R. (2000). Examining the social context of bullying behaviors in early adolescence. *Journal of Counseling and Development, 78,* 326–333.

Espelage, D. L. & De La Rue, L. (2013). Examining predictors of bullying and sexual violence perpetration among middle school female students. In Russell, B. (Ed), *Perceptions of female offenders: How stereotypes and social norms affect criminal justice responses* (pp. 25–46). New York: Springer.

Espelage, D. L., Green, H. D., & Polanin, J. (2012). Willingness to intervene in bullying episodes among middle school students: Individual and peer-group influences. *Journal of Early Adolescence, 32,* 776–801.

Espelage, D. L., & Holt, M. K. (2013). Suicidal ideation and school bullying experiences after controlling for depression and delinquency. *Journal of Adolescent Health, 53*(1), S27–S31.

Espelage, D. L., Holt, M. K., & Henkel, R. R. (2003). Examination of peer-group contextual effects on aggression during early adolescence. *Child Development, 74,* 205–220.

Espelage, D. L., Low, S., Polanin, J., & Brown, E. (2013). The impact of a middle-school program to reduce aggression, victimization, and sexual violence. *Journal of Adolescent Health, 53*(2) 180–186.

Espelage, D. L., Low, S., Rao, M. A., Hong, J. S., & Little, T. (2013). Family violence, bullying, fighting, and substance use among adolescents: A longitudinal transactional model. *Journal of Research on Adolescence.* Online first.

Espelage, D. L., Polanin, J., & Low, S. (2014). Teacher and staff perceptions of school environment as predictors of student aggression, victimization, and willingness to intervene in bullying situations. *School Psychology Quarterly, 29*(3), 387–305. http://dx.doi.org/10.1037/spq0000072

Fanti, K. A., & Kimonis, E. R. (2013). Dimensions of juvenile psychopathy distinguish "bullies," "bully-victims," and "victims." *Psychology of Violence, 3*(4), 396–409. doi:http://dx.doi.org/10.1037/a0033951

Faris, R., & Felmlee, D. (2011) Status struggles: Network centrality and gender segregation in same- and cross-gender aggression. *American Sociological Review, 76,* 48–73.

Farrington, D. P., & Ttofi, M. M. (2011). Bullying as a predictor of offending, violence and later life outcomes. *Criminal Behaviour and Mental Health, 21*(2), 90–98.

Fekkes, M., Pijpers, F. I. M., Fredriks, A. M., Vogels, T., & Verloove-Vanhorick, S. P. (2005). Do bullied children get ill, or do ill children get bullied? A prospective cohort study on the relationship between bullying and health-related symptoms. *Pediatrics, 117,* 1568–1574.

Fonagy, P., Twemlow, S., Vernberg, E., Mize, J., Dill, E., Little, T., & Sargent, A. J. (2009). A cluster randomized controlled trial of a child-focused psychiatric consultation and a school systems-focused intervention to reduce aggression. *Journal of Child Psychology and Psychiatry, 50*(5), 607–616.

Frey, K. S., Hirschstein, M. K., Snell, J. L., Edstrom, L.V., MacKenzie, E. P., & Broderick, C. J. (2005). Reducing playground bullying and supporting beliefs: An experimental trial of the Steps to Respect program. *Developmental Psychology, 41*, 479–491. doi:10.1037/0012-1649.41.3.479

Georgiou, S. N., & Fanti, K. A. (2010). A transactional model of bullying and victimization. *Social Psychology of Education, 13*(3), 295–311.

Gini, G., Albiero, P., Benelli, B., & Altoe, G. (2007). Does empathy predict adolescents' bullying and defending behavior? *Aggressive Behavior, 33*, 467–476. doi:10.1002/ab.20204

Gini, G., & Pozzoli, T. (2009). Association between bullying and psychosomatic problems: A meta-analysis. *Pediatrics, 123*, 1059–1065. doi:10.1542/peds.2008-1215

Gladden, R. M., Vivolo-Kantor, A. M., Hamburger, M. E., & Lumpkin, C. D. (2014). Bullying surveillance among youths: Uniform definitions for public health and recommended data elements, version 1.0. Atlanta, GA: National Center for Injury Prevention and Control, Centers for Disease Control and Prevention, and U.S. Department of Education.

Glew, G. M., Fan, M. Y., Katon, W., & Rivara, F. P. (2008). Bullying and school safety. *The Journal of Pediatrics, 152*, 123–128.

Greenberg, M. T., Weissberg, R. P., O'Brien, M. U., Zins, J. E., Fredericks, L., Resnik, H., & Elias, M. J. (2003). Enhancing school-based prevention and youth development through coordinated social, emotional, and academic learning. *American Psychologist, 58*, 466–474.

Hagelskamp, C., Brackett, M. A., Rivers, S. E., & Salovey, P. (2013). Improving classroom quality with the RULER approach to social and emotional learning: Proximal and distal outcomes. *American Journal of Community Psychology, 51*, 530–543. doi:10.1007/s10464-013-9570-x

Hawkins, J., Catalano, R. F., Kosterman, R., Abbott, R., & Hill, K. (1999). Preventing adolescent health-risk behaviors by strengthening protection during childhood. *Archives of Pediatrics and Adolescent Medicine, 15*(3), 226–234.

Hawkins, J. D., Smith, B. H., & Catalano, R. F. (2004). Social development and social and emotional learning. In J. E. Zins, R. P. Weissberg, M. C. Wang, & H. J. Walberg (Eds.), *Building academic success on social and emotional learning: What does the research say?* (pp. 135–150). New York, NY: Teachers College Press.

Hemphill, S. A., Kotevski, A., Herrenkohl, T. I., Bond, L., Kim, M. J., Toumbouro, J. W., & Catalano, R. F. (2011). Longitudinal consequences of adolescent bullying perpetration and victimisation: A study of students in Victoria, Australia. *Criminal Behaviour and Mental Health, 21*, 107–116.

Herba, C. M., Ferdinand, R. F., Stijnen, T., Veenstra, R., Oldehinkel, A. J., Ormel, J., & Verhulst, F. C. (2008). Victimisation and suicide ideation in the TRAILS study: Specific vulnerabilities of victims. *Journal of Child Psychiatry and Psychology, 49*, 867–876.

Hirschstein, M. K., Edstrom, L. V. S., Frey, K. S., Snell, J. L., & MacKenzie, E. P. (2007). Walking the talk in bullying prevention: Teacher implementation variables related to initial impact of the Steps to Respect programme. *School Psychology Review, 36*, 3–21.

Holt, M. K., & Espelage, D. L. (2007). Perceived social support among bullies, victims, and bully–victims. *Journal of Youth and Adolescence, 36*, 984–994.

Hong, J. S., & Eamon, M. K. (2011). Students' perceptions of unsafe schools: An ecological systems analysis. *Journal of Child and Family Studies, 21*(3), 428–438.

Hong, J. S., & Espelage, D. L. (2012). A review of research on bullying and peervictimization in school: An ecological systems analysis. *Aggression and Violent Behavior, 17*, 311–312.

Juvonen, J., Nishina, A., & Graham, S. (2000). Peer harassment, psychological adjustment, and school functioning in early adolescence. *Journal of Educational Psychology, 92*, 349–359.

Juvonen, J., Wang, Y., & Espinoza, G. (2011). Bullying experiences and compromised academic performance across middle school grades. *Journal of Early Adolescence, 31*, 152–173.

Kaltiala-Heino, R., Rimpela, M., Marttunen, M., Rimpela, A., & Rantanen, P. (1999). Bullying, depression, and suicidal ideation in Finnish adolescents. *British Medical Journal, 319*, 348–351.

Kaminski, J. W., & Fang, X. (2009). Victimization by peers and adolescent suicide in three U.S. samples. *Journal of Pediatrics, 155*, 638–688.

Kärnä, A., Voeten, M., Little, T. D., Poskiparta, E., Kaljonen, A., & Salmivalli, A. (2011). A large-scale evaluation of the KiVa Antibullying Program: Grades 4-6. *Child Development, 82*, 311–330.

Kelly, B., Longbottom, J., Potts, F., & Williamsom, J. (2004). Applying emotional intelligence: Exploring the promoting alterative thinking strategies. *Educational Psychology in Practice, 20*, 221–240. doi:10.1080/0266736042000251808

Kim, M. J., Catalano, R. F., Haggerty, K. P., & Abbott, R. D. (2011). Bullying at elementary school and problem behaviour in young adulthood: A study of bullying, violence and substance use from age 11 to age 21. *Criminal Behaviour and Mental Health, 21*(2), 136–144.

Kim, Y. S., & Leventhal, B. (2008). Bullying and suicide: A review. *International Journal of Adolescent Medicine and Health, 20*(2), 133–154.

Klomek, A., Marrocco, F., Kleinman, M., Schonfeld, I. S., & Gould, M. S. (2007). Bullying, depression, and suicidality in adolescents. *Journal of American Academy of Child and Adolescent Psychology, 46*, 40–49.

Klomek, A. B., Sourander, A., Niemela, S., Kumpulainen, K., Piha, J., Tamminen, T., Almqvist, F., & Gould, M. S. (2009). Childhood bullying behaviors as a risk for suicide attempts and completed suicides: A population-based birth cohort study. *Journal of American Academy of Child and Adolescence Psychology, 48*, 254–261.

Kumpulainen, K., Räsänen, E., & Puura, K. (2001). Psychiatric disorders and the use of mental health services among children involved in bullying. *Aggressive Behavior, 27*, 102–110.

Kusche, C. A., & Greenberg, M. T. (1994). *The PATHS curriculum.* South Deerfield, MA: Channing-Bete.

Laukkanen, E., Honkalampi, K., Hintikka, J., Hintikka, U., & Lehtonen, J. (2005). Suicidal ideation among help-seeking adolescents. *Archives of Suicide Research, 9*, 45–55.

Lee, C. H. (2009). Personal and interpersonal correlates of bullying behaviors among Korean middle school students. *Journal of Interpersonal Violence, 25*, 152–176.

Li, X., Feigelman, S., & Stanton, B. (2000). Perceived parental monitoring and health risk behaviors among urban low-income African-American children and adolescents. *Journal of Adolescent Health, 27*(1), 43–48.

Limber, S. P., Riese, J., Snyder, M. J., & Olweus, D. (2015). The Olweus Bullying Prevention Program: Efforts to address risks associated with suicide and suicide-related behaviors. In P. Goldblum, D. L. Espelage, J. Chu, & B. Bongar (Eds.), *The challenge of youth suicide and bullying*. New York, NY: Oxford University Press.

Low, S., & Espelage, D. L. (2013). Differentiating cyber bullying perpetration from other forms of peer aggression: Commonalities across race, individual, and family predictors. *Psychology of Violence, 3*, 39–52.

Low, S., & Espelage, D. L. (2014). Conduits from community violence exposure to bullying and victimization: Contributions of parental monitoring, impulsivity and deviancy. *Journal of Counseling Psychology, 61*(2), 221–231. doi:10.1037/a0035207

Low, S., van Ryzin, M. J., Brown, E. C., Smith, B. H., & Haggerty, K. P. (2013). Engagement matters: Lessons from assessing classroom implementation of steps to respect: A bullying prevention program over a one-year period. *Prevention Science, 15*(2), 165–176.

Merrell, K. W. (2010). Linking prevention science and social and emotional learning: The Oregon Resiliency project. *Psychology in the Schools, 47*(1), 55–70.

Miller, S., Williams, J., Cutbush, S., Gibbs, D., Clinton-Sherrod, M., & Jones, S. (2013). Dating violence, bullying, and sexual harassment: Longitudinal profiles and transitions over time. *Journal of Youth and Adolescence, 42*(4), 607–618.

Nakamoto, J., & Schwartz, D. (2010). Is peer victimization associated with academic achievement? A meta-analytic review. *Social Development, 19*(2), 221–242.

Nansel, T. R., Overpeck, M., Pilla, R. S., Ruan, W., Simons-Morton, B., & Scheidt, P. (2001). Bullying behaviors among U.S. youth: Prevalence and association with psychosocial adjustment. *Journal of the American Medical Association, 285*, 2094–2100.

Neal, J. W. (2007). Why social networks matter: A structural approach to the study of relational forms of aggression in middle childhood and adolescence. *Child and Youth Care Forum, 36*, 195–211.

Olweus, D. (1993). *Bullying at school: What we know and what we can do.* Oxford, UK: Blackwell.

Olweus, D. (2010). Understanding and researching bullying: Some critical issues. In S. R. Jimerson, S. M. Swearer, & D. L. Espelage (Eds.), *Handbook of bullying in schools: An international perspective* (pp. 9–34). New York, NY: Routledge.

Olweus, D., & Limber, S. (2010). Olweus Bully Prevention Program. In S. Jimerson, S. Swearer, & D. L. Espelage (Eds.), *International handbook of bullying*. New York, NY: Routledge.

Peguero, A. A. (2009). Victimizing the children of immigrants: Latino and Asian American student victimization. *Youth and Society, 41*, 186–208.

Polanin, J., Espelage, D. L., & Pigott, T. D. (2012). A meta-analysis of school-based bullying prevention programs' effects on bystander intervention behavior and empathy attitude. *School Psychology Review, 41* , 47–65.

Poteat, P., & Rivers, I. (2014). Suicide ideation among sexual minority youth: The effects of bullying and possible protective factors. In P. Goldblum, D. L. Espelage, R. Bonger, & J. Chu (Eds.), *Youth suicide and bullying: Challenges and strategies for prevention and intervention.* New York, NY: Oxford University Press.

Pozzoli, T., & Gini, G. (2010). Active defending and passive bystanding behavior in bullying: The role of personal characteristics and perceived pressure. *Journal of Abnormal Child Psychology, 38*(6), 815–827.

Puhl, R. M., Peterson, J. L., & Luedicke, J. (2013). Strategies to address weight-based victimization: Youths' preferred support interventions from classmates, teachers, and parents. *Journal of Youth and Adolescence, 42*(3), 315–327. doi:http://dx.doi.org/10.1007/s10964-012-9849-5

Qin, D. B., Way, N., & Rana, M. (2008). The "model minority" and their discontent: Examining peer discrimination and harassment of Chinese American immigrant youth. In H. Yoshikawa & N. Way (Eds.), *Beyond the family: Contexts of immigrant children's development* (pp. 27–42). Hoboken, NJ: Jossey-Bass.

Remafedi, G., French, S., Story, M., Resnick, M. D., & Blum, R. (1998). The relationship between suicide risk and sexual orientation: Results of a population-based study. *American Journal of Public Health, 88,* 57–60. doi:10.2105/AJPH.88.1.57

Rigby, K., & Slee, P. (1999). Suicidal ideation among adolescent school children, involvement in bully–victim problems and perceived social support. *Suicide and Life-Threatening Behavior, 29,* 119–130.

Rivers, S. E., & Brackett, M. A. (2011). Achieving standards in the English language arts (and more) using the RULER Approach to social and emotional learning. *Reading & Writing Quarterly, 27(1/2),* 75–100. doi:10.1080/10573569.2011.532715

Robers, S., Kemp, J., & Truman, J. (2013). Indicators of school crime and safety: 2012. NCES 2013-036/NCJ 241446. *National Center for Education Statistics.*

Robinson, J. P. & Espelage, D. L. (2011). Inequities in educational and psychological outcomes between LGBTQ and straight students in middle and high school. *Educational Researcher, 40,* 315–330.

Robinson, J. P., & Espelage, D. L. (2012). Bullying explains only part of LGBTQ-heterosexual risk disparities: Implications for policy and practice. *Educational Researcher, 41*(8), 309–319. doi: 10.3102/0013189X12457023

Rodkin, P. C., & Berger, C. (2008). Who bullies whom? Social status asymmetries by victim gender. *International Journal of Behavioral Development, 32,* 473–485.

Rodkin, P. C., Espelage, D. L., & Hanish, L. D. (under review). A relational perspective on the social ecology of bullying. *American Psychologist.*

Rose, C. A., Monda-Amaya, L. E., & Espelage, D. L. (2011). Bullying perpetration and victimization in special education: A review of the literature. *Remedial and Special Education, 32,* 114–130.

Russell, S. T., & Toomey, R. B. (2012). Men's sexual orientation and suicide: Evidence for US adolescent-specific risk. *Social Science & Medicine, 74*(4), 523–529.

Salmivalli, C. (2010). Bullying and the peer group: A review. *Aggression and Violent Behavior, 15,* 112–120.

Salmivalli, C., Poskiparta, E., Tikka, A., & Pöyhönen, V. (2009). *KiVa: Teacher's guide, unit 1* (Research into Practice Publication Series, No. 2). Turku, Finland: University of Turka, Psychology Department.

Salmivalli, C., Pöyhönen, V., & Kaukiainen, A. (2009). *KiVa: Teacher's guide, unit 2* (Research into Practice Publication Series, No. 3). Turku, Finland: University of Turka, Psychology Department.

Schwartz, D., Gorman, A. H., Dodge, K. A., Pettit, G. S., & Bates, J. E. (2008). Friendships with peers who are low or high in aggression as moderators of the link between peer victimization and declines in academic functioning. *Journal of Abnormal Child Psychology, 36*(5), 719–730.

Schwartz, D., Gorman, A. H., Nakamoto, J., & Toblin, R. L. (2005). Victimization in the peer group and children's academic functioning. *Journal of Educational Psychology, 97*(3), 425.

Ttofi, M. M., Farrington, D. P., Lösel, F., & Loebel, R. (2011). Do the victims of school bullies tend to become depressed later in life? A systematic review and meta-analysis of longitudinal studies. *Journal of Aggression Conflict and Peace Research, 3,* 63–73. doi:10.1108/17596591111132873

Twemlow, S., Fonagy, P., & Sacco, F. (2004). The role of the bystander in the social architecture of bullying and violence in schools and communities. *Annals of New York Academy of Sciences, 1036,* 215–232.

Twemlow, S., Fonagy, P., & Sacco F. (2005). A developmental approach to mentalizing communities: I. The Peaceful Schools experiment. *Bulletin of the Menninger Clinic, 69,* 265–281. doi:10.1521/bumc.2005.69.4.265

Twemlow, S. W., Fonagy, P., Sacco, F. C., Gies, M., Evans, R., & Ewbank, R. (2001). Creating a peaceful school learning environment: A controlled study of an elementary school intervention to reduce violence. *American Journal of Psychiatry, 158,* 808–810.

Varjas, K., Henrich, C. C., & Meyers, J. (2009). Urban middle school students' perceptions of bullying, cyberbullying, and school safety. *Journal of School Violence, 8,* 159–176.

Walker, H. M., & Shinn, M. R. (2002). Structuring school-based interventions to achieve integrated primary, secondary, and tertiary prevention goals for safe and effective schools. In M. R. Shinn, G. Stoner, & H. M. Walker (Eds.), *Interventions for academic and behavior problems: Preventive and remedial approaches* (pp. 1–21). Silver Spring, MD: National Association of School Psychologists.

Wilson, S. J., & Lipsey, M. W. (2007). School-based interventions for aggressive and disruptive behavior: Update of a meta-analysis. *American Journal of Preventive Medicine, 33,* S130–S143.

Ybarra, M., Espelage, D. L., & Mitchell, K. J. (2014). Differentiating youth who are bullied from other victims of peer-aggression: The importance of differential power and repetition. *Journal of Adolescent Health.* Online First. http://dx.doi.org/10.1016/j.jadohealth.2014.02.009

Zins, J. E., Weissberg, R. P., Wang, M. C., & Walberg, H. J. (Eds.). (2004). *Building school success through social and emotional learning.* New York, NY: Teachers College Press.

CHAPTER 11

Cyberbullying and Sexting: School Mental Health Concerns

SHERI BAUMAN

LEARNING OUTCOMES

On completion of this chapter, the reader should be able to:

- Identify the characteristics of cyberbullying and sexting
- Describe the potential mental health outcomes associated with victimization by cyberbullying and sexting
- Create a treatment plan for a student victimized by cyberbullying and/or sexting
- Discuss systemic interventions that are necessary to mitigate the effects of the victimization

Perhaps due to the sensational media coverage of incidents of cyberbullying and sexting with tragic outcomes, the general public may believe these behaviors are epidemic among young people. One example is an MTV/Associated Press study that surveyed 14–24-year-olds (47% of whom were aged 14–17) and reported that 56% of participants had experienced "digital abuse" and about a third of participants had engaged in sexting (Kaufman, 2011). Such data, when publicized through popular media outlets, raises alarm and has fueled efforts to legislate a solution. In reality, cyberbullying is less common than traditional bullying. However, this does not mean that it is not a problem, or that it can be ignored. In recent years, the attention of researchers has turned to these problems in an attempt to provide a factual basis upon which strategies to reduce the incidence of these behaviors can be developed.

Most definitions of "cyberbullying" apply the definition of traditional bullying to the digital environment, using the three defining characteristics of intentional aggression, repetition, and power imbalance between the perpetrator and the target, and including a phrase such as "using digital technology." However, there is not yet universal agreement on this definition (Levy et al., 2012), with some scholars asserting that much of the extant research is actually measuring cyber-aggression (intentional harm inflicted via digital technology, without reference to repetition or power imbalance; see Chapters 2–5 in Bauman, Cross, and Walker, 2013, for extended discussions of definitional questions). The term *sexting* refers to the practice of transmitting sexual content via digital technology and includes images, video, and text. Sexts may be sent by the creator, the recipient, or a third party, and they become cyberbullying when the messages or images are used to inflict harm on a target by causing humiliation and embarrassment. Cyberbullying and sexting are facilitated by the rapid expansion of cell phone ownership; from 2004 to 2009, the percentage of 12-year-olds owning a cell phone increased from 18% to 58%, while for 17-year-olds the increase was from 64% to 83% in the same period (Lenhart, 2009). More recently, smartphones (those that combine features of cell phones and Internet connectivity) have gained a large proportion of users among youth. In 2013, 37% of teens owned smartphones (Madden, Lenhart, Duggan, Cortesi, & Gasser, 2013); about 25% of teens access the Internet mostly from a phone, a higher rate than adults. Note that in many states, sexual images such as those transmitted via sexting can qualify as child pornography under the law (Wolak & Finkelhor, 2011). In states without a specific sexting law, sexting can be prosecuted under existing laws related to child pornography. Because of the harsh penalties such convictions can impose, states have been considering legislation that specifically targets sexting among minors; by 2012, 19 states had adopted such laws (www.criminaldefenselawyer.com/crime-penalties/juvenile/sexting.htm).

In Florida, sexting among minors is a crime, unless the person did not solicit the image in his or her possession, did not send it to others, and took steps to report the image to an appropriate authority (www.criminaldefenselawyer.com/resources/teen-sexting-florida.htm). In Illinois in 2010, an adolescent who took a nude "selfie" had created child pornography, a class 1 felony. If a youth asks a romantic partner, also a minor, to send a nude image, he or she could be found guilty of the class 4 felony of "indecent solicitation of a child." And in Illinois, those who were convicted of these crimes must register as a sex offender. Some states are concerned that young people engaged in sexting suffer unnecessarily harsh penalties and, accordingly, are enacting legislation to treat sexting differently from other sex offenses. An Illinois law proposed in 2010 would treat most sexting violations by classifying the young person as a minor in need of supervision. A recent Vermont law exempts individuals aged 13–18 from prosecution for child pornography for a first sexting offense, and Ohio has eliminated sex offender registry requirements for youth prosecuted for sexting (Herman, 2010). The interested reader can access sexting laws by state at www.criminaldefenselawyer.com/crime-penalties/juvenile/sexting.htm#states.

This chapter reviews what is known about cyberbullying and sexting, as well as how they are linked to mental health issues in young people, and then offers suggestions for prevention and intervention strategies.

CYBERBULLYING

Several experts point to unique features of cyberbullying that may make this form of bullying more harmful than traditional physical, verbal, and relational bullying. These features include the perception of anonymity (and commensurate absence of accountability for perpetrators), the online disinhibition effect (Suler, 2004) that encourages crueler behavior than occurs in face-to-face environments, the absence of time and space limitations on the behavior, the enormous size of the potential audience, the absence of nonverbal clues to the sender's intent, and the permanence of content posted online (Bauman, 2011).

Prevalence

Although prevalence estimates vary widely across studies, recent research suggests that cyberbullying impacts millions of children and adolescents worldwide. The highest rate of victimization was reported by Juvonen and Gross (2008), who recruited a sample of 1,454 12–17-year-olds online, 72% of whom reported at least one incident in which they had been victimized digitally. Note that this figure must be interpreted cautiously: The participants were all visitors to a popular teen website and are unlikely to be representative of the general adolescent population. Wachs (2012), using a strict criterion of "once a week or more often" and a reference period of the previous year, reported 6.2% cyberbullies, 5% cybervictims, and 4.2% both cyberbullies and victims in the sample of German students in grades 5–10. In a recent U.S. study, Kowalski and Limber (2013) assessed the prevalence of cyberbullying in a sample of youth ($N = 931$; grades 6–12). Their results indicated that 10% of youth reported being cyberbullied at least once during the previous 2 months, 6% admitted to cyberbullying others during this same timeframe, and slightly more than 5% reported that they were both the target and perpetrator of cyberbullying. Hinduja and Patchin (2012) noted that their review of 35 research articles yielded an average of 24% of youth who had been cyberbullied and 17% who cyberbullied others, and Mishna, Khoury-Kassabri, Gadalla, and Daciuk (2012) found over 50% of middle-school students involved in cyberbullying. Although we are unable to give a definitive estimate of prevalence, it is clear that the problem is not trivial and that it merits the attention of researchers and practitioners.

Consequences

In addition to being prevalent and distressing to victims, cyberbullying is associated with a range of negative academic and psychosocial outcomes. That is, studies have found that cyberbullying is associated with elevated rates of depression, sadness, poor self-concept, somatic complaints, delinquent behavior, and social anxiety, school absences, and lower levels of academic achievement (Bauman & Newman, 2013; Bonnano & Hymel, 2013; Dempsey, Sulkowski, Nichols, & Storch, 2009; Gradinger, Strohmeier, Schiller, Stefanek, & Spiel, 2012; Perren, Dooley, Shaw, & Cross, 2010; Wang, Iannotti, & Nansel, 2009; Ybarra, 2004). An additional concern is that several studies have established a link between being cyberbullied and suicidal behavior (e.g., Bauman, Toomey, & Walker, 2013; Bonnano & Hymel, 2013; Litwiller & Brausch, 2013; Patchin & Hinduja, 2010; Sinclair, Bauman, Poteat, Koenig, & Russell, 2012). For example, in a population-based study of adolescents ($N = 1,963$), Patchin and Hinduja (2010) found that youth who experienced cyberbullying as either an offender or a target reported more suicidal thoughts and more suicide attempts than their peers who had not been exposed to this form of aggression. Furthermore, Bonnano and Hymel (2013) found that involvement in cyberbullying was associated with suicidal ideation, although no such association was detected for physical or social bullying. In addition, in a recent review, Parris, Varjas, Meyers, and Cutts (2012) summarized the consequences of cyberbullying by noting that externalizing behaviors and suicidal behaviors were present in higher rates among students involved in cyberbullying than among their uninvolved peers. Recent research examined the elements of cyberbullying that increase distress in targets (Kuhlmann, Pieschl, & Porsch, 2013). These researchers considered the *number of incidents*, the *status of the perpetrator* (anonymous, popular, or unpopular), the *perpetrator's motive* (intent to harm, feeling superior, seeking approval of others, retaliating, or fun) as well as the *medium* (visual or written), the *degree of publicity* (private, semi-public, or public), and the type of cyberbullying incident (harassment, denigration, outing, impersonation, or exclusion) and found that publicity (public incidents), number, and type of incidents (outing) were the most distressing to targets. The six features of cyberbullying investigated in this study could be adapted for use as part of an assessment by mental health practitioners in understanding the emotional effects of an incident.

Risk Factors

The strongest predictors of bullying others in cyberspace are being a victim of cyberbullying and being a perpetrator of traditional bullying (Bauman, 2010; Bauman & Pero, 2011; Vandenbosch & Van Cleemput, 2009). Hemphill and colleagues (2012) found that relationally bullying others in seventh grade was a predictor of cyberbullying others in ninth grade. Other studies have determined that high use of the Internet and cell phones for social communication was associated with higher rates of cybervictimization, as was willingness to disclose personal information in digital settings. As with traditional bullying, associations have been found with involvement in cyberbullying and assorted psychosocial problems (Gradinger, Strohmeier, & Spiel, 2009; Sourander et al., 2010). These researchers found that conduct and hyperactivity problems predicted being classified as either cyberbully only or cyberbully–victim, and deficits in prosocial behavior predicted being a cyberbully only. Problems with peers and emotional problems predicted cybervictim only and cyberbully–victim status. Being a cyberbully–victim was the strongest risk factor for concurrent psychosocial problems, as is the case with traditional bullying.

An interesting study examined the relations among coping strategies, cybervictimization, and health complaints (both physical and mental) in 325 year 7 (ages 11 and 12 years) students in England. In the sample, 18% reported being bullied via cell phone and 24% via the Internet. Victimization was associated with more depressive symptoms and health complaints, but coping style affected those relations so that problem-focused coping (e.g., seeking social support) was associated with fewer depressive symptoms and health complaints, whereas the reverse was true for emotion-focused coping (e.g., crying, acting out; Völlink, Bolman, Eppingbroek, & Behue, 2013). This has important implications for prevention and education.

Overlap With Traditional Bullying

A link between cyberbullying and traditional bullying has been detected, such that many youth report being victimized and bullying others in both cyber and physical settings (Dempsey, Sulkowski, Dempsey, & Storch, 2011; Li, 2007). In one study, 51% of cyberbullies reported having been victims of conventional bullying, and many of these reported using cyberbullying to retaliate against those who had bullied them in conventional settings (Ybarra & Mitchell, 2004). Similarly, Hinduja and Patchin (2007) also found that experience with conventional bullying was related to experience with cyberbullying, and Juvonen and Gross (2008) reported that 85% of those who were involved in online bullying were also involved in traditional forms of bullying. The risk of cybervictimization was almost 10 times as high for traditional victims as for nonvictims in middle school students (Holfeld & Grabe, 2012); Monks, Robinson, and Worlidge (2012) found that being a traditional bully increased the odds of being a cyberbully by almost seven times. In addition to overlap between cyber- and traditional bullying, researchers have found a significant overlap between cyberbullies and cybervictims. This overlap is captured by Mishna et al. (2012), who observed that although in traditional bullying a small proportion of youth are both bullies and victims, in cyberbullying a much larger group is so classified (25.7%). When working with a victim of cyberbullying, it would be helpful to inquire whether the person had also been victimized by traditional bullying, as well as whether he or she engaged in bullying others technologically.

However, the link between traditional and cyberbullying is not yet firmly established (Menesini & Spiel, 2012; Raskauskas & Stoltz, 2007). For example, Ybarra, Diener-West, and Leaf (2007) found that 64% of victims of cyberbullying were not bullied by conventional means. Similarly, Mishna, Saini, and Solomon (2009), in a study conducted with Canadian students ($N = 2,000$; mean age = 14.1), found that 75% of online bullies did not bully their victims using conventional means, and Smith et al. (2008) reported that victims of cyberbullying used the Internet more often than those who were not victims. Thus, cyberbullies tend to be technologically savvy and may bully others in cyberspace as opposed to physical settings.

Gender and Age Differences

Findings on gender and age differences have been mixed, with some studies finding that boys were more likely to be cyberbullies as well as to be both cyber- and traditional bullies (Calvete, Orue, Estévez, Villardón, & Padilla, 2010; Gradinger et al., 2009; Topçu, Erdur-Baker, & Çapa-Aydin, 2012). Another group of studies found that boys were more likely to be perpetrators of cyberbullying, whereas girls were more likely to be targets (Dehue, Bolman, & V″ollink, 2008; Kowalski, Morgan, & Limber, 2012; Mishna et al., 2012; Wang, Iannotti, & Nansel, 2009). Mesch (2009) reported significantly higher rates of reported online victimization by girls (61%) than boys (39%). Holfeld and Grabe (2012) found that females in middle school were more likely to be involved in cyberbullying in all roles. However, Perren and Gutzwiller-Helfenfinger (2012) found that boys were significantly more likely to be involved in traditional bullying, but not cyberbullying, and Werner, Bumpus, & Rock (2010) found no gender differences in cyber-aggression. Thus, we cannot yet make any generalizations about gender differences in cyberbullying.

Risk Factors

Researchers are now beginning to look into individual factors that are associated with involvement in cyberbullying. Several studies, each using different measures of empathy, found that cyberbullies had lower scores on the measure of empathy than those who were not engaging in this behavior (Lazarus, Barkoukis, Ourda, & Tsorbatzoudis, 2013). Moral disengagement—a cognitive process by which persons allow themselves to act in ways that contradict their moral beliefs and values—has also been implicated in cyberbullying (Pornari & Wood, 2010), but such results have not been sufficiently replicated (Lazarus et al., 2013). Lazarus and colleagues collected data from 355 Greek youths (aged 13–17) in an attempt to describe a process model of cyberbullying. Contrary to their expectations, only three social cognitive variables were significant predictors of cyberbullying intentions (social norms, prototype similarity, and situational self-efficacy). Social norms refer to the belief about the extent to which a behavior is enacted by others in a given normative group, such as one's classmates, close friends, and age-mates in the general population. Prototypes refer to the typical characteristics of a person who engages in cyberbullying, and to one's similarity to that description. The more like the prototype the participant rated him or herself, the more likely he or she was to be a cyberbully. Situational self-efficacy describes the person's self-assessed ability to resist the temptation to engage in cyberbullying in a given context. Moral disengagement was also found to predict cyberbullying intentions, whereas empathy was not. The authors suggest that empathy may have a more indirect influence via other variables, rather than a direct association.

SEXTING

Sexting has only recently become a focus of attention; the majority of studies to date have attempted to determine the prevalence of this behavior. Much of the literature has concentrated on legal issues—whether individuals who sext should be criminally prosecuted or required to register as sex offenders. Only very recently have researchers turned their attention to other aspects of this phenomenon; findings at this point are tentative. Nevertheless, sexting is a form of cyberbullying that can be particularly harmful, and mental health providers must have an understanding of how it affects youth, particular as there is evidence that engaging in sexting is associated with mental health symptoms; targets of cyberbullying were twice as likely to have received treatment from a mental health professional. Targets of cyberbullying and young people involved in sexting had higher rates of suicidal thoughts than those who were not involved, and they also had higher rates of high-risk behaviors such as using alcohol and illegal drugs and stealing or shoplifting. (MTV/AP, 2009).

Given the range of behaviors that qualify as sexting, researchers focused on 550 cases that had been referred to law enforcement agencies in order to develop a typology of "youth-produced sexual images" (Wolak & Finkelhor, 2011, p. 1). They classified the incidents as either *aggravated* or *experimental*, with aggravated incidents characterized by adult involvement, illegal or abusive behavior by minors, malicious use of images following conflicts, or using images either without knowledge of the subject or despite the objections of the subject of the images. Most incidents of cyberbullying via sexting are among these incidents. *Experimental* incidents are those that emerge from adolescent exploration of sexuality, and represent efforts to flirt, attract romantic partners, experiment with sexual activity, and gain attention. Although less aggressive in nature, this does not mean that these behaviors should be ignored: It does provide practitioners with a better understanding of the motivation behind the behavior. This typology may be useful for deciding how to handle such incidents and the underlying issues that are supporting the behavior.

Regardless of whether an incident is considered cyberbullying, sexting can also be a felony in some states, which means a person convicted of this crime could receive a prison sentence or be required to register as a sex offender for many years (Diliberto & Mattey, 2009). This applies to the person who originally sent the image as well as to the recipient and is important information for youth to understand, especially because each state has its own legislation that defines the severity (misdemeanor or felony) and consequences (incarceration and registration as a sex offender).

Prevalence

One national study of a representative sample of U.S. youth ages 12–17 concluded that approximately 4% of these adolescents had created and sent images that would be considered sexting. The study did not inquire about sexually explicit texts (Wolak & Finkelhor, 2011). Another study gathered data from 1,560 Internet users aged 10–17 via telephone survey in 2011 and found that 2.5% had been involved in the creation of nude or nearly nude images, of which only 1% were considered sexually explicit. Regarding receiving such images, those rates were 7.1% and 5.9% respectively (Mitchell, Finkelhor, Jones, & Wolak, 2012). This indicates that many images are being seen by multiple viewers. The Pew Internet and American Life Projects surveyed a nationally representative sample of youth aged 12–17 and found that 4% of teens who owned a cell phone reported sending sexually suggestive images to someone else and 15% indicated they had received such messages. This behavior was more common among 17-year-olds (30% vs. 8% for younger participants), and among those who paid for their own phones (17% compared to 3% of those who did not pay for their own phones). Another study analyzed data from a racially diverse sample of high school students in one area of Texas; in this group, 28% indicated they had sent a naked photo to someone; 31% had requested such an image from someone else. In addition, 57% had received requests to send a sext and were bothered by the requests (Temple, Paul, van den Berg, Le, McElhany, & Temple, 2012). Youth in a representative sample of Los Angeles high school students reported sexting at a rate of 15%, with 54% saying they knew someone who had sexted.

Associated Characteristics

Temple et al. (2012) reported that no gender differences were detected in sending sexts, but males were more likely to ask for images and females were more likely to have received such requests. Those who reported sexting behaviors were more likely to be dating and to have had sexual intercourse than those who did not. An important concern is that girls who engaged in sexting behaviors were also more likely to have had multiple sexual partners and to use alcohol or other drugs before engaging in sex (Temple et al., 2012). Although the participants in the study were limited geographically, they were quite diverse racially. They also suggest that sexting may become more popular in a particular location; this is consistent with the findings of Rice et al. (2012), who observed that youth whose peers reported sexting were more likely to sext themselves. In addition, Rice and colleagues also found that homosexual youth reported sexting at higher rates than their heterosexual peers. These studies suggest that sexting occurs more often in those who engage in a variety of risky sexual behaviors (e.g., multiple partners, unprotected sex). This practice becomes an additional risk for an already vulnerable group of young people.

Although studies have reported increased sexting behaviors among older adolescents, most studies have asked about lifetime prevalence of the activity rather than using a specific reference period (such as in the last few months), so the findings regarding age must be considered cautiously (Harris, Davidson, Letourneau, Paternite, & Miofsky, 2013). Similarly, although gender differences have not been found for prevalence of sexting, some evidence points to a difference in dynamics between males and females: Girls are more likely to sext in response to pressure from boys than vice versa (Harris et al., 2013).

Cases Handled by Law Enforcement

Given the potential criminal nature of this behavior, Wolak, Finkelhor, and Mitchell (2012) surveyed a national sample of law enforcement agencies by mail (87% response rate) and conducted followup telephone interviews (response rate 65%) regarding 3,477 cases of sexting handled by these agencies in 2008–2009.

Using the typology described above, about 67% of cases were classified as *aggravated* due to adult involvement (36%) or malicious or abusive behavior by a minor (31%). Arrests were made in 62% of cases involving an adult, in 36% of youth instances of aggravated behavior, and in 18% of experimental cases. Of the images, 63% were transmitted by cell phone and did not appear on the Internet.

EVIDENCE-BASED RESEARCH AND PRACTICE

There is no standard of practice for providing services to those who are victimized by cyberbullying or sexting. Some attention has been paid to prevention strategies in the literature, but even if prevention programs were successful, it is unlikely that they would completely eradicate cyberbullying and sexting. This means there will always be perpetrators and victims (and sometimes both in the same person) who will need and potentially benefit from the provided services of a mental health professional in the school. The absence of any literature on how best to assist those involved in cyberbullying is a serious omission. Nevertheless, the current chapter represents a genuine attempt to establish a best practice foundation.

A thorough evaluation of the state of Internet Safety Education (ISE) efforts provides a useful way to gauge the current status of prevention program development, considering that ISE programs are designed to teach students how to avoid being victimized (Jones, Mitchell, & Walsh, 2013). These researchers did not have good news: They concluded that the approaches currently in use and under development did not include necessary components of effective prevention education. That is, they have not used messages grounded in research, they have not focused on skill-building, nor have they provided sufficient practice for skill development or devoted sufficient time to teach the needed skills. This means that victimized students may not have the benefit of a school climate that actively discourages cyberbullying. In such cases, it is imperative that mental health professionals advocate for systemic interventions, including education about cybersafety, and for a strong school ethos that does not allow for peer mistreatment.

Although students are usually quite adept at using digital technology, they are not always aware of strategies to protect themselves from harm and of actions they can take if they are targeted. It seems that systematic instruction on cybersafety is now a necessity, beginning at the elementary level (see Bauman & Tatum, 2009, for discussion of children's websites). For example, a recent study found that 76% of third graders visit YouTube.com and 17% post video on the site. Twenty percent of those third-graders had a Facebook account, despite the minimum age requirement of 13 (Bauman, Card, Erickson, & Williams, 2012). Essential content of instruction, presented in age-appropriate manner, includes how to protect one's privacy, how to report offenses, how to respond if targeted, what is illegal in addition to being disturbing, how to preserve information for evidence, and how to behave respectfully in cyberspace. Such instruction should include realistic scenarios, so that students can receive sufficient practice in the requisite skills. Older students can be effective at presenting information to younger students; such programs also support a school ethos demonstrating that students care about others.

In addition to students, teachers and other educators need training, particularly because many are less familiar with digital technology than are their students. Aside from receiving information about cyberbullying and sexting, teachers will benefit from opportunities to practice effective responses to offenders and targets, and clear guidance about the requirements and procedures for reporting incidents. Mental health providers can be instrumental in providing consultation and assistance to teachers.

Schools should have clear policies regarding cyberbullying and sexting, developed with input from all stakeholders: administrators, education professionals, students, parents, and community members. Schools demonstrate their commitment to these policies by publicizing them conspicuously, supporting the policy with appropriate instruction, and intervening as necessary to ensure that students abide by those policies. They also involve parents in the development of policies, in educational sessions designed for parents, and engaging parents of students who are involved in these behaviors. Finally, a school ethos that promotes a positive and inclusive environment can be reinforced with visual cues (e.g., posters as well as student-created videos such as the one at www.youtube.com/watch?v=waAqJ6727Hk), student-led programs (clubs, events, peer-instruction), and continual efforts to create a school climate that includes sufficient levels of both structure and support (Cornell, 2013).

A unique feature of cyberbullying is that because many of these incidents originate off campus or on a personal electronic devices, schools are often reluctant to intervene. An extensive discussion of this issue is beyond the scope of this chapter, but mental health providers in schools need to keep in mind that they may not be able to rely on the usual disciplinary practices to sanction the offender.

Depression, Anxiety, and CBT

If victims of cyberbullying exhibit clinically significant mental disorders, it is likely that they will experience depression or anxiety or both. Cognitive-Behavioral Therapy (CBT) is widely used in treating depression in adolescents, and despite some variation in effect sizes from studies using different methodologies, CBT is considered an effective treatment for adolescent depression (Klein, Jacobs, & Reinecke, 2007; Spirito, Esposito-Smythers,

Wolff, & Uhl, 2011; Weersing & Brent, 2006). CBT has also been found to be effective with suicidal adolescents (Spirito et al., 2011), which enhances its value for victims of cyberbullying. CBT is effective in treating anxiety disorders in children and adolescents (James, James, Cowdrey, Soler, & Choke, 2013; Seligman & Ollendick, 2011) as well. Thus it appears that a cognitive-behavioral approach is a reasonable framework for providing services to students involved in cyberbullying. Doll et al. (2012) point out that common cognitive distortions in children who are bullied traditionally are variations of "This will never stop," "There's no way to stop this from happening," and "This is so terrible that I would rather die than endure this any longer" (Doll, Swearer, Collins, Chadwell, Dooley, & Chapla, 2012). It is reasonable to assume that similar cognitions would be involved in victimization by cyberbullying or sexting.

CBT is based on Beck's theory of depression, which is based on the "cognitive triad," in which the depressed person has created mental models that include three elements "I am defective, worthless, unworthy, and so on," "The word is a dangerous place where people are waiting to hurt me," and "The future does not promise any improvement in my situation." That is, the depressed person has a negative view of self, the world, and the future. A key element of CBT is changing these cognitions.

There are several manualized programs for CBT with adolescents. Modifications to ensure attention to cyberspecific aspects are needed, but the framework provides a starting point. The most common components of CBT with this developmental stage are providing information about CBT and establishing a therapeutic alliance, cognitive restructuring, behavioral activation, and emotion regulation, along with social skills training, problem-solving skills, mood monitoring, and family involvement (Kennard et al., 2009). In the case of a victim of cyberbullying, it is imperative that mental health providers be familiar with digital technology so as to establish a shared understanding of the problem and to be able to assist the client in establishing attainable goals. It is easy for adults to minimize these incidents, particularly when they do not grasp the magnitude of the harm.

Self-monitoring of mood and other symptoms should be initiated early in treatment. It is also important to work on cognitive restructuring via identifying toxic automatic thinking or underlying negative schemas, identifying cognitive distortions related to the situation, and replacing those thoughts with more rational ones. However, this is particularly difficult for victims of cyberbullying. For example, the cognition "Everyone at my school knows about this" may not be a distortion; images and messages can be forwarded to huge numbers of persons in seconds. Nor is it an exaggeration to say, "Even if the site removes this, it could easily have been copied by someone and can reappear when I am applying to colleges or for a job."

Teaching problem-solving techniques is an important component of CBT for cyberbullying victims (see Verduyn, 2011, for an overview). As noted above, problem-solving responses to victimization were found to be less damaging psychologically than emotion-focused responses; these strategies can be taught and practiced. Assisting the client, who is likely to feel helpless and hopeless, in generating viable alternatives from which to generate an action plan requires knowledge and creativity on the part of the counselor. Professionals need to have a current understanding of how some actions might work. For example, if someone has made cruel remarks about someone on Facebook, the site is highly unlikely to remove it unless it violates their policies, which are strongly supportive of free speech. A recent court case, still in appeal at the time of this writing, involved a woman who sued the owner of the website thedirty.com for posts that were false and caused her significant distress. On this website, the owner receives anonymous posts, then decides whether to post them on the public site. He also at times adds his own comments (Myers, 2013). A federal law (Communications Decency Act of 1996) protects immunity from prosecution to website owners for content posted by users but encourages sites to monitor and remove offensive material. The law has been upheld in many suits, but this case is unusual in that it has been allowed to proceed. Jurors ruled in favor of the woman who had been maligned on the site and awarded a monetary compensation. On June 16, 2014, the judgment for Jones was reversed as a matter of law under the Communications Decency Act. Regardless of the outcome, most teens (and most individuals) do not have the resources to pursue lengthy and costly legal cases. Nevertheless, it is important that they report offensive content to the site and request prompt removal of that material; students must have realistic expectations, however, of the response to their request. It is also important that in some cases, students can report an incident to police if a law has been broken. It is illegal to harass someone (in person or via technology) based on membership in a protected status group (that is, if the harassment is based on gender, religion, national origin, disability status, and in some states, sexual orientation). In egregious cases, a student (with family support) might consider legal action against the perpetrator; although also a long process, it may be more successful than suing a website owner.

For someone whose reputation has been compromised via digital means, overcoming the negative publicity is not a simple task. It could be that the person can generate positive content (perhaps with the aid of teachers and friends) to balance the negative. The student could contact college admissions personnel to find out whether including something in his or her personal essay explaining the negative content would be advisable. Developing responses (retorts) to future harassment is also necessary, and roleplaying those responses until they feel natural to the student is helpful. Thus, the interventionist's understanding of both technology and the psychosocial impact of cyberbullying is prerequisite to working with these youth. In fact, it may be advisable to incorporate technology into the treatment plan (e.g., students could be sent texts to rate their mood at different times between meetings or could receive reminders about a task they agreed to do). Positive feedback could also be delivered electronically.

Behavioral interventions can be used to increase attendance at school and increasing commitment to academic pursuits. Behavioral interventions may also be helpful if the youth is obsessively re-reading cruel messages. CBT generally uses homework to assist clients in continuing the therapeutic work and applying skills; clinicians can assign tasks to reinforce in-session activities and help the client focus on the goals. Components to address anxiety can be included in the overall treatment plan, including relaxation techniques and systematic desensitization.

Working With Family

Many CBT interventions include a family component (Kennard et al., 2009), although this is not considered an essential ingredient of CBT. With cyberbullying and sexting, parents may be ill equipped to assist their child, due either to a lack of familiarity with the digital world or to a lack of understanding of the effects on an adolescent. It would be helpful to enlist the assistance of parents in supporting the student's efforts to overcome the practical and emotional consequences of the events, by providing education, and ensuring they closely monitor progress. This is a necessity if there are any concerns about suicidal thoughts or behaviors.

CASE STUDY

Reason for Referral

Sarah has been referred due to declining school performance and attendance, decreased attention to personal appearance, sad demeanor, social withdrawal, and disinterest in usual extracurricular activities.

Background/History

Sarah is a junior in high school who transferred to the school from out of state when her parents moved for a new employment opportunity. She had been a cheerleader at her previous school, has always been a good student, is attractive, and gets along well with her two younger siblings. At the beginning of the year, Sarah tried out and made the cheerleader squad at her new school. She also attracted the attention of a very popular senior boy, and they became a couple.

The cheerleaders did not welcome Sarah into their group and have made rude comments about her performance and excluded her from after-game get-togethers. As the year progressed, the girls escalated their torment, spreading rumors about her alleged sexual promiscuity and calling her derogatory names. This bullying moved online, and social media were used to further defame Sarah. In addition, she frequently receives texts that tell her no one likes her and that everyone knows she is a whore.

When her relationship with her boyfriend became more serious, he asked her to send him nude photos of her. She resisted at first, but he assured her that it was a token of their love, and that he would never show them to anyone else. Now, after an argument provoked in part by false rumors posted online, he sent the photos to many of his friends, who forwarded them to others, so most of the students at her school have seen them. The students have now escalated their online and in-person campaign to defame her and make her life miserable. She feels she has no friends, that her family would blame her for what happened, and that there is no way to recover from this humiliation.

Overview of Current Interventions

The school counselor recommended that Sarah's parents seek outside mental health counseling for Sarah. The school does not know whether that recommendation has been followed. The school attendance office has notified Sarah's parents of her absences, and several teachers have contacted them regarding Sarah's declining academic performance.

Conceptualization

From a cognitive-behavioral framework, Sarah seems to exhibit the *cognitive triad:* She believes that she is damaged beyond repair, that the world is cruel and inhospitable, and that the future is likely to get worse. In light of the effectiveness of CBT for depression in adolescents, that would be a likely approach to take in treatment. However, the first task would be to assess suicidality, and take steps to implement a safety plan if there is a risk.

Intervention Goals and Plan

1. To assist Sarah in identifying and disputing erroneous cognitions related to being victimized via cyberbullying and sexting.
2. To help Sarah develop a realistic menu of options she can use to respond to the current situation at school.
3. To provide emotional and informational support as Sarah works through these goals.
4. To enlist Sarah's family to support the therapeutic process.

Actions

1. Monitor suicidal behaviors (ideation, plans, and attempts) and inform others as necessary for her safety.
2. Administer a Beck Youth Inventory (2nd edition) to quickly assess depression, anxiety, anger, disruptive behavior, and self-concept. Develop specific goals for any clinically significant elevations.
3. Reduce depressive symptoms using cognitive restructuring. Identify cognitive schemas that foster depressive thinking, and generate more rational replacement cognitions. Be careful not to minimize the harm done; emphasizing resilience is essential. Identify persons who can provide emotional support at school and outside of school and create an action plan for eliciting and maintaining that support.
4. Brainstorm possible actions Sarah can take (e.g., contacting police, changing schools, closing social media accounts, joining antibullying groups) and assist her in evaluating each. Once a plan has been created, generate a timetable for Sarah to follow in implementing the selected strategies Monitor her progress.

Efficacy Measures

Re-administer inventories to measure change. Use school attendance and academic performance to assess the degree to which she has re-engaged in school.

Case Prognosis/Summary/Referral

These incidents can be difficult to address with only the individual victim. Hopefully, while a mental health specialist is working with Sarah, appropriate personnel are working with other involved students (and any bystanders) to enlist their cooperation in making things better for Sarah. The sexting material, depending on the state and age of the boy, could be referred to authorities for prosecution. At a minimum, the offender should understand the serious legal consequences that he could experience as a result of this behavior. The case of Phillip Alpert is a good example (see Richards & Calvert, 2009), and viewing a video of him talking about his experience (www.youtube.com/watch?v=FssnkvIBdgg) could be instructive. If restorative practices are available at the school, it is important that a restorative conference be held (Wachtel, O'Connell, & Wachtel, 2010), led by a well-trained facilitator, and any agreements reached be closely monitored. Restorative practices are a set of approaches to student misbehavior, particularly mistreatment of others, that are nonpunitive. The goal is to repair the damage to relationships caused by a student's behavior by conducting restorative circles (and restorative conferences for more serious offenses) that engage the school community in helping the offender take responsibility for his/her behavior and develop a plan to repair the harm caused to the target and the community. Interested readers are referred to www.iirp.edu/article_ detail.php?article_id=NTUx for an overview of this approach.

SUMMARY

Cyberbullying was defined as intentional harm of a target via digital technology. Although sexting is not always cyberbullying, there are many situations in which images intended to be private are circulated in order to damage the reputation and social standing of the target. In such situations, sexting becomes a means for cyberbullying. Although cyberbullying has been found to be less prevalent than traditional bullying, the nature of cyberspace creates an environment in which the potential for harm to targets is magnified. Further, in many cases those who are targeted by cyberbullying are also targeted in traditional bullying. Like traditional bullying, cyberbullying is associated with negative psychosocial consequences, including depression, anxiety, and suicidal behaviors, as well as declines in student attendance and academic performance.

Although some recommendations have been suggested for safety education, there is not an evidence-best practice protocol for responding to individuals affected by cyberbullying. In this chapter, an approach grounded in research on Cognitive-Behavioral Therapy with children and adolescents is presented as an initial guide for practitioners who respond to distressed students. Furthermore, the case study (a composite) provides an opportunity for readers to see how they might intervene with a serious case of cyberbullying or sexting.

RESOURCES

Books

Bauman, S. (2011). *Cyberbullying: What counselors need to know.* Alexandria, VA: American Counseling Association. Although other books are available on cyberbullying, this one was written for mental health professionals. It includes practical information on various forms of technology and includes a review of various nonpunitive strategies for responding to bullying. Developmental differences in the phenomenon are described, allowing users to adjust their approach to the appropriate developmental level.

Websites

Developed and maintained by researchers Justin Patchin and Sameer Hindjua, cyberbullying.us is frequently updated with current information and new developments. In the resources section, there are numerous useful guides for educators as well as parents and teens. Victims' stories are available on the site, which can be used to consider how helpers might respond to those students. It is an excellent one-stop site for information related to cyberbullying.

The website www.netsmartz.org is an excellent resource for parents, educators, law enforcement, and young people. They provide free curriculum resources for online safety at various age levels that can be used for classroom instruction. It includes video clips of true stories that can be used in training.

A short film called *Let's Fight It Together* can be streamed from www.digizen.org that is effective in presentations to students. It is unique in that in addition to the video, there are interviews with each of the characters (both youth and adults) that offer additional insights into their behavior. There is also a game based on the video and a "social networking detective" activity that gives students an opportunity to apply their learning. All the material is available for free download. A brief video about the nature of digital citizenship can serve as a stimulus for both adults and youth to discuss the topic. The site accepts student work, which can be an incentive for students to create and share content.

Although I rely on www.commonsensemedia.org for all types of information, its links on sexting include a number of thoughtful videos, articles, and information for educators that are very useful. Those who are interested in creating presentations for students on this topic will find very useful items here. Their cyberbullying links are also diverse and include a review of an iPad app called "Professor Garfield Cyberbullying" that parents might want to use to teach younger children how to respond to cyberbullies. A useful feature of this site is the ratings of materials, so the viewer can see what others thought about any given resource. One of the links has information specifically for school administrators.

REFERENCES

Bauman, S. (2010). Cyberbullying in a rural intermediate school: An exploratory study. *Journal of Early Adolescence, 30,* 803–833. doi:10.1177/0272431609350927

Bauman, S. (2011). *Cyberbullying: What counselors need to know.* Alexandria, VA: American Counseling Association.

Bauman, S., Card, N., Erickson, D., & Williams, R. (2012, June 29). Highlights from wave 1 data: A prospective longitudinal study of the emergence of cyberbullying from childhood to adolescence. Presentation at the COST conference, Paris, France.

Bauman, S., Cross, D., & Walker, J. (2013). *Principles of cyberbullying research: Definition, methods, and measures.* New York, NY: Routledge.

Bauman, S., & Newman, M. (2013). Testing assumptions about cyberbullying: Perceived distress associated with acts of conventional and cyber bullying. *Psychology of Violence, 3,* 27–38. doi:10.1037/a0029867

Bauman, S., & Pero, H. (2011). Bullying and cyberbullying among Deaf and hard of hearing students and their hearing peers. *Journal of Deaf Studies and Deaf Education, 16,* 236–253. doi:10.1093/deafed/enq043

Bauman, S., & Tatum, T. (2009). Websites for young children: Gateway to social networking? *Professional School Counseling, 13,* 1–10.

Bauman, S., Toomey, R., & Walker, J. (2013). Relations among bullying, cyberbullying and suicide in high school students. *Journal of Adolescence, 36,* 341–360. http://dx.doi.org/10.1016/j.adolescence.2012.12.001

Bonnano, R. A. & Hymel, S. (2013). Cyber bullying and internalizing difficulties: Above and beyond the impact of traditional forms of bullying. *Journal of Youth and Adolescence, 42,* 685–697. doi:10.1007/s10964-013-9937-1

Calvete, E., Orue, I., Estévez, A., Villardón, L., & Padilla, P. (2010). Cyberbullying in adolescents: Modalities and aggressors' profile. *Computers in Human Behavior, 26,* 1128–1135. doi:10.1016/j.chb.2010.03.017

Cornell, D. (2013, June). *Bullying and school climate.* Presentation at the Bullying Research Network Think Tank, Santa Barbara, CA.

Dehue, F., Bolman, C., & Völlink, T. (2008). Cyberbullying: Youngsters' experiences and parental perception. *CyberPsychology and Behavior, 11,* 217–223. doi:10.1089/cpb.2007.0008

Dempsey, A. G., Sulkowski, M. L., Dempsey, J., & Storch, E. A. (2011). Has cyber technology produced a new group of peer aggressors? *Cyberpsychology, Behavior, and Social Networking, 14,* 297–302. doi:10.1089/cyber.2010.0108

Dempsey, A. G., Sulkowski, M. L., Nichols, R., & Storch, E. A. (2009). Differences between peer victimization in cyber and physical settings and associated psychosocial adjustment in early adolescence. *Psychology in the Schools, 46,* 962–972. doi:10.1002/pits.20437

Diliberto, G. M., & Mattey, E. (2009). Sexting: Just how much of a danger is it and what can school nurses do about it? *NASN School Nurse, 24,* 262–267. doi:10.1177/1942602X09348652

Doll, B., Swearer, S. M., Collins, A. M., Chadwell, M. R., Dooley, K., & Chapla, B. A. (2012). Bullying and coercion: School-based cognitive-behavioral interventions. In R. M. Mennuti, R. W. Christner, & A. Freeman (Eds.), *Cognitive–behavioral interventions in educational setting: A handbook for practice* (2nd ed., pp. 339–379). New York, NY: Routledge.

Gradinger, P., Strohmeier, D., Schiller, E. M., Stefanek, E., & Spiel, C. (2012). Cyber-victimization and popularity in early adolescence: Stability and predictive associations. *European Journal of Developmental Psychology, 9,* 228–243. doi:10.1080/17405629.2011.643171

Gradinger, P., Strohmeier, D., & Spiel, C. (2009). Traditional bullying and cyberbullying: Identification of risk groups for adjustment problems. *Journal of Psychology, 217*(4), 205–213. doi:10.1027/0044-3409.217.4.205

Harris, A. J., Davidson, J., Letourneau, E., Paternite, C., & Miofsky, K. T. (2013). *Building a prevention framework to address teen sexting behaviors.* Report NCJ244001. Retrieved from https://www.ncjrs.gov/App/Publications/abstract.aspx?ID=266079

Hemphill, S. A., Kotevski, A., Tollit, M., Smith, R., Herrenkohl, T. I., Toumbourou, J. W., & Catalano, R. F. (2012). Longitudinal predictors of cyber and traditional bullying perpetration in Australian secondary school students. *Journal of Adolescent Health, 51*, 59–65. doi:10.1016/j.jadohealth.2011.11.019

Herman, J. D. (2010, April). Sexting: It's no joke, it's a crime. *Illinois Bar Journal, 98*, 192ff. Retrieved from http://www.isba.org/ibj/2010/04/sextingitsnojokeitsacrime

Hinduja, S. & Patchin, J. (2007). Offline consequences of online victimization. *Journal of School Violence, 6*, 89–112. doi:10.1300/J202v06n03_06

Hinduja, S., & Patchin, J. W. (2012). Cyberbullying: Neither an epidemic nor a rarity. *European Journal of Developmental Psychology, 9*, 539–543. doi:10.1080/17405629.2012.706448

Holfeld, B., & Grabe, M. (2012). Middle school students' perceptions of and responses to cyberbullying. *Journal of Educational Computing Research, 46*, 395–413.

James, A. C., James, G., Cowdrey, F. A., & Soler, A. (2013). Cognitive behavioural therapy for anxiety disorders in children and adolescents. *The Cochrane Library*. Retrieved from http://onlinelibrary .wiley.com/doi/10.1002/14651858.CD004690.pub3/abstract. doi:10.1002/14651858.CD004690.pub3

Jones, L. M., Mitchell, K. J., & Walsh, W. A. (2013). *Evaluation of Internet child safety materials used by ICAC task forces in school and community settings*. NIJ Evaluation Final Technical Report for Project Number 2009-SN-B9-0004.

Juvonen, J., & Gross, E. F. (2008). Extending the school grounds? Bullying experiences in cyberspace. *Journal of School Health, 78*(9), 496–502. doi:10.1111/j.1746-1561.2008.00335.x

Kaufman, G. (2011, September 27). Cyberbullying, sexting widespread, MTV/AP survey reveals. Retrieved from http://www.mtv.com/news/articles/1671547/cyberbullying-sexting-mtv-ap-survey .jhtml; www.eurekalert.org/pub_releases/2013-10/natu-mac102413 .php

Kennard, B. D., Clarke, G. N., Weersing, V. R., Asarnow, J. R., Shamseddeen, W., Porta, G., . . . Brent, D. A. (2009). Effective components of TORDIA cognitive–behavioral therapy for adolescent depression: Preliminary findings. *Journal of Consulting and Clinical Psychology, 77*, 1033–1041. doi:10.1037/a0017411

Klein, J. B., Jacobs, R. H., & Reinecke, M. A. (2007). Cognitive behavioral therapy for adolescent depression: A meta-analytic investigation of changes in effect-size estimates. *Journal of the American Academy of Child and Adolescent Psychiatry, 46*, 1403–1413. doi:10. 1097/chi.0b013e3180592aaa

Kowalski, R., & Limber, S. P. (2013). Psychological, physical, and academic correlates of cyberbullying and traditional bullying. *Journal of Adolescent Health, 53*, S13–S20. doi:10.1016/j.jadohealth.2012.09.018

Kowalski, R., Morgan, C. A., & Limber, S. P. (2012). Traditional bullying as a warning sign of cyberbullying. *School Psychology International, 33*, 505–519. doi:10.1177/0143034312445244

Kuhlmann, C., Pieschl, S., & Porsch, T. (2013). What aspects of cyber cruelty are judged most distressing? An adaptive conjoint study with two independent samples. In M. Knauff, M. Pauen, N. Sebanz, & I. Wachsmuth (Eds.), *Proceedings of the 35th Annual Conference of the Cognitive Science Society* (pp. 2784–2789). Austin, TX: Cognitive Science Society.

Lazarus, L., Barkoukis, V., Ourda, D., & Tsorbatzoudis, H. (2013). A process model of cyberbullying in adolescence. *Computers in Human Behavior, 29*, 881–887. doi:10.1016/j.chb.2012.12.015

Lenhart, A., (2009). *How and why minor teens are sending sexually suggestive nude or nearly nude images via text messaging.* Washington, DC: Pew Internet & American Life Project.

Levy, N., Cortesi, S., Gasser, U., Crowley, E., Beaton, M., Casey, J., & Nolan, C. (2012). *Bullying in a networked era: A literature review.* Research Publication No. 2-12-17. Cambridge, MA: Berkman Center for Internet and Society at Harvard University.

Li, Q. (2007). Bullying in the new playground: Research into cyberbullying and cyber victimisation. *Australasian Journal of Educational Technology, 23*, 435–454.

Litwiller, B. J., & Brausch, A. M. (2013). Cyber bullying and physical bullying in adolescent suicide: The role of violent behavior and substance use. *Journal of Youth and Adolescence, 42*, 675–684. doi:10.1007/s10964-013-9925-5

Madden, M., Lenhart, A., Duggan, M., Cortesi, S., & Gasser, U. (2013, March). Teens and technology 2013. Retrieved from http://www.pewinternet.org/Reports/2013/Teens-and-Tech.aspx

Menesini, E., & Spiel, C. (2012). Introduction: Cyberbullying: Development, consequences, risk and protective factors. *European Journal of Developmental Psychology, 9*, 163–167. doi:10.1080/17405629.2011.652833

Mesch, G. S. (2009). Parental mediation, online activities, and cyberbullying. *CyberPsychology and Behavior, 12*, 387–393. doi:10.1089/cpb.2009.0068

Myers, A. L. (2013, December 10). Internet giants weigh in on defamation lawsuit. *Arizona Daily Star*, p. A14.

Mishna, F., Khoury-Kassabri, M., Gadalla, T., & Daciuk, J. (2012). Risk factors for involvement in cyber bullying: Victims, bullies and bully–victims. *Children and Youth Services Review, 34*, 63–70. doi:10.1016/j.childyouth.2011.08.032

Mishna, F., Saini, M., & Solomon, S. (2009). Ongoing and online: Children and youth's perceptions of cyberbullying. *Children and Youth Services Review, 31*, 1222–1228. doi:10.1016/j.childyouth.2009.05.004

Mitchell, K. J., Finkelhor, D., Jones, L. M., & Wolak, J. (2012). Prevalence and characteristics of youth sexting: A national study. *Pediatrics, 129*, 13–20. doi:10.1542/peds.2011-1730

Monks, C. P., Robinson, S., & Worlidge, P. (2012). The emergence of cyberbullying: A survey of primary school pupils' perceptions and experiences. *School Psychology International, 33*, 477–491. doi:10.1177/0143034312445242

MTV/AP. (2009). *2009 AP-MTV digital abuse study.* Retrieved from http://www.athinline.org/MTV-AP_Digital_Abuse_Study_Executive_Summary.pdf

Parris, L., Varjas, K., Meyers, J., & Cutts, H. (2012). High school students' perceptions of coping with cyberbullying. *Youth Society, 44*(2), 284–306. doi:10.1177/0044118X11398881

Patchin, J., & Hinduja, S. (2010). Bullying, cyberbullying, and suicide. *Archives of Suicide Research, 14*, 206–211. doi:10.1080/13811118.2010.494133

Perren, S., Dooley, J., Shaw, T., & Cross, D. (2010). Bullying in school and cyberspace: Associations with depressive symptoms in Swiss and Australian adolescents. *Child and Adolescent Psychiatry and Mental Health, 4*, 1–10. doi:10.1186/1753-2000-4-28

Perren, S., & Gutzwiller-Helfenfinger, E. (2012). Cyberbullying and traditional bullying in adolescence: Differential roles of moral disengagement, moral emotions, and moral values. *European Journal of Developmental Psychology, 9*, 195–209. doi:10.1080/17405629.2011.643168

Pornari, C. D., & Wood, J. (2010). Peer and cyber aggression in secondary school students: The role of moral disengagement, hostile attribution bias, and outcome expectancies. *Aggressive Behavior, 36*, 81–94. doi:10.1002/ab.20336

Raskauskas, J., & Stoltz, A. D. (2007). Involvement in traditional and electronic bullying among adolescents. *Developmental Psychology, 43*, 564–575. doi:10.1037/0012-1649.43.3.564

Rice, E., Rhoades, H., Winetrobe, H., Sanchez, M., Montoya, J., Plant, A., & Kordic, T. (2012). Sexually explicit cell phone messaging associated with sexual risk among adolescents. *Pediatrics, 130*, 667–673. doi:10.1542/peds.2012-0021

Richards, R. D., & Calvert, C. (2009). *When sex and cell phones collide: Inside the prosecution of a teen sexting case.* Retrieved from http://comm.psu.edu/assets/pdf/pennsylvania-center-for-the-first-amendment/sexcellphones.pdf

Seligman, L. D., & Ollendick, T. H. (2011). Cognitive behavioral therapy for anxiety disorders in youth. *Child and Adolescent Psychiatric Clinics of North America, 20*, 217–238. doi:10.1016/j.chc.2011.01.003

Sinclair, K. O., Bauman, S., Poteat, V. P., Koenig, B., & Russell, S. T. (2012). Cyber and bias-based harassment: Associations with academic, substance use, and mental health problems. *Journal of Adolescent Health, 50*, 521–523. doi:10.1016/j.jadohealth.2011.09.009

Smith, P. K., Mahdavi, J., Carvalho, M., Fisher, S., Russell, S., & Tippett, N. (2008). Cyberbullying: Its nature and impact in secondary school pupils. *Journal of Child Psychology and Psychiatry, 49*, 376–385. doi:10.1111/j.1469-7610.2007.01846.x

Sourander, A., Klomek, A. B., Ikonen, M., Lindroos, J., Luntamo, T., Koskelainen, M., . . . Helenius, H. (2010). Psychosocial risk factors associated with cyberbullying among adolescents. *Archives of General Psychiatry, 67*(7), 720–728. doi:10.1001/archgenpsychiatry.2010.79

Spirito, A., Esposito-Smythers, Wolff, J., & Uhl, K. (2011). Cognitive–behavioral therapy for adolescent depression and suicidality. *Child and Adolescent Psychiatric Clinics of North America, 20*, 191–204.

Suler, J. (2004). The online disinhibition effect. *Cyberpsychology & Behavior, 7*, 321–326. doi:10.1089/1094931041291295

Temple, J. R., Paul, J. A., van den Berg, P., Le, V. D., McElhany, A., & Temple, B. W. (2012). Teen sexting and its association with sexual behaviors. *JAMA Pediatrics, 166*, 828–833. doi:10.1001/archpediatrics.2012.835

Topçu, C., Erdur-Baker, Ö., & Çapa-Aydin, Y. (2012). Examining of cyberbullying experiences among Turkish students from different school types. *CyberPsychology and Behavior, 11*, 643–648. doi:10.1089/cpb.2007.0161

Vandenbosch, H., & Van Cleemput, K. (2009). Cyberbullying among youngsters: Profiles of bullies and victims. *New Media and Society, 11*(8), 1349–1371. doi:10.1177/1461444809341263

Verduyn, C. (2011). Cognitive–behavioral therapy for depression in children and adolescents. *Tidsskrift for Norsk Psykologforening, 48,* 34–39.

Võllink, T., Bolman, C. A. W., Eppingbroek, A., & Behue, F. (2013). Emotion-focused coping worsens depressive symptoms in cyberbullied children. *Journal of Criminology,* article ID 416976. doi:10.1155/2013/416976

Wachs, S. (2012). Moral disengagement and emotional and social difficulties in bullying and cyberbullying: Differences by participant role. *Emotional and Behavioural Difficulties, 17,* 347–360. doi:10.1080/13632752.2012.704318

Wachtel, T., O'Connell, T., & Wachtel, B. (2010). *Restorative Justice conferencing: Real justice and the conferencing handbook.* Bethlehem, PA: International Institute for Restorative Practices.

Wang, J., Iannotti, R. J., & Nansel, T. R. (2009). School bullying among U.S. adolescents: Physical, verbal, relational, and cyber. *Journal of Adolescent Health, 45*(4), 368–375. doi:10.1016/j.jadohealth.2009.03.021

Weersing, V. R., & Brent, D. A. (2006). Cognitive behavioral therapy for depression in youth. *Child and Adolescent Psychiatric Clinics of North America, 15,* 939–957. doi:10.1016/j.chc.2006.05.008

Werner, N. E., Bumpus, M. F., & Rock, D. (2010). Involvement in Internet aggression during early adolescence. *Journal of Youth and Adolescence, 39,* 607–619.

Wolak, J., & Finkelhor, D. (2011, March). *Sexting: A typology.* Durham, NH: Crimes against Children Research Center.

Wolak, J., Finkelhor, D., & Mitchell, K. J. (2012). How often are teens arrested for sexting? Data from a national sample of police cases. *Pediatrics, 129,* 4–12. doi:10.1542/peds.2011-2242

Ybarra, M. L. (2004). Linkages between depressive symptomatology and Internet harassment among young regular Internet users. *CyberPsychology and Behavior, 7,* 247–257. doi:10.1089/109493104323024500

Ybarra, M. L., Diener-West, M., & Leaf, P. J. (2007). Examining the overlap in Internet harassment and school bullying: Implications for school intervention. *Journal of Adolescent Health, 41,* S42–S50.

Ybarra, M. L., & Mitchell, K. (2004). Online aggressor/targets, aggressors, and targets: A comparison of associated youth characteristics. *Journal of Child Psychology & Psychiatry, 45,* 1308–1316. doi:10.1111/j.1469-7610.2004.00328.x

CHAPTER 12

Suicide Prevention and Intervention

SCOTT POLAND

CHERYL KORNFELD

LEARNING OUTCOMES

On completion of this chapter, the reader should be able to:

- Know the incidence of youth suicide, and understand the liability issues regarding suicidal youth
- Understand the key role that a mental health professional can play in prevention, intervention, and postvention of suicide
- Know how to conduct a comprehensive suicide assessment, how to notify parents about their child's suicidal behavior, how to refer to community resources, and how to provide followup services at school
- Become an advocate for suicide prevention in schools

In 2010, 38,364 Americans died by suicide, accounting for 1.6% of deaths in the United States (Centers for Disease Control and Prevention [CDC], 2011). In that same year, Americans 10–24 years old completed 4,867 (12.6%) of those deaths by suicide (CDC, 2011). It is important to note that the number of reported suicides may be an underestimation of the actual number of deaths by suicide. Whereas the facts illustrate the dire need to focus on youth suicidal behavior, legislation pertaining to suicide prevention programs in schools serving K–12 has only been passed and enforced in few states (LaFleur & Poland, 2012). Thus it is essential that schools become a skilled setting that enhances knowledge and methods for assessing for suicidal risk, seeking appropriate support and care, and intervening with at-risk youth.

Practicing and future mental health professionals in the school play a critical role as a consultant and trainer to other school personnel to ensure proper suicide prevention measures are taken. This translates to the school psychologist, counselor, social worker, or mental health professional taking an active role in training the school staff on suicide screening, as well as in advocating for (and aiding in) the implementation of suicide prevention and intervention programs.

EVIDENCE-BASED RESEARCH AND PRACTICE

Risk Factors

There are numerous risk factors and trends for suicide among adolescents in the United States. These include, but are not limited to, gender; ethnicity; involvement in bullying; previous suicide attempts; a psychological disorder such as major depressive disorder or a substance abuse disorder; family history of suicide; family violence; sexual orientation minority/same-sex attraction; situational factors; and exposures to suicidal behavior of others, such as family members, peers, or the media (Lieberman, Poland, & Cassel, 2008). Furthermore, students who feel socially isolated or who feel a lack of connectedness to their peers or school are also at risk for suicidal ideation and behaviors (Miller, 2011).

There is an increased risk for suicide in adolescents with a mood disorder, most notably major depressive disorder and feelings of hopelessness (Miller, 2011). School mental health clinicians should use depression screenings as a means to detect students who are experiencing depression and are therefore more prone to suicidal ideation, plan, or intent. Additionally, impulsivity has a direct correlation with suicidal youth (Goldsmith, Pellmar, Kleinman, & Bunny, 2002). For instance, if a disciplinary action is not handled properly, an impulsive youth may turn to an impulsive suicidal act. Furthermore, adolescents with a depressed affect who use and abuse substances tend to be more impulsive and are also at a greater risk for suicidal behaviors. Mental illness, which affects up to 20% of the teen population (CDC, 2011), is a significant risk factor for suicide among teenagers, with a strong emphasis on depressive disorders, the presence of impulsivity, and substance use disorders (Dube et al., 2001).

School mental health professionals must be aware of familial psychiatric history and what might be going on in the student's home as to more accurately assess the student's suicide risk. It is unclear whether a family history of suicidal behaviors is linked to a genetic predisposition, to contagion (a known suicide serving as a "model" for a subsequent suicide), to gaining increased attention for such behaviors, or, more likely, to some combination of these (Burns & Patton, 2000; Henry, Stephenson, Hanson, & Hargett, 1993; Wagner, 1997). Four of the major problem areas of childhood adversity factors that school mental health professionals should be on the lookout for that are associated with elevated risk for suicidal behavior are (1) childhood maltreatment or victimization, (2) problematic parenting or family environment, (3) socioeconomic hardships, and (4) childhood adversities such as difficult peer relationships, legal problems, loss of a parent or caregiver, and a history of mental disorder or suicide attempts in the child or family members (Hardt, Johnson, Courtney, & Sareen, 2006). A school mental health professional should note the aforementioned risk factors/red flags for possible elevated suicidality in the student who is experiencing one or more of the aforementioned areas. If these risk factors are present for specific students, the school psychologists should take an active role in checking in with the student's teachers on a daily basis.

Furthermore, while antidepressant medication has proven to be successful at helping to treat depression in children and adolescents, a warning label stating that children and adolescents with depression (ages 5–17) are at an increased risk of suicidal ideation/behaviors created an adverse effect on the prescription of these drugs (U.S. Food and Drug Administration, 2004). However, antidepressant medications can be helpful is most situations. As with all medications, careful daily monitoring is needed along with a clear communication channel to the appropriate medical professional. The school mental health professional should be up to speed on the research for the best practices of treatment for adolescent suicidality. The school psychologist, guidance counselor, social worker, or other mental health professional should be aware of and make note on what psychotropic medications the at-risk student is taking while advocating for what the current research considers to be the best practice: a combination of therapy (cognitive-behavioral being the highest-regarded) and closely monitored medication. Those involved with the student's medication should engage in daily monitoring of the medication and should have clear communication with his or her psychiatrist in order to ensure compliancy and effectiveness. Speaking with parents/guardians regarding the positive benefits and risks of antidepressants allows for the mental health professional to aid the parents and teenager in overcoming stigma that often stops individuals from taking the medication as prescribed.

Gender and Developmental Factors

Research illustrates that death by suicide is the third leading cause of death after accidents and homicides for males and females between the ages of 10 and 24 across all ethnicities (CDC, 2012). Whereas males accounted for 84% of completed suicide in this age range in 2010, their same-age female peers are more likely to seriously contemplate suicide (females: 19.3%, males: 12.5%), make a suicide plan (females: 15%, males: 10.8%), and attempt suicide (females: 9.8%, males: 5.3%) (CDC, 2012). In other words, although females might contemplate, plan for, and attempt suicide at a rate two to three times higher than males, the rate at which males tend to complete suicide is about five times higher than the rate of female completed suicide within the same age group. Males are less likely to seek support when in need and are more likely to use more lethal means than their same-age female peers.

Research continuously indicates that 100–200 suicide attempts are made for every young person who dies by suicide (CDC, 2012). It is estimated that there are just about 1 million suicide attempts annually by young people. It appears as though the risk in suicide increases with age (higher for 15-year-olds than for those 10–14). Although the rate of suicide among youth 10–14 years old has steadily declined over the past few years, the overall rate of suicide in this population is still higher than it has been in previous decades and continues to be of concern (Miller, 2011; CDC, 2011; CDC, 2012; Lieberman, Poland, & Cassel, 2008).

Ethnicity and Cultural Factors

The prevalence of suicidal ideation and attempts also varies among individuals from different racial and ethnic backgrounds. American Indian and Alaska Natives have the highest rates of suicidal ideation, attempts, and planning among individuals between ages 15 and 19, followed by Hispanic, Caucasian, and African American individuals, respectively (CDC, 2012). The highest rate of completed suicide among youths is also within the American Indian and Alaska Natives, but Caucasian youth, non-Hispanic black youth, Asian/Pacific Islander youth, and Hispanic youth follow, respectively.

SEXUAL ORIENTATION

There has been a dramatic increase of media attention recently on the subject of the relationship between adolescents' sexual orientation and risk for suicidal behaviors (Hatzenbuehler, 2011). Though a question of mediating factors such as depression, hopelessness, and the social environment remains, lesbian, gay, bisexual, and transgender (LGBT) children and adolescents are at a higher risk for suicidal ideation and attempts than their heterosexual peers (Hatzenbuehler, 2011). Whereas 38.3% of LGBT children and adolescents with low family acceptance of their sexual orientation reported suicidal thoughts over the previous 6 months, only 18.5% of youth experiencing high family acceptance reported the same thoughts (Ryan et al., 2010). Reported lifetime suicide attempts reduced from 56.8% to 30.9% when a family engaged in high-acceptance behaviors/attitudes versus those families demonstrating low acceptance. Furthermore, suicide risk declines (as psychological well-being increases) in LGBT children and adolescents who experience family connectedness, school safety, strong and positive associations to the LGBT community, and perceived caring from other adults (Eisenberg & Resnick, 2006).

Children and adolescents who are questioning their sexual orientation are also more likely to be bullied than their heterosexual counterparts, and bullied children and adolescents are more likely to contemplate and to attempt suicide (Hatzenbuehler, 2011). Furthermore, a more supportive social environment significantly reduced the probability of a suicide attempt, especially those children and adolescents among the LGBT population, in comparison to a more negative environment (Hatzenbuehler, 2011).

Bullying

Dan Olweus, creator of the Olweus Bullying Prevention Program, defines bullying as occurring "when a person is exposed repeatedly, and over time, to negative actions on the part of one or more persons, and he or she has difficulty defending himself or herself" (Olweus, 1993, p. 9). A child or adolescent's connectedness to his or her peers can play a significant role in his or her risk for suicide, and a higher feeling of victimization or isolation may lead to a higher risk for suicidal ideation and behaviors. Children or adolescents involved in bullying, as a victim or bully, are at a significantly higher risk for depression and suicide. According to Lieberman and Cowan, (2011), "adolescents frequently cite interpersonal problems as a precipitant of suicidal behavior and, relevant to the issue of loss as a trigger, bullying causes a substantial loss of dignity and humanity" (p. 13). Furthermore, the more frequently an adolescent is involved in bullying, the more likely that he or she is depressed, has feelings of hopelessness, has serious suicidal ideation, or has attempted suicide (Gould & Kramer, 2011).

Students experiencing bullying in conjunction with higher social isolation, depressed feelings, or suicidal ideation are at higher risk for subsequent suicidal ideation 4 years later than students who experience one of the factors exclusively (i.e., bullying without feelings of depression/suicidality or feelings of depression/suicidality in the absence of bullying; Klomek et al., 2011). According to the Suicide Prevention Resource Center (2011) *Issue Brief on Suicide and Bullying*, there is a strong association between bullying and suicide, even suggesting that the children who are bullied are those who are at highest risk for suicide due to the commonality of risk factors.

As a dependence on technology is growing within U.S. culture, there is a significant need for school mental health professionals to be aware of the impact that technology, particularly cyberbullying, has on suicide risk among children, adolescents, and young adults. Cyberbullying can be viewed as any act of bullying (i.e., mean/hurtful comments, spreading rumors, physical threats, pretending to be someone else, and mean/hurtful pictures) through a cell phone text, e-mail, or any social media outlet or online source (Hinduja & Patchin, 2012). It is the role of the school mental health professional to be advocating for anti-bullying programs in their school to reduce suicide risk for the students and to be aware of any bullying, especially cyberbullying, that might be occurring. Students known by school personnel to be the victims of bullying should be questioned about suicidal thoughts and plans (see Chapter 11 on cyberbullying and sexting).

Situational Factors

A mental health worker's knowledge of the primary methods of suicide for young persons is important for effectively assessing one's suicidal risk. Whether or not a child or adolescent has an identifiable mental health disorder or other suicide risk factors, the presence of a firearm in a home, especially a loaded gun, is highly associated with an increased risk for youth suicide (American Foundation for Suicide Prevention, 2006). Firearms are reported to be the leading cause of death by suicide among individuals between the ages of 10 and 24, followed by hanging/ suffocation (CDC, 2011).

Situational crises are also situational factors that can dramatically increase suicide risk, as these crises can be precipitating incidents for suicidal behaviors among children or adolescents. While these acute incidents are not the actual cause of suicide attempt or completed suicide, they can lead to suicidal behaviors when in conjunction with other risk factors such as access to lethal means, substance use and abuse, depression, or past suicide attempts (Miller, 2011; Poland & Lieberman, 2002). Some specific examples of what constitutes a situational crisis include the following:

- breakup with a significant other
- trouble with authorities such as school staff or the police
- a death of a friend or loved one, the anniversary of a death of a friend or loved one
- an unwanted pregnancy or abortion
- embarrassment or humiliation in front of peers, relational/social/work/financial loss
- a serious injury or illness
- disappointment or rejection
- family conflict or dysfunction
- high demands placed on the individual at school or at home

- increased responsibilities of caretaking in the home
- increased community violence in the surrounding area

All these situational events can serve as trigger events and increase suicide risk for youth (Miller, 2011; Kalafat & Lazarus, 2002; Miller & McConaughy, 2005).

Protective Factors

Research that examines intrapersonal factors has found greater resilience among individuals with higher self-esteem (Sharaf, Thompson, & Walsh, 2009). In addition to this intrapersonal characteristic of resilience, interpersonal factors are also examined. When the availability of peer and family support is present, suicide risk decreases as self-esteem increases (Eisenberg & Resnick, 2006; Sharaf et al., 2009). Knowing that resilience can be defined as "the process of overcoming the negative effects of risk exposure, coping successfully with traumatic experiences, and avoiding the negative trajectories associated with risk" (Sharaf et al., 2009, pp. 160–161), increasing such protective factors (self-esteem and social support through peers and family) among youth in the United States is a helpful tactic in suicide prevention programs that need to be further explored.

Additionally, those students who feel as though they know adults who are trustworthy and capable of helping them with suicidal concerns maintain a positive attitude toward seeking help from school staff, are actively engaged in school/school activities, and are willing to potentially break promises of secrecy to talk with adults about suicidal ideation/behavior are major predictors of help-seeking behaviors for suicide (Eisenberg & Resnick, 2006; Pisani et al., 2012). As a result, these aforementioned studies suggest that designing suicide prevention strategies with the intent of strengthening self-esteem and social supports among students, as well as increasing their trust in school staff, should be effective in decreasing suicide risk among children and adolescents.

SUICIDE PREVENTION AND INTERVENTION PRACTICES

It is not only necessary for research to focus on a range of interventions for those at risk for suicide, but it is also important for mental health professionals in the school to understand the benefits of various prevention strategies. The numerous secondary intervention and postvention programs (i.e., those that play a significant role in aiding individuals who have been emotionally affected by a suicide) will, it is hoped, in turn help thwart subsequent suicide attempts.

A principal focus on primary prevention is essential for school mental health professionals. A multitiered model is based upon the severity and features of the suicidal risk, as well as the need for intervention. Each tier can each be thought of as follows: (a) low-risk: ideation; (b) moderate-risk: current ideation and previous attempts or behaviors; (c) high-risk: current plan and intent with access to means (Lieberman, Poland, & Cassel, 2008).

There are two major goals of suicide prevention programs (CDC, 1994). The first goal is to look at individuals who are already at risk to make appropriate referrals to outside professionals and to provide effective treatment. The second goal is to reduce risk factors in general. It is the role of the school psychologist, guidance counselor, counselor, or social worker to be the school's advocate, consultant, and trainer or implementer for such programs. School mental health professionals should play a principle role in advocating for and implementing gatekeeper training, suicide psychoeducation, and proper mental health treatment in the schools.

Gatekeeper training involves educating individuals in the respective contexts (school staff and community members such as clergy, recreational staff, clinical providers of healthcare to adolescents) to identify adolescents at-risk for suicide. Approaches using this framework also teach staff how to respond to suicidal individuals or other crises in their respective environments (American Foundation for Suicide Prevention, 2011).

General suicide psychoeducation (i.e., teaching students about suicide, warning signs, and how to seek help for self or others) should be implemented in the schools and this instruction fits well within a Tier 1 prevention/early intervention approach. These strategies often incorporate activities helping to boost the self-esteem of the adolescents involved. This framework can also be seen as one aspect of gatekeeper training, as the specified school staff members would be educated by a trained professional prior to educating the students on suicide. This education will hopefully be followed by screening programs. Screening programs (instruments or questionnaires) are highly regarded methods for helping to uncover those adolescents who are possibly at risk for suicide, which will then lead to the use of appropriate protocols and treatment.

Gatekeeper Training and Screening Programs

Prevention programs have been proven to be successful Tier 1 strategies that properly train and educate school staff in suicide, as well as effectively screen for possible suicide risk, reduce suicidal ideation, decrease suicide attempts, and increase coping skills (Aseltine, James, Schilling, & Glanovsky, 2007; Brown & Goldstein Grumet, 2009). Signs of Suicide is a suicide prevention program for youth that uses a screening of adolescents to determine their risk for depression and suicidal tendencies.

The evidence-based Signs of Suicide plan incorporates two frameworks: (a) increasing awareness through educating both students and school staff about recognizing the warning signs of depression and suicide and ways to intervene and (b) a screening that provides students with a short questionnaire to assess depression and suicide risk. This tool is used among eighth-grade and older students, and there is a distinct kit to use within each age group. Although no formal training is necessary, the school mental health professional is the appropriate staff member to serve as a key advocate and consultant for its implementation as well as train other staff members on the appropriate ways to handle depressed or potentially suicidal students. Thus, the school personnel will be better able to educate at-risk students and their peers so that those students at risk are apt to seek out or to be referred to the appropriate mental health services.

Although this suicide prevention tool is evidence-based, many schools wait or procrastinate implementing the plan. Unfortunately, it is all too often not used in a school setting until there have been one or more suicides. It is imperative that the school mental health professional take a firm stance on ensuring that a suicide prevention plan (preferably Signs of Suicide or another evidence-based practice) is put into place in the school prior to the occurrence of a suicide/suicides (visit www.mentalhealthscreening.org for more detailed information on the Signs of Suicide program and ways of implementing it in a school setting).

Identifying Suicidal Youth

It is imperative that schools put forth effort to identify adolescents who are at risk for suicide. Although many of such adolescents go unknown, the majority of them display warning signs and clues in some fashion that indicate they are contemplating suicide. Because children and adolescents do not often refer themselves to treatment, a school mental health professional's or other gatekeeper's effort to identify at-risk youth is vital. Warning signs can be understood as an acute risk factor such as a trait, attribute, or characteristic that has been found to be associated with suicidal ideation/behavior. There are various warning signs of youth suicide of which school mental health professionals should be aware (Poland & Lieberman, 2002; Rudd et al., 2006; Substance Abuse and Mental Health Services Administration, 2012):

- *Threats*: Can be either passive (e.g., "No one understands. What's the use?") or direct (e.g., "I wish I were dead"). Children and adolescents may use artistic outlets, such as creative writing or visual art pieces, to express thoughts of suicide. These threats may be made through cyber methods such as social media outlets or text messages. Whether direct or indirect communication, an individual who hears or reads such threats has the duty to take it seriously.

- *Plan/method/access*: The more specific the plan might be, the greater the probability for self-harming. Someone who has easier access to and is actively searching for access to means to hurt himself or herself with firearms, sharp objects, pills, drugs, and alcohol may be providing warning signs.
- *Final arrangements*: Someone who has a sense of purpose-lessness may begin to give away possessions and begin to write goodbye notes.
- *Sudden changes*: Dramatic changes in mood, behavior, friends, or personality should be looked at as a potential warning side of suicidal ideation/behaviors. Although it is common for adolescents to go through mood changes, a dramatic shift that continues for days may be an indication of possible suicidal ideation. Withdrawal from friends, family, and society may also be a warning side of suicide.

There are various methods of Tier 2 and Tier 3 interventions (selected and indicated strategies) that schools can use for suicidal youth, and it is important that each school plan in advance the steps to take with a potentially suicidal student. The Substance Abuse and Mental Health Services Administration (2012) toolkit strongly advocates for the placement of protocols at each school in order to specify which staff will handle each of the tasks in the event of a suicide risk, suicide attempt, or completed suicide. Two crucial components that should be in place in every school, even if the school does not provide further suicide prevention strategies, are "protocols for helping students at possible risk of suicide" and "protocols for responding to a suicide death (and thus preventing additional suicides)" (Substance Abuse and Mental Health Services Administration, 2012, p. 17).

The mental health professional in the school can take the lead role of developing a protocol to include necessary handouts and essential forms for documentation, risk assessment, notifying parents, providing referrals, and follow-up support. Some sample protocols for helping those students at risk that are provided within the toolkit include forms for parents and staff regarding at-risk adolescents; resources on properly assessing risk; information sheets for staff, students, and parents on various risk factors for youth suicide; suitable documentation examples; and methods for notifying parents of their child's suicide risk.

Through the use of self-report questionnaires and depression screening measures, school mental health professionals are more effective at screening for suicide potential, in addition to the presence of suicide risk factors, among students. These measures also aid in beginning to assess if a student's risk is at Tier 1, 2, or 3 for the school mental health professional to act accordingly.

Suicide Intervention Model

Understanding how to properly conduct a risk assessment and knowing how to appropriately respond based on the student's level of risk are both significant factors in suicide prevention and intervention. Because early detection is extremely important, suicide risk assessment must be done carefully and accurately. Effective guidelines, as provided by Poland (1995) for the school mental health professional to follow while assessing a student's suicide risk are (a) connect with student through providing empathy, support, and trust; (b) reflect feelings, remain nonjudgmental, and do not minimize the problems; (c) respect the student's developmental, cultural, and sexuality issues while collecting necessary information considering appropriate community referrals; (d) use an assessment worksheet; (e) be direct in questioning the student, staff member, and/or parents when collecting information; (f) never promise confidentiality; and (g) ensure that the school mental health professional is maintaining the chain of supervision at all times.

Asking a student if the student is thinking or has ever thought of suicide is vital, as it may lead to disclosure of risk that might otherwise have remained hidden. A multistage model can aid in early detection through the utilization of screenings and clinical interviews as listed in Table 12.1 (Reynolds, 1991). While screenings should be brief, well validated, and reliable, the follow-up clinical interview with the student and the student's support system should be thorough in assessing ideation, plan, intent, risk factors, warning signs, and protective factors. Questions, indicators levels of risk, and general interventions are summarized in Table 12.2.

Notifying Parents

The failure of the school mental health professional to notify parents/guardians when there is reason to suspect that the student is suicidal is quite a common source for lawsuits. The school mental

TABLE 12.1 Standardized Self-Report and Screening Scales for Assessment of Suicide

- The Columbia Suicide Severity Rating Scale (Posner et al., 2011)
- Beck Scale for Suicidal Ideation (Beck, 1991)
- The Suicidal Ideation Questionnaire (Reynolds, 1988; appropriate for students in grades 7–12)
- The Hopelessness Scale for Children (Kazdin, Rodgers, & Colbus, 1986)
- Signs of Suicide (www.mentalhealthscreening.org)
- Brief Suicide Risk Assessment Questionnaire (Miller & McConaughy, 2005)
- The Reynolds Adolescent Depression Scale–Second Edition (Osman et al., 2010)
- MAPS: Measure for Adolescent Potential for Suicide (Eggert, Thompson, & Herting, 1994)

Sources: Lieberman et al. (2008); Miller & McConaughy (2005); Substance Abuse and Mental Health Services Administration (2012).

TABLE 12.2 Questions, Indicators, Levels of Risk, and General Interventions

Tier 1: Low-risk (ideation)

- *Sample question to the student:* Have you ever thought about suicide or harming yourself?
- *Other possible indicators:* Current or recent thoughts; signs of depression; direct or indirect threats; sudden changes in personality, friends, or behaviors; evidence of self-harm in written or art work; dark Internet websites or social media posts
- *Actions:* Reassure and supervise the student; notify the parent; assist in connecting with school and community resources; suicide-proof environments; mobilize a support system; develop a safety plan that identifies caring adults, appropriate communication, coping skills, and resource numbers
- Document all actions

Tier 2: Moderate-risk (current ideation and previous behaviors)

- *Sample question to the student:* Have you ever tried to kill or harm yourself?
- *Other possible indicators:* Previous attempts; recent mental health hospitalizations; recent trauma (losses, victimization); recent medications for mood disorders; alcohol and substance addiction; running into traffic or jumping from high places; impulsivity; repetitive self-injury
- *Actions:* See Tier 3.

Tier 3: High-risk (current plan and access to method)

- *Sample question to the student:* Do you have a current plan to kill or harm yourself?
- *Other indicators:* Current plan with method/access; final arrangements; giving away prized possessions or written/e-mailed goodbye notes; refusal to agree to a safety plan
- *Actions:* Supervise the student at all times (including rest rooms); notify and release student only to (a) parent or guardian who commits to seek an immediate mental health assessment, (b) law enforcement, (c) psychiatric mobile responder; document all actions.
- *Prepare a reentry plan:* All students returning from mental health hospitalization should have a reentry meeting where parents, school, and community mental health personnel make appropriate follow-up plans.

health professional has an obligation to report any student who is suspected to be at risk for suicide based on foreseeability. In other words, even if a student denies suicidal ideation/intent, it is the duty of the school to notify the parents if the information available infers that the student is likely suicidal and would, furthermore, be considered negligence for school personnel to refrain from doing so (*Eisel v. Board of Education of Montgomery County*, 1991).

The importance of informing the parents of a possible suicidal child is not just to prevent a potential lawsuit. It is critical for parents or guardians to be notified in order to provide the best care for their child's safety (one caveat being if there are grounds to infer that the child would be abused or worsened by being in his or her home environment). After the appropriate school staff member is with the student, preferably the school mental health professional, it is vital that the staff member get in touch with the parents or guardians. It is then essential to gain any further information from the parents or guardians that might contribute to the assessment of the student's risk if they are available or cooperative (Lieberman et al., 2008). The Substance Abuse and Mental

Health Services Administration toolkit contains guidelines for notifying parents and for suicide prevention in high schools. It also provides a list of helpful steps for helping to engage parents and support them through this process.

In addition, three essential aspects of involving the parents of a potentially suicidal child are stressed (DiCara et al., 2009). First, a school staff member, such as the school mental health professional, should explicitly inform the parents or guardians that their child is at risk for suicide and explain the reasons why this is believed to be true. The school staff member(s) on this case should then explain the importance of removing access in the home to any lethal means.

Secondly, it is crucial to educate the parents/guardians on how to properly rid access to lethal means and ways in which to keep the child safe at home for the time being. Thirdly, appropriate referrals, with the level of care based on the severity of the case, should also be given to the child's parents/guardians at this time. For schools to provide best practices for suicide prevention, policies for parental notification should be in place for students who are suspected to be suicidal, even if the student denies suicidal intent.

When it comes time to warn parents that their child might be suicidal, some issues may arise. First, if the team collaboratively decides that it is more of a risk to inform the student's parents based on potential neglect/abuse in the home, the school staff should move to directly calling the state's child protective services instead. Second, some parents are uncooperative and may refuse to come to the school to talk and/or personally pick up their children to bring them home safely. We *strongly advise against* allowing students to walk or take the bus home alone, no matter what the parents suggest. If a parent or guardian refuses to ensure the safety of their child, refuses to seek out additional mental health services for their child, or does not take the suicide risk seriously, it is recommended that the school mental health professional or other school personnel call the state's respective child protective services.

Providing Referrals

School mental health professionals should keep a list of up-to-date community mental health resources to use as referrals for students who are possibly at risk for suicide in anticipation of suicidal crises. After an action plan is in place for the student and his or her parent(s) makes an appointment, it is important to strongly advocate for the family to sign a release of information for the school mental health professional to be able to directly communicate with any outside therapists/psychologists, psychiatrists, and/or medical doctors. It is recommended that the designated reporter or school mental health professional contact the agency/mental health professional in order to ensure that no relevant information be left out. Furthermore, various factors such as developmental, cultural, socioeconomic (potential need for provider who offers sliding scale rates), and sexuality issues should be considered when making such referrals (Lieberman, Poland, & Cowan, 2006).

The following case study will further explore the role of a mental health professional when he or she is presented with a student who is possibly suicidal. This case example is an actual instance of a tragic suicide. Names have been changed to protect confidentiality of the student as the school mental health professional and school system are in the process of being sued.

CASE STUDY

Mark, a 16-year old male student, was referred to the school counselor after he wrote a suicidal note and gave it to a friend. There was talk regarding a suicide pact including Mark, but he denied suicidal ideation or plan when interviewed by the counselor. Mark reported to the counselor that he was new to this school—he had enrolled only 5 weeks ago—and was sad that his friend, with whom he was rumored to be in a suicide pact, had attempted suicide that day. Mark reported being under stress, as he is facing felony charges, and said that he used to drink but that he has been "sober" for the past 2 weeks. Mark informed the school counselor that his mother attempted suicide the previous year and that she believes that he is likely to kill himself. Further, he stated that he lives with his grandmother (his legal guardian), with whom he gets along well, but not his mother, who "hates" him.

To take the appropriate actions to ensure Mark's safety, it is important that the counselor in the aforementioned situation assess the safety and suicide risk of Mark. First, the counselor should explore the current feelings of the student, the warning signs that initiated the referral, as well as Mark's current and past levels of depression and hopelessness. Following these questions, the counselor should discuss Mark's current or past thoughts of suicide as well as any previous attempts (identify the methods used if there have been any past attempts). Although Mark is denying any current suicidal ideation, plan, or intent; the school counselor should consult with Mark's teachers to assess for any warning signs that Mark may not be openly discussing. The counselor questions Mark's current and past substance abuse, moods, and stressors that may be attributing to the possible suicide risk. The counselor's assessment also included finding out about any past trauma (his mother's attempted suicide), considering a possible history of mental illness or familial mental illness, as well as determining Mark's support system—his grandmother, in particular. The counselor should also be uncovering Mark's reasons for living. Healthy answers to this question might indicate lower suicide risk. In this case, however, the risk factors (most notably the suicidal note) are so obvious that they must be taken very seriously no matter the protective factors that might be revealed.

Although Mark denies suicidality, the assessment should give the school counselor a better idea of the level of Mark's risk. Collaboration with school staff and crisis teams may be necessary. Difficult decisions made in such situations will be best made when discussed with and supported by other staff members, such as a nurse or other mental health professional, a school administrator, and other members of a school's crisis team. If the counselor/staff deem Mark a possible or probable risk to himself, his suicidal plan, ideation, or behavior must be disclosed to a third party, such as Mark's grandmother. The student should be told that disclosing such information to the people who care most about him is extremely important. Keeping Mark informed of what actions are to be taken is a way to empower him and help him to feel as though his concerns will be both heard and understood. Mark's having written a suicide note and being rumored to be in a pact are enough to necessitate notifying his grandmother. Because Mark reports sadness due to a friend's suicide attempt, and the rumors that Mark was in a suicide pact with this friend, it is also imperative that the school counselor not leave Mark alone—even just to walk down the hall to a bathroom. An adult should escort Mark throughout the day until his grandmother picks him up from school.

If the counselor does suspect Mark to be suicidal, it is a primary responsibility of the surrounding adults to remove access to lethal means. In addition to his grandmother ridding the environment of access to weapons or anything that has potential to cause physical pain/death, it can be beneficial for the school counselor to prompt Mark to commit to treatment. Although no-suicide contracts are sometimes used, research illustrates that the use of written, signed safety contracts might give mental health professionals and school mental health professionals a false sense of security—as well as encouraging undue reduction in clinical caution with the student (Miller, 2011). In lieu of a contract, a safety plan can be made in collaboration with the school mental health professional and Mark to ensure that he remains safe when he is feeling suicidal. This safety plan is to be used as a method of expressing direct, concrete, and nonsuicidal action. In conjunction with a safety plan, the school counselor should talk with Mark's grandmother to inform her of his probable suicidality and refer Mark to a therapist. Mark should be directly handed off to his grandmother to ensure that he is not alone. The school counselor should then follow up with Mark's grandmother to see whether they followed through with the recommendation(s).

Unfortunately, the school did not notify Mark's grandmother of Mark's suicidality. That same day, Mark received a low grade on his report card, resulting in an argument between his grandmother and himself. Mark later died by suicide. The grandmother further stated that had she known about his possible suicidality, she would not have argued with him as she did and would have taken a different approach to address her grandson's issues.

Documentation

Documenting every step of this process is a crucial aspect for clinical, legal, and ethical reasons. When possible, the documentation should be done on the day of the assessment/incident and important information collected through interviews and assessments should be written down verbatim. These documents are an essential step of Tier 3 support when a referral of a suicidal student is made and a crisis team is used. There should be specified forms available within each school district in order to ensure proper records are kept of their responses, actions taken, recommendations, and referrals made to a suicidal student or the student's parents (Lieberman et al., 2008).

Following Up and Providing Support

Whether or not the parents follow through with the school's referrals, it is important that follow-up services be offered for the student and his or her family. A school should monitor the student's progress and make any modification(s) to the student's plan when necessary to meet the primary goal of ensuring the student's future safety. Additionally, the school's effort to provide continuous support and resources is necessary in order to create a positive atmosphere for enhancing the student's success (Lieberman et al., 2008).

POSTVENTION

The term *postvention* refers to events and activities that are planned for schools to put into action following a suicide as a means to assess the overall impact, identify at-risk students, prevent a contagion effect from occurring, and support survivors who are emotionally affected by the death. Although schools are often unprepared to handle the aftermath of a suicide, what is implemented following a suicide is just as essential as the prevention efforts.

The American Foundation for Suicide Prevention and Suicide Prevention Resource Center (2011) created the *After a Suicide: A Toolkit for Schools*, which provides schools with appropriate postvention considerations and guidelines for addressing a suicide among the community. A strong collaboration between the school, parents, media, and community must exist to appropriately handle the situation at hand and minimize further suicide risk for others. Following a suicide, a collaborative effort is needed in order to provide the proper support to those survivors and to prevent contagion. Survivors of the suicide include friends, family, survivors of previous attempts, classmates, and the school mental health professional who might have worked with the student. Discussions and counseling for these survivors throughout the day following a suicide, as well as mental health referrals, are ways that schools can support staff and students.

To provide the best care to the school/community, this toolkit outlines specific actions to take (and not to take) following a suicide. The toolkit specifically states that schools should strive to treat all deaths the same—suicide or not. Almost any question that one could possibly have regarding postvention procedures is answered in the toolkit. Rather than waiting until after a suicide occurs, it is highly recommended that the toolkit be downloaded as soon as possible from www.sprc.org/sites/sprc.org/files/library/AfteraSuicideToolkitforSchools.pdf.

The postvention process can also be viewed as a prevention method or a Tier 1 level of support, as it is an important step in limiting imitative behaviors following a suicide. It is important for the community to highlight the positive contributions and aspects of the deceased's life rather than sensationalizing the cause of death. Also, a school district should attempt to limit the amount and type of information used by the media when discussing the student's suicide.

This process should be one that is empathizing and psycho-educational in nature, discussing ways of identifying and finding help for potentially suicidal individuals and those suffering from mental illness. Resources such as the *After a Suicide* toolkit and American Association of Suicidology (www.suicidology.org/home) provide letter templates and guidelines for the media and community to attempt to ensure that the suicide is handled properly to limit a contagion effect.

SUMMARY

Suicide is now the third leading cause of death in the United States for 10–24-year-olds. Many theories have been proposed to explain this increase: from the little black box on antidepressant medications to the explosion of social media, from economic strife to the trauma of military service, from the stigma surrounding having a mental illness to the stigma of asking for help. Undoubtedly, suicide remains a complex behavior, most often the result of numerous risk factors that come together in a perfect storm. Although research has revealed little in the identification of predictors, it has provided rich data on the complex relationships of suicide to bullying/cyberbullying, self-injury, depression, substance abuse, trauma, and parental rejection of LGBT youth. Despite these facts and statistics, the school mental health professional might be surprised to know that there is often resistance—even denial—from school administrations regarding implementing suicide prevention strategies.

It is critical that all school mental health professionals be familiar with all of the current aspects, data, and research of suicide risk and suicide intervention in schools. They must continue to work with administrators to ensure safe campuses for all students and prepare their school personnel to recognize and intervene with students who present at all levels of risk for suicide (including depression screenings). They must continue to work compassionately with parents on prevention and early intervention with children with mental health issues. They must continue to work collaboratively with their community mental health partners and law enforcement. School mental health professionals can make all the difference in the world by ensuring that their schools have in place prevention, intervention, and postvention strategies regarding suicidal youth.

RESOURCES

The American Foundation for Suicide Prevention and Suicide Prevention Resource Center's (2011) *After a Suicide: A Toolkit for Schools* (www.sprc.org/library/AfteraSuicideToolkitforSchools .pdf) provides a broad consensus regarding the best ways to deal with a tragic loss in a school community and to promote a coordinated crisis response in order to effectively manage the situation, provide opportunities for grief support, maintain an environment focused on normal educational activities, help students cope with their feelings, and minimize the risk of suicide contagion.

The Substance Abuse and Mental Health Services Administration's (2012) *Preventing Suicide: A Toolkit for High Schools* (store .samhsa.gov/product/Preventing-Suicide-A-Toolkit-for-High -Schools/SMA12-4669) assists high schools and school districts in designing and implementing strategies to prevent suicide and promote behavioral health. It includes tools to implement a multifaceted suicide prevention program that responds to the needs and cultures of students.

The Signs of Suicide Prevention Program (www.mentalhealth screening.org) aids students and teachers in identifying symptoms of depression in themselves as well as their peers. This evidence-based program is designed for middle-school and high-school students. It includes gatekeeper training and screening tools in its strategy to address risk and reduce suicide attempts among these age groups.

REFERENCES

American Foundation for Suicide Prevention. (2006). *About the cause: Suicide and depression facts.* New York, NY: Author.

American Foundation for Suicide Prevention and Suicide Prevention Resource Center. (2011). *After a suicide: A toolkit for schools.* Newton, MA: Education Development Center. Retrieved from http://www.sprc.org/library/AfteraSuicideToolkitforSchools.pdf

Aseltine, R. H., James, A., Schilling, E. A., & Glanovsky, J. (2007). Evaluating the SOS suicide prevention program: A replication and extension. *BMC Public Health 2007, 7*(161). Retrieved from http://www.biomedcentral.com/1471-2458/7/161

Beck, A. (1991). *Beck Scale of Suicidal Ideation.* San Antonio, TX: Harcourt Assessment.

Brown, M. M., & Goldstein Grumet, J. (2009). School-based suicide prevention with African American youth in an urban setting. *Professional Psychology: Research and Practice, 40,* 111–117. doi:10.1037/a0012866

Burns, J. M., & Patton, G. C. (2000). Preventive interventions for youth suicide: A risk factor–based approach. *Australian and New Zealand Journal of Psychiatry, 34*(3), 388–407. doi:10.1046/j.1440-1614.2000.00738.x

Centers for Disease Control and Prevention (CDC). (1994). Programs for the prevention of suicide among adolescents and young adults and suicide contagion and the reporting of suicide: Recommendations from a national workshop. *Morbidity and Mortality Weekly Report, 43*(6), 1–18.

Centers for Disease Control and Prevention (CDC). (2011). *Web-based injury statistics query and reporting system.* Atlanta, GA: National Centers for Injury Prevention and Control. Retrieved from http://cdc.gov/injury/wisqars/index.html

Centers for Disease Control and Prevention (CDC). (2012). *Youth risk behavior surveillance—United States, 2011. Surveillance summaries. Morbidity and Mortality Weekly Report, 61*(4), 1–162. Retrieved from www.cdc.gov/mmwr/pdf/ss/ss6104.pdf

DiCara, C., O'Halloran, S., Williams, L., & Canty-Brooks, C. (2009). *Youth suicide prevention, intervention, and postvention guidelines.* Augusta, ME: Maine Youth Suicide Prevention Program. Retrieved from http://www.maine.gov/suicide/docs/Guidelines%2010-2009--w%20discl.pdf

Dube, S. R., Anda, R. F., Felitti, V. J., Chapman, D. P., Williamson, D. F., & Giles, W. H. (2001). Childhood abuse, household dysfunction, and the risk of attempted suicide throughout the life span: Findings from the Adverse Childhood Experiences study. *Journal of the American Medical Association, 286,* 3089–3096. doi:10.1001/jama.286.24.3089

Eggert, L. L., Thompson, E. A. and Herting, J. R. (1994). A Measure of Adolescent Potential for Suicide (MAPS): Development and preliminary findings. *Suicide and Life-Threatening Behavior, 24,* 359–381.

Eisel v. Board of Education of Montgomery County. 324 Md. 376, 597 A. 2d 447 (Md Ct. App. 1991).

Eisenberg, M. E., & Resnick, M. D. (2006). Suicidality among gay, lesbian, and bisexual youth: The role of protective factors. *Journal of Adolescent Health, 39,* 662–668.

Goldsmith, S. K., Pellmar, T. C., Kleinman, A. M., & Bunny, W. E. (Eds). (2002). *Reducing suicide: A national imperative.* Washington, DC: National Academies.

Gould, M., & Kramer, R. A. (2011). Youth suicide prevention. *Suicide and Life-Threatening Behavior, 31,* 6–31. doi:10.1521/suli.31.1.5.6.24219

Hardt, J., Johnson, J. G., Courtney, E. A., & Sareen, J. (2006). Childhood adversities associated with risk for suicidal behavior. *Psychology Times, 23*(7), 1–2.

Hatzenbuehler, M. L. (2011). The social environment and suicide attempts in lesbian, gay, and bisexual youth. *Pediatrics, 127,* 896–903. doi:10.1542/peds.2010-3020

Henry, C. S., Stephenson, A. L., Hanson, M. F., & Hargett, W. (1993). Adolescent suicide and families: An ecological approach. *Adolescence, 28*(110), 291–308.

Hinduja, S., & Patchin, J. W. (2012). *School climate 2.0: Preventing cyberbullying and sexting one classroom at a time.* Thousand Oaks, CA: Sage.

Kalafat, J., & Lazarus, P. J. (2002). Suicide prevention in schools. In S. E. Brock, P. J. Lazarus, & S. R. Jimerson (Eds.), *Best practices in school crisis prevention and intervention* (pp. 211–223). Bethesda, MD: National Association of School Psychologists.

Kazdin, A. E., Rodgers, A., & Colbus, D. (1986). The hopelessness scale for children: Psychometric characteristics and concurrent validity. *Journal of Consulting and Clinical Psychology, 54,* 241–245.

Klomek, A. B., Kleinman, M., Altschuler, E., Marrocco, F., Amakawa, L., & Gould, M. S. (2011). High school bullying as a risk for later depression and suicidality. *Suicide and Life-Threatening Behavior, 41,* 501–516. doi:10.1111/j.1943-278X.2011.00046.x

LaFleur, G., & Poland, S. A. (2012). Schools can be the difference in preventing suicide. *Education Week News, 32*(9), 24–25.

Lieberman, R., & Cowan, K. C. (2011). Bullying and youth suicide: Breaking the connection. *National Association of Secondary School Principals: Principal Leadership, 12*(2), 12–17.

Lieberman, R., Poland, S., & Cassel, R. (2008). Best practices in suicide intervention. In A. Thomas & J. Grimes (Eds.), *Best practices in school psychology V* (pp. 1457–1473). Bethesda, MD: National Association of School Psychologists.

Lieberman, R., Poland, S., & Cowan, K. C. (2006). Suicide prevention and interventions: Best practices for principals. *National Association of Secondary School Principals: Principal Leadership, 7*(2), 11–15.

Miller, D. N. (2011). *Child and adolescent suicidal behavior: School-based prevention, assessment, and intervention.* New York, NY: Guilford.

Miller, D. N., & McConaughy, S. H. (2005). Assessing risk for suicide. In S. H. McConaughy (Ed.), *Clinical interviews for children and adolescents: Assessment to intervention* (pp. 184–199). New York, NY: Guilford.

Olweus, D. (1993). *Bullying at school: What we know and what we can do.* Malden, MA: Blackwell.

Osman, A., Gutierrez, P. M., Bagge, C. L., Fang, Q., & Emmerich, A. (2010). Reynolds adolescent depression scale–2nd edition: A reliable and useful instrument. *Journal of Clinical Psychology, 66,* 1324–1345.

Pisani, A. R., Schmeelk-Cone, K., Gunzler, D., Petrova, M., Goldston, D. B., Tu, X., & Wyman, P. A. (2012). Associations between suicidal high school students' help-seeking and their attitudes and perceptions of social environment. *Journal of Youth and Adolescence, 41,* 1312–1324.

Poland, S. (1995). Best practices in suicide intervention. In A. Thomas & J. Grimes (Eds.), *Best practices in school psychology III* (pp. 155–166). Washington, DC: National Association of School Psychologists.

Poland, S., & Lieberman, R. (2002). Best practices in suicide intervention. In A. Thomas & J. Grimes (Eds.), *Best practices in school psychology IV* (pp. 1151–1167). Bethesda, MD: National Association of School Psychologists.

Posner, K., Brown, G. K., Stanley, B., Brent, D. A., Yershova, K. V., Oquendo, M. A., . . . Mann, J. J. (2011). The Columbia–Suicide Severity Rating Scale (C-SSRS): Initial validity and internal consistency findings from three multi-site studies with adolescents and adults. *American Journal of Psychiatry, 168,* 1266–1277.

Reynolds, W. (1991). A school-based procedure for the identification of adolescents at risk for suicidal behaviors. *Family and Community Health, 14,* 64–75.

Reynolds, W. M. (1988). The suicidal ideation questionnaire: Professional manual. Odessa, FL: Psychological Assessment Resources.

Rudd, M. D., Berman, A. L., Joiner, T. E., Nock, M. K., Silverman, M., Mandrusiak, M., . . . Witte, T. (2006). Warning signs for suicide: Theory, research, and clinical applications. *Suicide and Life-Threatening Behavior, 36,* 255–262.

Ryan, C., Russell, S. T., Huebner, D. M., Diaz, R., & Sanchez, J. (2010). Family acceptance in adolescence and the health of LGBT young adults. *Journal of Child and Adolescent Psychiatric Nursing, 23,* 205–213. Retrieved from http://familyproject.sfsu.edu/files/FAP_Family%20 Acceptance_JCAPN.pdf

Sharaf, A. Y., Thompson, E. A., & Walsh, E. (2009). Protective effects of self-esteem and family support on suicide risk behaviors among at-risk adolescents. *Journal of Child and Adolescent Psychiatric Nursing, 22,* 160–168. doi:10.1111/j.1744-6171.2009.00194.x

Signs of Suicide. Retrieved from http://www.mentalhealthscreening.org

Substance Abuse and Mental Health Services Administration. (2012). *Preventing suicide: A toolkit for high schools* (HHS Publication No. SMA-12-4669). Rockville, MD: Author. Retrieved from http:// store.samhsa.gov/product/Preventing-Suicide-A-Toolkit-for-High Schools/SMA12-4669

U.S. Food and Drug Administration. (2004). *FDA launches a multi-pronged strategy to strengthen safeguards for children treated with antidepressant medications.* Washington, DC. Retrieved from http://www.fda.gov/ NewsEvents/Newsroom/PressAnnouncements/2004/ucm108363 .htm

Wagner, B. M. (1997). Family risk factors for child and adolescent suicidal behavior. *Psychological Bulletin, 121*(2), 246–298. doi:10.1037/0037/0033-2909.121.2.246

CHAPTER 13

Impact of Physical and Sexual Childhood Abuse

JENNIFER H. GREEN

TERRI L. MESSMAN-MOORE

LEARNING OUTCOMES

On completion of this chapter, the reader should be able to:

- Define childhood physical abuse and childhood sexual abuse
- Identify associated impairment in cognitive, emotional, behavioral, biological, interpersonal, and self-regulation domains that may affect social, emotional, behavioral, and academic functioning
- Identify effective therapeutic strategies to support students who have been abused, and evidenced-based prevention and treatment approaches for child maltreatment

Exposure to traumatic events is very common in the lives of children. In their lifetime, 80% of all children will be exposed to trauma, with 60% exposed each year (Finkelhor et al., 2009). Childhood abuse is one of many traumatic or negative events children may experience, and sexual or physical abuse may often occur in the context of other stressors including exposure to interparental (i.e., marital) conflict or violence, psychological maltreatment and neglect, poor parent–child relationship quality, and parental psychopathology. These types of childhood adversity within the family affect as many as 72% of all children (Chartier et al., 2010), with 37% experiencing two or more such adverse childhood experiences. Child abuse and other adverse childhood experiences have a cumulative effect, with the negative effects increasing with each additional type of abuse experienced (Dube et al., 2005; Finkelhor, 2008). Different types of childhood maltreatment often coexist, and thus many documented outcomes of childhood physical abuse (CPA) or childhood sexual abuse (CSA) may be indicative of cumulative effects of multiple types of child maltreatment (Dube et al., 2005). However, much of the research is limited by frequent focus on a single type of abuse or neglect in most studies. Although there are unique (i.e., specific) outcomes associated with CPA and CSA, different types of maltreatment often show common (i.e., similar) patterns of negative sequelae. Moreover, acts constituting childhood abuse are not always clear cut and often overlap with harsh parenting practices such as corporal punishment that may fall short of abuse. In essence, childhood abuse does not occur in a vacuum. Rather, it is influenced by cultural (i.e., cultural differences in accepted parenting practices such as corporal punishment), societal (i.e., community violence), situational (i.e., poverty), family (i.e., conflict, interparental violence), and parental factors (i.e., mental illness or substance abuse), which, alone or in concert with childhood abuse, may negatively influence children's functioning and behavior. Given extensive research that indicates childhood physical and sexual abuse are both associated with significant negative, deleterious, and pernicious effects on physical and mental health (Barnett et al., 2011; Berliner, 2010), these forms of abuse are the focus of the current chapter.

CHILDHOOD PHYSICAL ABUSE

CPA is typically defined as acts of violence by a parent or caregiver that cause some form of harm (i.e., observable injuries that last at least 48 hours) or possibility of endangerment (i.e., substantial risk for injury; U.S. Department of Health & Human Services, 1988). CPA thus involves behavior that may result in injury (e.g., punching, hitting with an object, burning). In some cases it is difficult to distinguish CPA from common forms of punishment (i.e., corporal punishment) that may be considered acceptable discipline, although such experiences also have negative consequences (Barnett et al., 2011). Thus, child protective agencies typically focus on the outcome of such acts. Although some discrepancies exist, most experts consider the following signs indicative of CPA: bruises, black eyes, welts, lacerations, or rope marks; open wounds, cuts, punctures, or untreated injuries in stages of healing; bone or skull fractures; and sprains, dislocations, or internal injuries/bleeding (Wiehe, 1997). When such signs are accompanied by sudden changes in the child's behavior, teachers and school personnel should consider CPA a likely explanation, especially when such injuries occur in conjunction with a child's report of abuse.

Official estimates of CPA suggest that it is experienced by 16–25% of children (Barnett, Miller-Perrin, & Perrin, 2011), although self-report surveys generally yield higher prevalence rates. In a comprehensive national population survey, 46.3% of children had experienced CPA; boys are slightly more likely than girls to experience CPA, with the peak of assaults occurring between 6 and 9 years of age (Finkelhor, Turner, Ormrod, Hamby, & Kracke, 2009). In a national survey of adults, almost half reported at least one physical assault by a caretaker, with acts ranging from relatively minor (e.g., being slapped or hit) to more serious forms (e.g., being threatened with a weapon), although most acts of CPA consisting of pushing, grabbing, shoving, slapping, hitting, or being hit with an object (Tjaden & Thoennes, 2000). Between 5% and 10% of children are victimized by severe physical abuse each year, whereas over 50% experience corporal punishment (Straus, Hamby, Finkelhor, Moore, & Runyan, 1998).

Most physical abuse of children occurs by parents or caregivers. Perpetrators of CPA tend to be male (62%). Female children are more likely to be abused by a biological parent, whereas male children are more likely to be abused by a nonbiological parent or parent's partner. CPA tends to occur in families marked by more verbal and physical conflict, higher levels of spousal disagreement and tension, and lower levels of family cohesion and emotional expressiveness. CPA is associated with depression, anger control problems, parenting difficulties, and neurobiological abnormalities in the abuser (Barnett et al., 2011). Younger children, those with difficult (i.e., acting out) behaviors, and those with physical and mental disabilities are at greatest risk for CPA. Children with an emotional disturbance, learning disability, physical health problems, or speech or language delay or impairment were almost twice as likely to experience physical abuse; in 47% of the cases, the disabilities were judged to contribute to child maltreatment (U.S. Department of Health & Human Services, 1993). Situational conditions associated with greater risk of CPA include single-parent households, large family size, parental unemployment, low socioeconomic status, and community violence. Although child maltreatment occurs in all socioeconomic groups, CPA occurs disproportionately among economically and socially disadvantaged families (Barnett et al., 2011).

Correlates of CPA

The most common correlates of CPA among children who have been abused include physical aggression, noncompliant and disruptive behaviors, irritability, and angry outbursts (Kolko, 2002). In most studies, physically abused children exhibit more aggression than nonabused children, even after controlling for poverty, family instability, and witnessing interparental violence (e.g., Springer et al., 2007). CPA is associated with cognitive problems in children, including lower intellectual and cognitive functioning (e.g., verbal facility, language, problem-solving skills, perceptual motor skills, memory, and dissociation), lower levels of school achievement and adjustment, and more learning disabilities (e.g., Halambie & Klapper, 2005). CPA is associated with heightened risk for psychological disorders in children, adolescents, and adults, including depression, bipolar disorder, attention deficit hyperactivity disorder (ADHD), posttraumatic stress disorder (PTSD), and anxiety (Ackerman et al., 1998; Runyon, Deblinger, & Schroeder, 2009).

TABLE 13.1 Domains of Impairment Associated with Childhood Physical and Sexual Abuse

Domain	Type of Impairment
Cognitive	Disorganized Easily distractible Difficulty learning Deficits in basic skills (reading, math, writing) Deficits in verbal abilities, memory, problem-solving, and perceptual-motor skills Attention and/or concentration problems Declining grades
Externalized Behavior	Tantrums Hyperactivity Impulsivity Aggression Noncompliance/acting out Conduct problems Excessive absences, school truancy Substance abuse Sexual risk-taking Sexualized behavior and preoccupation[†]
Emotion	Irritability Hostility/anger Anxious, fearful Afraid to go home Sadness Lack of motivation, hope, optimism Extreme passivity/compliance
Physical	Sleep disturbances and nightmares Stomachache Headaches Somatic symptoms Skins disorders Eating disturbance Enuresis, encopresis Genital pain, itching, odors[†] Problems walking, sitting[†]
Social	Social withdrawal Family/peer conflict Difficulty forming and/or maintaining friendships Peer rejection Difficulty trusting others Isolation/loneliness Insecurity, clinging Revictimization[†]

TABLE 13.1 Domains of Impairment Associated with Childhood Physical and Sexual Abuse (*continued*)

Domain	Type of Impairment
Self-Attributions	Low self-esteem Guilt Self-blame[†]
Psychological Symptoms	Posttraumatic Stress Disorder Depression Suicidal ideation Dissociation Anxiety Obsessions Tics ADHD Eating Disorder (e.g., bulimia) Oppositional Defiant Disorder Conduct Disorder Substance Use Disorder

Sources: Ackerman et al., 1998; Bernard-Bonnin, Herbert, Daignault, & Allard-Dansereau, 2008; Blaustein, 2013; Halambie & Klapper, 2005; Kendall-Tackett et al., 1993; Kolko, 2002; Runyon et al., 2009; Springer et al., 2007; Werkele & Wolfe, 2003

[†]Correlates associated with CSA and not associated with CPA.

Table 13.1 contains a more comprehensive list of correlates, symptoms, and diagnoses associated with CPA.

CHILDHOOD SEXUAL ABUSE

CSA typically involves sexualized interactions between a child below the legal age of consent (typically 14 to 18 years of age) and an adult that may include contact (e.g., kissing, fondling, genital penetration) or noncontact (e.g., exhibitionism, voyeurism, pornographic photography). In addition, CSA includes forced or coerced sexual acts by another child, including a sibling or same-aged peer (Berliner, 2010). Considering that sexual behavior can be consensual and that age of majority varies by state, studies do not consistently define age cutoffs for CSA; these can range from 12 to 18. Thus some studies of CSA may also encompass unwanted sexual experiences that occur during adolescence, including sexual victimization by dating partners, sexual harassment, sexual assault, and rape by peers. However, most researchers do not conceptualize CSA to include peer sexual assault during adolescence, which is often studied separately. Rates of CSA are difficult to determine seeing that abuse is not always reported to authorities. As such, most CSA prevalence estimates are obtained with retrospective surveys of adults, which range from 7% to 62% for women and from 3% to 16% for men, with higher rates in clinical and forensic samples. In national U.S. surveys, 25–32% of women and 14–16% of men report experiencing contact CSA

(Briere & Elliott, 2003; Dube et al., 2005). Unlike physical child abuse and neglect, CSA typically involves abuse by individuals outside the family. Fathers or stepfathers are the offenders in only 16% of cases, and familial sexual abuse (including all relatives) occurs in about one-third of cases (Hanson et al., 2006). CSA most often occurs with an acquaintance or someone the child or family knows (Berliner, 2010). When CSA occurs within the family, it often occurs in the context of other forms of child maltreatment (e.g., child physical abuse, emotional abuse, neglect), witnessing interparental conflict or violence, or other signs of familial distress and dysfunction, including parental impairment via mental illness or substance use (Berliner, 2010; Dube et al., 2005).

The majority of CSA victims are female, with girls at 2.5 to 3 times greater risk than boys (Putnam, 2003), whereas the majority of perpetrators are male (Dube et al., 2005). However, sexual minority youth are at significantly higher risk for CSA, with male and female sexual minority youth 4.9 and 1.5 times more likely, respectively, to report CSA compared to their sexual nonminority peers (Friedman et al., 2011). The mean age for the onset of CSA is 9 years old, although boys are typically older than girls when CSA occurs. Boys are more likely than girls to experience CSA by a female perpetrator and by a perpetrator who has abused other children (Berliner, 2010). Unlike other forms of child abuse, CSA is not associated with socioeconomic status, race, or ethnicity (Putnam, 2003). However, children who live without one of their biological parents, girls with a stepfather in the home, and children whose parents suffer some type of impairment, particularly maternal illness, alcoholism, or extended maternal absences, may be at greater risk for CSA either by a familial or non-familial perpetrator (Putnam, 2003). In addition, children with a physical, psychological, or cognitive disability also appear to be at greater risk for CSA (Berliner, 2010; Putnam, 2003).

Correlates of CSA

CSA has been correlated with psychological, physical, behavioral, sexual, and interpersonal problems in children and adults (Kendall-Tackett, Williams, & Finkelhor, 1993). As many as 40% of sexually abused children may present with few or no symptoms, although studies suggest children's functioning may deteriorate, with 10–20% of asymptomatic children developing symptoms within 12–18 months after discovery of abuse, a phenomenon called the "sleeper effect" (Putnam, 2003). The most common effects of CSA in children, adolescents, and adults include depression, anxiety (e.g., fears, phobias, panic attacks), symptoms of PTSD (i.e., flashbacks, nightmares, disturbed concentration), dissociation (e.g., feeling "spaced out" or out-of-body experiences), inappropriate sexual behavior in children or sexual risk-taking in adolescents and adults, behavioral regression in children (e.g., bed-wetting), and revictimization (Kendall-Tackett et al., 1993). Table 13.1 contains a more comprehensive list of correlates, symptoms, and diagnoses associated with CSA.

EFFECTS OF CHILDHOOD PHYSICAL AND SEXUAL ABUSE: A DEVELOPMENTAL PSYCHOPATHOLOGY FRAMEWORK

Children who have experienced CSA or CPA may exhibit symptoms or problematic behaviors across numerous domains in functioning (see Table 13.1). Researchers suggest that the most significant predictor of outcome is a child's "trauma burden," with the type of trauma being less important than the accumulation of a trauma history (Finkelhor, 2008). However, in studies of numerous types of childhood maltreatment, CSA is frequently associated with negative outcomes (Friedman et al., 2011; Putnam, 2003). The likelihood of serious psychological and health outcomes is higher when child abuse occurs in the context of other adverse childhood events, which increases the child's trauma burden (Dong et al., 2004). Negative outcomes of child maltreatment are more likely among children with preexisting anxiety disorders, among those with parental psychopathology, illness, or domestic violence, and among children who have experienced other traumatic events (Berliner, 2010).

Children who have experienced childhood physical or sexual abuse are at heightened risk for developing PTSD, although most children exposed to traumatic events do not develop the full-blown disorder (Copeland, Keeler, Angold, & Costello, 2007). However, children and adolescents who have experienced sexual trauma, particularly rape, have the highest rates of PTSD (Copeland et al., 2007). Although not all children meet criteria for PTSD, many children will show subclinical symptoms severe enough to interfere with functioning following a traumatic experience. Symptoms include anxiety reactions (e.g., extreme fear, startle response, hypervigilance), reexperiencing symptoms (e.g., general or trauma-related nightmares, flashbacks), behavioral regression (e.g., bedwetting, language regression/mutism), dissociation (e.g., zoning out), reenactment (e.g., via play or nightmares), and behavioral avoidance of trauma-related cues, emotional restriction, or numbing (e.g., depression, irritability; American Psychiatric Association, 2013). Considering that reactions consistent with a PTSD diagnosis are fairly uncommon in children and adolescents, some researchers argue that this diagnosis does not fully encapsulate the impact of traumatic events, particularly chronic, repeated events that often occur within the family (Copeland et al., 2007).

Developmental trauma disorder (van der Kolk, 2005) has been suggested as an alternative to PTSD to conceptualize the response of children who have experienced more chronic trauma within the family system (e.g., maltreatment, abandonment), as opposed to discrete traumatic events (e.g., car accident, single act of violence) that characterize the diagnosis of PTSD. Both the chronic nature of the trauma as well as the added developmental complications associated with experiencing a traumatic event at the hands of a caregiver who is supposed to be a source of protection, comfort, and regulation are components of this condition that are especially relevant to the maladaptive outcomes that frequently result from child maltreatment. The unpredictability in caregivers' behavior (e.g., one minute they may be warm and nurturing, the next violent and angry) is particularly damaging and has grave implications for the development of trust in others, self-regulation, and self-concept (van der Kolk, 2005).

Developmental trauma disorder (DTD) is characterized by disruptions in numerous aspects of functioning and development. Symptoms may overlap with PTSD and include a triggered pattern of repeated dysregulation in multiple domains, including affective (e.g., crying, fear responses), somatic (e.g., stomachaches, headaches), behavioral (e.g., traumatic reenactment, acting out), cognitive (e.g., confusion, dissociation, disrupted concentration), and social (e.g., disrupted peer relationships, clinging behavior) responses, as well as attributions regarding abuse (e.g., self-blame, self-hatred). In addition, children with DTD will display persistent negative expectations about others (e.g., distrust, anticipation of lack of protection or revictimization). This pattern of symptoms and beliefs can result in impairment in educational, familial, peer, legal, and vocational functioning (Ford et al., 2013; Teague, 2013; van der Kolk, 2005).

A developmental psychopathology framework (Toth & Cicchetti, 1999) is useful in conceptualizing the effects of child abuse on children's functioning and development in multiple domains (e.g., academic, social, emotional). The outcomes of child abuse will in part depend on the developmental processes active at the time the trauma occurs. Child abuse interrupts the process of development and can have far-reaching academic implications (e.g., concentration or behavior problems interfere with information processing and learning; attachment disruptions may degrade social relationships). Educators and school based mental health professionals can expect abuse sequelae to shift or emerge over time depending upon current biological, cognitive, emotional, and social development processes. The following examples highlight developmental processes prominent in different developmental stages.

Infancy and Early Childhood

In infancy and early childhood, child maltreatment can interrupt attachment relationships and may influence a child's ability to trust others in early childhood and beyond (Cole & Putnam, 1992).

In this developmental period, children are learning to regulate their own emotions and need scaffolding and support from caregivers through caregiver modeling of adaptive emotion regulation (Crockenberg & Leerkes, 2000). Experiences of child abuse challenge the acquisition of skills to regulate emotion and behavior for two reasons. First, abusive caregivers are often the source of a child's distress and thus are not in a role to provide soothing support to cultivate emotion regulation. Second, caregivers of abused children often lack effective self-regulation and emotion regulation skills and thus are unable to model or teach children this important skill. In early childhood, children are also internalizing behavioral expectations such as following adult (e.g., parents, teachers) instructions and exhibiting important social skills when interacting with peers (e.g., sharing, cooperation). Traumatic experiences may interfere with the acquisition of important developmental milestones, disrupting learning and social processes even if a child is no longer experiencing abuse by the time he or she enters school. Thus the effects of abuse in early childhood may linger due to missed developmental opportunities.

School-Aged Children

When children enter school, they must quickly adapt to behavioral expectations in terms of responding to directions, concentrating on academic work, and regulating activity level. Academic learning is paramount in terms of developmental processes in school age children. Child abuse can interfere with children's ability to concentrate, learn, and retain information (Macfie, Cicchetti, & Toth, 2001; U.S. Department of Health & Human Services, 2008). Behavioral conduct problems and aggression associated with abuse may contribute to school misconduct and interfere with learning. Furthermore, children experiencing abuse may have caregivers who are not able, available, or willing to support their academic development (e.g., helping with homework). Because academic concepts build on each other over time, missing basic skills will not only lead to low achievement at one point in time, but also will make it more difficult for children to catch up in the future.

Adolescents

In adolescence, peer relationships, romantic relationships, and identity formation are all important. Adolescents are conscious of what peers think of them and are knowledgeable about their own status, as compared with their peers', in terms of academics, athletics, and social status. Current or previous experiences of abuse may degrade self-esteem, identity formation, and expectations for romantic relationships or peer relationships. Abused adolescents, regardless of whether the abuse was sexual or physical, are more likely to engage in risky behavior, including substance use, sexual risk-taking, and delinquent behavior including truancy. Adolescents who have experienced CSA may experience heightened distress when understanding the stigma of abuse, particularly in cases of incest (Cole & Putnam, 1992). Among young women, a history of CSA (but not CPA) is associated with increased risk for revictimization in the form of rape in adolescence or adulthood (Messman-Moore & Brown, 2004). Among male and female adolescents, both forms of child abuse are risk factors for experiencing and perpetrating intimate partner violence in adulthood (Gomez, 2011).

Caveats: Correlates of Child Abuse

Educators and school based mental health professionals are encouraged to consider the broader context when considering whether abuse has occurred and how to respond to it. Although CPA and CSA have been associated with numerous negative outcomes in children and adults, it is critical to refrain from making causal assumptions regarding childhood abuse experiences and behavioral correlates. The presence of signs and symptoms associated with abuse does not necessarily indicate that a particular form of abuse, if any, actually occurred.

Relevant to the discussion of outcomes of child maltreatment, the concept of *equifinality* implies that there are multiple pathways that can result in a common outcome (Toth & Cicchetti, 1999). For example, experiencing maltreatment, the loss of a loved one, or parents' divorce could lead to concentration problems at school. The outcomes associated with child abuse are not necessarily unique or specific only to abuse, which means that the presence of symptoms or maladaptive behaviors are not necessarily a sign that maltreatment has occurred. It is helpful for teachers and school staff to be aware that the symptoms and problems discussed in this chapter are not specific to child maltreatment and could be caused by other etiological factors (e.g., poverty, parental conflict/divorce). The developmental psychopathology framework also implies a variety of possible outcomes for children who have been abused and neglected. The concept of *multifinality* suggests that any one experience (e.g., physical abuse) can lead to a variety of different outcomes (Toth & Cicchetti, 1999). For example, some children who experience maltreatment may respond with depression, others with anxiety, others with acting out, while some children may show high levels of resilience and maintain adaptive functioning. Protective factors, discussed below, can play an important role in promoting positive outcomes and reducing negative sequelae for children who have experienced maltreatment.

PROVIDING SUPPORT IN A SCHOOL CONTEXT TO CHILDREN WHO HAVE EXPERIENCED ABUSE

The experience of childhood abuse is nested in a context, including cultural, societal, community, and family factors that influence the unique effect on each individual child. Risk and protective factors occurring in concert with maltreatment will influence the effect and affect a child's response to and outcomes related to child abuse. Certain protective factors can promote resiliency, the notion that some children will have positive and adaptive outcomes even when faced with significant risk factors such as maltreatment (Masten & Coatsworth, 1998). Some of these protective factors can be cultivated in the school setting. For example, a child's feeling of connection to school, and having at least one adult outside the home that cares about the child, can promote resilience and reduce the likelihood of maladaptive outcomes in children who experience maltreatment (Masten & Coatsworth, 1998). Although such attributes are an aspect of positive school climate helpful for all students, promotion of these elements may be even more important for students who experience abuse. Although some students from high-risk backgrounds (e.g., maltreatment, poverty) may engage in behaviors that are challenging for teachers, it is precisely these students who need to know that adults at school care about them, recognize their strengths, and acknowledge their successes, especially in the classroom setting. The use of positive behavior supports serves as an effective tool in accomplishing this goal (Walker et al. 2005).

General Support Strategies

Given the information provided thus far, there are numerous important actions that teachers and school staff educators and school-based mental health professionals can take to provide support and enhance the educational experience of abused children. Based upon clinical practice below are guidelines to consider when responding to children who may be exhibiting problems in cognitive, emotional, behavioral, social, or other domains in the school setting.

- Respond with understanding and flexibility around homework and out of school projects. Students who have experienced maltreatment may be spending time in multiple homes/placements and may not have the materials or knowledgeable adults to help with homework. The family may be required to be engaged in multiple services and appointments (e.g., medical, counseling, legal system, children's services), which may make finding time for homework challenging.

- Stay abreast of student's living arrangements and primary caregiver. Maintain regular contact with primary caregivers about student's well-being at school and how caregivers can support academics at home. Help caregivers problem-solve around ensuring the student has necessary supplies, time, and space to complete homework.
- A student who does not have an individualized education plan (IEP) may need tutoring or extra structured time to complete schoolwork and homework. Extra support, presented in a positive way, can result in the student's feeling successful about completing schoolwork and feeling more connected to a caring adult. Find creative ways to support learning that don't stigmatize students or make them feel inadequate about needing extra help.
- Maintain an empathetic, warm, and caring attitude toward the student, even when addressing problematic behaviors. Expectations for safe and respectful behaviors can be communicated in ways that keep the student engaged and invested in school.
- Students who feel connected to their teacher are more likely to want to behave responsibly. Reinforcers (e.g., rewards) for desirable behaviors are more likely to be effective when they are delivered by an adult the student feels truly cares about him or her.
- Be aware that sudden and loud noises or raised voices may trigger a fear response or traumatic memories in students who have experienced maltreatment. The fear response may show itself as anxiety, dissociation (i.e., zoning out), agitation, or noncompliant behavior.
- Encourage and show support for mental health and therapy services that may require time away from classroom during academics. Addressing mental health through formal counseling or therapy may reduce nonacademic barriers to learning which will positively affect learning and academic achievement in the long run.
- If the school does not have mental health professionals with specialized training in treating trauma in children, refer families and students to community mental health providers who do.

Information presented about the implications of child abuse may also apply to students who are experiencing harsh parenting practices and discipline which does not meet the threshold for child abuse, but may also appear problematic. It is likely there are many students for whom abuse may not be confirmed who would benefit from teachers and school staff that respond to emotional, behavioral, and academic difficulties with empathy, warmth, and strength-based approaches that foster feelings of connectedness to school and awareness that adults care.

EVIDENCE-BASED PREVENTION AND TREATMENT

Intervention for abused children and their parents typically occurs along two lines: (1) prevention of child maltreatment and (2) intervention after abuse has occurred. Prevention of child abuse via focusing on changing harsh parenting practices is an important component of addressing the child abuse, and typically focuses on interventions with parents. Schools may be particularly interested in the prevention of child abuse as well as the promotion of more adaptive parenting practices as strategies to support readiness for learning in the school environment. However, if child abuse does occur, treatment focused on parenting behaviors and parent–child interactions or psychotherapy for PTSD and other trauma symptoms will be necessary.

Parent Training Programs—Intervention Focus across Tiers 1, 2, and 3

Parent training programs are frequently identified as effective practices to prevent child maltreatment, and to teach parents to replace abuse parenting patterns with adaptive parenting strategies. Although many of these programs were originally developed to target child disruptive behavior disorders, there is mounting evidence for their effectiveness in preventing child maltreatment and in changing existing abusive parenting practices. Evidence-based practices (EBP) are interventions that have shown effectiveness in the research literature through well-controlled empirical research studies. As there are a plethora of marketed intervention programs asserting to be effective educational parenting programs, school professionals are encouraged to review the empirical evidence for the effectiveness of any program before adopting or referring families to them. The resources section of this chapter contains links to reputable websites which evaluate specific programs and provide information about programs that have found to be effective in preventing and reducing child maltreatment. The following brief review of promising prevention and treatment strategies for child maltreatment will focus on interventions that are most likely to be accessible and useful in a school setting for school-age children.

Incredible Years–Parent Training (IY–PT) has been identified as a "probably efficacious treatment" for disruptive behavior in children (Eyberg, Nelson, & Boggs, 2008), earned a Scientific Rating of 1 (well-supported by research evidence) by the California Evidence-Based Clearinghouse for Child Welfare (www.cebc4cw .org/topic/parent-training/), and is listed in the SAMHSA's National Registry of Evidence Based Programs and Practices (www.nrepp.samhsa.gov/ViewIntervention.aspx?id=311). Considering that children with disruptive behavior problems are at higher risk for child maltreatment, the IY–PT program is relevant for preventing child maltreatment. The IY–PT program focuses on helping parents to understand the value of and successfully implement parenting behaviors such as child-directed play, delivering effective praise and rewards, social–emotional coaching, problem solving, consistent routines, and monitoring. Parents are also taught how to use nonviolent discipline strategies such as time-out when necessary. In general the IY–PT program has been shown to improve warm and nurturing parent–child interactions and to reduce harsh discipline and coercive parenting strategies and is an established child abuse prevention intervention (e.g., Webster-Stratton & Hammond, 1997; Webster-Stratton, Reid, & Hammond, 2004). Thus, referring high-risk families to community based IY–PT programs or offering IY–PT through the school constitute an effective child maltreatment prevention/ intervention strategy.

The IY model also contains programming (classroom-based and small group) for children focused on teaching skills such as identifying and coping with difficult feelings (e.g., anger, frustration, disappointment), problem-solving, and social skills (Webster-Stratton & Reid, 2003). The child interventions have been shown to be effective at preventing and reducing disruptive behavior disorders (Webster-Stratton & Reid, 2003), which in turn may decrease the likelihood of harsh parenting and child maltreatment. Furthermore, children who are the recipients of child abuse or harsh parenting strategies will benefit from learning skills in self-regulation that may promote adaptive behavior in the classroom.

In addition to child abuse prevention, the IY model is particularly well suited to changing parenting behaviors of those who have engaged in child maltreatment. As described by Webster-Stratton and Reid (2010), the group nature of the intervention makes it cost-effective to deliver in the child welfare system, reduces stigma, and increases supportive relationships among participants. Furthermore, the IY model emphasizes the importance of parent participation, discussion and engagement as opposed to direct instruction. The former strategic interactions leads to greater internalization of the content. One recent study demonstrated the effectiveness of the IY-PT intervention with families who have self-reported previous child maltreatment (Hurlburt, Nguyen, Reid, Webster-Stratton, & Zhang, 2013) and the IY-PT intervention has shown effectiveness in populations which include families with involvement in the child welfare system (Webster-Stratton, 1998; Webster-Stratton, Reid, & Hammond, 2001). Webster-Stratton and Reid (2010) provide information about specific adaptations to make with child welfare populations (e.g., increase focus on topics such as parent–child attachment and positive discipline; increase practice opportunities through additional role play, addition of home visits to coach parent–child interactions, educate caseworkers on IY principles).

The Triple P–Positive Parenting Program (Sanders, 1999) is another evidence-based parent training program that has been shown to prevent child maltreatment. Triple P takes a public health approach and applies multiple intervention levels to different segments of the population in providing parent training and family support (Sanders, 2008). Universal, community-level interventions such as media and broad-based communication strategies (e.g., newspaper articles, radio public service announcements) are provided to an entire community. More intensive, individualized services are offered to families with the greatest level of need (i.e., parents at risk of child abuse). The Triple P model emphasizes a reduction of stigma such that information and services are open to all families and are delivered through a variety of community organizations (e.g., schools, healthcare, child welfare, mental health care). The parent training aspect highlights five core principles of positive parenting: (1) safe and engaging environment, (2) positive learning environment, (3) assertive discipline, (4) realistic expectations, and (5) parental self-care. The Triple P model also attends to cultural differences such that the program includes culturally sensitive adaptations (Sanders, 2008).

Not only has research demonstrated the effectiveness of Triple P in improving parenting practices, but there is also evidence the intervention showed preventative effects for substantiated cases of child maltreatment, out of home placements, and serious injuries related to child maltreatment (Prinz, Sanders, Shapiro, Whitaker, & Lutzker, 2009). Triple P is identified as a "probably efficacious" treatment for disruptive behavior in children (Eyberg et al., 2008) and is identified by the Centers for Disease Control and Prevention as an effective program for stopping child maltreatment (www.cdc.gov/violenceprevention/childmaltreatment/prevention.html). The California Evidence-Based Clearinghouse for Child Welfare give Triple P a rating of 1 (well supported by research evidence; www.cebc4cw.org/topic/parent-training), and the Promising Practices Network lists Triple P as a Promising Program for addressing or preventing child emotional, physical or sexual abuse, or child neglect (www.promisingpractices.net/program.asp?programid=272).

Programs such as IY and Triple P may be most useful to schools in the context of helping parents learn adaptive parenting strategies that emphasize positive parent–child interactions, effective limit setting, nonphysical forms of discipline, problem solving, and self-regulation. The prevention of outright child maltreatment as well as shifting from harsh, inconsistent, and coercive parenting strategies to more positive interactions contributes to a positive effect on children's readiness for learning in the school environment.

Treatment for Children Who Have Experienced Abuse

Some victims of physical or sexual abuse demonstrate symptoms of posttraumatic stress disorder (PTSD) or complex developmental trauma disorder and will require more formalized, trauma-specific interventions to address symptomatology. Cognitive-Behavioral Intervention for Trauma in Schools (CBITS) and Trauma-Focused Cognitive-Behavioral Therapy (TF–CBT) have both received considerable empirical support for their effectiveness in addressing trauma symptoms in children and adolescents.

Implemented by a mental health professional in a school setting, CBITS is the best school-based approach for addressing symptoms of trauma in the school setting (Leenarts, Diehle, Doreleijers, Jansma, & Lindauer, 2013). CBITS includes group and individual sessions, parent educational sessions, and one teacher educational session, and utilizes standard cognitive-behavioral interventions such as psychoeducation about trauma, relaxation, coping skills, exposure, and social problem solving. CBITS has been shown to decrease self-report symptoms of PTSD and depression, and parent-report of psychosocial dysfunction at three-month follow up for children experiencing many different types of traumatic experiences (Stein et al., 2003). Both the CBITS and TF-CBT interventions were also shown to reduce symptoms of PTSD in school children in New Orleans 15 months after hurricane Katrina (Jaycox et al., 2010). CBITS is recommended for students who have experienced trauma such as maltreatment by the Centers for Disease Control and Prevention, SAMHSA's National Registry of Evidence-Based Programs and Practices, and the U.S. Department of Justice's Office of Juvenile Justice and Delinquency Prevention (cbitsprogram.org).

TF–CBT is another evidence-based treatment approach that is delivered outside the school setting by a mental health professional. A recent review identified TF-CBT as the treatment approach with the most empirical support for children who have experienced maltreatment (Leenarts et al., 2013) and is the only treatment approach to meet the criteria of "well established" in their review of evidence-based treatments for children exposed to traumatic events (Silverman et al., 2008). TF-CBT includes the following components: psychoeducation and skill building for children and parents about common responses to trauma; affect regulation and coping skills such as relaxation; exposure and processing of the traumatic event with a trauma narrative; and promotion of future safety and a positive developmental trajectory (Cohen, Mannarino, & Deblinger, 2006). TF–CBT is a recommended practice of the National Child Traumatic Stress Network and SAMHSA's National Registry of Evidence-Based Programs and Practices (Child Sexual Abuse Task Force and Research and Practice Core, National Child Traumatic Stress Network, 2004). The following case study illustrates the implementation of effective intervention for children exposed to abuse.

CASE STUDY

Reason for Referral

Abagail[1] was referred to the school counselor by her family due to disruptive behavior at home and growing disengagement at school.

Background

At the time of intervention, Abagail was an 8-year-old European American girl in the 2nd grade. Her family was of low socioeconomic status, and Abagail was living primarily with her maternal aunt, uncle, and two younger cousins because her mother was participating in an intensive outpatient substance abuse treatment program. She spent time with her mother for a few hours each weekend. Abagail's father had been in prison for the past two years on drug-related charges. Abagail desperately missed her mother and her father and talked about them frequently. Abagail had been exposed to domestic disputes between her parents and had also experienced intermittent neglect over the course of her life due to her parents' substance abuse. Her grandmother had helped with her care from the time of Abagail's birth until she was 5 years old but eventually became ill and had not participated in Abagail's care very much in the past three years, although the two visited a few times each month.

Abagail was sexually abused in her home by a 20-year-old male cousin at bedtime one to two times a week for about 3 months. The cousin resided outside the home, but had been spending the night at Abagail's home a few times a week for the past three years. Abagail eventually told her aunt, who believed her and immediately contacted the police. The family cut off all contact with the cousin, who denied the allegations and moved away. Child Protective Services investigated the allegations but did not find enough evidence to bring charges.

Abagail's aunt contacted the school counselor asking for support owing to an increase in aggressive behavior toward her cousins, aunt, and mother. Abagail had become more irritable and hit and pushed her cousins when they argued. These problems were most evident around bedtime. She refused to engage in the bedtime routine, requested to see her mother, and sometimes became aggressive when things did not go her way (e.g., if she was not able to choose the bedtime book or delay bedtime). Abagail awoke with nightmares two to four times a week, but could typically not recall their content.

Academic History

Abagail attended the same school for first and second grade. In first grade, her teacher described her as a quiet, sweet, and hard-working student. She started slightly behind her peers in reading and math but was performing at grade level by the end of the first year with her aunt's support. Abagail made friends in first grade but did not connect with peers outside of school. In second grade, her teacher expressed concern that Abagail was falling behind grade standards and described Abagail's work as variable (sometimes done well, at other times incomplete). She described Abagail as distant and unengaged in both her schoolwork and her peer relationships and noted that Abagail "completely zoned out" at times, staring off into space, mostly when students were working independently.

Goals and Course of Intervention

The school counselor referred the family to a psychologist in the community who had expertise in TF–CBT to address Abagail's symptoms and the problematic behavioral issues at home. Therapy focused on helping Abagail identify her feelings, develop coping strategies, and process the sexual abuse as well as her feelings of confusion and loss of her mother, father, and grandmother. The psychologist worked with Abagail's aunt to provide psychoeducation about CSA and appropriate behavior management strategies and supported Abagail as she explained the skills she was learning in therapy and suggestions about incorporating these into the home. Although her mother expressed a desire to be involved, she ultimately never attended therapy with Abagail and her aunt.

The psychologist recommended the identification of multiple adults in the school setting to connect with Abagail to increase her feelings of engagement in school and help her to catch up with her academic work. The school counselor reached out to Abagail's aunt and invited her to attend a meeting to discuss how the school could best support Abagail. Her aunt was open with the team about Abagail's family history, and the school team responded with compassion and a genuine desire to support Abagail's social, emotional, and academic needs. The school's intervention specialist offered to include Abagail in a reading group with other second graders that met three times a week. Abagail's homeroom teacher made special efforts to engage Abagail when she seemed to be zoning out by lightly touching her on the shoulder and kindly bringing her attention to her work. The homeroom teacher also invited Abagail to eat lunch with her and a peer in the classroom twice a week, socializing and working together on homework. The school counselor invited Abagail to join a friendship group of girls so that she could interact in a structured and small group setting with peers who were also needing support with social skills and opportunity for friendships. Finally, the team developed a system for the teacher to communicate with Abagail's aunt about school work and encouraged her to communicate with the teacher if therapy appointments or visits with her mother might interfere with homework completion.

Outcome Highlights

As a result of the strong collaboration between Abagail's family, therapist, and school professionals, Abagail demonstrated improvement in her social, emotional, and behavioral function at school and at home, as well as improvement in her academic performance. Her aunt's ratings on the Behavior Assessment System for Children–2nd edition (BASC-2) indicated positive change on the aggression, conduct problems, and anxiety scales, which all fell into the average range by the end of treatment. Abagail's aunt's qualitative reports indicated an improvement in behavior, especially around bedtime, and a decrease in aggressive behavior with her cousins. Abagail's aunt and therapist both noted improvements in Abagail's ability to verbalize her feelings and use coping strategies learned in therapy. Her teacher reported gradual increases in Abagail's engagement with peers and classroom activities. Abagail developed friendships with a few of her peers to whom she was introduced in the context of the multiple school interventions. Finally, her teacher was very pleased to report substantial improvement in her reading skills. By the end of second grade, Abagail was reading with 98% accuracy at leveled text, level M/DRA 28. Her AIMSWeb scores also showed significant improvement.

This case highlights a number of important issues related to supporting children who have experienced maltreatment:

- Children who experience maltreatment often have challenging family situations beyond abuse that put them at risk for negative outcomes. For example, it was important to address Abagail's experiences of loss in addition to the CSA in the context of TF-CBT.
- TF-CBT aims to engage parents in therapy. However, if not feasible, therapy is adapted to include the child's primary caregiver, in this case her aunt.
- Therapy is one of several forms of intervention for children who have experienced abuse. Teachers and other school personnel are vital members of the support team and can provide critical support in emotional, social, and academic domains in a naturalistic environment. Attention to the child's emotional, social, and academic

functioning can significantly positively affect future functioning and developmental trajectory.
- Ongoing communication, mutual respect, and a positive
relationship between the family and school personnel are
essential ingredients for supporting a child who experienced abuse.

SUMMARY

Educators and school personnel may benefit from using a developmental psychopathology framework to understand the cognitive, behavioral, emotional, interpersonal, and psychological
difficulties that are associated with a history of child physical or
sexual abuse. Children who exhibit difficulties in these domains
may benefit from interventions that provide opportunities for
fostering attachment to nurturing adults, acquisition or enhancement of self-regulation skills (which may improve attention, concentration, and subsequently improve academic performance),
and direct, tailored academic support and accommodations.
CSA and CPA are each associated with a diverse array of difficulties that may interfere with learning and socialization. Because
numerous types of childhood adversity including abuse are often
experienced within the home, the school can be an important
safe setting in which to foster supportive and nurturing relationships with children while also providing a structure to intervene
directly with parents or caregivers to promote more adaptive and
effective parenting strategies.

RESOURCES

California Evidence-based Clearinghouses for Child Welfare
(www.cebc4cw.org). This website provides a database of evidence-based programs that can be used by professionals that
serve children and families served by the child welfare system.

Centers for Disease Control and Prevention (CDC) Child
Maltreatment (www.cdc.gov/violenceprevention/childmal-
treatment/index.html). This website contains general information about child maltreatment.

Centers for Disease Control and Prevention (CDC) Child
Maltreatment Prevention Strategies (www.cdc.gov/violencepre-
vention/childmaltreatment/prevention.html). This section of
the CDC Child Maltreatment website contains descriptions of
effective programs for preventing and stopping maltreatment
(Prevention Strategies section).

Cognitive Behavioral Intervention for Trauma in Schools (CBITS;
cbitsprogram.org). This website provides information and free
resources about the CBITS program, a school-based intervention

designed to reduce symptoms of PTSD, improving academic and social/emotional functioning of students 5th through 12th grade who have witnessed or experienced traumatic events.

Promising Practices Network (www.promisingpractices.net). This website provides research-based information about best practices and effective programs designed to improve child well-being in physical and mental health, academic success, and economic security.

The Incredible Years Training Series (incredibleyears.com). This website provides information about the Incredible Years programs, which include evidence-based programming for parents, children, and teachers. The goal of the IY model is to prevent and treat young children's behavior problems and promote their social, emotional, and academic competence.

The National Child Traumatic Stress Network (NCTSN; www .nctsnet.org). This website provides information and resources for parents and caregivers, school and mental health professionals, policymakers, and the media about the impact of trauma on children, evidence-based treatment, networking and funding opportunities. The mission of the NCTSN is to raise the standard of care and improve access to services for traumatized children, their families, and communities throughout the United States.

SAMHSA's National Registry of Evidence-based Programs and Practices (www.nrepp.samhsa.gov). This website is a registry of more than 320 evidence-based substance abuse and mental health interventions.

Triple P Positive Parenting Program (www.triplep-america .com/glo-en/home). This website provides information about the Triple P Positive Parenting Program, a parenting and family support program designed to prevent and treat behavioral and emotional problems in children and adolescent.

NOTE

1. This case description is an amalgam of several cases involving child abuse, mental health, and school-based intervention. Aspects of the case, including the child's name (Abagail is a pseudonym), have been changed to preserve anonymity.

REFERENCES

Ackerman, P. T., Newton, J. O., McPherson, W., Jones, J. G., & Dykman, R. A. (1998). Prevalence of post-traumatic stress disorder and other psychiatric diagnoses in three groups of abused children (sexual, physical, and both). *Child Abuse and Neglect, 22*(8), 759–774. doi:10.1016/S0145-2134(98)00062-3

American Psychiatric Association (2013). *Diagnostic and statistical manual of mental disorders* (5th ed.). Arlington, VA: Author.

Barnett, O., Miller-Perrin, C. L., & Perrin, R. D. (2011). *Family violence across the lifespan* (3rd ed.). Thousand Oaks, CA: Sage Publications.

Berliner, L. (2010). Child sexual abuse: Definitions, prevalence and consequences. In J. E. B. Myers (Ed.), *APSAC handbook on child maltreatment* (pp. 215–232). Thousand Oaks, CA: Sage Publications.

Bernard-Bonnin, A. C., Hebert, M., Daignault, I. V., & Allard-Dansereau, C. (2008). Disclosure of sexual abuse and personal and familial factors as predictors of post-traumatic stress disorder symptoms in school-aged girls. *Pediatrics and Child Health, 13,* 479–486.

Blaustein, M. E. (2013). Childhood trauma and a framework for intervention. In E. Rossen & R. Hull (Eds.), *Supporting and educating traumatized students: A guide for school-based professionals* (pp. 3–21). New York, NY: Oxford University Press.

Briere, J., & Elliott, D. M. (2003). Prevalence and psychological sequelae of self-reported childhood physical and sexual abuse in a general population sample of men and women. *Child Abuse and Neglect, 27,* 1205–1222.

Chartier, M. J., Walker, J. R., & Naimark, B. (2010). Separate and cumulative effects of adverse childhood experiences in predicting adult health and health care utilization. *Child Abuse and Neglect, 34,* 454–464.

Child Sexual Abuse Task Force and Research & Practice Core, National Child Traumatic Stress Network. (2004). *How to implement trauma-focused cognitive behavioral therapy.* Durham, NC and Los Angeles, CA: National Center for Child Traumatic Stress.

Cohen, J. A., Mannarino, A. P., & Deblinger, E. (2006). *Treating trauma and traumatic grief in children and adolescents.* New York, NY: Guilford.

Cole, P. M., & Putnam, F. W. (1992). Effect of incest on self and social functioning: A developmental psychopathology perspective. *Journal of Consulting and Clinical Psychology, 60,* 174–184.

Copeland, W. E., Keeler, G., Angold, A., & Costello, E. J. (2007). Traumatic events and posttraumatic stress in childhood. *Archives of General Psychiatry, 64,* 577–584.

Crockenberg, S. & Leerkes, E. (2000). Infant social and emotional development in family context. In C. H. Zeanah, Jr. (Ed.), *Handbook of infant mental health* (2nd ed., pp. 60–90). New York, NY: Guildford.

Dong, M., Anda, R. F., Felitti, V. J., Dube, S. R., Williamson, D. F., Thompson, T. J., et al. (2004). The interrelatedness of multiple forms of childhood abuse, neglect, and household dysfunction. *Child Abuse and Neglect, 28,* 771–784.

Dube, S. R., Anda, R. F., Witfield, C. L., Brown, D. W., Felitti, V. J., Dong, M., et al. (2005). Long-term consequences of childhood sexual abuse by gender of victim. *American Journal of Preventive Medicine, 28,* 430–438.

Eyberg, S., Nelson, M., & Boggs, S. (2008). Evidence-based psychosocial treatments for children and adolescents with disruptive behavior disorder. *Journal of Clinical Child and Adolescent Psychology, 37*(1), 215–237.

Finklehor, D. (2008). *Childhood victimization: Violence, crime, and abuse in the lives of young people.* New York, NY: Oxford University Press.

Finkelhor, D., Turner, H., Ormrod, R. K., Hamby, S. L., & Kracke, K. (2009). *Children's exposure to violence: A comprehensive national survey.* Washington, DC: U.S. Department of Justice (OJJDP/CDC). Retrieved from http://www.ojp.usdoj.gov

Ford, J. D., Grasso, D., Greene, C., Levine, J., Spinazzola, J., & van der Kolk, B. (2013). Clinical significance of a proposed developmental trauma disorder diagnosis: Results of an international survey of clinicians. *Journal of Clinical Psychiatry, 74*(8), 841–849. doi:10.4088/JCP.12m08030

Friedman, M. S., Marshal, M. P., Guadamuz, T. E., Wei, C., Wong, C. F., Saewyc, E., & Stall, R. (2011). A meta-analysis of disparities in childhood sexual abuse, parental physical abuse, and peer victimization among sexual minority and sexual nonminority individuals. *American Journal of Public Health, 101,* 1481–1494.

Gomez, A. M. (2011). Testing the cycle of violence hypothesis: Child abuse and adolescent dating violence as predictors of intimate partner violence in young adulthood. *Youth and Society, 43,* 171–192.

Halambie, A. M., & Klapper, S. A. (2005). The impact of maltreatment on child development. In *Child welfare law and practice: Representing children, parents and state agencies in abuse, neglect, and dependency cases.* (pp. 53–77). Denver, CO: Bradford.

Hanson, R. F., Self-Brown, S., Fricker-Elhai, A., Kilpatrick, D. G., Saunders, B. E., & Resnick, H. S. (2006). The relationship between family environment and violence exposure among youth: Findings from the National Survey of Adolescents. *Child Maltreatment, 11,* 3–15.

Hurlburt, M. S., Nguyen, K., Reid, J., Webster-Stratton, C., & Zhang, J. (2013). Efficacy of the Incredible Years group parent program with families in Head Start who self-reported a history of child maltreatment. *Child Abuse and Neglect, 37*(8), 531–543. doi:10.1016/j.chiabu.2012.10.008

Jaycox, L. H., Cohen, J. A., Mannarino, A. P., Walker, D. W., Langley, A. K., Gegenheimer, K. L., . . . Schonlau, M. (2010). Children's mental health care following Hurricane Katrina: A field trial of trauma-focused psychotherapies. *Journal of Traumatic Stress, 23*(2), 223–231.

Kendall-Tackett, K. A., Williams, L. M. & Finkelhor, D. (1993). Impact of sexual abuse on children: A review and synthesis of recent empirical studies. *Psychological Bulletin, 113,* 164–180.

Kolko, D. J. (2002). Child physical abuse. In J. E. B. Myers, L. Berliner, J. Briere, C. T. Hendrix, C. Jenny, & T. A. Reid (Eds.), *The APSAC handbook on child maltreatment* (2nd ed., pp. 21–54). Thousand Oaks, CA: Sage.

Leenarts, L. W., Diehle, J., Doreleijers, T. H., Jansma, E. P., & Lindauer, R. L. (2013). Evidence-based treatments for children with trauma-related psychopathology as a result of childhood maltreatment: A systematic review. *European Child and Adolescent Psychiatry, 22*(5), 269–283. doi:10.1007/s00787-012-0367-5

Macfie, J., Cicchetti, D. & Toth, S. L. (2001). The development of dissociation in maltreated preschool-aged children. *Development and Psychopathology, 13,* 233–254.

Masten, A. S., & Coatsworth, J. D. (1998). The development of competence in favorable and unfavorable environments. *American Psychologist, 53,* 205–220.

Messman-Moore, T. L., & Brown, A. L. (2004). Child maltreatment and perceived family environment as risk factors for adult rape: Is child sexual abuse the most salient experience? *Child Abuse and Neglect, 28,* 1019–1034.

Prinz, R. J., Sanders, M. R., Shapiro, C. J., Whitaker, D. J., & Lutzker, J. R. (2009). Population-based prevention of child maltreatment: The U.S. triple P system population trial. *Prevention Science, 10*(1), 1–12. doi:10.1007/s11121-009-0123-3

Putnam, F. W. (2003). Ten-year research update review: Child sexual abuse. *Journal of the American Academy of Child and Adolescent Psychiatry, 42,* 269–278.

Runyon, M. K., Deblinger, E., & Schroeder, C. (2009). Pilot evaluation of outcomes of combined parent–child cognitive-behavioral therapy for families at risk for child physical abuse. *Cognitive and Behavioral Practice, 16,* 101–118.

Sanders, M. R. (1999). The Triple P–Positive parenting program: Towards an empirically validated multilevel parenting and family support strategy for the prevention of behavior and emotional problems in children. *Clinical Child and Family Psychology Review, 2*(2), 71–90.

Sanders, M. R. (2008). Triple P–Positive parenting program as a public health approach to strengthening parenting. *Journal of Family Psychology, 22,* 506–517.

Silverman, W. K., Ortiz, C. D., Viswesvaran, C., Burns, B. J., Kolko, D. J., Putnam, F. W., & Amaya-Jackson, L. (2008). Evidence-based psychosocial treatments for children and adolescents exposed to traumatic events. *Journal of Clinical Child and Adolescent Psychology, 37*(1), 156–183. doi:10.1080/15374410701818293

Springer, K. W., Sheridan, J., Kuo, D., & Carnes, M. (2007). Long-term physical and mental health consequences of childhood physical abuse: Results from a large population-based sample of men and women. *Child Abuse and Neglect, 31,* 517–530.

Stein, B. D., Jaycox, L. H., Kataoka, S. H., Wong, M., Tu, W., Elliott, M. N., & Fink, A. (2003). A mental health intervention for schoolchildren exposed to violence: A randomized controlled trial. *Journal of the American Medical Association, 290*(5), 603–611. doi:10.1001/jama.290.5.603

Straus, M. A., Hamby, S. L., Finkelhor, D. Moore, D. W., & Runyan, D. (1998). Identification of child maltreatment with the Parent-Child Conflict Tactics Scales: Development and psychometric data for a national sample of American parents. *Child Abuse and Neglect, 22,* 249–270.

Teague, C. M. (2013). Developmental trauma disorder: A provisional diagnosis. *Journal of Aggression, Maltreatment & Trauma, 22*(6), 611–625. doi:10.1080/10926771.2013.804470

Tjaden, P., & Thoennes, N. (2000). *Full report of the prevalence, incidence, and consequences of violence against women: Findings from the National Violence Against Women Survey* (NCJ Publication No. 183781). Washington, DC: U.S. Department of Justice.

Toth, S. L., & D. Cicchetti (1999). Developmental psychopathology and child psychotherapy. In S. W. Russ & T. H. Ollendick (Eds.), *Handbook of psychotherapies with children and families* (pp. 15–44). New York, NY: Kluwer Academic.

U.S. Department of Health & Human Services. (2008). *Child Maltreatment.* Washington, DC: DHHS, Office of the Inspector General.

U.S. Department of Health & Human Services, Administration on Children, Youth and Families. (1988). *Study findings: Study of national incidence and prevalence of child abuse and neglect* (DHHS Publication No. ADM 20-01099). Washington, DC: Government Printing Office.

U.S. Department of Health & Human Services, Administration on Children, Youth and Families. (1993). *A report on the maltreatment of children with disabilities* (DHHS Publication No. 105-89-1630). Washington, DC: Government Printing Office.

van der Kolk, B. A. (2005). Developmental trauma disorder. *Psychiatric Annals, 35,* 401–408.

Walker, B., Cheney, D., Stage, S., Blum, C., & Horner, R. (2005). School-wide screening and positive behavior supports. *Journal of Positive Behavior Interventions.* 7, 4, 194–204.

Webster-Stratton, C. (1998). Preventing conduct problems in Head Start children: Strengthening parenting competencies. *Journal of Consulting and Clinical Psychology, 66*(5), 715–730.

Webster-Stratton, C., & Hammond, M. (1997). Treating children with early-onset conduct problems: A comparison of child and parent training interventions. *Journal of Consulting and Clinical Psychology, 65,* 93–109.

Webster-Stratton, C., & Reid, M. J. (2003). Treating conduct problems and strengthening social and emotional competence in young children: The Dina dinosaur treatment program. *Journal of Emotional and Behavioral Disorders, 11*(3), 130–143.

Webster-Stratton, C., & Reid, M. J. (2010). Adapting the Incredible Years, an evidence-based parenting programme for families involved in the child welfare system. *Journal of Children's Services, 5,* 25–42.

Webster-Stratton, C., Reid, M. J., & Hammond, M. (2001). Preventing conduct problems, promoting social competence: A parent and teacher training partnership in Head Start. *Journal of Clinical Child Psychology, 30*(3), 283–302.

Webster-Stratton, C., Reid, M. J., & Hammond, M. (2004). Treating children with early-onset conduct problems: Intervention outcomes for parent, child, and teacher training. *Journal of Clinical Child and Adolescent Psychology, 33,* 105–124.

Werkele, C., & Wolfe, D. A. (2003). Child maltreatment. In E. J. Mash & R. A. Barkley (Eds.), *Child psychopathology* (2nd ed., pp. 632–684). New York, NY: Guildford.

Wiehe, V. R. (1997). *Sibling abuse: Hidden physical, emotional, and sexual trauma* (2nd ed.). Thousand Oaks, CA: Sage.

CHAPTER 14

Substance Abuse

JOSHUA HERSH

LEARNING OUTCOMES

On completion of this chapter, the reader should be able to:

- Recognize the prevalence of substance use and abuse among children and adolescents
- Know how children's behavior in school may be affected by substance use
- Know basic evidence-based treatment modalities for abuse
- Understand basic elements and processes of substance use
- Understand ways that schools can educate about and play a role in substance prevention

Nearly half of high school students surveyed by Columbia University's National Center on Addiction and Substance Abuse (CASA) revealed that they are using alcohol or drugs (CASA, 2012). In addition, the abuse of prescription drugs has also been dramatically increasing, with estimates as high as 24% of high school students reporting the misuse of prescription drugs (Partnership for a Drug-Free America, 2012).

Many of these students who are using alcohol and drugs meet the *Diagnostic and Statistical Manual of Mental Disorders* (5th ed.; *DSM-5*; American Psychiatric Association, 2013) criteria for a substance use disorder. A substance use disorder can include recurrent cravings, using a substance despite adverse consequences (such as legal or medical consequences), tolerance (needing to use more of the substance), and withdrawal symptoms (uncomfortable and even life threatening symptoms that occur when a substance is discontinued; American Psychiatric Association, 2013).

Because substance use disorders are viewed as mental disorders in children and adolescents, it becomes impossible to fully understand mental health issues in the schools without understanding these disorders. Therefore, it is essential to review how students self-administer substances, as well as the common substances students select. It is also helpful to be familiar with evidenced-based approaches to the prevention and treatment of substance use problems in children and adolescents. This chapter is designed to help in regard to acquiring this knowledge.

ROUTES OF ADMINISTRATION

When a drug is swallowed, it must be absorbed through the digestive tract and then be filtered in the liver. The body views all drugs as "poisons," and the liver is our best defense against these poisons. This is kind of like our own internal security guard. When a drug is swallowed, only a small percentage of the drug reaches the brain. When a drug is snorted, smoked, or injected, it avoids the liver (the security guard), and a much higher percentage of the drug is ingested.

When a child or adolescent attempts to abuse a substance to experience psychoactive effects, there is often an attempt to bypass the stomach and the liver. That is why most substance use disorders involve children using substances by routes of administration other than swallowing. These routes include smoking (through the lungs), intranasal (snorting through the nose), injection (using a syringe to inject directly in the blood), and sublingual (under the tongue). Less common ways have also recently gained some notoriety in the media, such as intravaginal and rectal administration (Lovett & Mcniff, 2012). While these less common administrative modes are harder to detect, school-based mental health providers need to be aware of all substance administration avenues and listen to "talk on the street—or in the halls" about trends of administration (as well as slang for drugs) among youth in local schools.

TOLERANCE, CROSS-TOLERANCE, REBOUND, AND WITHDRAWAL

Another way the body protects itself against "poisons" is through the concept of tolerance and cross-tolerance. This is kind of like the internal security guard getting familiar with certain threats and being more prepared to fight them. Basically, after repeated use, the same amount of drug is insufficient to cause the desired effect, and thus more drug is need to have the same effect.

Cross-tolerance occurs when an individual has become tolerant to a drug and requires higher than normal doses of a similar drug to have its effects. This can be compared to our internal security guard's becoming familiar with certain threats that are similar to each other. An example of this occurs when someone uses one stimulant (such as caffeine) and experiences tolerance to other stimulants (such as nicotine or cocaine).

Drug rebound is also important to understand. This can occur after only one dose of a drug. It usually lasts for a short time, and symptoms are often opposite the drug response. Some examples of rebound are the "hangover" after using alcohol or the "crash" after using caffeine.

Drug withdrawal shares similarities with rebound but only occurs after long term use of a drug. The onset of withdrawal depends on the half-life of the drug. Drugs that have short half-lives can start a withdrawal syndrome within hours, but drugs that have very long half-lives will not start their withdrawal syndrome for days or even weeks. Withdrawal symptoms can be lethal such as in the case of alcohol withdrawal.

Coadministration

Many children or adolescents that are using alcohol or drugs are often not taking the substances alone. A study done in adults in 2006 reported that 39% of all patients admitted for alcohol or drug treatment reported problems with more than one substance (Substance Abuse and Mental Health Services Administration, Office of Applied Studies, 2007). Often these combinations of substances are more harmful than taking only one substance. Many celebrity deaths have been attributed to the combination of different classes of substances ("Death by Drugs: Fatal Celebrity Drug and Alcohol Addictions," 2010). Not only is the rate of overdose increased with co-administration, but also treatment becomes more difficult. Signs and symptoms of intoxication and withdrawal also become more confusing and difficult to sort out.

COMMONLY ABUSED SUBSTANCES

Given the prevalence and dangers inherent within substance abuse, it is critical for mental health professionals in educational settings to become aware of the substances that are likely used by youth. Tables 14.1 and 14.2 highlight commonly used substances according to the National Institute of Drug Abuse (www .drugabuse.gov), and the next section discusses each substance in further detail.

Alcohol

Alcohol is one of the most commonly used substances by teens. The most common route of administration is usually oral (drinking), but other routes include intravaginal and rectal use. Because of the multitude of problems created by alcohol use, extensive interventions at the local, state, and federal levels have been developed toward the prevention and treatment of alcohol problems in children and adolescents (CASA, 2009). These interventions have been correlated with a reduction in alcohol use among teens to historically low levels. Between 2006 and 2011, heavy drinking declined from 9% to 6% among 8th-graders, from 20% to 15% among 10th-graders, and from 25% to 22% among 12th-graders (Johnston, O'Malley, Bachman, & Schulenberg, 2013). This reduction is welcomed, but what signs surface among youth who abuse alcohol?

Signs of Intoxication

Alcohol causes a general slowing of most brain functions. Symptoms of alcohol intoxication include decreased anxiety, sleepiness, decreased motor coordination, and slurred speech. Because the part of the brain that inhibits inappropriate impulses is also slowed, children and adolescents intoxicated with alcohol can get mentally or physically aggressive and sexually inappropriate. If a child or adolescent consumes a large amount of alcohol, he or she can experience signs and symptoms of alcohol poisoning, such as vomiting, confusion, decreased breathing, inability to maintain wakefulness, and possible death.

Rebound Effects

Rebound symptoms from alcohol are often known as a "hangover" and include headache, nausea, diarrhea, sensitivity to light and noise, lethargy, thirst, depression, and anxiety. These symptoms usually begin the morning after consuming heavy amounts of alcohol.

Binge Drinking

Binge drinking, defined as drinking five or more alcoholic drinks in a row in the previous 2 weeks, was reported by 5 % of 8th-graders, 16% of 10th-graders, and 24% of 12th-graders (Johnston et al., 2013). Binge drinking can be associated with risky sexual behavior, academic problems, and legal problems. Binge drinking also contributes to alcohol associated deaths. It is reported that 5,000 people each year under age 21 die from alcohol-related injuries, including motor vehicle crashes, homicides, and suicides (Centers for Disease Control and Prevention [CDC], 2010).

Tolerance and Withdrawal

Tolerance to alcohol implies that more alcohol is needed to produce the desired effect. If alcohol is consumed on a daily basis over months or years, withdrawal symptoms can also occur when alcohol is abruptly discontinued. Withdrawal symptoms include fever, tremors, rapid heart rate, and elevated blood pressure. Withdrawal from alcohol can lead to seizures or delirium tremens, which can be fatal. It has been estimated that 1.3% of adolescents meet the *DSM-IV* criteria for alcohol dependence, a condition in which adolescents usually experience signs of tolerance and withdrawal (Swendsen et al., 2012). The diagnosis of alcohol dependence has been removed from the *DSM-IV* in favor of a substance use disorder, mild, moderate, and severe (American Psychiatric Association, 2013).

Benzodiazepines and Hypnotics

Benzodiazepines are commonly prescribed medications for anxiety and include alprazolam (Xanax), lorazepam (Ativan), and clonazepam (Klonopin; see Figure 14.1). Hypnotics are commonly prescribed sleep medication and include zolpidem (Ambien) and escopliclone (Lunesta). Benzodiazepines and hypnotics are usually prescribed to take orally or sublingually, and they can be both in a tablet and a liquid form. When abused, children and adolescents will usually use them orally, intranasally, or inject them. Signs of intoxication, rebound, and dependence from benzodiazepines are very similar to alcohol use. If a child appears intoxicated, it is often hard to tell the difference between alcohol intoxication and intoxication with a benzodiazepine.

The main difference between alcohol and the different benzodiazepines is the length of time each chemical stays in the bloodstream. The half-life of a drug is the amount of time it takes for half the drug to leave the body. The half-life of alcohol is very short, and after drinking a drink of alcohol, much of the drink leaves the bloodstream within hours. The half-life of benzodiazepines is much longer; it can even take days for the substance to leave the body. This long half-life can cause a prolonged rebound effect and a prolonged withdrawal syndrome. This also contributes to increased lethality in overdose, especially in combination with other substances such as opiates or alcohol.

Stimulants

Stimulants are commonly used substances by children that come in many forms, both legal and illicit. Common stimulants include nicotine, caffeine, prescription stimulants, cocaine, and methamphetamine.

| Xanax | Klonopin | Ativan | Ambien |

FIGURE 14.1 Examples of benzodiazepines and hypnotic substances.

Sources: Connecticut Department of Consumer Protection (2013a, 2013b); National Institutes of Health (2013a).

Signs of Intoxication

Stimulants mainly work by increasing adrenaline and engaging the "fight or flight" response which contributes to increased heart rate, euphoria, and increased alertness. When taken in higher doses, they can cause cardiac toxicity, rapid heart rate, high blood pressure, and possible heart attack or stroke. Stimulant intoxication can cause unpredictable behavior including paranoia and delusions. "Runs" are uninterrupted sequences of stimulant abuse to extend the high and postpone the crash. During the "runs," a child or adolescent may remain missing for days.

Rebound Effects

Rebound effects with stimulants are commonly referred to as the "crash." These often occur as the stimulant is wearing off. Symptoms include fatigue, lethargy, depression, and an increase in hyperactivity. The onset of the crash and the length of time it lasts depends on the half-life of the stimulant.

Tolerance and Withdrawal

Like other substances, children and adolescents who use stimulants on a regular basis can experience tolerance and withdrawal symptoms. Withdrawal symptoms occur when, after a long period of daily use, stimulants are stopped abruptly. The withdrawal symptoms of stimulants are similar to rebound symptoms and include fatigue, depression, lethargy, hypersomnolence, increased appetite, weight gain, and headache.

Caffeine

Caffeine is one of the most commonly used stimulants. The half-life of caffeine is 5–6 hours. It is located in many substances, such as coffee, tea, energy drinks, energy supplements, and pills. All forms of caffeine are legal for teens to buy. Caffeine is usually consumed orally, but other forms are becoming more popular, such as sublingual use. Caffeine also is commonly mixed with alcohol in order to allow people to stay up longer and become more intoxicated. Deaths have been attributed to caffeine use and the U.S. Food and Drug Administration (FDA) is examining the impact of caffeine use and may make some forms of caffeine age-restricted or illegal (Meier, 2012).

Nicotine

Nicotine is another very commonly used stimulant. It is found exclusively in the tobacco plant (*Nicotiana tabacum*). Tobacco is made into snuff, chewing tobacco, pipe tobacco, cigars, and cigarettes. Nicotine has also been isolated from tobacco and is used in electronic inhalers (e-cigarettes), patches, and gum. The most common routes of administration of nicotine are smoking, sublingual, intranasal, and transdermal. Nicotine has a typical half-life of about 30 minutes and thus has a fast onset of action and fast onset of rebound and withdrawal effects.

Similar to alcohol, extensive resources have been spent on decreasing nicotine use by children (CASA, 2009). In 2010, the purchase of tobacco by a person under age 18 was made illegal and vendors may suffer a fine for selling an underaged person tobacco products. Like alcohol use, efforts to reduce tobacco use in children and adolescents have been correlated with decreased tobacco use. Cigarette smoking peaked in 1996–1997 and has declined continuously since then (Johnston et al., 2013).

Cocaine

Cocaine is a white powder stimulant found in the coca plant (see Figure 14.2). Cocaine is illegal and is usually smuggled into the United States from Mexico. It is snorted, smoked, or injected and has a typical half-life of about 60–90 minutes. Crack cocaine is a form of cocaine that is created with baking soda and that is usually smoked; it brings a quicker high of shorter duration. Also, crack cocaine is typically less expensive than powdered cocaine. Cocaine use has slowly decreased in children and adolescents. The use of cocaine by 12th-graders dropped from 5.2% to 2.7% from 2007 to 2012 (Johnston et al., 2013). Some of this reduction may be attributed to increased educational efforts, but some of it may be the shifting of use to prescription stimulants, which are considered easier to obtain by children and adolescents (Boyd, McCabe, Cranford, & Young, 2007).

Prescription Stimulants

Commonly abused prescription stimulants include methyphenidate (Ritalin), amphetamine mixed salts (Adderall), amphetamine extend release (Concerta), and lisdexamfetamine (Vyvanse; see Figure 14.3). Their half-life and potency depends on their dosage and formulation. Prescription stimulants are mostly used by adolescents for the purpose of increasing the ability to study. However, they are also used to help stay up and drink longer, for weight loss, and for performance enhancement in athletics

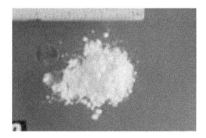

FIGURE 14.2 Cocaine in powder form.
Source: U.S. Drug Enforcement Administration (2013a).

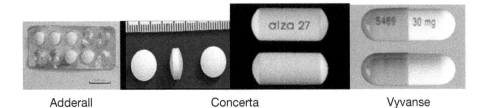

FIGURE 14.3 Stimulants: Adderall, Concerta, and Vyvanse.

Sources: U.S. Food and Drug Administration (2012); National Institutes of Health (2013b).

(Gomes, Song, Godwin, & Toriello, 2011). Prescription stimulants are typically swallowed, snorted, or injected.

Adolescents using prescription stimulants are also using other substances of abuse, such as alcohol and marijuana (Arria et al., 2008). Like other stimulants, use of prescription stimulants can lead to a variety of mental and physical consequences. The rate of increase in use and complications of prescription stimulants is evidenced in the increasing emergency room visits. Between 2005 and 2010, the number of emergency department (ED) visits involving stimulant medications increased from 13,379 to 31,244 visits (Substance Abuse and Mental Health Services Administration, Drug Abuse Warning Network, 2010).

Methamphetamine

Methamphetamine is a highly addictive drug that is often created in "home meth labs" from over-the-counter ingredients such as pseudoephedrine (Sudafed). Crystal meth is the most common form of methamphetamine and is usually smoked in glass pipes, similar to how crack cocaine is used. It may be injected (either dry or dissolved in water), snorted, swallowed, or inserted into the anus or urethra. The annual prevalence in adolescents appears to be decreasing and is currently at about 1.1% in 8th-graders and 1.6% in 12th-graders (Johnston et al., 2013).

The process of creating crystal meth can be very dangerous. Many people suffer injuries and die each year from chemical burns, chemical inhalation, and fires at meth labs (CDC, 2011a). Another of the unique dangers of meth use includes a condition informally known as "meth mouth." For many reasons, crystal meth users experience rapid tooth and gum decay (Hasan & Ciancio, 2004; Shaner, 2002; see Figure 14.4).

Opiates

Opiates include prescription opiates such as acetaminophen/hydrocodone (Vicodin), acetomenophin/oxycodone (Percocet), oxymorphone (Opana), and heroin (see Figure 14.5). Many children and adolescents who misuse opiates start with prescription

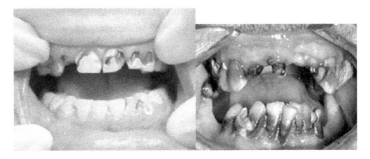

FIGURE 14.4 The impact of methamphetamine use on oral health.
Source: U.S. Department of Justice (2013).

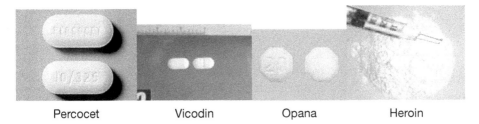

Percocet   Vicodin   Opana   Heroin

FIGURE 14.5 Opiates: Percocet, Vicodin, Opana, and heroin.
Sources: Connecticut Department of Consumer Protection (2013c); U.S. Department of Justice (2006); U.S. Drug Enforcement Administration (2013b).

opiate use. Prescription painkiller overdoses were implicated in the deaths of nearly 15,000 people in the United States in 2008 (CDC, 2011b). Oral prescription opiate use often leads to intranasal prescription opiate use, which leads to intranasal heroin use and ultimately to injecting heroin (Lankenaua et al., 2012). Injecting heroin leads to an increased mortality due to Hepatitis C, HIV, overdose, and other complications.

Signs of Intoxication

Opiates work by binding to opiate receptors in the brain, which exist to help modulate pain. The mental effects of opiate intoxication include euphoria, slowed movement, sedation, pain-killing effects, and calmness. The physical effects include bradycardia, low body temperature, pinpoint pupils, slurred speech, low blood pressure, and constipation. When overdosed, people often die from respiratory depression.

Withdrawal

Opiate withdrawal is considered the most uncomfortable withdrawal syndrome of all drugs of abuse. Although not life-threatening, the mental and physical symptoms include restlessness, anxiety, dilated pupils, increased pulse rate, yawning, chills, tearing, sweating, gooseflesh, insomnia, muscular aches, nausea, vomiting, diarrhea, and dehydration.

Cannabinoids

Cannabinoids bind to the cannabinoid receptors in the brain and body and produce a variety of effects. Marijuana is the most commonly used cannabinoid (see Figure 14.6). Tetrahyocannabinol (THC) is the chemical in marijuana that binds to the cannabinoid receptors and produces the psychoactive effects. Smoking marijuana is the common route of administration and causes 50% of cannabinoids to enter the lungs. Holding the smoke in the lungs maximizes absorption. THC is not absorbed well when swallowed, but children and adolescents do use marijuana orally and often mix it with sweet foods such as brownies. New forms of marijuana such as "oils" and "waxes" are becoming more popular and increase the potency.

Marijuana use by adolescents declined from the late 1990s until the mid- to late 2000s but has been on the increase since then. In 2012, 6.5% of 8th-graders, 17.0% of 10th-graders, and 22.9% of 12th-graders had used marijuana in the preceding month. This is a 3–4% increase in 10th- and 12th-graders since 2007. Daily use has also increased. 6.5% of 12th-graders now use marijuana every day, compared to 5.1% in the 2007 (Johnston et al., 2013).

Synthetic marijuana is a new and major concern. Also known as "spice" or "K2," synthetic marijuana refers to herbal mixtures laced with synthetic cannabinoids, chemicals that act in the brain similarly to THC. These mixtures could be obtained legally until recently. In 2011, approximately 11% of 12th-graders reported using K2 (Johnston et al., 2013).

Signs of Intoxication and Withdrawal

Signs of intoxication from cannabinoids include euphoria followed by relaxation, impaired memory, poor concentration, conjunctiva injection (red eyes), loss of coordination, vivid

Marijuana   K2 (spice; synthetic marijuana)

FIGURE 14.6 Cannabinoids.

Sources: Alaska Department of Public Safety (2013); U.S. Drug Enforcement Administration (2013c).

enhancement of most senses, insomnia, increased appetite (munchies), hyperactivity, sensory exaggeration, and mood exaggerations. Signs of withdrawal can include insomnia, hyperactivity, and decreased appetite.

MDMA (3,4-methylenedioxy-N-methylamphetamine)

MDMA is commonly known as "ecstasy" or "Molly" and was synthesized from methamphetamine in 1985 (see Figure 14.7). MDMA is commonly used in the "rave" scene in which teens get together in large groups, listen to electronic music, and use drugs such as MDMA and hallucinogens. MDMA is seeing a significant drop among teens. Past-year use of ecstasy by 12th-graders decreased from 5.3% in 2011 to 3.8% in 2012, and among 10th- and 8th-graders, it dropped from 4.5 to 3.0% and from 1.7 to 1.1%, respectively (Johnston et al., 2013).

Signs of Intoxication

Signs of intoxication from MDMA include subjective feelings of openness, empathy, energy, euphoria, and well-being. Sensations are enhanced for some users, making physical contact with others more pleasurable. Heart rates and blood pressure are increased, and there is a risk of permanent heart damage. MDMA can also cause impaired muscular coordination, chills, confusion, dehydration, jaw clenching, and hyperthermia.

Hallucinogens

Hallucinogens include LSD, psilocybin, mescaline, ketamine, PCP, and 2C-E (see Figure 14.8). Hallucinogens are commonly experimented with but are not as commonly used on a regular basis. According to the 2012 Monitoring the Future study, 1.9 % of 8th-graders and 4.0% of 12th-graders had admitted to trying LSD once in their lifetime. In addition, 7.8% of high school seniors had used hallucinogens other than LSD at least once in their lifetime (Johnston et al., 2013).

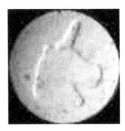

FIGURE 14.7 MDMA (ecstasy).
Source: U.S. Drug Enforcement Administration (2013c).

| LSD | Psilocybin | 2C-E |

FIGURE 14.8 Hallucinogens.
Sources: U.S. Department of Justice (2001); U.S. Drug Enforcement Administration (2011); U.S. Drug Enforcement Administration (2013d).

Signs of Intoxication

Hallucinogens may cause euphoria, changes in mood, depersonalization, illusions, visual hallucinations, time and visual distortions, and synesthesias (sensory confusion). They may also cause nausea, dilated pupils, increased heart rate and blood pressure, hyperthermia, and tremors. Children and adolescents can exhibit dangerous behavior while intoxicated with hallucinogens. In addition, children and adolescents can also experience "bad trips" that can result in anxiety, paranoia, and psychosis that can last for months after use (Nichols, 2004).

Bath Salts

Bath salts are newer designer drugs that were legal until 2012. They are chemicals designed for intranasal use and were packaged in containers that were for sale at gas stations and specialty stores. They are a variety of synthesized chemicals, called substituted cathinones, that can act as both stimulants and hallucinogens. Users of bath salts have reported experiencing symptoms including headaches, heart palpitations, nausea, cold fingers, hallucinations, paranoia, and panic attacks. Deaths have been associated with the use of bath salts (Prosser and Nelson, 2012; see Figure 14.9).

Solvents/Inhalants

Inhalants include volatile solvents, aerosols, anesthetic agents, amyl, butyl, and isobutyl nitrite. They are often available in household products that children and adolescents have easy access to, such as cleaners and glues. Inhalants are one of the most dangerous drugs owing to their ability to cause direct damage to the structures of the brain. Fortunately, inhalant use is at its lowest levels in survey history. Past-year inhalant use by younger teens dropped significantly between 2007 and 2012, from 8.3% of 8th-graders and 6.6% of 10th-graders to 6.2% and 4.1%, respectively (Johnston et al., 2013).

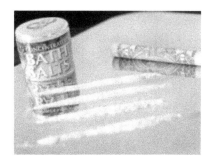

FIGURE 14.9 Bath salts.
Source: Griffo (2011).

Signs of Intoxication

At low doses, inhalants cause marked euphoria and dizziness, slurred speech, ataxia, impaired judgment and euphoria, and possible perceptual distortions. At high doses, they have generalized depressant effects upon the central nervous system similar to sedative hypnotics such as alcohol or benzodiazepines.

See Tables 14.1 and 14.2 for a complete list of substances.

RISK FACTORS FOR SUBSTANCE USE IN CHILDREN AND ADOLESCENTS

To create effective prevention strategies and to treat substance use disorders effectively, it is important to understand the risk factors that contribute to substance in children and adolescents.

Societal and Neighborhood Risk Factors

Different countries have different rates of substance use, but the United States is the society with the highest level of illegal drug use in the world (Degenhardt et al., 2008). Societal risk factors include legality, social acceptability, and availability of substances. Alcohol is the most commonly used drug in the United States, and it has been found that legal restrictions on the purchase of alcohol, decreased availability of alcohol, and societal norms unfavorable toward alcohol use are associated with a lower prevalence of alcohol abuse. Decreasing availability of other substances in society also reduces use of the substance (Hawkins, Catalano, & Miller, 1992).

Certain neighborhoods or schools are more associated with use of substances than others. Neighborhoods that include poverty and disorganization are more likely to have problems with substance use (Degenhardt et al., 2008). Neighborhoods may also differ from geographical differences regarding access to different drugs (Substance Abuse and Mental Health Services Administration, 2012). For instance, predominately Caucasian rural schools

TABLE 14.1 Commonly Abused Drugs

Substances: Category and Name	Examples of Commercial and Street Names	DEA Schedule*/How Administered**	Acute Effects/Health Risks
Tobacco			
Nicotine	Found in cigarettes, cigars, bidis, and smokeless tobacco (snuff, spit tobacco, chew)	Not scheduled/ smoked, snorted, chewed	*Increased blood pressure and heart rate/chronic lung disease; cardiovascular disease; stroke; cancers of the mouth, pharynx, larynx, esophagus, stomach, pancreas, cervix, kidney, bladder, and acute myeloid leukemia; adverse pregnancy outcomes; addiction*
Alcohol			
Alcohol (ethyl alcohol)	Found in liquor, beer, and wine	Not scheduled/ swallowed	*In low doses, euphoria, mild stimulation, relaxation, lowered inhibitions; in higher doses, drowsiness, slurred speech, nausea, emotional volatility, loss of coordination, visual distortions, impaired memory, sexual dysfunction, loss of consciousness/increased risk of injuries, violence, fetal damage (in pregnant women); depression; neurologic deficits; hypertension; liver and heart disease; addiction; fatal overdose*
Cannabinoids			
Marijuana	Blunt, dope, ganja, grass, herb, joint, bud, Mary Jane, pot, reefer, green, trees, smoke, sinsemilla, skunk, weed	I/smoked, swallowed	*Euphoria; relaxation; slowed reaction time; distorted sensory perception; impaired balance and coordination; increased heart rate and appetite; impaired learning, memory; anxiety; panic attacks; psychosis/cough; frequent respiratory infections; possible mental health decline; addiction*
Hashish	Boom, gangster, hash, hash oil, hemp	I/smoked, swallowed	
Opioids			
Heroin	*Diacetylmorphine:* smack, horse, brown sugar, dope, H, junk, skag, skunk, white horse, China white; cheese (with OTC cold medicine and antihistamine)	I/injected, smoked, snorted	*Euphoria; drowsiness; impaired coordination; dizziness; confusion; nausea; sedation; feeling of heaviness in the body; slowed or arrested breathing/ constipation; endocarditis; hepatitis; HIV; addiction; fatal overdose*
Opium	*Laudanum, paregoric:* big O, black stuff, block, gum, hop	II, III, V/swallowed, smoked	

	Commercial and street names	DEA schedule/how administered	Acute effects/health risks
Stimulants			
Cocaine	Cocaine hydrochloride: blow, bump, C, candy, Charlie, coke, crack, flake, rock, snow, toot	II/snorted, smoked, injected	*Increased heart rate, blood pressure, body temperature, metabolism; feelings of exhilaration; increased energy, mental alertness; tremors; reduced appetite; irritability; anxiety; panic; paranoia; violent behavior; psychosis/weight loss; insomnia; cardiac or cardiovascular complications; stroke; seizures; addiction* **Also, for cocaine**—nasal damage from snorting **Also, for methamphetamine**—severe dental problems
Amphetamine	Biphetamine, Dexedrine: bennies, black beauties, crosses, hearts, LA turnaround, speed, truck drivers, uppers	II/swallowed, snorted, smoked, injected	
Methamphetamine	Desoxyn: meth, ice, crank, chalk, crystal, fire, glass, go fast, speed	II/swallowed, snorted, smoked, injected	
Club Drungs			
MDMA (methylenedioxymethamphetamine)	Ecstasy, Adam, clarity, Eve, lover's speed, peace, uppers	I/swallowed, snorted, injected	*MDMA—mild hallucinogenic effects; increased tactile sensitivity, empathic feelings; lowered inhibition; anxiety; chills; sweating; teeth clenching; muscle cramping/sleep disturbances; depression; impaired memory; hyperthermia; addiction* *Flunitrazepam—sedation; muscle relaxation; confusion; memory loss; dizziness; impaired coordination/addiction* *GHB—drowsiness; nausea; headache; disorientation; loss of coordination; memory loss/unconsciousness; seizures; coma*
Flunitrazepam***	Rohypnol: forget-me pill, Mexican Valium, R2, roach, Roche, roofies, roofinol, rope, rophies	IV/swallowed, snorted	
GHB***	Gamma-hydroxybutyrate: G, Georgia home boy, grievous bodily harm, liquid ecstasy, soap, scoop, goop, liquid X	I/swallowed	
Dissociative Drugs			
Ketamine	Ketalar SV: cat Valium, K, Special K, vitamin K	III/injected, snorted, smoked	*Feelings of being separate from one's body and environment; impaired motor function/anxiety; tremors; numbness; memory loss; nausea* **Also, for ketamine**— *analgesia; impaired memory; delirium; respiratory depression and arrest; death* **Also, for PCP and analogs**—*analgesia; psychosis; aggression; violence; slurred speech; loss of coordination; hallucinations* **Also, for DXM**—*euphoria; slurred speech; confusion; dizziness; distorted visual perceptions*
PCP and analogs	Phencyclidine: angel dust, boat, hog, love boat, peace pill	I, II/swallowed, smoked, injected	
Salvia divinorum	Salvia, Shepherdess's Herb, Maria Pastora, magic mint, Sally-D	Not scheduled/chewed, swallowed, smoked	
Dextromethorphan (DXM)	Found in some cough and cold medications: Robotripping, Robo, Triple C	Not scheduled/swallowed	

(continued)

TABLE 14.1 Commonly Abused Drugs (*continued*)

Substances: Category and Name	Examples of Commercial and Street Names	DEA Schedule*/ How Administered**	Acute Effects/Health Risks
Hallucinogens			Altered states of perception and feeling; hallucinations; nausea
LSD	*Lysergic acid diethylamide*: acid, blotter, cubes, microdot, yellow sunshine, blue heaven	I/swallowed, absorbed through mouth tissues	**Also, for LSD and mescaline**—increased body temperature, heart rate, blood pressure; loss of appetite; sweating; sleeplessness; numbness; dizziness; weakness; tremors; impulsive behavior; rapid shifts in emotion
Mescaline	Buttons, cactus, mesc, peyote	I/swallowed, smoked	**Also, for LSD**—Flashbacks, Hallucinogen Persisting Perception Disorder
Psilocybin	Magic mushrooms, purple passion, shrooms, little smoke	I/swallowed	**Also, for psilocybin**—nervousness; paranoia; panic
Other Compounds			**Steroids**—no intoxication effects/hypertension; blood clotting and cholesterol changes; liver cysts; hostility and aggression; acne; in adolescents—premature stoppage of growth; in males—prostate cancer, reduced sperm production, shrunken testicles, breast enlargement; in females—menstrual irregularities, development of beard and other masculine characteristics
Anabolic steroids	*Anadrol, Oxandrin, Durabolin, Depo-Testosterone, Equipoise*: roids, juice, gym candy, pumpers	III/injected, swallowed, applied to skin	
Inhalants	Solvents (*paint thinners, gasoline, glues*); gases (*butane, propane, aerosol propellants, nitrous oxide*); nitrites (*isoamyl, isobutyl, cyclohexyl*): laughing gas, poppers, snappers, whippets	Not scheduled/inhaled through nose or mouth	**Inhalants** (varies by chemical)—stimulation; loss of inhibition; headache; nausea or vomiting; slurred speech; loss of motor coordination; wheezing/cramps; muscle weakness; depression; memory impairment; damage to cardiovascular and nervous systems; unconsciousness; sudden death

Source: National Institute on Drug Abuse (2011).

* Schedule I and II drugs have a high potential for abuse. They require greater storage security and have a quota on manufacturing, among other restrictions. Schedule I drugs are available for research only and have no approved medical use; Schedule II drugs are available only by prescription (unrefillable) and require a form for ordering. Schedule III and IV drugs are available by prescription, may have five refills in 6 months, and may be ordered orally. Some Schedule V drugs are available over the counter.

** Some of the health risks are directly related to the route of drug administration. For example, injection drug use can increase the risk of infection through needle contamination with staphylococci, HIV, hepatitis, and other organisms.

*** Associated with sexual assaults.

TABLE 14.2 Commonly Abused Prescription Drugs

Substances: Category and Name	Examples of Commercial and Street Name	DEA Schedule*/How Administered	Intoxication Effects/ Health Risks
Depressants			*Sedation/drowsiness, reduced anxiety, feelings of well-being, lowered inhibitions, slurred speech, poor concentration, confusion, dizziness, impaired coordination and memory/slowed pulse, lowered blood pressure, slowed breathing, tolerance, withdrawal, addiction; increased risk of respiratory distress and death when combined with alcohol*
Barbiturates	*Amytal, Nembutal, Seconal, Phenobarbital:* barbs, reds, red birds, phennies, tooies, yellows, yellow jackets	II, III, IV/injected, swallowed	
Benzodiazepines	*Ativan, Halcion, Librium, Valium, Xanax, Klonopin:* candy, downers, sleeping pills, tranks	IV/swallowed	*for barbiturates—euphoria, unusual excitement, fever, irritability/life-threatening withdrawal in chronic users*
Sleep Medications	*Ambien (zolpidem), Sonata (zaleplon), Lunesta (eszopiclone)*	IV/swallowed	
Opioids and Morphine Derivatives**			*Pain relief, euphoria, drowsiness, sedation, weakness, dizziness, nausea, impaired coordination, confusion, dry mouth, itching, sweating, clammy skin, constipation/slowed or arrested breathing, lowered pulse and blood pressure, tolerance, addiction, unconsciousness, coma, death; risk of death increased when combined with alcohol or other CNS depressants*
Codeine	*Empirin with Codeine, Fiorinal with Codeine, Robitussin A-C, Tylenol with Codeine:* Captain Cody, Cody, schoolboy; (with glutethimide: doors & fours, loads, pancakes and syrup)	II, III, IV/injected, swallowed	
Morphine	*Roxanol, Duramorph:* M, Miss Emma, monkey, white stuff	II, III/injected, swallowed, smoked	*for fentanyl—80–100 times more potent analgesic than morphine*
Methadone	*Methadose, Dolophine:* fizzies, amidone, (with MDMA: chocolate chip cookies)	II/swallowed, injected	*for oxycodone—muscle relaxation/twice as potent analgesic as morphine; high abuse potential*
Fentanyl and analogs	*Actiq, Duragesic, Sublimaze:* Apache, China girl, dance fever, friend, goodfella, jackpot, murder 8, TNT, Tango and Cash	II/injected, smoked, snorted	*for codeine—less analgesia, sedation, and respiratory depression than morphine*
Other Opioid Pain Relievers: Oxycodone HCL Hydrocodone Bitartrate Hydromorphone Oxymorphone Meperidine Propoxyphene	*Tylox, Oxycontin, Percodan, Percocet:* Oxy, O.C., oxycotton, oxycet, hillbilly heroin, percs *Vicodin, Lortab, Lorcet:* vike, Watson-387 *Dilaudid:* juice, smack, D, footballs, dillies *Opana, Numorphan, Numorphone:* biscuits, blue heaven, blues, Mrs. O, octagons, stop signs, O Bomb *Demerol, meperidine hydrochloride:* demmies, pain killer *Darvon, Darvocet*	II, III, IV/chewed, swallowed, snorted, injected, suppositories	*for methadone—used to treat opioid addiction and pain; significant overdose risk when used improperly*

329

TABLE 14.2 Commonly Abused Prescription Drugs (*continued*)

Substances: Category and Name	Examples of Commercial and Street Name	DEA Schedule*/How Administered	Intoxication Effects/ Health Risks
Stimulants			*Feelings of exhilaration, increased energy, mental alertness/increased heart rate, blood pressure, and metabolism, reduced appetite, weight loss, nervousness, insomnia, seizures, heart attack, stroke*
Amphetamines	*Biphetamine, Dexedrine, Adderall:* bennies, black beauties, crosses, hearts, LA turnaround, speed, truck drivers, uppers	II/injected, swallowed, smoked, snorted	*for amphetamines—rapid breathing, tremor, loss of coordination, irritability, anxiousness, restlessness/delirium, panic, paranoia, hallucinations, impulsive behavior, aggressiveness, tolerance, addiction*
Methylphenidate	*Concerta, Ritalin:* JIF, MPH, R-ball, Skippy, the smart drug, vitamin R	II/injected, swallowed, snorted	*for methylphenidate—increase or decrease in blood pressure, digestive problems, loss of appetite, weight loss*
Other Compounds			Euphoria, slurred speech/increased heart rate and blood pressure, dizziness, nausea, vomiting, confusion, paranoia, distorted visual perceptions, impaired motor function
Dextromethorphan (DXM)	*Found in some cough and cold medications:* Robotripping, Robo, Triple C	not scheduled/ swallowed	

Source: National Institute on Drug Abuse (2011).

*Schedule I and II drugs have a high potential for abuse. They require greater storage security and have a quota on manufacturing, among other restrictions. Schedule I drugs are available for research only and have no approved medical use. Schedule II drugs are available only by prescription and require a new prescription for each refill. Schedule III and IV drugs are available by prescription, may have five refills in 6 months, and may be ordered orally. Most Schedule V drugs are available over the counter.

** Taking drugs by injection can increase the risk of infection through needle contamination with staphylococci, HIV, hepatitis, and other organisms. Injection is a more common practice for opioids, but risks apply to any medication taken by injection.*

may show more use of methamphetamine, whereas urban schools may show more use of crack cocaine (Raptopoulos, 2008). More academically competitive schools may have more prescription stimulant abuse (McCabe, Knight, & Teter, 2005). Understanding the climate and context for your school puts you in a better position to craft an appropriate intervention and education for students.

Family Risk Factors

Children and adolescents are also more likely to use a substance if their family carries several risk factors. For example, if another member of the family, such as a parent or sibling, uses a substance, then the child is also more likely to use a substance (Ary, Tildesley, Hops, & Andrews, 1993). It has also been found that lack of maternal involvement in activities with children, lack of consistent parental discipline, and low parental educational aspirations for their children predict initiation of drug use (Kandel & Andrews, 1987).

Genetic inheritance from family members also likely plays a role in substance use. Adoption studies in Denmark and the United States have provided evidence for genetic transmission of alcoholism in males, reporting increased rates of alcoholism for the adopted sons of alcoholics compared with adopted males without a biological alcoholic parent (Goodwin, Schulsinger, Hermansen, Guze, & Winokur, 1973; Pickens et al., 1991). Studies have also suggested that inheritance plays a role in drug use. Data collected by telephone interview from 3,372 twin pairs of the Vietnam-Era Twin Registry found a significant difference between concordance rates for monozygotic (26.2%) versus dizygotic (16.5%) twins on drug use disorder inheritance (Tsuang et al., 1996).

The enzyme aldehyde dehydrogenase (ALDH) is important in the metabolism of ethanol. Levels and types of this enzyme are inherited and are known to vary in certain populations. For instance, many Asians have a form of this enzyme that contributes to flushing after drinking and may also affect the ability to feel the euphoria from alcohol use. Studies suggest that levels and type of ALDH contribute to different rates of alcoholism (Schuckit, 1987; Higachi, Matsushita, Murayama, Takagi, & Hayashida, 1995). Equipping youth and families with this information in addition to other knowledge may be helpful in mediating alcohol use and abuse.

Individual Risk Factors

In addition to societal and family risk factors, each child and adolescent has his or her own risk factors that contribute to substance use. Poor impulse control in childhood predicts frequent marijuana use at age 18 (Shedler & Block, 1990). Aggressiveness in boys as early as age 5 has been found to predict later antisocial behavior including frequent drug use in adolescence (Fleming, Kellam, & Brown, 1982). Failure in school and low degree of commitment to education has been identified as a predictor of adolescent drug abuse (Jessor, 1976; Robins, 1984). Surveys of high school students have found significantly lower substance use among students who expect to attend college than among those who do not plan to go on to college (Johnston, O'Malley, & Bachman, 1985). Finally, "peer pressure" is known to influence substance use. Peer use of substances has been found to have a significant effect on substance use in adolescents (Barnes & Welte, 1986; Kandel, Simcha-Fagan, & Davies, 1986; Steinberg, Fletcher, & Darling, 1994).

PREVENTION OF SUBSTANCE USE DISORDERS

To decrease substance use in the schools, a tiered intervention model that provides support along three tiers can be extremely beneficial. Tier 1 involves universal education programs that support the drug-free development of all students, Tier 2 involves targeted small group substance abuse interventions, and Tier 3 involves individual treatment of students with substance use issues.

Most prevention strategies involve Tier 1 and Tier 2 interventions. Tier 1 interventions are designed to expose students to the knowledge of the harmful effects of substances and help to reinforce positive behaviors among students. Life skills training (LST) curriculum is an example of a Tier 1 intervention. LST is designed to teach students to educate students about substance abuse and about how to resist peer pressure, develop greater self-esteem, and cope with anxiety (Belcher & Shinitzky, 1998; Botvin & Griffin, 2000; Komro et al., 2001). Other Tier 1 interventions that have been studied include Project ALERT (Belcher & Shinitzky, 1998) and Project Northland (Komro et al., 2001; Tobler et al., 2000). Ellickson et al. (1990, 2003) found the Project ALERT program to be effective for prevention and use reduction in school-age children.

Tier 2 interventions involve selected interventions to target specific students. Tier 2 interventions often involve student support teams (SST) consisting of educators, administrators, psychologists, and social workers. These teams help to match high-risk students with appropriate individual and group interventions. These interventions may involve programs such as small psychoeducational groups, harm reduction programs, drama workshops, and mentoring. The SST may also refer to more intensive individualized Tier 3 treatment. Examples of successful SST programs exist in the literature (Ervin, Schaughency, Matthews, Goodman, and McGlinchey, 2007).

Tier 1 and Tier 2 prevention programs can be started as early as preschool. The Incredible Years program is an example of a prevention program that starts at a very young age and is designed to help children with problem-solving strategies, managing anger, practicing friendship, and exhibiting appropriate classroom behaviors. Long-term follow-up of children who underwent the Incredible Years program indicates a decrease in substance use and other problematic behaviors when they reach adolescence (Webster-Stratton, 2011) .

It has been suggested that both Tier 1 and Tier 2 prevention programs should not only focus on one substance, but instead target the wide variety of substances (National Institute on Drug Abuse, 2003). When prevention programs focus on one specific drug, such as alcohol or tobacco, they may decrease the use of that drug but in turn increase the use of other substances. For instance, alcohol and tobacco use have been decreasing even as marijuana, prescription drug, and opiate use increase. Thus, prevention programs should likely address all forms of substance use previously mentioned, including alcohol, prescription drugs, and illicit drugs.

Although prevention programs should provide education on all drugs, it also has been suggested that prevention programs should target the specific substances that are problematic in the local community. For example, certain educational settings may find themselves especially plagued by cocaine and crack marketing and use; these settings may benefit from enhanced efforts to educate about this substance. Other settings may be plagued by prescription stimulants, and education should be geared towards these drugs (National Institute on Drug Abuse, 2003).

Finally, it should be noted there is evidence to suggest that research-based prevention programs can be cost effective. Research shows that for each $1 invested in prevention, a savings of up to $10 in treatment for alcohol or other substance abuse can be seen (Aos, Phipps, Barnoski, & Lieb, 2001).

IDENTIFICATION OF STUDENTS WITH SUBSTANCE USE ISSUES

Prevention is not always effective, and it is important for all professions that work with children, such as psychologists, educators, administrators, counselors, and peers, to understand how to identify a student with a substance use problem. Symptoms common in children and adolescents with substance use issues include moodiness, irritability, and evasiveness. Signs of intoxication or withdrawal from substances may also be noticed. Children and adolescents with a substance use disorder also have an increased likelihood of having another psychiatric disorder, such as depression, anxiety, attention deficit hyperactivity disorder (ADHD), and conduct disorder (Shrier, Harris, Kurland, & Knight, 2003).

Children and adolescents with substance use disorders may also show tardiness, absences, and/or a change in performance in school. There may be secretive or suspicious behavior and increased secrecy about possessions or activities. Parents and teachers may notice a change in clothing choices or new fascination with clothes that highlight drug use (PAM Organizers' Packet, 2013). They may also start to associate with known drug users (Lundborg, 2006). There may be an unexplained need for money, an increase in borrowing money, and possible stealing of items or money. They may be caught with items that suggest drug use such as pipes and rolling papers. Breath mints may be used to cover up the smell of alcohol, and eyedrops may be used to eliminate redeye from marijuana. The student may also start to have legal issues related to their alcohol or drug use (Mulvey, Schubert, & Chassin, 2010). Legal issues may be a result of being caught with illicit drugs or related to crime associated with obtaining the drugs.

Screening Students for Substance Use Issues

Screening for substance abuse problems is another way to identify students with substance use issues. Screening should be developmentally, age-, gender-, and culturally appropriate for the child or adolescent. Any person conducting screening and involved with the screening process should be qualified and appropriately trained. Common screening instruments for children and adolescents include the Adolescent Drinking Index (ADI), Adolescent Obsessive-Compulsive Drinking Scale (A-OCDS), Rutgers Alcohol Problem Index (RAPI), Drug Abuse Screening Test–Adolescents (DAST-A), Adolescent Alcohol and Drug Involvement Scale (AADIS), Assessment of Substance Misuse in Adolescence (ASMA), CRAFFT, and Personal Experience Screening Questionnaire (PESQ). See Table 14.3 for a list of commonly used screening instruments in children and adolescents (Substance Abuse and Mental Health Services Administration, 2011).

Treatment of Substance Use Disorders

Once a student is identified as having a substance use disorder, Tier 3 interventions that involve specific treatments can be used. Counseling can be done at the school or by a variety of public and private agencies. Substance Abuse and Mental Health Services Administration (SAMSHA) offers a treatment locator at www.findtreatment.samhsa.gov. Agencies can be contacted and asked whether they have substance abuse treatment and mental health services for children and adolescents. In addition, information about peer support groups such as Alcoholics Anonymous (AA) and Narcotics Anonymous (NA) can be found online (see the Resources section of this chapter).

Readiness for Help

To begin substance use treatment, it is important to identify a child or adolescent's readiness for help. One way this can be done is using the transtheoretical model for behavioral change. The transtheoretical model describes five stages of change including precontemplation, contemplation, preparation, action, and maintenance.

Children or adolescents in the precontemplation stage of a substance use problem have not even started to think about stopping their substance use. This affects their willingness to engage in treatment. Children or adolescents in the contemplation stage are usually willing to engage in at least a discussion about the advantages and disadvantages of using substances. They are starting to think about stopping their substance use but have not made a commitment to take action. Children or adolescents in the preparation stage are starting to be ready for change. These individuals have a plan of action such as attending counseling, peer support groups, or making environmental changes.

Children or adolescents in the action stage have made specific changes to decrease their substance use in the past 6 months. They are often engaging in treatment and have made environmental changes such as changing their peer group. Once the changes have been sustained for at least 6 months, they move to the maintenance stage. Children or adolescents in the maintenance stage are working to prevent relapse. They are less tempted to relapse and are increasingly confident that they can continue their change (Glanz & Rimer, 2008).

Confidentiality Issues

When children or adolescents enter treatment, one of their foremost concerns is confidentiality. They may be concerned about people obtaining their treatment records or their parents and their peers knowing that they have a problem. While it may be uncomfortable for families to accept and contrary to common school practice, it can be explained to children age 12 or older that they can seek outpatient substance abuse treatment without parent or guardian notification. They can also request that substance abuse treatment records be kept from their parents or legal guardian. Their parents cannot be notified unless the safety of the teen is in question (Electronic Code of Federal Regulations, 2013). As regards more specific medical treatment (such as inpatient treatment or medication), a child 18 years or younger must have the permission of a parent or guardian.

TABLE 14.3 Matrix of Substance Use/Abuse Screening Tools

Tool Characteristics	Alcohol Use/Abuse Screening Tools			Drug Use/Abuse Screening Tools	Substance Use/Abuse Screening Tools for Adolescents			
	Adolescent Drinking Index (ADI)	Adolescent Obsessive-Compulsive Drinking Scale (A-OCDS)	Rutgers Alcohol Problem Index (RAPI)	Drug Abuse Screening Test-Adolescents (DAST-A)	Adolescent Alcohol and Drug Involvement Scale (AADIS)	Assessment of Substance Misuse in Adolescence (ASMA)	CRAFFT	Personal Experience Screening Questionnaire (PESQ)
Target Conditions	Alcohol Use problem severity	Craving and problem drinking; differentiates drinkers from experimenters or abusers	Alcohol Use severity	Drug use problem severity	Alcohol and drug use problem severity	Drug use problem severity	Alcohol and drug use problem severity	Chemical dependency, psychosocial problems, and faking
High-Risk Items* Included	Yes	Yes	Yes	Yes—Includes drug-related risks, such as blackouts, withdrawal, and illegal activities	Yes	Yes	Yes—Also includes driving with a driver who has been drinking or is high	Yes—Drug use and certain psychosocial challenges
Informants or Youth Age Range	Youth ages 12–17 years	Youth ages 14–20 years	Adolescents	Adolescents	Youth ages 14–20 years	Adolescents	Adolescents	Youth ages 12–18 years
Format (Self-administered unless stated otherwise)	Paper & pencil, (group or Individual)	Paper & pencil	Paper & pencil interview	Paper & pencil	Paper & pencil or structured interview	Paper & pencil	Interview	Paper & pencil
Usual Administration Time	5 minutes	5–10 minutes	10 minutes	5 minutes	5 minutes	5 minutes	5 minutes	10 minutes
Reading Level Required	5th grade	5th grade†	6th–7th grade	6th grade	Not specified	Not specified	Appropriate for youth with poor reading skills	4th grade

	(p. 155)	(p. 157)	(p. 176)	(p. 167)	(p. 154)	(p. 160)	(p. 163)	(p. 174)
Translations		Adult Spanish version could be easily adapted by a bilingual provider					English version could be easily adapted by a bilingual provider	French, Spanish, and Portugese; English version adapted for Alaskans and Native Americans
Settings Where Tool Has Been Studied (Note: Tools may have been used successfully in settings where they have not been researched.)								
Primary Care						X	X	
Schools		X (College)				X	X	X
Early Care								
Child Welfare								
Juvenile Justice						X	X	X
Shelters			X	X				
Mental Health Treatment	X							
Substance Abuse Treatment	X			X		X	X	X
Cost	$100 for manual and 25 test booklets	Free	Free	Free or nominal cost	Free	Free	Free	$60 for manual; $43 for 25 forms; $99 for a kit that includes the manual and 25 forms
Appendix B page #	Page 155	Page 157	Page 176	Page 167	Page 154	Page 160	Page 163	Page 174

* High-risk items are those that identify acute mental health or substance use conditions warranting a prompt response. Examples of such conditions are suicidal thoughts, plans for self-harm, or abuse of substances. Specific high-risk items are listed for some tools.

† As Indicated in Deas, Roberts, Randall, and Anton (2001).

Psychotherapy for Substance Use

Several psychotherapies have been studied in children and adolescents with substance use disorders and have evidence to support their effectiveness. Motivational Enhancement Therapy (MET) involves increasing motivation to reduce substance use in one to five targeted sessions. Often a list is made of the positive and negative effects of using substances. This form of therapy is often targeted at children and adolescents in the precontemplation and contemplation stages. It is designed to help them move into the preparation and action stages of treatment. Several studies have found MET to have efficacy in treating adolescents and young adults with substance use disorders (Monti et al., 1999; Borsari & Carey, 2000; Marlatt et al., 1998).

Cognitive-Behavioral Therapy (CBT) involves modifying thought processes, beliefs, and behaviors associated with substance use. It usually involves stimulus control, which attempts to reduce environmental triggers associated with substance use. Examples of stimulus control include ending relationships with substance using peers and avoiding television shows that depict substance use. Studies have demonstrated the effectiveness of CBT in adolescents with substance use disorders (Kaminer, Burleson, & Goldberger, 2002).

Family therapy is also used to treat substance use disorders in children and adolescents. Family therapy examines the interdependent nature of family relationships. The goal of family therapy is to intervene in these relationships and to alter them in ways that bring about productive change for the entire family. Studies have also demonstrated effectiveness of family therapy in adolescents. (Ozechowski & Liddle, 2000).

Group therapy is also commonly used to treat substance use disorders. Group therapy provided by treatment centers is often psychoeducational in nature. In psychoeducational groups, children and adolescents are educated about different substances and the harms associated with them. They also are taught coping skills to deal with emotions such as anxiety and depression and how to deal with stressful situations. Finally, they are often given information on how to change peer relationships and avoid contact with other students that are using substances. One study done comparing four types of interventions suggested that group therapy is the most cost-effective treatment in adolescents (French et al., 2008).

Peer Support Groups

Peer support groups for children and adolescents include AA and NA. These programs rely primarily on the 12-step model for recovery. The 12-step model includes admitting that one cannot control one's addiction or compulsion, recognizing a higher power that can give strength, and making amends for past errors. Children and adolescents attending peer support group will often find a sponsor who helps guide their journey through the steps. (Substance Abuse and Mental Health Services Administration, 2011).

Peer support groups also exist for parents of children with substance use disorders. Al-Anon and Nar-Anon are two commonly attended peer support groups. Topics frequently discussed at these groups include education for parents about different substances, how to reduce enabling behaviors, and how to keep prescription medications safe from children. Several studies have shown peer support groups to be effective in treatment of substance use disorders (Humphreys et al., 2004). Most peer support groups have meeting locators and educators should be familiar with how to refer students and families to these locators.

Medication-Assisted Treatment

Several medications are FDA-approved to treat substance use issues. These medications have not been well tested in children, but they are being used off label in children. For nicotine dependence, nicotine replacement (gum, patch, e-cigarette) is used to decrease cravings and withdrawal symptoms from cigarettes. Buproprion (Zyban) and Varenicline (Chantix) are medications that have been FDA-approved for smoking cessation. Both buproprion and varencycline have been found to decrease cravings, and varencycline also helps with withdrawal symptoms and blocks the euphoria of nicotine.

Medications have also been FDA-approved to treat opiate dependence. Research shows the combination of medication assisted treatment and psychotherapy works better than psychotherapy alone for opiate dependence (Marsch, 2007). Naltexone (Vivitrol) is a medication which blocks the effects of opiates and can be given as a once-monthly injection. Methadone is an opiate that can only be dispensed at designated clinics and that acts as long-acting replacement for heroin and pain pills. Buprenorphine (Suboxone) is a partial opioid agonist that also acts as a long-acting replacement for heroin and pain pills that does not require daily dispensing. Both methadone and buprenorphine have been proven to reduce mortality from opiate addiction (Gibson et al., 2008). Naloxone (Narcan) is an opioid antagonist used to block the actions of opioids in a life-threatening situation of opioid overdose.

Medications have also been FDA-approved to treat adults with alcohol dependence. Disulfuram (Antabuse) is a medication that causes patients to experience an uncomfortable reaction when they drink alcohol. Naltrexone (vivitrol) is used to treat cravings and block the high from alcohol use. Acamprosate calcium (Campral) is thought to help alleviate cravings and withdrawal symptoms.

Levels of Treatment

The American Society of Addiction Medicine (ASAM) has outlined four levels of treatment for adolescents. Level I consists of outpatient treatment (such as individual therapy, family therapy, and group counseling) not totaling more than 6 hours per week. Level II consists of intensive outpatient treatment (IOP) of more than 6 hours per week. Level III and level IV consist of different forms of inpatient treatments ranging from half-way houses and supportive living environments to medically monitored inpatient units (ASAM, 2007).

Referrals to each level of care should involve thoughtful consideration. Children and adolescents who do not require medical supervision and do not experience withdrawal symptoms should be considered for Level I or II treatment. Children and adolescents who are chemically dependent on a substance (experience withdrawal symptoms) should be considered for medically monitored inpatient treatment. Students who need a more structured living environment should be considered for longer-term residential treatment facilities.

Legal Issues

Mandatory Drug Testing

In 2002, the U.S. Supreme Court allowed the public schools to perform mandatory drug testing on all students. Approximately 25% of districts now have a student drug-testing policy. It has been suggested that mandatory urine testing can help guide more students into treatment, but there are also privacy, disciplinary, and legal concerns (Butler, 2012).

Alternatives to Suspension and Prosecution

Many students with substance use disorders have violated codes of conduct at schools in addition to state and federal laws. Students caught with illegal substances will often face charges through the school's disciplinary system and through the legal system. Many schools suspend or expel students that have violated the code of student conduct as a result of their substance use disorder.

Many professionals have expressed concerns about long-term consequences for students who are expelled or convicted. To address these concerns, two programs have been developed. Alternative to Suspension (ATS) is a program adopted by schools that specifically targets a behavior that violates school policy and procedure (i.e., alcohol and drugs use) with a goal of altering behavior, fostering accountability, and reducing recidivism. If a student is caught with a substance, a mandated treatment is developed, often involving periodic drug screens (urine testing) and appropriate inpatient or outpatient treatment. Drug court has been developed by the legal system with a similar purpose. By entering drug court, offenders can obtain treatment and urine screening in order to have alcohol and drug charges dropped.

CASE STUDY

Reason for Referral

Brandon was referred due to excessive tardiness to morning classes and because his grades were in decline in all subjects.

Background/History

Brandon is a 16-year-old high school sophomore who has been referred to the school counselor due to academic difficulty and tardiness. He has been a solid academic student (GPA 3.0), but his grades have slipped dramatically this quarter. Currently, he has a C to D average for all subjects. His teacher spoke to his mother, Mrs. Tucker, about his grades and tardiness, and his mother was surprised. However, she acknowledged "he has not been himself for the last 2 months." His mother stated that he is hanging around "Tyler" and they think that Tyler is "bad news" and "always getting into trouble." According to Mrs. Tucker, Brandon does not keep a regular schedule and is out late most of the week and weekends. When asked, his mother did not think her son was using drugs but appeared to have little knowledge about different drugs and referred to all drugs as "crack." She did state that Brandon's father is in recovery from alcoholism and that he would "kill" Brandon if he was "smoking crack." Both his teacher and Brandon's mother agree that he would benefit from seeing the school counselor and/or the school psychologist on a weekly basis. They are hoping that Brandon's particular issues can be better defined and identified through this process.

Case Conceptualization

The school counselor/school psychologist established weekly appointments with Brandon. In an attempt to operationally define Brandon's specific problem(s), the possibility of drug usage, among other issues (e.g., depression, anxiety), was discussed. At first Brandon denied that there were any problems with drugs. The counselor reassured Brandon that sharing a substance use problem would be confidential. Over the course of the month, Brandon admitted that he was given "Percocet" from Tyler 3 months ago, and he is now using "Percocets" and

"Opanas" daily. He states he was swallowing the pills, but in the last few weeks he found the pills haven't been working when he swallows them. He has started to snort them. He is having frequent cravings and is starting to experience sweating and restlessness when he goes a day without using pain medications. He wants help, but he states, "My dad would kill me if he found out about this."

Brandon scores high on the AADIS (Moberg, 1991) that shows he has a problem with substances. He exhibits symptoms consistent with an opiate use disorder, moderate to severe. He is experiencing tolerance to opiates (needing more to have the same effect) along with withdrawal symptoms. Risk factors for use include Brandon's peer relationship with Tyler and his family history of addiction. He is assessed as being in the contemplation stage of change. He wants to stop using pain medications but is worried about his parents' finding out about his use.

Intervention Goals and Plan

The school counselor and school psychologist met regularly with Brandon in order to address his substance use disorder. The immediate therapy goal was to help Brandon communicate his problem to his parents so he can consider participating in more intense structured outpatient treatment. In particular, Brandon was more communicative with his mother about his drug problem. As maternal involvement increased, Mrs. Tucker was directed toward Nar-Anon to be more directly educated about prescription opiate use. She was then given a list of treatment providers for opiate dependence, including outpatient and inpatient treatment centers. The option of medication assisted treatment was discussed.

Intervention Assessment

Once Brandon received formal treatment for opiate dependency, he was monitored for signs of continued use. Physical signs of intoxication or withdrawal were also carefully monitored, and the outpatient weekly sessions were continued in order to determine how he was tolerating the substance abuse treatment and to make sure he is relapse free. The school-based weekly sessions were continued to monitor his academic progress, grades, and attendance at school.

Case Prognosis

Research suggests that the combination of medication and psychotherapy for opiate dependence is effective in children (Marsch, 2007). If treated before it progresses to significant drug dependency (e.g., I.V. heroin use), the life expectancy of a child or adolescent with opiate dependence improves dramatically.

Brandon's intervention success, as is true for all youth, is directly related to his level of parental support, his ability to engage in treatment, and his ability to change peer relationships.

SUMMARY

When resources are spent on prevention programs for children and adolescents, such as in the case of alcohol and tobacco, the results are positive. Therefore, educators, administrators, and mental health professionals should be familiar with research backed prevention strategies to target substance use. As new substances invade the schools, educational and mental health professionals should continually educate themselves on the different substances being used. They should be familiar with typical signs of intoxication and withdrawal from these substances. They should also be able to identify signs that children have developed substance use disorders. When children and adolescents are identified as having a problem, educators and mental health providers should be able to confer with family members and also be familiar with how to refer children and adolescents to research backed treatments for substance use disorders. Finally, consult with area treatment specialists to determine what school-based support intervention may be needed for youth identified with substance disorders.

RESOURCES

The websites for Alcoholics Anonymous (www.aa.org) and Narcotics Anonymous (www.na.org) have a wealth of information about drug and narcotic treatment.

The National Institute on Drug Abuse has produced a "brief" that outlines prevention principles to assist parents and educators with understanding risk and protective factors related to drug use (www.drugabuse.gov/publications/preventing-drug-abuse-among-children-adolescents/prevention-principles).

This U.S. Department of Health and Human Services child welfare information gateway provides a wealth of information for families about substance abuse prevention (www.childwelfare.gov/systemwide/substance/prevention/#1).

This National Institute on Drug Abuse document provides up-to-date information on drug use trends of high school youth (www.drugabuse.gov/publications/drugfacts/high-school-youth-trends).

DrugWarFacts.org (www.drugwarfacts.org/cms/Drug_Usage#MTF-C) provides data on drug use and provides information about "war on drug prevention initiatives."

REFERENCES

Alaska Department of Public Safety. (2013). Retrieved from http://dps .alaska.gov/CrimeLab/controlledsubstances.aspx

American Psychiatric Association. (2013). *Diagnostic and statistical manual of mental disorders* (5th ed.). Arlington, VA: Author.

Aos, S., Phipps, P., Barnoski, R., and Lieb, R. (2001). The comparative costs and benefits of programs to reduce crime. Vol. 4 (1-05-1201). Olympia, WA: Washington State Institute for Public Policy.

Arria, A. M., Caldeira, K. M., O'Grady, K. E., Vincent, K. B., Johnson, E. P., & Wish, E. D. (2008). Nonmedical use of prescription stimulants among college students: Associations with attention-deficit-hyperactivity disorder and polydrug use. *Pharmacotherapy, 28*(2), 156–169.

Ary, D., Tildesley, E., Hops, H., & Andrews, J. (1993). The influence of parent, sibling and peer modeling and attitudes on adolescent use of alcohol. *International Journal of the Addictions, 28*, 853–880.

ASAM PPC-2R. (2007). *ASAM Patient Placement Criteria for the Treatment of Substance-Related Disorders* (2nd ed.).

Barnes, G. M., & Welte, J. W. (1986). Patterns and predictors of alcohol use among 7–12th-grade students in New York State. *Journal of Studies on Alcohol, 47*(1), 53–62.

Belcher, H. M. E., & Shinitzky, H. E. (1998). Substance abuse in children. *Archives of Pediatrics and Adolescent Medicine, 152*, 952–960.

Borsari, B. & Carey, K. (2000). Effects of a brief motivational intervention with college student drinkers. *Journal of Consulting and Clinical Psychology, 68*, 728–733.

Botvin, G. J., & Griffin, K. W. (2000). Preventing substance use and abuse. In K. M. Minke & G. G. Bear (Eds.), *Preventing school problems-promoting school success: Strategies that work* (pp. 259–298). Bethesda, MD: National Association of School Psychologists.

Boyd, C. J., McCabe, S., Cranford, J.A., & Young A. (2007). Prescription drug abuse and diversion among adolescents in a southeast Michigan school district. *Archives of Pediatric and Adolescent Medicine, 161*(3), 276–281.

Butler, F. (2012). Urine trouble: Drug testing of students and teachers in public schools. *Current Issues in Education, 15*(1). Retrieved from http://cie.asu.edu/ojs/index.php/cieatasu/article/view/805

Centers for Disease Control and Prevention (CDC). (2010). Alcohol-related disease impact (ARDI). Atlanta, GA: Author.

Centers for Disease Control and Prevention (CDC). (2011a). Acute Public Health Consequences of Methamphetamine Laboratories. Retrieved from www.cdc.gov

Centers for Disease Control and Prevention (CDC). (2011b). Vital signs: Overdoses of prescription opioid pain relievers—United States, 1999–2008. *MMWR, 60*, 1–6.

Connecticut Department of Consumer Protection. (2013a). Retrieved from http://www.ct.gov/dcp/cwp/view.asp?Q=525038

Connecticut Department of Consumer Protection. (2013b). Retrieved from http://www.ct.gov/dcp/cwp/view.asp?Q=525042

Connecticut Department of Consumer Protection. (2013c). Retrieved from http://www.ct.gov/dcp/cwp/view.asp?a=1620&Q=525166& PM=1

Death by drugs: Fatal celebrity drug and alcohol addictions. (2010). Retrieved from http://www.gatehouseacademy.com/research/articles/celebrity-drug-and-alcohol-addictions

Degenhardt, L., Chiu, W., Sampson, N., Kessler, R., Anthony, J., Angermeyer, M., . . . Wells, E. (2008). Toward a global view of alcohol, tobacco, cannabis, and cocaine use: Findings from the WHO World Mental Health surveys. *PLoS Medicine, 5*(7), e141.

Electronic Code of Federal Regulations. (2013). §2.14. Retrieved from http://www.ecfr.gov/cgi-bin/text-idx?c=ecfr&tpl=/ecfrbrowse/Title42/42cfr2_main_02.tpl

Ellickson, P. L. & Bell, R. M. (1990). Drug prevention in junior high: A multi-site longitudinal test. *Science, 247*, 1299–1305.

Ellickson, P. L. , McCafferty, D. F., Ghosh-Dastidar, B., & Longshore, D. L. (2003). New inroads in preventing adolescent drug use: Results from a large-scale trial of Project ALERT in middle schools. *American Journal of Public Health, 93*(11), 1830–1836.

Ervin, R. A., Schaughency, E., Matthews, A., Goodman, S. D., & McGlinchey, M. T. (2007). Primary and secondary prevention of behavior difficulties: Developing a data-informed problem-solving model to guide decision making at a school-wide level. *Psychology in the Schools, 44*, 7–18.

Fleming, J. P., Kellam, S. G., & Brown, C. H. (1982). Early predictors of age at first use of alcohol, marijuana, and cigarettes. *Drug and Alcohol Dependence, 9*(4), 285–303.

French, M. T., Zavala, S. K., McCollister, K. E., Waldron, H. B., Turner, C. W., & Ozechowski, T. J. (2008). Cost-effectiveness analysis of four interventions for adolescents with a substance use disorder. *Journal of Substance Abuse Treatment, 34*(3), 272–281.

Gibson, A., Degenhardt, L., Mattick, R., Ali, R., White, J., & O'Brien, S. (2008). Exposure to opioid maintenance treatment reduces long-term mortality. *Addiction, 103*(3), 462–468.

Glanz, K. & Rimer, B. (Eds). (2008). The transtheoretical model and stages of change. In *Health Behavior and Health Education: Theory, Research, and Practice* (4th ed.). New York, NY: Jossey-Bass.

Gomes, J., Song, T., Godwin, L., & Toriello, P. J. (2011). Prescription stimulant abuse on university campuses. *Journal of Human Behavior in the Social Environment, 21*, 822–833.

Goodwin, D. W., Schulsinger, F., Hermansen, L., Guze, S. B., & Winokur, G. (1973). Alcohol problems in adoptees raised apart from alcoholic biological parents. *Archives of General Psychiatry, 28*, 238–243.

Griffo, J. A. (2011). Griffo's law banning dangerous products masquerading as bath salts goes to governor. Retrieved from http://www.nysenate.gov/press-release/griffos-law-banning-dangerous-products-masquerading-as-bath-salts-goes-governor

Hasan, A., & Ciancio, S. (2004). Relationship between amphetamine ingestion and gingival enlargement. *Pediatric Dentistry, 26*(5), 396–400.

Hawkins, J., Catalano, R., & Miller, J. (1992). Risk and protective factors for alcohol and other drug problems in adolescence and early adulthood: Implications for substance abuse prevention. *Psychological Bulletin, 112*(1), 64–105.

Higachi, S., Matsushita, S., Murayama, M., Takagi, S., & Hayashida M. (1995). Alcohol and aldehyde dehydrogenase polymorphisms and the risk for alcoholism. *American Journal of Psychiatry, 152*(8), 1219–1221.

Humphreys, K., Wing, S., McCarty, D., Chappel, J., Gallant, L., Haberle, B., & Weiss, R. (2004, April). Self-help organizations for alcohol and drug problems: Toward evidence-based practice and policy. *Journal of Substance Abuse Treatment, 26*(3), 151–158.

Jessor R. (1976). Predicting time of onset of marijuana use: A developmental study of high school youth. *Journal of Consulting and Clinical Psychology, 44*(1), 125–134.

Johnston, L. D., O'Malley, P. M., Bachman, J. G., & Schulenberg, J. E. (2013). *Monitoring the Future national results on adolescent drug use: Overview of key findings, 2012.* Ann Arbor, MI: Institute for Social Research, The University of Michigan.

Johnston, L. D., O'Malley, P. M., & Bachman, J. G. (1985). Use of licit and illicit drugs by America's high school students: 1975–1984. DHHS Publication No. [ADM] 85-1394. Rockville, MD: National Institute on Drug Abuse.

Kaminer, Y., Burleson, J. A., & Goldberger, R. (2002). Cognitive–behavioral coping skills and psychoeducation therapies for adolescent substance abuse. *Journal of Nervous and Mental Disease, 190*(11), 737–745.

Kandel, D., & Andrews, K. (1987). Process of adolescent socialization by parents and peers. *International Journal of Addictions, 22,* 319–342.

Kandel, D., Simcha-Fagan, O., & Davies, M. (1986). Risk factors for delinquency and illicit drug use from adolescence to young adulthood. *Journal of Drug Issues, 16,* 67–90.

Komro, K. A., Perry, C. L., Williams, C. L., Stigler, M. H., Farbakhsh, K., & Veblen-Mortenson, S. (2001). How did Project Northland reduce alcohol use among young adolescents? Analysis of mediating variables. *Health Education Research, 16*(1), 59–70.

Lankenaua, S. E., Teti, M., Silva, K., Bloom, J. J., Harocopos, A., & Treese, M. (2012). Initiation into prescription opioid misuse amongst young injection drug users. *International Journal of Drug Policy, 23,* 37–44.

Lovett, E., & McNiff, E. (2012). Five shocking ways your kids try to get drunk. Retrieved from http://abcnews.go.com/Health/shocking-ways-kidsdrunk/story?id=17281602#.Ubdpf_lkxdJ

Lundborg, P. (2006). Having the wrong friends? Peer effects in adolescent substance use. *Journal of Health Economics, 25*(2), 214–233.

Marlatt, G. A., Baer, J. S., Kivlahan, D. R., Dimeff, L. A., Larimer, M. E., Quigley, L. A., Somers, J. M. & Williams, E. (1998). Screening and brief intervention for high-risk college student drinkers: Results from a 2-year follow-up assessment. *Journal of Consulting and Clinical Psychology, 66,* 604–615.

Marsch, L. A. (2007). Combined behavioral and pharmacological treatment of opioid-dependent adolescents: A randomized, controlled trial. *Progress in Neurotherapeutics and Neuropsychopharmacology, 1,* 251–264.

McCabe, S., Knight, J., & Teter, C. (2005). Non-medical use of prescription stimulants among US college students: Prevalence and correlates from a national survey. *Addiction, 100,* 96–106.

Meier, B. (2012, November 15). Caffeinated drink cited in reports of 13 deaths. *New York Times,* p. B1.

Moberg, D. P. (1991). Adolescent Drug Involvement Scale. *Journal of Adolescent Chemical Dependency, 2,* 75–88.

Monti, P. M., Colby, S. M., Barnett, N. P., Spirito, A., Rohsenow, D. J., Myers, M., . . . Lewander, W. (1999). Brief intervention for harm reduction with alcohol-positive older adolescents in a hospital emergency department. *Journal of Consulting and Clinical Psychology, 67,* 989–994.

Mulvey, E. P., Schubert, C. A., & Chassin, L. (2010). Substance use and delinquent behavior among serious adolescent offenders. *Juvenile Justice Bulletin,* Rockville, MD.

The National Center on Addiction and Substance Abuse at Columbia University (CASAColumbia™). (2009). *Shoveling up II: The impact of substance abuse on state budgets.* New York, NY: Author.

The National Center on Addiction and Substance Abuse at Columbia University (CASAColumbia™). (2012). *National survey of American attitudes on substance abuse XVII: Teens.* New York, NY: Author.

National Institute on Drug Abuse. (2003). *Preventing drug abuse among children and adolescents: A research-based guide for parent, educators, and community leaders* (2nd ed.). Bethesda, MD: Author.

National Institute on Drug Abuse. (2011). Commonly abused drugs. Retrieved from http://www.drugabuse.gov/sites/default/files/cadchart_2.pdf

National Institutes of Health. (2013a). Retrieved from http://pillbox.nlm.nih.gov/pillimage/search_results.php?s=20&getingredient=Zolpidem&submit=Search

National Institutes of Health. (2013b). Retrieved from http://pillbox.nlm.nih.gov/pillimage/search_results.php?getingredient=Vyvanse&submit=Search

Nichols, D. (2004). Hallucinogens. *Pharmacology and Therapeutics, 101*(2), 131–181.

Ozechowski, T. J., & Liddle, H. A. (2000). A family-based therapy for adolescent drug abuse: Knowns and unknowns. *Clinical Child and Family Psychology Review, 3*(4), 269–298.

PAM Organizers' Packet. (2013). Is my child using alcohol, tobacco, or other drugs? For parents, caregivers, and other adults. Retrieved from http://www.preventionnetwork.org/Data/Sites/1/pampacket/left2013/ismychildusingalcohol,tobacco,orotherdrugs.pdf

Partnership for a Drug-Free America. (2006). *The Partnership Attitude tracking study.* New York, NY: Author.

Pickens, R. W., Svikis, D. S., McGue, M., Lykken, D. T., Heston, L. L., & Clayton, P. J. (1991). Heterogeneity in the inheritance of alcoholism: A study of male and female twins. *Archives of General Psychiatry, 48,* 19–28.

Prosser, J., & Nelson, L., (2012). The toxicology of bath salts: A review of synthetic cathinones. *Journal of Medical Toxicology, 8*(1), 33–42.

Raptopoulos, K. (2008). *Differences in methamphetamine users and crack cocaine users* (Graduate school thesis). University of Arkansas at Little Rock.

Robins, L. N. (1984). The natural history of adolescent drug use. *American Journal of Public Health, 74*(7), 656–657.

Schuckit, M. A. (1987). Biological vulnerability to alcoholism. *Journal of Consulting and Clinical Psychology, 55,* 301–309.

Shaner, J. (2002). Caries associated with methamphetamine abuse. *The Journal of the Michigan Dental Association, 84*(9), 42–47.

Shedler, J., & Block, J. (1990). Adolescent drug use and psychological health. A longitudinal inquiry. *American Psychologist, 45*(5), 612–630.

Shrier, L., Harris, S. K., Kurland, M., & Knight, J. R. (2003). Substance use problems and associated psychiatric symptoms among adolescents in primary care. *Pediatrics, 111*, e699–e705.

Steinberg, L., Fletcher, A., & Darling, N. (1994). Parental monitoring and peer influences on adolescent substance use. *Pediatrics, 6*, 1060–1064.

Substance Abuse and Mental Health Services Administration, Office of Applied Studies. (2007). *Treatment Episode Data Set (TEDS) Highlights—2006 National Admissions to Substance Abuse Treatment Services.* OAS Series #S-40, DHHS Publication No. (SMA) 08-4313, Rockville, MD.

Substance Abuse and Mental Health Services Administration, Drug Abuse Warning Network. (2010). *National estimates of drug-related emergency department visits* (HHS Publication No. (SMA) 12-4733, DAWN Series D-38). Rockville, MD: Substance Abuse and Mental Health Services Administration.

Substance Abuse and Mental Health Services Administration. (2011). Identifying mental health and substance use problems of children and adolescents: A guide for child-serving organizations (HHS Publication No. SMA 12-4670). Rockville, MD: Author.

Substance Abuse and Mental Health Services Administration. (2012). Results from the 2011 National Survey on Drug Use and Health: Summary of National Findings, NSDUH Series H-44, HHS Publication No. (SMA) 12-4713. Rockville, MD: Author.

Swendsen, J., Burstein, M., Case, B., Conway, P., Dierker, L., He, J., & Merikangas, K. (2012). Results of the National Comorbidity Survey–Adolescent Supplement. *Archive of General Psychiatry, 69*(4), 390–398.

Tobler, N. S., Roona, M. R., Ochshorn, P., Marshall, D. G., Streke, A. V., & Stackpole, K. M. (2000). School-based adolescent drug prevention programs: 1998 meta-analysis. *The Journal of Primary Prevention, 20*, 275–336.

Tsuang, M. T., Lyons, M. J., Eisen, S. A., Goldberg, J., True, W., Lin, N., Meyer, J. M., Toomey, R., Faraone, S. V., & Eaves, L. (1998). Genetic influences on *DSM-III-R* drug abuse and dependence: A study of 3,372 twin pairs. *American Journal of Medical Genetics, 67*, 473–477.

U.S. Department of Justice. (2001). Retrieved from http://www.justice.gov/archive/ndic/pubs0/665/index.htm

U.S. Department of Justice. (2006). Retrieved from http://www.justice.gov/archive/ndic/pubs3/3843

U.S. Department of Justice. (2013). Retrieved from www.justice.gov/archive/olp/methawareness

U.S. Drug Enforcement Administration. (2011). Drugs of abuse. Retrieved from http://www.justice.gov/dea/docs/drugs_of_abuse_2011.pdf

U.S. Drug Enforcement Administration. (2013a). Retrieved from www.justice.gov/dea/pr/multimedia-library/image-gallery/images_cocaine.shtml

U.S. Drug Enforcement Administration. (2013b). Retrieved from http://www.justice.gov/dea/pr/multimedia-library/image-gallery/images_narcotics.shtml

U.S. Drug Enforcement Administration. (2013c). Retrieved from http://www.justice.gov/dea/pr/multimedia-library/image-gallery/images_ecstasy.shtml

U.S. Drug Enforcement Administration. (2013d). Retrieved from http://www.justice.gov/dea/pr/multimedia-library/image-gallery/images_lsd.shtml

U.S. Food and Drug Administration. (2012). Retrieved from http://www.fda.gov/NewsEvents/Newsroom/PressAnnouncements/ucm305932.htm

Webster-Stratton, C., Rinaldi, J., & Reid, J. M. (2011). Long-term outcomes of Incredible Years parenting program: Predictors of adolescent adjustment. *Child and Adolescent Mental Health, 16*(1), 38–46.

Psychopharmacology

JOSHUA HERSH

LEARNING OUTCOMES

On completion of this chapter, the reader should be able to:

- Identify the most commonly prescribed psychotropic medications within the school context
- Recognize the important elements that ensure medication efficacy with children and adolescents
- Know how children's behavior in school may be affected by taking medication
- Understand the controversies inherent with prescribing medications
- Understand the intersection of psychotherapy and medication use

Jacob is a 10-year-old boy in the fifth grade noticed by his teacher as being very sleepy in class over the past few weeks. The teacher asks the student about his sleepiness, and Jacob simply says, "I'm tired." To gather further information, the teacher contacts the student's mother, "Mrs. Matthews." Mrs. Matthews states that she took Jacob to her family doctor 2 weeks ago because he wasn't falling asleep at night and he was "having severe" tantrums during the day. She states her family doctor diagnosed Jacob with "bipolar disorder" and started Jacob on "Zyprexa." She believes "Zyprexa" is a "miracle drug" and states that he is falling asleep much faster and is not having as many tantrums at home. She states that she has noticed that Jacob is a "little sleepy" but did not realize that he was sleeping during classes.

Stories such as Jacob's are being seen more and more by teachers, psychologists, and administrators in the school setting. For the last 15 years, the use of psychotropic medications (medications that affect the brain and behavior) in children and adolescents has been increasing. A recent study found that between 1993 and 2002, prescriptions for psychotropic meds in children and adolescents increased 60% (Morris & Stone, 2011). These medications are now prescribed by many different providers, including psychiatrists, pediatricians, family practice doctors, and nurse practitioners.

Because of the increasing use of psychotropic medications in children, it is becoming more and more important for the team of people working with children (teachers, psychologists, social workers, and administrators) to become familiar with pediatric psychopharmacology. This includes an understanding of basic pharmacology, important neurotransmitters, and commonly used psychotropic medications in children and adolescents. Furthermore, it includes a discussion of controversies in pediatric psychopharmacology and a discussion of how best to integrate medication prescribing with other forms of treatment. These issues are all addressed in this chapter.

BASIC PHARMACOLOGY CONCEPTS

There are some basic pharmacology concepts that affect how psychiatric medications are prescribed to children and adolescents. The weight of a child is a very important determinant of dosage, and medications are often prescribed to children and adolescents in mg/kg (milligrams of drug per weight in kilograms of child). Weight of a child or adolescent often changes over time and therefore dosage needs to be constantly adjusted. The route of administration is also a very important indicator of dosage and frequency. Common routes of administration of psychiatric medications include oral (swallowing), sublingual (under the tongue), and intramuscular (arm injection).

The half-life of a drug also affects the dosage and frequency of the medications. The "half-life" of a drug is how long it takes for half the medications to leave the body. Many factors can affect the half-life of drugs, including presence of enzymes, age, nutrition, sex, and disease. Finally, the prescribing of psychotropic drugs may be affected by buildup of tolerance. Tolerance has been found to occur in psychiatric medication when a dosage of a medication is no longer effective. For example, it has been suggested that up to 33% of patients treated for depression experience tolerance to antidepressants (Katz, 2011).

Neurotransmitters

The brain is made up of neurotransmitters or substances that communicate a message from one neuron to another. These neurotransmitter substances can be viewed like parts of a car that all work together to make the car drive from point A to point B. Psychotropic medications are chemicals that basically manipulate parts of the car. These medications induce their effects by helping the neurotransmitters function better (agonists) or impairing the neurotransmitter (antagonists). In other words, agonists help the car parts function better, whereas antagonists stop them from functioning. A summary of the basic neurotransmitters affected by psychotropic medications is found below. (See Table 15.1.)

Norepinephrine

Norepinephrine is part of the sympathetic nervous system. The sympathetic nervous system is basically like pressing down on the gas pedal of a car. It's not pressed all the time, but when it's pressed, the car moves faster. The sympathetic nervous system is turned on during the "fight or flight" response to threatening situations. This may include a physical threat (such as a fight) or a mental threat (such as an upcoming exam). There are receptors for the norepinephrine (called α and β receptors) located on the heart, lungs, and intestines and throughout the brain. When norepinephrine is released (when the gas pedal is pushed) the body reacts by increasing heart rate and blood pressure, increasing lung capacity, inhibiting digestion, and increasing arousal and focus. These functions help us to survive stressful situations.

Many psychotropic medications work to simulate the effect of norepinephrine (press the gas pedal) or block the effect (take the foot off the pedal). For instance, stimulants such as methylphenidate (Ritalin) or amphetamine mixed salts (Adderall) increase release of norepinephrine, whereas beta-blockers such as propranolol (Inderal) block its effects.

Dopamine

Dopamine is also part of the sympathetic nervous system. It also helps the car move faster. It has receptors located in the heart, kidney, and brain. It is involved in increasing cardiac output and in increasing focus and arousal. Dopamine hyperactivity in the brain has been implicated in psychosis (brain on overdrive).

Dopamine not only is involved in the sympathetic nervous system, but also has a few separate functions. It is involved in the reward system in the brain and helps us to experience pleasure (not unlike the pleasure one feels when driving a nice car). Dopamine also helps in regulating complex muscle movements (similar to how an engine communicates through the gears and wheels of a car to make it move).

Many psychiatric medications target the various functions of dopamine. Stimulants increase stimulation of dopamine, which increases focus and arousal. Addictive drugs contribute to dopamine release in the pleasure center of the brain. Addiction may occur by direct or indirect stimulation of dopamine. Antipsychotics antagonize dopamine in order to treat psychosis. Unintended consequences of antipsychotic blockade of dopamine include dysphoria and muscle movement problems.

Acetylcholine

Acetylcholine is part of the parasympathetic nervous system. The parasympathetic nervous system allows normal digestion to take place by increasing saliva production and facilitating intestinal contractions. The normal digestive cycle is like the fuel cycle of a car. A car needs time to stop, fill up on fuel, and then release the burned fuel through the exhaust system. Other activities of acetylcholine include skeletal muscle contraction and facilitating memory. There are really no current psychotropic medications used in children designed to specifically increase acetylcholine. However many medications antagonize acetylcholine unintentionally and cause side effects such as dry mouth, constipation, and memory problems. Side effects caused by these medications are called anticholinergic side effects. The school team, especially school nurses, should pay attention to any student complaints about such side effects.

Serotonin

Serotonin is kind of like the oil to the engine of car. It makes sure the engine runs smoothly. Most serotonin is in the intestine and is involved in normal intestinal movements. Serotonin is also involved in regulation of mood, anxiety, aggression, body temperature, sexuality, and appetite. Medications commonly used that affect serotonin are the selective serotonin reuptake inhibitors (SSRIs) such as fluoxetine (Prozac) and sertraline (Zoloft). SSRIs can all have gastrointestinal side effects owing to the large amount of serotonin in the intestines. In the opening of this chapter, our student Jacob was prescribed Zyprexa, which blocks, among other transmitters, serotonin. MDMA, or "ecstasy," is an illegal drug that increases serotonin in the brain. Ecstasy can contribute to feelings of increase sexuality and changes in mood. It also can cause dangerously elevated body temperature (much like a car engine overheating).

Gamma Amino Butyric Acid (GABA)

Gamma Amino Butyric Acid (GABA) is produced throughout the brain and is the general inhibitory neurotransmitter of the brain. It's similar to the friction of the road. When driving a car,

TABLE 15.1 National Institute of Mental Health (NIMH)—Identification of Neurotransmitters

Neurotransmitter	Body and Brain Functions	Psychiatric Medications That Increase Effect	Psychiatric Medications That Block Effect
Norepinephrine	Focus and arousal	Stimulants SNRIs	Beta-blockers Alpha-agonists
Dopamine	Focus and arousal Experience pleasure Muscle movements	Stimulants Buproprion (Wellbutrin) Addictive substances	Antipsychotics
Acetylcholine	Memory Saliva production Intestinal contractions	None	Tricyclics Atypical antipsychotics Antihistamines Benzotropine (Cogentin)
Serotonin	Sexuality Emotional regulation Body temperature Aggression Appetite	SSRIs SNRIs Some tricyclics Buspirone	
GABA	General inhibitor	Benzodiazepines Mood Stabilizers	
Histamine	Wakefulness		Antihistamines

friction of the road is there all the time. With no friction, a car would slide off the edge; with too much friction, the car would move very slowly. Drugs that facilitate GABA cause a general slowing of brain functions. These include the benzodiazepines like lorazepam (Ativan) and the mood stabilizers like valproic acid (Depakote).

Histamine

Histamine is involved in the immune response and also helps us stay awake. One can compare histamine to the car ignition. When histamine is active, the car is turned on, and when histamine is blocked, the car is turned off. Drugs that block histamine usually cause sleepiness and decrease anxiety.

COMMONLY USED PSYCHOTROPIC MEDICATIONS IN CHILDREN AND ADOLESCENTS

Categories of psychotropic medications have been formed for multiple reasons (often historical or political) and can often be confusing to those learning about them. For instance, why are antidepressants and antipsychotics often used for anxiety? It is important to understand the drugs more in terms of their mechanisms of action and not by category. It will then be easier to understand when and why drugs are used for certain reasons.

Antidepressants

Medications labeled as antidepressants are used for a variety of conditions, including depressive disorders, anxiety disorders, pain disorders, and impulse control disorders. It is generally accepted that most antidepressants take about 3–4 weeks to reach full effect. However, in chronic or more severe depression, there is evidence that they may take longer to reach their full effect (Kornstein & Schneider, 2001).

The National Center for Health Statistics says that 5% of American 12- to 19-year-olds use antidepressants (Qiuping, Dillon, & Burt, 2010). Like most medications in children, use of antidepressants is controversial. One frequently cited large multisite clinical trial, the National Institute of Mental Health (NIMH)-funded Treatment for Adolescents with Depression Study (TADS), studied adolescents aged 12 to 17 and found that antidepressant medication was significantly more effective for depressive symptoms than placebo (TADS, 2009). This study contrasts with data gathered by the authors of a meta-analysis that looked at several smaller clinical trials and did not find much difference between antidepressants and placebo in treating depression (Jureidini et al., 2004).

In addition to controversy about effectiveness, there is also controversy regarding the safety of antidepressants in children. In 2004, a Food and Drug Administration (FDA) joint advisory committee voted to recommend that a "black box" warning label be required for antidepressant drugs, indicating that they increase the risk of suicidal thinking and behavior in pediatric patients (Food and Drug Administration, 2004). Despite the FDA warning, some researchers have found evidence that there is no increased risk of suicide in children while taking antidepressants. One group of authors looked at suicide data and actually found a decrease in suicides in children and adolescents on antidepressants (Gibbons, Hur, Bhaumik, & Mann, 2006). Despite the uncertainty about the increase in suicidal thoughts and behavior, the FDA warning has affected prescribing rates of antidepressants in children. Antidepressant use in children and adolescents was at its peak in 2004 and decreased after the FDA warning (Singh, Prakash, Rais, & Kumari, 2009). As a school mental health professional, you may wish to monitor for suicidal thoughts and other changes in behavior following medication initiation.

Selective Serotonin Reuptake Inhibitors (SSRIs)

SSRIs are the most commonly prescribed antidepressants in children. They are thought to work by inhibiting the reuptake of serotonin, which causes increases in serotonin and leads to changes in the brain that affect mood and anxiety regulation. Like other antidepressants, the effects are not immediate and usually take about a month to show themselves. SSRIs are

TABLE 15.2 National Institute of Mental Health (NIMH)—Medications Organized by
Trade Name: Antidepressants

Trade Name	Generic Name	FDA-Approved Age
Antidepressant Medications (also used for anxiety disorders)		
Anafranil (tricyclic)	clomipramine	10+ (for OCD only)
Asendin	amoxapine	18+
Aventyl (tricyclic)	nortriptyline	18+
Celexa (SSRI)	citalopram	18+
Cymbalta (SNRI)	duloxetine	18+
Desyrel	trazodone	18+
Effexor (SNRI)	venlafaxine	18+
Elavil (tricyclic)	amitriptyline	18+
Emsam	selegiline	18+
Lexapro (SSRI)	escitalopram	18+ 12–17 (for major depressive disorder)
Ludiomil (tricyclic)	maprotiline	18+
Luvox (SSRI)	fluvoxamine	8+ (for OCD only)
Marplan (MAOI)	isocarboxazid	18+
Nardil (MAOI)	phenelzine	18+
Norpramin (tricyclic)	desipramine	18+
Pamelor (tricyclic)	nortriptyline	18+
Parnate (MAOI)	tranylcypromine	18+
Paxil (SSRI)	paroxetine	18+
Pexeva (SSRI)	paroxetine-mesylate	18+
Pristiq	desvenlafaxine (SNRI)	18+
Emsam	selegiline	18+
Lexapro (SSRI)	escitalopram	18+ 12–17 (for major depressive disorder)
Prozac (SSRI)	fluoxetine	8+
Remeron	mirtazapine	18+
Sarafem (SSRI)	fluoxetine	18+ (for premenstrual dysphoric disorder [PMDD])
Sinequan (tricyclic)	doxepin	12+
Surmontil (tricyclic)	trimipramine	18+
Tofranil (tricyclic)	imipramine	6+ (for bedwetting)
Tofranil-PM (tricyclic)	imipramine pamoate	18+
Vivactil (tricyclic)	protriptyline	18+
Wellbutrin	bupropion	18+
Zoloft (SSRI)	sertraline	6+ (for OCD only)

commonly prescribed for depression and anxiety disorders including panic disorder and obsessive–compulsive disorder. They are also prescribed for aggression and developmental disorders. They are safe in overdose, which is one of the reasons why they are commonly prescribed instead of older antidepressants such as tricyclics and monoamine oxidase inhibitors.

Examples of SSRIs include fluoxetine (Prozac), sertraline (Zoloft), citalopram (Celexa), fluvoxamine (Luvox), and paroxetine (Paxil). Most SSRIs are used off label in children and adolescents, which means they have not been FDA-approved to prescribe to children and adolescents. Treating off label, while controversial, is perfectly legal and is common practice in medicine. There are a few exceptions to the off-label use. Fluoxetine (Prozac) has been FDA-approved to treat pediatric depression and obsessive compulsive disorder (OCD). Sertraline (Zoloft) and fluvoxamine (Luvox) have also been FDA-approved to treat OCD in children.

Common side effects of SSRIs can include gastrointestinal distress, sleepiness, and sexual dysfunction. SSRIs do differ slightly in their side effect profiles. For instance, paroxetine tends to cause more sleepiness than other antidepressants (Pae & Patkar, 2007). SSRIs can have severe withdrawal symptoms when treatment is abruptly stopped that include flulike symptoms, anxiety, and gastrointestinal disturbance (Tamam & Ozpoyraz, 2002).

SSRIs show differences in their half-lives that affect how they are dosed and how quickly they should be tapered when discontinued. Close monitoring of children and adolescents prescribed SSRIs is crucial.

Serotonin Norepinephrine Reuptake Inhibitors (SNRIs)

Serotonin norepinephrine reuptake inhibitors (SNRIs) are thought to work by inhibiting the reuptake of serotonin and norepinephrine leading to increases in these two neurotransmitters in the brain. SNRIs are not FDA-approved in children but are commonly used off label to treat depression. They are often used in treatment resistant depression, because a few studies suggest that the dual effect may be helpful in treatment resistant depression (Nemeroff, 2007).

Examples of SNRIs include vanlafaxine (Effexor), Desvenlafaxine (Pristiq), and duloxetine (Cymbalta). Duloxetine (Cymbalta) is also approved for both depression and chronic pain in adults. It has been suggested that both serotonin and noepinephrine help modulate pain, and by affecting both neurotransmitters, SNRIs can significantly help with pain (Marks et al., 2009). Vanlafaxine (Effexor) and duloxetine both have relatively short half-lives and can have severe drug withdrawal if not tapered slowly.

Norepinephrine Dopamine Reuptake Inhibitors (NDRIs)

Another class of antidepressant drugs are norepinephrine dopamine reuptake inhibitors (NDRIs). NDRIs work by inhibiting the reuptake of norepinephrine and dopamine, which results in increased levels of these two neurotransmitters in the brain. The only NDRI that is currently FDA-approved to treat depression in adults is bupropion (Wellbutrin). Bupropion tends to cause more stimulation of the sympathetic nervous system than SSRIs or SNRIs and is often used to help with energy when symptoms of fatigue, low motivation, or sleepiness are present. Some studies have suggested that it can also be effective for symptoms of attention deficit hyperactivity disorder (ADHD; Reimherr, Hedges, Strong, Marchant, & Williams, 2005). It also has FDA approval when used in adults to help with smoking cessation (Zyban).

Bupropion is not approved for treatment of anxiety disorders and may exacerbate anxiety or insomnia. Other common side effects include decreased appetite and headache. Unlike SSRIs and SNRIs, buproprion does not cause sexual dysfunction. There is also an increased risk of seizures, especially for those who have a seizure disorder.

Tricyclics

The use of tricyclic antidepressants has decreased since the development of newer antidepressants such as SSRIs. Their mechanism of action is thought to include increasing levels of norepinephrine or serotonin in the brain. They can have a number of uncomfortable anticholinergic side effects such as constipation and dry mouth. They can also be fatal in overdose, mostly because of heart arrhythmia. Examples of tricyclic antidepressants include imipramine (Tofranil) and nortriptyline (Pamelor). Tricyclics are frequently used in adults with chronic pain and for insomnia. Clomipramine (Anafranil) is a tricyclic approved to treat OCD in children.

Monoamine Oxidase Inhibitors—MAOIs

MAOIs are thought to work by preventing degradation of norepinephrine and serotonin. Like NDRIs they stimulate the sympathetic nervous system and are often used for symptoms of hypersomnolence, lack of motivation, and lethargy. They are used rarely nowadays owing to severe drug and dietary interactions that can be fatal. Examples include phenelzine (Nardil) and tranlcypromine (Parnate). Although MAOIs are rarely prescribed for children, if used, most physicians will caution parents or caregivers about a wide range of dietary and potential physical complications along with use of MAOIs with common cold medication (especially those containing dextromethorphan; Krans & Krucik, 2013).

Other Antidepressants

A few other antidepressants do not fall into the other categories and are worth mentioning. Trazodone (Desyrel) is a commonly used medication in children for insomnia. It is a heterocyclic antidepressant but is not typically used for depression owing to anticholinergic side effects. Mirtazepine (Remeron) is an alpha-2 antagonist that is also commonly used for insomnia. When used as an antidepressant, it tends to cause sleepiness and weight gain owing to antihistamine effects. Vilazodone (Viibryd) is a newer medication that is thought to have extra serotonin activity at the 5HT-1a receptor. The significance of this additional serotonin activity is unknown (Laughren et al., 2011). (For a list of all antidepressants, see Table 15.2.)

Mood Stabilizers

Mood stabilizers are drugs mainly used to treat bipolar disorder but are also used for conduct disorder and impulse control disorders. The mood stabilizers include lithium and a number of anticonvulsants. Mood stabilizers have been studied in children with mood disorders and have been found to be effective in most studies (Liu et al., 2011). Like the antidepressants, there is also a concern about suicidality with the mood stabilizers. The FDA issued a warning in 2008 about the risk for suicidality associated with use of anticonvulsant medications such as valproate and carbamazepine (Food and Drug Administration, 2009).

Lithium

Lithium was the first medication to be approved by the FDA for the treatment of mania in youth ages 12 to 17 years. Despite its FDA approval, lithium has a number of side effects that can make it difficult to tolerate and leads to a high dropout rate in studies (Liu et al., 2011). Side effects of lithium include sleepiness, stomach upset, acne, and frequent urination. Lithium also has drug interactions with diuretics (drugs used to treat high blood pressure) and over-the-counter pain medications such as ibuprofen. These interactions increase the chance of lithium toxicity, a condition in which the lithium blood level gets too high. Lithium toxicity includes confusion, tremors, and balance problems. A study that suggests that children under age 7 may be more at risk for toxicity from lithium and should avoid taking it (Hagino et al., 1995). Because of concerns about toxicity, children and adolescents taking lithium need to get blood levels checked frequently.

Valproic Acid (Depakote)

Valproic acid has been commonly used in children despite lack of FDA approval for use in treating bipolar disorder in children. It is FDA-approved to treat for seizures down to age 10 and for mania in adults. The results of studies of valproic acid in children have been conflicting but most show some effectiveness (Liu et al., 2011). The mechanism of action of valproic acid is thought to work by facilitating GABA. Common side effects from valproic acid include sleepiness, weight gain, tremor, and hair loss. As when treating with lithium, blood levels are frequently monitored by prescribers. Although valproic acid is usually safe in children, there can be rare complications, such as blood count abnormalities, pancreatitis, and liver failure.

Carbamazepine (Tegretol)

Carbamazepine (Tegretol) has also been commonly used in children despite lack of FDA approval for use in treating bipolar disorder in children. A few studies suggest the effectiveness of carbamazepine in children (Liu et al., 2011). Common side effects from carbamazepine include sleepiness, headaches, migraines, motor coordination impairment, and gastrointestinal problems. Carbamazepine can make birth control ineffective and can lead to unwanted pregnancies. In rare cases, carbamazepine can cause aplastic anemia, a condition in which the immune system is impaired. Like lithium and valproic acid, blood levels should be monitored and patients should be monitored for potential complications. Oxcarmazepine (Trileptal) is a newer form of carbamazepine that doesn't require blood work but has not been as well studied in children for bipolar disorder.

Lamotrigine (Lamictal)

The FDA has approved lamotrigine for maintenance therapy for bipolar disorder in adults. It is also approved for seizure disorders in children. Like most other mood stabilizers, it is used off label for the treatment of bipolar disorder in children and adolescents. The dose of lamotrigine needs to be increased slowly in children to prevent the occurrence of a fatal rash, called Stevens-Johnson syndrome, which occurs at higher rates in children and adolescents than in adults. In addition, if lamotrigine is taken with valproic acid, it may bring increased risk of Stevens-Johnson syndrome.

Other Anticonvulsants

Several other anticonvulsants have been used off label to treat bipolar disorder, conduct disorder, and impulse control disorders. Gabapentin (Neurontin) was used quite frequently for bipolar disorder until studies found it ineffective. Several lawsuits were initiated in the last decade regarding off-label promotion of gabapentin. In 2004, the drug company Pfizer pled guilty and agreed to pay more than $430 million to settle charges that it had illegally marketed Gabapentin for unapproved uses.

Topiramate (Topamax) has also been studied for bipolar disorder in adults. A few studies of adults with bipolar disorder suggest that topiramate is not effective for the treatment of bipolar disorder (Liu et al., 2011). However, it is still occasionally

TABLE 15.3 National Institute of Mental Health (NIMH)—Medications Organized by Trade Name: Mood Stabilizing and Anticonvulsant Medications

Trade Name	Generic Name	FDA-Approved Age
Mood Stabilizing and Anticonvulsant Medications		
Depakote	divalproex sodium (valproic acid)	2+ (for seizures)
Eskalith	lithium carbonate	12+
Lamictal	lamotrigine	18+
lithium citrate (generic only)	lithium citrate	12+
Lithobid	lithium carbonate	12+
Neurontin	gabapentin	18+
Tegretol	carbamazepine	any age (for seizures)
Topamax	topiramate	18+
Trileptal	oxcarbazepine	4+

used off label. Common side effects include cognitive problems and decreased appetite. Because its effect on appetite, it is also occasionally used as a weight loss drug. Topamax, when used with children, is used for treatment of seizures. (For a list of all mood stabilizers, please see Table 15.3.)

Antipsychotics

Antipsychotics, also called neuroleptics, are FDA-approved for the treatment of schizophrenia, and many are also becoming approved for the treatment of mania. They are often divided into typical (conventional) antipsychotics and atypical (newer) antipsychotics. Both typical and atypical antipsychotics work by blocking the dopamine receptor. While blocking the dopamine receptor can help with psychotic symptoms, it can also lead to a number of uncomfortable side effects, such as sleepiness, inability to experience pleasure, and slowed thinking. This may contribute to the low continuation rates of antipsychotics. One well-known large study looking at real-life adult patients with schizophrenia called the Clinical Antipsychotic Trials for Intervention Effectiveness (CATIE) found that only about 25% of adult patients voluntarily stay on antipsychotics after 18 months (Manschreck & Boshes, 2007).

Antipsychotics can cause a permanently disabling condition called tardive dyskinesia. This condition is characterized by repetitive, involuntary, purposeless movements. Some examples of these types of involuntary movements include grimacing, tongue protrusion, and lip smacking. Tardive dyskinesia is rare in children and adolescents and is typically only seen after long-term use of antipsychotics.

Typical Antipsychotics

Typical antipsychotics were commonly used during the 1900s, but their use has decreased since then. They have been commonly used for the treatment of psychotic disorders, anxiety disorder, bipolar disorder, impulse control disorders, and aggression. They are also commonly used today for acute agitation in emergency rooms and psychiatric hospitals.

Typical antipsychotics are known to frequently cause extrapyramidal side effects (EPS) such as pseudoparkinsonism. Parkinson's disease, caused by depletion of dopamine in the brain, consists of tremor, slow movements, and rigidity. Pseudoparkinsonism is caused by blockage of dopamine in the brain by typical antipsychotics and has similar symptoms. In addition, children and adolescents are also at risk for experiencing an acute dystonic reaction. An acute dystonic reaction involves a tightness in the jaw or other muscles such as the diaphragm or eye muscles, which can be life threatening if not treated. EPS is usually treated with an anticholinergic medication such as benzotropine (Cogentin).

Atypical Antipsychotics

The use of atypical antipsychotics has increased dramatically in the last 20 years. Between 1993 and 2009, there was approximately an eightfold increase in atypical antipsychotic prescriptions written for children and adolescents. Most of these prescriptions were given for disruptive behavior disorders (Olfson, Blanco, Liu, Wang, & Correll, 2012). Placebo-controlled trials support the effectiveness of atypicals in decreasing psychotic symptoms of schizophrenia in adolescents and manic symptoms of bipolar disorder in children and adolescents (Vitiello et al., 2009). The FDA has approved several atypical antipsychotics for the acute treatment of manic and mixed episodes in children and adolescents.

Atypical antipsychotics are called atypical because they do not cause the EPS symptoms as commonly as the typical antipsychotics. This may be because their mechanism of action also involves blocking dopamine receptors in the brain but they do not block them as tightly. This also may be owing to strong anticholinergic side effects that help with EPS. Despite the lower amount of EPS symptoms, atypical antipsychotics still can cause tardive dyskinesia. However, according to one study, rates are lower with the atypicals at 3.9% as opposed to the typicals at 5.5% (Correll & Schenk, 2008).

Olanzapine (Zyprexa)

Olanzapine is a commonly used atypical antipsychotic. Like most atypical antipsychotics, it is often used for schizophrenia and other psychotic disorders, bipolar disorder, aggression, anxiety, and depression. It is also only FDA-approved to treat acute manic/mixed episodes of bipolar disorder in children. Olanzapine has strong anticholinergic effects leading to low EPS rates. The most common side effects of olanzapine include sleepiness, dizziness, fatigue, dry mouth, constipation, blurred vision, increased appetite, and weight gain.

The weight gain caused by olanzapine and other antipsychotics has been a source of controversy. The weight gain can contribute to a metabolic syndrome that is associated with the development of diabetes. Several lawsuits have been filed against the makers of olanzapine and other atypical antipsychotics related to the development of diabetes in patients. The FDA now requires all atypical antipsychotics to include a warning about the risk of developing hyperglycemia and diabetes.

Quetiapine (Seroquel)

Quetiapine is another commonly used atypical antipsychotic. Like olanzapine, it is only FDA-approved to treat acute manic/mixed episodes of bipolar disorder in children and adolescents but is commonly used off label to treat other conditions. Like olanzapine, quetiapine also has strong anticholinergic side effects.

Risperidone (Risperdal)

Risperidone is another commonly used atypical antipsychotic. Risperidone has been FDA-approved for the treatment of 13- to 17-year-old adolescents with schizophrenia and of 10- to 17-year-old youths with bipolar mania or mixed episode. It is also been FDA-approved to treat irritability and aggression in children with autism. It is also commonly used off label for other disorders. In August 2012, Johnson & Johnson agreed to pay $181 million to 36 U.S. states to settle claims that it had promoted risperidone for nonapproved uses, including dementia, anger management, and anxiety (Hill, 2012).

Common side effects include sleepiness, weight gain, restlessness, and dizziness. Risperidone is more likely than olanzapine or quetiapine to cause EPS symptoms similar to the typical antipsychotics (Leucht, Pitschel-Walz, Abraham, & Kissling, 1999). Risperdal can also lead to elevated levels of prolactin, which can cause breast milk secretion even in males.

Ziprazadone (Geodon)

Ziprazidone is not approved for children and adolescents but is often used off label in similar ways to the other antipsychotics. It has an intramuscular injection form that is FDA-approved for acute agitation in schizophrenic patients. There are some concerns about heart rhythm abnormalities and an EKG is recommended when starting ziprazidone. Ziprazidone is frequently marketed to cause lower weight gain than other atypical antipsychotics.

TABLE 15.4 National Institute of Mental Health (NIMH)—Medications Organized by Trade Name: Antipsychotic Medications

Trade Name	Generic Name	FDA-Approved Age
Combination Antipsychotic and Antidepressant Medication		
Symbyax (Prozac, Zyprexa)	fluoxetine, olanzapine	18+
Antipsychotic Medications		
Abilify	aripiprazole	10+ for bipolar disorder, manic or mixed episodes 13–17 for schizophrenia and bipolar
Clozaril	clozapine	18+
Fanapt	iloperidone	18+
fluphenazine (generic only)	fluphenazine	18+
Geodon	ziprasidone	18+
Haldol	haloperidol	3+
Invega	paliperidone	18+
Loxitane	loxapine	18+
Moban	molindone	18+
Navane	thiothixene	18+
Orap (for Tourette syndrome)	pimozide	12+
perphenazine (generic only)	perphenazine	18+
Risperdal	risperidone	13+ for schizophrenia 10+ for bipolar mania and mixed episodes 5–16 for irritability associated with autism
Seroquel	quetiapine	13+ for schizophrenia 18+ for bipolar disorder 10–17 for treatment of manic and mixed episodes of bipolar disorder.
Stelazine	trifluoperazine	18+
thioridazine (generic only)	thioridazine	2+
Thorazine	chlorpromazine	18+
Zyprexia	olanzapine	18+ 13–17 as second-line treatment for manic or mixed episodes of bipolar disorder and schizophrenia

Aripiprazole (Abilify)

Aripiprazole has been FDA-approved for the treatment of 13- to 17-year-old adolescents with schizophrenia and of 10- to 17-year-old youths with bipolar mania or mixed episodes. It is also approved to treat irritability in children with autism. Common side effects include sleepiness, agitation, blurred vision, constipation, headache, and increased salivation.

Other Antipsychotics

Clozapine (Clozaril) is an atypical antipsychotic that is considered very effective but is not frequently used in children owing to risk of low blood counts and need for frequent blood monitoring. Paliperidone (Invega), Lurasidone (Latuda), Iloperidone (Fanapt), and Asenapine Maleate (Saphris) are antipsychotics that have entered the market since 2009. These drugs are marketed to cause less weight gain in adults. They have not been approved yet for children. (For a list of all antipsychotics, see Table 15.4.)

Anxiolytics

Anxiolytics include medications designed to help with anxiety. These include buspirone, antihistamines, and benzodiazepines.

Buspirone (Buspar)

Buspirone is a medication approved to treat generalized anxiety disorder (GAD) in adults. Buspirone is thought to work by stimulating 5-HT1a serotonin receptors. It has no FDA approval in children but is commonly used off label for anxiety and as an add on to antidepressants for depression. It has relatively few side effects, including dizziness and dry mouth. There is no addictive potential, so it is often used in patients if there are concerns about addiction.

Antihistamines

Antihistamines include (Benadryl) and hydroxyzine (Vistaril). Antihistamines work by blocking histamine, which results in lower anxiety levels. Hydroxyzine is FDA-approved for the treatment anxiety in children. Common side effects of antihistamines include sleepiness and anticholinergic side effects, such as dry mouth, blurred vision, and constipation. Antihistamines have low addictive potential.

Benzodiazepines

Benzodiazepines include lorazepam (Ativan), clozazepam (Klonopin), and diazepam (Valium). Benzodiazepines work by facilitating GABA, which slows down most brain functions. They are commonly used for panic attacks, specific phobias, insomnia, and other forms of anxiety. Although benzodiazepines are not approved for specific psychiatric disorders in children and adolescence, they often have indications for anxiety in children. For example, lorazepam is FDA-approved for the treatment of anxiety in age 12 and older. Cross-tolerance of benzodiazepines occurs with alcohol, so benzodiazepines are also commonly used for alcohol detoxification.

Benzodiazepines are schedule IV controlled substances. They have risk of abuse and dependency and patients with a history of addiction need to be monitored closely. They also

TABLE 15.5 National Institute of Mental Health (NIMH)—Medications Organized by Trade Name: Antianxiety Medications

Trade Name	Generic Name	FDA-Approved Age
Antianxiety Medications (All these antianxiety medications are benzodiazepines except for BuSpar.)		
Ativan	lorazepam	18+
BuSpar	buspirone	18+
Klonopin	clonazepam	18+
Librium	chlordiazepoxide	18+
oxazepam (generic only)	oxazepam	18+
Tranxene	clorazepate	18+
Valium	diazepam	18+
Xanax	alprazolam	18+

can have a potentially lethal withdrawal syndrome. Therefore, many clinicians suggest trying nonaddictive medications such as antidepressants, antihistamines, and buspirone before using benzodiazepines for anxiety disorders (Longo & Johnson, 2000). (For a list of all benzodiazepines, see Table 15.5.)

Hypnotics

Hypnotics are mainly used for the treatment of insomnia. Examples include zolpidem (Ambien) and zalaplon (Sonata). The mechanisms of action of hypnotics are very similar to benzodiazepines and involve facilitation of GABA. They are not FDA-approved in children but are frequently used off label. Like benzodiazepines, they are schedule IV controlled substances and have potential for abuse and dependence.

There is evidence that treatment of insomnia with hypnotics can lead to tolerance and dependence in the long term. Therefore, it is often recommended that hypnotics not be used long-term. Cognitive-behavioral interventions and "sleep hygiene" for insomnia are effective long term (Kirkwood, 1999).

Stimulants

Stimulants are FDA-approved drugs to treat ADHD and are the most widely used psychotropic medications in children. An estimated 3.5% of U.S. children received stimulant medication in 2008, up from 2.4% in 1996. Over the period 1996 to 2008, use increased consistently at an overall annual growth rate of 3.4% (Zuvekas & Vitiello, 2012). Stimulants are thought to work by increasing norepinephrine and dopamine levels in the brain.

A number of studies have documented the effectiveness of stimulants for ADHD (Charach, Ickowicz, & Schachar 2004). Stimulants have a relative fast onset of action and last for several hours to an entire day depending on formulation. Common stimulants include methylphenidate (Ritalin), amphetamine mixed salts (Adderall), methylphenidate extended-release tablets (Concerta), and Lisdexamfetamine dimesylate (Vyvanse).

Side effects from stimulants can include insomnia, decreased appetite, anxiety, and worsened tics. Stimulants are schedule II controlled substances. They are listed by the Drug Enforcement Agency (DEA) as having a "high potential for abuse" that "may lead to severe psychological or physical dependence" (DEA Drug Fact Sheet). In order to minimize potential for tolerance and dependence, drug holidays may be encouraged. Drug holidays are periods when children and adolescents go off stimulants on summers, weekends, holidays, and breaks (Yanofski, 2011).

There is controversy surrounding growth suppression and cardiac safety from stimulants. A few studies report long-term growth suppression with children taking stimulants. One study found that after 3 years on the ADHD drug methylphenidate (Ritalin), children are about 1 inch shorter and 4.4 pounds lighter than their peers (Swanson et al., 2007). Another study showed no such growth suppression (Biederman, Spencer, Monuteaux, & Faraone, 2010). Some physicians encourage drug holidays to avoid growth suppression.

When it comes to cardiac safety, there are also conflicting reports (Hammerness, Perrin, Shelley-Abrahamson, & Wilens, 2011). In 2006, the FDA required labeling that advised that sudden death has been reported with stimulant treatment in children and adolescents with structural cardiac abnormalities or other serious heart problems. The FDA suggested that stimulants not be used in such patients (Smith, 2006).

Because of stimulants' widespread use and effectiveness, it is quite likely that school-based mental health professionals will interact with school-age children and families who are using stimulant regimens. It is critical that both family and school be familiar with the treatment plan, monitor use and side effects, and communicate about the effects the medication is having on behavior at school and at home. In addition, at times, treatment may involve dosage changes or on/off schedule of doses. These schedules can be a point of discussion between the school-based mental health/health team and family.

Atomoxetine (Strattera)

Atomoxetine is an FDA-approved as a nonstimulant medication to treat ADHD. Its mechanism of action is thought to also include increased norepinephrine and dopamine levels in the brain. Unlike stimulants, the effects of atomoxetine are not immediate and take several weeks to occur. Furthermore, atomoxetine has a low addictive potential and may be preferable in children and adolescents with a history of addiction. Nausea and sedation are common side effects, and there are possible liver problems when combined with alcohol.

Alpha2-Agonists

Alpha2-agonists have been used off label in children and adolescents to treat Tourette syndrome, aggression, insomnia, ADHD, and developmental disorders. They include clonidine (Catapress) and guanfacine (Tenex, Intuniv). Intuniv is an extended-release alpha-agonist FDA-approved in 2009 to treat children and adolescents with ADHD ages 6 to 17.

Alpha2-agonists cause inhibition of norepinephrine release in the brain. Reducing norepinephrine levels in the brain may contribute to these medications' ability to decrease anxiety,

TABLE 15.6 National Institute of Mental Health (NIMH)—Medications Organized by Trade Name: ADHD Medications

Trade Name	Generic Name	FDA-Approved Age
ADHD Medications **(All these ADHD medications are stimulants except for Intuniv and Straterra.)**		
Adderall	amphetamine	3+
Adderall XR	amphetamine (extended-release)	6+
Concerta	methylphenidate (long-acting)	6+
Daytrana	methylphenidate patch	6+
Desoxyn	methamphetamine	6+
Dexedrine	dextroamphetamine	3+
Dextrostat	dextroamphetamine	3+
Focalin	dexmethylphenidate	6+
Focalin XR	dexmethylphenidate (extended-release)	6+
Intuniv	guanfacine	6+
Metadate ER	methylphenidate (extended-release)	6+
Metadate CD	methylphenidate (extended-release)	6+
Methylin	methylphenidate (oral solution and chewable tablets)	6+
Ritalin	methylphenidate	6+
Ritalin SR	methylphenidate (extended-release)	6+
Ritalin LA	methylphenidate (long-acting)	6+
Strattera	atomoxetine	6+
Vyvanse	lisdexamfetamine dimesylate	6+

insomnia, and hyperactive symptoms of ADHD. It has also been suggested that Alpha2-agonists may work on receptors in the prefrontal cortex of the brain. This may contribute to its benefit on inattentive ADHD symptoms (Scahill, 2009). Side effects of alpha2-agonists can include sleepiness, fatigue, and decrease in blood pressure.

Beta-Blockers

Beta-blockers have been used to treat anxiety in adults and their benefit has been established in several clinical trials (Neppe, 1989). They include propranolol (Inderal) and atenolol (Tenormin). Their mechanism of action involves blocking norepinephrine at the beta receptor. This may decrease the "fight or flight" response to stressful situations. Research is lacking in children, but these medications are used off label for anxiety, aggression, and ADHD. Beta blockers are also very commonly used for performance anxiety. (For a list of all ADHD medications, see Table 15.6.)

Psychiatric Controversies

The use of psychotropic medication in children is one of the most controversial topics in medicine today. A newspaper article search reveals numerous articles highlighting this controversy such as a *New York Times* article entitled "Debate over Children and Psychiatric Drugs" (Carey, 2007). This article discussed the case of Rebecca Riley, a 4-year-old who died from the combined effects of multiple psychiatric medications taken for bipolar disorder and ADHD. The prosecutor charged her parents with deliberately poisoning their daughter by giving her overdoses of prescription drugs to sedate her. Both her parents were convicted of murder and were sentenced to life in prison.

Overprescribing of Medication

There is a great deal of controversy surrounding the overprescribing of medication to children. Many educators and psychologists believe that overprescribing medication minimizes psychotherapy and environmental changes that may be more helpful in the long term. Also, such as in the case of Rebecca Riley, there are concerns about parents misusing the drugs (taking the drugs themselves or overmedicating their children to sedate them). Over the last few decades, there has been a large increase in deaths and poisonings in children and adolescents related to psychotropic medication (Wysowski , 2007).

There are particular concerns that certain populations are vulnerable to being overprescribed. The Government Accountability Office (GAO) report found that foster children were prescribed psychotropic drugs at rates up to nearly five times higher than nonfoster children. In addition, foster children were much more likely to be prescribed five or more medications at one time (Abdelmalek, Adhikari, Koch, Diaz, & Weinraub, 2011). The developmentally disabled are also vulnerable to being overprescribed. A nonprofit agency in New York was recently cited for 11 violations in 6 years related to misusing drugs in the developmentally disabled to control behavior (Hakim, 2011).

School mental health professionals can aid in this area by serving as major education and resource conduits for families, readily having school nurses available to facilitate conversations between families and school officials relating to the child's school-based behavior and medication. In addition, developing a partnership with area pediatricians and psychiatrists with school-based mental health professionals to provide "information sessions" is important. Monitoring regimens closely is the key to efficacy and safety.

Long-term Harmful Effects of Medication

Another topic of controversy is the long-term effects of psychotropic medication in children. There is concern about long-term damage to the brain and development, growth suppression, and damage to other organ systems such as the heart and liver. These effects are difficult to measure owing to the large number of variables that affect development and behavior. A few scientists have looked at postnatal exposure to SSRIs and childhood exposure to antipsychotics in mice and rats. These scientists did find some long-term changes in development in both groups (Oberlander, Gingrich, & Ansorge, 2009; Milstein et al., 2013). It is difficult to know whether these results can be generalized to humans.

Diagnosing Bipolar Disorder in Children

Since the 1990s, the diagnosis of bipolar disorder in children has been increasing dramatically (Moreno et al., 2007). Controversy arises because many of these children and adolescents who are diagnosed with bipolar disorder do not clearly fit into the diagnosis of bipolar disorder according to the *Diagnostic and Statistical Manual of Mental Disorders* (4th ed.; *DSM-IV*; American Psychiatric Association, 1994; Parens & Johnston, 2010). These children are often treated with mood stabilizers and antipsychotics. There is evidence that the pharmaceutical industry may play a role in increasing the diagnosis of bipolar disorder in children to sell more psychiatric drugs (Healy, 2006).

In order to help solve this controversy, prescribers have advocated that the *DSM-IV* diagnosis of bipolar disorder be rewritten to apply to children and adolescents (Parens & Johnston, 2010). The fifth edition of the *DSM (DSM-5*; American Psychiatric Association, 2013) responded to this criticism with the creation of a new diagnosis called disruptive mood dysregulation disorder. It is unknown whether this new diagnosis will help to diminish the controversy.

Integrating Psychotherapy with Psychopharmacology

Many children and adolescents are now working within a treatment team that includes educators, social workers, school psychologists, counseling psychologists, and prescribers. In a 1980s survey, 63% psychiatrists and 79% psychologists had patients in treatment with more than one mental health provider (Chiles, Carlin, Benjamin, & Beitman, 1991). Since then, the number of mental health providers per child has likely increased. Each one of these providers may have his or her own theoretical background and approach to treatment. Children might get advice from one provider to take medication and another provider to stop medication. This can be confusing to children and families and may interfere with treatment.

Because of these issues, mental health professionals have discussed ways to integrate psychotherapy and psychopharmacology that will be helpful to children. As mentioned earlier, one suggestion is that regular communication occur between treatment providers. Specifically, during this communication, diagnostic impressions and treatment plans should be discussed and agreed upon, treatment goals or expectations shared, roles clarified, and understanding about ongoing communication and any issues that arise during treatment be discussed. In addition, any attempts by patients or families to drive treatment providers against one another should be curtailed (Beitman, Blinder, Thase, Riba, & Safer, 2003). A strong and transparent professional alliance between all treatment partners is best for the child and family.

When integrated, many studies also suggest that the combination of therapy and medication is superior to each alone. The frequently cited TADS study of depression in children and adolescents showed that combination therapy of medication and psychotherapy is the most effective treatment for depression (TADS, 2009). Another study showed that combination of medication and psychotherapy is the most effective treatment for anxiety (Compton et al., 2010). Finally, a clinical trial of treatment strategies for ADHD found that although combined treatment with medication and behavioral therapy (such as positive reinforcement and study skills) did not yield significantly greater benefits than medication management for core ADHD symptoms, it provided modest advantages for non-ADHD symptoms and positive functioning outcomes (The MTA Cooperative Group, 1999).

With an understanding of psychotropic medication types, application, use, and counterindications, let's explore a case to integrate this information.

CASE STUDY

Reason for Referral

Max was referred owing to poor grades and easy distraction in class.

Background/History

Max is a 14-year-old high school freshman who has been noticed by his teacher being easily distracted in class. He appears to be daydreaming often and is forgetting assignments or turning them in late. The teacher talks to Max, but he does not know why his performance has decreased. His teacher then contacts his mother, Mrs. Cane, who says that she thinks that his ADHD medication is no longer working. She says that Max has always had difficulties "paying attention, losing things, and waiting until the last minute." However, they took him to his pediatrician 2 years ago when his middle school academic performance and conduct were reported as poor, at which time he was started on Vyvanse. She states that Vyvanse worked great during middle school, but now it does not appear to be helping. His inattentiveness, inability to focus, and related behaviors have increased at home and apparently at school. Max is reported to have no illicit drug use, is involved in two school-based activities, and appears to engage in typical social interactions for his age.

Overview of Current Intervention

Max is being prescribed Vyvanse for ADHD by his pediatrician. It does not appear to be helping. Currently, it is unclear what interventions are being leveraged by school-based personnel.

Conceptualization

Max appears to be having symptoms consistent with ADHD that include trouble sustaining attention and difficulty organizing things. He was started on Vyvanse in middle school, which was effective, but now it is no longer working. There are several possibilities why the medication is no longer effective. He may have grown in size and weight, and this may affect dosage. There is also a possibility that he has developed a degree of tolerance to the medication. Furthermore, it is possible that the high school requires more sustained focus and better organizational skills than middle school, and this has affected his ability to stay focused and complete his work on time.

Intervention Goals and Plan

Max is referred for weekly sessions with an academic counselor. These weekly sessions focus on helping Max keep a planner in order to keep track of deadlines and plan out assignments. Max is encouraged to use his study halls effectively, especially while the medication's effect is most pronounced. Max's parents are involved in helping Max by providing accountability and positive reinforcement.

Max's pediatrician is contacted for follow-up assessment. An integrated treatment plan is discussed with all mental health providers. Max's pediatrician may decide to increase the medication or to encourage drug holidays to improve medication effectiveness. Max's pediatrician should also be in regular contact with parents and the academic counselor about Max's progress.

Intervention Assessment

Max's progress can be assessed by ADHD rating scales completed by himself, his parents, and his teachers (e.g., Vanderbilt ADHD Diagnostic, SNAP-IV, ADHD Rating Scale-IV). He can also be assessed by his grades, his ability to complete assignments, and his consistent usage of a planner.

Case Prognosis

Max's success is most likely dependent on medication effectiveness, his ability to integrate behavioral strategies, communication between his treatment providers, and parental support. He has no comorbidities, and that will likely improve his outcome. With this interdisciplinary approach, his prognosis is good.

SUMMARY

Despite the controversy surrounding the use of psychotropic medications with children and adolescents, the use of the psychotropic medications is increasing. Some medications have been FDA-approved in children and adolescents, but most are still used off label. An understanding of issues in pediatric psychopharmacology can help educators, administrators, and mental health professionals recognize when psychotropic medication issues arise. By recognizing these issues, communication can then occur with prescribers. After communication occurs with a prescriber, an integrated treatment plan can be formed, and regular issues can be discussed within the school setting. This will allow for the most effective comprehensive care of children and adolescents taking psychotropic medications.

RESOURCES

The MedlinePlus Drug Information website, which is associated with the National Library of Medicine (www.nim.nih.gov/medlineplus/druginformation.html), provides information about a variety of prescription and over-the-counter medications. Drugs can be searched for alphabetically, and standard information about each identified drug, including its designed effect, along with side effects, is provided. Information on herbs and supplements is also available. A search box exists (type in "illegal drugs") from which numerous articles, statistics, and general findings can be generated.

The Foundation for a Drug-Free World (www.drugfreeworld.org) is a nonprofit public benefit corporation dedicated to providing accurate, factual information about drugs and their effects on human behavior, especially on children and young adults. Personal stories, educational videos, as well as resources/tools for educators are provided. Free DVD kits for educators are also provided. This site is accessible in over 15 different languages.

KidsHealth (www.kidshealth.org) is sponsored by the Nemour Foundation Center for Children's Health Media. This user-friendly site provides a simple, straightforward way to access health information. The site consists of four separate sites each designed for parents, children, teens, and educators. Typing "drugs" in the search box provides a wide variety of related responses (e.g., stress reduction, prescription drug abuse, stimulant effects, signs of addiction).

REFERENCES

Abdelmalek, M., Adhikari, B., Koch, S., Diaz, J., & Weinraub, C. abcnews. com. Nov. 30, 2011. Retrieved from http://abcnews.go.com/US/study-shows-foster-children-high-rates-prescription-psychiatric/story?id=15058380#.UbjWjPlkxdI.

American Psychiatric Association. (1994). *Diagnostic and statistical manual of mental disorders* (4th ed.). Washington, DC: Author.

American Psychiatric Association. (2013). *Diagnostic and statistical manual of mental disorders* (5th ed.). Washington, DC: Author.

Beitman, B. D., Blinder, B. J., Thase, M. E., Riba, M., & Safer, D. L. (2003). *Integrating psychotherapy and pharmacotherapy: Dissolving the mind–brain barrier*. New York, NY: W. W. Norton.

Biederman, J., Spencer, T. J., Monuteaux, M. C., & Faraone, S. V. (2010). Naturalistic 10-year prospective study of height and weight in children with attention deficit hyperactivity disorder grown up: Sex and treatment effects. *Journal of Pediatrics, 157*(4), 635–640.

Carey, B. (2007). Debate over children and psychiatric drugs. *New York Times.* Retrieved from http://www.nytimes.com/2007/02/15/us/15bipolar.html?_r=0

Charach, A., Ickowicz, A., & Schachar, R. (2004). Stimulant treatment over five years: Adherence, effectiveness, and adverse effects. *Journal of the American Academy of Child and Adolescent Psychiatry, 43*(5), 559–567.

Chiles, J. A., Carlin, A. S., Benjamin, G. A., & Beitman, B. D. (1991). A physician, a nonmedical psychotherapist, and a patient: The pharmacotherapy-psychotherapy triangle. In B. D. Beitman & G. L. Klerman

(Eds.), *Integrating pharmacotherapy and psychotherapy* (pp. 105–118). Washington, DC: American Psychiatric Press.

Compton, S. N., Walkup, J. T., Albano, A. M., Piacentini, J. C., Birmaher, B., Sherrill, J. T., & March, J. S. (2010). Child/Adolescent Anxiety Multimodal Study (CAMS): Rationale, design, and methods. *Child and Adolescent Psychiatry and Mental Health, 4*(1), 1–15.

Correll, C. U., & Schenk, E. M. (2008). Tardive dyskinesia and new antipsychotics. *Current Opinion in Psychiatry, 21*(2), 151–156.

DEA Drug Fact Sheet. Amphetamines. Retrieved from http://www.justice.gov/dea/druginfo/all_fact_sheets.pdf

Food and Drug Administration. (2004). Revisions to product labeling. Retrieved from http://www.fda.gov/downloads/Drugs/DrugSafety/Informationby DrugClass/UCM173233.pdf

Food and Drug Administration. (2009). Suicidal behavior and ideation and antiepileptic drugs. Retrieved from http://www.fda.gov/Drugs/DrugSafety/PostmarketDrugSafetyInformationforPatientsandProviders/ucm100190.htm

Gibbons, R. D., Hur, K., Bhaumik, D. K., & Mann, J. (2006). The relationship between antidepressant prescription rates and rate of early adolescent suicide. *American Journal of Psychiatry, 163,* 1898–1904.

Hagino, O. R., Weller, E. B., Weller, R. A., Washington, D., Fristad, M. A., & Kontras, S. B. (1995). Untoward effects of lithium treatment in children aged four through six years. *Journal of the American Academy of Child and Adolescent Psychiatry, 34*(12), 1584–1590.

Hakim, D. (2011, December 23). Abused and used: In treating disabled, potent drugs and few rules. *New York Times,* p. A1.

Hammerness, P. G., Perrin, J. M., Shelley-Abrahamson, R. & Wilens, T. E. (2011). Cardiovascular Risk of Stimulant Treatment in Pediatric Attention-Deficit/Hyperactivity Disorder: Update and Clinical Recommendations. *Journal of the American Academy of Child and Adolescent Psychiatry, 50*(10), 978–990.

Healy D. (2006). The latest mania: Selling bipolar disorder. *PLoS Med, 3*(4), e185.

Hill, Michael. (2012, August 30). NY AG: Janssen pays $181M over drug marketing. *Seattle Times.*

Jureidini, J. N., Doecke, C. J., Mansfield, P. R., Haby, M. M., Menkes, D. B., & Tonkin, A. L. (2004). Efficacy and safety of antidepressants for children and adolescents. *British Medical Journal, 328*(7444), 879–883.

Katz, G. (2011). Tachyphylaxis/tolerance to antidepressive medications: A review. *The Israel Journal of Psychiatry and Related Science, 48*(2), 129–135.

Kirkwood, C. K. Management of insomnia. (1999). *Journal of the American Pharmaceutical Association, 39*(5), 688–696.

Kornstein, S. G., & Schneider, R. K. (2001). Clinical features of treatment-resistant depression. *Journal of Clinical Psychiatry, 62*(suppl 6), 18–25.

Krans, B., & Krucik, G. (2013). What are MAO inhibitors? Help for Depression. Cleveland Clinic, July 13, 2013. Retrieved from http://www.helpfordepression.com/slidshiow/drugs-and-medications/what-are-mao-inhibitors

Laughren, T. P., Gobburu, J., Temple, R. J., Unger, E. F., Bhattaram, A, Dinh, P. V., . . . Zineh, I. (2011). Vilazodone: Clinical basis for the U.S. Food and Drug Administration's approval of a new antidepressant. *Journal of Clinical Psychiatry, 72*(9), 1166–1173.

Leucht, S., Pitschel-Walz, G., Abraham, D., & Kissling, W. (1999). Efficacy and extrapyramidal side-effects of the new antipsychotics olanzapine, quetiapine, risperidone, and sertindole compared to conventional antipsychotics and placebo. A meta-analysis of randomized controlled trials. *Schizophrenia Research, 35*(1), 51–68.

Liu, H. Y., Potter, M. P., Woodworth, K. Y., Yorks, D. M., Petty, C. R., Wozniak, J. R., & Biederman, J. (2011). Pharmacologic treatments for pediatric bipolar disorder: A review and meta-analysis. *Journal of the American Academy of Child and Adolescent Psychiatry, 50*(8), 749–762.e39

Longo, L. P. & Johnson, B. (2000). Addiction: Part I. Benzodiazepines—side effects, abuse risk and alternatives. *American Family Physician, 61*(7), 2121–2128.

Manschreck, T., and Boshes, R. A. (2007). The CATIE schizophrenia trial: Results, impact, controversy. *Harvard Review of Psychiatry, 15*(5), 245–258.

Marks, D. M., Shah, M. J., Patkar, A. A., Masand, P. S., Park, G., & Pae, C. (2009). Serotonin-norepinephrine reuptake inhibitors for pain control: Premise and promise. *Current Neuropharmacology, 7*(4), 331–336.

Milstein, J. A., Elnabawi, A., Vinish, M., Swanson, T., Enos, J. K., Bailey, A. M., . . . Frost , D. O. (2013). Olanzapine treatment of adolescent rats causes enduring specific memory impairments and alters cortical development and function. *PLoS One, 8*(2), e57308.

Moreno, C., Laje, G., Blanco, C., Jiang, H., Schmidt, A. B., & Olfson M. (2007). National trends in the outpatient diagnosis and treatment of bipolar disorder in youth. *Archives of General Psychiatry, 64*(9), 1032–1039.

Morris, J. & Stone, G. (2011). Children and psychotropic medication: A cautionary note. *Journal of Marital and Family Therapy, 37*(3), 299–306.

The MTA Cooperative Group. (1999). Multimodal treatment study of children with ADHD. *Archives of General Psychiatry, 56*(12), 1073–1086.

Nemeroff, C. B. (2007). Prevalence and management of treatment-resistant depression. *Journal of Clinical Psychiatry, 68*(Suppl 8), 17–25.

Neppe, V. M. (1989). *Innovative psychopharmacotherapy*. New York, NY: Raven.

Oberlander, T. F., Gingrich, J. A., & Ansorge, M. S. (2009). Sustained neurobehavioral effects of exposure to SSRI antidepressants during development: Molecular to clinical evidence. *Clinical Pharmacology and Therapeutics, 86*(6), 672–677.

Olfson, M., Blanco, C., Liu, S., Wang, S., & Correll, C. U. (2012). National trends in the office-based treatment of children, adolescents, and adults with antipsychotics. *Archives of General Psychiatry, 69*(12), 1247–1256.

Pae, C. U., & Patkar, A. A. (2007). Paroxetine: Current status in psychiatry. *Expert Review of Neurotherapeutics, 7*(2), 107–120.

Parens, E. & Johnston, J. (2010). Controversies concerning the diagnosis and treatment of bipolar disorder in children. *Child and Adolescent Psychiatry and Mental Health, 4*, 9.

Pfizer. Geodon (ziprasidone HCl) Dear Healthcare Professional Letter, Mar. 2002. MedWatch. Food and Drug Administration. Retrieved from http://www.fda.gov/Safety/MedWatch/SafetyInformation/SafetyAlertsforHumanMedicalProducts/ucm170899.htm

Qiuping, G., Dillon, C. F., & Burt, V. L. (2010). Prescription drug use continues to increase: U.S. prescription drug data for 2007–2008. NCHS Date Brief. no 42. Hyattsville, MD: National Center for Health Statistics.

Reimherr, F. W., Hedges, D. W., Strong, R. E., Marchant, B. K., & Williams, E. D. (2005). Bupropion SR in adults with ADHD: A short-term, placebo-controlled trial. *Neuropsychiatry Disease and Treatment,* *1*(3), 245–251.

Scahill, L. (2009). Alpha-2 adrenergic agonists in children with inattention, hyperactivity and impulsiveness. *CNS Drugs, 23*(1 suppl.), 43–49.

Singh, T., Prakash, A., Rais, T., & Kumari, N. (2009). Decreased use of antidepressants in youth after U.S. Food and Drug Administration black box warning. *Psychiatry (Edgmont), 6*(10), 30–34.

Smith, M. (2006). Cardiovascular safety warning added for stimulants for ADHD. Medpage. Today.com. www.medpagetoday.com/Psychiatry/ADHD-ADD/3987

Swanson, J. M., Elliott, G. R., Greenhill, L. L., Wigal, T., Arnold, L. E., Vitiello, B., . . . Volkow, N. D. (2007). Effects of stimulant medication on growth rates across 3 years in the MTA follow-up. *Journal of the American Academy of Child and Adolescent Psychiatry, 46*(8), 1015–1027.

TADS Team. (2009). The Treatment for Adolescents with Depression Study (TADS): Outcomes over one year of naturalistic follow-up. *American Journal of Psychiatry, 166*(10), 1141–1149.

Tamam, L., & Ozpoyraz, N. (2002). Selective serotonin reuptake inhibitor discontinuation syndrome: A review. *Advances in Therapy, 19*(1), 17–26.

Vitiello, B., et al. (2009). Antipsychotics in children and adolescents: Increasing use, evidence for efficacy and safety concerns. *European Neuropsychopharmacology, 19*(9), 629–635.

Wysowski, D. K. (2007). Surveillance of prescription drug-related mortality using death certificate data. *Drug Safety, 30*(6), 533–540.

Yanofski, J. (2011). The dopamine dilemma—Part II. Could stimulants cause tolerance, dependence, and paradoxical decompensation? *Innovations in Clinical Neuroscience, 8*(1), 47–53.

Zuvekas, S. H., & Vitiello, B. (2012). Stimulant medication use among U.S. children: A twelve-year perspective. *American Journal of Psychiatry, 169*(2), 160–166.

Student Threat Assessment

DEWEY G. CORNELL

LEARNING OUTCOMES

On completion of this chapter, the reader should be able to:

- Consider the risk of school violence from a factual, base rate perspective
- Distinguish threat assessment from other violence prevention strategies
- Use threat assessment guidelines to differentiate transient from substantive threats
- Understand the role of mental health professionals in evaluating student threats of violence

THE RISK OF VIOLENCE IN U.S. SCHOOLS

The perceived risk of school shootings has had far-reaching effects on American education (Borum et al., 2010). For nearly two decades, periodic news reports of school shootings—typically accompanied by frightening images of students fleeing schools and tearful interviews with grieving family members and friends—have aroused great concern and distress about the safety of our schools. Each highly publicized school shooting stimulates nationwide demands for new security measures such as fortifying building entrances and installing video cameras and alarm systems. Students are now required to participate in school lockdown drills, and SWAT teams are trained to storm school buildings. All of these changes reinforce the common misperception that schools are dangerous places where students and staff are at risk for a violent attack.

Accompanying the fear of school shootings is heightened sensitivity to student misbehavior, particularly when students make threats of violence or engage in behavior that raises concern about the potential for violence. A typical response by school authorities is to suspend these students from school and refer them for a mental health evaluation. These are high-stakes evaluations that pose many challenges for the mental health clinician working individually or as part of a threat assessment team. What kind of evaluation should a mental health professional/ team conduct, and what kind of recommendations should be made to school authorities? In a climate of fear, school authorities may want to err on the side of safety and suspend or expel a student rather than risk underreacting to a possible attacker. In order to conduct a reasonably objective and unbiased assessment, the school mental health professional should have a good understanding of the base rates for violent crime in schools. He or she should be armed with facts to reassure authorities about the fundamental safety of schools. Because aggressive behavior can range from severe, but rare, acts of criminal violence to relatively minor, but commonplace, verbal teasing, there are multiple base rates to consider.

The very low base rates for serious violent crime at school should make clinicians exceedingly careful about concluding that there is a substantial risk of homicide or injury in any particular school. According to the Centers for Disease Control and Prevention, approximately 14 to 34 youth aged 5 to 18 are victims of homicide at school in a typical year. Although such cases are often highly publicized, they represent less than 2% of the 1,300 to 2,900 total homicides for this age group (Robers, Kemp, Rathbun, & Morgan, 2014). In others words, youth are at least 50 times more likely to be murdered somewhere other than school.

Another report estimated that with an average of 21 student homicides distributed across 125,000 schools, the typical U.S. school can expect a student to be murdered about once every 6,000 years (Borum et al., 2010). Security measures intended to prevent student murders would seem to be based on an unrealistic appraisal of danger and failure to consider the much higher prevalence of violent crime in other settings.

The United States has one of the highest rates of gun violence in the world, so there is certainly cause for concern about violent crime in general (Alpers & Wilson, 2013). Gun violence generates approximately 31,000 deaths and 78,000 nonfatal injuries in the general population every year (American Psychological Association, 2013), which translates to approximately 300 shootings every day. Again, base rate data show the low incidence of shootings in schools. An analysis of data from the National Incident Based Reporting System (NIBRS) found that homicide shootings most frequently occur in residences (53%), on roads (23%), and in parking lots or garages (6%), but only a fraction (0.3%) occur in schools (this category includes colleges as well as primary and secondary schools; Nekvasil, Cornell, & Huang, 2013). Shootings in schools command national attention, which gives them a prominence that is unjustified by their incidence in comparison to the daily barrage of shootings in other locations.

The National Crime Victimization Survey (NCVS) provides base rate information on nonfatal violent crimes (Robers et al., 2014). This ongoing national program interviews representative samples of the U.S. population to determine the prevalence of criminal victimization and is independent of law enforcement or school records, so it is presumed to be a more inclusive and complete assessment. Analyses of a subgroup of students (aged 12–18) permits a comparison of criminal victimization at school versus away from school. The rate of serious violent victimization (rape, sexual assault, robbery, and aggravated assault) was 3.5 per 1,000 students at school (including travel to and from school) and 5.4 per 1,000 students away from school. Moreover, serious violent crime has declined substantially from a peak of 22.1 per 1,000 in 1992 to 3.5 per 1,000 in 2011. Objectively, schools are much safer today than they were 20 years ago.

The base rates are much higher for less serious forms of violent victimization. The NCVS category for all violent crime includes both serious violent crimes and the broad category of simple assault, which includes threats and attacks without a weapon or serious injury. For the more inclusive category of all violent crime, victimization rates range from a low of 17 victimizations per 1,000 students at school in 2010 to 91 in 1993. Rates of violent victimization are typically higher away from school (with the exception of 2011, when the rate at school was 24, compared to 17 away from school). The rates for violent victimization are twice as high among 12- to 14-year-olds (34 in 2011) as 15- to 18-year-olds (14), likely owing to the high rate of fighting among early adolescent youth.

Another source of base rate information is anonymous student surveys such as the Youth Risk Behavior Survey (YRBS; Robers et al., 2014). Anonymous surveys have the advantage of allowing students to report behaviors they might otherwise not want to admit, but there is also the potential for a small group of students to inflate reports of violent behavior through dishonest or careless reporting (Cornell, Lovegrove, & Baly, 2013). According to YRBS data, approximately 16% of boys and 8% of girls in grades 9 to 12 reported being in a physical fight at school at least once in the previous 12 months. Approximately 8% of boys and 2% of girls reported carrying a weapon on school property during the previous 30 days (Robers et al., 2014).

Teachers are also potential targets of violence. Approximately 8% of teachers reported being threatened with injury, and approximately 4% reported being physically attacked by a student during the previous 12 months (Robers et al., 2014).

However, teachers are much more likely to experience abusive or disrespectful language from a student. A statewide sample of Virginia high school teachers found that 43% reported receiving obscene remarks or gestures from and 84% reported being spoken to in a rude or disrespectful manner by a student during the school year (Gregory, Cornell, & Fan, 2012).

EVIDENCE-BASED RESEARCH AND PRACTICE

After the 1999 shooting at Columbine High School in Colorado, reports by the Federal Bureau of Investigation (FBI; O'Toole, 2000) and U.S. Secret Service and Department of Education (Fein et al., 2002) recommended that schools adopt a threat assessment approach to violence prevention. Although threat assessment was an unfamiliar concept to most educators and mental health professionals at the time, it has become widely recognized as a valuable strategy for preventing acts of targeted violence such as those seen in mass shootings in schools, shopping centers, business places, and other settings. Threat assessment is used by the U.S. Secret Service, the U.S. State Department, and the U.S. Marshal Service to prevent violence to federal officials and is a recommended practice for the prevention of workplace violence (American Psychological Association, 2013; ASIS International, 2011).

Threat assessment is a specialized form of risk assessment that is conducted when an individual threatens to commit a violent act or engages in threatening behavior. (The term "behavioral threat assessment" is sometimes used to distinguish this process from a physical assessment of a facility's vulnerability to attack.) The concept of threat assessment has evolved to include the identification, assessment, and management of persons who have communicated threats of violence or engaged in some form of threatening behavior (Borum, Cornell, Modzeleski, & Jimerson, 2010). Threat assessment can be regarded as a problem-oriented approach to violence prevention, because it recognizes that people threaten violence when they are frustrated and distressed over a conflict or problem that they cannot resolve. Even if the individual does not currently pose a threat (i.e., not actively planning or preparing to carry out an attack), an important goal is to help the individual resolve the underlying conflict or problem so that the situation does not escalate.

In school settings, a threat assessment is concerned with understanding why a student made a threat or engaged in threatening behavior, and then identifying appropriate interventions that address the underlying problem or concern that motivated the threat. For example, a student may be bullied by peers or feel mistreated by school authorities. The threat assessment process includes efforts to stop bullying or resolve conflicts as appropriate to the situation. In many cases, the student's threat is merely a transient expression of frustration or defiance that does not pose a serious, substantive threat to safety. In cases in which there is imminent danger, the threat assessment response includes protective actions such as warning potential victims and contacting law enforcement.

It is important to recognize that verbal threats of violence are a relatively common event in schools. A survey of 4,400 high school students found that approximately 14% reported being threatened with harm by another student in the past 30 days (Nekvasil & Cornell, 2012). Of the students who reported that they had been threatened, nearly three-quarters did not believe the threat was serious. Even among the students who regarded the threat as serious, only about one-third reported that the aggressor attempted to carry out the threat. Although student threats occur frequently, few come to the attention of school authorities. Among the students who felt the threat was serious, fewer than one-quarter informed a teacher or other school staff member.

The dilemma for school authorities is that when a threat comes to their attention, they must make a decision about its seriousness without overreacting or underreacting. Mental health professionals must recognize that from a base rate perspective, a verbal threat alone has little prognostic value. Instead, the clinician should conduct an evaluation and formulate a prevention plan using a threat assessment approach.

Threat Assessment Teams

Most authorities recommend that threat assessments be conducted by multidisciplinary teams rather than a single individual (O'Toole, 2000; Fein et al., 2002). A team is typically composed of representatives from three domains: administration, law enforcement, and mental health. The team is usually led by a school administrator, such as principal or assistant principal, who is responsible for school disciplinary matters.

The law enforcement representative may be a school resource officer (SRO) or another police officer who is available to work with the school. The SRO can advise the team whether a student's behavior has violated the law and can conduct a criminal investigation and take appropriate action in the most serious cases. Such cases are rare in most schools, and the SRO's everyday role is to be a member of the school community who encourages law-abiding behavior and establishes positive relationships with students. School resource officers can take a preventive approach to crime by identifying and monitoring potentially volatile conflicts between students or groups of students.

Depending on the school's staffing pattern, a threat assessment team should include one or more mental health professionals (school counselor, school psychologist, social worker, etc.). A mental health professional may be involved at multiple stages in a threat assessment. In the most serious cases, a school psychologist or other suitably qualified staff member conducts an evaluation of the student with two main objectives. The first objective is to screen the student for mental health problems that demand immediate attention, such as psychotic symptoms or suicidality. The second objective is to assess why the student made the threat and make recommendations for dealing with the problem or conflict that stimulated the threatening behavior.

Mental health professionals also may conduct interventions such as counseling a distressed student or resolving conflicts between students. There is a large body of evidence that school-based interventions can reduce aggressive behavior (Wilson & Lipsey, 2007). There are several comprehensive lists of evidence-based programs, such as the National Registry of Evidence-Based Programs and Practices (Substance Abuse and Mental Health Services Administration, 2014) and Blueprints for Healthy Youth Development (formerly Blueprints for Violence Prevention; Center for the Study and Prevention of Violence, 2014), that provide examples of effective programs in areas such as social competence training, cognitive-behavioral counseling to improve social interaction and problem-solving skills, and conflict resolution programs. In all cases, there should be follow-up monitoring to ensure that a plan is working.

A school-based team is preferable to an external team for multiple reasons. First, a threat assessment requires an immediate response. School authorities cannot wait for a team of outside experts to assemble and begin an investigation. In some school systems, students have been suspended from school for weeks awaiting an evaluation by an external team. Second, threat assessment requires careful consideration of contextual and situational factors that are familiar to school personnel who know the students and school climate. Third, most student threats are not serious enough to warrant the assembly of an outside team. Many cases involve rash or foolish statements that are routinely resolved by a school administrator or counselor. Finally, threat assessment should not be limited to an initial assessment but should involve an ongoing process of intervention and reassessment. An effective threat assessment team will implement a response to a serious threat that is intended to reduce the risk of violence and will continue to monitor the student's status. Nevertheless, in a complicated case involving a serious threat of violence, the school-based team may want to draw upon the expertise of mental health experts and other resources in the community.

Virginia Student Threat Assessment Guidelines

Many school systems have developed their own threat assessment procedures, but there is little research on their effectiveness (e.g., Van Dreal, 2011; Van Dyke & Schroeder, 2006). The Virginia

Student Threat Assessment Guidelines is the only threat assessment program that is recognized as an evidence-based practice in the National Registry of Evidence-based Programs and Practices (NREPP, 2013; www.nrepp.samhsa.gov/ViewIntervention.aspx?id=263). The Virginia Guidelines were developed in 2002 (Cornell & Sheras, 2006) and have been the subject of a series of studies involving hundreds of schools. The first two studies of the Virginia Guidelines were field tests that demonstrated that school-based teams could carry out threat assessments in a practical, efficient manner without violent outcomes (Cornell et al., 2004; Strong & Cornell, 2008). Notably, almost all of the students were permitted to return to school, and few of the students received long-term suspensions or transfers to another school. Students receiving special education services made more threats than students in general education, but they did not receive disproportionately higher rates of school suspension (Kaplan & Cornell, 2005).

Key to the threat assessment approach is training school-based multidisciplinary teams to take a flexible, but systematic and investigative approach to evaluating student threats rather than pursue a more rigid zero-tolerance approach that does not consider the context and meaning of the student's behavior. Several studies have shown that staff training in the Virginia Guidelines has a substantial effect on the attitudes and knowledge of school personnel across disciplines (Allen, Cornell, Lorek, & Sheras, 2008; Cornell, Allen, & Fan, 2012; Cornell, Gregory, & Fan, 2011; Cornell, Sheras, Gregory, & Fan, 2009; Cornell et al., 2004; Strong & Cornell, 2008). These studies have found substantial changes in knowledge and attitudes regarding school violence, school discipline, and threat assessment. School personnel showed a decrease in fears of school violence and a shift in attitudes consistent with a threat assessment perspective. For example, they were willing to adopt a problem-solving approach to student conflicts and reduced their endorsement of a zero-tolerance approach. These changes were observed across groups of school principals, psychologists, counselors, social workers, and school-based police officers.

Four controlled studies have been conducted to date. The first controlled study was a retrospective comparison of 95 high schools reporting use of the Virginia Guidelines, 131 schools reporting use of locally developed procedures, and 54 schools reporting no use of a threat assessment approach (Cornell et al., 2009). Students at schools using the Virginia Guidelines reported less bullying in the past 30 days, greater willingness to seek help for bullying and threats of violence, and more positive perceptions of school staff members than students in either of the other two groups. In addition, there were one-third fewer long-term suspensions, after controlling for school size, minority composition and socioeconomic status of the student body, neighborhood violent crime, and the extent of security measures in the schools (Cornell et al., 2009).

The second controlled study examined changes in suspension rates and bullying infractions 1 year before and 1 year after 23 high schools implemented the Virginia Guidelines (Cornell, Gregory, & Fan, 2011). The high schools using the Virginia Guidelines experienced large reductions in long-term suspensions and bullying infractions, but 26 control group schools showed little change. For long-term suspensions, the control group had no change, but schools using the Virginia Guidelines experienced a 52% decline. For bullying infractions, the control group had a slight increase, whereas schools using the Virginia Guidelines had a decline of 79%.

The third study was a randomized controlled study of 40 schools where half of the schools were randomly assigned to receive threat assessment training and 20 delayed training for 1 year and served as a control group. During 1 school year, there were 201 students identified as making threats of violence. The incidence of student threats that came to the attention of school authorities was nearly the same in both groups of schools (100 in intervention schools and 101 in control schools). The critical issue was how school authorities would respond to these threats and the extent to which they would rely on school suspension or transfer as a response. Three outcomes were assessed: (1) use of counseling and mental health services to resolve conflicts, (2) involvement of parents in response to the threat, and (3) return of students to school without long-term suspension or alternative school placement. A potential fourth outcome was to examine whether the students carried out their threat of violence, but as found in previous studies (Cornell et al., 2004; Strong & Cornell, 2008), so few students carried out their threats that meaningful group comparisons were not possible. Compared with control students, students in schools using the Virginia Guidelines were approximately four times more likely to receive counseling services and two-and-a-half times more likely to receive a parent conference. Notably, students in the intervention group were about one-third as likely to receive a long-term suspension and one-eighth as likely to be transferred to a different school.

The fourth study examined suspension rates in secondary schools that had adopted the Virginia Guidelines across the state of Virginia (JustChildren and Cornell, 2013). Among Virginia's 663 secondary schools (middle, high, or combined schools), the 398 schools that used the Virginia Guidelines recorded 15% fewer short-term suspensions and 25% fewer long-term suspensions per year than the other 265 schools. This study was particularly concerned with the racial disparity between black and white students, because black students across all schools were twice as likely as white students to be suspended from school.

A noteworthy finding was that short-term and long-term suspension rates were lower for both white and black students in schools using the Virginia Guidelines, and the lower rate for black students substantially reduced the racial disparity in long-term suspensions. The following case study illustrates how a threat assessment is conducted using the seven-step decision tree.

CASE STUDY

Reason for Referral

Adam was an 8th-grade student referred to the school's threat assessment team after several classmates reported to a teacher that he had threatened to "blow you all away with my shotgun." According to the Virginia Guidelines, a threat is defined as any communication of intent to harm someone. When a threat is reported by anyone to the school principal or any member of the school's threat assessment team, one or more members of the team begins a threat assessment.

Referrals are initiated when a student makes a threat or engages in clear threatening behavior. Students should not be screened for dangerousness based on a checklist of warning signs or a psychological profile. Law enforcement and mental health authorities have consistently cautioned against the use of checklist and profiling approaches to identify presumably dangerous students. The FBI's profiling experts concluded that "trying to draw up a catalogue or 'checklist' of warning signs to detect a potential school shooter can be shortsighted, even dangerous. Such lists, publicized by the media, can end up unfairly labeling many nonviolent students as potentially dangerous" (O'Toole, 2000, p. 2). The basic problem with warning signs and checklists used to profile school shooters is that although they may seem compelling, the identified risk factors are widely found in the general population and are not specific indicators of violence. Characteristics such as "history of discipline problems" and "feelings of being picked on and persecuted" (Dwyer, Osher, & Warger, 1998) represent legitimate concerns that merit intervention as counseling issues, but are not reliable predictors of imminent violence. School professionals should be leery of checklists and other profiling approaches (including computer software) that purport to predict such an extraordinarily rare event as a homicidal act.

Both the FBI and Secret Service studies of school shootings found that most student attackers communicated or leaked their intentions to others before their violent act (O'Toole, 2000; Vossekuil, Fein, Reddy, Borum, & Modzeleski, 2002). This observation supports the conclusion that shootings could be prevented by investigating students who communicated a threat or engaged in some other threatening behavior. The threat assessment process can be distinguished from profiling because it is initiated in response to the student's own threatening behavior and focuses on ascertaining whether this behavior indicates serious intent (Reddy et al., 2001).

THREAT ASSESSMENT PROCESS

The Virginia threat assessment process is guided by a seven-step decision tree (see Figure 16.1) that is designed to help the team distinguish transient threats that can be easily resolved from substantive threats that require more extensive assessment and protective action. A transient threat is an expression of anger, frustration, or humor that does not represent a sustained intent

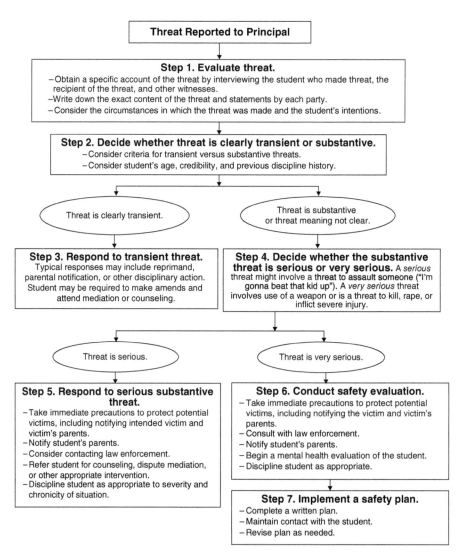

FIGURE 16.1 Decision tree for student threat assessment.

to harm someone. Because most threats in schools are transient threats, the decision tree begins with a triage process to determine whether the threat can be quickly and easily resolved as a transient threat or will require more extensive evaluation and protective action as a substantive threat.

A team member begins at Step 1 by gathering information about the reported threat from witnesses and from the student who allegedly made the threat, using a standard but flexible set of questions. The focus is on understanding the context of the threat, that is, what the student meant and intended in making the threat. For example, the statement, "I'm going to kill you," could convey a serious threat, but in most cases it is nothing more than a figure of speech. The student's account is compared with what other witnesses report and how they experienced the threat.

At Step 2, the team decides whether the threat is transient or substantive. Transient threats are defined as behaviors that can be readily identified as expressions of anger, frustration, or humor that dissipate when the student has time to reflect on the meaning of what he or she has said. The defining feature of a transient threat is that the student does not have a sustained intention to harm someone. In contrast, a substantive threat involves a sustained intent to harm someone beyond the immediate incident. If there is doubt, the threat is regarded as substantive. Several features are used to help identify substantive threats:

- The threat includes plausible details, such as a specific victim, time, place, and method of attack.
- The threat involves preparation, such as acquiring weapons or making a plan of attack.
- There are efforts to recruit accomplices or invite an audience.

There are no absolute indicators that a threat is substantive, but any one of these features may lead the team to treat the threat as substantive, at least until there is sufficient information to resolve the threat.

A transient threat is resolved at Step 3 when it is clear that the student has no intention to harm anyone. Usually the student offers an explanation and apology that clarifies the situation. The student might be reprimanded or disciplined in some way if his or her behavior was disruptive or violated school rules, and in some cases the student may be referred for counseling if there is a conflict or problem that merits attention.

After the teacher reported Adam's alleged threat to the assistant principal, he initiated the threat assessment process by interviewing each of the students identified by the teacher. The assistant principal took notes and asked a series of questions to clarify the nature of the threat and the circumstances in which it was made. The first student, Megan, said that Adam had told her that he had a "hit list" with her name on it. Megan said that she had recently dated Adam and "he's mad at me for breaking up with him." The assistant principal then interviewed two boys, Jason and Kyle, who said that Adam had threatened to shoot them with his shotgun. Both boys professed that they had no idea why Adam had threatened him.

When the assistant principal interviewed Adam, he appeared uncomfortable and embarrassed, but defensive and uncooperative. Adam admitted that he was angry with Megan and the two boys, but denied that he had threatened them. If Adam had admitted his behavior, apologized, and explained that he was merely angry with his classmates, the assistant principal might have been able to treat the threat as transient and not serious. He or another team member could have reviewed the conflict that precipitated the threat and found that it was possible to resolve it. However, Adam's uncooperativeness and denial of the threat made it impossible to resolve as a transient threat.

Substantive Threats

The Virginia Guidelines indicate that whenever a threat cannot be resolved as a transient threat, it is considered a substantive threat, which means that there is some risk that the threat might be carried out. At Step 4, the team distinguishes two levels of substantive threats: Serious substantive threats involve a threat to hit, fight, or assault someone, and very serious substantive threats are threats to kill, rape, or use a weapon to injure someone. If the case involved a serious substantive threat, the team would proceed to Step 5. At this stage, the school team would take appropriate protective action to prevent the threat from being carried out. Typically, the team would monitor the student and keep him or her separated from the threatened individual. They would counsel the student about the consequences of his or her behavior and seek some alternative way to resolve the conflict. They would notify the student's parents of the threat. They would also notify the threatened individual, and if this individual was a minor, the minor's parent or guardian. In all of these contacts, the team's emphasis would be on uncovering the reason for the threat and seeking a resolution to the problem or conflict that generated it.

In cases of very serious substantive threats, there would be some additional team actions at Step 6. The team should take appropriate protective action to ensure that the threat is not carried out. Adam was detained in the principal's office until his parents could be summoned. His parents were informed of the alleged threat and the school's policy and procedures for responding to a very serious substantive threat. Although the threat assessment guidelines discourage use of school suspension, in the case of a very serious substantive threat, it is advisable to use a short-term suspension until the team can complete a more comprehensive assessment and devise a plan. It is a matter of safety for the student as well as others for the student to be removed from school for a few days. A longer suspension, however, is rarely needed.

Information Sharing

The team also contacted the parents of the students who were threatened. They described the threat, disclosed the name of the student who made the threat, and reviewed their school policies and procedures for dealing with threats. They stressed the need to work cooperatively with the parents to resolve the situation.

Some school authorities mistakenly believe that the Family Educational Rights Privacy Act (FERPA) forbids them from releasing the names of students or sharing other confidential information regarding a threat. After the 2007 shootings at Virginia Tech, the U.S. Department of Education (2007) issued a series of clarifying statements about FERPA. One important clarification is that student information, including student names, can be disclosed in a health or safety emergency. Furthermore, school authorities should understand that FERPA applies only to student educational records, and there is no federal restriction on information that is based on the personal observation or knowledge of school personnel that is not based on school records. For example, if a teacher observes a student making a threat, or a student admits to a school counselor that he threatened someone, this information is not restricted by FERPA.

FERPA also permits schools to maintain threat assessment records that are not part of a student's educational record and thus not restricted by FERPA (U.S. Department of Education, 2007). Records maintained for safety or security purposes are deemed "law enforcement unit" records and can be disclosed to others when it is considered appropriate by school authorities. Although student confidentiality is an important concern and should be safeguarded in most circumstances, it is secondary to safety, and confidentiality must not keep school authorities from taking reasonable action to prevent a serious act of violence.

Law Enforcement Actions

In very serious substantive cases, the school resource officer may conduct an investigation of the threat to determine whether any laws have been violated and whether the student has acquired weapons or engaged in other plans to carry out the threat. The officer also provides advice on school security, should that be a concern. In Adam's case, his parents told the police officer that Adam did not own a shotgun and to their knowledge had never fired a shotgun. Although the officer did not have a search warrant, she could inspect Adam's home if the parents gave their permission. They gave permission for the officer to come to their house and look through Adam's room to confirm that he did not have firearms there. On the grounds that he had reasonable suspicion that Adam might have a weapon, the school principal opened Adam's locker and searched his book bag. The school resource officer observed these searches and could take a more active role if a firearm was found.

Mental Health Evaluation

In very serious substantive cases, the school psychologist (or another designated mental health professional) should begin a mental health evaluation of the student as soon as possible, with the initial goal of assessing the student's mental state and need for immediate mental health services. This evaluation can begin before the parents are contacted if necessary, much as a mental health professional will evaluate a student for suicide risk as promptly as possible. However, after parents are contacted, the mental health professional will want to obtain parental permission to continue. In Adam's case, the assistant principal and school psychologist explained to the parents that school policy required them to conduct a mental health evaluation in order to determine whether it was safe for him to return to school. The psychologist explained to Adam's parents the purpose of the evaluation, that she would include their input in the evaluation, and that she would share the results of the evaluation with them. The parents asked whether they could obtain an independent evaluation from someone in the community and they were informed that this was their prerogative, but that it would supplement rather than replace the need for a school-based evaluation.

The mental health assessment is central to very serious substantive threats, but its purpose is different from the evaluations often requested by school authorities who do not use a threat assessment approach. In many cases, school authorities will not allow a student to return to school without a report from a mental health professional certifying that the student is safe. It is unreasonable for school authorities to want an unequivocal prediction whether a student will carry out a threat, because predictions of violence tend to be unreliable and prone to error. Under the Virginia Guidelines, the school psychologist or other mental health professional should follow a risk reduction or risk management approach rather than a predictive approach. The goal of threat assessment is always to reduce risk through interventions aimed at the problems that led to the threat. Rather than make uncertain and questionable predictions, school mental health professionals are asked to apply their skills in working with troubled students and helping them resolve personal problems and conflicts in their relationships.

The Virginia Guidelines provide a detailed description of the process and content for an assessment of a student who has made a very serious substantive threat. The first goal of this evaluation is to assess the student's mental state and need for immediate mental health services. For example, does the student have delusional ideas that are motivating the threat? Is the student so depressed or suicidal that he or she might act without concern for the consequences? A second goal is to recommend strategies addressing the problem or conflict underlying the threat. For example, is the student a victim of bullying or involved in some other peer conflict?

The Virginia Guidelines (Cornell & Sheras, 2006) provide a detailed outline of topics for mental health professionals to cover in their evaluation. As in the case of Adam, the interviewer begins by explaining that the purpose of the interview is to understand what happened from the student's perspective. Adam was asked specifically to describe the alleged threat incidents, but the interviewer was careful to use open-ended questions that were not judgmental or leading. For example, the school psychologist asked Adam "What happened today in the hallway with Megan?" rather than "Why did you threaten Megan in the hallway?". The school psychologist tried to find out as much as possible about the incidents, but also explore Adam's motives. She made a point of encouraging Adam to explain his actions, asking questions such as "I know you must have had some reason to say that, what led up to it?"

Initially, Adam denied threatening Megan or the two boys, but eventually related his story that Megan had broken up with him unexpectedly and that he felt devastated and cried. She laughed at his tears and told the two boys, who were mutual friends. The boys sided with Megan and repeatedly made fun of him for crying. The interviewer's supportive and sympathetic approach encouraged Adam to acknowledge that he had made threats. He related that their "crybaby" taunts angered him and he decided to retaliate by threatening to kill all three of them. He was quick to emphasize that the threats were "not real, just a way to get back at them."

The school psychologist also investigated Adam's understanding of the consequences of carrying out the threat, how others would be affected, and what would happen to him. It is useful to assess how much empathy and understanding a student has of the effects of his actions on his targets as well as others, such as their families and his family. In this case, Adam recognized the seriousness of his actions and realized that he had made a terrible mistake to threaten them, even though he was angry and felt they deserved some kind of retribution.

After gaining as much information as possible about the threat incidents, the school psychologist reviewed Adam's current behavioral and emotional status. In all cases, it is important to inquire about symptoms of depression and anxiety, as well as feelings of irritability and anger. It is necessary to look for indications of delusions or hallucinations, or any other indication of deterioration into serious mental illness that might not be immediately apparent. The emergence of mental illness can be insidious and not easily detected. A frightened, mistrustful, or paranoid adolescent might not admit to hearing voices or having delusional ideas.

Another area of inquiry is the presence of risk factors that might be directly connected to the threat situation, such as the availability of weapons, especially access to firearms, and experiences of being bullied or teased by peers. Adam possessed no firearms and had invented the idea that he had a shotgun, based on a movie he had seen. It is also useful to review the student's history of aggressive behavior, delinquency, school discipline problems, and exposure to violence. Adam did not have a history of fighting or misbehaving at school. He had not been exposed to violence in the home.

Along with risk factors, the interview should cover protective factors and coping capacity. Adam has reasonably good family support and peer support, although the teasing by his two friends was a blow to his self-esteem. He did have other friends who were sympathetic, and he did not see himself as alienated from all of his peers. It can be especially useful to assess whether the student feels pessimistic or hopeless about the future, or can conceive of a positive outcome. Adam recognized that his situation was not hopeless, that eventually he would get over the loss of his girlfriend, and that the teasing would stop. He realized that he had gotten caught up in the situation and acted impulsively by making threats without thinking about the consequences. In contrast, the threats of students who feel they have nothing to lose or nothing to look forward to in the future are cause for concern.

Risk Scores

Psychologists in particular look for tests or scales that can quantify student characteristics. Although a number of risk assessment instruments have been developed for specific populations, such as prison inmates or sex offenders, there is little research on the risk of imminent violence in student populations. Many of the risk factors commonly identified in the literature are associated with general risk for violence that could be years in the future, rather than immediate risk to carry out a specific threat. Even youth who score high on risk assessment instruments do not engage in frequent acts of violence. This makes these scores of doubtful value in determining whether a student is going to carry out a threat in the immediate future. As a result, mental health professionals should be cautious about using instruments that reduce the risk of violence to a single score or categorical determination. No psychological test or instrument can replace the professional judgment that is essential to making decisions about interventions to prevent violence (Borum et al., 2002; Heilbrun, Dvoskin, & Heilbrun, 2009).

One resource for interviewing youth about general risk factors is the Structured Assessment of Violence Risk in Youth (SAVRY; Borum et al., 2002). SAVRY can be used as an assessment tool in conjunction with a threat assessment, but it is not a formal test. SAVRY purposely does not produce a risk score, because the risk for violence is much more situational and transitory than risk scores imply (Borum et al., 2002). Risk scores, as well as classifications of risk (e.g., high, medium, low) are static designations that ignore the variability in youth behavior and their responsiveness to their immediate environment. A youth who is low-risk when he is calm may be much more dangerous when he is angry, intoxicated, or surrounded by peers who encourage aggressive behavior. A student's level of risk rises when the student moves from a supervised classroom into the hallway between classes, and then rises again when he or she leaves school in the afternoon.

The mental health evaluation may include additional information obtained from parents, teachers, and other informed sources (e.g., if the student is receiving mental health services or special education services). In Adam's case, space limitations preclude a more complete summary of the evaluation process. Overall, his evaluation lessened concern about Adam's potential for violence and suggested some strategies for intervention.

Case Resolution

At Step 7, the results of the mental health evaluation, law enforcement investigation, and any other sources of information are used to develop an intervention plan designed to reduce the risk of violence and, when appropriate, return the student to school. In Adam's case, he was willing to admit his mistakes and apologize for his threatening behavior. The three students targeted by his threats apologized for their behavior toward him and the two boys, although not the girl, resolved to renew their friendship with Adam. Adam and his parents agreed that school authorities could share information with the parents of the targeted students to explain the situation and the school's decision to permit Adam to return to school under certain conditions. Adam also agreed that he would attend a series of counseling sessions and that he would contact an adult at school if there were further problems in getting along with his peers. Upon his return to school, Adam checked in with the school counselor initially on a daily basis and then at longer intervals. There were no further problems.

SUMMARY

Public attention to school shootings has contributed to an exaggerated perception of the risk of school violence. In contrast, mental health professionals who evaluate students for violence risk should keep in mind the low base rates for serious violent crime in schools. Student threat assessment is a problem-solving approach to violence prevention that gives schools a flexible and practical alternative to zero tolerance discipline. A series of studies have found that the Virginia Student Threat Assessment Guidelines allow school authorities to resolve student threats and keep students in school. School mental health professionals can work with a multidisciplinary team to reduce the risk of violence by addressing the problem or conflict that generated the student's threatening behavior.

RESOURCES

The National Center for Education Statistics publishes an annual *Indicators of School of School Crime and Safety* report that compiles results from various studies of school safety conditions (www.bjs.gov/index.cfm?ty=tp&tid=974).

The National Registry of Evidence-based Programs and Practices (NREPP) provides a comprehensive list of mental health intervention programs (nrepp.samhsa.gov).

Information on the Virginia Student Threat Assessment Guidelines is available from the Youth Violence Project at the Curry School of Education, University of Virginia (curry.virginia.edu/research/labs/youth-violence-project).

REFERENCES

Allen, K., Cornell, D., Lorek, E., & Sheras, P. (2008). Response of school personnel to student threat assessment training. *School Effectiveness and School Improvement, 19*, 319–332.

Alpers, P., & Wilson, M. (2013, August 14). *Global impact of gun violence: Firearms, public health and safety.* Retrieved from http://www.gunpolicy.org/firearms/region

American Psychological Association. (2013). *Gun violence: Prediction, prevention, and policy.* Retrieved from http://www.apa.org/pubs/info/reports/gun-violence-prevention.aspx

Appalachian State University. (n.d.). *Counseling for Faculty and Staff.* Retrieved from http://cfs.appstate.edu/index.php?module=page smith&uop=view_page&id=20

ASIS International and Society for Human Resource Management. (2011). *Workplace violence prevention and intervention: An American standard* (ASIS/SHRM WVP.1-2011). New York, NY: American National Standards Institute.

Borum, R., Bartel, P., & Forth, A. (2002). *Manual for the Structured Assessment of Violence Risk in Youth (SAVRY)*. Lutz, FL: Psychological Assessment Resources.

Borum, R., Cornell, D. Modzeleski, W., & Jimerson, S. R. (2010). What can be done about school shootings? A review of the evidence. *Educational Researcher, 39*, 27–37.

Center for the Study and Prevention of Violence (2014). Blueprints for Healthy Youth Development. Retrieved from http://www.blue printsprograms.com

Cornell, D., Allen, K., & Fan, X. (2012). A randomized controlled study of the Virginia Student Threat Assessment Guidelines in grades K–12. *School Psychology Review, 41*, 100–115.

Cornell, D., Gregory, A., & Fan, X. (2011). Reductions in long-term suspensions following adoption of the Virginia Student Threat Assessment Guidelines. *Bulletin of the National Association of Secondary School Principals, 95*, 175–194.

Cornell, D. G., Lovegrove, P. J., & Baly, M. W. (2013, November 11). Invalid survey response patterns among middle school students. *Psychological Assessment*. Advance online publication. doi:10.1037/a0034808

Cornell, D. & Sheras, P. (2006). *Guidelines for responding to student threats of violence*. Longmont, CO: Sopris West.

Cornell, D., Sheras, P., Gregory, A., & Fan, X. (2009). A retrospective study of school safety conditions in high schools using the Virginia Threat Assessment Guidelines versus alternative approaches. *School Psychology Quarterly, 24*, 119–129.

Cornell, D., Sheras, P., Kaplan, S., McConville, D., Douglass, J., Elkon, A., McKnight, L., Branson, C., & Cole, J. (2004). Guidelines for student threat assessment: Field-test findings. *School Psychology Review, 33*, 527–546.

Dwyer, K., Osher, D., & Warger, C. (1998). *Early warning, timely response: A guide to safe schools*. Washington, DC: U.S. Department of Education.

Fein, R. A., Vossekuil, B., Pollack,W. S., Borum, R., Modzeleski,W., & Reddy, M. (2002). *Threat assessment in schools: A guide to managing threatening situations and to creating safe school climates*. Washington, DC: U.S. Secret Service and U.S. Department of Education.

Gregory, A., Cornell, D., & Fan, X. (2012). Teacher safety and authoritative school climate in high schools. *American Journal of Education, 118*, 401–425.

Heilbrun, K., Dvoskin, J., & Heilbrun, A. (2009). Toward preventing future tragedies: Mass killings on college campuses, public health, and threat/risk assessment. *Psychological Injury and Law, 2*, 93–99.

JustChildren, and Cornell, D. (2013). *Prevention v. punishment: Threat assessment, school suspensions, and racial disparities*. Legal Aid Justice Center, Charlottesville, VA. Retrieved from https://www.justice4all. org/wp-content/uploads/2013/12/UVΛ-and-JustChildren-Report-Prevention-v.-Punishment.pdf

Kaplan, S., & Cornell, D. (2005). Threats of violence by students in special education. *Behavioral Disorders, 31*, 107–119.

National Registry of Evidence-Based Programs and Practices (NREPP). (2013). Virginia Student Threat Assessment Guidelines. Retrieved from http://www.nrepp.samhsa.gov/ViewIntervention.aspx?id=263

Nekvasil, E., & Cornell, D. (2012). Student reports of peer threats of violence: Prevalence and outcomes. *Journal of School Violence, 11*, 357–375.

Nekvasil, E., Cornell, D., & Huang, F. (2013). *Prevalence and offense characteristics of multiple casualty homicides: Is school fortification needed?* Unpublished manuscript, University of Virginia, Charlottesville.

O'Toole, M. E. (2000). *The school shooter: A threat assessment perspective.* Quantico, VA: National Center for the Analysis of Violent Crime, Federal Bureau of Investigation.

Reddy, M., Borum, R., Berglund, J., Vossekuil, B., Fein, R. A., & Modzeleski, W. (2001). Evaluating risk for targeted violence in schools: Comparing risk assessment, threat assessment, and other approaches. *Psychology in the Schools, 38*, 157–172.

Robers, S., Kemp, J., Rathbun, A., & Morgan, R. E. (2014). *Indicators of school crime and safety: 2013* (NCES 2014-042/NCJ 243299). Washington, DC: National Center for Education Statistics, U.S. Department of Education, and Bureau of Justice Statistics, Office of Justice Programs, U.S. Department of Justice.

Strong, K., & Cornell, D. (2008). Student threat assessment in Memphis City Schools: A descriptive report. *Behavioral Disorders, 34*, 42–54.

Substance Abuse and Mental Health Services Administration. (2014). SAMHSA's National Registry of Evidence-based Programs and Practices. U. S. Department of Health and Human Services. Retrieved from http://nrepp.samhsa.gov/Index.aspx

U.S. Department of Education. (2007). *Balancing student privacy and school safety: A guide to the family educational rights and privacy act for elementary and secondary schools.* Retrieved from http://www2.ed.gov/policy/gen/guid/fpco/brochures/elsec.pdf

Van Dreal, J. (2011). *Assessing student threats: A handbook for implementing the Salem-Keizer system.* Lanham, MD: Rowman and Littlefield.

Van Dyke, R., & Schroeder, J. (2006). Implementation of the Dallas Threat of Violence Risk Assessment. In S. R. Jimerson & M. J. Furlong (Eds.), *The handbook of school violence and school safety* (pp. 603–616). Mahwah, NJ: Erlbaum.

Vossekuil, B., Fein, R., Reddy, M., Borum, R., & Modzeleski, W. (2002). *The final report and findings of the Safe School Initiative: Implications for the prevention of school attacks in the United States.* Washington, DC: U.S. Secret Service and U.S. Department of Education.

Wilson, S. J., & Lipsey, M. W. (2007). School-based interventions for aggressive and disruptive behavior: Update of a meta-analysis. *American Journal of Preventive Medicine, 33*, 130–143. doi:10.1016/j.amepre.2007.04.01

CHAPTER 17

School Crisis Prevention and Intervention: Emergency Preparedness and Response

AMANDA B. NICKERSON
TODD A. SAVAGE
SCOTT A. WOITASZEWSKI

LEARNING OUTCOMES

On completion of this chapter, the reader should be able to:

- Identify ways schools can work to prevent crises from happening and to mitigate the potential negative consequences that may result when a crisis does occur
- Outline how the characteristics of crisis events, one's exposure to a crisis, and individual vulnerability and protective factors affect the potential for a person to develop trauma subsequent to a crisis
- Recognize reactions that may require school crisis intervention
- Define school crisis intervention and its various aspects and levels, particularly within a multitiered systems of support framework
- Become familiar with the PREPaRE model of crisis prevention and intervention and its specific application to schools

The topic of school crisis prevention and intervention has received much attention in the literature, in the media, and in the minds of all persons connected to the system of education in the United States, given highly visible crisis events that have taken place throughout the past 20 or more years. Paducah, Jonesboro, Littleton,

Newtown, and Arapahoe all conjure up images of shock, disbelief, and grief following the shootings committed by adolescent boys or young men at schools in each of these communities, among others. Although planning for a quick and effective response to an active school shooter is an important aspect of a school safety plan, the focus of this chapter will be more comprehensive. School mental health professionals, administrators, and other educators are encouraged to develop and address a full range of crisis prevention, preparedness, and crisis response skills. School safety plans, as mandated by federal and state legislation, should include evidence-informed preventative strategies along with multiple tiers of service that address multiple hazards. School-based crises could include everything from a non-fatal playground injury to events of terrorism. A full range of crises must be considered, yet schools will be best served through attempts to prevent and be prepared for crises that are most likely for that school location and environment. A structured system for preventing, preparing for, and responding to school crises is covered next.

EVIDENCE-BASED RESEARCH AND PRACTICE

Research conducted over the past several decades has advanced our understanding of the impact of trauma on children's functioning, as well as approaches that work best to prevent, mitigate, and intervene in crisis situations. Crisis prevention and preparedness are critical to creating school environments that minimize the likelihood of a crisis occurring in the first place, while ensuring that staff, students, and the community are prepared for the multiple crises that could occur (e.g., natural disasters, accidents, violent deaths). Using evidence-based, comprehensive models of school-wide positive behavioral support is associated with reduced problem behaviors and improvements in student academic performance, school organizational health, and perceptions of safety (Sprague & Horner, 2012). In addition, social and emotional learning (SEL) programming builds social competences, reduces problem behavior, and improves academic outcomes (Durlak, Weissberg, Dymnicki, Taylor, & Schellinger, 2011). Preventing crises requires that multidisciplinary school and district safety teams attend to both physical and psychological safety by developing, exercising, and evaluating crisis plans that are based on careful vulnerability assessments (Brock, Nickerson, Reeves, Jimerson, Lieberman, & Feinberg, 2009; U.S. Department of Education, Office of Elementary and Secondary Education, Office of Safe and Healthy Students, 2013). Training staff to identify and intervene with threats of suicide and violence toward others is also critical in preventing crises (see Chapter 12, "Suicide Prevention and Intervention").

Some crisis events are more likely to generate psychological trauma than others (Nooner et al., 2012) depending on factors such as predictability, consequences, duration, and intensity.

Natural disasters and accidents tend to be less traumatic than human-caused or intentional crises, such as assaultive violence (Charuvastra & Cloitre, 2008). It is also clear individuals are differentially affected by crises depending on characteristics of the event, exposure (i.e., physical and emotional proximity), and individual risk and protective factors (Brock et al., 2009). With regard to *physical proximity* (i.e., direct exposure), children who sustain injuries (Kolaitis et al., 2003) or who are witness or are otherwise exposed to death or injury (Eksi et al., 2007) are more likely to exhibit posttraumatic stress symptoms. In addition, *emotional proximity* (e.g., knowing the victim, especially in the case of the death of a friend or relative) is associated with negative mental health outcomes for children (Kolaitis et al., 2003), such as complicated grief, depression, and symptoms of posttraumatic stress disorder (PTSD; Cohen & Mannarino, 2004; Melhem et al., 2004).

Beyond the traumatizing potential of an event based on exposure, it is also important to consider other variables that may increase or decrease the likelihood of adverse outcomes following a crisis. Prior traumatization is a well-documented risk factor (Nader, Pynoos, Fairbanks, & Frederick, 1990; Olff, Langeland, & Gersons, 2005), with children from impoverished backgrounds being more likely to have experienced prior traumatic events and trauma-related psychopathology (Buka, Stichick, Birdthistle, & Earls, 2001). Coping, a complex process of cognitive, behavioral, and emotional responses to stress, is an important contributor to children's adjustment after a crisis (Pfefferbaum, Noffsinger, & Wind, 2012). Although assessment typically involves examining coping strategies used in a crisis (with avoidant coping being more problematic if used as a long-term strategy; Krause, Kaltman, Goodman, & Dutton, 2008), it is also important to understand children's (a) coping styles used across and within stressful situations; (b) cognitive appraisals of the threat; (c) perceived effectiveness of their coping styles and self-efficacy, or capacity to manage effectively in similarly stressful future event; and (d) source, type, and availability of external resources and their function in stimulating coping (Pfefferbaum et al., 2012).

Part of what makes children particularly vulnerable to developing PTSD, affective disorders, and disrupted learning after a crisis is their lack of experience implementing effective coping and decision-making skills in crisis situations, as well as their generally less well-developed emotion regulation abilities (Lonigan, Phillips, & Richey, 2003; National Commission on Children and Disasters, 2010). In addition, the presence of social support is associated with a lower likelihood of developing PTSD (Ozer, Best, Lipsey, & Weiss, 2003), whereas lack of emotional and practice support from families due to parental distress, mental illness, or poor coping strategies is associated with more negative mental health outcomes for children following a crisis (Caffo & Belaise, 2003; Green et al., 1991).

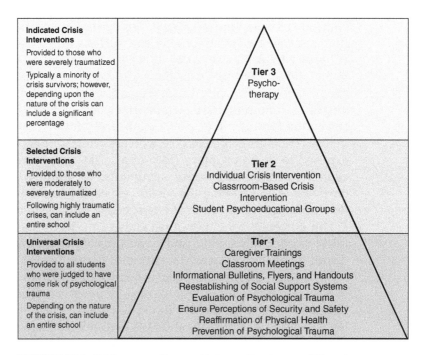

FIGURE 17.1 Crisis prevention and intervention in a multitiered framework.

Adapted from the chapter "Best Practices for School Psychologists as Members of Crisis Teams: The PREPaRE Model" by S. E. Brock, A. B. Nickerson, M. A. Reeves, and S. R. Jimerson (2008). In A. Thomas and J. Grimes (Eds.), *Best Practices in School Psychology* (5th ed.; p. 1495). Bethesda, MD: National Association of School Psychologists.

A consistent research finding is that healthy recovery is to be expected for most people following crises, even without psychological intervention (McNally, Bryant, & Ehlers, 2003). In most cases, given reunification with loved ones or other healthy social supports, a high percentage of school students and staff will recover relatively quickly. The aforementioned research on the differential impact of crisis events and risk and protective factors serves as the foundation for best practice in crisis prevention and intervention. An increasingly important role in the provision of mental health services is the use of a multitier public health model (Merrell, Ervin, & Gimpel Peacock, 2012; Shinn & Walker, 2010), which has been applied to crisis prevention and intervention (Brock et al., 2009; see Figure 17.1).

Tier 1

The first tier, universal crisis interventions, are provided to all students and tailored to the nature of the crisis. These approaches are focused on preventing and mitigating risk for all individuals. Therefore, this includes crisis prevention and preparedness activities. Clearly, preventing violence and other more preventable crisis events is critical. It is also important for schools to prepare for multiple crisis events (e.g., natural disasters, unexpected deaths, accidents) with comprehensive crisis plans and crisis teams that use the U.S. Department of Homeland Security's (2008) Incident Command System (see Nickerson, Brock, & Reeves, 2006).

Once a crisis event occurs, there are a number of universal crisis interventions that should be followed to decrease the risk of developing psychological trauma and other adverse reactions. First and foremost, physical health must be affirmed by carefully executing the crisis plan. After the danger has passed, it is important to ensure that individuals are given accurate reassurances about their safety. Indeed, adult reactions are important influences on children's perceptions of threat in crisis situations (DeVoe, Klein, Bannon, & Miranda-Julian, 2011) and social support is a critical factor influencing the psychological adaptation of children exposed to trauma (Caffo & Belaise, 2003; Ozer et al., 2003). Therefore, one of the oldest and arguably most effective crisis intervention strategies is to help children access their natural social supports through reunification with primary caregivers, providing opportunities for peer support, and reestablishing routines (Brock et al., 2009).

It is also critical to provide psychoeducation, or information about the event, children's typical responses, and effective coping strategies. Psychoeducational interventions involve relaying facts related to the crisis and do not involve sharing of intense experiences or feelings between individuals. This psychoeducation can be done though informational bulletins and handouts and meetings or trainings with caregivers (e.g., parents/guardians, school staff). The goal of such informative interventions is to provide accurate information about what occurred and did not occur, and to provide information about how to access available resources. In these trainings, teachers can also be provided with the guidance necessary to conduct a classroom meeting with students, in which the teacher informs the students about the facts of the crisis situation, typically through a script prepared by the crisis team, and allows students to ask questions (Reeves, Kanan, & Plog, 2010). Sharing this information, particularly when used as part of comprehensive interventions, is associated with better coping (Howard & Goelitz, 2004; Pynoos, Goenjian, & Steinberg, 1998) and reduced mental health symptoms (Berger, Pat-Horencyzk, & Gelkopf, 2007; Gelkopf & Berger, 2009) after a crisis. When provided with quick and accurate information about what has occurred as well as guidance about where to seek out additional support, students often perceive their school to be safe and the school staff as ready and in control.

As stated previously, crises have a differential effect on people depending on several variables; therefore, individuals will require different interventions (Watson, Brymer, & Bonanno, 2011). A critical universal prevention strategy is to evaluate risk of trauma through psychological triage to decide who may need more intensive interventions and, importantly, who may not need to be provided with additional interventions beyond the universal strategies. It is important to note that the initial identification of students or staff who may need more intensive interventions happens simultaneously with the provision of other universal crisis interventions (for example, during a classroom, meeting a teacher may identify a child or group of children who are ruminating about the event). Like any human experience or behavior, assessing student need following a crisis can be a complex process. Educators are discouraged from assuming that all students will have similar needs. Rather, careful consideration of variables known to increase psychological trauma will be an important component of an effective triage. We turn to those evidence-informed practices next.

Tier 2

Based on the psychological triage that identifies individuals who may need more intensive interventions based on their physical or emotional proximity to the crisis, previous risk and protective factors, and more immediate crisis reactions, the school-based mental health professional may select a more intensive individual or group crisis intervention (Brock et al., 2009). The factors that influence psychological trauma most are the individual's physical proximity to the incident and emotional proximity to victims. To that end, crisis team members responsible for evaluating student needs following a crisis will be able to respond most effectively by determining (a) who was there (physical proximity), (b) where were they relative to the incident (physical proximity), and (c) who are the family, friends, teammates, and so forth of the victim (emotional proximity). The answers to these questions will likely drive initial intervention efforts, but students and staff may require immediate and intense intervention even without being physically or emotionally proximal to the crisis. Individual vulnerability factors such as the recent loss of a loved one prior to the crisis or isolation from family or peers may increase the likelihood of psychological trauma after a school crisis. Culture may also be a contributing factor in the development of trauma (Brock et al., 2009). Although it is beyond the scope of this chapter to outline all of the different cultural ways people from a variety of backgrounds will react to crises, it is imperative that school staff and crisis team members be aware of the cultural backgrounds present in the school population and have access to cultural brokers to help determine what is typical of terms of how people react to events so they do not misinterpret or mislabel those reactions. Regardless, the goal of these more intense Tier 2 interventions is to provide guidance to help individuals who have experienced a crisis to take independent actions to mitigate traumatic stress (Sahin, Yilmaz, & Batigun, 2011), such as promoting social support and facilitating approach-oriented coping (Frazier, Tashiro, Bennan, Steger, & Long, 2004).

Although the Tier 2 student psychoeducational group intervention is similar to Tier 1 psychoeducation, it differs in that instead of providing information about the crisis event and allowing for questions, it also provides an opportunity for group leaders to identify common crisis reactions and teach strategies for managing stress (Brock et al., 2009). In contrast to the brief classroom meetings, which are often conducted with all students in a school, the student psychoeducational group would be delivered to a classroom or group of students who are at higher risk of trauma owing to their physical or emotional proximity to the event or their preexisting vulnerabilities.

The next level of intervention at Tier 2, which is similar to the psychoeducational group except it goes a step further to help students actively explore and process their individual crisis experiences and reactions, is called the classroom-based (or group-based) crisis intervention (Brock et al., 2009). It should be noted that elements of this intervention, particularly the sharing of experiences during the crisis event, are controversial. Therefore, it is essential this intervention not focus on reliving or recounting details of the experience, but rather allow students with similar exposure to the crisis to share their experiences and reactions so that these can be normalized, so that coping and stress management can be taught, and so that those in need of more intensive intervention can be identified (Brock et al., 2009). Several studies have demonstrated one-time psychological debriefing sessions with adult emergency workers fail to prevent posttraumatic stress disorder and may relate to increased symptomatology (e.g., Bisson, 2003; Deahl, 2000), suggesting that brief exposure sessions in the absence of other treatments may leave individuals emotionally aroused and more sensitive to the traumatic experience (Yule, 2001). In a randomized controlled trial of psychological debriefing with children and adolescents involved in traffic accidents, Stallard and colleagues (2006) found the youth exposed to this and the comparison condition both showed significant reductions on all measures of traumatic stress several months later. Taking into account this research, Brock and colleagues (2009) offered several suggestions and cautions when using this group-based crisis intervention. First, these groups should be conducted by a mental health professional (in collaboration with the classroom teacher and other support for a 1:8 adult:child ratio) with a group of no more than 25–30 students who were not physically injured or acutely traumatized but who do share similarities in degree of crisis exposure and experience, crisis impact, and developmental level. This composition is important so that students are not placed in an intervention with other students who were not as seriously traumatized, in light of the potential for secondary trauma (Motta, 2012). Additionally, effective classroom-based or group-based psychological interventions may need to be as long as 2 to 3 hours and include the possibility of follow-up sessions. Although this type of group intervention is not considered to be long-term therapy, it will likely need to be more intense than one brief session.

The most intense and directive Tier 2 crisis intervention is individual crisis intervention. Clearly, the group setting is not appropriate for highly traumatized students (e.g., those who are very depressed, guilt-ridden, physically injured), and individuals in crisis are best addressed with a basic problem-solving model to help reestablish immediate coping. This is also referred to as psychological first aid, and readers are encouraged to consult Brymer and colleagues' (2006) detailed psychological first aid field manual through the National Child Traumatic Stress Network Center website (www.nctsn.org/content/psychological-first-aid) for more details about this approach. The core actions in this individualized crisis intervention include making psychological contact (i.e., establishing rapport), ensuring physical and psychological safety and comfort, providing emotional support to contain distress and stabilize the individual, gathering information to identify crisis-generated problems, supporting adaptive coping and problem solving through practical assistance, connection with social support, and providing information on coping. In addition, the practitioner assesses trauma risk and provides linkages with appropriate assistance (Brock et al., 2009; Brymer et al. 2006). Throughout crisis response interventions, the facilitators of the interventions must continue to monitor student need (i.e., "secondary triage"). Some students originally identified as high-need may improve quickly or may not have been as negatively affected as initially assessed. In contrast, other students may not be identified as high need until well beyond the end of the crisis event.

Tier 3

Each of the crisis interventions described thus far is short-term and occurs in the immediate aftermath of a crisis situation. Clearly, these interventions will be only the first step in a longer-term psychotherapeutic treatment process for more severely traumatized individuals who may warrant individual and group treatments. In a recent meta-analysis, Rolfsnes and Idsoe (2011) found that of the 16 Cognitive-Behavioral Therapy interventions implemented in school settings, 11 of the studies yielded effect sizes in the medium to large range, showing reductions in PTSD and many comorbid symptoms. Cognitive-Behavioral Intervention for Trauma in Schools (CBITS; Jaycox, 2003) is a 10-session, manualized treatment designed for inner-city schools to use with multicultural populations who have experienced trauma. CBITS focuses on common reactions to crisis, relaxation, restructuring negative thoughts, coping with the traumatic event through exposure (e.g., drawing, talking, writing), social problem-solving skills, and relapse prevention (Jaycox, 2003). Studies of CBITS have revealed that students in the intervention have reduced PTSD scores relative to wait-list controls (Kataoka et al., 2003; Stein et al., 2003), results that are consistent even with cultural modifications (Morsette et al., 2009) and implementation of certain elements in a curriculum-style format by teachers and school counselors (Jaycox et al., 2009). Treatment for PTSD and other disorders that may stem from or be exacerbated by a crisis event is beyond the role of most school-based practitioners, so it is important for schools to be able to make referrals to the appropriate community-based professionals who can implement evidence-based treatments such as Trauma-Focused Cognitive-Behavioral Therapy (Cohen, Berlinger, & Mannarino, 2000; Leenarts, Diehle, Doreleijers, Jansma, & Lindauer, 2013) and Cognitive-Behavioral Therapy for Childhood Traumatic Grief (Cohen & Mannarino, 2004; Cohen, Mannarino, & Staron, 2006).

CASE STUDY

No single action for addressing school crises is likely to be sufficient. Options that narrowly address one portion of school crisis efforts (e.g., remodeling a school building to promote physical safety; focus planning efforts around the possibility of school intruders or school shooters)—if deemed appropriate through a school vulnerability assessment—are best viewed as one component of a larger, more far-reaching plan. In short, there is no school crisis prevention and intervention panacea. Rather, schools must embrace a comprehensive model of safety and crisis planning, inclusive of phases spanning from prevention to recovery, collaboration between multiple agencies, consideration of multiple hazards, and multiple tiers of service (Reeves, Kanan, & Plog, 2010). This evidence-informed approach has been recommended throughout this chapter and, ideally, is one that is best integrated into an existing school system of tiered academic, behavioral, and mental health service delivery.

To assist educators in the development of a comprehensive school crisis prevention and intervention system, the following case study summary is offered. The case study facilitates crystallization of vital chapter content and includes ideas for how the case could be handled within a wide-ranging model. For purposes of full disclosure, the case presented here is an amalgam of real-life cases from the field, though it does not represent any one particular case. The response and discussion of Charlie's case can help school crisis teams plan for a comprehensive crisis prevention and intervention system but it is not intended to be prescriptive. Indeed, through self-evaluation and reflection following Charlie's case, the crisis team determined several steps for improvement, which are noted at the end of this discussion. A brief summary of Charlie's case follows.

Charlie, a 14-year-old middle school student in a suburban community, was feeling increasingly isolated at school. He was evaluated for special education services in first grade, but did not qualify and no other services beyond the general education curriculum had been provided to him. More recently, Charlie had struggled to fit in socially, contributing to both bully perpetration and victimization experiences. Although he was "on the radar" of the school administration and some teachers, Charlie was generally viewed as a student who quietly went about his business. Last week he posted cryptic messages on an online social networking site, indicating anger toward his peers and self, as well as comments suggesting a growing fascination with previous violent events. Shortly after arriving to school today, three of Charlie's peers found him unconscious in a restroom stall. An open bottle of pills and a significant amount of blood were visible on the floor nearby. Charlie recovered from this incident, but the crisis team and broader school community are now moving quickly to determine how this happened and what needs to happen next.

Crisis Prevention and Preparedness (Tier 1)

Emergency responders were called immediately, and Charlie was rushed to the hospital with self-inflicted cut wounds to his arms and what was later discovered to be a prescription drug overdose. While the school was not able to prevent this particular incident, being prepared with a comprehensive plan began to pay off. Six months prior to Charlie's case, the school crisis team had conducted a tabletop exercise with local police, the school's resource officer, and other emergency responders. Crisis team members from the school and from multiple community agencies were able to practice responding collaboratively to a mock crisis while becoming familiar with each other, crisis response timing, and necessary resources. At the onset of Charlie's case, community responders and school professionals were able to capitalize on this preparedness by using the terminology of the required Incident Command Structure (ICS), leading to a quicker and more efficient response. Additionally, subsequent analysis of Charlie's case revealed evidence that the crisis team response had been keenly observed by other students and staff in Charlie's school. The crisis team's quick and calm response reflected organized adult leadership, reinforcing student and staff perceptions of physical and psychological safety. Such preparedness can drive a strong message of well-being immediately after a crisis incident and can be a foundation for future prevention.

Two members of the middle-school crisis team, the building principal (in the role of Incident Commander as part of the ICS) and the school psychologist (serving as the Mental Health Division supervisor under the Operations—Student Care section of the ICS), were on the scene quickly in Charlie's case and were able to begin the evaluation and intervention process. Although the causes of Charlie's injuries were not immediately and completely clear, they were fairly confident that this was a suicide attempt and that there was no additional threat to others. As a first step to recovery, the school psychologist reaffirmed the physical safety of the three young boys who discovered Charlie in the restroom. Considering that Charlie had two younger siblings attending the local elementary school, and taking into account the belief that students in that school may require crisis intervention, the principal quickly estimated that a moderate amount of overall psychological trauma was likely and that a district-level response would in all probability be needed (i.e., from options including minimal response, building level, district level, or regional response). Helping professionals in other school buildings in the district were notified immediately as additional crisis team members began arriving at the middle school to begin the triage process.

Furthermore, in preparation for various crises, the crisis team had previously developed several electronic psychoeducational handout templates for parents, caregivers, and school staff. Thanks to this prior preparation, the school principal was quickly able to modify a prepared template to be disseminated to parents and staff. The handout briefly outlined what was known about Charlie's case at that point and included a summary of common developmentally appropriate reactions to crises as well as where to find additional coping resources. A script of known facts was provided to teachers to read to their classes.

Within about 3 hours of the incident, a one-page incident action plan was created, outlining how the district planned to respond to Charlie's case. As appropriate, several of the students who were physically proximal, emotionally proximal, and who were deemed vulnerable in other ways were reunited with home-based caregivers or connected to established school-based supports. Reestablishing social support was viewed as critical to keeping psychological trauma minimized. The evaluation of and planning for more intense Tier 2 or Tier 3 interventions was now just beginning.

Evaluating Psychological Trauma and Providing School-Based Interventions (Tier 2)

The well-planned triage process helped ensure evaluation of potential psychological trauma among students and staff in the school. One week after Charlie's incident, a school counselor, as part of her role in student care in the Operations Section of the ICS, was able to assist the three boys who found Charlie by means of a classroom-based (group) crisis intervention (based on the physical proximity risk factor). The boys were provided an opportunity to share their stories about and reactions to the event (e.g., difficulty sleeping and concentrating), and the counselor was able to normalize these common reactions to crises as well as to teach coping strategies. During this intervention, the school-based mental health professional was reminded that one of the three boys who found Charlie had recently experienced the sudden death of a sibling, making him particularly susceptible to considerable psychological trauma (addressing the need to evaluate personal vulnerability factors and conduct secondary triage). That student began receiving an individual crisis intervention, in which the school counselor met with him alone to further assist his adaptive coping, distress containment, and his connection to resources. A second school counselor intervened with Charlie's younger siblings (addressing emotional proximity) at their elementary school and provided a similar group crisis intervention. In addition, the team quickly identified several other students in the building who were believed to be vulnerable to psychological trauma (e.g., students who tended to be socially isolated, who experienced significant family dysfunction, or who had a history of other trauma). With awareness of the contagion effect after a suicide or suicide attempt (Reeves et al., 2011) the crisis team formed two different homogenous classroom-based intervention groups from those individuals evaluated as susceptible to psychological trauma. The recipients of those services were fluid for awhile, as the secondary triage process continued for several days and even weeks.

Intervention for the Several Traumatized (Tier 3)

As Charlie was reintegrated into school, he received weekly and sometimes daily individualized support from a school-based counselor. His school counselor helped ensure Charlie's safety in school, while assisting him with general school-based coping and problem solving. Additionally, Charlie began services through a community-based therapist the crisis team had previously identified as being skilled with crisis recovery and psychological trauma (Tier 3 crisis intervention). Finally, through ongoing triage efforts, the boy who found Charlie, and who also had experienced a recent sibling death, was referred for Tier 3 community-based psychotherapy. While his school-based support was helpful and continued for a short period of time, the crisis team determined he could benefit from more intense psychological support.

Team Evaluation

As with any crisis, the crisis team at Charlie's school took time to evaluate its crisis prevention and intervention efforts following Charlie's case. In the ensuing months, the school safety team was enhanced through increased membership and further comprehensive crisis training. With Charlie's case prompting additional urgency, the safety team began meeting more frequently and quickly began reflecting on its current practices. Existing in a relatively small district with limited resources, the crisis team determined that its crisis prevention and intervention approaches could be more effective and efficient if integrated into its emerging tiered models for academic and behavioral service delivery. A single leadership team began monitoring and addressing all aspects of academic, behavioral, and mental health development in the school, with crisis prevention and intervention being considered a common thread in each. The team began reflecting on the literature indicating connections between mental health, academic achievement, and crisis prevention (e.g., Collaborative for Academic, Social, and Emotional Learning, 2008; Durlak et al., 2011), and they completed a school vulnerability assessment within 1 month of Charlie's case (see Reeves et al., 2011, Handout #6). From those reflections, the team shaped several action steps for improved crisis prevention and intervention services. The following processes gained increased prominence in the school's safety plan:

a) Annual vulnerability assessment, from which the physical and psychological safety aspects of a school building, grounds, and overall environment can be evaluated for susceptibility (Reeves et al., 2011).

b) Development of additional psychological safety strategies, including augmentation of school-wide systematic services (e.g., Positive Behavior Supports [PBS]) as well as new simple and cost-effective strategies (e.g., working to ensure that each student in the school has a positive relationship with at least one adult staff member). Given improved team awareness of how crises can and do occur, Charlie and other students with mental health vulnerabilities were provided enhanced adult connections, both formally and informally.

c) Increased monitoring of school-wide climate data to guide resource allocation and instructional/intervention design. Students and staff in Charlie's school began completing brief, electronically disseminated school climate surveys each semester. The team was able to begin addressing specific student and school ecology challenges (e.g., common bullying locations), potentially contributing to the prevention of future school crises.

d) Ongoing analysis of building physical safety, to include increased supervision of susceptible hallways and bathrooms, as well as structural enhancements of school bathrooms (e.g., removal of outer doors, removal of bathroom stall hooks), all of which could contribute to cases like Charlie's.

e) Development of an anonymous student reporting system, where students are able to inform school leaders of suspected peer behavioral or mental health concerns. In Charlie's case, it was discovered that several warning signs were apparent to his peers, including verbalized and online threats to self and others. This outcome could also be paired with the development of procedures and a training module targeting followup assessment for risk of harm to self or others (Reeves et al., 2010).

f) Improved care for caregivers. In the immediate aftermath of Charlie's case, one school counselor and two other school staff members had begun struggling psychologically after Charlie's case. Heavy workloads and personal variables probably contributed to the stress. The school safety team added safety plan content ensuring future crisis response caregivers would be monitored for vulnerabilities, stress, and burnout, none of which were part of team culture before Charlie's case (Brock et al., 2009).

SUMMARY

Crises, ranging from a child with a sprained ankle on the playground to natural disasters that destroy property and lives, can put stress on any system, especially schools. As such, crisis prevention, mitigation, preparation, and intervention have become necessary and critical tasks at all levels of the educational hierarchy. Schools must do everything they can to prevent and minimize a potential crisis from occurring while preparing for those situations that cannot be avoided. When a crisis does happen, school-based mental health professionals need to reaffirm the physical health and safety of all students and staff and begin the process of triage to route people to the appropriate level of intervention they may require. Knowing that recovery is the norm, reestablishing social supports (e.g., reunifying people with their loved ones) and providing basic psychoeducation may be all the intervention most students and staff will need. Others, owing to their physical and emotional proximity to the crises or to affected individuals as well as personal vulnerabilities, may require more in-depth, school-based psychological intervention or individual psychotherapy beyond the educational setting to help them recover from a crisis. Although schools may need to embrace the need for a "new normal" after some crises, ongoing triage and followup are necessary to ensure that people have indeed bounced back from the crisis, optimizing their potential to meet successfully the academic, behavioral, and social/emotional demands of the schooling process.

Throughout this chapter, the various components and levels of interventions associated with the PREP_aRE curriculum have been emphasized. The PREP<u>a</u>RE model is unique in that it was developed by school-based mental health professionals to be applied specifically to school settings. As data-based decision makers, school-based mental health professionals should always use the data to which they have access to drive their actions in addressing the needs of their constituents, whether it is academic programming or crisis prevention and intervention efforts. The PREP<u>a</u>RE model is an evidence-informed, comprehensive approach to making schools as safe as can be and in providing the range of services needed to accomplish this goal. Although no one wishes to incur any type of crisis in schools, knowing what to do and how to do it will not only help schools return to the business of education more quickly, it conveys the message to all that the dedicated professionals associated with a building or district have things "under control," thereby augmenting the resilience and the psychological safety of the entire school community.

RESOURCES

Books

Brock, S. E., & Jimerson, S. R. (Eds.). (2012). *Best practices in school crisis prevention and intervention* (2nd ed.). Bethesda, MD: National Association of School Psychologists. This edited volume provides a comprehensive review of best practices in the area of school crisis prevention and intervention. Content includes general crisis intervention issues as well as response and intervention for specific crisis events.

Brock, S. E., Nickerson, A. B., Reeves, M. A., Jimerson, S. R., Feinberg, T., & Lieberman, R. (2009). *School crisis prevention and intervention: The PREP<u>a</u>RE model.* Bethesda, MD: National Association of School Psychologists. This book complements the PREP<u>a</u>RE School Crisis Prevention and Intervention Training Curriculum and provides a review of the empirical supports of the PREP<u>a</u>RE model discussed in this chapter.

Reeves, M. A, Kanan, L. M., & Plog, A. E. (2010). *Comprehensive planning for safe learning environments: A school professional's guide to integrating physical and psychological safety—prevention through recovery.* New York, NY: Routledge. This book provides educational professionals with guidance on how to establish a comprehensive safe learning environment within a multi-tiered approach. It addresses not only physical safety, but psychological safety, as well.

Websites

The PREP<u>a</u>RE: School Crisis Prevention and Intervention Training Curriculum homepage (www.nasponline.org/prepare/index .aspx) at the National Association of School Psychologists website (www.nasponline.org) presents information on the curriculum itself, in addition to information on how to become trained in the curriculum, how to bring the curriculum to a school building or district, and how to become a trainer, in addition to other crisis prevention and intervention resources.

The National Child Traumatic Stress Network (www.nctsn.org).

Readiness and Emergency Management for Schools Technical Assistance Center (rems.ed.gov).

REFERENCES

Berger, R., Pat-Horencyzk, R., & Gelkopf, M. (2007). School-based intervention for prevention and treatment of elementary-students' terror-related distress in Israel: A quasi-randomized controlled trial. *Journal of Traumatic Stress, 20*, 541–551. doi:10.1002/jts.20225

Bisson, J. I. (2003). Single-session early psychological interventions following traumatic events. *Clinical Psychology Review, 23*, 481–499. doi:10.1016/S0272-7358(03)00034-5

Brock, S. E., Nickerson, A. B., Reeves, M. A., & Jimerson, S. R. (2008). Best practices for school psychologists as members of crisis teams: The PREPaRE Model. In A. Thomas & J. Grimes (Eds.), *Best practices in school psychology V* (vol. 4, 5th ed., pp. 1487–1504). Bethesda, MD: National Association of School Psychologists.

Brock, S. E., Nickerson, A. B., Reeves, M. A., Jimerson, S. R., Lieberman, R. A., & Feinberg, T. A. (2009). *School crisis prevention and intervention: The PREPaRE model.* Bethesda, MD: National Association of School Psychologists.

Brymer, M. J., Jacobs, A., Layne, C., Pynoos, R. S., Ruzek, J., Steinberg, A., . . . Watson, P. (2006). *Psychological first-aid: Field operations guide* (2nd ed.). Los Angeles, CA: Author. Retrieved from http://www.ptsd.va.gov/professional/manuals/psych-first-aid.asp

Buka, S. L., Stichick, T. L., Birdthistle, I., & Earls, F. J. (2001). Youth exposure to violence: Prevalence, risks, and consequences. *American Journal of Orthopsychiatry, 71*, 298–310. doi:010.1037/F0002-9432.71.3.298

Caffo, E., & Belaise, C. (2003). Psychological aspects of traumatic injury in children and adolescents. *Child and Adolescent Psychiatric Clinics of North America, 12*, 493–535. doi:10.1016/S1056-4993(03)00004-X

Charuvastra, A., & Cloitre, M. (2008). Social bonds and posttraumatic stress disorder. *Annual Review of Psychology, 59*, 301–328. doi:10.1146/annurev.psych.58.110405.085650

Cohen, J. A., Berlinger, L., & Mannarino, A. P. (2000). Treating traumatized children: A research review and synthesis. *Trauma, Violence, and Abuse, 1*, 29–46. doi:10.1177/1524838000001001003

Cohen, J. A., & Mannarino, A. P. (2004). Treatment of childhood traumatic grief. *Journal of Clinical Child and Adolescent Psychology, 33*, 819–831. doi:10.1207/s15374424jccp3304_17

Cohen, J. A., Mannarino, A. P., & Staron, V. R. (2006). A pilot study of modified Cognitive–Behavioral Therapy for Childhood Traumatic Grief (CBT-CTG). *Journal of the American Academy of Child and Adolescent Psychiatry, 45*, 1465–1473. doi:10.1097/01.chi.0000237705.43260.2c

Deahl, M. (2000). Psychological debriefing: Controversy and challenge. *Australian and New Zealand Journal of Psychiatry, 34*, 929–939. doi:10.1080/F000486700267

DeVoe, E. R., Klein, T. P., Bannon, W., Jr., & Miranda-Julian, C. (2011). Young children in the aftermath of the World Trade Center attacks. *Psychological Trauma: Theory, Research, Practice, and Policy, 3*, 1–7. doi:10.1037/a0020567

Durlak, J. A., Weissberg, R. P., Dymnicki, A. B., Taylor, R. D. and Schellinger, K. B. (2011). The impact of enhancing students' social and emotional learning: A meta-analysis of school-based universal interventions. *Child Development, 82*, 405–432. doi:10.1111/j.1467-8624.2010.01564.x

Eksi, A., Braun, K. L., Ertem-Vehid, H., Peykerli, G., Saydam, R., Toparlak, D., & Alyanak, B. (2007). Risk factors for the development of PTSD and depression among child and adolescent victims following a 7.4 magnitude earthquake. *International Journal of Psychiatry in Clinical Practice, 11*, 190–199. doi:10.1080/13651500601017548

Frazier, P., Tashiro, T., Bennan, M., Steger, M., & Long, J. (2004). Correlates of levels and patterns of positive life change following sexual assault. *Journal of Consulting and Clinical Psychology, 72*, 19–30. doi:10.1037/0022-006X.72.1.19

Gelkopf, M., & Berger, R. (2009). A school-based, teacher-mediated prevention program (ERASE-Stress) for reducing terror-related traumatic reactions in Israeli youth: A quasi-randomized controlled trial. *Journal of Child Psychology and Psychiatry, 50*, 962–971. doi:10.1111/j.1469-7610.2008.02021.x

Green, B. L., Korol, M., Grace, M. C., Vary, M. G., Leonard, A. C., Gleser, G. C., & Smitson-Cohen, S. (1991). Children and disaster: Age, gender, and parental effects on PTSD symptoms. *Journal of the American Academy of Child and Adolescent Psychiatry, 30*, 945–951. doi:10.1097/00004583-199111000-00012

Howard, J. M., & Goelitz, A. (2004). Psychoeducation as a response to community disaster. *Brief Treatment and Crisis Intervention, 4*, 1–10. doi:10.1093/brief-treatment/mhh001

Jaycox, L. (2003). *Cognitive–behavioral intervention for trauma in schools.* Longmont, CO: Sopris West.

Jaycox, L. H., Langley, A. K., Stein, B. D., Wong, M., Sharma, P., Scott, M., & Schonlau, M. (2009). Support for Students Exposed to Trauma: A pilot study. *School Mental Health, 1*, 49–60. doi:10.1007/s12310-009-9007-8

Kataoka, S. H., Stein, B. D., Jaycox, L. H., Wong, M., Escudero, P., Tu, W., Zaragoza, C., & Fink, A. (2003). A school-based mental health program for traumatized Latino immigrant children. *Journal of the American Academy of Child and Adolescent Psychiatry, 42*, 311–318. doi:10.1097/00004583-200303000-00011

Kolaitis, G., Kotsopoulos, J., Tsiantis, J., Haritaki, S., Rigizou, R., Zacharaki, L., . . . Katerelos, P. (2003). Post-traumatic stress reactions among children following the Athens earthquake of September 1999. *European Child and Adolescent Psychiatry, 12*, 273–280. doi:10.1007/s00787-003-0339-x

Krause, E. D., Kaltman, S., Goodman, L. A., & Dutton, M. A. (2008). Avoidant coping and PTSD symptoms related to domestic violence exposure: A longitudinal study. *Journal of Traumatic Stress, 21*, 83–90. doi:10.1002/jts.20288

Leenarts, L. E., Diehle, J., Doreleijers, T. A., Jansma, E. P., & Lindauer, R. J. (2013). Evidenced-based treatments for children with trauma-related psychopathology as a result of childhood maltreatment: A systematic review. *European Journal of Child and Adolescent Psychiatry, 22,* 269–283. doi:10.1007/s00787-012-0367-5

Lonigan, C. J., Phillips, B. M., & Richey, J. A. (2003). Posttraumatic stress disorder in children: Diagnosis, assessment, and associated features. *Child and Adolescent Psychiatric Clinics of North America, 12,* 171–194. doi:10.1016/S1056-4993(02)00105-0

McNally, R. J., Bryant, R. A., & Ehlers, A. (2003). Does early psychological intervention promote recovery from post-traumatic stress? *Psychological Sciences in the Public Interest, 4,* 45–80. doi:10.1111/1529-1006.01421

Melhem, N. M., Day, N., Shea, M., Day, R., Reynolds, C. F., III, & Brent, D. (2004). Predictors of complicated grief among adolescents exposed to a peer's suicide. *Journal of Loss and Trauma, 9,* 21–34. doi:10.1080/15325020490255

Merrell, K. W., Ervin, R. A., & Gimpel Peacock, G. (2012). *School psychology for the 21st century: Foundations and practices* (2nd ed.). New York, NY: Guilford.

Morsette, A., Swaney, G., Stolle, D., Schuldberg, D., van den Pol, R., & Young, M. (2009). Cognitive Behavioral Intervention for Trauma in Schools (CBITS): School-based treatment on a rural American Indian reservation. *Journal of Behavior Therapy and Experimental Psychiatry, 40,* 169–178. doi:10.1016/j.jbtep.2008.07.006

Motta, R. W. (2012). Secondary trauma in children and school personnel. *Journal of Applied School Psychology, 28,* 256–269. doi:10.1080/15377903.2012.695767

Nader, K., Pynoos, R., Fairbanks, L., & Frederick, C. (1990). Children's post-traumatic stress disorder reactions one year after a sniper attack at their school. *American Journal of Psychiatry, 147,* 1526–1530. http://ajp.psychiatryonline.org/journal.aspx?journalid=13

National Commission on Children and Disasters. (2010, October). *2010 Report to the President and Congress* (AHRQ Publication No. 10-M037). Rockville, MD: Agency for Healthcare Research and Quality.

Nickerson, A. B., Brock, S. E., & Reeves, M. A. (2006). School crisis teams within an incident command system. *The California School Psychologist, 11,* 51–60.

Nooner, K. B., Linares, O., Batinjane, J., Kramer, R. A., Silva, R., & Cloitre, M. (2012). Factors related to posttraumatic stress disorder in adolescence. *Trauma Violence Abuse, 13,* 153–166. doi:10.1177/1524838012447698

Olff, M., Langeland, W., & Gersons, B. P. R. (2005). The psychobiology of PTSD: Coping with trauma. *Psychoneuroendocrinology, 30,* 974–982. doi:10.1016/j.psyneuen.2005.04.009

Ozer, E. J., Best, S. R., Lipsey, T. L., & Weiss, D. S. (2003). Predictors of post-traumatic stress disorder and symptoms in adults: A meta-analysis. *Psychological Bulletin, 129,* 52–73. doi:10.1037//0033-2909.129.1.52

Pfefferbaum, B., Noffsinger, M. A., & Wind, L. H. (2012). Issues in the assessment of children's coping in the context of mass trauma. *Prehospital and Disaster Medicine, 27,* 272–279. doi:10.1017/S1049023X12000702

Pynoos, R. S., Goenjian, A. K., & Steinberg, A. M. (1998). A public mental health approach to the postdisaster treatment of children and adolescents. *Child and Adolescent Psychiatric Clinics of North America, 7*, 195–210. doi:10.1046/j.1440-1819.1998.0520s5S129.x

Reeves, M. A, Kanan, L. M., & Plog, A. E. (2010). *Comprehensive planning for safe learning environments: A school professional's guide to integrating physical and psychological safety—prevention through recovery.* New York, NY: Routledge.

Reeves, M. A., Nickerson, A. B., Conolly-Wilson, C. N., Susan, M. K., Lazzaro, B., Jimerson, S. R., & Pesce, R. C. (2011). *Crisis prevention and preparedness: Comprehensive school safety planning (PRE-PaRE Workshop 1).* Bethesda, MD: National Association of School Psychologists.

Rolfsnes, E. S., & Idsoe, T. (2011). School-based intervention programs for PTSD symptoms: A review and meta-analysis. *Journal of Traumatic Stress, 24*, 155–165. doi:10.1002/jts.20622

Sahin, N. H., Yilmaz, B., & Batigun, A. (2011). Psychoeducation for children and adults after the Marmara earthquake: An evaluation study. *Traumatology, 17*, 41–49. doi:10.1177/1534765610395624

Shinn, M. R., & Walker, H. M. (Eds.). (2010). *Interventions for achievement and behavior problems in a three-tier model including RtI.* Bethesda, MD: National Association of School Psychologists.

Sprague, J. R., & Horner, R. H. (2012). School-wide positive behavioral interventions and supports. In S. R. Jimerson, A. B., Nickerson, M. J. Mayer, & M. J. Furlong (Eds.), *Handbook of school violence and school safety: International research and practices* (2nd ed., pp. 447–462). Mahwah, NJ: Erlbaum.

Stallard, P., Velleman, R., Salter, E., Howse, I., Yule, W., & Taylor, G. (2006). A randomized controlled trial to determine the effectiveness of an early psychological intervention with children involved in road traffic accidents. *Journal of Child Psychology and Psychiatry, 47*, 127–134. doi:10.1111/j.1469-7610.2005.01459.x

Stein, B. D., Jaycox, L. H., Kataoka, S. H., Wong, M., Tu, W., Elliot, M. N., & Fink, A. (2003). A mental health intervention for school children exposed to violence: A randomized controlled trial. *The Journal of the American Medical Association, 290*, 603–611. doi:10.1001/jama.290.5.603

U.S. Department of Education, Office of Elementary and Secondary Education, Office of Safe and Healthy Students. (2013). Guide for developing high-quality school emergency operations plans. Washington, DC: Author. Retrieved from http://rems.ed.gov/docs/REMS_K-12_Guide_508.pdf

U.S. Department of Homeland Security. (2008, December). *National incident management system.* Washington, DC: Author. www.fema.gov/sites/default/files/orig/fema_pdfs/pdf/emergency/nims/NIMS_core.pdf

Watson, P. J., Brymer, M. J., & Bonanno, G. A. (2011). Post-disaster psychological intervention since 9/11. *American Psychologist, 66*, 482–494. doi:10.1037/a0024806

Yule, W. (2001). Posttraumatic stress disorder in the general population and in children. *Journal of Clinical Psychiatry, 62*, 23–28. www.crossref.org/guestquery

CHAPTER 18

Mental Health Intervention Case Studies

G. SUSAN MOSLEY-HOWARD
MONA BURTS-BEATTY

LEARNING OUTCOMES

On completion of this chapter, the reader should be able to:

- Recognize the importance of multidisciplinary partici- pation in mental health intervention within Response to Intervention (RTI)
- Understand the role of schools in the mental health inter- vention process
- Integrate evidence-based strategies into tiered interven- tion approaches
- Recognize effective tiered intervention strategies based upon the presented cases

MENTAL HEALTH INTERVENTION: WHAT IS A SCHOOL TO DO?

Throughout this book readers have been provided with a glimpse of numerous key issues facing schools today as they attempt to address the mental health needs of K–12 students. School staff understand the importance of (a) assessing and intervening with students who are at risk for school failure or underachievement; (b) remaining up to date about medication that students may be taking; (c) adhering to school-based ethical, legal, and policy man- dates; (d) building a safe climate while being ready for emergency response; and (e) attending to the academic, social, and mental health issues children bring to school each day. This serves as one underlying reason for this book. Schools that wish to aid students in meeting their academic and interpersonal needs must rely on interdisciplinary teams to leverage Response to Intervention (RTI), evidence-based practice (EBP), and a system of care that contains strategies designed to target various behavioral issues (Splett & Maras, 2011).

Even though most of today's youth are thriving, research and public discourse highlight a myriad of behavioral problems presented by today's youth. Even "well adjusted" youth face typical developmental challenges as a part of growing up. For those youth who present with chronic behavioral difficulty, most agree that the behaviors presented can hinder these students in reaching their full potential whether in the academic or interpersonal arena (Beyer et al., 2012; Weist et al., 2007). One dilemma for families, educators, and mental health professionals attempting to support these youth is how to distinguish normative developmental "acting out" from maladaptive features. These distinctions need to be made within a developmental context. For example, what may be typical for a 3- to 4-year-old is not typical for a 12- to 13-year-old, and vice versa. Screening and assessment are important components in distinguishing these differences. Chapter 1 (RTI mental health intervention) and Chapter 5 (culturally sensitive mental health services) also highlight common dysfunctional behaviors observed among youth in the United States today. We encourage all educators to be mindful of the developmentally appropriate and nonappropriate behavioral milestones or conditions that exist among children in schools and adjust expectations, and instructional and behavioral approaches accordingly. (The reader is referred to the Centers for Disease Control and Prevention's [CDC] annual Youth Risk Behavior Survey and the following references for more information about youth development trends: American Psychological Association, 2002; Harrison et al., 2012; Office of Child Development Special Report, 2005; Spear, 2000.) In this chapter we present case studies that highlight the process, tools, and evidence-based intervention strategies either used in schools to either prevent behaviors that hinder student progress or used with students already exhibiting behavioral or socioemotional conditions deemed as negatively impacting academic progress.

EVIDENCE-BASED PRACTICE AND INTERDISCIPLINARY TEAMS

The importance of using EBP has been well established, and mental health practitioners and educators alike attempt to ensure that students receive the highest level of care (Kazak et al., 2010; Kratochwill et al., 2012; Meyer, Finn, Eyde, Kay, Moreland et al., 2001). Combining EBP with an interdisciplinary approach is critically important in schools.

The team approach has been advanced within health care and mental health for some time and is not new to schools. Academic collaboration across subject matter is a common aspiration in schools (Brownell, Adams, Sindelar, & Waldron, 2006). However, emphasizing this practice and implementing it are not necessarily easy. Kazak et al. (2010) highlight the power and importance of leveraging every disciplinary skill set for comprehensive, efficient, and effective behavioral treatment outcomes. Schools employ a variety of highly trained nurses, counselors, speech pathologists, psychologists, police officers, teachers, and administrators. Using all of their skill sets to enhance student outcomes is key to academic achievement and social adjustment. Facilitating student outcomes requires the aforementioned professions on the school team to maintain mutual respect, be knowledgeable about each team member's role, have a well-defined team approach, and work within a school system designed for such an approach. Team approaches, however, don't just happen; they must be intentionally crafted. Resources used to develop this process emphasize issues such as role definition; sharing of skill sets and knowledge; managing and ameliorating turf battles; using processes for student problem identification, referral, and case coordination; and effectively leveraging prevention programs and intervention approaches (Bronstein, Anderson, Terwilliger, & Sager, 2012; Weist, Ambrose, & Lewis, 2006). The involvement of all professional disciplines (e.g., nursing, speech pathologists, counselors, social workers, pediatrician, school psychologists, teachers) along with parents and community-based agencies is critical.

The EBP and team approaches can then be implemented within the RTI framework. This framework can be thought of in terms of instructional implementation and/or direct mental health intervention. In addition, the knowledge base of school teams can be enhanced with exposure to mental health awareness raising (e.g., Youth Mental Health First Aid, National Council for Behavioral Health, 2014; see Resources section). Based upon broad exposure or screening assessment, children who do not gain the intended treatment outcomes or respond in the desired fashion are provided additional support. For those children (again determined through assessment processes) who do not benefit from the more intensive support, they are afforded a more targeted individual intervention (Bradley, Danielson, Doolittle, 2005; Kratochwill, Clements, Kalymon, 2007). So the question emerging for schools is how can we integrate and leverage the best practices emerging in the field of school-based mental health using the breath of school professionals to optimize results for all children? The following case studies aim to demonstrate some possibilities.

SCHOOL-BASED CASE STUDIES

The following cases are framed using case conceptualization features in order to assist the reader with evaluating and making sense of the case. Case conceptualization is a tool for observing, understanding, and conceptually integrating student behaviors, thoughts, feelings, and physiology from a behavioral intervention perspective. The cases presented here loosely rely on the process advanced by Neukrug and Schwitzer (2006), which are to (1) *evaluate* a student's concerns by observing, assessing, and measuring his or her behaviors; (2) *organize* these observations, assessments, and measures into *patterns and themes* regarding the student's concerns; and (3) select a *theoretical orientation* to interpret, explain, or make intervention judgments.

In these cases, evidence-based best practices are used and where appropriate, the decisions and collective work of the school staff, mental health professionals, and those aligned with the schools is featured. Ideally, the school-based team should examine the case and have a picture of what has led to the student's concerns and what features are maintaining or perpetuating the problem (sustaining factors). Understanding these factors will then lead to intervention planning, which uses the case conceptualization to decide how to best address, reduce, manage, or resolve the student's issues. However, despite this process, we understand that in a school setting the cases do not always unfold in this fashion, nor can they be handled strictly by best practice—yet every effort must be made to adhere to this format.

The cases within this chapter fall within the second and third tiers of RTI intervention. Briefly, Tier 1 interventions are designed for all students (i.e., schoolwide) to enhance a targeted skill or issue; Tier 2 is usually designed for an identified small group who, through assessment, was deemed to need more support beyond the Tier 1 experience. And for those who show intensive behavioral needs, an individualized intervention plan is followed (Tier 3). Each case study is based upon a real situation reported from a school, but the identity of the child and school setting, as well as select details about the case, have been masked or changed to protect identities. The case format is generally organized as follows: (1) reason for referral, (2) background/case history, (3) case conceptualization, (4) overview of behavioral/mental health intervention, and (5) goals and course of intervention. Three cases are covered here. Case 1 focuses on a middle-school boy exhibiting social anxiety disorder (SM; Tier 3 intervention), Case 2 focuses on a boy exhibiting conduct issues (Tier 3 intervention), and Case 3 focuses on a middle-school girl struggling with her parent's divorce (Tier 2 intervention).

CASE 1: KYM: SOCIAL ANXIETY (SELECTIVE MUTISM)

Reason for Referral

The counselor and educators are concerned that Kym's academic performance and social development are being increasingly hindered by his social anxiety. His upcoming transition to high school is a concern as well in light of the level of expected social engagement (e.g., class participation, extracurricular social interactions, ability to actively work toward his academic goals and aspirations).

Case Background

Background/history	• Lives in the northeast U.S.
	• Male
	• Chinese nationality—immigrated to United States at age 7
	• 8th-grade student (age 13)
	• Family history:
	  o Blue-collar background with income $25,000–$30,000
	  o Two-parent home, one younger sibling, one older cousin in home (bilingual)
	  o Parents do not speak English

Presenting behaviors	• Quiet child (nonculturally related) • Diagnosed (private practitioner) with social anxiety disorder—selective mutism[1] • Refusal to speak began 5 years ago with move to United States
Evidence-based practices used	Evidence-based supports included, but were not limited to, the New York University Child Study Center Clinic and Child Mind Institute (www.aboutourkids.org; www.childmind.org) intervention program, which includes a multiphased EBP process, much of which is presented below in case details—e.g., stress reduction breathing, voice recording
Academically relevant information	*Cognitive skills:* Based upon school records, average range *Academic skills:* Achieving at academic rates consistent with same-aged typically developing peers *Communication:* Proficient command of English, but chooses not to communicate
School-based services and processes used	*RTI* • Tier 1: Psychoeducational whole-class social skills session (middle school) • Tier 2: Social skills group (middle school for more intensive support) • Tier 3: Speech–language intervention (initiated during elementary school to date) • Tier 3: Counseling (during middle school—focus of this case study—embedded in the following)
IDEA-based identification (if applicable) for services	*N/A*
Length of time case was in process	The entire scope of the intervention has occurred over 3 academic years This current academic year has focused on mental health counseling intervention

Goals, Case Conceptualization, and Overview of Mental Health Intervention

The overarching goal is to have Kym be able to speak with his teachers when needed. This intervention involves the counselor, teachers, school psychologists, speech interventionist, and parents.

Academic performance is a high priority for Kym, and any decrease in grades adds to his anxiety and affects self-efficacy. Kym reported seeing himself as someone who just doesn't speak and doesn't have the social skills to engage or be "liked." Kym reported lots of social fear (fear of rejection, speaking), yet maintained a fairly flat affect during early portions of the intervention. However, as the initial 4 weeks of intervention progressed, he developed a desire for social interaction and showed much more emotion, often laughing and smiling. Kym reported being especially happy toward the end of the intervention process after speaking with a peer (this peer may be chosen to serve as a social partner in high school next school year).

While Kym currently reports a positive outlook, he appears to be having difficulty transferring the more positive thoughts discussed in sessions to the outside world when he thinks of speaking to others outside of intervention time. The targeted approach is to use a combination of Cognitive-Behavioral Therapy (CBT) techniques to address his thoughts, feelings, and fears, relaxation techniques to help reduce his anxiety, behavioral techniques to help Kym begin speaking again, and lots of positive praise to help him feel good about himself.

Brief Summary Notes of Intervention Session Content

Initial Sessions (sessions 1–5, first month)

- Use of a cultural informant process added to this intervention (refer to Chapter 5 for more information about this role), and use of EBP strategies from the New York University Child Study Center Clinic and Child Mind Institute were important (see link in this chapter's Resources section). Rapport building via playing games, creating art work, and identifying his likes and dislikes were emphasized at this stage. Introduction to the tape recorder as a way to communicate his thoughts about school and social interaction came next. He described some of his feelings (*nervous, anxious*) and thoughts (*he would sound funny to peers*). Introduction of anxiety reduction strategies (breathing, relaxation) was phased in next.

Early Working Sessions (sessions 6–10)

- Paired stress reduction exercises with a tape recorder as a vehicle to respond to verbal conversation prompts, used scaling to communicate his anxiety levels during practices, used shaping, scaffolding, approximal steps to arrive at speaking (speaking in recorder while alone in room, speaking while not facing the mental health interventionist [MHI], then speaking and facing the MHI, etc.), began to use charting of behaviors and thoughts. Highlighted differences between accents in U.S.–global accents from around the world in schools. Worked with cultural informant to identify Kym's values and topics Kym may wish to discuss.

Middle Working Sessions (sessions 11–14)

- Focus shifted to speaking with others, such as trusted teachers then counselor. Levels of anxiety were charted with each verbal interaction. He also used breathing and other reduction techniques, used email and phone (with scripted conversation then impromptu) to start connection with teachers, and then transitioned to speaking live, identifying his feelings about the interactions both pre and post the intervention.

Later Working Sessions (sessions 14–18)

- Next, he contrasted how his voice sounds to him on the recorder versus how he thought it would sound, moving toward speaking to people while in the room with him (not looking at each other) . . . reviewed breathing and visualization again, focused on building more extended interactions with the math teacher (subject he enjoys discussing), then moved the conversations with her to the math classroom (while they were alone in the classroom). Focus on positives that may come out of talking with teachers and peers . . . pondering what is a "big deal"' versus a "little deal" . . . confronting the "awfulizing" in terms of his fears.

Final Working Sessions (sessions 19–25)

- Moved conversations with the MHI and teachers to hallways where other students were present . . . after multiple attempts began charting behavior, using relaxation strategies, finally transferred this to speaking with a peer. Began preparation for Kym's transition to the 9th-grade building by visiting that site with him. Assigned a "social partner" and held a parent meeting including the cultural informant. A case conference was called with the high school counselor, key teachers, speech pathologist, parents (accompanied by cultural informant to aid with language barriers), and school psychologist in preparation for Kym's transition. Summer homework focused on targeted social interactions being assigned to Kym and seeing a community-based mental health professional.

Goals, Course of Intervention, and Summary

Kym made considerable progress toward the goal of being able to speak with teachers over the course of the year. He began the year not being able to speak to anyone and over time was able to communicate via writing then speaking, and moving from speaking with the MHI to teachers to peers. Kym also reported feeling proud of himself for accomplishing difficult tasks. When the MHI began working with Kym, he found it difficult to express affect and identify fears about speaking and reported high anxiety, and now he has been able to identify some of his fears related to speaking and his reduced anxiety.

Summary

Throughout the intervention, Kym's score on an anxiety scale modeled on the Liebowitz (1987) Social Anxiety Scale (24 items scaled 0–3, where 0 = none, 1 = mild, 2 = moderate, 3 = severe; Balon, 2005; Storch et al., 2006) declined from the 70/80 range (severe social phobia) to the 40/50 range (moderate phobia). These score changes caused Kym to realize his progress, but it was recommended that he remain in treatment to make more progress. He must also continue to confront his fear, challenge negative thoughts, and maintain behavioral practice in various settings. Kym would also benefit from praise regarding this success and positive attributes he possesses. Transitioning to the high school will set the stage for future successes with appropriate support, so a well-defined transition plan is recommended.

CASE 2: RYAN DIAGNOSED WITH AUTISM, CONDUCT, AND SOCIAL SKILL ISSUES

Reason for Referral

Ryan is the focus of this intervention because of disruptive behavior (demonstrated by, e.g., arguing, crying, teasing) exhibited in the classroom that hinders his academic progress and negatively impacts the classroom climate. The school team completed a functional behavioral assessment to aid in better understanding the nature of his disruptive classroom behaviors.

Case Background

Background/history	• Lives in the U.S. Midwest • Male • Caucasian • 5th-grade student (age 10) • Little family history information available
Presenting behaviors	*Social defiance and disruptive behaviors (physical aggression, argumentative;* in fall 2012, Ryan was suspended for pushing his gifted intervention teacher while upset)
Evidence-based practices used	Evidence-based supports included but were not limited to social skills tools from programs such as Project ACHIEVE—Stop and Think; educators provided verbal praise, social skills instruction, extended time to gather materials, parking lot sheet for questions, problem-solving strategies when frustrated

Academically relevant information	*Received Gifted Instruction* *Cognitive skills:* Described as "bright," logical thinker, excels in math *Academic skills:* Achieving above same-aged typically developing peers (per psychologist assessment), loves to read (especially in areas of interest), works well independently *Communication:* Writing can be very sophisticated, as can his verbal responses, but engages in unacceptable (antisocial) pragmatic language skills when he is frustrated and angry
School-based services and processes used	• *RTI* • Initially qualified for special education and related services under the preschool category of speech and language disability (2006) • While in kindergarten, continued to qualify for disability services under the school-age category of speech and language (2007) • Reevaluated again to determine whether he qualified for disability services in the area of emotional disturbance due to his escalating behaviors interfering with educational performance (January 2008) • Reevaluated and diagnosed with autism[2] by independent psychologist (June 2008)
IDEA-based identification (if applicable) for services	• Presently receiving services under the disability category of autism (2012)
Length of time case was in process	6 academic years: All phases of services 1 academic year: Social intervention skills intervention

Goals, Case Conceptualization, and Overview of Mental Health Intervention

The overarching goal for Ryan is to determine the pattern of Ryan's disruptiveness and begin to provide the social skills for him to self-regulate and reduce his inattention and disruptions in class. This intervention involved a team of teachers, a private psychologist (provided diagnostic data), an intervention specialist, and the school psychologist.

To begin the assessment process, Ryan's teachers were asked to divide their classroom routines into segments and rate the likelihood of Ryan exhibiting problematic behaviors within these segments. That analysis was completed in the form of a functional behavioral assessment[3] (FBA) and is provided in Appendix A at the end of this chapter.

As the FBA data show, teachers frequently rated Ryan as disruptive, insubordinate, aggressive, and argumentative toward teachers. Teachers also reported that he seeks attention from peers and often wants immediate gratification; is emotional (cries, yells, stomps); perceives classroom situations and rules as unfair; is unable or unwilling to accomplish classroom tasks; and creates tension and conflict for himself.

To determine the nature and patterns of Ryan's behavior the mental health intervention team posed the following questions:

1. What events predict when the problem behavior(s) will occur?

Based upon the FBA, Ryan appears to exhibit the most difficulties during transitions, unstructured play time, lunch, and during whole group and small group instruction. When Ryan wants attention from peers, he may behave in a way that attracts it, typically negative (laughing at others, teasing others, arguing with others). Ryan often wants to be with others, yet he demands that the other children engage in activities based upon his rules or his perceptions at the time. When Ryan has a question in the classroom, he frequently blurts out and requests that his question either be heard or answered immediately. When Ryan becomes fixed on a topic, then transitions are more difficult for him. At other times, Ryan becomes inattentive to instruction and becomes absorbed in his own thoughts. At these times, he may be writing in his journal, sneaking some reading time in a book, or just "zoning out."

2. What consequences appear most likely to maintain the problem behavior(s)?

Ryan responds when his abilities are regarded and rewarded with attention and when he feels affirmed. He needs constant engagement structure and stimulation. Self-regulatory feedback, expectations, and guidance are helpful.

What follows now are the team's proposed strategies for addressing the behaviors.

Intervention Strategies Used to Control Problem Behavior

Calm ("if–then") explanations have been attempted by all staff to diffuse a potential problem. Ryan often writes his feelings in a journal and takes this home for parent support. Social demands and the extent of social learning/peer-assisted learning opportunities have been decreased with more opportunity for individual work. Additionally, Ryan is often redirected or prompted to attend to a lesson and engage in the activity. Maintaining his attention to a topic that he cares little about has been a challenge.

Next, the team examined Ryan's mechanism of motivation. They examined whether behavior was exhibited to obtain sensory input (sensory); whether behavior was exhibited to escape or avoid something unpleasant or nonpreferred (escape); whether behavior was exhibited for attention, whether from adults or peers (attention); and whether behavior was exhibited to obtain a reward or a preferred activity (tangible; see Appendix B at the end of this chapter).

According to teacher ratings, Ryan is rated highest in the areas of tangibles and escape. Ryan also misbehaves to upset or annoy teachers when they do not pay attention to him. In addition, teachers note that he misbehaves when told that he can't do something that he has wanted to do or when a request is made of him that he does not want to perform. The balance of teacher ratings of Ryan's behavior suggests that he has a need for escape, tangibles, and attention.

Overall Conceptualization of Ryan's Behavior

Ryan's inattentiveness and disruptive behavior is potentially tied to his need for attention. In addition, Ryan has difficulties with perspective—taking or putting himself in the shoes of another person. He finds it difficult to understand the viewpoints of others. He does not process when others are annoyed by his attempts to get their attention. His thinking tends to be centered on himself and often remains inflexible. Ryan does not understand that others, whether peers or the adults in the school environment, may interpret rules differently and have different perspectives. Ryan has difficulties understanding social rules within the school and classroom. He also has difficulties being patient when he has a question or an issue. He typically wants his needs met immediately or the problem solved immediately. When a resolution is not offered, he typically reacts by arguing, blurting out, crying, pushing, or shoving at times. If Ryan perceives a response as being unfair, he may react more intensely. When he puts himself in a hierarchical role (I'm in the gifted math class), and attempts to direct his teacher(s), he gets the attention and the authority he is seeking by disrupting class and calling attention to his perspectives, wants, and needs. He sometimes enjoys calling attention to his abilities.

Goals, Course of Intervention, and Summary

Based upon this assessment process (functional assessment checklist and motivation assessment scale), a specific plan was constructed for Ryan that establishes specific incremental steps needed to reach the overarching goal of attentiveness and reduction of disruption. This plan will be implemented by Ryan's teachers and intervention specialist. The desired behaviors and strategies of the plan are outlined below (elements of Reality Therapy–Choice Theory are used here as referenced in Chapter 8).

Desired Behaviors

Ryan will comply with teacher requests and directives.
Ryan will engage in social situations peacefully.
Ryan will pay attention to instruction, as evidenced by
    1. Active listening (eyes on speaker)
Ryan will complete his classroom work, as evidenced by
    1. Engagement in the assignment, whether in-group or by himself, and checked by teacher(s), submitted as requested

Proactive and Interactive Strategies

To increase the desired behavior, the following are recommended:

1. Staff will keep Ryan's needs in mind and use Wants, Direction, Self-Evaluation Plan (WDEP) analysis (see Chapter 8).

2. Staff will establish firm limits pertaining to classroom behaviors and attentiveness.

3. Staff will provide individual instruction on classroom rules (nonnegotiable) using such procedures as modeling, drill and practice, visuals (note cards), and verbal reasoning options.

4. Staff will praise Ryan often when he is exhibiting positive behaviors and remaining engaged and attentive (refrain from providing attention when disruptive).

5. Staff will provide direct social skills instruction on an "as needed" basis; topics include playing fair, courtesy rules, unwritten social rules, and so forth. Ryan needs to learn and accept that certain behaviors will not be tolerated and that being polite is appropriate in any situation. Remind Ryan that being polite and having good manners will gain him entry into group social interactions.

6. Assist Ryan to think more flexibly. Help him work through more literal, black and white thinking patterns.

7. Staff will allow Ryan several extra minutes (up to 5) to gather his materials before transitioning to another classroom.

Reactive Strategies

To address Ryan's argumentativeness and classroom disruption,

1. Staff will verbally restate the directions, up to three times.

2. When Ryan becomes disruptive in the classroom and wants a question answered immediately (raising hand and saying "Excuse me, excuse me"), staff will state "Not now, Ryan," but will allow him extra time at the end of instruction to ask the question of his teacher directly. (A "parking lot" sheet for Ryan's questions will be provided to him—he can post his questions there with color priority rating dots—to be reviewed by teacher during breaks).

3. When Ryan becomes angry with a peer or peers, and becomes agitated, staff will state a scripted message to indicate to Ryan that he needs to control his emotions, stop crying, and take a "social time out."

4. Staff will maintain a neutral demeanor without showing an emotional reaction.

Plan Evaluation

To assess Ryan's progress multiple rating scales along with skill and behavior monitoring will be used over the course of the semester.

Case Prognosis, Summary, and Future Direction

Progress was made in Ryan's case. Ryan's family was deeply involved and provided consistent modeling at home. The adults in Ryan's environment benefited from remembering what drove Ryan's needs and helped Ryan see whether his disruptive behavior was getting him what he needed. Continuing to partner with the consulting psychologist for continued intensive intervention outside of school was valuable as well. Finally, the intervention team shared this plan with middle-school staff to assist in Ryan's transition for the elementary school–to–middle school transition process for the subsequent school year.

CASE 3: MARIA AND HER PARENTS' DIVORCE

Reason for Referral

Maria, a 7th-grade Latina child, is referred by her parents and teachers to participate in a group designed for children whose parents recently divorced. Concern stemmed from an observed decrease in academic performance, moodiness at home, loss of interest in school, and Maria reporting being upset over her parents' divorce. Her intervention plan was based on the Children of Divorce Intervention Program (CODIP; Pedro-Carroll, Sutton, & Wyman, 1999). This program has been successful with reducing the negative impact of parental divorce on children (Alpert-Gillis, Pedro-Carroll, & Cowen, 1989; Pedro-Carroll et al., 1992; Pedro-Carroll & Jones, 2005.)

Case Background

Background/history	<ul><li>Lives in the U.S. Southwest</li><li>Female</li><li>Latina</li><li>7th-grade student (age 12)</li><li>Family history:<ul><li>Both working parents with income $30,000–$40,000</li><li>Parents divorced</li><li>Oldest of three children, well-adjusted child, no reported medical issues, and no previous academic challenges; involved in scouting and her church; before the divorce, Maria's parents lived (along with the maternal grandmother) in a modest home</li></ul></li></ul>
Presenting behaviors	Upon reporting the upcoming divorce, Maria's mother reported <ul><li>Moodiness, withdrawal, and "clinging behavior" unusual for her</li><li>Declining grades, loss of interest in school</li><li>Reports of feeling less confident and sad</li></ul>
Evidence-based practices used	<ul><li>Evidence-based supports included, but were not limited to, materials from the Children of Divorce Intervention Program (embedded within this case study; CODIP; Alpert-Gillis et al., 1989)</li></ul>

Academically relevant information	*Cognitive skills:* Above-average performance since preschool *Academic skills:* Achieving at academic rates consistent with that of same-aged typically developing peers; performed well on all school-based assessments and standardized tests *Communication:* Above-average in written and oral skills; previous compliant classroom demeanor and behavior, current detachment
School-based services and processes used	• *RTI* • Tier 2: Psychoeducational counseling group for children whose parents are divorcing
IDEA-based identification (if applicable) for services	*N/A*
Length of time case was in process	Fall term of 2012 academic year

Goals, Case Conceptualization, and Overview of Mental Health Intervention

Maria was included in a divorce group comprising 10 7th- and 8th-graders. The 12- to 14-week program is designed to (1) increase an understanding of divorce, (2) minimize behavioral and emotional problems connected with parental divorce, (3) build coping skills (problem solving, communication, relaxation, impulse control) and confidence using CBT approaches, and (4) provide support and increase academic engagement. The group was co-led by the school counselor and school psychologist for weekly sessions.

Course of Intervention

- Referral information was received from teachers and parents, consent was secured, and screening interviews were completed with all children (including Maria).
- In conjunction with this program for students, the school provided information to parents about an 11-session "New Beginnings" Parent Group (CBT group). This program is effective at improving the parent–child relationship, effective discipline, divorce stressors, interparent conflict, and child mental health issues (Wolchik et al., 2002).
- The student group sessions included the following sequential topics:

  1. Getting Acquainted
  2. Developing Group Trust: The Lifeline Exercise
  3. Sharing Experiences: "Tender Places"
  4. Understanding Divorce-Related Feelings
  5. Developing a Group Newsletter

6. Developing Problem-Solving Skills
7. Addressing Divorce Related Problems
8. Learning to Communicate Effectively
9. Dealing Effectively with Anger
10. Resolving Conflict
11. Understanding Families
12. Panel of Experts on Family Changes
13. Building Self-Esteem
14. Saying Goodbye

Goals, Course of Intervention, and Summary

Maria responded well to the group sessions based upon her session exercise results. Based on parent and teacher reports and school psychologist observation, Maria began the sessions exhibiting high levels of self-blame, sadness, and withdrawal. Maria also reported feeling disinterested in school and unable to cope with her parents divorce. She engaged fully in the group sessions and connected well with group members. The goal of the Tier 2 group intervention was to provide Maria with the tools to express her feelings, provide her with information about divorce, regain her interest in school, and acquire skills to cope with the divorce situation. Based upon all measures, she accomplished these goals. The group also provided Maria with the assurance that she is not the only youth experiencing divorce. She also obtained support from peers.

Summary

Throughout the intervention, Maria's responses to session exercises suggested that she was developing skills and an understanding about divorce that provided a new framework from which she could cope. Her pre and post scores on measures modeled after Pedro-Carroll's Children's Divorce Adjustment Scale (CDAS; 3-point scale—usually yes, sometimes, usually no—measures feelings about self, family, and coping), the Children's Family Adjustment Scale (CFAS; 3-point scale—yes, sometimes, no—measures feelings about self, family, and support), and parent and teacher ratings (4-point scale—from very true for child to not at all true for child) on motivation and school performance improved. Maria's divorce adjustment rating scores returned to a normative range. She is currently reengaged with school, and her grades have risen to prior levels (As and Bs).

Maria also benefits from sessions or conversations with her parents to further her understanding of their continued concern and care for her. As she continues throughout adolescence, Maria's parents and teachers have been encouraged to monitor her progress and provide appropriate support.

Case Prognosis, Summary, and Future Direction

According to progress made to date, Maria has a very good chance of continuing to adapt and respond in healthy ways to her family dynamics and changes. She can also be a good support for her siblings as they cope with the family issues. Maria is rediscovering her sense of self, focusing more on school, and reconnecting with her parents.

SUMMARY

This chapter presented authentic examples (case studies) of how mental health intervention in the schools is enhanced by the use of evidence-based response-to-intervention practice. An effective RTI approach relies on direct measures or screening of student performance/behavior to identify further need for intervention, the use of research-based strategies, and monitoring of student performance with an end goal in mind. The push to use evidence driven methods to examine the mental health status of our youth is growing.

Youth today face academic and mental health challenges long before age 18, and the earlier we intervene, the more promising the outcome (Merikangas et al., 2011). School is one of the primary places where mental health issues can be addressed. Being aware of issues such as brain development, the prevalence of depression and anxiety in youth, the rates of substance use and abuse, and the dynamics of social struggles or bullying provides professionals who work in schools with a perspective on the life of youth today. If schools can establish the systems needed to address these issues, we stand a chance of ameliorating them (Adelman & Taylor, 2011, 2007). Leveraging broad-based behavioral supports along with more targeted interventions can go a long way toward enhancing the resiliency and coping capacity of children, thus enhancing their academic and social success.

NOTES

Case names were changed, and some aspects of the case augmented to protect subjects' identities and enhance the scope of the case.

1. Selective mutism (SM) is viewed as a "specifier" within social anxiety disorder (social phobia)] in the *Diagnostic and Statistical Manual of Mental Disorders* (5th ed.; *DSM-5*; American Psychiatric Association, 2013) that is marked by fear or anxiety in social contexts to the extent that it effects functioning, creates avoidance or failure to speak (in social contexts as required/expected), and does not result from a physiological, other medical, or mental health disorder.
2. Autism spectrum disorder (ASD) as defined by the *DSM-5* (American Psychiatric Association, 2013) is a persistent deficit in social communication and interaction in multiple contexts and a presence of restricted or repetitive behavior patterns, interests, or activities.

These behaviors must be seen in early childhood and cause significant impairment in social, occupational or other areas of functioning (not explained by intellectual disability or delay).

3. Functional behavioral assessment (functional behavioral analysis) is an approach or set of strategies used to determine the underlying function or purpose of behavior. By diagnosing the scope and causes of the target behaviors, interventions can be identified to address the problem behaviors. Steps include identifying and describing the target behavior; collecting data (e.g., rating scales, observations) on the presence of behavior and the antecedent or consequent events controlling the behavior; developing a hypothesis about the behavior and testing that hypothesis; and then creating interventions designed to augment the behavior and monitor effects.

APPENDIXES

APPENDIX A. RYAN'S FUNCTIONAL BEHAVIORAL ASSESSMENT REPORT

Problem Schedule	Teacher/ Subject	Activity	Likelihood of Problem Behavior on Scale From 1 (not likely) to 6 (highly likely)	Specific Behavior
9:20–9:30	Smith/ Reading	Transition	5	Verbally inappropriate
9:30–9:35	"	Vocab. practice	5	Unresponsive
9:35–9:55	"	Listening comp	5	Inattentive, work not done
9:55–10:35	"	Reading comp	2 and 4	Work not done; becomes more inattentive as the morning progresses
10:35–10:45	"	Word power	6	Inattentive
10:45–10:50	"	Clean up	1	Quick to exit for math
11:00–11:15	Richards/ Math	Homework	1 and 5	Disruptive if no homework or better if reading independently
11:15–11:30		Announcements agenda	6	Interruption
11:30–12:00		Whole-class instruction	5	Reading book, disruption (talking out)
12:00–12:25		Work time	5	Aggression, disruptions, individual or group work not done, insubordination, free time

(continued)

APPENDIX A *(continued)*

Problem Schedule	Teacher/ Subject	Activity	Likelihood of Problem Behavior on Scale From 1 (not likely) to 6 (highly likely)	Specific Behavior
12:25–12:30		Homework	5	Rushes out of room clean up; leaves early
12:35–1:05	Lunch/ Recess	Lunch/Recess	1 and 5	Seeks negative attention (tries to make peers laugh) when peers do not follow his lead, or plays by himself and walks around
1:25–1:45	Smith/ Social Studies	Video presentation	4	Not doing work; inattentive
1:45–2:05		Work time	4	Not doing work; inattentive
2:05–2:10	Birdsong/ Science	Entrance	5	Tardy—lingers in previous class, talks out to whole class
2:10–2:30		Instruction	4	Interruption— "excuse me" out loud
2:30–2:50		Prepare for dismissal and specials	4	Lingers with teacher

APPENDIX B. RYAN'S MOTIVATION ASSESSMENT RATINGS

Motivation Assessment Scale				
Teachers	Shaffer	Richards	Birdsong	Smith
Scale Dimensions				
Sensory	10	5	11	4
Escape	14	10	13	15
Attention	18	11	18	4
Tangible	12	10	19	20

Note: Higher score indicates greater tendency in that area.

RESOURCES

This section includes an extended list of resources focusing on content related to the chapter case studies, but also general references connected with evidence-based practice and RTI approaches.

Places to Find Evidence-Based Practice and RTI Information

General Intervention Resources

> Center for Response to Intervention at American Institutes for Research (www.rti4success.org).

> Substance Abuse and Mental Health Services Administration's National Registry of Evidence-Based Programs and Practices (NREPP; www.nrepp.samhsa.gov).

> National Council for Behavioral Health, Washington, DC. Youth Mental Health First Aid (www.mentalhealthfirstaid .org).

> What Works Clearinghouse (ies.ed.gov/ncee/wwc).

Social Anxiety

> Social Anxiety and Selective Mutism: Krysanski 2003 (p. 33) and Silva, Gallagher, and Minami (2006) highlight various mental health interventions used in the treatment of SM. The most efficacious course of treatment for SM involves behavioral interventions using contingency management, shaping, self-modeling, desensitization, stimulus fading with some cognitive strategies (depending upon the age of the child), and medication (Bogels et al., 2010; Krysanski, 2003).

> The resource by Mitchell and Kratochwill (2013), "Treatment of Selective Mutism: Applications in the Clinic and School Through Conjoint Consultation," proves to be a very helpful tool for collaborative interventions.

> To find additional courses of treatment for SM, consult the New York University Child Study Center Clinic and Child Mind Institute (www.aboutourkids.org; www.childmind.org).

Autism

> The Autism Speaks website provides comprehensive information about autism, research on autism, and resources to assist with treatment and education (www.autism speaks.org).

> The CDC (Centers for Disease Control and Prevention) provides extensive information and evidence based treatment options for autism spectrum disorder (www.cdc.gov/ ncbdd/autism/index.html).

Divorce Groups

> Authored by Janice L. DeLucia-Waack (2006), *Leading Psychoeducational Groups for Children and Adolescents* (Sage) provides directions on how to implement groups for children experiencing a parental divorce (ISBN 978-1-4129-1401-7).

Children of Divorce Intervention Program (CODIP; JoAnne Pedro-Carroll) is a well-documented 12- to 15-session group counseling program for children aged 5 to 13. Four field-tested curricula have been developed for use with grades K–8. Efficacy has been shown in numerous controlled studies (www.childrensinstitute.net/programs/codip). Contact Joanne Pedro-Carroll, PhD, through the Children's Institute, 274 North Goodman, Suite D103 Rochester, NY 14607. jpcarroll@childrensinstitute.net.

SAMHSA's National registry of evidence-based programs and practices offers a helpful summary of the COPID program (www.nrepp.samhsa.gov/viewintervention.aspx?id=220).

A helpful parent guide is also posted on the Help Guide website. It provides tips for parents on how to support children during the divorce process (www.helpguide.org/mental/children_divorce.htm).

Other resources:

- New Beginnings Parent Resource (www.blueprintsprograms.com/evaluationAbstracts.php?pid=ae694b0755cd5eed5886ec4d8e658bde9639331d).
- Vocabulary and schedules to assist with normalizing both homes/domiciles (school, homework, chores, etc.) are available at www.divorcehq.com.
- The game "My Two Homes," published by Childswork/Childsplay (1994), is designed for children aged 6 to 12 who are having difficulty adjusting to their parents' divorce. The game allows children to address questions about divorce and supports children with communication, feeling identification, and coping through play.
- Social stories address living in two different homes and blended families. "Real-life calls for real books: Literature to help children cope with family stressors," by Sherron Killingsworth Roberts and Patricia A. Crawford, in *Beyond the Journal: Young Children on the Web* (September 2008) chronicles multiple story-based resources that can be used to assist children with life situations including parental divorce. This can be accessed through the National Association for the Education of Young Children at www.naeyc.org/files/yc/file/200809/crawford.pdf.
- Journaling/writing tools can be used to support children with self-expression. These tools can be accessed through "Creative interventions for children of divorce," by Liana Lowenstein, in *Play Therapy* (2009) at www.a4pt.org.

Social Skills

The Stop and Think Social Skills Program (EBP per U.S. Department of Health and Human Services–SAMHSA) to assist children with interpersonal, problem-solving, and conflict resolution skills can be accessed through www .projectachieve.info/stop-think/social-skills-program .html.

Reality Therapy

Two scholarly explorations, one by Cynthia Mason and Jill Duba (2009), "Using Reality Therapy in schools" (*International Journal of Reality Therapy, 29*(2), 5–12) and the second by Jamie Yarbrough and Charles Thompson (2002), "Using single-participant research to assess counseling approaches on children's off-task behaviors" (*Professional School Counseling, 5*(5), 308–314), highlight the utility and effectiveness of RT within the counseling context.

Implementation of RT strategies in schools can be examined by visiting www.wglasser.com and www .realitytherapywub.com.

REFERENCES

Adelman, H. S., & Taylor, L. (2011). Expanding school improvement policy to better address barriers to learning and integrate public health concerns. *Policy Futures in Education, 9*, 431–436.

Adelman, H. S., & Taylor, L. (2007). Systemic change and school improvement. *Journal of Educational and Psychological Consultation, 17*, 55, 77.

Alpert-Gillis, L. J., Pedro-Carroll, J. L., & Cowen, E. L. (1989). The children of divorce intervention program: Development, implementation, and evaluation of a program for young urban children. *Journal of Consulting and Clinical Psychology, 57*, 583–589.

American Psychiatric Association. (2013). *Diagnostic and statistical manual of mental disorders* (5th ed.). Arlington, VA: Author.

American Psychological Association. (2002). *Developing adolescents: A reference for professionals.* Washington, DC: Author.

Balon, R. (2005). Measuring anxiety: Are we getting what we need? *Depression and Anxiety, 22*(1), 1–10.

Bogels, S. M., Alden, L., Beidel, D. C., Clark, L. A., Pine, D. S., Stein, M. B., & Voncken, M. (2010). Social anxiety disorder: Questions and answers for the *DSM-V. Depression and Anxiety, 27*, 168–189.

Beyer, T., Postert, C., Muller, J., & Tilman, F. (2012). Prognosis and continuity of child mental health problems from preschool to primary school: 4-year study. *Child Psychiatry Human Development, 43*, 533–543.

Bradley, R., Danielson, L., & Doolittle, J. (2005). Response to intervention. *Journal of Learning Disabilities, 38*(6), 485–486.

Brownell, M. T., Adams, A., Sindelar, P., & Waldron, N. (2006). Learning from collaboration: The role of teacher qualities. *Council for Exceptional Children, 72*(2), 169–185.

Bronstein, L. R., Anderson, E., Terwilliger, S. H., & Sager, K. (2012). Evaluating a model of school-based health and social services: An interdisciplinary community-university collaboration. *Children and Schools, 34*(3), 155–165.

Harrison, J. R., Vannest, K., Davis, J., & Reynolds, C. (2012). Common problem behaviors of children and adolescents in general education classrooms. *Journal of Emotional and Behavioral Disorders, 20*(1), 55–64.

Kazak, A. E., Hoagwood, K. A., Weisz, J. R., Hood, K., Kratochwill, T. R., Vargas, L. A., & Banez, G. A. (2010). A meta-systems approach to evidence-based practice for children and adolescents. *American Psychologist, 65*(2), 85–97.

Kratochwill, T. R., Hoagwood, K. A., Kazak, A. E., Weisz, J. R., Hood, K., Vargas, L. A., & Banez, G. A. (2012). Practice-based evidence for children and adolescents: Advancing the research agenda in schools. *School Psychology Review, 41*(2), 215–235.

Kratochwill, T. R., Clements, M. A., & Kalymon, K. M. (2007). Response to intervention: Conceptual and methodological issues in implementation. In S. R. Jimerson, M. K. Burns, & A. M. VanDerheyden (Eds.), *Handbook for Response to Intervention: The science and practice of assessment and intervention.* New York, NY: Springer Publishing Company.

Krysanski, V. L. (2003). A brief review of selective mutism literature. *The Journal of Psychology, 137*(1), 29–40.

Liebowitz, M. R. (1987). Liebowtiz Social Anxiety Scale. *Modern Problems in Pharmacopsychiatry, 22,* 141–173.

Merikangas, K. R., He, J., Burstein, M. E., Swendsen, J., Avenevoli, S., Case, B., Georgiades, K., Heaton, L., & Olfson, M. (2011). Service utilization for lifetime mental disorders in U.S. adolescents: Results from the national co-morbidity survey adolescent supplement (NCS-A). *Journal for the American Academy of Child and Adolescent Psychiatry, 50*(1), 32–45.

Meyer, G. J., Finn, S. E., Eyde, L. D., Ky, G. G., Moreland, K. L., Dies, R. R., Elsman, E. J., Kubiszyn, T. W., & Reed, G. M. (2001). Psychological testing and psychological assessment: A review of evidence and issues. *American Psychologist, 56*(2), 128–165.

Mitchell, A. D., & Kratochwill, T. R. (2013). Treatment of selective mutism: Applications in the clinic and school through conjoint consultation. *Journal of Educational and Psychological Consultation, 23*(1), 36–62.

National Council for Behavioral Health. (2014). Retrieved from http://www.mentalhealthfirstaid.org

Neukrug, E. S., & Schwitzer, A. M. (2006). *Skills and tools for today's counselors and psychotherapists: From natural helping to professional counseling.* New York, NY: Thompson/Brooks/Cole.

Office of Child Development (OCD) Special Report (July, 2005). *Understanding common problem behaviors in young children.* University of Pittsburgh. 1–4. Retrieved from http://www.ocd.pitt.edu/Files/PDF/sr2005-07.pdf

Pedro-Carroll, J. L., Alpert-Gillis, L. J., & Cowen, E. L. (1992). An evaluation of the efficacy of a preventive intervention for 4th- and 6th-grade urban children of divorce. *Journal of Primary Prevention, 13,* 115–130.

Pedro-Carroll, J. L., & Jones, S. H. (2005). A preventative play intervention to foster children's resilience in the aftermath of divorce. In L. A. Reddy, T. M. Files-Hall, & C. E. Schaefer (Eds.), *Empirically based play interventions for children* (pp. 51–75). Washington, DC: American Psychological Association.

Pedro-Carroll, J. L., Sutton, S. E., & Wyman, P. A. (1999). A two-year follow up evaluation of a preventive intervention program for young children of divorce. *School Psychology Review, 28*, 467–476.

Silva, R. R., Gallagher, R., & Minami, H. (2006). Cognitive-behavioral treatment for anxiety disorders in children and adolescents. *Primary Psychiatry, 13*(5), 68–76.

Spear, L. P. (2000). The adolescent brain and age-related behavioral manifestations. *Neuroscience and Biobehavioral Reviews, 24*, 417–463.

Splett, J. W., & Maras, M. (2011). Closing the gap in school mental health: A community-centered model for school psychology. *Psychology in the Schools, 48*(4), 385–399.

Storch, E. A., Masia-Warner, C., Heidgerken, A. D., Fisher, P. H., Pincus, D. B., & Liebowitz, M. R. (2006). Factor structure of the Liebowtiz social anxiety scale for children and adolescents. *Child Psychiatry and Human Development, 37*(1), 25–37.

Weist, M. D., Rubin, M., Moore, E., Adelsheim, S., & Wrobel, G. (2007). Mental health screening in schools. *Journal of School Health, 77*(2), 53–58.

Weist, M. D., Ambrose, M. G., & Lewis, C. P. (2006). Expanded school mental health: A collaborative community-school example. *Children and Schools, 28*(2), 45–50.

Wolchik, S. A., Sandler, I. N., & Millsap, R. E. (2002). Six-year follow up of preventive interventions for children of divorce: A randomized controlled trial. *The Journal of the American Medical Association, 288*(15), 1874–1881.

Index

abuse (of minors). *See* child abuse
academic outcomes, of bullying
    victims, 214–215
acetylcholine, 354
ADAPT-ITT cultural adaptation
    model, 116
administrative law, 65. *See also* legal
    system
African American youths
    health risks, 108, 109–110
    Strong African American Families
        Program, 115–116
After a Suicide: A Toolkit for Schools,
    280–281, 282
after-school programs, resources from, 40
Al-Anon (peer support group), 339
alcohol. *See* drug and alcohol use
Alcoholics Anonymous, 338–339
aldehyde dehydrogenase, 331
Alpha2-agonists, 369–370
American Counseling Association,
    VISTAS Online, 98
Americans with Disabilities Act (1990), 83
Americans with Disabilities
    Amendments Act (2008), 83,
    85, 101
antidepressants
    commercial products, 357
    monoamine oxidase inhibitors, 359
    norepinephrine dopamine reuptake
        inhibitors, 359
    selective serotonin reuptake
        inhibitors, 356, 358
    serotonin norepinephrine reuptake
        inhibitors, 358
    tricyclics, 359

antidiscrimination statutes. *See*
    Americans with Disabilities
    Act (1990); Americans with
    Disabilities Amendments Act
    (2008); Rehabilitation Act,
    Section 504
antihistamines, 366
anxiolytics, 317, 366–367
Asian American youths, 109–110
Atomoxetine (Strattera), 368–369
attention deficit hyperactivity disorder
    (ADHD)
    among ethnic minority youths, 108
    case study treatment, 373–374

Baltimore School Mental Health
    Technical Assistance and
    Training Initiative, 55
bath salts, 324
Behavioral and Emotional Screening
    System, 24–25
Behavior Assessment System for
    Children-2, 24
behavior exploration, 175–176
benzodiazepines, 317, 366–367
beta-blockers, 370
bipolar disorder diagnosis, 371–372
Brown v. Board of Education (1954), 66–67
Buckley Amendment. *See* Family
    Educational Rights and Privacy
    Act (1974, FERPA)
bullying. *See also* cyberbullying
    academic outcomes impact, 214–215
    definition, 214
    social–ecological model of, 217–221
    suicide risk, 215–217, 269–270